Major Problems in American Sport History

MAJOR PROBLEMS IN AMERICAN HISTORY SERIES

GENERAL EDITOR

THOMAS G. PATERSON

Major Problems
in American Sport History

DOCUMENTS AND ESSAYS
EDITED BY

STEVEN A. RIESS
NORTHEASTERN ILLINOIS UNIVERSITY

HOUGHTON MIFFLIN COMPANY   BOSTON   NEW YORK

Address editorial correspondence to:

Houghton Mifflin Company
College Division
222 Berkeley Street
Boston, MA 02116-3764

Editor-in-Chief: Jean L. Woy
Senior Associate Editor: Frances Gay
Editorial Assistant: Joanne Markow Cavanaugh
Editorial Production Coordinator: Carla Thompson
Production/Design Coordinator: Deborah Frydman
Marketing Associate: Amanda Rappaport
Director of Manufacturing: Michael O'Dea

Cover Art: Harvey Dinnerstein. *The Wide Swing*. 1974. Oil on canvas. 24 × 32 in. The Butler Institute of American Art, Youngstown, Ohio. Phil Desind Collection.

Cover Design: Alwyn Velasquez, Lapis Design

Text credits begin on page 435.

Printed in the U.S.A.

Library of Congress Catalog Card Number: 96-76951

ISBN: 0-669-35380-9

123456789-DH-00 99 98 97 96

For Jocelyne and Jacquelyne,
our first dividends

Preface

During the 1996 summer Olympics in Atlanta, 200 million Americans watched the festival of international sport on television. Televised sport is so popular that it has become the cornerstone of superstations like TBS, WOR, and WGN, and it has spurred the rise of the highly successful all-sports network ESPN. The longest-running prime-time television show is "Monday Night Football." An adult fitness fad has flourished, as people are exercising, cycling, and jogging to keep healthy and youthful. Our preeminent American heroes are not politicians, business executives, or scientists, but sport figures like Muhammad Ali, Michael Jordan, and the new star Kerri Strug, whose Olympic performance thrilled the world.

How did sport become such an important aspect of American life? When and why did this happen? These are some of the questions the study of American sport history explores. Let's start with a definition. Jockeys, baseball players, competitive dart throwers, and marathoners are athletes, but chess and bridge players are not, because sports in modern society are defined as competitive, rule-based pastimes that require physical dexterity. Participants in sports are athletes who compete against themselves, another individual, or an established record, or as members of a team. Competitors may be amateurs, who play purely for enjoyment, "sport for sport's sake," in front of no one or 100,000 paying spectators, or they may be professionals, athletes who are compensated for their efforts and exhibit their skills before a paying audience.

American sport history examines the development over time of athletic activities, particularly the emergence of specific sports with their own rules and institutions. Why, for example, are there eleven players on a football team? Why does major league baseball consist of two leagues? The study of sport also entails analyzing the relationship between sports and social institutions, political and economic structures, geography, and group and individual behavior. Why, for example, is baseball the national pastime? How did American society and its subcommunities shape the development of sport? What has been the role of government in sport? How did the loss of public space influence the rise of sport? Finally, the study of sport also involves considering how sport has influenced American values and social behavior.

Until recently, historians rarely studied sport because it seemed intrinsically trivial, because they considered other topics to be more important, or because they were snobs. Scholars believed that sport and its institutions were well understood by the public—after all, ten-year-old boys were assumed to have a great command of esoteric statistics—and that their analysis would not foster any new knowledge or explain any broad historical problems. Furthermore, historians who wanted to study sport were often deterred by the fear that they could never get a job if they wrote dissertations on sport. Even noted historians who wanted to study sport were worried that writing about it would mark them as students of the frivolous.

Academic interest in sport history emerged in the early 1970s as a result of such factors as the rise of the New Social history; student demands for a more relevant curriculum; the growing importance of interdisciplinary history, especially as influenced by cultural anthropology; the democratization of the historical profession; and the establishment of the North American Society for Sport History (1972), an association that created a supportive intellectual community for historians interested in sport, and that founded the *Journal of Sport History* in 1974. However, the fundamental factor that encouraged sport scholarship was that historians began to realize that the analysis of the internal history of sport and the history of sport's interaction with the broader society elucidated certain central themes of American history, particularly class, ethnicity, race, and gender issues. One product of this growing awareness was Ken Burns's 18½-hour documentary *Baseball,* first broadcast on national television in 1995. Burns saw that analyzing baseball's myths, realities, symbols, and rituals provided an excellent vehicle for examining and understanding American mores, values, and beliefs.

From very modest origins, sport history has expanded into a booming field, and by the late 1980s there was a flood of high-quality scholarship, especially on baseball and boxing. Sport history is no longer simply social history but may also be economic history, urban history, political history, educational history, or cultural history, depending on the topic and the questions under consideration.

Major Problems in American Sport History combines primary documents and historical essays to examine central problems from a variety of viewpoints. The book is organized chronologically and topically from the colonial era to the present. The first chapter introduces different approaches to and ways of thinking about the history of sport. The next chapter explores the origins of sport in colonial America; it is followed by a chapter on sport in premodern nineteenth-century America and another on the making of a modern sporting culture at midcentury. Next are several chapters that examine sport in the period from about 1870 to the decades between the two world wars, when urbanization, industrialization, and immigration dominated U.S. life. This second section includes chapters on higher education, urban space, social class, professionalization, gender, ethnicity and race, and athletic heroes. The final section discusses the shaping of contemporary sport, which became truly national and far more democratic than before, and also the escalating commercialization and professionalization of sport. These last three chapters analyze the increase in women's participation, the racial question, and the growth of sport into a contemporary big business.

As in other books in this series, each chapter opens with a brief introduction that sets the scene and defines the central issues of the topic. Specific introductory headnotes for the documents and essays in each chapter also provide guidance.

These chapters do not by any means cover all the major problems in sport history. It has been necessary to limit the book's length to fit the format of most courses in the field. For example, if length had not been a consideration, I would have included a chapter on sport and foreign relations (especially cultural diffusion and diplomacy). The emphasis in selecting documents and essays, especially for the first several chapters, has been on sport in the Northeast, particularly New York

City, which for many years was the national center of sport as well as finance, trade, and communications. Sporting activities in New York since the early 1800s received disproportionate attention from the media until relatively recently, when sport became more national in scope. Thus it is understandable that New York has been the major focus of sport scholars, including many of those whose works are included in this volume.

In a project of this nature, many people have helped me along the way, and it is a pleasure to thank them. Several historians made available to me copies of their syllabi early in this project, especially Margaret Costa, California State University, Long Beach; Lynne Emery, California State Polytechnic University, Pomona; Stephen Hardy, University of New Hampshire; and Mary Lou LeCompte, University of Texas, Austin. Detailed and extremely helpful written reviews of draft tables of contents were also provided by Melvin Adelman, Ohio State University; Linda Borish, Western Michigan University; Richard Crepeau, University of Central Florida; Robert Curtin, Northeastern University; Stephen Hardy, University of New Hampshire; George Kirsch, Manhattan College; John Marszalek, Mississippi State University; Patrick Miller, Northeastern Illinois University; Donald Mrozek, Kansas State University; Stephen Norwood, University of Oklahoma; Jeffrey Sammons, New York University; and Nancy Struna, University of Maryland, College Park. They all made useful suggestions, and I believe this book is much better for their astute critiques. I want to thank Howard Chudacoff for recommending me to Thomas Paterson, the series editor, whose guidance has been useful right from the start. The project began when the series was published by D. C. Heath, and I want to thank history editor James Miller, managing editor Sylvia Mallory, and her successor, Patricia Wakeley, for their help. As the project moved on to Houghton Mifflin, I received superb guidance and assistance from senior associate editor Frances Gay and from Joanne Markow Cavanaugh and Carla Thompson, who managed the production of the book.

S. A. R.

Contents

CHAPTER 1
What Is Sport History?
Page 1

CHAPTER 2
Sport in Colonial America
Page 21

CHAPTER 3
Traditional Sport, Modern Sport, and the Male Bachelor Subculture, 1800–1860
Page 49

CHAPTER 4
The Making of a Modern Sporting Culture, 1840–1870
Page 82

CHAPTER 5
Sport and Higher Education in America, 1865–1910
Page 112

CHAPTER 6
Sport and the Rise of the Industrial Radial City, 1870–1920
Page 140

CHAPTER 7
Sport and Class, 1870–1920
Page 169

CHAPTER 8
The Commercialization and Professionalization of Sports, 1870–1920
Page 205

P H O T O G R A P H   E S S A Y
Uniforming Sportswomen
Page 239

C H A P T E R   1 1
Sports Heroes and American Culture, 1890–1940
Page 309

C H A P T E R   1 2
Sport and American Women Since 1930
Page 338

C H A P T E R   1 3
Sport and Race in America Since 1945
Page 370

C H A P T E R   1 4
The Business of Sport, 1945–1990
Page 400

Major Problems in American Sport History

What Is Sport History?

The analysis of American sport history is a relatively new area of scholarly inquiry. Intellectuals in general, including historians, all but ignored sport as a suitable field of inquiry. Articles and books were written on sporting subjects, but most were written by journalists for a general audience. The academic lack of interest in sport was particularly remarkable because the United States had a rich sporting heritage, which dated back to pre-Columbian American Indians. The earliest English colonists participated in athletic competitions, especially southerners who became renowned for their horse racing. The United States, following the example of Great Britain, became a major sporting nation in the mid-nineteenth century that supported important amateur and professional traditions. Sport in the United States was at first primarily a participatory recreation, but by the late nineteenth century, it became increasingly professionalized and popular as a spectatorial entertainment.

Nonetheless, prior to 1960, only three scholarly books had been written on American sport history. Historians avoided the topic for several reasons. The primary reason was they believed there were more important subjects to examine such as political or diplomatic history, and that studying sport would not provide any broader understanding of American history. In addition, they disdained studying popular culture. They remained either indifferent to or defensive about the great importance of sport both as a major force on their college campuses and as a growing commercial enterprise. Lastly, professors were afraid their careers would be adversely affected by writing on sport.

Academic interest in sport history emerged in the early 1970s among younger scholars reacting to the democratization of the historical profession, to the rise of the New Social history, to student demands for a more relevant curriculum, and to the growing recognition by historians that sport and its interplay with society could inform us about the American experience. Scholars began by studying the history of individual sports, but they also examined sport in terms of society's political, economic, cultural, and social history. Sport history helped them analyze the behavior, values, and culture of social classes, ethnic groups, and races, and it is becoming an important vehicle for understanding gender issues.

⚾ E S S A Y S

The first essay in this section, written by Elliott J. Gorn, professor of history and American studies at Miami University, Ohio, and Michael Oriard, an English scholar at Oregon State University, analyzes why the study of sport needs to be taken seriously. Their critical commentary is drawn from the "Point of View" column in a 1995 issue of the *Chronicle of Higher Education.* The next two essays help illustrate how historians have analyzed the development of American sport history.

The first major scholarly article on American sport history was Frederick L. Paxson's "The Rise of Sport," published in 1917 in the *Mississippi Valley Historical Review (MVHR).* He argued that the rise of sport in the late nineteenth century was a response to the rise of cities where Americans were deprived of a rigorous rural and frontier life. A student of the renowned Western historian, Frederick Jackson Turner, Paxson asserted that with the loss of the frontier, Americans needed the new safety valve that sport represented to help residents of congested heterogeneous cities to cope with their problems and tensions and to sustain harmony. It would be thirty-six years before another essay on sport appeared in the prestigious *Journal of American History* (the former *MVHR*). Paxson's influential deprivation thesis was slightly modified by Arthur M. Schlesinger, Sr.'s *The Rise of the City, 1878–1898* (1938), which attributed the athletic boom to a reaction against restricting urban life. Urbanites were deprived of traditional fresh air recreations, and they turned to spectator sports to experience rural life vicariously. The deprivation model was reinforced by Foster Rhea Dulles, *America Learns to Play: A History of Popular Recreation* (1940), who noted that crowded urban conditions and the pace of industrial work made traditional village pleasures impractical; therefore, urbanites turned to escapist spectatorial entertainments as outlets for their "surplus energy and suppressed emotions."

A more sophisticated alternative paradigm was established by John R. Betts in "The Rise of Organized Sport in America" (Ph.D. diss., 1951). He argued that American sport was not a romantic reaction against industrialization and urbanization but rather an urban product of post–Civil War industrialization.

Contemporary interpretations for the rise of American sport emphasize the importance of American modernization or else the related process of urbanization. In the second essay in this section, entitled "Capitalism, Protestantism, and the Rise of Modern Sport," Allen Guttmann critiques Marxist and neo-Marxist analyses of sport and posits a Weberian interpretation that stresses how the modernization of sport was a product of the rationalization of society. Guttmann, a distinguished professor of American studies at Amherst College, is our most prolific historian of sport. In 1975 he published an innovative book entitled *Ritual and Record: The Nature of Modern Sport,* from which this selection is drawn. In it he created a classification system to distinguish the primary characteristics of premodern and modern sport. Guttmann described modern sports as secular, highly specialized, rationalized, bureaucratized, and obsessed with records and record keeping, traits exactly opposite to premodern sport.

The third essay in this section was written by Stephen Hardy, a professor in the Department of Kinesiology at the University of New Hampshire, who is well known for his imaginative scholarship. He proposes a slightly different interpretation for the emergence and growth of American sport that stresses the shaping influence of urbanization. Hardy sees the city as more than merely the site for the development of sport, but as a dynamic force comprised of physical structures, social organizations, and value systems whose interaction over the course of time helped mold American sporting institutions, values, and behavior.

Taking Sports Seriously

ELLIOTT J. GORN AND MICHAEL ORIARD

The West Indian scholar C. L. R. James's 1963 work, *Beyond a Boundary*, is a remarkable book of history and memory. It is about the game of cricket. More, it is about the West Indies, poverty, being black, and colonialism. Cricket is James's microscope, and through it he magnifies whole areas of life and thought. He presents cricket as both sport and metaphor, the property of colonizers and colonized, in which struggles over culture, power, hegemony, and resistance are played out. Many scholars consider *Beyond a Boundary* to be the most profound and moving book ever written about sports. . . .

Despite the obvious importance of sports in American life, only a small number of American academics have made a specialty of analyzing the relationship between athletics and culture, and their work remains ghettoized. Historians, sociologists, psychologists, anthropologists, and even philosophers and literary scholars have established subspecialties on sports, but their work hovers at the margins of their disciplines.

Moreover, the booming field of cultural studies seems oblivious to the work done on athletics. This is ironic, because cultural studies—the interdisciplinary analysis of history, cultural expression, and power—is exactly where the study of sports is most needed. Where is there a cultural activity more freighted with constructions of masculinity than football, more deeply inscribed with race than boxing, more tied in the public mind to the hopes and hopelessness of inner-city youths than basketball? Gender, race, and power are central theoretical and methodological concerns of cultural studies.

Despite the continuing discussion in American studies of "the body" (of how human beings conceive of themselves physically), athletes' bodies remain curiously off-limits. Yet power and eroticism meet most conspicuously in the athletic body—Florence Griffith-Joyner's, Greg Louganis's, or Michael Jordan's.

Is "the body" as conceived in cultural studies a rhetorical construction, while the bodies of athletes are too palpably real? Are we, as intellectuals, just uncomfortable with physicality, because our own bailiwick is the life of the mind? Could it be that professors are creatures of words while the language of athletics is fundamentally non-verbal? Or are we simply playing out the long-standing faculty antagonism to the distorted priorities of universities with multimillion-dollar athletics programs?

Furthermore, although critical scholarship about television's place in American life is an important part of cultural studies, amazingly little of that scholarship is concerned with televised sports. Yet the mass media have always depended on athletics to reach large audiences, from the invention of the sports pages in the first large-circulation metropolitan newspapers in the 1880's and 1890's, to the

---

From Elliott J. Gorn and Michael Oriard, "Taking Sports Seriously," *Chronicle of Higher Education,* March 24, 1995, A52.

first World Series radio broadcasts in the early 1920's, to the baseball and football games and boxing matches telecast at the beginning of the television age. Today, international broadcasts via satellite, cable superstations, and pay-per-view television all thrive on sporting events. Sports have been the cash cow of the increasingly pervasive (some would say invasive) entertainment media.

In an age that (properly) embraces multiculturalism, athletics represent both our diversity and our common culture. It is almost a cliché to mention that sports are the *lingua franca* of men talking across divisions of class and race. Sports also reveal just how interdependent particular subcultures and the larger consumer culture can be. Think, for example, of the symbiotic ties between inner-city playground basketball and the National Basketball Association championships.

Sports keep bringing us back to the ever-shifting relationship between commercialized mass culture (the Olympics come immediately to mind) and subcultures of difference (the Gay Games, for example).

Sports also are clearly about gender, although, until recently, this often has been overlooked. Certainly athletics have shaped American masculinity. One hundred years ago, in an essay called "The American Boy," Theodore Roosevelt exhorted young men to follow the same principles in life as in football: "Hit the line hard; don't foul and don't shirk, but hit the line hard."

For women, organized sports became available as feminism grew and they gained access to higher education and other areas from which they had previously been excluded. Even as Roosevelt wrote his essay, women at Vassar, Smith, Mount Holyoke, and Wellesley Colleges were playing baseball—not softball; baseball. By the turn of the century, a particularly aggressive form of basketball had become a source of pride and passion at women's colleges and on countless playgrounds. We are just beginning to ask what such facts say about definitions of feminism and femininity.

The general banishment of sports from cultural studies is not merely an omission of an important expressive form; leaving out sports distorts our view of culture. Sports present unique challenges to theories about cultural power and personal freedom, which cultural-studies scholars discuss using such categories as "representation," "commodification," "hegemony," and "subversion." One of the challenges is that sports differ from movies, novels, music, and television shows, all of which scholars view as wholly "constructed." Sports, however, are essentially "unscripted." They are real contests, in which many people have participated, at least at an amateur level.

This makes sports different from the other forms of entertainment, which are packaged by their creators. Knowledgeable fans can understand the games on their own terms and ignore the silly prattle of the "color" commentators. Baseball officials cannot script a "Cinderella season" on demand. What sports "mean" to their vast audiences cannot be ordained by either owners or media pundits.

The great virtue of cultural studies has been to take seriously the idea of "otherness," a concept that, in part, relates to how a group defines itself by the images that it creates of outsiders. But otherness is a slippery term. To many scholars— whose values are cosmopolitan, whose politics are progressive, and whose incomes are upper middle class—the "other" is not necessarily the same as for most Americans. Young, verbally dexterous, and entrepreneurial rappers—modern-day rebels against a narrow-minded and prissy culture—may be far less alien to hip young intellectuals than the gifted and disciplined athlete. "Otherness," for scholars, may reside even more in the polyester-clad fan who drinks with his buddies and roots for the home team, or in the middle-aged woman out bowling in her weekly league game. What, in the eyes of many in the academy, could be more unhip, uncool, "other" than American working-class pleasures?

Some scholars have suggested that, after Martin Luther King, Jr., Jackie Robinson may well have been the most influential black American of the past 50 years. Not everyone would agree with this proposition, but it is plausible, and it speaks volumes about American culture that the artistry, grace, fierce will, and embattled restraint of a baseball player could become a symbol of courage and strength to so many people. There is no getting around it: For African Americans, sports have been a fount of creativity, of art, of genius. Sports have also been a source of respect for black Americans among people of all races. Any list of the most culturally influential African Americans of the 20th century would have to include Robinson, as well as Jesse Owens, Joe Louis, Jack Johnson, Wilma Rudolph, and Muhammad Ali.

C. L. R. James was so convinced of the importance of sports that he declared cricket and soccer to be "the greatest cultural influences in 19th-century Britain." Although a bit hyperbolic, James's point is well taken. That athletics have remained so far beyond the boundary of most intellectual discourse is beyond belief. As James so brilliantly demonstrated, the study of sport can take us to the very heart of critical issues in the study of culture and society.

Capitalism, Protestantism, and the Rise of Modern Sport

ALLEN GUTTMANN

Modern sport, a ubiquitous and unique form of nonutilitarian physical contests, took shape over a period of approximately 150 years. . . . Modern sports were born in England and spread from their birthplace to the United States, to Western Europe, and to the world beyond. The origins of modern sports have been chronicled in hundreds of books and articles and particular sports have had their industrious historians, but only a handful of scholars, mostly Europeans, have attempted to *explain* the rise of modern sports. The most persuasive explanations have been stimulated by the insights of Karl Marx and Max Weber, neither of whom wrote very much about sports.

From Allen Guttmann, "Capitalism, Protestantism, and Modern Sport," in *From Ritual to Record: The Nature of Modern Sports* (New York: Columbia University Press, 1978), 57–89.

1. A Marxist Interpretation

Marxist interpretations of the rise of modern sports begin with the materialist conception of history. In the Marxist view, sports are invariably related to the organization of the modes of production. . . . Medieval sports mirrored feudal society and modern sports are the product of Liberal capitalism, that is, of bourgeois society. . . . I shall, for the rest of this section, write from their point of view. . . .

Medieval sports served the interest of the feudal nobility which was the effective ruling class of the Middle Ages. Sports were of many kinds; even the peasants had their rude games, their running, wrestling, fighting with staves, their rough-and-tumble version of what eventually became modern soccer. The sports of the peasantry tended to be those which kept them physically fit for the strenuous tasks of agricultural labor. . . .

The sports of the nobility also bore the marks of their origins in the world of work. On the one hand, there were hunting, fishing, and hawking. . . . In addition to the "field sports" which evolved directly from the world of productive work, there were sports immediately related to the realities of political power. There were tournaments and jousts, the first a miniature battle between a large number of armored horsemen, the second a combat between two mounted knights. In a world based on rule by physical force, play itself symbolized the relationship between classes. The tournament was mock warfare, sport, a demonstration of martial ability, and a subtle warning to those who might dream of a more egalitarian social order.

The class relationships of capitalist society are governed by different modes of production from those of the Middle Ages. Different social imperatives led to different kinds of sports and, more importantly, to different conceptions of the nature of sports.

The gross disparities in the distribution of wealth obtained from industrial and financial capitalism led to increased differentiation in the kinds of sports enjoyed by the rich and the poor. The lords of the land became landlords, and they laid aside the weapons of a feudal age. Sports lost their directly political function—it is impossible to crush a rebellion with a golf club—and certain sports became the expression of a leisured class. Golf and tennis continued to be the prerogative of the ruling class, but there was no longer any need to confine them to the wealthy by royal edict or by threats of dire punishment. Economic cost sufficed. . . .

In capitalist society, sports like soccer and baseball are reserved for the laboring classes. These sports have as their major goal the maintenance of a maximally productive work-force. . . . It is also necessary to provide some kind of compensation for the cramped physical conditions of assembly-line production, lest illness reduce the worker's labor power to zero.

The sports of the elite are means of socialization by which the rulers can develop those traits of character and leadership necessary for dominion at home and abroad. The sports of the proletariat, on the other hand, are vehicles for a different sort of socialization. They tend to be team sports which inculcate subordination and acceptance of authority, authority symbolized most immediately in the person of the coach. They initiate youth into the routines of the industrial system and they act to divert potentially revolutionary energies from politics.

It was inevitable, therefore, that England, the homeland of industrial capitalism, was also the birthplace of modern sports. The astonishing readiness of the English . . . to wager on horses, cocks, bears, ships, and pugilistic butchers paralleled the increased willingness to risk venture capital in the development of England's expanding industry. . . .

In the nineteenth century, public schools like Rugby, Eton, Harrow, and Winchester joined with Oxford and Cambridge to create an ethos of fair play, good sportsmanship, and business acumen. . . . From Oxford and Cambridge the energetic British soldier, civil servant, or businessman went forth to Vancouver, Madras, Cape Town, or Melbourne. And brought with him the marvels of modern sports. . . .

The receptivity of a nation to the ecological invasion of modern sport is in itself an index of that nation's industrial development. Despite the accidents of historical transmission and all the other uncertainties of such an investigation, it is nonetheless remarkable how the spread of modern sports organizations correlates with the rise of industrialism. . . .

In the early nineteenth century, modern sports were—like capitalism itself—a progressive force, more democratic than the medieval sports they superseded, but the development of industrial capitalism led to forms of exploitation which were even grimmer than those of feudalism. Sports began to play an increasingly conservative and reactionary role. One sign of this has been the intense commercialization of sports everywhere outside the orbits of the Soviet Union and the People's Republic of China. The tendency to transform human behavior into transactions of the marketplace has made sports into a matter of profit and loss. The structure of amateur sports demands on ticket sales to college games and to meets sponsored by sports organizations like the AAU. The sporting goods and recreation industries are large and complex. The structure of professional sports is openly rather than covertly commercial. Corporations and wheeler-dealer millionaires own teams and take advantage of the tax laws to profit economically while complaining all the while of the unprofitability of their franchises. . . . The result? Teenagers sell themselves into semibondage for millions of dollars, "amateur" athletes earn enough *sub rosa* to grumble about their losses when they become professionals, drug-abuse accompanies the desperate desire to share in the winner's bonus. All in all, an unattractive picture.

In addition to commercialism, Western sports have increasingly been vehicles for the inculcation of militarism, nationalism, and imperialism. In the 1920s and 1930s, the leaders of sports were ready to welcome Fascism. . . .

The final stage of historical development comes with the emergence of socialism, which eliminates the exploitative relationship between the capitalist and the worker. Since the mode of production is transformed, it is inevitable that sports too are transformed. In the Soviet Union and in the nations of Eastern Europe, sports continue to be a means of socialization. . . . In addition to their recreational function, sports are elements in national security and economic productivity. In the Soviet Union there is an entire system of physical culture, beginning with compulsatory exercises for preschool children and including organized sports within the schools and universities as well as in factories and offices. . . .

In line with this policy, Ministers of Sport and Tourism urge the people of every Communist country to maintain their physical fitness through calisthenics and sports in order to raise the level of industrial output and to contribute to the defense of socialist society. . . . A less official but scarcely less prominent goal is competition with athletes from capitalist nations in order to demonstrate the superiority of the socialist way of life.

Under socialism, sports are available as never before to both sexes, to all races, and to all classes. "Universal sport," comments a leading Polish sociologist, "requires the removal of all kinds of social divisions. . . . Sport for all assumes the abolition of every social, national, class-linked, sexual, and racial discrimination." Sports cease to be associated with nationalism and imperialism. They contribute to the creation of what Marxists refer to as "New Socialist Man." . . .

2. The Neo-Marxist Critique

The Marxist interpretation of the rise of modern sports begins in more or less objective analysis and ends in polemics. The closer the discussion comes to the present, the less disinterested, the more passionate. The Neo-Marxist critique commences with the fundamental criticism of Western sports made by Marxist scholars and extends the criticism into a wholesale indictment not simply of the alleged perversions of sport under contemporary capitalism but of the very idea of sports. . . . While American radicals such as Jack Scott and Harry Edwards expose the authoritarianism and racism of the "sports establishment" of the United States, the Neo-Marxists are still more radical. They reject not merely the abuses of the institution but the institution itself. They hold that sports in their *ideal* form—sports as described by coaches, physical educators, and administrators—are a perversion of the human spirit.

The theoretical sources of Neo-Marxism lie partly in Marx, especially in the early, more philosophical writings, and partly in Freud, whose theory of the unconscious is a necessary element in the argument that workers (or athletes) who seem satisfied with the status quo are victims of "false consciousness," i.e., they do not really understand their own interests. Institutionally, Neo-Marxism flourished in the 1920s at Frankfurt's *Institut für Sozialforschung*, where Theodor Adorno, Max Horkheimer, and Herbert Marcuse labored in fruitful collaboration. Although none of the great figures of prewar Neo-Marxism has devoted an entire book to the phenomenon of sports, passages in Adorno's *Prismen* (1955) and *Erziehung zur Mündigkeit* (1970) have been an important stimulus for Bero Rigauer, Gerhard Vinnai, Jean-Marie Brohm, and other spokesmen for the Neo-Marxist critique of sports which sprang up in Germany and France in the 1960s. . . .

Of the seven characteristics of modern sports, the Neo-Marxists are quite ready to accept the first two—secularism and equality—but specialization represents the beginnings of evil. Consider, for instance, the field-goal kicker of an American football team. Is there a more absurd symbol of specialization in modern sports? . . . Consider, similarly, the single-minded dedication necessary to become the world's best highjumper or hammer-thrower. Consider the months and the years of rigorous training, the abnegations, the self-discipline, the asceticism, the cultivated one-sidedness. . . .

Simultaneously with the advent of specialization, man becomes mechanical, the athlete is metamorphosed into a cog in the machinery of sports. . . . The final result of specialization is, paradoxically, a mechanical perfection with no human quirks to hinder replacement or substitution.

Rationalization in sports is equally incompatible with spontaneity and inventivenesss. There is no modern sport which does not have codified rules and regulations, but why shouldn't we play whatever game we want to play, in whatever manner and spirit we choose? . . .

There is more to rationalization than the coercion of the spontaneous impulses of *Homo ludens.* Bourgeois theorists boast that sports offer a model of fair play through adherence to the rules of the game. The Neo-Marxists maintain that society's rules are exploitative, grossly unfair, and immoral. . . .

Bureaucratic organization? The phrase itself reeks of inhumanity. Individual athletes become helpless pawns in the hands of a power structure composed of retired athletes, government functionaries, or wealthy businessmen with an interest in (and frequently a profit from) sports. . . .

Quantification? . . . In a capitalist society, the human personality becomes a salary, a serial number, a batting average. Despite the elegant rhetoric about playing the game rather than thinking about the numbers, the spectator's attention becomes fixed in a relentless search for quantification. There is no time left for consideration of grace, no room for fair play, no chance to respond to the kinesthetic sense of physical exuberance. . . .

The extreme form of this tendency is, as we have seen, the emphasis on records, on the most repressive form of quantification. The fetish of achievement is no longer satisfied by victory in the contest itself. . . . Almost everyone, except the handful of athletes who set the (always temporary) records, is left with a sense of frustration and failure.

To the Marxist critique of sports under capitalism and to the rejection of the distinguishing characteristics of modern sport, the followers of Adorno and Marcuse add specific charges about the insidious function of sports. The most important charge is that sports are designed as sexual sublimation. Sports release sexual impulses in the form of aggression. If these impulses had been left repressed, they might have exploded in the form of political revolution. . . .

. . . Sexual repression produces aggression and it is aggression that is directly released through sports, aggression which might otherwise destabilize the entire system of political control. . . . Sexuality appears in sports as sexuality— but only in the forms of perversion, as sadism, masochism, narcissism, and homosexuality. . . .

In short, sport is "the capitalistically distorted form of play." Sport is not an escape from the world of work but rather an exact structural and functional parallel to the world of work. Sport does not offer compensation for the frustrations of alienated labor in capitalist society; it seduces the luckless athlete and spectator into a second world of work more authoritarian and repressive and less meaningful than the economic sphere itself. Capitalist society is essentially achievement-oriented and competitive and sports present to us the purest model of that society—and that is just what is wrong with sports. What society needs is not greater pressure for more achievement, but freedom from the incessant demands for achievement, from the "inhumane absurdity . . . of the will to win." What society needs is not sports but play. . . .

3. A Critique of Critiques

. . . The Marxists and the Neo-Marxists agree that the evolution of modern sports can be explained by the development of industrial capitalism. Supported by the undeniable fact that England was the birthplace of both modern sports and the industrial revolution, the theory has a great deal to recommend it, but I am prepared to advocate an alternative explanation. It is important, however, that we know exactly why we cannot accept the Marxist and the Neo-Marxist interpretations *in toto*.

The Marxist claim that the nature of sport is determined by the means of production is not persuasive. Despite its wealth of detailed information, this analysis remains vague about the exact relationship between a given sport and a given economic system. . . . If the political purposes of the ruling class are the clue to the kinds of sports in medieval society, then we must ask why the English ruling class persistently emphasized *archery* as the preferred sport for the yeomanry. Was it sensible to encourage the disadvantaged to practice the very weapon which was to end the supremacy of the mounted knight?

More vague and less persuasive still are the arguments made about the specific kinds of sports practiced in the modern world. . . . What is the exact relationship between industrial capitalism and the game of soccer? The game itself can be traced back to medieval times. It is popular today in countries which remain almost entirely agricultural as well as in the most industrial cities of Europe. . . . If the game of soccer by its internal structure contributes to the exploitation of the working class, then it is difficult to see that the enthusiastic players of the Soviet Union are exempt from the same exploitation as those of São Paulo and Liverpool. . . .

Equally unpersuasive is the allegation that Western sports have been schools of nationalism and imperialism. . . . Considerable empirical evidence points to the conclusion that militarism and nationalism are more strongly associated with the sports of Communist than with those of non-Communist countries. . . . Nonetheless, we must not mistakenly assume that commercialism is solely responsible for all the ills of modern sports. There are many evils specific to commercialism: the neglect of sports that do not prove profitable, excessive costs which limit access to facilities that should be available to all, the mutilation of televised games and meets by advertisements, and the manipulation of scheduling in order to cash in on "prime-time" television audiences. Most of the diseases of modern sports, however, have infected all modern societies. . . .

. . . The characteristics of modern sports are essentially invariant in every modern society, whether that society is Liberal, socialist, or Communist. Differences do exist, . . . but these differences are minor in comparison with those distinguishing modern from primitive, ancient, and medieval sports. This fact seriously undercuts the Neo-Marxist critique. . . . To the thesis that modern sports alienates the athlete from himself, Hans Lenk has countered that there is less alienation in sport than elsewhere in the modern world. Sports remain a subdivision of the realm of freedom in that the athlete chooses whether or not to participate. . . . In the achievements of sports one can experience a sense of wholeness denied else-where. . . .

Unless we are to assume that men and women are so victimized by "false con-sciousness" that they have lost all awareness of their own emotions, we must pay attention to what people say about their athletic experiences. . . . [Roger] Bannister tried to portray his emotional state as he neared the end of the first four-minute mile:

> I had a moment of mixed joy and anguish, when my mind took over. It raced well ahead of my body and drew my body compellingly forward. I felt that the moment of a lifetime had come. There was no pain, only a great unity of movement and aim. The world seemed to stand still, or did not exist. . . . I felt at that moment that it was my chance to do one thing supremely well. I drove on, impelled by a combination of fear and pride. . . .

At least one aspect of the Neo-Marxist critique is susceptible to an empirical test. The argument that sports function to render apathetic and to divert from polit-ical activity can be invalidated by the evidence. Numerous studies have demon-strated a strong correlation between active and passive sports participation. Those who participate directly in sports are more likely than nonparticipants to be specta-tors, both in person and through the electronic media. Since active participants are invariably a minority of the total population of a society, this does *not* mean that most spectators are also active participants. They *are,* however, more likely to be participants than their fellow citizens who avoid the spectator's role. . . .

. . . If sport *in general* is repressive, alienating, and apathy-inducive, which is the Neo-Marxist thesis, then we must conclude that the ruling class of modern so-ciety has decided to alienate itself rather than those whom they most oppress. There is overwhelming evidence to demonstrate conclusively that managers and professionals participate in sport at higher rates than members of the working class; the educated participate at a higher rate than the uneducated; men participate more than women. These relationships hold for Communist as well as non-Com-munist countries and they hold more strongly for highly competitive than for more recreational sport. If sport is an engine of alienation, we can only conclude that the advantaged have turned it upon themselves rather than upon the disadvantaged.

4. A Weberian Interpretation

The critique of the Marxist and Neo-Marxist critiques brings us once again to the fact that there is undoubtedly some relationship between the rise of modern sports and the development of modern society. What relationship? The answer must, in-evitably, be a generalization of a rather large order. Such generalizations are cer-tainly subject to close scrutiny and hard questions about detailed interactions, but there is at least one interpretation which does not founder upon the shoals of blatant contradiction of theory by fact.

The entire discussion of the difference between primitive and modern sports was informed by . . . Max Weber's analysis of the transition from traditional to modern society. . . .

One great advantage of the Weberian model is that it enables one to see in the microcosm (modern sports) the characteristics of the macrocosm (modern society) secularism, equality, specialization, rationalism, bureaucratic organization, and quantification. These six characteristics, plus the quest for records which appears even more strikingly in sports than in the rest of the social order, are interdependent, systematically related elements of the ideal type of a modern society. They derive from the fundamental Weberian notion of the difference between the ascribed status of traditional society and the achieved status of a modern one.

Another advantage of the Weberian interpretation is that it does not reduce explanation to . . . economic determinism. . . . The trouble with economic determinism in this particular case is that the explanatory factor, industrialization, does not explain enough. Although the first nations to industrialize were, indeed, the first to develop national organizations for modern sports, other countries, like Bulgaria and Cuba, have reached impressive levels of athletic achievement without extensive industrialization (not to speak of industrial *capitalism*). Industrialism no longer seems to be the key, if it ever was.

A recent statistical study by Hilmi Ibrahim attempts to correlate national success in Olympic competition, on a points-per-capita basis, with industrialization as measured by Robert Marsh's Index of Societal Differentiation, which ranks nations by the percentage of their nonagricultural labor and the level of their energy consumption. With these admittedly imperfect variables, Ibrahim found that nations high on Marsh's scale have done well at the Olympics, but less industrialized nations have often done better, especially in recent years. Using Ibrahim's data, we can calculate the Spearman rank-order correlation for Olympic success and industrialization. If the rank order in the first category is the same as in the second, the correlation is 1.0. If the order is reversed, the correlation is -1.0. For the top five medal-winners in 1968, the correlation of athletic success to level of industrialism was actually $-.8$.

Economic factors remain, however, absolutely essential to any satisfactory interpretation of the nature of modern sport. In every modern society, for instance, the middle class is overrepresented in its active and passive participation in sports. This overrepresentation cannot be unrelated to economic factors like wealth and income and occupational category. Marxist scholarship has alerted us to this relationship. But it is also true of modern sports that the young are more intensely involved than the old, men more than women, the educated more than the uneducated, Protestants more than Catholics, and the upwardly mobile more than the downwardly mobile. Class is important, but age, sex, education, religion, and mobility are also important factors which cannot be neglected if we seek to comprehend the nature of modern sports. Once again, the common thread that ties these factors together is the emphasis on achievement. If status is awarded on the basis of age or sex or religious affiliation, then social mobility—if there is any—will hardly be a function of achievement and the educational process will not stress individual effort as the route to success. Obviously, we do *not* now and never will live entirely in what the psychologist David McClelland calls "the achievement society." Not even in the achievement-oriented world of sports are the influences of ascribed status completely absent. Coaches will always play favorites and officials will never be completely unbiased. But the Weberian model is more congruent with social reality than is any other model. The congruence is especially close in modern sports.

For a Weberian interpretation, however, the relation of sports to religion is a particularly sticky wicket. . . . We know that modern sports spread from Protestant England and that they spread more quickly to Protestant than to Catholic countries (although France is an important exception here). We also know that Protestants are more likely than Catholics to be involved in sports and also more likely to be athletes of international calibre (which is not to deny that Catholics are overrepresented in some sports, like American professional football). . . . We are tempted to seize upon Weber's own concept of "secular asceticism" and to explain disparities in the rate of participation and achievement by the self-discipline of physical training, which is therefore the equivalent of the deferred gratification necessary for the accumulation of capital and the reinvestment of profits.

Unfortunately for this line of reasoning, we quite properly think of the English and American Puritans as among the most Protestant of Protestants and we know that the Puritans were bitterly hostile to sports. . . . The Puritans of Massachusetts and Connecticut "banned dice, cards, quoits, bowls, nine-pins, 'or any other unlawful game in house, yard, garden, or backside,' [singling] out for special attention 'the Game called Shuffle Board, in howses of Common Interteinment, whereby much precious time is spent unfruitfully.'" . . .

James I of England urged in his *Book of Sports* (1618) that the people of his realm should not be disturbed "from any lawfull Recreation: Such as dauncing, either men or women, Archeries for men, leaping, vaulting or other harmless Recreation . . . ," but the Puritans of the Commonwealth had the hangman burn the king's book. Dennis Brailsford, in a history of sport and society from Queen Elizabeth to Queen Anne, sums up the Puritan view: "The Puritans saw their mission to erase all sport and play from men's lives." . . . Other historians have commented on the sudden revival of English sports in 1660 when Charles II, "the Merry Monarch," returned to restore the banished pleasures of the stage and the turf. There is ample evidence of Protestantism's reluctance, before the twentieth century, to look favorably upon modern sports.

This hostility poses one problem. Another arises when we ponder the enthusiasm for modern sports in the Soviet Union and in Japan, two nations quite definitely out of the orbit of Protestantism, nor can we explain the achievements of Polish, Cuban, Bulgarian, and Hungarian athletes by references to Protestantism any better than by assertions about the imperatives of capitalist development. The clue of this explanatory labyrinth may well be found in Robert Merton's famous essay, "Puritanism, Pietism, and Science" (1936). In this essay, Merton demonstrated that Protestants were much more likely than Roman Catholics to have been partisans of the "new science" of the seventeenth century:

> . . . It is evident that through the psychological compulsion toward certain modes of thought and conduct this value-complex made an empirically-founded science commendable rather than, as in the medieval period, reprehensible, or at best acceptable on sufferance.

The implication for our present purpose is that the correlation between Protestantism and participation in sports disguises the fundamental causal relationship between these two dependent variables and the independent variable which acts upon them. The basic explanatory factor is the scientific world-view which has since been espoused by the Japanese and by every Marxist society. . . .

In other words, the mathematical discoveries of the seventeenth century were popularized in the eighteenth century, at which time we can observe the beginnings of our modern obsession with quantification in sport. . . . The emergence of modern sports represents neither the triumph of capitalism nor the rise of Protestantism but rather the slow development of an empirical, experimental, mathematical *Weltanschauung.* England's early leadership has less to do with the Protestant ethic and the spirit of capitalism than with the intellectual revolution symbolized by the names of Isaac Newton and John Locke and institutionalized in the Royal Society . . . (1662).

This interpretation was suggested by Hans Lenk: "Achievement sport, i.e., sport whose achievements are extended beyond the here and now through measured comparisons, is closely connected to the scientific-experimental attitudes of the modern West." The suggestion was further developed by Henning Eichberg in *Der Weg des Sports in die industrielle Zivilisation.* Equipped with this insight into the role of the scientific *Weltanschauung* in the rise of modern sports, we can satisfactorily account for the post-World-War-II surge of athletic achievement in the nations of Eastern Europe, where the vestiges of premodern social organization and ideology were suddenly, even ruthlessly, challenged by a relentlessly modern attitude.

To the degree that religious tradition induces a nonscientific or even an antiscientific orientation, the transition from folk-games to modern sports will be inhibited and retarded, but the reason for this inhibition and retardation has less to do with the positive in religious faith than with the negative assessment of modern science. This can be seen in the case of Canadian sport, where the French population has been drastically underrepresented. . . . In France itself, modern sports appeared early and developed fairly quickly. . . . Catholicism seems to have encouraged a kind of parochial antagonism to the modern world, a negativism which appears in the statistics on sports participation. Although roughly 30 percent of Canada is ethnically French, this group has provided only 8.1 percent of the 4,297 athletes representing Canada at the Commonwealth, Pan-American, and Olympic games. Since we know that economic factors play an important role in rates of participation in modern sports, we cannot simply say that religion alone is responsible for this striking disparity, but it would be a mistake to discount the powerful influence of the Catholic Church in Quebec. . . .

Henning Eichberg has pointed to the importance of a mathematical-empirical world-view, but he has also, less persuasively, attempted to find a correlation between the rise of modern sports and the Romantic Revolution which swept over much of Europe and America at the end of the eighteenth and the beginning of the nineteenth centuries. It is, in my view, more probable that Romanticism, with its pervasive antiscientific bias, encouraged the survival of pre-modern sports like hunting and fishing and hindered the emergence of modern sports. . . .

. . . In our search for the roots of modern sport, we have moved in an explanatory regression from abstractions like the Industrial Revolution and the Reformation to a still more abstract formulation—the scientific world-view. And now we confront a paradox. The quest for records is in itself one of the most remarkable forms of the Faustian drive, one of the most extraordinary manifestations of the Romantic pursuit of the unattainable. Sports themselves, originating in the spontaneous expression of physical energy, have their source in the irrational. We are all familiar with the frenzy of an athletic encounter, with the atavistic enthusiasm of football fans, with the naked aggression of the boxer's punch, with the inexplicable determination of the entranced runner who staggers on despite the spasms of his tortured body. Paradox, yes. Contradiction, no. Sports are an alternative to and, simultaneously, a reflection of the modern age. They have their roots in the dark soil of our instinctive lives, but the form they take is that dictated by modern society. Like the technological miracle of Apollo XI's voyage to the moon, they are the rationalization of the Romantic.

Urbanization and the Rise of Sport

STEPHEN HARDY

. . . Historians have recognized the importance of the city as the cradle of modern sport, and have essentially agreed that America's transition from a rural-agricultural to an urban-industrial nation played a pivotal role in the expansion of activities such as we have described for Boston. Not only have these historians viewed the city as the fountainhead for the flood of pastimes that swept the country, they have also suggested that elements of a new urban order *caused* the deluge. In brief, they have argued that recreation and sport were both reactions to negative features of city life and products of the city's technological, economic, and social advantages.

An article written in 1917 attempted to link the rise of sports with the closing of the frontier. As the freelands were filled, the author argued, Americans searched for substitute "safety valves" that might vent the pressures generated in a modern industrial society. Urban congestion "stimulated the need" for outlets such as the pioneer life had once provided. As Foster Rhea Dulles later concluded, sports offered "a new outlet for an inherently restless people" who suffered under "the restrictions of urban living." The simple diversions of rural Americans could not adapt to the urban environment. The countryside was inaccessible to most city dwellers. But before succumbing to what John Higham called "the frustrations, the routine, and the sheer dullness of an urban-industrial culture," Americans discovered and nurtured games and pastimes that let off steam and at the same time strengthened their bodies and spirits for another round of city life.

These insights are essentially antiurban; they concentrate on the negative features of urban living, such as congestion or the sedentary routines of work and free time. By themselves, they do not explain the material forces that enabled new

From Stephen Hardy, "The City and the Rise of Sport," in *How Boston Played: Sport, Recreation, and Community, 1865–1915* (Boston: Northeastern University Press, 1982), 14–20.

leisure pursuits to develop and thrive. In considering this question, a number of historians have cast the city in a more positive light. In this view, the heightened interest in parks, playgrounds, baseball, and bicycles was not merely a reaction to the oppression of the modern city; it was a product of an environment that nurtured industry, innovation, and opportunity.

As the principal architect of this argument notes, the city's contributions were multiple. Improved transportation increased the scope of competition and enabled more residents to participate or watch. A higher standard of living, more free time, and more discretionary income improved the recreation opportunities of an ever wider segment of the urban population. Swifter, cheaper modes of communication like the telegraph and the penny press helped to whip up enthusiasm for sports and games. Larger, more concentrated populations alone meant a greater market of consumers for sporting equipment, entertainment, and information.

The two interpretations are not mutually exclusive. They can be blended to present a general outline that links the rise of recreation and sports to the modern urban complex. Simplified, it suggests that as cities grew in size, population, and density, their inhabitants felt a longing for the outdoor life and recreational pastimes that were being swallowed up by the stultifying regime of the machine age. Just as things appeared bleakest, however, urban economic, technological, and demographic conditions formed the foundation for an arena of new leisure forms, adapted to the pace and lifestyle of America's cities.

These themes have carried us some distance in understanding the development of American recreation and sports. At the same time, though, it is clear that the arguments contain some serious limitations. For one, they often suggest that mankind possesses what Lucas and Smith call an "unquenchable play instinct . . . universal and timeless." But as one critic of this notion contends, "labelling a behavior as the product of an instinct is not the same as explaining that behavior." Indeed, the idea that a specific sport like football or baseball grew as a result of some inborn need for play seems somehow overly simplistic. There is an additional problem about the idea that sports fulfilled a natural urge or served as a social safety valve. The middle and upper classes, who dominated these activities throughout the nineteenth century, were the classes with greatest access to the pure outdoor life itself, via country homes or vacations to the shore or the mountains. Why, then, would social elites have experienced a need for modern sports? At the same time, why was it inevitable that improved transportation and communication, or increased leisure time and income, would result in a proliferation of something like athletic clubs or schoolboy sports?

Questions like these have prompted historians to reexamine the relationship between the modern city and its recreational life. The results have been thoughtful and imaginative. For instance, a recent book on the rise of "modern city culture" maintains that baseball helped to fuse the fragmented groups which had divided cities by wealth, occupation, language, and ancestry. First, baseball offered all classes and ethnic groups a sense of common history in the form of team records and statistics; people who were otherwise alienated could communicate through the language of box scores and batting averages. Second, baseball taught all residents the proper use of rules and regulations to get ahead; in business as in baseball one could stretch the rules as long as he didn't break them. It was winning that counted most. Finally, a professional ball game demonstrated the importance of meeting exact performance standards; the properly executed work skill, like the perfectly placed squeeze bunt, was the individual's contribution to group performance.

But did the lessons in baseball reach all the people? Perhaps not. A detailed study of professional baseball during the late nineteenth and early twentieth centuries underscores the fact that baseball was limited in the degree to which it actually integrated the public. Admission prices and Sunday laws kept the ball park beyond the reach of most working-class urbanites. Because of this, baseball remained a middle-class sport. Nonetheless, much of its popularity lay in the belief, however false, that it was democratic and integrative.

Other recent studies suggest other reasons for the increase in urban participants and spectators. Sports clubs were an important source of identity in a dense and diversified population. Similarly, teams and heroes could act as symbolic representatives who acted out the struggle of life on behalf of a particular group or even the city as a whole. James B. Connolly's Olympic victory was thus a victory for all Bostonians, and more so for all Irish Bostonians. Along different lines, new forms of leisure sometimes appeared to offer temporary escape from the noise, congested, and strain of downtown. (But there were ironies to this. Some sources of escape, like Coney Island, presented their patrons with a more frantic, noisier din than they had left!) Finally, many team sports promised to instill values of self-discipline, character, and sacrifice for the good of the group. Many reformers jumped at the chance to organize the games of immigrant children; they would learn on the playground what they didn't get in the classroom.

Boston, like most large cities in the United States, grew and changed rapidly during the late nineteenth and early twentieth centuries. As a modern city, Boston experienced more than increased population, cramped housing, and attendant "social" problems. It became, in the words of Ralph Turner, "a developing structure of thought and behaviour, that effectively altered and transformed traditional patterns of social life." This dynamic process was manifested in a number of concrete ways, such as "in new social services, in new amusements . . . in new standards of consumption, in new relationships of the sexes and the members of families," and in new circumstances affecting health, disease, and death. . . .

Development and change in a city like Boston can be analyzed from three interrelated "perspectives," which were first outlined by Louis Wirth. First, the city can be viewed as a *physical structure*. One can examine the changing functions and forms of various sections of the city, changes brought on by population flow, shifts in technology and economy, uncontrolled land development, or urban planning. In other words, what caused the evolution of specialized business districts, shopping districts, slums, recreation areas, and suburbs?

Next, the city can be considered as a *social organization*. One can focus on the dynamics of its social groups, social institutions, and social relationships. Of interest are the sharper distinctions between income and status groups, the change from traditional social ties like kinship or neighborhood to modern ties like political parties, and finally the rise of specialized agencies to control education, economic production, and recreation.

Wirth's third perspective treats the city as a *state of mind,* or value system, and examines the emotional adjustments of individuals and groups to city life, or the effects of changing social relationships on the urban personality. Here one might consider the ideologies and attitudes that have developed in response to perceptions of the city—how the city affects man's way of perceiving himself and others. Man, in turn, gives the city a personality, as "Big Apple," "jungle," or both.

The first perspective examines the city's anatomy, the second its physiology, and the third, its soul. The distinctions between the groupings are seldom clear-cut; indeed, they are often interrelated. Oscar Handlin demonstrates, for instance, that Irish immigration before the Civil War radically altered Boston's physical structure. The North End became the Irish ghetto, as older residents fled to other residential districts. At the same time, it affected Boston's social relationships and its citizens' beliefs that their city was totally "Yankee."

Sports too can be analyzed as physical structures, social organizations, or states of mind. As physical structures, they transcend the game to include the facilities and environments upon which their existence depends. As social organizations, they are filled with numerous and changing forms of social groups, social behavior, social relationships, and social order. Some are unique to sport, some are reflections of their parent cultures and societies, some are mixtures. Finally, like the city, sport or recreation may be a state of mind, a reified idea, a concept treated as if it were a material thing. In this perspective, advocates have ballyhooed certain pastimes like baseball as panaceas for society's psychic and physical ills. Opponents have condemned other sports as contributors to social decay.

It is clear that as physical structure, social organization, and state of mind, recreation and sport have been integral parts of the process of urban growth. For instance, within the last decade, new civic centers and arenas—physical structures—have often been a central element both in the revitalization of downtown areas and in the improvement of a city's image, its state of mind. In 1972, Indianapolis Mayor Richard Lugar offered great hope for the remedial effects of the new Market Square project: "It will offer new hope for the heart of the city. Sports, along with the theater and the arts, must be a focal point for the renewal of the city." Similarly, Robert Abrams, borough president of the Bronx, defended Yankee Stadium's costly renovation during the city's economic crisis by emphasizing that "Yankee Stadium is part of the chemistry of life in this town." At the same time, however, critics have questioned whether the benefits of arenas accrue less to the city and its inhabitants than to the owners of the sports teams involved.

If the sport facility can alter a city, the opposite can be equally true, with devastating effect. Racial migrations and their ensuing social tensions have transformed recreation areas like the South Side beaches of Chicago or Carson Beach in Boston into powder kegs of violence that erupt at the slightest spark, as happened in Chicago during the summer of 1919. Thus, urban social processes have the power to convert sporting areas, designed as asylums of leisure and relaxation, into symbols of struggles over "turf" or, worse, into bloody fields of racial strife.

As a social organization, sport can affect the mechanisms of social status in the city. This holds true particularly in the case of elite sporting club membership.

As one study concludes, "in cities, people rate their fellow citizens by superficial evidence and by symbols such as residential address, occupational titles, and club memberships." Research in Kansas City has shown that the clearest index of that city's upper class is membership in an elite country club like the First Jackson or the Missoukana. In turn, the location of the country club can become the most desirable area for upper-class residence.

Along related lines, one baseball historian has uncovered the close relationships between politicians, trolley companies, real estate speculation, and ball clubs. Local bosses were often either club owners or close associates. They offered the teams preferential treatment on matters like municipal services or taxation; they provided inside information on potential developments in real estate or transportation. In return the politicians "used the franchise as a source of honest graft and patronage, as an inducement to encourage people to travel on the traction routes they operated, and to improve their public image." In other words, baseball helped to cement the structures of urban political power, a fact not overlooked by Boss Tweed in New York or Boss Cox of Cincinnati.

Finally, much of the rationale of organized sport, its state of mind or value system, grew as a reaction to the physical environment of the city and to perceptions of suffering and degradation caused by cramped housing and industrial pollution. At the same time, public parks, which were a product of this reaction, altered the physical development of the city by countering unchecked urban growth, by redirecting transportation lines, and by deflecting the patterns of residential land speculation.

While the "perspectives" of the city or sport as physical structures, social organizations, and value systems can help us to make sense of broad relationships, it is necessary that we consider the precise circumstances, events, and personalities which affected them in Boston. If, through analyzing how Boston played, we can bring to life some fragments of her sporting past, and organize them in a framework of change, perhaps we can also reveal something about the meaning of life in the city.

☒ F U R T H E R   R E A D I N G

Larry Gerlach, "Not Quite Ready for Prime Time: Baseball History, 1983–1993," *Journal of Sport History* 21 (Summer 1994), 103–37

Elliott Gorn and Warren Goldstein, *A Brief History of American Sports* (1993)

Allen Guttmann, *From Ritual to Record: The Nature of Modern Sports* (1978)

Allen Guttmann, *Sports Spectators* (1986)

Allen Guttmann, *A Whole New Ball Game: An Interpretation of American Sports* (1988)

Stephen Hardy, "The City and the Rise of American Sport, 1820–1920," *Exercise and Sports Sciences Reviews* 9 (1981), 183–229

Roberta J. Park, "A Decade of the Body: Researching and Writing About the History of Health, Fitness, Exercise and Sport, 1983–1993," *Journal of Sport History* 21 (Spring 1994), 59–82

Benjamin G. Rader, *American Sports: From the Age of Folk Games to the Age of Televised Sports*, 3rd ed. (1995)

Steven A. Riess, *City Games: The Evolution of American Urban Society and the Rise of Sports* (1989)
Steven A. Riess, "From Pitch to Putt: Sport and Class in Anglo-American Sport," *Journal of Sport History* 21 (Summer 1994), 138–84
Jeffrey Sammons, " 'Race' and Sport: A Critical, Historical Examination," *Journal of Sport History* 21 (Fall 1994), 203–78
Patricia Vertinsky, "Gender Relations, Women's History, and Sport History: A Decade of Changing Enquiry, 1983–1993," *Journal of Sport History* 21 (Spring 1994), 1–24

Sport in Colonial America

Sporting activities in what became the United States were first played by American Indians for religious, medicinal, and commercial purposes (gambling). However, in contrast to what occurred in Canada, native sports had little impact on the pastimes of overseas immigrants. How then did sport develop in colonial America? What was the impact of the settlers' culture (athletic traditions, morality, and religious customs) and the problems of living in a new and often dangerous environment? How did the character of their communities (Puritan Boston vs. Anglican Jamestown) shape their experience as it relates to sport? The colonists' favorite sports were drawn mainly from the frontier and rural character of their surroundings, although colonial villages, towns, and cities provided the primary sites for major sporting contests, for the first athletic clubs, and for the rudimentary commercialization of sport.

Seventeenth-century Puritans permitted lawful sports that were enjoyed in moderation and were recreational (i.e., improved participants' capabilities to perform their worldly duties). They barred blood sports, gambling activities, Sunday amusements, and any pleasures identified with Catholic or pagan rituals. However, as New England's population became more mixed in the eighteenth century and as its social structure widened, it became harder to limit sport. In the Anglican South, on the other hand, a livelier English sporting culture was maintained. Gambling sports like cockfighting and especially horse racing were extremely popular and reflected the manliness of the participants and spectators. Horse racing in the late seventeenth century, which consisted of impromptu short contests, reflected the elevated status of the great tobacco planters who dominated the land. By the middle of the eighteenth century, the gentry began importing thoroughbreds that could race for miles. Scheduled races supervised by elite jockey clubs were held at enclosed tracks in cities like Charlestown, Annapolis, and Williamsburg.

DOCUMENTS

The documents illuminate several perspectives on colonial sports and record evidence of the premodern sport enjoyed by early Americans. The first document, generally known as King James I's *Book of Sports* (1618), was issued by the Crown as a political ploy. James sought to increase his popularity with the masses by sustaining traditional pastimes in the face of opposition by Puritan magistrates, while in the meantime, he wanted to undermine their growing power. The second document is a law passed by the General Court of Massachusetts on October 19, 1658, to restrict Sunday recreations. The third document reports the agreements made in preparation for a late seventeenth-century Virginia horse race and the court case that followed when one participant did not complete the contract. Horse racing agreements were considered legally binding contracts. The fourth document is a review of Virginia racing in 1772 by a British traveler. By this time the elite of America had been racing thoroughbreds for over a generation at formal racetracks. The fifth document is the report of a cockfight attended by Elkanah Watson in 1787 shortly after he had purchased a 640-acre plantation in Virginia. The final document is an account by George Catlin, the noted painter and ethnographer of American Indians, of a lacrosse match he witnessed being played among the Choctaws during the 1830s. Such matches had been played well before the coming of Europeans, making American Indians the first people in what is now the United States to play team ball sports.

King James I Identifies Lawful Sports in England, 1618

"Whereas upon our returne the last yere out of Scotland, we did publish our Pleasure touching the recreations of Our people in those parts under Our hand. For some causes Us thereunto mooving, Wee have thought good to command these Our Directions then given in Lancashire with a few words thereunto added, and most appliable to these parts of Our Realmes, to bee published to all Our Subjects.

'Whereas wee did justly in Our Progresse through Lancashire, rebuke some Puritanes and precise people, and tooke order that the like unlawfull carridge should not bee used by any of them hereafter, in the prohibiting and unlawfull punishing of Our good people for using their lawful recreations, and honest exercises, after the afternoone Sermon or Service: Wee now finde that two sorts of people, wherewith that countrey is much infected (Wee meane Papists and Puritanes), have maliciously traduced and calumniated those Our just and honourable proceedings. And, therefore, lest Our reputation might, upon the one side (though innocently), have some aspersion layd upon it, and that, upon the other part, Our good people in that Countrey be misled by the mistaking and misinterpretation of Our meaning: We have, therefore, thought good hereby to cleare and make Our pleasure to be manifested to all Our good People in those parts.

'It is true that at Our first entry to this Crowne, and Kingdome, We were informed, and that too truely, that Our County of Lancashire abounded more in Popish Recusants than any County of England, and thus hath still continued since, to Our great regreet, with little amendment, save that now of late, in Our last riding through Our said County, Wee find both by the report of the Judges, that there is some amendment now daily beginning, which is no small contentment to Us.

'The report of this growing amendment amongst them, made Us the more sorry, when with Our own eares We heard the general complaint of Our people,

From King James I, " 'The Kinges' Majesties Declaration Concerning Lawfull Sports," in *The King's Book of Sports,* ed. L. A. Govett (London: Elliott Stock, 1890).

that they were debarred from all lawful Recreation, and exercise upon the Sundayes afternoone, after the ending of all Divine Service, which cannot but produce two evils: The one, the hindering of the conversion of many, whom their Priests will take occasion hereby to vexe, persuading that no honest mirth or recreation is lawful or tolerable in Our Religion, which cannot but breed a great discontentment in Our people's hearts, especially of such as are, peradventure, upon the point of turning; The other inconvenience is, that this prohibition barreth the common and meaner sort of people from using such exercises as may make their bodies more able for warre, when Wee, or Our Successors, shall have occasion to use them. And, in place thereof, sets up filthy tiplings and drunkennesse, and breeds a number of idle and discontented speeches in their Ale houses, For when shall the common people have leave to exercise, if not upon the Sundays and holy daies, seeing they must apply their labour, and win their living in all working daies?

'Our expresse pleasure therefore is, that the lawes of Our Kingdome, and Canons of Our Church be as well observed in that Countie, as in all other places of this Our Kingdome. And on the other part, that no lawfull Recreation shall bee barred to Our good People, which shall not tend to the breach of our aforesayd Lawes, and Canons of our Church: which, to expresse more particularly, Our pleasure is, That the Bishop, and all other inferiour Churchmen, and Churchwardens, shall, for their part, bee carefull and diligent, both to instruct the ignorant, and convince and reforme them that are misled in Religion, presenting them that will not conform themselves, but obstinately stand out, to our Judges and Justices, Whom We likewise command to put the Law in due execution against them.

'Our pleasure therefore is, That the Bishop of that Diocesse take the like straight order with all the Puritanes and Precisians within the same, either constraining them to conform themselves, or to leave the County according to the Lawes of Our Kingdome, and Canons of our Church, and so to strike equally on both hands, against the contemners of our Authority, and adversaries of Our Church. And as for Our good people's lawfull Recreation, Our pleasure likewise is, Our good people be not disturbed, . . . or discouraged from any lawfull recreation, Such as dancing, . . . Archery, . . . leaping, vaulting, or any other such harmlesse Recreation, nor from having of May Games, Whitson Ales, and Morrisdances, and the setting up of Maypoles, and other sports therewith used, so as the same be had in due and convenient time, without impediment or neglect of Divine Service: . . . But withall we doe here account still as prohibited all unlawfull games to bee used upon Sundayes onely, as Beare and Bullbaitings, Interludes, and at all times, in the meaner sort of people, by Law prohibited, Bowling: And likewise we barre from this benefite and liberty, all such knowne Recusants, either men or women, as will abstaine from comming to Church or Divine Service, that will not first come to the Church and serve God: Prohibiting, in like sort, the said Recreations to any that, though conform in Religion, are not present in the Church at the Service of God, before their going to the said Recreations.

'Our pleasure likewise is That they to whom it belongeth in Office, shall present and sharpely punish all such as in abuse of this Our liberty, will use these exercises before the ends of all Divine Services for that day. And we likewise straightly command, that every person shall resort to his owne Parish Church to hear Divine Service, and each Parish by itselfe to use the said Recreation after Divine Service.

'Prohibiting likewise any offensive weapons to bee carried or used in the said times of Recreations, And Our pleasure is That this, Our Declaration, shall bee published by order from the Bishop of the Diocesse, through all the Parish Churches, and that both Our Judges of Our Circuit, and Our Judges of Our Peace be informed thereof.

Restrictive Sabbath Statutes of Colonial Massachusetts, 1658

Whereas by too sad experience it is observed, the sunn being sett, both euery Saturday & on the Lords day, young people & others take liberty to walke & sporte themselves in the streets or feilds in the seuerall tounes of this jurisdiction, to the dishonor of God and the disturbance of others in theire religious excercises, and too frequently repajre to publicque houses of enterajnement, & there sitt drincking, all which tends, not only to the hindering of due preparation for the Saboath, but asmuch as in them ljes renders the ordinances of God altogether vnprofitable, & threatnes rooting out of the power of godljnes, and procuring the wrath & judgments of God vpon vs and our posteritje, for the prevention whereof itt is ordered by this Courte & the authoritje thereof, that if any person or persons henceforth, either on the Saturday night or Lords day night after the sunne is sett, shallbe found sporting in the streets or feilds of any toune in this jurisdiction, drincking, or being in any house of entertajnement, (vnlesse straingers or sojourners, as in theire lodgings,) & cannot giue a sattisfactory reason to such magistrate or comissioner in ye seuerall tounes as shall haue the cognizance thereof, euery such person so found, complajned of, & prooved transgressing shall pay fiue shillings for euery such transgression, or suffer corporall punishment, as authoritje aforesajd shall determine.

A Henrico County, Virginia, Horse Race Contract, 1698

At a Court held at Varina, Ap'l 1st, 1698, Richard Ward complains against John Stewart, Jun'r, in a plea of debt for that, that is to say the s'd plaintiff & defendant did on the 12th day of June Last, covenant and agree in the following words:

"It is Covenspied and agreed this 12th day of June, 1697, Between Mr. Richard Ward of the one part, in Henrico Co'ty, & John Steward, Jun'r, of ye

From Nathaniel B. Shurtleff, ed., *Records of the Governor and the Company of the Massachusetts Bay,* vol. 4, bk. 1 (Boston: William White Press, 1853), 347.

From Henrico County Records, 1677–99, in William C. Stanard, "Racing in Colonial Virginia," *Virginia Magazine of History and Biography* 2 (1894–1895): 296–98.

other part in ye same Co'ty: Witnesseth, that the aforesaid Mr. Richard Ward doth hereby covenant, promise & agree to run a mare named Bony, belonging to Thomas Jefferson, Jun'r [Grandfather of the President], ag'st a horse now belonging to Mr. John Hardiman, named Watt, the said horse & mare to Run at the race-place commonly called ye Ware, to run one quarter of a mile. And ye said John Steward, Jun'r, doth hereby Coven't & agree to Run a horse now belonging to Mr. Jno. Hardiman, of Cha: City Co'ty, the said horse named Watt to Run ag'st a mare belonging to Thomas Jefferson, Jun'r, named Bony. The s'd horse to give the s'd mare five horse Lengths, Vizt: that is to say ten yards. And it is further agreed upon by the parties above s'd, that the s'd horse & mare are to Run on the first day of July next Ensuing the date hereof. And it is further agreed upon by the parties above s'd that if the s'd mare doth come within five Lengths of the fores'd Horse, the fores'd John Steward to pay unto Mr. Rich'd Ward the sum of five pounds Sterling on Demand, & the s'd Richard Ward doth oblige himself that if the afores'd horse doth come before s'd mare five Lengths, then to pay unto the afores'd John Steward, Jun'r, the sum of six pounds Sterling on Demand. It is further agreed by the p'ties aforesaid, that there be fair Rideing & the Riders to weigh about one-hundred & thirty Weight, to the true p'formance of all & singular the p'misses, the p'ties above s'd have hereunto set their hands the day and year above written."

"And the plaintiff in fact saith, That pursuant to the afores'd agreement, The s'd horse & mare . . . were by the s'd pl't'f & Def'd't brought upon the afores'd Ground to Run upon the first day of July, and the word being given by the person who was appointed to start the s'd horse & mare, The afores'd mare, with her Rider who weighed about one hundred & thirty weight, Did Leap off, and out running the afores'd horse came in first between the poles which were placed at the comeing in of the s'd Race, commonly called the Ware, one quarter of a mile distance from the starting place appointed; and was by the s'd mare, with her Rider of about one hund'd & thirty weight as afores'd, fairly Run.

"Wherefore the afores'd pl't'f saith that the afores'd Mare, Bony, with fair Running & Rideing, according to agreement, Did beat the s'd horse Watt, and that according to the true meaning of the s'd agreem't he, the s'd plaintiff, hath Woon the wager, to-witt: the sum of five pounds sterling of the afores'd John Steward. And thereupon he brings suit ag'st the afores'd John Steward, Jun'r, & demands Judgem't for the afores'd sum of five p'ds Sterl., with Co'ts, &c. To which the Defend't, by Mr. Bartholomew Fowler, his attorney, appears and upon oyer of the plaintiff declaracon pleads that he oweth nothing by the covenants, &c., and thereof puts himself upon ye country & ye pl't'f likewise.

"Whereupon, it is ordered that a Jury be impanelled & sworn to try the issue. . . .

"Who Returned this Verdict: We find for the plaintiff. Upon the motion of the plaintiffs' attorney the s'd Verdict is Recorded, & Judgment is awarded the s'd pl't'f against the Def'd't for the sum of five pounds Sterling, to be p'd with Costs, als Ex'o."

An Englishman's Positive Impressions of Virginia Racing, 1772

"There are races at Williamsburg twice a year; that is, every spring and fall, or autumn. Adjoining to the town is a very excellent course, for either two, three, or four mile heats. Their purses are generally raised by subscription, and are gained by the horse that wins two four-mile heats out of three; they amount to an hundred pounds each for the first days runing, and fifty pounds each every day after; the races commonly continueing for a week. There are also matches and sweepstakes very often, for considerable sums. Besides these at Williamsburg, there are races established annually, almost at every town and considerable place in Virginia; and frequent matches, on which large sums of money depend; the inhabitants, almost to a man, being quite devoted to the division of horse-racing.

Very capital horses are started here, such as would make no despicable figure at Newmarket; nor is their speed, bottom, or blood inferior to there appearance; the gentlemen of Virginia sparring no pains, trouble or expence in importing the best stock, and improving the excellence of the breed by proper and judicious crossing.

Indeed, nothing can be more elegant and beautiful than the horses had here, either for the turf, the field, the road, or the coach; and they have always fine, long, full, flowing tails; but their carriage horses seldom are possessed of that weight and power, which distinguish those of the same kind in England.

Their stock is from old Cade, old Crab, old Partner, Regulus, Babraham, Bosphorus, Devonshire Childers, the Cullen Arabian, &c., in England; and a horse from Arabia, which was imported into America, and is now in existance.

In the southern part of the colony, and in North Carolina, they are much attached to *quarter-racing,* which is always a match between two horses, to run one quarter of a mile straight out, being merely an exertion of speed; and they have a breed that perform it with astonishing velocity, beating every other for that distance, with great ease; but they have no bottom. However, I am confident that there is not a horse in England, nor perhaps the whole world, that can excel them in rapid speed: and these likewise make excellent saddle-horses for the road. The Virginians, of all ranks and denominations, are excessively fond of horses, and especially those of the race breed. The gentlemen of fortune expend great sums on their race studs, generally keeping handsome carriages, and several elegant sets of horses, as well as others for the race and road; even the most indigent person has his saddlehorse, which he rides to every place, and on every occasion; for in this country nobody walks on foot the smallest distance, except when hunting; indeed a man will frequently go five miles to catch a horse to ride only one mile upon afterwards. In short, their horses are their pleasure and their pride.

From John F. D. Smyth, *A Tour in the United States of America* (London: G. Robinson, 1784), as quoted in William C. Stanard, "Racing in Colonial Virginia," *Virginia Magazine of History and Biography* 2 (1894–1895): 300–301.

Elkanah Watson's Misgivings on Cockfighting, 1787

In one of these excursions, I accompanied a prominent planter at his urgent solicitation, to attend a cock-fight in Hampton County, Virginia, a distance of twenty miles. We reached the ground about ten o'clock the next morning. The roads, as we approached the scene, were alive with carriages, horses, and pedestrians, black and white, hastening to the point of attraction. Several houses formed a spacious square, in the centre of which was arranged a large cock-pit; surrounded by many genteel people, promiscuously mingled with the vulgar and debased. Exceedingly beautiful cocks were produced, armed with long, sharp, steel-pointed gaffs, which were firmly attached to their natural spurs.

The moment the birds were dropped, bets ran high. The little heroes appeared trained to the business, and not the least disconcerted by the crowd or shouting. They stepped about with great apparent pride and dignity; advancing nearer and nearer, they flew upon each other at the same instant with a rude shock, the cruel and fatals gafts being driven into their bodies, and at times, directly through their heads. Frequently one, or both, were struck dead at the first blow, but they often fought after being repeatedly pierced, as long as they were able to crawl, and in the agonies of death would often make abortive efforts to raise their heads and strike their antagonists. I soon sickened at this barbarous sport, and retired under the shade of a wide-spread willow, where I was much better entertained in witnessing a voluntary fight between a wasp and spider.

In viewing the crowd, I was deeply astonished to find men of character and intelligence giving their countenance to an amusement so frivolous and scandalous, so abhorrent to every feeling of humanity, and so injurious in its moral influence, by the inculcation of habits of gambling and drinking, in the waste of time, and often in the issues of fighting and duelling.

George Catlin Describes a Choctaw Lacrosse Match, c. 1830s

"Monday afternoon at three, o'clock, I rode out with Lieutenants S. and M., to a very pretty prairie, about six miles distant, to the ball-play-ground of the Choctaws, where we found several thousand Indians encamped. There were two points of timber about half a mile apart, in which the two parties for the play, with their respective families and friends, were encamped; and lying between them, the prairie on which the game was to be played. . . . Each party had their goal made with two upright posts, about 25 feet high and six feet apart, set firm in the ground, with a pole across at the top. These goals were about forty or fifty rods apart; and at a point just half way between, was another small stake, driven down, where the

From Elkanah Watson, *Men and Times of the Revolution; or Memoirs of Elkanah Watson*, ed. Winslow C. Watson (New York: Dana and Co., 1856), 261–62.

From George Catlin, *Letters and Notes on the Manners, Customs, and Conditions of the North American Indians*, vol. 2 (London: David Bogue, 1844), 124–26.

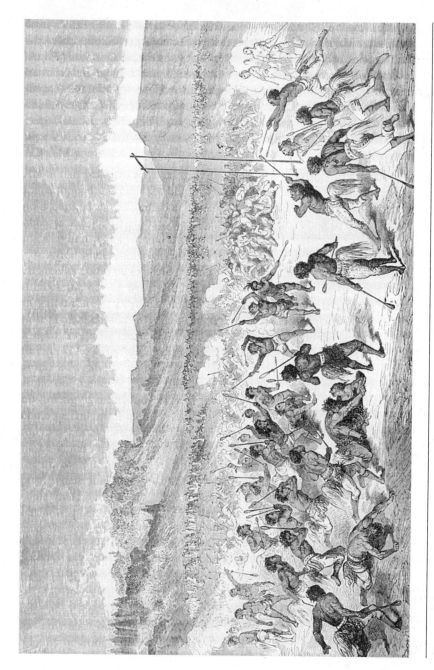

Choctaw lacrosse. This ball-and-stick game had some forty variations. Note the multitude of participants. (Stock Montage, Inc.)

ball was to be thrown up at the firing of a gun, to be struggled for by the players. All this preparation was made by some old men, who were, it seems, selected to be the judges of the play, who drew a line from one bye to the other; to which directly came from the woods, on both sides, a great concourse of women and old men, boys and girls, and dogs and horses, where bets were to be made on the play. The betting was all done across this line, and seemed to be chiefly left to the women, who seemed to have martialled out a little of everything that their houses and fields possessed. Goods and chattels—knives—dresses—blankets—pots and kettles—dogs and horses, and guns; and all were placed in the possession of *stake-holders,* who sat by them, and watched them on the ground all night, preparatory to the play.

The sticks with which this tribe play, are bent into an oblong hoop at the end, with a sort of slight web of small thongs tied across, to prevent the ball from passing through. The players hold one of these in each hand, and by leaping into the air, they catch the ball between the two nettings and throw it, without being allowed to strike it, or catch it in their hands. . . .

. . . In every ballplay of these people, it is a rule of the play, that no man shall wear moccasins on his feet, or any other dress than his breech-cloth around his waist, with a beautiful bead belt, and a "tail," made of white horsehair or quills, and a "*mane*" on the neck, of horsehair dyed of various colours.

This game had been arranged and "made up," three or four months before the parties met to play it, and in the following manner:—The two champions who led the two parties, and had the alternate choosing of the players through the whole tribe, sent runners, with the ball-sticks most fantastically ornamented with ribbons and red paint, to be touched by each one of the chosen players; who thereby agreed to be on the spot at the appointed time and ready for the play. The ground having been all prepared and preliminaries of the game all settled, and the bettings all made, and goods all "staked," night came on without the appearance of any players on the ground. But soon after dark, a procession of lighted flambeaux was seen coming from each encampment, to the ground where the players assembled around their respective byes; and at the beat of the drums and chaunts of the women, each party of players commenced the "ball-play dance." Each party danced for a quarter of an hour around their respective byes, in their ball-play dress; rattling their ball-sticks together in the most violent manner, and all singing as loud as they could raise their voices; whilst the women of each party, who had their goods at stake, formed into two rows on the line between the two parties of players, and danced also, in an uniform step, and all their voices joined in chaunts to the Great Spirit; in which they were soliciting his favour in deciding the game to their advantage; and also encouraging the players to exert every power they possessed, in the struggle that was to ensue. In the mean time, four old *medicine-men,* who were to have the starting of the ball, and who were to be judges of the play, were seated at the point where the ball was to be started; and busily smoking to the Great Spirit for their success in judging rightly, and impartially, between the parties in so important an affair.

This dance was one of the most picturesque scenes imaginable, and was repeated at intervals of every half hour during the night, and exactly in the same manner; so that the players were certainly awake all the night, and arranged in their appropriate dress, prepared for the play which was to commence at nine o'clock the next morning. In the morning, at the hour, the two parties and all their friends, were drawn out and over the ground; when at length the game commenced, by the judges throwing up the ball at the firing of a gun; when an instant struggle ensued between the players, who were some six or seven hundred in numbers, and were mutually endeavoring to catch the ball in their sticks, and throw it home and between their respective stakes; which, whenever successfully done, counts one for game. In this game every player was dressed alike, that is, *divested* of all dress, except the girdle and the tail, which I have before described; and in these desperate struggles for the ball, when it is *up* (where hundreds are running together and leaping, actually over each other's heads, and darting between their adversaries' legs, tripping and throwing, and foiling each other in every possible manner, and every voice raised to the highest key, in shrill yelps and barks)! there are rapid succession of feats, and of incidents, that astonish and amuse far beyond the conception of any one who has not had the singular good luck to witness them. In these struggles, every mode is used that can be devised, to oppose the progress of the foremost, who is likely to get the ball; and these obstructions often meet desperate individual resistance, which terminates in a violent scuffle, and sometimes in fisticuffs; when their sticks are dropped, and the parties are unmolested, whilst they are settling it between themselves; unless it be by a general *stampedo,* to which they are subject who are down, if the ball happens to pass in their direction. Every weapon, by a rule of all ball-plays, is laid by in their respective encampments, and no man allowed to go for one; so that the sudden broils that take place on the ground, are presumed to be as suddenly settled without any probability of much personal injury; and no one is allowed to interfere in any way with the contentious individuals.

There are times, when the ball gets to the ground, and such a confused mass rushing together around it, and knocking their sticks together, without the possibility of any one getting or seeing it, for the dust that they raise, that the spectator loses his strength, and everything else but his senses; when the condensed mass of ball-sticks, and shins, and bloody noses, is carried around the different parts of the ground, for a quarter of an hour at a time, without any one of the mass being able to see the ball; and which they are often thus scuffling for, several minutes after it has been thrown off, and played over another part of the ground.

For each time that the ball was passed between the stakes of either party, one was counted for their game, and a halt of about one minute; when it was again started by the judges of the play, and a similar struggle ensued; and so on until the successful party arrived to 100, which was the limit of the game, and accomplished at an hour's sun, when they took the stakes; and then, by a previous agreement, produced a number of jugs of whiskey, which gave all a wholesome drink, and sent them all off merry and in good humour, but not drunk.

☾ *E S S A Y S*

The following essays compare the sporting experience of two distinctly different colonial communities—the plantation society of the Anglican Chesapeake region, and the less stratified society of bourgeois Puritan Boston. In the first monograph, Timothy

Breen, a renowned colonial historian at Northwestern University, employs the methods of cultural anthropology to analyze late seventeenth-century Virginia horse racing and to explain the significance of gambling among leading tobacco planters. He describes a society that was highly individualistic, materialistic, and honor-bound. Elite plantation owners utilized horse racing to certify social status, to express dominant values like risk taking, and to deflect potential social conflicts through their agreements and conventions that facilitated the horse races. In the second essay, Nancy Struna, of the University of Maryland, author of a forthcoming book, tentatively titled *People of Prowess,* examines how the changing values of successive generations of Puritans shaped their recreational experiences. Struna points out that contrary to conventional wisdom, there were proper times and places for moral sport in Puritan society. A confident first generation of true believers fighting for survival in the wilderness gave way to a second generation of doubters. By the third generation, community leadership was passing from the ministers to merchants, whose differing values influenced recreational patterns.

The Cultural Significance of Gambling Among the Gentry of Virginia

TIMOTHY H. BREEN

. . . In late seventeenth- and early eighteenth-century Virginia, gentlemen spent a good deal of time gambling. During this period, in fact, competitive gaming involving high stakes became a distinguishing characteristic of gentry culture. Whenever the great planters congregated, someone inevitably produced a deck of cards, a pair of dice, or a backgammon board; and quarter-horse racing was a regular event throughout the colony. Indeed, these men hazarded money and tobacco on almost any proposition in which there was an element of chance. . . .

The great planters' passion for gambling, especially on quarter-horse racing, coincided with a period of far-reaching social change in Virginia. Before the mid-1680s constant political unrest, servant risings both real and threatened, plant-cutting riots, and even a full-scale civil war had plagued the colony. But by the end of the century Virginia had achieved internal peace. Several elements contributed to the growth of social tranquility. First, by 1700 the ruling gentry were united as they had never been before. . . . A sizable percentage of the Virginia gentry, perhaps a majority, had been born in the colony. The members of this native-born elite—one historian calls them a "creole elite"—cooperated more frequently in political affairs than had their immigrant fathers. They found it necessary to unite in resistance against a series of interfering royal governors [and] . . . successfully consolidated their control over Virginia's civil, military and ecclesiastical institutions. They monopolized the most important offices; they patented the best lands.

From Timothy H. Breen, "Horses and Gentlemen: The Cultural Significance of Gambling Among the Gentry of Virginia," *William and Mary Quarterly* 34 (April 1977): 329–47.

A second and even more far-reaching element in the creation of this remarkable solidarity among the gentry was the shifting racial composition of the plantation labor force. Before the 1680s the planters had relied on large numbers of white indentured servants to cultivate Virginia's sole export crop, tobacco. These impoverished, often desperate servants disputed their masters' authority and on several occasions resisted colonial rulers with force of arms. In part because of their dissatisfaction with the indenture system, and in part because changes in the international slave trade made it easier and cheaper for Virginians to purchase black laborers, the major planters increasingly turned to Africans. The blacks' cultural disorientation made them less difficult to control than the white servants. . . . By the beginning of the eighteenth century Virginia had been transformed into a relatively peaceful, biracial society in which a few planters exercised almost unchallenged hegemony over both their slaves and their poorer white neighbors.

The growth of gambling among the great planters during a period of significant social change raises important questions not only about gentry values but also about the social structure of late seventeenth-century Virginia. Why did gambling, involving high stakes, become so popular among the gentlemen at precisely this time? Did it reflect gentry values or have symbolic connotations for the people living in this society? Did this activity serve a social function, contributing in some manner to the maintenance of group cohesion? Why did quarter-horse racing, in particular, become a gentry sport? And finally, did public displays such as this somehow reinforce the great planters' social and political dominance?

In part, of course, gentlemen laid wagers on women and horses simply because they enjoyed the excitement of competition. . . . Another equally acceptable explanation for the gentry's fondness for gambling might be the transplanting of English social mores. . . . While both views possess merit, . . . the widespread popularity of gambling among the gentry indicates that this type of behavior may have had deeper, more complex cultural roots than either of these explanations would suggest.

In many societies competitive gaming is a device by which the participants transform abstract cultural values into observable social behavior. In his now-classic analysis of the Balinese cockfight Clifford Geertz describes contests for extremely high stakes as intense social dramas. These battles not only involve the honor of important villagers and their kin groups, but also reflect in symbolic form the entire Balinese social structure. Far from being a simple pastime, betting on cocks turns out to be an expression of the way the Balinese perceive social reality. The rules of the fight, the patterns of wagering, the reactions of winners and losers—all these elements help us to understand more profoundly the totality of Balinese culture.

The Virginia case is analogous to the Balinese. When the great planter staked his money and tobacco on a favorite horse or spurred a sprinter to victory, he displayed some of the central elements of gentry culture—its competitiveness, individualism, and materialism. In fact, competitive gaming was for many gentlemen a means of translating a particular set of values into action, a mechanism for expressing a loose but deeply felt bundle of ideas and assumptions about the nature of society. The quarter-horse races of Virginia were intense contests involving personal honor, elaborate rules, heavy betting, and wide community interest; and just as the cockfight opens up hidden dimensions of Balinese culture, gentry gambling offers an opportunity to improve our understanding of the complex interplay between cultural values and social behavior in Virginia.

Gambling reflected core elements of late seventeenth- and early eighteenth-century gentry values. . . . Virginia gentlemen placed extreme emphasis upon personal independence. This concern may in part have been the [product] of the colony's peculiar settlement patterns. The great planters required immense tracts of fresh land for their tobacco. Often thousands of acres in size, their plantations were scattered over a broad area from the Potomac River to the James. The dispersed planters lived in their "Great Houses" with their families and slaves, and though they saw friends from time to time, they led for the most part isolated, routine lives. . . . Some planters were uncomfortably aware of the problems created by physical isolation. . . .

Yet despite such apparent cultural privation, [planters] refused to alter their life styles in any way that might compromise their freedom of action. . . . Some of these planters even saw themselves as lawgivers out of the Old Testament. . . . Whatever the origins of this independent spirit, it bred excessive individualism in a wide range of social activities. While these powerful gentlemen sometimes worked together to achieve specific political and economic ends, they bristled at the least hint of constraint. . . .

The gentry expressed this uncompromising individualism in aggressive competitiveness, engaging in a constant struggle against real and imagined rivals to obtain more lands, additional patronage, and high tobacco prices. Indeed, competition was a major factor shaping the character of face-to-face relationships among the colony's gentlemen, and when the stakes were high the planters were not particular about the methods they employed to gain victory. In large part, the goal of the competition within the gentry group was to improve social position by increasing wealth.

Some gentlemen believed that personal honor was at stake as well. Robert "King" Carter, by all accounts the most successful planter of his generation, expressed his anxiety about losing out to another Virginian in a competitive market situation. "In discourse with Colonel Byrd, Mr. Armistead, and a great many others," he explained, "I understand you [an English merchant] had sold their tobaccos in round parcels and at good rates. I cannot allow myself to come behind any of these gentlemen in the planter's trade." Carter's pain arose not so much from the lower price he had received as from the public knowledge that he had been bested by respected peers. He believed he had lost face. This kind of intense competition was sparked, especially among the less affluent members of the gentry, by a dread of slipping into the ranks of . . . the "common Planters.". . . The efforts of "these mighty dons" to outdo one another were almost certainly motivated by a desire to disguise their "originals" to demonstrate anew through competitive encounters that they could legitimately claim gentility.

Another facet of Virginia gentry culture was materialism. This certainly does not mean that the great planters lacked spiritual concerns. Religion played a vital role in the lives of men like Robert Carter and William Byrd II. Nevertheless, piety was largely a private matter. In public these men determined social standing not by a man's religiosity or philosophic knowledge but by his visible estate—his lands, slaves, buildings, even by the quality of his garments. . . .

The gentry were acutely sensitive to the element of chance in human affairs, and this sensitivity influenced their attitudes toward other men and society. Virginians knew from bitter experience that despite the best-laid plans, nothing in their lives was certain. Slaves suddenly sickened and died. English patrons forgot to help their American friends. Tobacco prices fell without warning. Cargo ships sank. Storms and droughts ruined the crops. The list was endless. [William] Fitzhugh warned an English correspondent to think twice before allowing a son to become a Virginia planter, for even "if the best husbandy and the greatest forecast and skill were used, yet ill luck at Sea, a fall of a Market, or twenty other accidents may ruin and overthrow the best Industry." Other planters, even those who had risen to the top of colonial society, longed for greater security. . . . However desirable such certainty may have appeared, the planters always put their labor and money into tobacco, hoping for a run of luck. One simply learned to live with chance. . . .

Gaming relationships reflected these strands of gentry culture. In fact, gambling in Virginia was a ritual activity. It was a form of repetitive, patterned behavior that not only corresponded closely to the gentry's values and assumptions but also symbolized the realities of everyday planter life. This congruence between actions and belief, between form and experience, helps to account for the popularity of betting contests. The wager, whether over cards or horses, brought together in a single, focused act the great planters' competitiveness, independence, and materialism, as well as the element of chance. It represented a social agreement in which each individual was free to determine how he would play, and the gentleman who accepted a challenge risked losing his material possessions as well as his personal honor.

The favorite household or tavern contests during this period included cards, backgammon, billiards, nine-pins, and dice. The great planters preferred card games that demanded skill as well as luck. Put, piquet, and whist provided the necessary challenge, and Virginia gentlemen . . . regularly played these games for small sums of money and tobacco. These activities brought men together, stimulated conversation, and furnished a harmless outlet for aggressive drives. They did not, however, become for the gentry a form of intense, symbolic play such as the cockfight in Bali. . . .

Horse racing generated far greater interest among the gentry than did the household games. Indeed, for the great planters and the many others who came to watch, these contests were preeminently a social drama. To appreciate the importance of racing in seventeenth-century Virginia, we must understand the cultural significance of horses. By the turn of the century possession of one of these animals had become a social necessity. Without a horse, a planter felt despised, an object of ridicule. Owning even a slowfooted saddle horse made the common planter more of a man in his own eyes as well as in those of his neighbors; he was reluctant to venture forth on foot for fear of making an adverse impression. . . . Such behavior seems a waste of time and energy only to one who does not comprehend the symbolic importance which the Virginians attached to their horses. A horse was an extension of its owner; indeed, a man was only as good as his horse. Because of the horse's cultural significance, the gentry attempted to set its horsemanship apart from that of the common planters. Gentlemen took better care of their animals, and, according to John Clayton, who visited Virginia in 1688, they developed a distinctive riding style. "They ride pretty sharply," Clayton reported, "a Planter's Pace is a Proverb, which is a good sharp hand-Gallop." A fast-rising cloud of dust far down a Virginia road probably alerted the common planter that he was about to encounter a social superior.

The contest that generated the greatest interest among the gentry was the quarter-horse race, an all-out sprint by two horses over a quarter-mile dirt track. The great planters dominated these events. . . . Members of the House of Burgesses, including its powerful speaker, William Randolph, were frequently mentioned in the contests that [came] before the courts. On at least one occasion the Rev. James Blair, Virginia's most eminent clergyman and a founder of the College of William and Mary, gave testimony in a suit arising from a race run between Capt. William Soane and Robert Napier. The tenacity with which the gentry pursued these cases, almost continuations of the race itself, suggests the victory was no less sweet when it was gained in court.

Many elements contributed to the exclusion of lower social groups from these contests. Because of the sheer size of wagers, poor freemen and common planters could not have participated regularly. . . .

The gentry actively enforced its exclusive control over quarter-horse racing. When James Bullocke, a York County tailor, challenged Mr. Mathew Slader to a race in 1674, the county court informed Bullocke that it was "contrary to Law for a Labourer to make a race being a Sport for Gentlemen" and fined the presumptuous tailor two hundred pounds of tobacco and cask. . . .

In most match races the planter rode his own horse, and the exclusiveness of these were two ways to set up a challenge. The first was a regularly scheduled affair usually held on Saturday afternoon. By 1700 there were at least a dozen tracks, important enough to be known by name, scattered through the counties of the Northern Neck and the James River valley. The records are filled with references to contests held at such places as Smith's Field, Coan Race Course, Devil's Field, Yeocomico, and Varina. No doubt, many races also occurred on nameless country roads or convenient pastures. On the appointed day the planter simply appeared at the race track and waited for a likely challenge. . . . A second type of contest was a more spontaneous challenge. When gentlemen congregated over a jug of hard cider or peach brandy, the talk frequently turned to horses. The owners presumably bragged about the superior speed of their animals, and if one planter called another's bluff, the men cried out "done, and done," marched to the nearest field, and there discovered whose horse was in fact the swifter.

Regardless of the outcome, quarter-horse races in Virginia were exciting spectacles. The crowds of onlookers seem often to have been fairly large, as common planters, even servants, flocked to the tracks to watch the gentry challenge one another for what must have seemed immense amounts of money and tobacco. . . . Attendance at race days was sizable enough to support a brisk trade in cider and brandy. . . .

The magnitude of gentry betting indicates that racing must have deeply involved the planter's self-esteem. Wagering took place on two levels. The contestants themselves made a wager on the outcome, a main bet usually described in a written statement. In addition, side wagers were sometimes negotiated between spectators or between a contestant and spectator. Of the two, the main bet was far the more significant. From accounts of disputed races reaching the county courts we know that gentlemen frequently risked very large sums. The most extravagant contest of the period was a race run between John Baker and John Haynie in Northumberland County in 1693, in which the two men wagered 4000 pounds of tobacco and 40 shillings sterling on the speed of their sprinters, Prince and Smoaker. Some races involved only twenty or thirty shillings, but a substantial number were run for several pounds sterling and hundreds of pounds of tobacco. While few, if any, of the seventeenth-century gentlemen were what we would call gambling addicts, their betting habits seem irrational even by the more prudential standards of their own day: in conducting normal business transactions, for example, they would never have placed so much money in such jeopardy.

To appreciate the large size of these bets we must interpret them within the context of Virginia's economy. Between 1660 and 1720 a planter could anticipate receiving about ten shillings per hundred-weight of tobacco. Since the average grower seldom harvested more than 1500 pounds of tobacco a year per man, he probably never enjoyed an annual income from tobacco in excess of eight pounds sterling. For most Virginians the conversion of tobacco into sterling occurred only in the neat columns of account books. They themselves seldom had coins in their pockets. Specie was extremely scarce, and planters ordinarily paid their taxes and conducted business transactions with tobacco notes—written promises to deliver to the bearer a designated amount of tobacco. The great preponderance of seventeenth-century planters were quite poor, and even the great planters estimated their income in hundreds, not thousands, of pounds sterling. . . . The Baker-Haynie bet—to take a notable example—amounted to approximately £22 sterling, more than 7 percent of Fitzhugh's annual cash return. It is therefore not surprising that the common planters seldom took part in quarter-horse racing: this wager alone amounted to approximately three times the income they could expect to receive in a good year. Even a modest wager of a pound or two sterling represented a substantial risk.

Gentlemen sealed these gaming relationships with a formal agreement, either a written statement laying out the terms of the contest or a declaration before a disinterested third party of the nature of the wager. In either case the participants carefully stipulated what rules would be in effect. Sometimes the written agreements were quite elaborate. . . .

Virginia's county courts treated race covenants as binding legal contracts. If a gentleman failed to fulfill the agreement, the other party had legitimate grounds to sue; and the county justices' first consideration during a trial was whether the planters had properly recorded their agreement. The Henrico court summarily dismissed one gambling suit because "noe Money was stacked down nor Contract in writing made[,] one of wch in such cases is by the law required." Because any race might generate legal proceedings, it was necessary to have a number of people present at the track not only to assist in the running of the contest but also to act as witnesses if anything went wrong. The two riders normally appointed an official starter, several judges, and someone to hold the stakes.

Almost all of the agreements included a promise to ride a fair race. Thus two men in 1698 insisted upon "fair Rideing"; another pair pledged "they would run fair horseman's play." By such agreements the planters waived their customary right to jostle, whip, or knee an opponent, or to attempt to unseat him. During the last decades of the seventeenth century the gentry apparently attempted to substitute riding skill and strategy for physical violence. The demand for "fair Rideing" also suggests that the earliest races in Virginia were wild, no-holds-barred affairs that afforded contestants ample opportunity to vent their aggressions.

The intense desire to win sometimes undermined a gentleman's written promise to run a fair race. When the stakes were large, emotions ran high. One man complained in a York County court that an opponent had interfered with his horse in the middle of the race, "by meanes whereof the s[ai]d Plaintiff lost the said Race." Joseph Humphrey told a Northumberland County court that he would surely have come in first in a challenge for 1500 pounds of tobacco had not Capt. Rodham Kenner (a future member of the House of Burgesses) "held the defendt horses bridle in running his race." Other riders testified that they had been "Josselled" while the race was in progress. . . .

Planters who lost large wagers because an opponent jostled or "hollowed" them off the track were understandably angry. Yet instead of challenging the other party to a duel or allowing gaming relationships to degenerate into blood feuds, the disappointed horsemen invariably took their complaints to the courts. Such behavior indicates not only that the gentlemen trusted the colony's formal legal system—after all, members of their group controlled it—but also that they were willing to place institutional limitations on their own competitiveness. Gentlemen who felt they had been cheated or abused at the track immediately collected witnesses and brought suit before the nearest county court. The legal machinery available to the aggrieved gambler was complex; and no matter how unhappy he may have been with the final verdict, he could rarely claim that the system had denied due process.

The plaintiff brought charges before a group of justices of the peace sitting as a county court; if these men found sufficient grounds for a suit, the parties—in the language of seventeenth-century Virginia—could "put themselves upon the country." In other words, they could ask that a jury of twelve substantial freeholders hear the evidence and decide whether the race had in fact been fairly run. If the sums involved were high enough, either party could appeal a local decision to the colony's general court, a body consisting of the governor and his council. Several men who hotly insisted that they had been wronged followed this path. For example, Joseph Humphrey, loser in a race for 1500 pounds of tobacco, stamped out of a Northumberland County court, demanding a stop to "farther proceedings in the Common Law till a hearing in Chancery.". . . All the men involved in these race controversies took their responsibilities seriously, and there is no indication that the gentry regarded the resolution of a gambling dispute as less important than providing a will or punishing a criminal. It seems unlikely that the colony's courts would have adopted such an indulgent attitude towards racing had these contests not in some way served a significant social function for the gentry.

Competitive activities such as quarter-horse racing served social as well as symbolic functions. As we have seen, gambling reflected core elements of the culture of late seventeenth-century Virginia. Indeed, if it had not done so, horse racing would not have become so popular among the colony's gentlemen. These contests also helped the gentry to maintain group cohesion during a period of rapid social change. After 1680 the great planters do not appear to have become significantly less competitive, less individualistic, or less materialistic than their predecessors had been. But while the values persisted, the forms in which they were expressed changed. During the last decades of the century unprecedented external pressures, both political and economic, coupled with a major shift in the composition of the colony's labor force, caused the Virginia gentry to communicate these values in ways that would not lead to deadly physical violence or spark an eruption of blood feuding. The members of the native-born elite, anxious to preserve their autonomy over local affairs, sought to avoid the kinds of divisions within their ranks that had contributed to the outbreak of Bacon's Rebellion. They found it increasingly necessary to cooperate against meddling royal governors. Moreover, such earlier unrest among the colony's plantation workers as Bacon's Rebellion and the plant-cutting riots had impressed upon the great planters the need to present a common face to their dependent laborers, especially to the growing number of black slaves who seemed more and more menacing as the years passed.

Gaming relationships were one of several ways by which the planters, no doubt unconsciously, preserved class cohesion. By wagering on cards and horses they openly expressed their extreme competitiveness, winning temporary emblematic victories over their rivals without thereby threatening the social tranquility of Virginia. These non-lethal competitive devices, similar in form to what social anthropologists have termed "joking relationships," were a kind of functional alliance developed by the participants themselves to reduce dangerous, but often inevitable, social tensions.

Without rigid social stratification racing would have lost much of its significance for the gentry. Participation in these contests publicly identified a person as a member of an elite group. Great planters raced against their social peers. They certainly had no interest in competing with social inferiors, for in this kind of relationship victory carried no positive meaning: the winner gained neither honor nor respect. By the same token, defeat by someone like James Bullocke, the tailor from York, was painful, and to avoid such incidents gentlemen rarely allowed poorer whites to enter their gaming relationships—particularly the heavy betting on quarter horses. The common planters certainly gambled among themselves. Even the slaves may have laid wagers. But when the gentry competed for high stakes, they kept their inferiors at a distance, as spectators but never players.

The exclusiveness of horse racing strengthened the gentry's cultural dominance. By promoting these public displays the great planters legitimized the cultural values which racing symbolized—materialism, individualism, and competitiveness. These colorful, exclusive contests helped persuade subordinate white groups that gentry culture was desirable, something worth emulating; and it is not surprising that people who conceded the superiority of this culture readily accepted the gentry's right to rule. The wild sprint down a dirt track served the interests of Virginia's gentlemen better than they imagined.

The Sporting Life in Puritan America

NANCY STRUNA

Year after year the historical, or hysterical, battle has raged over the New England Puritans and their sport. Did they, or did they not sport? Did they forbid others within society to sport? Upon what bases did they accept or reject sport? . . .

A developmental examination of sport within the first century of Puritan society in Massachusetts Bay can perhaps more adequately provide the necessary societal perspective. In Massachusetts Bay, the initial Puritan enterprise in the new world, three generations appeared in the course of the first one hundred years, 1630–1730. During this century a transformation occurred within the value system as structured and interpreted by those Puritans. Initiated as a Puritan attempt to preserve the visible church, the colonial enterprise coalesced as a mercantile outpost of the British empire.

As a behavioral form defined in terms of the seventeenth century, sport becomes a vehicle for the observation of changes in societal attitudes and institutions. Thus, the habits of participation and attitudes in Massachusetts Bay achieve greater clarity as these emerge within the context of that dynamic society, and as they represent similarities and differences among three generations.

The Plan for Society, 1630–1730

The initial generation of Puritans who settled in Massachusetts Bay resolved to establish a society dedicated to the preservation of the visible church and bound by a philosophy which clearly defined man's role and niche in the world. As descendants of Adam, the Puritans recognized themselves as corrupt men who had been given a second chance to achieve salvation. To escape the experiences of the disorderly, ungodly world, the Puritans established a "city upon a hill" in Massachusetts Bay. John Winthrop, the first governor of the Massachusetts Bay Company in the new world, identified for his colonists the values which God had ordained for all his creations. Hierarchy, inequality, mutality, variety, and order were all observable in nature. Conformity to the rest of God's works demanded the implanting of these values in society. Only through self-consciousness of one's emotions and attitudes toward behavior could a Puritan hope to entertain a godly mind.

A few years before the journey to New England, John Downame advised his congregation of the lifetime service required by God and, though possibly inadvertently, of the place that sport might hold in the Puritan value system:

> Wee must constantly and continually, in everything, and at everytime, performe service unto God in all our actions and throughout our whole course and conversation . . . in

From Nancy Struna, "Puritans and Sport: The Irretrievable Tide of Change," *Journal of Sport History* 4 (Spring 1977): 1–21.

> the meanest duties of the basest calling, yea even in our eating and drinking, lawful
> sports and recreations, when as wee doe them in faith.

Sport might thus be as mutually beneficial to man as eating and drinking, especially if pursued in lawful forms and attentive to order. . . .
. . . Winthrop struggled with the occurrence of sport in his life:

> When I had some tyme abstained from suche worldly delights as my heart most desired, I grewe melancholick and uncomfortable, for I had been more careful to refraine
> from an outward conversation in the world, than to keepe the love of the world out of
> my heart, or to uphold my conversation in heaven . . . I grewe unto a great dullnesse
> and discontent: which being at last perceived, I examined my heart, and findinge it
> needfull to recreate my minde with some outward recreation, I yielded unto it, and by a
> moderate exercise herein was much refreshed. . . .

Abstention had created disorder in Winthrop's life; melancholy and discomfort had detracted from his attention to God. Yet to ensnare his "heart so farre in worldly delights" forced him to cool "the graces of the spirit by them."

Moderation, Downame had called the key to order in one's life. Winthrop discovered a similar sense of sobriety when "outward recreation" was necessary. The mind dominated God's gifts to man, but activities of the body might refresh an overworked mind. The maintenance of order necessitated mutual operations between mind and body. Moderation in sport, in its recreative sense, provided a balancing factor ordained by God. . . .

Members of the Company realized that men were corrupt and that few, if any, could adhere to the strict behavioral code every moment of his life. To this end the Puritans employed the civil government, wherein elected magistrates covenanted with freeholding church members to govern according to "God's laws and man's.". . .

As the epitome of right thinking men and guardians of the churches, the magistrates had to insure the sanctity of the Sabbath. The Court of Assistants in 1630 ordered that John Baker ". . . shalbe whipped for shooteing att fowle on the Sabbath day." The implication is that the Court punished Baker for his inattention to the Sabbath, rather than for his fowling. Within five years all [persons] absent from church meetings faced fines or imprisonment. The records indicate that church absentees engaged in sport less frequently than they drank, labored unnecessarily, or traveled. Sport apparently maintained its position in the delicate hierarchy on the Sabbath.

Magistrates similarly restricted sport, or more precisely the occasion for sport, when this detracted from the economic success of the colony and social order. Perhaps the underlying theme of the first generation was the promotion of the public good. Thomas Hooker warned against the designs and devices of individuals whose selfish activities would precipitate "the distraction and desolation of the whole" and "prejudice the publike good." In a society without institutions to care for the poor, the criminals, and other societal malcontents, the magistrates had to prevent such unstabilizing germs, rather than wait to treat the products. . . .

In many respects the inns and common houses of entertainment disrupted the orderly arrangement of society. Though necessary for the housing of travelers, these houses encountered rigid surveillance of visitor tenure, volume and price of liquors and tobacco, and activities permitted on the premises. The General Court scrutinized the taverns primarily because:

> . . . it hath appeared unto this court, upon many sad complaints, that much drunkenness, wast of the good creatures of God, mispence of precious time, & other disorders have frequently fallen out in the inns. . . .

Since people could not legally enjoy gaming in their own residences, apparently some traveled to the inns for that opportunity. Not until 1647 did the General Court outlaw shovel-board, and shortly after bowling and gaming in general, ". . . whereby much pcious time is spent unfruitfully, & much wast of wine & beare occasioned thereby . . ." The delay in banning these games, as well as the emphasis on unprofitability and drunkenness, suggest that the magistrates did not intend to denounce the nature of the game, but rather to attack overspending and inebriation.

Aside from the desire, in varying degrees, for economic stability and order in society, sport reflected other values and habits of Puritan life. In 1639 the first military company organized and depended upon physical exercise, marksmanship and athletic contests, and mock battles as the core of the training day. Competitive matches emerged as tests of skill.

Military leaders sometimes restricted other occasions for sport. Near Salem in 1636, three men vacated their posts to go fowling. Instead of being happily diverted by birds, they fell prey to lurking Indians. Only one man returned to face the wrath of the lieutenant whose orders had been countered.

Sport provided a means by which some men could support both the hierarchical composition of society and the public welfare. On the *Arbella* Winthrop had announced that ". . . in all times some must be rich, some poor; some high and eminent in power and dignity; others mean and in subjection." In the first decade alone two men seemingly tried to replicate the English game preserve. In 1632 John Perkins reserved two areas in which he could ". . . take Fowle wth netts." From the town of Salem in 1639, Emmanuell Downing received five hundred acres for the ". . . takeing wild foule by way of duck coy." The General Court, ". . . being desiros to encourage the & others, in such designs as tend to publike good . . .", forbade all others to shoot within a half mile of the pond.

The experience of Downing and Perkins suggests that sport provided some occasions for society to focus upon the individual, especially when the needs of the individual and the community coincided. By 1641 the rights of freemen appeared printed as the Body of Liberties. One of the articles insured householders of their rights to fish and fowl for sport or livelihood within the limits of their towns. . . .

Thus, in the first two decades of Puritan life in Massachusetts Bay, the occurrence of sport was very real, reflecting both values and diversity within that society. Frequently the occasions for sport detracted from societal values, at least as conceived of by magistrates. Magistrates sought to limit these occasions and, in effect, may have restricted participation. Yet, when Samuel Maverick described Boston, he noted that its streets were . . . ". . . full of Girles and Boys sporting up and down, with a continued concourse of people."

Imposed Homogeneity, 1650–1690

Maverick's approving comments on the progress of society do not in any way predict the crisis which befell the Puritans after [midcentury]. As members of the second generation came of age, fewer of them joined the congregations. In their failure either to experience or relate conversion experiences and thus become baptized members, they threatened the original mission of the colony to preserve the church. Ministers and magistrates reacting to the decline in membership, which reached a record low in the 1650's and continued through the 1680's, transformed their mission into one of preserving an entire people. They isolated groups within society and attacked heterogeneous attitudes. In a miscalculated effort to resurrect the supposedly homogeneous society of the first generation, they succeeded only in arousing hostility, some guilt, and greater diversity.

Ministers believed that the key to the survival of the pure church lay within the grasp of the children. . . . Youths over the age of fourteen and strangers, ". . . the reputed great provokers of the high displeasure of Almightly God," apparently seized upon sport and other socializing activities as alternatives to Sabbath solitude.

The General Court decried the youths who took the ". . . liberty to walke & sporte themselves in the streets or feilds . . .", disturbed the religious preparations of others, and ". . . too frequently repajre to publique houses of entertainment & there sitt drincking . . ." Apparently the Court sought to enforce a rigid homogeneity within a society which had already become diverse. In an effort to preserve the efficacy of the congregations, the Court legislated against religious disturbances and excessive drinking. . . .

One must realize, however, that within society a common acceptable focus on sport must have existed. Without a sporting vernacular and some recognized values, there would have been no basis for the apparent divisions which arose. John Cotton and Increase Mather concurred that one's perspective determined the efficacy of the activity. In nearly the same breath in which he denounced gaming, the second generation Mather admitted that "For a Christian to use Recreation is very lawful, and in some cases a great Duty. . . ."

Ministers generally applied to sport the dictates of service to God. Some Puritans observed that sport provided desirable opportunities for socialization, for military preparedness, or for recreation and catharsis. Whether in London or Boston, Samuel Sewall swam, fished, and recognized bowling greens. In 1679 John Richardson exhorted the militia men to attain greater skill:

> Victory is the Mark that skill aims at; Skill of hand, Strength of body, & Courage of mind do make a compleat Champion.

Harvard College officials even allotted a minimum two and one-half hours for sport among their students after 1655.

A man relaxed and refreshed through sport could function more efficiently in his calling. If this calling fulfilled the needs of the community, the benefit to all was obvious. Puritans continued to respond to the communal ideal so obvious during the first twenty years in Massachusetts Bay. However, the degree of commitment to that response varied. Whereas once Winthrop had to judge only for himself and record in his own diary how much sport he might enjoy, now Cotton defined and printed for others similar limitations. Ministers at training days seemingly cajolled, or at least challenged, recruits to strive for skill and to distinguish the play of boys from that of men. Yet, no longer did they act and speak simply to vindicate their own actions. They could not stamp out the heterogeneous attitudes toward sport. Even the Reverend Peter Thatcher of Milton purchased " 'a pack of ninepins and bowle'." Soldiers on active duty during King Philip's War in 1675 lost their arms while gaming.

Those who attempted to dictate the acceptable values of sport probably did not fear that men would sport, but rather certain occasions for sport and the aftermath of some of these. The laws and sermons of the second generation anticipated God's wrath, for the most part, because of the largely misunderstood decline in church membership. By instilling order, a sense of conforming order ascertained by more and more artificial officers and institutions, these leaders hoped to return their people to the path of God. The gradual increase in population, Indian threats to a more distant frontier, and vacillating periods of economic expansion and contraction presented new problems to second generation leaders.

In an attempt to enforce uniformity, Harvard College had actually reacted in a positive sense by permitting sport on campus and not allowing students to venture off campus. Magistrates, however, did not so readily solve the problems of filling the churches and preserving the communities. Taverns continually irritated those who tried to order society. Leaders among the second generation became ever more concerned about the opportunities these taverns provided. Shuffleboard and bowling had already become forbidden, at least partly because of the gaming element. In 1651 the General Court forbade dancing at weddings in taverns because ". . . there are many abuses and disorders by dancing in ordinaryes . . ." . . .

On other occasions as well, sport constituted a threat to the safety of the colonists and to the order of society in general. In Boston the selectmen and the council reacted to the dangers of football:

> Forasmuch as sundry complaints are made that several persons have received hurt by boys and young men playing at football in the streets, these are therefore to enjoin that none be found at that game in any of the streets, lanes, or enclosures of this town, under penalty of twenty shillings for every such offense.

By 1662 cases of "violent rideing in the streets" of Boston occurred so frequently that the General Court railed against the effect of ". . . indaingering the bodies and lives of many persons . . ." Apparently, by 1672, the danger had not abated. Coupled with the economic disasters attendant upon horse racing for money, the Court of Assistants cited the "Hazard of their limbs and lives" as reasons for refusing to permit this sport within four miles of any town.

Men carrying cocks offered an exciting pastime for some Bostonians. Samuel Sewall described one such incident:

> Jos. Maylem carries a Cock at his back, with a Bell in 's hand, in the Main Street; several follow him blindfold, underpretence of striking him or 's cock, with great cartships strike passengers, and make great disturbance.

Judge Sewall ordered the constables to ". . . take effectual care to suppress and dissipate all unlawful Assemblies or tumultuous gatherings . . ." arising from ". . . Shailing or throwing at Cocks and such like Disorders, tending to the disturbance of their Magesties liege People, and breach of the peace." Governor Bradford himself signed the order. Though the magistrates uttered not a word against cock scaling itself, they condemned the dangers to the community inherent in the situation. . . .

Two primary factors appeared to negate, or at least limit, the effectiveness of the laws and the desired conformity to first generation values. The first of these was the declining ability of the family to instill discipline and thus preserve social order. To offset this decline, magistrates had to instill more artificial institutions and officers to carry out what were once family responsibilities. By 1655 the General Court had established houses of correction. It empowered constables and selectmen to ". . . take notice of comon coasters, unprofitable fowlers, and other idle psons . . .", as well as to restrain the "Vnreuerent carriage and behavior of divers young psons." . . .

The second emanated from inconsistencies within the calling doctrine and stewardship of wealth concept. Some Puritans envisioned financial gain to be derived from sporting ventures. Yet the speculation involved in gaming or providing dancing lessons was not recognized by the authorities as a legitimate and fruitful economic venture. . . .

The second generation society, at least the Puritan leaders among them, did not preserve a Christian utopia in Massachusetts Bay, nor did they succeed in impressing a homogeneous character upon the ruled. By singling out distinct groups, the ministers marked an actual fragmentation in society. Laws involving sport illustrate the merging of concerns for sin, economy, and order.

For many members of society, sport retained much of its original essence. Sport provided diversion, recreation, competitive skill training, and healthful exercise. Henryson even rationalized that an illegal sporting activity might indeed provide the same essential benefits. Others began to envision economic opportunities.

The Fracturing of Society, 1690–1730

As the second generation merged with the third, this fragmenting process continued. A new English administration and interference with Massachusetts introduced several variables into the predominantly Puritan culture of Massachusetts. More direct colonial contact with England and greater proximity to British society at home and abroad helped to diversify colonial society. As a result of both external and internal factors, Massachusetts society generated a greater degree of attitudinal and role change than it ever had previously. Sport was both affected by and reflected this transformation. Opportunities for the recreational and economic functions of sport increased, while positive and negative attitudes solidified. Newspaper advertisements of sporting events appeared and laws regulating sport as a behavior declined in frequency.

After 1690 external factors enhanced the religious fluctuations within Massachusetts. In the aftermath of the Glorious Revolution, the English parliament had passed the Act of Toleration. To the Anglican population and other sects in Massachusetts, coupled with a franchise based on financial qualifications, this meant greater freedom from Puritan religious restraint. Ministers reacted intensely to their loss of domination and to the failures of their own congregation members to exhibit conversion experiences. The treatment of sport by the ministers illustrates their confused and frequently reactionary opinions and attitudes.

At militia trainings, always a natural forum with an isolated audience, ministers frequently used metaphors of sport to praise, inspire, and harangue the men. The christian soldier, who vigilantly protected his god and his society, warranted great praise. "Indeed men of Martial Spirits and Skill ought to be Encouraged. These Trainings and Exercises are very commendable . . .", emphasized Peter Thatcher. Benjamin Wadsworth cited biblical injunctions and maneuvers for artillery men and grenadiers. More importantly, however, Boone differentiated between classes in society. He warned the private soldier to avoid drunkenness and gaming, but to gentlemen and commanders he spoke in terms of "healthful Exercise", so becoming to their stations in life.

Joseph Belcher reminded his listeners of the spiritual purpose of one's calling. He urged his comrades to battle effectively, to win the prize, and to obtain victory, and he portrayed the Apostle Paul as the epitome of the ultimate victor in heaven. Possibly Belcher believed that the utilization of talent and training for success in one's particular calling had finally superseded the societal goal of unity and the attainment of heaven. "You are not called to quit your pleasures, only change the objects of them," Belcher advised the militia.

The militia sermons and attitudes toward training days represent a mingling of concerns. At times the ministers appeared as a conservative force trying to revitalize the essence of community with God as the focus. Sport was useful to them as a medium for instilling discipline, cooperation, and the will to struggle. Almost simultaneously however, they recognized other, more personal interpretations of the same elements which could and did exist. The ministers helped to consummate a class society by speaking to gentlemen in a different tone than to others. They advocated rational thought and efficiency of body, mind, and spirit.

The minister's treatment of the family and children is similarly reflective of the struggle to accommodate the style of a fluctuating society to the values of their fathers and grandfathers. For some, such as Cotton Mather and Benjamin Wadsworth, sport provided a medium through which they could regulate and educate their children. Mather even translated sporting phrases into Latin for his son Sam to study. . . .

In 1709 Increase Mather authored a simmering "Advice to a Young Man" distinguishing between lawful, moderate sporting and the indulgence in "sinful sports and pastimes". William Cooper published an entire sermon dedicated to "How and Why Young People Should Cleanse Their Way". . . .

As had been the practice of their fathers and grandfathers, the ministers after 1690 turned to magistrates for legitimate support of their position on behavior. The General Court retained its duty to protect the churches throughout the seventeenth century and well into the eighteenth. "An Act for the better Observation and Keeping the Lords-Day," published a minimum of four times between 1692 and 1727, prohibited people from engaging in any unnecessary aspects of their ordinary callings, to travel, or to ". . . use any Game, Sport, Play or Recreation."

The frequency with which this law appeared, the appearance of penalties for second offenders in 1716, and the additions of proscribed activities suggest, among other ideas, that the laws were disobeyed, ignored, or unknown. These factors may help to explain the continuous appearance of lotteries, sport, and drinking at taverns. . . .

Inns and taverns continued to be closely scrutinized by the General Court. To limit incentives for people to misspend or misuse time and money, the magistrates prohibited ". . . Dice, Cards, Tables, Bowles, Shuffleboard, Billiards, Coyts, Cales, Logats, or any implements used in Gaming." Unfortunately for the gamesters, who now bore the brunt of fines and punishment, many could not afford the luxury of gaming, while the state could not bear the expense of paupers. . . .

This idea of proper choices permeated society and became a very personal consideration when one's safety became endangered. Citizens of Boston, in reacting to the bodily harm inflicted by young boys sporting in the streets, restricted opportunities for throwing foot-balls, squibs, snowballs, and long bullets. Throwing the long bullet, made of iron, lead, brass, wood, or stone, resulted in ". . . divers Inconveniencies and may be of the Pernicious Consequence. . . ."

The disapproval of foot-ball seems to relate directly to the site of its occurrence. Away from the confines of town streets and yards, players presumably did not endanger spectators or passersby. John Dunton, an English traveler, described the circumstances of such a game in Rowley:

> . . . there was that day a great game of Foot-ball to be play'd with their feet, which I thought was very odd; but it was upon a broad Sandy Shoar, free from stones, which made it more easy. Neither were they so apt to trip up one anothers heels and quarrel, as I have seen 'em in England.

The players maintained a sense of fair, competitive play and apparently had chosen to disallow any raucous behavior.

Apparently public recalcitrance to other sport forms diminished as some patrons of horse racing, bear baiting, and billiards removed these from the streets and taverns. Particularly after 1715, newspapers advertised rules, weights, wagers, and prizes, often to "gentlemen and others." The designs of racing competition became increasingly complex, as exemplified by this notice in the *Boston Gazette* in 1725:

> This is to give notice to all gentlemen and others that there is to be Thirty Pounds in Money run for . . . by Six Horses, Mares or Geldings, Two miles . . . to carry 9 stone Weight, the Standard to be 14 hands high . . . Each one that Runs to have their Number from 1 to 6, to be drawn, and to run by 2 . . . , the 3 first Horses to run a second Heat . . .

The colonists who wrote and read this and other notices apparently knew how to organize sporting events and understood a concept of competition. Horses of fairly equal stature frequently ran for symbols of wealth and esteem, not merely for money purses. The prize signified the achievement of status for a single winner, an individual who relied upon his own talents to his own benefit rather than always for that of the community. . . .

A 1714 advertisement in the *Boston Newsletter* of a bowling green includes several intriguing comments about the society of that day. Daniel Stevens, the owner of the British Coffee House, invited men according to their position in society, ". . . all Gentlemen, Merchants, and others, that have a mind to Recreate themselves, shall be accomodated . . ." By accommodating these men Stevens apparently sought to provide a service, in the form of recreation, to three distinct and recognized social groupings. Further, as the owner of the British Coffee House, Stevens was not bound by laws regulating sporting activities in inns or taverns. Either the laws did not apply to coffee houses, or they were simply ineffective.

The Stevens' case is only one of many that reveals how far in practice the third generation had strayed from the ideal values established by the first. Economic success and social position, rather than the authority of God, reckoned the hierarchical organization of society. Individual initiative and a worldly competitive spirit replaced the older sense of mutuality, as the welfare of the individual superseded that of the community in many instances. Rational thought, particularly in matters of economic stability and personal safety, not revelation, helped to transform the concept of order. Men relied upon themselves rather than God for the plan of society.

Even the ministers could not stem the tide of change. Verbal vengeance became their weapon against practices which they did not completely understand or for which they assumed primarily negative consequences. To them the contraction of family responsibilities in maintaining order meant only that the family unit was disintegrating and negating its function in society. Few, if any, ministers realized that this transformation within the family might actually produce a more stable one, with members bound by love rather than fear.

Both Puritans and non-Puritans within the first century in Massachusetts Bay did sport and, undoubtedly, with increasing frequency as the century progressed. Several primary factors have arisen to at least partially explain this phenomenon. Perhaps the most obvious is that the Puritans were human and, as such, they demanded refreshment, relaxation, socialization, and competition, all of which sport provided. Secondly, is the fact that from the onset of the colony the immigrants never formed a uniform society, either in purpose or in action. Consequently, the interpretations of values and social mores varied widely among those possessing authority and those without such. Time and money served both God and men; however, the use of such by men did not always conform to religious dictates or civil enactments. What was idleness to some apparently represented the economic use of time to others.

Throughout this century the initially Puritan-oriented society diversified ever further. Non-Puritan immigrants speeded changes within towns and countryside. Massachusetts gradually turned to the world, especially to that of mercantile Britain. The occasions for sport now fit the needs of the world of Daniel Stevens rather than that of John Winthrop.

Thus, the enigmatic status of sport in Puritan society emerges slightly less puzzling when viewed in the perspective of the first century society in Massachusetts Bay. Diverse sporting habits and attitudes existed because of the demands placed on sport and the roles devised for sport by the Puritans themselves. As a behavioral form, sport mirrored developments within Massachusetts Bay and, in turn, was affected by the transformation and diversification of that society. Individuals sported and groups sported, but only in the context of the entire society do their activities and attitudes begin to fit as pieces of an interlocking puzzle.

F U R T H E R   R E A D I N G

Kendall Blanchard, *The Mississippi Choctaws at Play* (1981)

Jane Carson, *Colonial Virginians at Play* (1965)

Stewart Culin, *Games of the North American Indians* (1907)

William C. Ewing, *The Sports of Colonial Williamsburg* (1937)

John Hervey, *Racing in America, 1665–1865,* vol. 1 (1944)

J. Thomas Jable, "Pennsylvania's Blue Laws: A Quaker Experiment in the Suppression of Sport and Amusements," *Journal of Sport History* 1 (1974), 107–21

Bonnie S. Ledbetter, "Sports and Games of the American Revolution," *Journal of Sport History* 6 (Winter 1979), 29–40

H. Telfer Mook, "Training Day in New England," *New England Quarterly* 2 (December 1938), 675–97

R. E. Powell, "Sport, Social Relations and Animal Husbandry: Early Cock-Fighting in North America," *International Journal of Sport History* 5 (1993), 361–81

William C. Stanard, "Racing in Colonial Virginia," *Virginia Magazine of History and Biography* 2 (1894–1895), 293–302

Nancy Struna, "The Formalizing of Sport and the Formation of an Elite," *Journal of Sport History* 13 (Winter 1986), 212–34

Nancy Struna, "Gender and Sporting Practice in Early America, 1750–1810," *Journal of Sport History* 18 (Spring 1991), 10–30

Nancy Struna, "The North-South Races: American Thoroughbred Racing in Transition, 1823–1850," *Journal of Sport History* 8 (Summer 1981), 28–57

Nancy Struna, "Sport and Society in Early America," *International Journal of the History of Sport* 5 (December 1988), 292–311

Hans Peter Wagner, *Puritan Attitudes Towards Recreation in Early Seventeenth-Century New England* (1982)

Traditional Sport, Modern Sport, and the Male Bachelor Subculture, 1800–1860

In the days of the Early Republic, about 95 percent of the population lived in rural or frontier areas, and as late as the Civil War, 80 percent of Americans still lived in rural areas. Farmers and frontiersmen enjoyed traditional pastimes that required strength and skill and reflected their manliness and honor. Sports in the early nineteenth century were all premodern and exhibited little in the way of organization, specialization, rationalization, information, rules, or records. Sportsmen formed a male bachelor subculture whose traditional sports dominated American athletics into the 1840s. Their favorite sports included boxing, gouging (no-holds-barred fighting), horse racing, hunting, and cockfighting. Some of these sports, notably gouging, died out. Boxing and cockfighting went largely underground, and horse racing virtually collapsed in the North after 1845, though it survived in the South.

What accounted for this? Had the United States become "civilized"? What was the impact of the Second Great Awakening and the reform impulse of the Jacksonian Era? How did the rise of cities hinder traditional sports? What was the impact of the new, moral sporting pastimes that competed successfully for public interest and the new sporting ideology that justified those new games? Harness racing was one sport that emerged in the early nineteenth century and successfully adapted to the requirements of an increasingly rational society. How was it able to adjust to an increasingly urban environment to become the first fully modern sport and the most popular spectator sport at the middle of the nineteenth century?

DOCUMENTS

The first document comprises the reminiscences of John Bernard, an English comedian and theater manager who moved to Virginia and the Carolinas in 1799 and 1800. He recounts here some successful and some not so successful evening deer hunts. The second document, drawn from a short novel by James Hall, is a description of a vile billiard parlor in the 1820s. The third document is the report in the *American Turf Register and Sporting Magazine* of the first great footrace in American history, a match sponsored in 1835 by sportsman John Cox Stevens at Long Island's Union Course. Stevens had bet that a man could run ten miles in under sixty minutes, and he sponsored the race to prove it. The fourth document examines the brutality of prize fighting. In 1842 the renowned pugilist Yankee Sullivan arranged a fight between Christopher Lilly and Thomas McCoy, which was attended by 1,500 spectators in Hastings, New York. The fight lasted for two hours and forty-three minutes, when McCoy died in the ring. Sullivan and two other men who had arranged the match were convicted of fourth-degree manslaughter. The document consists of a report of the fight and an editorial from Horace Greeley's *New York Tribune*. The fifth document consists of a Boston policeman's report about a rat-baiting match he attended. Rat baiting was one of the vilest sports of the subterranean male bachelor subculture. The sixth document, drawn from the *New York Herald*'s front page coverage, reports the Fashion-Peytona horse race of 1845, attended by well over 50,000 spectators. It was the fifth and last Great Intersectional race that dated from the Sir Henry–Eclipse match of 1823. The reporter examines the ambiance of this major contest as well as the behavior of the huge crowd.

A Traveler Belittles Hunting in Virginia, 1799, and the Carolinas, 1800

The last and least frequent mode of passing time that I partook of in Virginia was hunting. It was a curious thing that, with few or none of the domestic tastes of the mother-country, the slave states alone were decidedly English in their public amusements. Whether the importation of these had been generally beneficial to so young a country is another question. The planters had wealth and leisure, two incentives to enjoyment, besides a greater than either—a warm climate. Climate, in fact, makes all the difference. It is an easy thing to be a stoic in a cold one, the absence of temptation always leading a man to flatter himself into a belief of his superior goodness. However, hunting, . . . could not come under the ban of even the "Blue Laws." It was a healthy recreation and served to increase a man's knowledge of topography. . . .

But hunting in Virginia, like every other social exotic, was a far different thing from its English original. The meaning of the latter is simple and explicit. A party of horsemen meet at an appointed spot and hour, to turn up or turn out a deer or a fox, and pursue him to a standstill. Here a local peculiarity—the abundance of game—upsets all system. The practice seemed to be for the company to enter the wood, beat up the quarters of anything, from a stag to a snake, and take their chance for a chase. If the game went off well, and it was possible to follow it through the thickets and morasses, ten to one that at every hundred yards up sprung so many rivals that horses and hunters were puzzled which to select, and every

From John Bernard, *Retrospections of America, 1797–1811,* ed. Mrs. Bayle Bernard (New York: Harper, 1887), 156–57, 206–7.

buck, if he chose, could have a deer to himself—an arrangement that I was told proved generally satisfactory, since it enabled the worst rider, when all was over, to talk about as many difficulties surmounted as the best. . . .

* * * *

. . . [Planters'] diversions were varied by an excursion for deer-killing. A party well-armed with guns and brandy sallied into the woods, preceded by a nigger carrying some lighted charcoal in a pan. The victims were so fascinated by the light that they always stared at it transfixed, while its reflection on their eyeballs gave the sportsman an unerring aim. . . .

Sometimes, also, very ludicrous mistakes occurred from the multiplying faculty of the shooter's vision, the amount of game being frequently determined by his amount of brandy; so that, after an immense deal of devastation, when the blacks were sent to collect the spoil, they would proclaim, with a convulsion of laughter, the identity of the dead deer with certain stumps and bushes.

I once heard of the joke ending seriously for a host who piqued himself on his superior eye and rifle. He was entertaining a party one evening with a history of his feats, when they expressed a wish to witness a specimen. Stimulated by two kinds of spirit—love of glory and rum—he ordered the necessary preparations, and led the way with his lauded weapon, his friends laying a heavy wager that he would not kill ten deer in twice as many minutes. Now it happened, all unknown to him, that his cattle had been turned into the woods a few hours previously, and he stumbled upon just the spot where they had made a rendezvous. Pitchy darkness, swimming heads, and the order to lie close prevented discoveries till extermination had commenced. The planter, surrounded by blacks who loaded his guns and kept the fire in a bright flame, in less than ten minutes had doubled the required number. At the moment, however, that his triumph and his party's consternation were rising to a climax, a venerable cow, whose back had been grazed by a bullet, felt impelled to get up and send forth a long moan of remonstrance. The mistake was instantaneously revealed; right and left the dead or dying tenants of his meadows were identified. The betters burst into an uproar of laughter; the negroes, fearing that his gun would next be levelled at themselves, threw down the light and scampered. Choked with vexation, but overpowered by drams, the planter raved, swore, and jumped about in the darkness like a demon. Nor did the return home tend to allay his irritation, for a mile's scramble through the woods in the gloom of Erebus usually divested the wanderer of his hat, boots, or skirts, as well as some portion of his beauty. . . .

James Hall Depicts a Low-life Billiard Parlor, 1828

It was a large apartment, indifferently lighted, and meanly furnished. In the centre stood the billiard table, whose allurements had enticed so many on this evening to forsake the quiet and virtuous comforts of social life, and to brave the biting blast,

---

From James Hall, *The Western Souvenir, A Christmas and New Year's Gift for 1829* (Cincinnati: N. & G. Guilford, 1828), 194–211.

and the not less "pitiless peltings" of parental or conjugal admonition. Its polished mahogany frame, and neatly brushed cover of green cloth, its silken pockets, and party-colored ivory balls, presented a striking contrast to the rude negligence of the rest of the furniture; while a large canopy suspended over the table, and intended to collect and refract the rays of a number of well trimmed lamps, which hung within its circumference, shed an intense brilliancy over that little spot, and threw a corresponding gloom upon the surrounding scene. Indeed, if that gay alter of dissipation had been withdrawn, the temple of pleasure would have presented rather the desolate appearance of the house of mourning.

The stained and dirty floor was strewed with fragments of segars, playbills, and nut shells; the walls blackened with smoke seemed to have witnessed the orgies of many a midnight revel. A few candles, destined to illumine the distant recesses of the room, hung neglected against the walls—bowing their long wicks, and marking their stations by streams of tallow, which had been suffered to accumulate through many a long winter night. The ceiling was hung with cobwebs, curiously intermingled with dense clouds of tobacco smoke, and tinged by the straggling rays of light which occasionally shot from the sickly tapers. A set of benches attached to the walls, and raised sufficiently high to overlook the table, accommodated the loungers, who were not engaged at play, and who sat or reclined, solemnly puffing their segars, idly sipping their brandy and water, or industriously counting the chances of the game, but all observing a profound silence which would have done honor to a turbaned divan, and was well suited to the important subjects of their contemplation. Little coteries of gayer spirits laughed and chatted aside, or made their criticisms on the players in subdued accents—any remarks on that subject being forbidden to all but the parties engaged; while the marker announced the state of the game, trimmed the lamps, and supplied refreshments to the guests.

The Great Foot Race of 1835

The great trial of human capabilities, in going ten miles within the hour, for $1,000, to which $300 was added, took place on Friday, on the Union Course, Long Island; and we are pleased to state, that the feat was accomplished twelve seconds within the time, by a native born and bred American farmer, Henry Stannard, of Killingworth, Connecticut. Two others went the ten miles—one a Prussian, in a half a minute over; the other an Irishman, in one minute and three quarters over the time.

As early as nine o'clock, many hundreds had crossed the river to witness the race, and from that time until near two, the road between Brooklyn, and the course presented a continuous line; (and in many places a double line) of carriages of all descriptions, from the humble sand cart to the splendid barouche

From *American Turf Register and Sporting Magazine* (June 1835): 518–20.

and four; and by two o'clock, it is computed that there were at least from sixteen to twenty persons on the course. The day, though fine, being windy, delayed the start until nineteen minutes before two, when nine candidates appeared in front of the stand, dressed in various colors, and started at the sound
of a drum.

The following are the names, &c. of the competitors . . . :

Henry Stannard, a farmer, aged twenty-four, born in Killingworth, Connecticut. He is six feet one inch in height, and weighed one hundred and sixty-five
pounds. He was dressed in black silk pantaloons, white shirt, no jacket, vest, or
cap, black leather belt and flesh colored slippers.

Charles R. Wall, a brewer, aged eighteen years, born in Brooklyn. . . .

Henry Sutton, a house painter, aged twenty-three years, born in Rahway, New
Jersey. . . .

George W. Glauer, rope-maker, aged twenty-seven, born in Elberfeldt,
Prussia. . . .

Isaac S. Downes, a basket-maker, aged twenty-seven, born at Brookhaven,
Suffolk county. . . .

John Mallard, a farmer, aged thirty-three, born at Exeter, Otsego Co. New
York. . . .

William Vermilyea, shoemaker, aged twenty-two years, born in New York. . . .

Patrick Mahony, a porter, aged thirty-three, born in Kenmar county, Kerry,
Ireland. . . .

John M'Cargy, a butcher, aged twenty-six, born at Harlaem. . . .

There was a tenth candidate, a black man, named Francis Smith, aged twenty-
five, born in Manchester, Virginia. Mr. Stevens was willing that this man should
run; but as he had not complied with the regulation requiring his name to be entered by a certain day, he was excluded from contesting the race.

The men all started well, and kept together for the first mile, except Mahony,
who headed the others several yards, and Mallard, who fell behind after the first
half mile. At the end of the second mile, one gave in; at the end of the fourth mile,
two more gave up; in the fifth, a fourth man fell; at the end of the fifth mile, a fifth
man gave in; during the eighth mile, Downes, one of the fastest, and decidedly the
handsomest runner, hurt his foot, and gave in at the termination of that mile, leaving but three competitors, who all held out the distance.

Stannard, the winner, we understand, has been in good training for a month.
He is a powerful stalwart young man, and did not seem at all fatigued at the termination of the race. He was greatly indebted to Mr. Stevens, for his success; Mr. S.
rode round the course with him the whole distance, and kept cheering him on, and
cautioning him against over-exertion in the early part of the race; at the end of the
sixth mile, he made him stop and take a little brandy and water, after which his foot
was on the mile mark just as the thirty-six minutes were expired; and as the trum-
pet sounded he jumped forward gracefully, and cheerfully exclaimed. "Here am I
to time;" and he was within the time every mile. After the race was over, he
mounted a horse and rode round the course in search of Mr. Richard Jackson, who
held his overcoat. He was called up to the stand and his success (and the reward of
$1,300) was announced to him, and he was invited to dine with the Club; to which

he replied in a short speech thanking Mr. Stevens, and the gentlemen of the Club for the attention shewn to the runners generally throughout the task. . . .

Horace Greeley Decries the Slaughter of Boxer Thomas McCoy, 1842

. . . Christopher Lilly, by whose hands McCoy met his death, is a young man of English parentage and 'sporting' habits, about 23 years old. He lately fought a pugilistic battle with one Murphy, and came off victor. He has since been engaged in sparring exhibitions in the Bowery, where he met Thomas McCoy, a Whitehall boatman, only 20 years old, of Irish parentage, and it seems a young man of fine character, marred by a fondness for pugilistic display and for the company and the scenes to which this taste introduced him. These two young men had been old acquaintances, and there was an unsettled grudge between them. They met at one of the flash groggeries where pugilism is the staple of excitement, soon after Lilly's victory over Murphy, which was the theme of general applause, in which McCoy refused to join. Being challenged for his opinion, he gave it against Lilly's achievement. This nettled the champion, who asked him to put on the gloves and try a round with him; McCoy refused, and instantly Lilly struck him a blow which laid him on the floor. He rose and rushed at the assailant, but they were separated and a regular fight instantly agreed on by their respective friends; $200 being the original stakes, but thousands were afterwards bet upon the result. The day was fixed, and the parties went directly into training.

On Tuesday morning last, being the day agreed on, the pitted boxers, their seconds, doctors, friends, judges, &c., and some thousands eager to be spectators, left in two steamboats for the selected battleground, near the little village of Hastings, in Westchester Co., 20 miles from this City. . . .

McCoy had been sick, and was evidently in an inferior condition for such an affray. . . . He was also too high on flesh, showing that he had not been carefully trained for such brutality. . . .

Let none say that his death was accidental. He openly avowed, on starting to the battleground, that he went to *"win or die."* He tied a *black* handkerchief to his post in the ring as his colors, to evince the same determination. Not one of the fifteen hundred who quietly looked on could have been ignorant that his life was the fearful stake of the contest. . . .

. . . Lilly was cool, cautious and husbanded his strength; McCoy rash, eager, probably smarting under a sense of wrong, exposing himself constantly, and wasting his energy in furious, ineffective lunges. His *seconds* and backers had not even sense enough to caution him against his errors until he was virtually beaten. They saw him sweat like rain, and their only expedient was to deluge him repeatedly in

From Horace Greeley, "The Slaughter of McCoy," *New York Tribune*, September 19 and 20, 1842.

cold water! The judges twice decided that Lilly struck 'foul,' giving the battle to McCoy; but his principal backer waived the 'advantage,' as he called it, and suffered the fight to go on! And their beautiful *doctor!* who was there, if for any thing, to save the life of their champion in extremity, saw the murder perfected without a word, only interpolating to *lance the eyes* of the victim, as directed, when they had been entirely closed by the blows of his antagonist!

It is of course understood that McCoy was a willing victim. He probably sought—he certainly did not shun—the conflict. At the opening of the fight, he drew from his pocket two $100 bills, and bet them on the result with his opponent. He evidently fought throughout under the influence of personal feeling. . . .

Where were his seconds? his doctor? and the fifteen hundred spectators? The first urging on the fight; the second doing nothing; of the last a few murmured and two or three remonstrated aloud, but not one stirred to rescue him from inevitable death! . . .

How shall we speak of the getters up and encouragers of this fight?—the gamblers, the brothelmasters, and keepers of flash groggeries, who were ever the chief patrons of 'the ring,' and who were the choice spirits of this festival of fiends? They were in raptures as the well-aimed, deadly blows descended heavily upon the face and neck of the doomed victim, transforming the image of God into a livid and loathsome ruin; *they* yelled with delight as the combatants went down—often on their heads—with a force that made the earth tremble around them—as the blood spirted in rills from the fated sacrifice, or as his conqueror came down heavily upon him and lay there to beat the breath out of him, until taken off by the seconds! They enlivened the shocking scene, as McCoy's eyes closed beneath the blows of his antagonist, with "Shutters up! There's a death in the family!", "Finish him, Chris!" "Knock out his eye!" &c. . . .

—But why linger on the dreadful scene? At the *one hundred and twentieth* round, McCoy stood up as erect as ever, but with his eyes closed in funeral black, his nose destroyed, his face gone, and clots of blood choking the throat which had no longer power to eject them. He could barely walk, but still sparred with some spirit, though unable to get in a blow at his still vigorous antagonist, though the latter was evidently suffering severely from blows in his body. The fight had now lasted *two hours and forty-three minutes,* McCoy had received not less than *one hundred* square blows, and had been thrown or been knocked down *eighty-one times,* his opponent falling heavily as possible upon him. For the last time was this repeated; and, when Lilly was lifted off, McCoy was found lifeless, and sank inanimate as lead in his second's arms. 'Time' was called, but for him Time was no more! Lilly was declared victor, and, appearing little hurt and less disfigured, jumped with a cry of exhultation [*sic*] and sprang out of the ring! McCoy still gasped for breath, sucking his remnants of lips far back into his mouth by the violence of the effort. A moment more, and his struggles ceased—the widow's darling child had been immolated on the alter of *"Sport!"*—he was dead! And even in that moment of freezing horror—when it would seem that the blood of the hardiest ruffian must have curdled with conscious guilt and remorse, and a shadow darkened the most indurated brow—even then, in reference to the fact that *another* fight had been arranged to come off on this occasion, one voice was raised in the crowd, exclaiming, "Come, *carry off your dead, and produce your next man!*"—thus closed the fight at Hastings and the life of Thomas McCoy!

The Slaughter of McCoy, Its Causes, &C.

. . . In the first place, we rejoice to know that the originators and fosterers of pugilism in this country are almost entirely foreigners by birth. This species of ruffianism is not native here, nor is our atmosphere congenial to it. To say nothing of the combatants; the seconds, trainers, &c. of this fight, as of former fights, are, with hardly an exception, from abroad. . . . This is encouraging. This horrid vice— alas that we must more correctly say, this *form* of a horrid vice—has but a sickly hold on our soil, and may be wholly extirpated if proper exertions are made at the proper time. That time, we need not state, is now.

But again: the principal patrons of the pugilistic *science!* among us are the keepers of drinking-houses of the very worst description, professional gamblers, and a few who unite with one or both of these highly reputable and useful callings the keeping or protecting of brothels! To this rule there is hardly an exception. The three seconds who have run away were all keepers or drunkards at least; we believe one or more of them added to this one or both of the other vocations. The principal promoters and backers of the fight were what are called 'king gamblers'—keepers of faro banks, roulette tables, and the like. We believe the world might be safely challenged to produce a single patron of 'the ring' who lives by industry in any useful calling.

We have now a few questions to ask, which we trust will be answered to the public satisfactorily and speedily. They are these: Who licenses foreigners of at best suspicious character to keep houses of public entertainment in our city? If those pugilistic grog shops are kept without licenses, whose duty is it to close them? Why is it not done? . . .

A Policeman Visits the Dissipated Rat Pits of Boston, c. 1860

A rat pit is one of those under-ground novelties occasionally seen in Boston by gaslight. The whereabouts, however, is not always exactly known to the uninitiated, the proprietors generally not choosing to either advertise or hang out a shingle to indicate the locality, . . . nor when found is the establishment such as would be likely to impress the mind with an idea of grandeur or sublimity. . . .

For many years one of these subterranean establishments was kept at "North End," which I have sometimes been called on to visit in my official capacity. The establishment consisted of a bar-room on the first floor from the street, not wide but deep, the counter running the whole length on one side. Behind this counter

From Edward H. Savage, *A Chronological History of the Boston Watch and Police, From 1631 to 1865; Together with the Recollections of a Boston Police Officer, or, Boston by Daylight and Gaslight, From the Diary of an Officer Fifteen Years in the Service* (Boston, 1873), 160–62.

stood females, with *vermilion* cheeks and low-necked dresses, ready to deal out New York gin and cabbage-leaf cigars to all who had the *dosh*. . . .

In passing through this room, (which was generally filled with pickpockets, petty knucks, fumes of tobacco, smoke and bad gin,) at the further end you find a trap-door leading down a flight of stairs to the *rat pit* below.

The pit consists of a broad crib of octagon form in the centre of the cellar, about eight feet in diameter and three and one half feet high, tightly secured at the sides. On three sides of the cellar are rows of board seats, rising one above the other, for the accommodation of spectators. On the other side, stands the proprietor and his assistant and an empty flour barrel, only it is half full of live rats, which are kept in their prison-house by a wire netting over the top of the cask. The amphitheatre is lighted with oil lamps or candles. . . . Spectators are admitted at twenty-five cents a head, and take their seats, when preparations for the evening's entertainment commence. The proprietor carefully lifts the edge of the wire netting over the rat barrel, and with an instrument looking much like a pair of curling tongs, he begins fishing out his game, rat by rat, depositing each carefully inside the pit until the requisite number are pitted. The assistant has brought in the dog, *Flora*, a favorite ratter, which he is obliged to hold fast by the nape of the neck, so eager is she for the fray. Then commences the betting, which runs high or low according to the amount of funds in the hands of the sports.

"A dollar. She kills twenty rats in twelve seconds!" "I take that!" "Half a dollar on the rats!" "Don't put in them small rats!" "Two dollars on Flora in fifteen seconds!" "Done, at fourteen!" "No, you don't!" "Don't put in all your big rats at once!" "Five dollars on the rats in ten seconds!" (no takers.) . . .

The bets having been arranged, time is called, and Flora is dropped into the ring. Flora evidently understands that her credit is at stake; but the growling and champing, and squealing, and scratching is soon over, and the twenty rats lie lifeless at the feet of the bloodthirsty Flora, when time is again called, and the bets decided, and all hands go up and liquor. This exhibition is repeated several times, with different dogs and lasts as long as the live rats hold out. . . .

The *New York Herald* Reports on "The Great Contest: Fashion *v.* Peytona," 1845

It was an exciting, but very beautiful morning, exciting because the contest between the North and the South for the dominion of the turf was to be settled, before the shades of evening closed on the well-trodden race ground. It is well understood that the ambiguity of the relative pretensions of the two great sections of the country to this honor, is the natural result of former well balanced successes. . . . In addition to the sectional feeling and the strong rivalry of sportsmen, and in one sense partizans—the vast sums of money pending on the race, attached a degree of

---

From *New York Herald*, May 5, 1845.

absorbing interest to the result, quite proportionate to the great demonstration that took place.

More than three thousand persons crossed the South Ferry . . . before 8 o'clock for the races. As the morning progressed, the crowd increased rapidly, and a sense of tumult, disorder and confusion ensued. . . . All seemed eager to reach the ground. Long trains of carriages, filled with all sorts of people, reaching to Broadway, lined Whitehall Street. Here was the magnificent barouche of the millionaire, full of gay, laughing, dark-eyed *demoiselles,* jammed in between a Bowery stage and a Broadway hack—here were loafers and dandies, on horseback and on foot . . . Southerners . . . with anxious faces, but hearts full of hope. . . . [A]ll business seemed laid aside . . . Omnibuses of all dimensions, cabriolets, chariots, drays, wagons, and every description of vehicle were put in requisition. . . .

By twelve o'clock about 30,000 persons had passed over the south and 20,000 over Fulton ferries.

We saw many distinguished sporting characters, politicians, editors, reporters, managers, actors, printers, devils, &c. . . .

The first train started from the terminus of the railway, Brooklyn, at 7 o'clock, followed by others at 8, 9¼, 9¾, and 10½ o'clock. With each of these trains one of our corps started, to not only note whatever might occur . . . , and also because it is fitting that the *Herald* should be represented, if not identified with all marvelous progressive movements of our race. A terrific rush from the ferry boats to the cars was the work of a moment. . . . A large number of cars had been fitted up with temporary seats . . . , however, happy was the wight who got a seat . . . for forty minutes or so, for the lawful consideration of twenty-five cents. . . .

* * * *

The enclosed area, whose circumference of a mile formed the Course, was the resort of the carriages and horsemen. . . . Immediately on the right of the Judge's stand, and opposite to the great stand for spectators, on the other side of the course, a dense mass of vehicles of all descriptions congregated. Among these the most striking were a number of the city omnibuses, which had been engaged for the day by a full complement of passengers, who from the roofs . . . were enabled to have a capital view of the race. As may be expected, the occupants of them were of a more mixed class than those who lolled in private carriages, or those engaged *special* for the occasion. . . .

* * * *

On the stand there could be fewer than thirty thousand persons; every train added countless hosts, for the first race of everybody who obtained admission, was to the grand stand, and the solicitude to secure places increased in the direct ratio of the difficulty of finding them, so that the onset of the last was impetuous in the extreme. A harder day's labor no men performed that day, than those who had charge of the stairs. We saw several altercations with fellows who attempted to get on the stand without tickets, but they were invariably foiled. . . . The lower portion of the stand was occupied by refreshment tables on one side and faro and roulette, and all sorts of gaming tables on the other. Betting and gambling and guzzling went on at a rapid rate. . . .

At about 2 o'clock the excitement . . . was tremendous. In the vicinity of the judges' stand, and the enclosed space before the grand stand the multitude heaved and fell like the bellows of the ocean in a mighty storm, and from amidst this excited throng, looking up at the stands, the immense sea of faces, and the hoarse murmur of expectation that spread through the thronged buildings, was one of the most extraordinary scenes that can well be imagined. Here might be seen representatives from all parts of the Union. . . . In one corner might be heard the Bowery boy arranging his final bet with a Northern blood, for some cool hundreds on Peytona. In the general eagerness to obtain a favorable position to view the coming race, many, at the peril of life and limb, were climbing on the different parts of the buildings, and the efforts of those who, though "not shaped for sportive tricks," still persisted in climbing to the roof eaves. . . . Two tall trees that stand toward the head of the course were filled with those who, proba-bly not relinquishing the idea of paying for grand stand or jockey club tickets, selected the commanding situation, and patiently waited in their perches for hours. . . . The track all round was lined inside by vehicle of every description and shape, from the rickety oyster cart . . . to the aristocratic turn-out of the "upper ten thousand". . . .

On the Course itself there was the utmost difficulty in preserving the track clear from intruders, and to the efficiency of a few may be ascribed the compara-tive order which was at length established. A young gentleman, mounted on a black horse, was quite conspicuous in the part he took, riding up and down, and most fearlessly charging the intruding multitude with his whip. The indomitable Captain Isaiah Rynders, mounted on his famous white charger, rendered most valuable services, and never have we seen such perfect self-possession and invin-cible good humor as was displayed on this occasion by the leader of the Empires. He was loudly cheered by the members of the Jockey Club, and by his address to the crowd, appealing to their feelings of pride as northerners, to show the southern-ers assembled that fair play could be given to their horse, succeeded in obtaining a clear course. . . . Yankee Sullivan, and others, including Bill Harrington, who with the rest . . . , most ably seconded the efforts of the rest. Justice Matsell, by his ap-pearance, was of most essential service, and where-ever a notorious character, or suspicious-looking individual, fell under the influence of his eye, their stay was short. . . .

We observed Mr. Prescott Hall in the Judge's stand exerting his lung to the ut-most preserve order, but beyond that we did not see any particular action on his part . . . but the exertions requisite appeared to have been left entirely to the twenty or thirty constables who were expected to control the hundred thousand people on the Course.

The booths and temporary stands with refreshments that were erected outside were crowded during the whole day. . . . The gambling fraternity were by no means inactive on the occasion, and the extraordinary force of example that al-ways tempts people to gamble at a race course was fully followed here. Roulette, sweat-cloth, thimble-rig and all the usual games were in full operation during the whole day. . . . There was one feature we noticed with pleasure, which was the almost universal absence of all the gross scenes of intemperance that used for-merly to disgrace our racecourses, and despite all the attraction for the various drinkables in the different booths, the crowd generally seemed to partake more of the eatables and the different temperance beverages of soda water, lemonade and the like. . . .

The Race

About half past two o'clock, the bugle sounded to bring forth the horses. . . . Mr. J. Laird topped the pig-skin across Fashion, dressed in a purple jacket and red and gold cap. The "indomitable Barney" mounted Peytona. Two finer animals and abler jockies . . . there is not in the States. Having gone to the scales, Laird made his weight to 125 lbs.; and Barney his to 118. . . .

After some endeavors on the part of those in authority, the track was well cleared as could be expected under the circumstances. . . . At 33 minutes past two o'clock the horses were saddled and mounted, and at the first tap they went forth in gallant style, Peytona having the pole, but a most beautiful start—nose and nose. They kept thus together round the bottom, Peytona gently falling off, but yet keeping her nose close to the tail of her rival. . . . They kept thus to the first quarter, the same to the half. At the third quarter they were close together, Peytona . . . at the drawgate . . . came in front, and led to the judges stand a length and a half in front. For the second mile they appeared to keep in this position round the bottom, but owing to the clouds of dust prevailing just then, only an occasional glimpse could be caught of them; but they seemed to maintain a similar position round the top to the drawgate, where Fashion appeared to come in front, but on reaching the judge's chair, Fashion's nose was close up with that of Peytona, on the inside. For the third mile they kept well thus together round, to the nearing of the half mile post, where the heavy patch before alluded to occurs, Fashion appeared to gain somewhat, but shortly after Peytona reached her flank, nipping her hard, but Fashion appeared immediately afterwards to make the gap wider. At the drawgate, Fashion appeared two lengths in front, but on nearing the judge's stand, Peytona had her nose close on the flank of her opponent. It was not pretty evident that Barney had it all his own way, and could do just as he pleased with the affairs, and faces became elongated, while others could scarce keep their feet. . . . Round the bottom they kept well together, but owing to dust, &c., there was no seeing further, until they reached the drawgate towards home, where Fashion appeared to have the lead, but it was immediately taken from her, and Peytona came home two lengths in front, making the first heat in 7m. 39s., amid the most unbounded of cheers. . . .

After the interval of twenty minutes the horses were again ready, and the crowd resumed their positions round the course; this time wound up to the pitch of frenzy. . . .

✴ ✴ ✴ ✴

At the first attempt they did not go forth, and were pulled up short, owing to what appeared a rather premature tap. They returned and commenced again, *de novo*. At the second attempt they went forth Peytona leading a neck, Laird well up round the bottom to the quarter; on approaching the half Fashion went in front, and led to the three-quarter. Here the crowd broke in at the lower drawgate, which caused some confusion for a few moments, but owing to the vigilance of those now engaged, was soon got under. Fashion led to the drawgate, where they came together to the Judge's chair, head and head, no telling who had the lead. For the second mile Fashion appeared to have the lead to the quarter, the other well up they kept so up the back stretch; at the three-quarter it was just so. Fashion still kept the lead, closely waited upon by Peytona; it was thus round the top, but at the drawgate they were again well together, Fashion having the track, but at the end of the second mile, notwithstanding Fashion's advantage Peytona led to the Judge's stand a head in front. For the third mile they kept so to the quarter; a table cloth might have covered the pair to the half-mile post. They kept just so to the three-quarters; at the drawgate Fashion led on the inside, but Peytona had got her and led her home a length in advance. "Now comes the tug of war." Peytona maintained her position, both well together, she gained a little on her round the bottom, but apparently with little effect; at the half they were well together, which was maintained to the three-quarters, but here the mob closed in so as to obscure sight from the club stand.— Fashion appeared to have the lead, but on approaching the drawgate, notwithstanding the mob closing on the track, Peytona led a way clear length in advance in 7.45 ¼.

We have only time to say that it was quite a waiting race; "Barney" knew what he had to do, and did it nobly, and doubtless more he would have done if it had been required.

⚾ *E S S A Y S*

In the first essay, Elliott J. Gorn, of Miami (Ohio) University, employs his expertise in folklore, working-class culture, and gender relations to illuminate the meaning of gouging. This "rough-and-tumble" fighting in the early nineteenth-century frontier provided an important means to display one's courage, manliness, and honor. In the second essay, Melvin L. Adelman of Ohio State University examines the rise of harness racing (trotting). Adelman points out that when thoroughbred racing died out in the North during the 1840s because of economic reasons, it was supplanted by the more democratic equestrian sport of harness racing. This, unlike thoroughbred racing, had urban roots, was relatively democratic, and was a very useful sport because it improved the breeding of working horses. Adelman argues that harness racing became the first modern sport. It began as a sport in the 1820s that had little organization, simple unwritten rules, local competition, no role differentiation, records, or publicity, and it evolved into a more sophisticated organized sport that by 1870 had specialized roles, national competition, uniform rules, and extensive record keeping.

The Social Significance of Gouging in the Southern Backcountry

ELLIOTT J. GORN

"I would advise you when You do fight, Not to act like Tygers and Bears as these Virginians do—Biting one anothers Lips and Noses off, and *gowging* one another—that is, thrusting out one anothers Eyes, and kicking one another on the Cods, to the Great damage of many a Poor Woman." Thus, Charles Woodmason, an itinerant Anglican minister born of English gentry stock, described the brutal form of combat he found in the Virginia backcountry shortly before the American Revolution. Although historians are more likely to study people thinking, government, worshiping, or working, how men fight—who participates, who observes, which rules are followed, what is at stake, what tactics are allowed—reveals much about past cultures and societies.

As early as 1735, boxing was "much in fashion" in parts of Chesapeake Bay, and forty years later a visitor from the North declared that, along with dancing, fiddling, small swords, and card playing, it was an essential skill for all young Virginia gentlemen. The term "boxing," however, did not necessarily refer to the comparatively tame style of bare-knuckle fighting familiar to eighteenth-century Englishmen. In 1746, four deaths prompted the governor of North Carolina to ask for legislation against "the barbarous and inhuman manner of boxing which so much prevails among the lower sort of people." The colonial assembly responded by making it a felony "to cut out the Tongue or pull out the eyes of the King's Liege People." Five years later the assembly added slitting, biting, and cutting off noses to the list of offenses. Virginia passed similar legislation in 1748 and revised these statutes in 1772 explicitly to discourage men from "gouging, plucking, or putting out an eye, biting or kicking or stomping upon" quiet peaceable citizens. By 1786 South Carolina had made premeditated mayhem a capital offense, defining the crime as severing another's bodily parts. . . .

. . . Not [only] assaults on persons or property but slights, insults, and thoughtless gestures set young southerners against each other. To call a man a "buckskin," for example, was to accuse of the poverty associated with leather clothing, while the epithet "Scotsman" tied him to the low-caste Scots-Irish who settled the southern highlands. . . .

Descriptions of these "fist battles," as [Philip] Fithian called them, indicate that they generally began like English prize fights. Two men, surrounded by onlookers, parried blows until one was knocked or thrown down. But there the similarity ceased. Whereas "Broughton's Rules" of the English ring specified that a round ended when either antagonist fell, southern bruisers only began fighting at this point. Enclosed not inside a formal ring—the "magic circle" defining a special place with its own norms of conduct—but within whatever space the

From Elliott J. Gorn, " 'Gouge and Bite, Pull Hair and Scratch': The Social Significance of Fighting in the Southern Backcountry," *American Historical Review* 90 (February 1985): 18–43.

spectators left vacant, fighters battled each other until one called enough or was unable to continue. Combatants boasted, howled, and cursed. As words gave way to action, they tripped and threw, gouged and butted, scratched and choked each other. . . .

Around the beginning of the nineteenth century, men sought original labels for their brutal style of fighting. "Rough-and-tumble" or simply "gouging" gradually replaced "boxing" as the name for these contests. Before two bruisers attacked each other, spectators might demand whether they proposed to fight fair—according to Broughton's Rules—or rough-and-tumble. Honor dictated that all techniques be permitted. Except for a ban on weapons, most men chose to fight "no holts barred," doing what they wished to each other without interference, until one gave up or was incapacitated.

The emphasis on maximum disfigurement, on severing bodily parts, made this fighting style unique. Amid the general mayhem, however, gouging out an opponent's eye became the sine qua non of rough-and-tumble fighting, much like the knockout punch in modern boxing. The best gougers, of course, were adept at other fighting skills. Some allegedly filed their teeth to bite off an enemy's appendages more efficiently. Still, liberating an eyeball quickly became a fighter's surest route to victory and his most prestigious accomplishment. To this end, celebrated heroes fired their fingernails hard, honed them sharp, and oiled them slick. " 'You have come off badly this time, I doubt?' " declared an alarmed passerby on seeing the piteous condition of a renowned fighter. " 'Have I,' says he triumphantly, shewing from his pocket at the same time an eye, which he had extracted during the combat, and preserved for a trophy."

As the new style of fighting evolved, its geographical distribution changed. Leadership quickly passed from the southern seaboard to upcountry counties and the western frontier. . . . Rough-and-tumbling was best suited to the backwoods, where hunting, herding, and semisubsistence agriculture predominated over market-oriented, staple crop production. . . .

The social base of rough-and-tumbling also shifted with the passage of time. Although brawling was always considered a vice of the "lower sort," eighteenth-century Tidewater gentlemen sometimes found themselves in brutal fights. These combats grew out of challenges to men's honor—to their status in patriarchal, kin-based, small-scale communities—and were woven into the very fabric of daily life. . . . Although they valued hierarchy, individual status was never permanently fixed, so men frantically sought to assert their prowess—by grand boasts over tavern gaming tables laden with money, by whipping and tripping each other's horses in violent quarter-races, by wagering one-half year's earnings on the flash of a fighting cock's gaff. . . .

Piety, hard work, and steady habits had their adherents, but in this society aggressive self-assertion and manly pride were the real marks of status. Even the gentry's vaunted hospitality demonstrated a family's community standing, so conviviality itself became a vehicle for rivalry and emulation. Rich and poor might revel together during "public times," but gentry patronage of sports and festivities kept the focus of power clear. Above all, brutal recreations toughened men for a violent social life in which the exploitation of labor, the specter of poverty, and a fierce struggle for status were daily realities.

During the final decades of the eighteenth century, however, . . . many in the planter class now wanted to distinguish themselves from social inferiors more by genteel manners, gracious living, and paternal prestige than by patriarchal prowess. They sought alternatives to brawling and found them by imitating the English aristocracy. A few gentlemen took boxing lessons from professors of pugilism or attended sparring exhibitions given by touring exponents of the manly art. More important, dueling gradually replaced hand-to-hand combat. The code of honor offered a genteel, though deadly, way to settle personal disputes while demonstrating one's elevated status. . . .

* * * *

By the early nineteenth century, rough-and-tumble fighting had generated its own folklore. Horror mingled with awe when residents of the Ohio Valley pointed out one-eyed individuals to visitors, when New Englanders referred to an empty eye socket as a "Virginia Brand," when North Carolinians related stories of mass rough-and-tumbles ending with eyeballs covering the ground, and when Kentuckians told of battle-royals so intense that severed eyes, ears, and noses filled bushel baskets. Place names like "Fighting Creek" and "Gouge Eye" perpetuated the memory of heroic encounters, and rustic bombast reached new extremes with estimates from some counties that every third man wanted an eye. As much as the style of combat, the rich oral folklore of the backcountry—the legends, tales, ritual boasts, and verbal duels, all of them in regional vernacular—made rough-and-tumble fighting unique.

It would be difficult to overemphasize the importance of the spoken word in southern life. Traditional tales, songs, and beliefs—transmitted orally by blacks as well as whites—formed the cornerstone of culture. Folklore socialized children, inculcated values, and helped forge a distinct regional sensibility. . . . Southern society was based more on personalistic, face-to-face, kin-and-community relationships than on legalistic or bureaucratic ones. Interactions between southerners were guided by elaborate rituals of hospitality, demonstrative conviviality, and kinship ties—all of which emphasized personal dependencies and reliance on the spoken word. Through the antebellum period and beyond, the South had an oral as much as a written culture.

Boundaries between talk and action, ideas and behavior, are less clear in spoken than in written contexts. Psychologically, print seems more distant and abstract than speech, which is inextricably bound to specific individuals, times, and places. . . . Literate peoples separate thought from action, pigeon-holing ideas and behavior. Nonliterate ones draw this distinction less sharply, viewing words and the events to which they refer as a single reality. In oral cultures generally, and the Old South in particular, the spoken word was a powerful force in daily life, because ideation and behavior remained closely linked.

The oral traditions of hunters, drifters, herdsmen, gamblers, roustabouts, and rural poor who rough-and-tumbled provided a strong social cement. Tall talk around a campfire, in a tavern, in front of a crossroads store, or at countless other meeting places on the southwestern frontier helped establish communal bonds between disparate persons. . . . But words could also divide. . . . Men were so touchy about their personal reputations that any slight required an apology. This failing, only retribution restored public stature and self-esteem. "Saving face" was not just a metaphor. . . .

The oral narratives of the southern backcountry drew strength from these national traditions yet possessed unique characteristics. Above all, fight legends portrayed backwoodsmen reveling in blood. Violence existed for its own sake, unencumbered by romantic conventions and claiming no redeeming social or psychic value. Gouging narratives may have masked grimness with black humor, but they offered little pretense that violence was a creative or civilizing force. . . .

The danger and violence of daily life in the backwoods contributed mightily to sanguinary oral traditions that exalted the strong and deprecated the weak. Early in the nineteenth century, the Southwest contained more than its share of terrifying wild animals, powerful and well-organized Indian tribes, and marauding white outlaws. Equally important were high infant mortality rates and short life expectancies, agricultural blights, class inequities, and the centuries-old belief that betrayal and cruelty were man's fate. . . .

Rather than be overwhelmed by violence, acquiesce in an oppressive environment, or submit to death as an escape from tragedy, why not make a virtue of necessity and flaunt one's unconcern? To revel in the lore of deformity, mutilation, and death was to beat the wilderness at its own game. The storyteller's art dramatized life and converted nameless anxieties into high adventure; bravado helped men face down a threatening world and transform terror into power. To claim that one was sired by wild animals, kin to natural disasters, and tougher than steam engines—which were displacing rivermen in the antebellum era—was to gain a momentary respite from fear, a cathartic, if temporary, sense of being in control. Symbolically, wild boasts overwhelmed the very forces that threatened the backwoodsmen. . . .

* * * *

More than realism or fantasy alone, fight legends stretched the imagination by blending both. As metaphoric statements, they reconciled contradictory impulses, at once glorifying and parodying barbarity. In this sense, gouging narratives were commentaries on backwoods life. The legends were texts that allowed plain folk to dramatize the tensions and ambiguities of their lives: they hauled society's goods yet lived on its fringe; they destroyed forests and game while clearing the land for settlement; they killed Indians to make way for the white man's culture; they struggled for self-sufficiency only to become ensnared in economic dependency. Fight narratives articulated the fundamental contradiction of frontier life—the abandonment of "civilized" ways that led to the ultimate expansion of civilized society. . . .

. . . Although rough-and-tumble fighting appears primitive and anarchic to modern eyes, there can be little doubt that its origins, rituals, techniques, and goals were emphatically conditioned by environment; gouging was learned behavior. Humanistic social science more than sociobiology holds the keys to understanding this phenomenon.

What can we conclude about the culture and society that nourished rough-and-tumble fighting? The best place to begin is with the material base of life and the nature of daily work. Gamblers, hunters, herders, roustabouts, rivermen, and yeomen farmers were the sorts of persons usually associated with gouging. Such hallmarks of modernity as large-scale production, complex division of labor, and regular work rhythms were alien to their lives. . . .

Boatmen, hunters, and herdsmen were often separate from wives and children for long periods. More important, backcountry couples lacked the emotionally intense experience of the bourgeois family. They spent much of their time apart and found companionship with members of their own sex. The frontier town or cross-roads tavern brought males together in surrogate brotherhoods, where rough men paid little deference to the civilizing role of women and the moral uplift of the domestic family. On the margins of a booming, modernizing society, they shared an intensely communal yet fiercely competitive way of life. Thus, where work was least rationalized and specialized, domesticity weakest, legal institutions primitive, and the market economy feeble, rough-and-tumble fighting found fertile soil.

Just as the economy of the southern backcountry remained locally oriented, the rough-and-tumblers were local heroes, renowned in their communities. . . . Legendary champions were real individuals, tested gang leaders who attained their status by being the meanest, toughest, and most ruthless fighters, who faced disfigurement and never backed down. . . .

Given the lives these men led, a world view that embraced fearlessness made sense. Hunters, trappers, Indian fighters, and herdsmen who knew the smell of warm blood on their hands refused to sentimentalize an environment filled with threatening forces. It was not that backwoodsmen lived in constant danger but that violence was unpredictable. Recreations like cockfighting deadened men to cruelty, and the gratuitous savagery of gouging matches reinforced the daily truth that life was brutal, guided only by the logic of superior nerve, power, and cunning. With families emotionally or physically distant and civil institutions weak, a man's role in the all-male society was defined less by his ability as a breadwinner than by his ferocity. The touchstone of masculinity was unflinching toughness, not chivalry, duty, or piety. Violent sports, heavy drinking, and impulsive pleasure seeking were appropriate for men whose lives were hard, whose futures were unpredictable, and whose opportunities were limited. Gouging champions were group leaders because they embodied the basic values of their peers. The successful rough-and-tumbler proved his manhood by asserting his dominance and rendering his opponent "impotent.". . . And the loser, though literally or symbolically castrated, demonstrated his mettle and maintained his honor. . . .

Above all, the ancient concept of honor helps explain this shared proclivity for violence. According to the sociologist Peter Berger, modern men have difficulty taking seriously the idea of honor. American jurisprudence, for example, offers legal recourse for slander and libel because they involve material damages. But insult—publicly smearing a man's good name and besmirching his honor—implies no palpable injury and so does not exist in the eyes of the law. Honor is an intensely social concept, resting on reputation, community standing, and the esteem of kin and compatriots. To possess honor requires acknowledgment from others; it cannot exist in solitary conscience. Modern man, Berger has argued, is more responsive to dignity—the belief that personal worth inheres equally in each individual, regardless of his status in society. Dignity frees the evangelical to confront God alone, the capitalist to make contracts without customary encumbrances, and the reformer to uplift the lowly. Naked and alone man has dignity; extolled by peers and covered with ribbons, he has honor.

Anthropologists have also discovered the centrality of honor in several cultures. According to J. G. Peristiany, honor and shame often preoccupy individuals in small-scale settings, where face-to-face relationships predominate over anonymous or bureaucratic ones. Social standing in such communities is never completely secure, because it must be validated by public opinion whose fickleness compels men constantly to assert and prove their worth. Julian Pitt-Rivers has added that, if society rejects a man's evaluation of himself and treats his claim to honor with ridicule or contempt, his very identity suffers because it is based on the judgment of peers. Shaming refers to that process by which an insult or any public humiliation impugns an individual's honor and thereby threatens his sense of self. By risking injury in a violent encounter, an affronted man—whether victorious or not—restores his sense of status and thus validates anew his claim to honor. Only valorous action, not words, can redeem his place in the ranks of his peer group.

Bertram Wyatt-Brown has argued that this Old World ideal is the key to understanding southern history. Across boundaries of time, geography, and social class, the South was knit together by a primal concept of male valor, part of the ancient heritage of Indo-European folk cultures. Honor demanded clan loyalty, hospitality, protection of women, and defense of patriarchal prerogatives. Honorable men guarded their reputations, bristled at insults, and, where necessary, sought personal vindication through bloodshed. The culture of honor thrived in hierarchical rural communities like the American South and grew out of a fatalistic world view, which assumed that pain and suffering were man's fate. It accounts for the pervasive violence that marked relationships between southerners and explains their insistence on vengeance and their rejection of legal redress in settling quarrels. Honor tied personal identity to public fulfillment of social roles. Neither bourgeois self-control nor internalized conscience determined status; judgment by one's fellows was the wellspring of community standing.

In this light, the seemingly trivial causes for brawls . . . —name calling, subtle ridicule, breaches of decorum, displays of poor manners—make sense. If a man's good name was his most important possession, then any slight cut him deeply. "Having words" precipitated fights because words brought shame and undermined a man's sense of self. Symbolic acts, such as buying a round of drinks, conferred honor on all, while refusing to share a bottle implied some inequality in social status. Honor inhered not only in individuals but also in kin and peers; when members of two cliques had words, their tested leaders or several men from each side fought to uphold group prestige. Inheritors of primal honor, the southern plain folk were quick to take offense, and any perceived affront forced a man either to devalue himself or to strike back violently and avenge the wrong.

The concept of male honor takes us a long way toward understanding the meaning of eye-gouging matches. But backwoods people did not simply acquire some primordial notion without modifying it. Definitions of honorable behavior have always varied enormously across cultures. The southern upcountry fostered a particular style of honor, which grew out of the contradiction between equality and hierarchy. Honorific societies tend to be sharply stratified. Honor is apportioned according to rank, and men fight to maintain personal standing within their social categories. Because black chattel slavery was the basis for the southern hierarchy, slave owners had the most wealth and honor, while other whites scrambled for a bit of each, and bondsmen were permanently impoverished and dishonored. Here was a source of tension for the plain folk. Men of honor shared freedom and equality; those denied honor were implicitly less than equal—perilously close to a slave-like condition. But in the eyes of the gentry, poor whites as well as blacks were outside the circle of honor, so both groups were subordinate. Thus, a herdsman's insult failed to shame a planter since the two men were not on the same social level. Without a threat to the gentleman's honor, there was no need for a duel; horsewhipping the insolent fellow sufficed.

Southern plain folk, then, were caught in a social contradiction. Society taught all white men to consider themselves equal, encouraged them to compete for power and status, yet threatened them from below with the specter of servitude and from above with insistence on obedience to rank and authority. Cut off from upper-class tests of honor, backcountry people adopted their own. A rough-and-tumble was more than a poor man's duel, a botched version of genteel combat. Plain folk chose not to ape the dispassionate, antiseptic, gentry style but to invert it. While the gentleman's code of honor insisted on cool restraint, eye gougers gloried in unvarnished brutality. In contrast to duelists' aloof silence, backwoods fighters screamed defiance to the world. As their own unique rites of honor, rough-and-tumble matches allowed backcountry men to shout their equality at each other. And eye-gouging fights also dispelled any stigma of servility. Ritual boasts, soaring oaths, outrageous ferocity, unflinching bloodiness—all proved a man's freedom. Where the slave acted obsequiously, the backwoodsman resisted the slightest affront; where human chattels accepted blows and never raised a hand, plain folk celebrated violence; where blacks could not jeopardize their value as property, poor whites proved their autonomy by risking bodily parts. Symbolically reaffirming their claims to honor, gouging matches helped resolve painful uncertainties arising out of the ambiguous place of plain folk in the southern social structure.

Backwoods fighting reminds us of man's capacity for cruelty and is an excellent corrective to romanticizing premodern life. But a close look also keeps us from drawing facile conclusions about innate human aggressiveness. Eye gouging represented neither the "real" human animal emerging on the frontier, nor nature acting through man in a Darwinian struggle for survival, nor anarchic disorder and communal breakdown. Rather, rough-and-tumble fighting was ritualized behavior—a product of specific cultural assumptions. Men drink together, tongues loosen, a simmering old rivalry begins to boil; insult is given, offense taken, ritual boasts commence; the fight begins, mettle is tested, blood redeems honor, and equilibrium is restored. Eye gouging was the poor and middling white's own version of a historical southern tendency to consider personal violence socially useful—indeed, ethically essential.

Rough-and-tumble fighting emerged from the confluence of economic conditions, social relationships, and culture in the southern backcountry. Primitive markets and the semisubsistence basis of life threw men back on close ties to kin and community. Violence and poverty were part of daily existence, so endurance, even callousness, became functional values. Loyal to their localities, their occupations, and each other, men came together and found release from life's hardships in strong drink, tall talk, rude practical jokes, and cruel sports. They craved one another's recognition but rejected genteel, pious, or bourgeois values, awarding esteem on the basis of their own traditional standards. The glue that held men together was an intensely competitive status system in which the most prodigious drinker or strongest arm wrestler, the best tale teller, fiddle player, or log roller, the most daring gambler, original liar, skilled hunter, outrageous swearer, or accurate marksman was accorded respect by the others. Reputation was everything, and scars were badges of honor. Rough-and-tumble fighting demonstrated unflinching willingness to inflict pain while risking mutilation— all to defend one's standing among peers—and became a central expression of the all-male subculture.

Eye gouging continued long after the antebellum period. As the market economy absorbed new parts of the backcountry, however, the way of life that supported rough-and-tumbling waned. Certainly by mid-century the number of incidents declined, precisely when expanding international demand brought ever more upcountry acres into staple production. Towns, schools, churches, revivals, and families gradually overtook the backwoods. In a slow and uneven process, keelboats gave way to steamers, then railroads; squatters, to cash crop farmers; hunters and trappers, to preachers. The plain folk code of honor was far from dead, but emergent social institutions engendered a moral ethos that warred against the old ways. For many individuals, the justifications for personal violence grew stricter, and mayhem became unacceptable.

Ironically, progress also had a darker side. New technologies and modes of production could enhance men's fighting abilities. "Birmingham and Pittsburgh are obliged to complete . . . the equipment of the 'chivalric Kentuckian,' " Charles Agustus Murray observed in the 1840s, as bowie knives ended more and more rough-and-tumbles. Equally important, in 1835 the first modern revolver appeared, and manufacturers marketed cheap, accurate editions in the coming decade. Dueling weapons had been costly, and Kentucky rifles or horse pistols took a full minute to load and prime. The revolver, however, which fitted neatly into a man's pocket, settled more and more personal disputes. Raw and brutal as rough-and-tumbling was, it could not survive the use of arms. Yet precisely because eye gouging was so violent—because combatants cherished maimings, blindings, even castrations—it unleashed death wishes that invited new technologies of destruction.

With improved weaponry, dueling entered its golden age during the antebellum era. Armed combat remained both an expression of gentry sensibility and a mark of social rank. But in a society where status was always shifting and unclear, dueling did not stay confined to the upper class. The habitual carrying of weapons, once considered a sign of unmanly fear, now lost some of its stigma. As the backcountry changed, tests of honor continued, but gunplay rather than fighting tooth-and-nail appealed to new men with social aspirations. Thus, progress and technology slowly circumscribed rough-and-tumble fighting, only to substitute a deadlier option. Violence grew neater and more lethal as men checked their savagery to murder each other.

Harness Racing: The First Modern American Sport, 1825–1870

MELVIN L. ADELMAN

Historians have assigned the rise of sport in America to the last three decades of the nineteenth century. Although they found antecedants to this development in the antebellum period, especially during the 1850s, they presented the era as one of limited sporting activity. This perspective of the pre-Civil War years is unfortunately based on only a handful of studies and most of these examine the changing attitudes toward athletics. The sporting patterns in New York City between 1820 and 1870 revealed, however, a much more active sporting life than was heretofore thought to have existed at that time. Far from mere prefigurings, the framework of modern sport was established during this half century.

The modernization of harness racing between 1825 and 1870 exemplifies the growth and transformation of sport during this period. An examination of the modernization of trotting can proceed by employing two ideal sporting types: one premodern and the other modern. These ideal sporting types need not be perfect representations of actual historical stages, but they may be distinguished by six polar characteristics (see Table 1). The modernization of sport entails the movement of the activity in the direction of the modern ideal type. This movement is generally, although not always, accompanied by a shift in the playing arena from an open to a closed one, the increasing presence of spectators and the commercialization of the sport.

Prior to 1825, harness racing was a premodern sport. Trotting consisted primarily of informal road contests which took place mainly in the northeastern section of the country. The sport was unorganized, lacked standardized rules, attracted limited public attention and possessed no permanent records. By 1870, harness racing had become a modern sport. The creation of the National Trotting Association in that year indicates the development of harness racing into a highly organized sport, with fairly uniform rules and with contests taking place throughout the country. The modernization of trotting is further illustrated by the coverage harness racing received in the daily and sporting press, the emergence of statistics and records and the appearance in 1871 of the first stud book devoted exclusively to trotting. Finally, harness racing emerged as the first sport to be successfully commercialized. By the mid-nineteenth century, trotting replaced thoroughbred racing as this country's number one spectator sport. Not until after the Civil War did base-

From Melvin L. Adelman, "The First Modern Sport in America: Harness Racing in New York City, 1825–1870," *Journal of Sport History* 8 (Spring 1981): 5–32.

ball challenge the supreme position of trotting; but by 1870, if not for awhile longer, harness racing remained the nation's leading spectator sport.

The contention that harness racing was the first modern sport in America does not mean that it was the initial sport to assume modern characteristics. Thoroughbred racing began to modernize during the eighteenth century when permanent jockey clubs were established. The modernization of this sport reached its pre-Civil War peak during the 1830s when the sport enjoyed a period of unprecedented growth and prosperity. By the mid-1840s, however, the process grounded to a halt when the sport collapsed throughout the North. With horse racing confined mainly to the South during the subsequent two decades, the modernization of the sport remained dormant until the revival of thoroughbred racing in the North in the years immediately following the Civil War. By 1870, nevertheless, the gestalt of horse racing was not as yet modern despite the significant steps in this direction during the antebellum period.

Conversely, the claims that harness racing had become a modern sport by 1870 does not mean to suggest that the modernization of trotting was complete by this date. Rather a key point of this article is that a certain stage is reached as a sport moves along the continuum from the premodern to the modern ideal form in which modern characteristics are sufficiently present to shape the structure and direction of the sport. At this juncture, the sport presents a modern configuration, one

Table 1.   The Characteristics of Premodern and Modern Ideal Sporting Types

PREMODERN SPORT	MODERN SPORT
1. ORGANIZATION—is either non-existent or at best informal and sporadic. Contests are arranged by individuals directly or indirectly (e.g., tavern-owners, bettors) involved.	1. ORGANIZATION—formal organizations, institutionally differentiated at the local, regional and national level.
2. RULES—are simple, unwritten and based upon local customs and traditions. Variations exist from locale to locale.	2. RULES—are formal, standardized and written. Rules are rationally and pragmatically worked out and legitimized by organizational means.
3. COMPETITION—locally meaningful contests only: no chance for national reputation.	3. COMPETITION— national and international superimposed on local contests; chance to establish national and international reputation.
4. ROLE DIFFERENTIATION—low role differentiation among participants and loose distinction between playing and spectating roles.	4. ROLE DIFFERENTIATION—high role differentiation; emergence of specialists (professionals) and strict distinctions between playing and spectating roles.
5. PUBLIC INFORMATION—is limited, local and oral.	5. PUBLIC INFORMATION—is reported on a regular basis in local newspapers as well as national sporting journals. The appearance of specialized magazines, guidebooks, etc.
6. STATISTICS AND RECORDS—non-existent.	6. STATISTICS AND RECORDS—are kept, published on a regular basis and are considered important measure of achievement. Records are sanctioned by national associations.

which shares more in common with its future than its premodern past. It is in this sense that harness racing had become America's first modern sport by 1870.

Harness racing conjures up a rural image, the sport of the county fair. Trotting was, however, an urban product. The sport first emerged on urban roads and developed its most salient modern characteristics in the city. New York played a more critical role in the development of harness racing than any other city. As early as 1832, the *Spirit of the Times* recognized that New York was the premier city in the breeding and training of trotting horses. Nearly a quarter of a century later, one frequent correspondent to this sporting journal maintained that trotting was indigenous to the Empire City and that there were "more fine horses here than can be found any where else in the world." The importance of New York to the growth of the sport did not derive solely from the concentration of the best stock in the metropolitan region. New York was the hub of harness racing throughout the period 1825 to 1870. In the nation's most populated city, there were more trotting tracks, more races, including a disproportionate number of the leading contests, and more prize money offered than in any other place in the country. Equally significant, the characteristics of modern harness racing initially appeared in New York. Here the sport was first organized and commercialized. As a result, New York set the pattern that was to be followed on a national scale.

* * * *

Harness racing emerged as a popular pastime in New York and in other parts of the northeast in the first quarter of the nineteenth century. . . .

. . . Trotting emerged at this time because improvements in the roads now made the sport possible. One historian noted that "it was only natural that the speed of the harness horse found its first testing ground upon the smooth hard roads whose networks radiated from the northeastern cities . . . especially those of the Boston–New York–Philadelphia regions."

Sportsmen began racing their "roadsters" (as street trotters came to be called) because it provided them with an amusement which was convenient, participatory and relatively inexpensive. Third Avenue quickly emerged as New York's major trotting area. Beginning outside the residential portion of the city at that time, the approximately five mile road was perfectly suited for these informal trials of speed. In close proximity to the homes of the horsemen, it was a convenient location for these contests which started upon the completion of the day's work and which usually lasted until dark. Moreover, numerous taverns dotted the highway where reinsmen could stop, arrange contests and discuss the latest sporting developments.

These impromptu contests appealed to the city's horsemen because they allowed personal participation. Unlike thoroughbred racing, where the owner and the rider of the horse had long been separated, trotting permitted the sportsman to demonstrate the prowess of his horse, as well as his own skill as a reinsman. Finally, the pastime did not require the capital outlay of thoroughbred racing. The trotter was not a "pure breed," but rather a horse drawn from the common stock that had the ability to trot. The plebian horses that engaged in these road races, moreover, were almost always used by their owners in their day-to-day activities.

Although early nineteenth-century trotting consisted almost exclusively of these impromptu contests, permanent structures began to emerge. The first trotting tracks in the New York metropolitan region were mere extensions of the courses used for thoroughbred racing. The most significant of these tracks was located in Harlem, and the first recorded performance by an American trotter took place there in 1806. Several years later, the first track constructed exclusively for trotting was built in Harlem next to the Red House Tavern. The course was the major resort for the Third Avenue road racing crowd and the track was probably constructed for their benefit. While racing took place on both courses, these tracks remained essentially training grounds for the city's roadsters. . . .

The formation of the New York Trotting Club (NYTC) in the Winter of 1824–1825 marks the first critical step in the modernization of harness racing. The first organized trotting club in America, there is no information on its members, although most were probably drawn from the men who raced their roadsters on Third Avenue and other roads in the New York metropolitan region. The creation of the NYTC was inspired by the success thoroughbred racing had enjoyed in New York after the State revoked its anti-racing legislation in 1821. The NYTC drew its objectives and methods heavily from the experience of horse racing. Similar to the racing organization of its sister sport, the NYTC justified its association on utilitarian grounds (the sport's contribution to the improvement of the breed); instituted regular meetings twice yearly; and, constructed a race course (in Centerville, Long Island) to facilitate the growth of the sport.

Trotting in New York made significant advances as both a participatory and spectator sport in the two decades following the formation of the NYTC. In 1835, the *Spirit* noted that the "number of fast horses for which our city is so celebrated is steadily accumulating." With some exaggeration, one contemporary observer claimed that "there was scarcely a gentleman in New York who did not own one or two fast (trotting) horses." The rising cost of good roadsters further indicated the increasing appeal of the sport. During the 1830s, the price of the best trotting horses doubled. In addition, trotting races on the city's tracks, especially the major ones, generated considerable excitement among New York's sporting crowd. In 1838, the *New York Herald* reported that the contest between *Dutchman* and *Ratner* created "as much interest in our city and neighborhood" as the intersectional horse race between *John Bascombe* and *Post Boy* held in New York two years earlier.

The emerging commercialization of trotting most accurately dramatizes the growth of the sport. By the mid-1830s, entrepreneurs began to tap the public interest in harness races that took place on New York's streets and tracks. The experience of the Beacon Course in nearby Hoboken, New Jersey, illustrates the early introduction of the profit motive into trotting. This course was constructed in 1837 for thoroughbred racing. When the sport proved unprofitable the following year, the proprietors of the track started to promote harness racing for the sole purpose of reaping the financial rewards from the gate receipts. By the early 1840s, businessmen had replaced the original sponsors of trotting—the road runners and their associations—as the major promotors of the sport. . . .

As thoroughbred racing collapsed throughout the North in the decade following the Depression of 1837, the sporting press took increasing note of the activities of the trotting horse. By the early 1840s, they suggested that the "ugly duckling" had become the legitimate rival of her more respected sister. . . .

Contemporaries claimed that the corresponding fates of the two turf sports were closely linked to the characteristics associated with the two different horses. In contrast to the aristocratic and foreign thoroughbred, the trotter was perceived as the democratic, utilitarian, and, by logical extension, the American horse. Implicit was the belief that harness racing surpassed horse racing as the leading turf sport because it more accurately captured the spirit of the American experience. . . .

. . . While contemporaries grossly exaggerated the extent to which the masses owned trotters, ownership of these plebeian and relatively inexpensive horses was far more widespread than thoroughbreds. . . . The evidence indicates that only a small number of trotting men came from the "upper crust." Conversely, the cost and upkeep of trotting horses were still sufficiently high to generally exclude individuals who fell below the middle class. While broad parameters still exist, it appears that trotting owners came from the more prosperous segments of the middle class—men who lived a comfortable, but hardly opulent, lifestyle. . . .

. . . The growth of harness racing did reflect shifting patterns of travel. With the improvement of roads and wagons, the driving horse increasingly replaced the saddle horse as the basic means of convoy in the northeastern and Middle Atlantic states. . . .

Since Americans believed that the true nature of the trotter—democratic and utilitarian—could only be developed in this country, they perceived the trotter as a native product. . . . The assumptions may be passed off as American chauvinism, but the contention that both the horse and the sport were indigenous products does contain merit. Harness racing had been a popular pastime in England, but its emergence as a sport first occurred in the United States. Similarly, the establishment of a distinct breed of trotting race horse was an American creation, although this process was not completed until the late nineteenth century. More significantly, it was the perception of the trotter as the American horse, more than the reality, which was of critical importance to the growth of the sport. . . .

. . . Trotting's supreme position in the turf world can be more productively analyzed in terms of three interacting forces: the increasing potential for commercialized amusements made possible by urban and economic expansion; the greater susceptibility of trotting to commercialization than any of its sporting counterparts; and, the more innovative nature of trotting.

The absence of surplus wealth and concentrated populations traditionally restricted the development of commercialized amusements. During the antebellum period, these two major barriers began to dissolve under the impact of urban and economic growth. . . .

The plebeian character of the trotter and its relatively inexpensive price made the sport more susceptible to commercialization. Since the trotter cost less than the thoroughbred, the prize money offered by track proprietors did not have to be as great for the owners of the trotters to cover their cost and make a profit. As late as 1860, purses in New York rarely exceeded $250 and contests could be run for as low as $10. . . .

The nature of the trotter facilitated the commercialization of the sport by making more races possible. Whereas a good thoroughbred might race six or seven times a year, the more durable trotter started at least twice as many races annually. Furthermore, a trotter's career lasted longer, many racing into their teens. More importantly, the trotter came from the common horse stock. Consequently, there were simply more of them to race. The impact of the greater numbers can be seen in terms of the respective racing sessions in New York. There were at most three weeks of thoroughbred racing in the city annually; but hardly a week would pass, except in the winter months, without a trotting match taking place somewhere in the New York metropolitan region.

Finally, harness racing was not bogged down in the "aristocratic" trappings which characterized horse racing. In 1843, the *Spirit* recognized that trotting men were more innovative and aggressive than their horse racing counterparts. As a result of their greater "enterprise, industry and go *aheadiveness,*" the sporting journal predicted, harness racing "will soon be a formidable rival to thoroughbred racing in the North." . . .

Trotting was more innovative than horse racing in two critical ways. The first was a product of the different social backgrounds of those involved in the respective sports. Engaged in thoroughbred racing were wealthy men and/or people from established families. Most of the owners of trotting horses and the proprietors of trotting tracks, however, appeared to have been middle-class in origin. The different social origins affected the entire tone of the two turf sports. While thoroughbred racing was run for and by the upper class, harness racing enticed a broader segment of the populace. The commercially minded proprietors of trotting tracks catered more readily to all ticket holders than those involved in their sister sport. . . .

In addition, trotting was more innovative because the comparatively new sport was not inhibited by tradition. By the 1840s, horse racing in America had a long heritage on how a thoroughbred race should be conducted. The absence of institutional confinements made it easier for trotting to adjust to commercialization. Similar to their horse racing counterparts, trotting men initially valued a horse which combined speed and endurance. Early trotting contests were raced in heats from one to five miles. By the early 1840s, trotting men broke with this pattern. Most major contests were now one mile heats with the winner required to win three heats. Since the new system placed less strain on the trotter, the horse could race more frequently and thereby more races were possible. Furthermore, harness racing contests took place in a wider variety of styles, giving the sport greater diversity and interest.

Harness racing surged to the forefront of not only the turf world but modern sport in general, because more than any other sport of the day it captured the flow of the American experience. In common with other forms of popular entertainment, the emergence of trotting as a spectator sport was a product of the two dynamic forces—urbanization and economic expansion—transforming and modernizing American life. The impact of these agents of change would have been far less had not trotting possessed properties which predisposed it toward commercialization. Here the nature of the horse played a critical role. Of equal significance was the fact that those who governed trotting, at least from the standpoint of sport, internalized the values of modern society. As such, they put a greater premium on innovation rather than tradition, and cash rather than class.

Harness racing progressed rapidly as a popular spectator sport both in New York and throughout the country in the two decades preceding the Civil War. While the change in the social and economic conditions, discussed in the previous section, created the setting for the growth of the sport, performers attracted the crowds. During the early years of organized trotting, numerous horses left their mark on the history of the sport, but it was *Lady Suffolk* who set the standard of excellence and was the sport's first hero. The fifteen year career of *Lady Suffolk* (1838–1853), moreover, illustrates the condition and development of trotting during this period.

Foaled in 1833, *Lady Suffolk* was . . . a descendant of imported *Messenger,* the founding father of the American trotter, but no preparation was made for the trotting career. As a weanling she was sold for $60, then resold as a two year old for $90. At age four she was pulling a butcher or oyster cart when David Bryan purchased her for $112.50 for use in his livery stable. The prowess of the horse went undiscovered until none other than William T. Porter by chance rented her for a tour of the Long Island tracks. The editor of the *Spirit* was impressed with the *Lady's* speed and good gait. He told Bryan that she had too much potential as a racer to be wasted in his stable. . . .

. . . Bryan was the embodiment of the professional ethic which came to dominate the sport. As one historian wrote, "For Bryan, his *Lady Suffolk* . . . was a mint of money, a nugget of rich metal to be melted by him in the heat of competition and struck off into dollars." Bryan raced his grey mare mainly in the New York metropolitan area because this is where he lived and, even more importantly, because the city's courses provided the best financial opportunities. Similar to other professional trotting men of his day, however, Bryan campaigned with *Lady Suffolk* on the growing number of tracks throughout the country, going as far west as St. Louis and as far south as New Orleans. . . . He entered the *Lady* in 162 races, and won between $35,000 and $60,000. The ability of *Lady Suffolk* to achieve victory, despite the clumsy and inept driving of her owner, derived from her saintly patience, an unbreakable spirit and a remarkable endurance. . . .

Harness racing had emerged as the nation's leading spectator sport by the time *Lady Suffolk* was retired in the early 1850s. During this decade, the sport emerged as an integral part of the county fair, and the public's desire to see harness races resulted in the creation of an ever increasing number of trotting tracks throughout the country. By 1858, one sporting journal estimated that over seventy trotting courses existed in America. . . .

. . . While trotting men had always been preoccupied with "time" as a measure of their horses' abilities and performances, statistics and records took on new importance when horsemen began touring the increasing number of tracks in search of fame and fortune. That these measurements served the interest of track promoters and fans of the sport was to a large extent responsible for their expanding value. Since a trotter might visit a city only once a year, proprietors of the courses could use the statistical reputation of a horse to encourage people to come to see the race even though they may have never seen him perform. Similarly, statistics nourished fan interest by providing them with a method of evaluating a horse in the absence of personal observation or witnessing the horse race on only a handful of occasions.

Trotting men were not only familiar with unsurpassed performances but were already cognizant of the concept of the record. In 1860, for example, *Flora Temple,* who succeeded *Lady Suffolk* as the "princess of the turf," sought to break *Dutchman's* record (7:32.5) for three miles. . . .

New York continued to dominate the development of harness racing even though the sport expanded nationally. At least seven trotting tracks existed in the metropolitan region, with three—Union, Fashion and Centerville Courses—hosting first class contests. More significantly, with the ever increasing importance of gate receipts, trotting in the Empire City drew the largest number of spectators. Between six and eight thousand spectators were usually present at each of the four to six leading matches held annually. However, when *Flora Temple* raced, attendance could jump into double figures. . . .

The growth of harness racing as a sports spectacle did not occur without problems. As the commercial and professional ethic came to dominate the sport, suspicions of irregularities on the trotting track markedly increased. The question of the integrity of harness racing produced the first extensive discussion and concern about the honesty of professional-commercial sport. . . .

The nature of professional athletics made creditable the assertion that races were fixed. Since the major purpose of the contest for the professional athlete is to make money, what guarantees exist that he would not manipulate the event to maximize his profit? A certain class bias against the professional athlete accentuated the suspicions inherent within the professional system. While no monolithic view of either the professional athlete or professional athletics existed, the prevailing attitude was that the public was assured honest contests only when the "better class governed the sport."

The strong temptations confronting the professional athlete went far in explaining why the press so vehemently opposed what was known as "hippodroming"—the making of contests for the sole purpose of splitting the gate receipts (in contrast to racing for stakes and purses). With no money depending on the outcome, and therefore with no incentive to win, these "concocted affairs" were perfect races to rig. . . .

The development of hippodroming was a legitimate response to the financial considerations of both the owners of the horses and the proprietors of the courses rather than being the product of evil intent. . . . It emerged from the inadequacy of the prevalent winner-take-all system. The new arrangements made it possible for a horse to be defeated and the owner still be able to cover part of his cost and possibly emerge with a profit. Consequently, it gradually facilitated an expansion in both the number of trotters and races. Equally important for the proprietors, it guaranteed the presence of the super horses that drew the huge crowds. . . .

Serious doubts must be raised of the prevalent view that widespread manipulation of races followed on the heels of the growth of professional-commercial harness racing. While dishonest contests occurred in New York, they were the exception rather than the rule. Nevertheless, professionalization did significantly alter the character of these contests. The emphasis of amateur turfmen on style and sportsmanship yielded to the sole objective of success as jockies adopted tricks and tactics which, if not outright violations of the rules, permitted the drivers to get all he could within them. . . .

While commercialization became harness racing's leading characteristic by the 1850s, informal trials of speed persisted on New York's streets. With the growth of the city, however, severe restrictions began to be placed on the roadster. By the early 1860s, New York's road runners had moved from Third Avenue to Harlem Lane in the upper part of Manhattan. This location shortly began to succumb to the forces of progress. Dismayed by the prospect of the loss of New York's last good driving area, the editor of *Wilkes' Spirit* believed that it "was incumbent upon the city's authorities to supply the vacancy created by the occupation of Harlem Lane." As the headquarters of the fast trotter, anything less, he suggested, "would be a national loss, as well as a municipal sham and disgrace."

The call for government intervention might be considered a "far sighted" approach, but trotting men took steps more typical of the period. They established private organizations which bought or rented their own tracks. Unlike earlier trotting or jockey clubs, these organizations did not sponsor public or private races, although club members could and probably did arrange contests amongst themselves and their guests. Rather, they were formed to perpetuate an informal pastime no longer possible in the more formalized urban setting. The first of these clubs was the Elm Park Pleasure Grounds Association established in the late 1850s. The majority of the 400 members were prosperous businessmen, although there were a handful of men of considerable wealth, most notably Cornelius Vanderbilt and Robert Bonner.

. . . Robert Bonner . . . amassed his fortune by the time he was thirty as the owner of the *New York Ledger,* a weekly family journal. In 1856, his physician advised him to find an outdoor recreation for health reasons. Bonner then bought a horse and began driving it on New York's speedways. There he had a few brushes with Vanderbilt. What emerged was a friendly rivalry between these two for the ownership of the best trotters. The Bonner-Vanderbilt duel . . . symbolized and gave impetus to an already existing process.

In the battle between the two giants, Bonner emerged as the king of the road. He spent lavishly in purchasing some of the best trotters of his era. Between 1859 and 1870, Bonner bought thirteen horses at a total cost of $162,000. His prize purchase was *Dexter,* clearly the number one trotter of his day. By the time he retired in 1890, the newspaper magnate had spent nearly half a million dollars for his horses, including $40,000 each for his stars *Maud S.* and *Pocahontas.*

Bonner's reputation as a horseman did not derive solely from his ownership of possibly the largest and best stable. A more significant reason, as the *New York Tribune* pointed out, was that he "did more to lift the trotting horse from disrepute to respectability than any other man." According to the universally accepted perspective, prior to Bonner's involvement, acceptable society viewed the owners of trotting horses as fast men "who spent their afternoons trotting from tavern to tavern . . . (and) had too much money in their pockets." Bonner was the critical figure in altering this negative impression. A man of unimpeachable character, . . . he so violently opposed gambling that he refused to enter his horses in public places. Consequently, Bonner could bring a dignity to the sport that other wealthy *nou-*

veaux, such as the salty Vanderbilt, never could. Through Bonner's influence, the ownership of trotting horses won an acceptable position in society. . . .

Nouveaux riche New Yorkers became involved in trotting, as they would in other sports, as a means of status confirmation. Interesting differences existed, however, between trotting and other sporting activities. In the prevailing pattern, new wealth asserted its position by patronizing those sports which had an upper class heritage and/or could be afforded only by men of wealth. In the early years of trotting, the sport shared none of these characteristics. [For trotting] to function as other upper class sports, therefore, exclusiveness had to be created. Two interrelated processes accomplished this transformation: the purchasing of the best trotters at lavish prices and the rationalization of the breeding industry.

The willingness of wealthy men to pay premium prices resulted in their monopoly of the best trotters by the 1870s. The soaring cost of trotters was in part a product of the growth of the sport and the increasing number of bidders for what is a relatively fixed market. . . . The fabulous sums trotting horses attracted was a critical part of the status game. To have obtained the best horses at anything less than these fantastic sums would have not satisfied the needs of these *parvenus* to demonstrate their wealth and status.

The rationalizations of the breeding industry further encouraged the concentration of good trotting horses in the hands of the wealthy. In the mid-nineteenth century, this business required little capital, organization or promotion. Some attention was paid to pedigree; however, lineage was usually guesswork, if not outright falsification. The small scale on which the business was run was not conducive to finely selective breeding, but its random nature had the valuable result of diffusing the blood of the best stock widely throughout the country. . . .

Within two or three decades, small breeders yielded to the larger stables owned by wealthy men for pleasure, profit or both. These well capitalized stock farms gathered the best trotters. Similar to other American industries in the latter part of the nineteenth century, the concentration of talent and wealth permitted the breeding of trotting horses to become a more rationalized process. For the small breeder, the swift trotter was essentially a sideline, although an important one, to the general stud services his horses provided. Above all, the major objective was the procreation of the race and the overall improvement of the breed. In the large stables, speed was the sole objective. . . .

During the 1870s, four more critical steps were taken to rationalize the breeding industry: (1) the creation of the first turf register devoted exclusively to the trotting horse (1871); (2) the appearance of the first sporting journal, *Wallace's Monthly Magazine,* concerned primarily with trotting affairs (1875); (3) the formation of the National Association of Trotting Horse Breeders (1876); and, (4) the establishment of a standard breed of trotting horse (1879). By the end of this decade, the rationalization of the breeding industry solidified the ownership of the leading trotters in the hands of wealthy men. Unable to compete with the big farms, the horses of the smaller breeders found themselves confined to tracks at county fairs. The day that a horse could be removed from a butcher's cart and became a world's champion was relegated to dime novels and serials in popular magazines.

Neither the shift in the social composition of the owners of trotting horses nor changes in the breeding industry undermined the popularity of harness racing. Since the initial growth of the sport was strongly linked to the inexpensive cost of the trotter and its broadly based ownership, why did trotting continue to enjoy widespread popular appeal in the aftermath of these profound alterations? The persistent perception of the trotter as the democratic and utilitarian horse, despite the changes, played a contributory role. . . .

The symbiotic relationship that already developed between the growth of harness racing, the changes in the breeding industry and the commercialization of the sport was an even more important factor. This linkage made it virtually impossible for the wealthy owners of trotters to create a sport run solely for their own class. While considerations of status contributed to elite involvement in this sport, financial concern, for the overwhelming majority of these turfmen, were always present. To offset the surging cost of trotting horses required a corresponding expansion of the economic side of the sport. Consequently, trotting men continued to welcome the public and their money from gate receipts and gambling as a means of defraying their expenses and making a profit. The ongoing willingness of harness racing to cater to a broad segment of the population resulted in the perpetuation of trotting as the "people's pastime."

Harness racing underwent tremendous growth as a commercial-spectator sport in New York in the 1860s. . . . The rapid expansion of harness racing not only in New York but throughout the nation during this decade, and especially after the Civil War, gave rise to several problems. . . . [In response,] delegates from forty-six tracks in fifteen states established the National Trotting Association (NTA). . . .

The dual objectives of the NTA were the creation of uniform government and the prevention and punishment of fraud. To facilitate the former goal, the NTA adopted rules which would be used at all tracks in the association. To expedite the later aim, the NTA attempted to buttress the power of local authorities by creating a board of appeals which would rule on all kinds of infractions. To give muscle to this court, it made the suspension on one track applicable to all courses within the federation. . . .

The formation of the NTA can be more appropriately examined as a response to what were the major problems of the turf: the inefficiency of uncoordinated local organizations and local rules to meet the needs of the proprietors of the courses and the owners of the horses. . . . Only with the tremendous expansion of trotting in the years following the Civil War, however, did the extant institutional structures of harness racing become incapable of meeting the requirements of the sport. . . . The creation of the NTA, to borrow a popular historical phrase, was part of harness racing's "search for order."

Trotting had long been governed solely by local rules. . . . Moreover, races began to be handicapped to maintain competitive balance between the increasing number of trotters present on the course. In the early 1860s, New York tracks began handicapping by weight, but not until the next decade was the more efficient system of time-classification introduced. The increase in the number of tracks throughout the country was far more significant in producing homogeneity in the rules. To facilitate the easy movement of horses from course to course, standardization of the rules and regulations became necessary. . . .

Besides the necessity of uniform rules, the expansion of harness racing made it imperative that the various tracks be coordinated. For New York's major courses it was not so much a question of the need to synchronize their respective schedules as it was the growing competition from the increasing number of tracks emerging outside of Manhattan. With these courses offering good prize money to attract top notch horses to their meetings, even New York lacked the financial resources to meet the combined competition of these tracks. While New York remained the sport's capital, the virtual monopoly it had of the best horses in former days was undermined. In the years immediately following the Civil War. . . . to guarantee the presence of the best talent, the enlarged market necessitated the creation of some form of systematic scheduling to avoid conflicting engagements. . . .

The formation of the NTA symbolized the transformation of harness racing from a premodern to a modern sport. In contrast to the informal road contests which took place in the northeastern section of the country a half century earlier, harness racing evolved into a highly organized sport, with relatively uniform rules and with contests taking place in all sections of the nation. The emergence of a trotting literature (stud books and *Wallace's Monthly Magazine*) and developments in the breeding industry (the formation of the National Association of Trotting Horse Breeders and the creation of a standard breed) in the 1870s further demonstrated the centralizing and modernizing forces at work in the sport. By this decade, one social historian noted, harness racing "had grown to such mammoth proportions and won a greater share of the public attention than any other public pastime which contributed to the enjoyment of the people."

FURTHER READING

Melvin L. Adelman, *A Sporting Time: New York City and the Rise of Modern Athletics, 1820–1870* (1986)

Dwight Akers, *Drivers Up! The Story of American Harness Racing* (1938)

Jack W. Berryman, "Sport, Health, and the Rural-Urban Conflict: Baltimore and John Stuart Skinner's American Farmer, 1819–1820," *Conspectus of History* 1 (1982), 43–61

John Dizikes, *Sportsmen and Gamesmen* (1981)

Elliott Gorn, *The Manly Art: Bare-Knuckle Prize Fighting in America* (1986)

Jennie Holliman, *American Sport, 1785–1835* (1931)

Peter Levine, "The Promise of Sport in Antebellum America," *Journal of American Culture* 2 (1980), 623–34

Edwin A. Miles, "President Adams' Billiard Table," *New England Quarterly* 45 (1972), 31–43

George Moss, "The Long Distance Runners in Ante-Bellum America," *Journal of Popular Culture* 8 (1974), 370–82

David K. Wiggins, "Sport and Popular Pastimes: Shadow of the Slavequarter," *Canadian Journal of the History of Sport and Physical Education* 11 (May 1980), 61–88

Norman W. Yates, *William T. Porter and the Spirit of the Times* (1957)

The Making of a Modern Sporting Culture, 1840–1870

❂

American sport began a dramatic transformation in the mid-nineteenth century, a period when sport was premodern and primarily participatory. Sport at that time defined manly behavior as aggressive, vigorous, courageous, and unchildlike. However, during this era, sport began to modernize, and the stage was set for the sporting boom of the post–Civil War period.

How was this achieved? How important was it to transform sport from a morally suspect amusement into a respectable and progressive recreation? What was the role of the new positive sporting creed and the development of modern sports?

The United States in the 1830s and 1840s was in the midst of the Second Great Awakening, a religious revival that anticipated the Second Coming of Christ. The movement raised the religious consciousness of middle-class evangelical Protestants who strongly opposed the pastimes of the male bachelor subculture on moral grounds. Secular reformers who felt that such uncivilized behavior was inappropriate for citizens of a Great Republic also opposed traditional amusements. They chastised gambling and blood sports for attracting the worst elements in society, teaching idleness and debauchery, and for not recreating participants and spectators.

Religious and secular reformers joined forces during the Jacksonian Era to create the first great period of American social reform when they sought to raise moral standards, fight slavery, promote democracy, and cope with problems of urban growth such as slums, drunkenness, rising crime rates, and epidemics. Many of these reformers, like Thomas Wentworth Higginson and Catharine Beecher, envisioned physical culture and clean outdoor sports as a potential answer to many social problems.

A positive sports creed emerged that recognized the possibility that clean sports could provide an alternative to vile games and promote public health, improve morality, and develop character. Good role models were provided by immigrant sports organizations like the German Turnverein, which emphasized gymnastics. Several sports became popular, including cricket, croquet, and cycling, but the most important was the new team game of baseball, which soon became the national pastime. Base-

ball and cricket particularly seemed to fit in well with the requirements of the new positive sports creed. Cricket and baseball, as baseball became more difficult and dangerous to play, were perceived as manly sports that promoted health, built character, and promoted morality. The sports creed not only promoted sports but also influenced the growing park movement, which in turn encouraged municipalities to set aside public space to facilitate healthful, uplifting recreations. The first such space was Central Park in New York, which was completed in 1858 and designed to include special places for games like baseball and cricket. However, park planner Frederick Law Olmsted, who supervised the construction of Central Park, personally preferred receptive (inactive) recreation that protected the park's grounds over active (sporting) recreation, and his vision had a great impact on the park's early use.

⚾ D O C U M E N T S

The first document is drawn from the classic essay "Saints and Their Bodies," written in 1858 by the Rev. Thomas Wentworth Higginson, a Boston brahmin and a leading social reformer. He, like many other reformers, was a champion of physical fitness. Higginson was a "muscular Christian" who advocated the union of a sound mind, body, and spirit. The second document is by Catharine Beecher, a member of a famous New England family, an early feminist, and one of the leading advocates of athletic activity for women. Beginning in 1832 with *Course of Calisthenics for Young Ladies,* Beecher had long encouraged physical fitness by recommending walking, swimming, horseback riding, and exercises to alleviate women's frailty. In *Letters to the People on Health and Happiness* (1855), she evaluated American women and offered suggestions for alleviating their ill health. The third document describes the benefits women derive from horseback riding. The fourth document describes the newly popular co-ed sport of ice skating at Central Park. The fifth document is an 1859 editorial from the *New York Herald* that compares baseball and cricket. The editor lauded both sports but explains why baseball had more popular appeal. The sixth document is an essay from the *Spirit of the Times* that praised the formation of the first major nonethnic athletic society in America, the New York Athletic Club, which became the model for future high-status athletic clubs in the United States.

Thomas W. Higginson Analyzes the American Clergy and Their Need for Physical Fitness, 1858

. . . There is in the community an impression that physical vigor and spiritual sanctity are incompatible. . . . But, happily times change. . . . Our moral conceptions are expanding to take in that "athletic virtue" of the Greeks. . . . The modern English "Broad Church" aims at breadth of shoulders, as well as of doctrines. . . . [Kingsley's] critics charge him with laying down a new definition of the saint, as a man who fears God and can walk a thousand miles in a thousand hours. . . .

From Thomas W. Higginson, "Saints and Their Bodies," *Atlantic Monthly* 1 (1858): 82–95.

. . . One of the most potent causes of the ill-concealed alienation between the clergy and the people, in our community, is the supposed deficiency, on the part of the former, of a vigorous, manly life. . . . What satirists upon religion are those parents who say of their pallid, puny, sedentary . . . offspring, "He is born for a minister," while the ruddy, the brave and the strong are as promptly assigned to a secular career! . . .

Physical health is a necessary condition of all permanent success. To the American people it has a stupendous importance, because it is the only attribute of power in which they are losing ground. Guarantee us against physical degeneracy, and we can risk all other perils,—financial crisis, Slavery, Romanism, Mormonism, Border Ruffians, and New York assassins. . . . Guarantee us health, and Mrs. Stowe cannot frighten us with all the prophesies of Dred; but when her sister Catharine informs us that in all the vast female acquaintance of the Beecher family there are not a dozen healthy women, we confess ourselves a little tempted to despair of the republic.

The only drawback to satisfaction in our Public-School System is the physical weakness which it reveals and helps to perpetuate. . . . The teacher of a large school in Canada went so far as to declare to us, that she could recognize the children born this side of the line by their invariable appearance of ill-health. . . .

There are statistics to show that the average length of human life is increasing; but it is probable that this results from the diminution of epidemic disease, rather than from any general improvement in *physique*. . . . Indeed, it is generally supposed that any physical deterioration is . . . peculiar to the United States. . . .

No one can visit Canada without being struck with the spectacle of a more athletic race of people than our own. On every side one sees rosy female faces and noble manly figures. . . .

Who, in this community, really takes exercise? Even the mechanic commonly confines himself to one set of muscles. . . . But the professional or business man, what muscles has he at all? . . . Even to ride sixty miles in a day, to walk thirty, to run five, or to swim one, would cost most men among us a fit of illness, and many their lives. Let any man test his physical condition, we will not say by sawing his own cord of wood, but by an hour in the gymnasium or at cricket, and his enfeebled muscular apparatus will groan with rheumatism for a week. Or let him test the strength of his arms and chest by raising and lowering himself a few times upon a horizontal bar, or by hanging by the arms to a rope, and he will probably agree with Galen in pronouncing it *robustum validumque laborem.* Yet so manifestly are these things within the reach of common constitutions, that a few weeks or months of judicious practice will renovate his whole system, and the most vigorous exercise will refresh him like a cold bath.

To a well-regulated frame, mere physical exertion . . . is a great enjoyment, which is, of course, enhanced by the excitement of games and sports. To almost every man there is joy in the memory of these things; they are the happiest associations of his boyhood. . . .

But, as far as there is a deficiency in these respects among us, this generation must not shrink from the responsibility. It is unfair to charge it on the Puritans. They are not even answerable for Massachusetts; for there is no doubt that athletic exercises, of some sort, were far more generally practiced in this community before the Revolution than at present. A state of almost constant Indian warfare then created an obvious demand for muscle and agility. At present there is no such immediate necessity. And it has been supposed that a race of shopkeepers, brokers, and lawyers could live without bodies. Now that the terrible records of dyspepsia and paralysis are disproving this, we may hope for a reaction in favor of bodily exercises.

. . . In one way or another, American schoolboys obtain active exercise. The same is true, in a very limited degree, even of girls. They are occasionally, in our larger cities, sent to gymnasiums,—the more the better. . . . A fashionable young lady is estimated to traverse her three hundred miles a season on foot; and this needs training. But out-door exercise for girls is terribly restricted, first by their costume, and secondly by the remarks of Mrs. Grundy. . . . Still, there is a change going on, which is tantamount to an admission that there is an evil to be remedied. Twenty years ago, if we mistake not, it was by no means considered "proper" for little girls to play with their hoops and balls on Boston Common; and swimming and skating have hardly been recognized as "lady-like" for half that period of time.

* * * *

. . . American men, how few carry athletic habits into manhood! The great hindrance, no doubt, is absorption in business; and we observe that this winter's hard times and consequent leisure have given a great stimulus to outdoor sports. But in most places there is the further obstacle, that a certain stigma of boyishness goes with them. So early does this begin, that we remember, in our teens, to have been slightly reproached with juvenility, because, though a Senior Sophister, we still clung to football. Juvenility! We only wish we had the opportunity now.

Catharine Beecher Criticizes Women's Frailty and Recommends What Should Be Done About It, 1855

You have read often of the Greeks. Some twenty centuries ago . . . they were remarkable, not only for their wisdom and strength, but for their great beauty, so that the statues they made to resemble their own men and women have, ever since, been regarded as the most perfect forms of human beauty.

The chief reason why they excelled . . . was the great care they took in educating their children. They had two kinds of schools—the one to train the minds, and the other to train the bodies of their children. And though they estimated very

From Catharine Beecher, *Letters to the People on Health and Happiness* (New York: Harper & Bros., 1855), 9, 107–8, 120–33, 172.

highly the education of the mind, they still more valued that part of school training which tended to develop and perfect the body. . . .

But the American people have pursued a very different course. It is true that a large portion of them have provided schools for educating the minds of their children; but instead of providing teachers to train the bodies of their offspring, most of them have not only entirely neglected it, but have done almost every thing they could do to train their children to become feeble, sickly, and ugly. And those, who have not pursued so foolish a course, have taken very little pains to secure the proper education of the body for their offspring during the period of their school life.

In consequence of this dreadful neglect and mismanagement, the children of this country are every year becoming less and less healthful and good-looking. There is a great change in reference to this matter within my memory. When young, I noticed in my travels the children in school-houses, or on Sunday in the churches almost all of them had rosy cheeks, and looked full of health and spirits. But now, when I notice the children in churches and schools, both in city and country, a great portion of them either have sallow or pale complexions, or look delicate or partially misformed. . . .

* * * *

Every year I hear more and more complaints of the poor health that is so very common among grown people, especially among women. And physicians say that this is an evil that is constantly increasing, so that they fear ere long, there will be no healthy women in the country.

. . . A change is possible. . . . Nothing is needed but a *full knowledge* of the cause, and then the *application of that practical common-sense and efficiency to this object.* . . .

I have been led to this effort by many powerful influences. More than half of the mature years of my own life have been those of restless debility and infirmities, that all would have been saved by the knowledge contained in this work.

. . . The more I traveled, and the more I resided in health establishments, the more the conviction was pressed on my attention that there was a terrible decay of female health all over the land, and that this evil was bringing with it an incredible extent of individual, domestic, and social suffering, that was increasing in a most alarming ratio. . . .

In my own family connection, I have nine married sisters and sisters-in-law, all of them either delicate or invalids, except two. I have fourteen married female cousins, and no one of them but is either delicate, often ailing, or an invalid. In my wide circle of friends and acquaintance all over the land out of my family circle, the same impression is made. In Boston I can not remember but one married female friend who is perfectly healthy.

. . . The thing which has pained and surprised me the most is the result of inquiries among the country-towns and industrial classes in our country. I had supposed that there would be a great contrast between the statements gained from persons from such places, and those furnished from the wealthy circles, and especially from cities. But such has not been the case. . . .

* * * *

Next to pure air, *healthful exercise and amusements* are the most important remedies for the evils set forth.

American Agriculturist Applauds
Ladies on Horseback, 1862

Learning that our article on Saddle Horses, a few months ago, interested many, and was the occasion of benefiting several invalids, the writer will now present a few hints on female equestrianism. As a mere accomplishment for young ladies, it ranks high. Perhaps in no place do female charms appear more fascinating, than in the saddle. You may think it is the jaunty cap and plume our Belle wears, or her flowing dress, or the fresh color which riding brings into her cheek, and the sparkle it gives her eye; you may say it is the spirited motion of her palfrey, or the contrast between his rugged strength and her delicate beauty. Analyze it as you please, it will yet be confessed, (certainly by every young man open to conviction) that Belle never looks so charming as when on horseback. We have heard of more than one susceptible youth who has lost his peace of mind by witnessing such a sight. Indeed, to old or young, it is very pleasing. And then, if to this sight you add several young ladies and gentlemen in different colored dresses, prancing along the highway together, you make a picture worth looking at.

The healthfulness of this exercise, few will question. It tends to give a young lady an erect posture; it strengthens her arms, chest, limbs; expands the lungs, gives tone to the stomach, and clearness to the brain. If the digestion is impaired, it will restore it much quicker and better than pills or bran-bread. The fine effect it has upon the spirits is enough to recommend it. How much more enlivening it is than rolling luxuriously over a smooth road in a modern, spring-seated, close-covered, velvet-cushioned carriage! Yet, many of our sighing young misses prefer the latter, 'it is so much more refined!' They think their complexions of satin softness and lily whiteness, would suffer from the exposure of horseback riding! Did you but know it, young lady, nine out of ten young gentlemen would be more pleased with you, if your complexion had the healthier tinge that comes from vigorous exercise in the open air. Who has not known or heard of invalids so weak that they had, at first, to be lifted into the saddle, but who, by steadily pursuing horseback riding for a period of weeks and months, have recovered vigorous health? All of us have known invalids with pulmonary affections, who, having tried the prescriptions of doctors of every school in vain, and having traveled to the sunny South to little purpose, have at last resorted to the saddle, and gained therein more advantage than from all things beside. Many a lady needs out-door exercise, but is too feeble to walk a great distance. Mount your horse, then, not your luxurious carriage. Mount your saddle, and you will find your weak back strengthened, your nerves braced, your head-ache dissipated, and every part of your system toned and invigorated. Your horse will do the hard work for you, and yet give you all needful exercise. He will bear you over the hills and far away into the woods, to gather flowers, and see the birds, and if you like, down yonder gorge to see a waterfall, and over the bridge to a certain farm-house to visit some friend, and see her pleasant occupations. Wherever you will, you can ride, and then come home refreshed and inspirited with new health. In England the ladies ride horseback more than in the northern United States. It often forms part of their education to learn to sit in the saddle gracefully, and to manage a horse with skill. In the southern states of this country, it has long been a very common practice. The writer of these lines has often raced with Virginia lasses, leaping brooks and ditches, and low fences, side by side with them, and he confesses that he generally (gallantly?) came off second best in the contest—as in duty bound. We are happy to know that female equestrianism is becoming, of late, more popular among us. In many of our cities, riding schools have been established, and along our parks and broad thoroughfares, many a gay company of lady-riders can be seen almost any fair day. So too in the country generally, there is an increasing fondness for this exercise.

The *New York Times* Recommends Skating at Central Park, 1859

Such a throng of skaters and spectators as collected yesterday at the Central Park has never before been equaled. The City cars were absolutely insufficient to accommodate the crowds that flocked to the skating carnival. From daylight until after dark the stream of visitors was continuous, including all ages, sexes and conditions in life, from the ragged urchin with one broken skate, to the *millionaire* in his richly-robed carriage. The Park presented a scene of brilliancy and animation more enlivening than on any day of the popular Saturday afternoon concerts, while the healthful glow on every cheek was a flattering testimonial to the efficacy of this noble breathing-spot of the City. Although the early comers had no very good skating to boast of, they certainly had a decided advantage over those who deferred the visit until late in the afternoon, for long before mid-day the ice was in a most deplorable condition.

The Caledonia Club, and their rivals in the manly sport of curling, were among the first on the pond, and were for a time busily engaged in practicing for their contemplated match. But, as the crowd increased, it was found impossible to keep a place sufficiently clear for them, while the cracking, cutting-up, sinking and melting ice finally compelled an abandonment of the match for the day. But the skaters, to the number of several thousands, in the face of obstacles that would have deterred any but New Yorkers, and perhaps even them on any other day, persisted in their evolutions, rejoiced in their gyrations, and exhibited their skill by

From "The Skating Carnival: Great Rush to the Central Park" [editorial], *New York Times,* December 27, 1859.

tortuous meanderings through the crowd,—presenting an exhilarating scene equal to the liveliness of a thousand ball-rooms. The collisions, the tumblings down, the wetting of clothing, the uncertain foothold of the beginners, as well as the skill of amateurs, afforded ample recreation to all and especially to the thousands who lined the banks. The drives commanding a view of the pond were crowded throughout the day, while at one time as many as an hundred carriages were drawn up near the shore to afford the occupants an extended view.

The number of ladies in vehicles and on foot was quite remarkable, and it was a common sight to see a gentleman with two pairs of skates on one arm, and a bundle of crinoline on the other. But few ladies, however, participated in the skating, partly owing to the bad condition of the ice on the pond appropriated to their use, and partly from the fact that they prefer to enjoy the sport by moonlight, when they are not so conspicuous. Had the ice permitted yesterday, a class of ladies would have been instructed in the art; but as it was, they had to postpone their lesson. Their diminutive ponds were flooded in the afternoon, so that the first cold snap will atone for yesterdays disappointment.

The condition of the ice in the afternoon was a source of general regret, but did not prevent the majority from attempting the fun in spite of the lowering of the signals that the pond was in good condition. So great was the crowd on the narrower and southern position of the pond, that about 1 P.M., the Police had orders to clear it. This was no easy task, for the skaters had rather the advantage of their pursuers, and darted hither and thither with a celerity that baffled the authority of the meagre force of the Central Park Police. At length a string of laborers was stretched across the pond, and, advancing, cleared nearly all before them—those who sifted through being captured by the officers, and the unruly ones taken to the station-house. In this way that portion of the pond was cleared in three quarters of an hour, most of the people leaving quietly upon request. But the effort to pursue the same plan on the larger portion of the pond, above the new iron bridge, signally failed. The agile skaters dodged the Police line easily, for the sweeping-machine could not be made to extend the width of the pond. If the sweepers went in the middle, the skaters nimbly slid by at the ends. If the sweepers undertook to spread out, the skaters sailed fleetly under their hands.

In vain did the officers of the law become indignant and exasperated and irate. The plan wouldn't work; and they finally gave up in sheer despair, contenting themselves with the reflection that if the people would run the risk of getting soaked, or even drowned, it wasn't their fault. So the skating went on unmolested, and the little boys took especial pains to collect in crowds near the signs of "danger." Yet no serious accident occurred, as there doubtless would have been had the facilities for getting on the pond been greater. Fortunately the sinking of the ice at the edges left a circuit of water about two inches deep and three feet wide, which made all without skates run the risk of wet feet before joining the crowd of skaters. It is to be hoped that either the Croton Board or the thaw will allow the pond to be speedily flooded so that ice may be formed which will not be as rough as a mill-stone.

One thing the skaters ought to understand and appreciate, and that is, that the police regulations are for their own comfort and safety, and should be obeyed with that alacrity which has characterized the orderly conduct of the great majority of visitors to the Central Park.

The *New York Herald* Compares Cricket and Baseball, 1859

Cricket . . . has not extended much . . . for two reasons: first, because base ball—an American national game—was in possession, and was too like cricket to be superceded by it, and secondly, in the points on which it differs from cricket it is more suited to the genius of the people. It is rapid and simple. Even if there were no base ball in existence cricket could never become a national sport in the America—it is too slow, intricate and plodding a game for our go ahead people.

Base ball has been from time immemorial a favorite and popular recreation in this country; but it is only within the last fifteen years that the game has been systematized and clubs formed for the purpose of playing at stated periods and under a code of written laws. The Knickerbocker Club, for New York, organized in 1845, was the first and since then numerous clubs have sprung up in this city and Brooklyn, and throughout the country. But the great increase has been within the last three or four years. . . .

The good effect produced on the health and strength and morals of the young men engaged in this outdoor exercise is the theme of all who are conversant with them. It has taken them from the unhealthy haunts of dissipation indoors, and given them a taste for manly sport which cannot fail to have a beneficial effect, not only in the physical development of our citizens, but on the national character. No 'refreshments' are allowed on the occasion of matches, which are visited by thousands of spectators, including a large number of ladies.

. . . . There is great art in pitching and the pitcher's position in base ball corresponds with the bowler's in cricket, though not quite so important. The ball must be pitched, not jerked, nor thrown, that is, the hand is held down to the hip or below it, and it must be aimed for the centre of the home base, or at the batman. It must not touch the ground before it reaches the batman, but the art of pitching consists in throwing it with such force that the batman has not time to wind his bat to hit it hard or so close to his person that he can only hit a feeble blow. . . . The batman strikes overhand at the ball. In cricket, he strikes underhand, because the ball is thrown low, and must strike the ground before it reaches the batman.

. . . . In cricket the batman is never compelled to run till he thinks proper, so that he has rarely any risk in making at least one run of sixty feet between the two wickets. . . . If he has time he runs back again, and counts another, and so on. . . .

From "Comparing Cricket and Baseball" [editorial], *New York Herald,* October 16, 1859.

Hence the English game is so slow and tame, and the American so full of life. In the latter the player is compelled to go. If the ball is caught, either flying or on the first bound from the earth, after being struck with the bat, the batman is put out without counting; or if it is held by the adversary on the first base before the striker touches it, or if at any time he is touched by the ball in the hands of an adversary without some part of his person being on the base. Formerly it was sufficient to strike the adversary with the ball by throwing it at him. This practice is now abolished as it was dangerous and unnecessary to the game. . . .

The base ball bat must be round. . . . The cricket bat is flat. . . . In cricket the batman has his legs cased in leather for protection, and so has the wicketkeeper who stands behind him to catch the ball after it glides off his bat or hand. The wicketkeeper has also strong gloves. Behind the batman in base ball stands a catcher, who, if he catches the ball flying or on the first hop puts out the batman. Thus the batman in both games correspond, also the pitcher corresponds with the bowler, and the catcher with the wicketkeeper, and these three are the men who, in both games, do the principal part of the work. In both games each man on each side must take the bat, in turn; in both games a bowler and a pitcher, a wicket keeper and a catcher are selected for their peculiar skill, and they play those parts throughout. . . .

In base ball the game centres around the bases; in cricket it centres around the wickets. In base ball the batman, when he runs, is put out by being touched with the ball when he is off his base. In cricket the batman is put out if he is caught outside of an enclosure in front of the wicket by his adversary, who does not touch him with the ball, but knocks down his wicket either by throwing the ball at it or by throwing it to the wicket keeper or any other player, who, with ball in hand, knocks it down. Thus running and throwing and catching are equally important in both games.

In the game of cricket the wicket consists of three round stakes, called stumps, placed upright in a row, twenty-seven inches out of the ground, and on the top is placed a small piece of wood called a bail . . . , which . . . with the least touch given to it or the stumps, it comes off, and puts the batman out. There are two of these wickets, pitched opposite to each other, at a distance of twenty-two yards . . . ; at each of these stands a batsman to defend them with the bat against being knocked down by the ball . . . Cricket is played by eleven on each side. The eleven who go in—that is, get first possession of the wickets and bats . . . , send two of their number to take those positions, and the remaining nine continue out of play till they are called in succession . . . until the whole eleven are thus put out. . . . Each side has two innings. . . . The object of the batman is to score by runs between the wickets; the object of his adversaries is to prevent him, by knocking down his wicket with the ball. The attack is made on the wicket which he has both to defend and make the runs as best he can. If his wicket is fairly down he is put out, and another . . . takes his place. The bowler from beside one of the wickets bowls at the opposite one to knock it done. The batman stops the ball with his bat or strikes it away. In this consists the greatest art of the game. The ball must be bowled, and . . . the hand must not be above the shoulder when delivering the ball . . . Sometimes the bowler bowls it with great force and very low, direct for the wicket. . . . Sometimes the artful bowler throws the ball . . . at an angle, in order to deceive, and gives it a twist when leaving his hand, which makes it come right to the wicket. . . . If the batman drives the ball out of the bounds, it is called a "lost ball," and counts six for him without running. . . . If a ball is caught in the air without touching the ground no run is reckoned, but the striker is not put out. . . .

. . . . There is only one bowler on the ground . . . but after every fourth ball the bowler changes over and bowls at the other wicket. The batman who guards that wicket which is not bowled has the privilege of making his run to the other wicket, when the ball is struck, just the same as the striker, and they generally run together, crossing each other.

The only points in which the base ball men would have any advantage over the cricketers, in a game of ball, are two—first, in the batting, which is overhand, and done with a narrower bat, and secondly in the fact of the ball being more lively, hopping higher, and requiring a different mode of catching. But the superior activity and practice of the Eleven in fielding would amply make up for this, even if they have not already practiced base ball. . . .

In cricket a very smooth ground is wanted on account of the bowling as the ball must strike the ground before it reaches the batman or strikes the wicket, and every obstruction on the surface would spoil the bowling. In base ball very smooth ground is not required, but a rather larger space than is necessary for cricket. . . .

. . . . It occupies on an average about two hours to play a game of base ball—two days to play a game of cricket.

From the foregoing description and comparison for the two games, the reader will see that base ball is better adapted for popular use than cricket. It is more lively and animated, gives more exercise, and is more rapidly concluded. Cricket seems very tame and dull after looking at a game of base ball. It is suited to the aristocracy, who have leisure and love ease; base ball is suited to the people. Cricket is the better game for warm weather, base ball when it cold. In cricket, those actually engaged except three—the bowler, the batman and the wicket-keeper—do little or nothing three-fourths of the time; and for half the day, sometimes longer, nine out of one side are not on the field at all. In the American game the ins and outs alternate by quick rotation, like our officials, and no man can be out of play longer than a few minutes. Still, the game of cricket is one of great merit and skill, and we should be glad to see it cultivated by all who have sufficient time for the purpose. Both games seem suited to the national temperament and character of the people among whom they respectively prevail.

The *Spirit of the Times* Examines the Founding of the New York Athletic Club, 1868

We have very great satisfaction in announcing that the first semi-annual games of the New York Athletic Club will take place upon November 11th. It is a gratifying fact that healthy and strengthening pastimes are daily growing into greater favor with the community, which the vitality and the increasing prosperity of the athletic organizations in this city amply testify. We believe that the benefit of such institutions as that to whose exhibition we have alluded can not be too highly appreciated by any class of the people; but we would more especially urge their value on the youth of our cities and colleges, whose business pursuits and recreations are unexceptionally of a sedentary character. To those young men who are for many hours of the day excluded from air and exercise, the cultivation of their physical power becomes a necessity if they would escape the doom of early senility; and it must necessarily be through their exertion and combined support if these organizations are to become permanent and flourishing. . . .

The New York Athletic Club, although but in its infancy, shows remarkable promise of becoming the leading institution of its kind in this country, and will, doubtlessly, in course of time, fill the same position in this country occupied by the London Athletic Club in England. The club was founded some few months ago by a number of gentlemen who were fully aware of the benefits to be derived from such an organization, and foresaw the probable advantage to be subsequently gained from it by the young men of New York. The prospects are undoubtedly encouraging, and give considerable assurances of success; but we would suggest that, in order to complete the organization and render it perfect, those designing to become members (who hesitate, thinking the club insufficiently formed) should at once join and put their shoulder to the wheel, and in a very short time every obstacle will be no more. It cannot be expected that a club like the present can become an accomplished fact without some little difficulties have been wrestled with and successfully overcome. It is the intention of the members of the club to extend its patronage to all species of gymnastics, rowing, swimming, and skating; but at present the funds of the organization being unequal to the fulfillment of these designs, it has been determined to institute a series of semi-annual games, in which pedestrianism is to take the prominent position. . . . In the spring of 1869 the procural of grounds for the club is designed by its members, on which a running track will be constructed and the necessary buildings erected. In its efforts to acquire stability and strength, the New York Athletic Club has our hearty support and cordial approval, believing as we do, that in such recreations becoming dear to the young men of the nation, we have an additional safeguard against the truth of the dismal doctrine of the degeneration of the human species.

From *Spirit of the Times* 19 (October 10, 1868): 121.

In the approaching games the various Caledonian clubs of this city have been invited to contest, so that a very interesting exhibition may be looked for with confidence. The exercises comprise jumping, leaping, racing, putting the shot, and throwing the hammer. Naturally enough, the Caledonian Club, which has for so long occupied the most prominent position as an athletic club in this city, will strain every nerve to keep ahead of its friendly but vigorous rival. . . . For its approaching exhibition the club has secured the Empire City Skating Rink, an enormous structure with a ground-floor and raised seats, having a capacity to accommodate an audience of at least ten thousand persons. As the display will take place by gaslight, a very large attendance may be anticipated.

❿ *E S S A Y S*

The first essay by Linda Borish, a historian at Western Michigan University, examines the ideas of moral reformers Catharine Beecher and Rev. Thomas Wentworth Higginson, one of the first "muscular Christians," on physical fitness. They both found antebellum Americans extremely unhealthy and offered their own recommendations for improvement—Beecher for women and Higginson for men—which would create healthy individuals prepared to assume their intended cultural and social roles. The second essay, by George B. Kirsch of Manhattan College, examines the growth of baseball as a spectator sport as it evolved from an amateur to a professional game. The first recorded game of baseball was played in 1845, and a decade later there were over 125 teams in metropolitan New York. Kirsch gives particular attention to the behavior and social composition of baseball crowds.

Catharine Beecher and Thomas W. Higginson on the Need for Physical Fitness

LINDA J. BORISH

In the mid-nineteenth century two articulate middle-class social reformers, Catharine Esther Beecher (1800–78) and Thomas Wentworth Higginson (1823–1911), criticized the condition of the social, physical and moral health of American citizens. Beecher and Higginson each envisioned an ideal American society based upon robust health and physical activity. Yet both were convinced that *ante bellum* Americans possessed strikingly poor health. Beecher and Higginson diagnosed the same problem of ill health, set forth its serious consequences and suggested a remedy, but each articulated the issues in gender-specific ways. The analogous, complementary perspectives of Beecher and Higginson on the health concerns, the gloomy scenarios resulting from frail health, and their solutions suggest that just as

From Linda J. Borish, "The Robust Woman and the Muscular Christian: Catharine Beecher, Thomas Higginson, and Their Vision of American Society, Health and Physical Activities," *International Journal of the History of Sport* 4 (September 1987): 139–51.

women were bound by cultural definitions of womanhood, so men were bound by cultural definitions of manhood in nineteenth-century America.

Examining Beecher's concept of womanhood, 'the cult of domesticity' and 'of true womanhood', and Higginson's concept of manhood, 'Muscular Christianity', reveals the workings of gender in their interpretations of health and physical exercise in American society. Architected as the culturally defined gender-based ideals, Beecher's robust woman and Higginson's muscular Christian expressed the proper social behaviour of women and men. Beecher intended to prepare women as cultural progenitors and social reproducers, while Higginson expected men to develop as cultural opportunists and cultural partakers.

As members of the New England, educated, urban middle class, Beecher and Higginson represented female and male voices for *ante bellum,* white, Anglo-Saxon, Protestant culture. They witnessed and responded to the broad transformation of American society in the nineteenth century. As both products and agents of their culture, each reformer prescribed the social behavior of women and men in order to adapt to the developing urban, industrial culture. America moved from a rural, agricultural, traditional nation to an urban, industrial, modern nation through the application of science and technology. This process altered the economic, social and political landscape of American culture. Reformers tried to articulate what ought to be done to ensure the future glory of the nation and the citizenry.

The economic growth provided contemporary reformers with problems that needed solving. In particular, cities became ripe for moral crusades. Population in the cities burgeoned dramatically. Immigrants poured into cities. Reformers regarded the urban areas as horrible pockets of vice, disease, and misery filled with poor foreigners. Indeed, as reformers, Beecher and Higginson pondered the process of urbanization and social change; as middle-class spokespersons, they expressed fears about the impact of immigration, industrialization, family disruption, religious changes and deepening class divisions on *ante bellum* culture. In particular, fears about declining physical debility in *ante bellum* America greatly alarmed Beecher and Higginson as they perceived collective robust health of Americans as essential to the preservation of American culture. Reforming society, according to these two outstanding individuals, must involve the regeneration of physical and moral health.

Trying to rid American society of its blemishes, Beecher and Higginson acted upon their culture. Several reform movements existed—abolition, women's rights, communitarianism, and labour reform—but these two reformers perceived the simultaneous perfection of individual and national health as a requisite for upholding the special promise of American culture. Beecher and Higginson launched a coherent and articulate campaign to save the nation by combating the ill health of its citizenry. The health reform movement exhibited all the characteristics of a fully fledged moral crusade. Every individual, health reformers asserted, had a responsibility and the power to overcome physical imperfections. Health became linked with promoting Christian society. Thus, health advocates presented good hygiene as a moral obligation. Whether the obligation was to God, to the race, the nation, nature or the self, failure to fulfil the laws of health constituted immorality. Bad hygiene represented an evil, and a disease represented a sin.

A millennial spirit pervaded the health reform ideas of the *ante bellum* period. Religious enthusiasm and optimism and a deep concern about the future of America shaped the effort to reform Americans' health. In their critique of American's frail health, Beecher and Higginson captured the public mood. They preached perfectionism and faith in the improvement of human beings in hopes of bringing about the Second Coming of Christ to reign on earth for a thousand years. Strong health thus became essential to achieving salvation. Physical degeneration represented a spiritual and medical problem. In the health reform ideology, renovating the spiritual and physical condition of Americans became essential for bettering individuals and the nation alike.

In anticipating the millennium, health reformers offered several approaches to curing ill health. Some health advocates promoted vegetarianism and temperance. Other antidotes for poor health included pure air, dress reform, physical education, and the water cure. Like other reformers in the health crusade, such as Lydia Maria Child, Sylvester Graham and William Alcott, Beecher and Higginson emphasized the importance of achieving sound health. In particular, Beecher and Higginson promoted a plan of self-help—healthful sporting activities—as a means for women and men to gain physical vigour. Self-help assumed that following specific rules and guidelines for daily living, all healthy, produced physical improvement. In their writings, Beecher and Higginson prescribed acceptable physical exercise and sport as part of the programme of self-help to perfect individual and national health. Indeed, as a form of self-help, sporting endeavours had an important role in their gospel of health.

An intimate connection existed between Beecher's and Higginson's concerns about Americans' health and their promotion of physical exercise and sport for males and females. For both like-minded New England reformers, health represented a central component of their view of American culture. Assumed Anglo-Saxon degeneracy, individual, familial and national decline, the close relationship between physical vigour and moral virtue, and settling the West all became linked to the condition of Americans' health. Indeed, alarmed at the prospects of doom and destruction resulting from the feeble health of the citizenry, Beecher articulated the concerns in female terms, whereas Higginson articulated the concerns in male terms.

Beecher decried the deterioration of American health. . . . As evidence of this physical decline Beecher cited the universal impression of foreigners when they arrived in America and observed the health of the inhabitants. Foreigners witnessed 'the proportion of sallow, thin, and unhealthful countenances . . . the directly opposite impression when our countrymen encounter the ruddy, healthful countenances to be met in England'. Americans appeared physically unfit when compared with their ancestors.

Beyond such general concerns, Beecher documented the particular decline of American women's health. Everywhere she looked, she noticed evidence of their ill health. To her audience she offered a grave diagnosis. In *Letters to the People on Health and Happiness,* Beecher declared:

> If a plan *for destroying female health,* in all the ways in which it could most effectively
> be done were drawn up, it would be exactly the course which is now pursued by a large

portion of this nation, . . . the results of such a course have been an amount of domestic unhappiness and individual suffering in all classes in our land that is perfectly frightful, and that these dreadful evils are constantly increasing. . . .

Such physical degeneration especially alarmed Beecher since she linked physical health for women to the fulfilment of the ideal of what historians have termed 'the cult of domesticity' and 'the cult of true womanhood'. Vigorous health, in short, became integrated with woman's proper sphere—the home. In the nineteenth-century doctrine of separate spheres, the home served as a redemptive counterpart to the chaotic, hectic world. While woman preserved morality in the home, man pursued roles in business and politics in the world.

A 'true' woman, according to Beecher, one possessing the virtues of piety, purity, domesticity, and submissiveness, needed robust health. To perform her roles of mother, wife, moral guardian, healthkeeper and housekeeper, a true woman required physical and moral energy. The physically debilitated mother could not carry out her womanhood role or reproductive function. 'It is well known,' Beecher contended, 'that the constitution of children depends on the health of the mother.' Preserving the physical fitness of the mother also went hand in hand with the social health of America. Future mothers, as well as fathers, depended on mothers for acquiring physical energy and moral character. . . .

Conveying the links between health and individuals, families, and the nation, Beecher clearly emphasized how woman's physical vigour provided the cornerstone of the warm, joyful, tranquil home. Woman's delicate health only brought melancholy to the home. Beecher lamented: 'When the wife and mother is suffering from the debility and pain of ill health, it not only ends her enjoyment of life, but a cloud of gloom settles over the whole family circle'. With the mother as a perpetual invalid, no longer did the home represent a haven. Women's frail health destroyed domestic happiness.

Not only activities within the home but the successful westward movement of population depended on the physical and moral energy of American women. The settling of the West represented an important part of Beecher's vision of America's march towards progress. . . . According to Beecher, only hearty women could endure and spread their moral attributes and the seeds of democracy in the American West. Beecher described the feeble women of the East who, accompanying their husbands on the frontier trail, strove to become 'heroines of the West'. Because of the delicacy of their constitution, however, these women could not survive the rigours of pioneer life. . . . The pioneer woman of robust health who performed her own domestic and outdoor labour represented the ideal woman in Beecher's thought. Yet, in Beecher's worst possible scenarios of ill health, women failed to fulfil the cultural ideal of womanhood. Beecher, however, provided an antidote to the problem of American woman's physical decline.

As a remedy for poor health, Beecher promoted physical activity and sport for women. Through such endeavors, women not only renovated their health but also became further exposed to their own proper sphere. For example, Beecher praised household tasks as an enjoyable physical activity capable of restoring women's health. She endorsed 'the gentle exercise and *amusement* of housekeeping'. Women should do the sweeping, dusting and laundry to improve their physical condition. Beecher asserted that a young lady who 'will spend two hours a day at the wash-tub, or with a broom, is far more likely to have rosy cheeks, and finely moulded form, and a delicate skin, than one who lolls all day in her parlor or chamber, or only leaves girt in tight dresses to make fashionable calls'. . . .

In addition to domestic labour, Beecher promoted callisthenics and gymnastics as suitable sports for women. Next to domestic exercises, callisthenics represented the best method of securing a healthy constitution. Callisthenic exercises had a therapeutic orientation, designed to remedy female physical problems. In *Callisthenic Exercises, for Schools, Families, and Health Establishments* Beecher divided the exercises into categories for specific areas of the body that needed to be strengthened. These included 'Exercises for the Chest and Lungs', 'Exercises to Perfect the Muscles of the Arms and Hands', 'Exercises for the Muscles of the Trunk', 'Exercises for the Calisthenic Hall. Walking, Skipping, Exercises with Weights'.

. . . To make the callisthenics more challenging and effective, Beecher even recommended the use of cloth bags filled with kernels of corn which the female pupils tossed or manipulated. To be sure, Beecher's regime of callisthenics excluded strenuous athletic exercises 'suited to the stronger sex, but not suited to the female constitution'.

Beecher did encourage a few outdoor physical activities such as walking and riding in the pure open air. These sports, along with exercises done with a horse and carriage, Beecher considered to be safe for women. Of course, these activities also enabled women to escape the confines of an indoor setting. Beecher believed fresh air to be so important to woman's physical development that she argued that young women should never be confined at any task for a long period of time. Any confinement should be followed 'by sports in the open airs. Such accommodations should be secured that, at all seasons, and in all the weathers, the teacher can send out a portion of her school, every half hour for sports'. Participating in sport outdoors, a woman accrued more benefits. . . .

Higginson criticized the health of Americans, especially in his *Atlantic Monthly* articles. He found it wanting. Writing about men's health in 'Saints, and Their Bodies', Higginson lamented that no robust saints existed in America. Not only saints, but shopkeepers, brokers, and lawyers also lived without healthy bodies. He witnessed the 'deficiency of physical health in America and the need of a great amendment'. . . .

. . . Higginson focused on his own gender with some cross-over to write about women. For example, in 'Barbarism and Civilization', he echoed Beecher's findings. In America, he observed that:

> every man grows to maturity surrounded by a circle of invalid female relatives, that he later finds himself the husband of an invalid wife and the parent of invalid daughters, and that he comes to regard invalidism . . . as the normal condition of that sex.

He wrote that among lower animals there seemed to be no inequality between the sexes as to strength and endurance. Yet in America, the ill health of women not only far exceeded that of men, but 'it still remains unquestionable that in every distinctive attribute of physical womanhood the barbarian has the advantage'. . . .

. . . Higginson agreed with Beecher that women needed physical well-being for duties in their own proper sphere. He preached that women must secure health in order for the country to be safe. . . .

Higginson believed that the fulfilment of men's roles required physical fitness. In their prescribed roles such as businessman, politician and preacher, men required formal education consisting of physical training as well as intellectual training. Indeed, Higginson thought that physical exercises and sports ought to become a training ground for manhood. Drawing on the physical, mental and moral education for English boys revealed in Thomas Hughes' *Tom Brown's School Days,* Higginson remarked: 'The charm which all have found in Tom Brown's "School Days at Rugby" lies simply in the healthy boy's life which it exhibits and in the recognition of physical culture which is so novel to Americans'. Higginson embraced the essential benefits of robust health for manhood acquired in boyhood.

Physical strength was a requisite for men's activities. Higginson stressed that the great deeds of the world could not be done by sickly men: 'Physical health is a necessary condition of all permanent success'. In short, full-grown men should take far more active exercise than boys. Connecting male fitness with the professions, he decried: 'When one sees a bookworm in his library, an anxious merchant-prince in his counting room, tottering feebly about, his thin underpinning scarcely able to support what he has already crammed into that heavy brain of his—and still piling in more—one feels disposed to cry out, "Unsafe passing here! Stand from under!" ' . . .

In his efforts to preserve the physical fitness of males Higginson promoted 'muscular Christianity'. Muscular Christianity originated as an English philosophy asserting the compatibility of robust physical activity and Christian moral rectitude. The term first became associated with the English novelist Charles Kingsley when a critic coined the term in 1857 in a review of Kingsley's book *Two Years Ago.* In addition to Kingsley, English novelist Thomas Hughes in his account of the popular fictional hero Tom Brown in *Tom Brown's School Days* in 1858 spread the muscular Christianity ideal in England and the United States. Muscular Christianity referred to the belief that physical health, achieved through vigorous physical activity and sport, contributed significantly towards the development of moral character, virtue, discipline and patriotism, and that these experiences could be transferred to other institutions in society. According to some historians Higginson viewed sport in this manner and can thus be termed a 'muscular Christian'. An organic relationship existed between health, spiritual morality and business success in muscular Christianity. Thus, this gospel encompassed Higginson's concern that men needed strong health for their careers just as Beecher believed that women needed strong health for *their* careers. By perfecting the body through athletics for the glory of God, man in turn fulfilled his duties in the world.

The manly task of settling the West required men's vigorous health. Yet for Higginson, man's need for physical health on the frontier differed from woman's. Whereas women needed firm health to set up a home and perform domestic duties on the frontier, Higginson believed men needed firm health to fulfil the task of conquering the wilderness, a 'feat of labor and endurance which may be matched without fear against any historic deed'. . . .

Marching westward, Americans could spread to the new territories their Anglo-Saxon supremacy which rested upon their energetic health. Vigorous American health, in fact, went hand in hand with maintaining Anglo-Saxon supremacy in Higginson's thought. Higginson indeed asserted that for Anglo-Saxons, 'The triumph of civilization over Barbarism is the only Manifest Destiny of America'. As a Civil War colonel in command of the first American regular army regiment of freed slaves in South Carolina, Higginson recorded his experiences in *Army Life in a Black Regiment.* The physical condition of the blacks had particular significance for Higginson. He remarked, 'In speaking of the military qualities of blacks . . . the only point where I am disappointed is . . . their physical condition'. Comparing black soldiers with white soldiers, he described how blacks often looked magnificent to his gymnasium-trained eye, but blacks suffered from pulmonary weakness, and guard duty injured them more than whites. About his soldiers he concluded, 'I think that neither their physical nor moral temperament gave them that toughness, that obstinate purpose of living, which sustains the more materialistic Anglo-Saxon'. Having compared blacks and whites, Higginson asserted white superiority and claimed that physical vigor represented the key to Anglo-Saxon superiority. He warned that feeble health 'must be amended, or the American race fails'. In his vision of civilization, Higginson thus contended, 'We can only say that there is an inexplicable step in progress . . . it is the development of mankind into a sufficient maturity of strength to keep the peace and organize institutions'. In settling the West, Americans upheld important cultural values as long as they survived the physical hardships of pioneer life. . . .

In Higginson's view, health represented the pillar of American society. Since men suffered from feeble health, however, Higginson wanted to redress this situation to avoid his grave prognosis for American culture.

As an antidote to men's physical ill health, Higginson highly recommended active exercises and sports, especially outdoor ones. In his autobiography, *Cheerful Yesterdays,* he reasoned that 'every boy of active tastes—and mine were eminently such—must become the one thing or the other, either a sportsman or a naturalist'. He urged Americans to go walking, riding, boating, sailing, rowing, swimming and skating. In fact, 'The most important portion of a boy's life', Higginson wrote, 'is perhaps his outdoor training, since to live out of doors is to be forever in some respects a boy'.

Higginson enthusiastically endorsed outdoor competitive team sports for men. Football, he wrote, 'is the most glorious of all games to those whose animal life is sufficiently vigorous to enjoy it'. Having played football at Harvard as an undergraduate, Higginson described why he loved the game: 'the very thud of the ball, the scent of bruised grass, the mighty rush of a hundred men, the swift and cool defense'. Men should also play baseball and cricket, games in which the players became exposed to the competition and discipline that carried over into worldly pursuits. As Higginson revealed, 'We love to encounter in the contests of manhood those whom we first met at football.' . . . Higginson 'kept up habits of active exercise, played football and baseball, swam in the river in summer' while pursuing his career at Harvard Divinity School. In addition, as president of a gymnastic club, a skating club and a cricket club, he participated in several athletic exercises.

Although some of his contemporaries considered competitive sports a frivolous use of time for businessmen, Higginson answered their criticisms. For example, he observed the game between his friends of the 'Union' and the 'Excelsior' Base-ball clubs, and narrated the events to his friend Dolorosus. Dolorosus, however, did not share Higginson's passion for the game. . . . Comparing Dolorosus's weak physical state with the 'manly figures and handsome, eager faces' of the baseball players, Higginson thought Dolorosus, not the baseball players, misused his time by spending long hours in his counting-room. . . .

To be sure, boyhood games and sports ought to be incorporated into manhood, in Higginson's view. 'Athletic sports are "boyish", are they? Then they are precisely what we want', Higginson insisted, at least for males. An intimate connection existed between healthy boyhood and manhood. As a boy when he learned to swim in the river, he experienced 'a sense of conquest and achievement so delicious'. In manhood, his swimming became an essential part of his Civil War military exploits described in *Army Life in a Black Regiment*. Undertaking a personal reconnaissance by swimming, Higginson recounted his experiences in 'A Night in the Water':

> I do not remember ever to have experienced a greater sense of exhilaration then when I slipped noiselessly into the placid water, and struck out into the smooth, eddying current for the opposite shore. The water was my ground, where I, too, had been at home from boyhood. . . . [I] was able to make some additional observations . . . then, turning my back upon the mysterious shore which had thus far lured me, I sank softly below the surface, and swam as far as I could under water.

Moreover, from boyhood, Higginson enjoyed boats. When for the first time he found himself at sea as commodore of a fleet of armed steamers, he revealed, 'I placidly accepted my naval establishment, as if it were a new form of boat-club, and looked over the charts, balancing between one river and another, as if deciding whether to pull up or down Lake Quinsigamond'. Drawing on his boyhood experiences of sport, then, helped to prepare Higginson for his military opportunities.

Clearly espousing the value of manly vigour, Higginson once again commented on the female constitution, observing females' inability to sustain the hearty athletic life of males in boyhood and manhood. In 'The Health of Our Girls', he contended that a girl could not be 'turned loose, cannot be safely left with boyish freedom to take her fill of running, rowing, riding, swimming, skating,—because life-long injury may be the penalty of a single excess'. Girls who undertook too little or too much exercise experienced a fatal situation. Higginson asserted:

> Some of the strongest and most athletic girls among us have lost their health and become invalids for years, simply by being allowed to live the robust, careless, indiscreet life on which boys thrive so wonderfully. . . . From the negative condition proceeds her inability to endure accidents which to an active boy would be trivial. Who ever hears of boy's incurring a lame knee for a year by slipping on ice, or spinal disease for a lifetime by a fall from a sled?

Without enough physical energy secured in sporting endeavours, the prospects appeared dim for a young girl to fulfil her responsibilites of womanhood. Sports for men and women became differentiated, similar to their roles in American culture.

Beecher and Higginson, then, clearly shared some views about the health of Americans; but for each, gender contoured the vision. For Beecher, physical health for women became linked to the fulfilment of the ideal of 'the cult of domesticity' and 'the cult of true womanhood'; for Higginson, physical health for men became linked to man's role and muscular Christianity. Beecher and Higginson, alarmed at the startlingly unhealthy state of Americans, urged Americans to renew their health by pursuing sporting activities. An organic relationship existed between health, sporting activities, and sex roles in each reformer's vision of the ideal American society. Each one, focusing on her or his own gender, with some cross-over by Higginson, presented a diagnosis of the problem of degenerated health, its consequences and a solution to the problem. Indeed, Beecher and Higginson expressed analogous concerns as each analysed the same problem for women and men, the same terrible scenario and the same remedy but in gender-specific terms.

For Beecher, robust health, achieved through appropriate sport, enabled woman to perform her role in the home as mother, wife and moral protector. Sport functioned to make women fit *for,* rather then detracting *from,* domestic duties. In Beecher's 'cult of domesticity', her 'cult of true womanhood', woman needed good health to fulfil her duties in her own proper sphere. For Higginson, on the other hand, robust health, achieved through appropriate sport, enabled man to perform his role as a businessman and leader in the world. The career preparation for men therefore included sport. Higginson's muscular Christian needed health to fulfil his role outside the home. Men, then, like women, lived within the context of culturally defined gender ideals.

While each reformer urged Americans to engage in more physical exercise, the specific exercises each promoted indicate how sport was intertwined with gender concepts. Beecher advised women to engage in housework, callisthenics, walking, riding and gardening—all individual, non-competitive activities—in preparation for their prescribed domestic role. In Beecher's thought, woman's physical health and physical exercise represented a constraining experience training women for their role in the home, for 'the building of a glorious temple.' For Beecher, sport went hand in hand with women's profession, 'embracing the three departments of *teaching, health,* and *domestic economy* . . . as distinct as and as important as those of law, medicine, and theology for man. For Higginson, sport also became a part of role preparation. The competition, hard work and values men became exposed to in such sports as boating, football, baseball, cricket and gymnastics prepared men to experience the world off the playing fields. In Higginson's thought, man's physical health and physical exercise represented a liberating experience, so that 'the heart of manhood is born again' in training men for their role in the world. Whereas in Beecher's domestic ideology sport for women had the narrow function of making women healthy to be homemakers, in Higginson's muscular Christianity sport for men had a broad function, making men healthy to be cultural participants of the world outside the home. Beecher's robust woman and Higginson's muscular Christian indeed encompassed the social behaviours of woman's and man's separate spheres. The robust woman would be fit to be a social reproducer and cultural progenitor, while the muscular Christian would be fit to partake of cultural opportunities in business and politics.

In Beecher's and Higginson's vision of the ideal American society, robust health represented a pillar of American national culture. Lack of sound social, moral, and physical health of the nation's citizenry meant the unfulfilled promise of American culture. Physical degeneration of Americans, of course, needed to be remedied. Yet ill health for women required womanly solutions while ill health for men required manly solutions. When physically fit for their prescribed duties, healthy men and women contributed to the improvement and progress of American culture for future generations. In fact, for Beecher and Higginson, energetic health, gained in sporting endeavours, went hard in hand with reform efforts to better American culture. Improving mid nineteenth-century American culture rested upon the sound health of both the robust woman and the muscular Christian. With health as the medium of analysis, Beecher's 'cult of domesticity' and Higginson's 'muscular Christianity' suggest how gender-based ideals shaped women as well as men in nineteenth-century America.

Baseball Spectators, 1855–1870

GEORGE B. KIRSCH

On August 23, 1860 about 15,000 people packed themselves around the Putnam Base Ball Club's grounds in Brooklyn to witness the deciding game of the championship series between that city's two crack clubs—the Atlantics and the Excelsiors. These teams had split the other two contests—the Excelsiors won the first easily, but lost the next by a single run. The excitement among the baseball fraternity was intense before the climactic encounter, as rumors circulated that the Excelsiors would not be allowed to win a close contest. During the early play one of the Atlantics agitated part of the crowd by refusing to yield immediately to an umpire's call. In the top of the sixth, with the Excelsiors ahead, 8–6, a group of rowdies renewed their "insulting epithets and loud comments on the decision of the umpire." At that point Captain Joseph Leggett of the Excelsiors warned the spectators that his team would withdraw if the hooting continued. Members of the Atlantics then appealed to their supporters to permit the game to continue, as 100 policemen tried to restrain the unruly onlookers. But when the roughs increased their yelling and abuse of the umpire and the Excelsiors, Leggett ordered his players off the field. As they left, a large crowd pursued them, "alternately groaning the Excelsiors and cheering the Atlantics." The mob menaced the Excelsiors, and pelted their omnibus with stones as they drove off. The newspapers blamed the disorders and interference on gambling, and condemned the behavior of those spectators

---

From George B. Kirsch, "Baseball Spectators, 1855–1870," *Baseball History* 3 (Fall 1987): 4–18.

who had disrupted the contest. The *Brooklyn Daily Eagle* commented: "It might be supported that clubs could meet for exercise without creating a morbid excitement like that attending the contest of international pugilists." It concluded that "a little further decadence will reduce the attendance at ball matches to the level of the prize ring and the race course," and lamented that "sports which are healthful and respectable in themselves should be rendered disreputable by their surroundings."

This celebrated episode in antebellum American sport provides a dramatic example of the importance of spectators during the formative years of baseball. Interclub and special all-star matches were more than just competitions among the players. They were also public entertainments and major events in the recreational life of thousands of city and town dwellers. In order to fully understand the cultural meaning of the creation of modern sports in the United States, it is necessary to examine their audiences. In particular, it is important to know who attended these contests, why they came, how they experienced them, and how they influenced the games and the sports themselves. . . .

During the early years of team sports in America, amateur clubs generally did not restrict attendance at their matches. An early "Manual of Cricket" defined the policy that baseball officials also observed: "It is always a proper courtesy, and tends to the popularity of this noble exercise, to allow any respectable and quiet strangers to come on the ground to witness either play or practice; but it is always good policy, likewise to have it understood by the visitors that it is a privilege, not a right." Before the 1860s promotors charged admission fees only for the all-star baseball games and international cricket contests. Since people also had to pay for their transportation to these special matches, they tended to attract mostly middle- and upper-class spectators, but when leading teams played interclub games on neighborhood ball grounds (especially in Brooklyn, Newark, and Jersey City), the attendance included members of the lower classes as well. When the Knickerbockers played the Excelsiors before about 6,000 people in August 1859, "a means of rational enjoyment was offered freely to all who chose to avail themselves of it, the only passport requisite being, orderly conduct while on the ground, thus giving to those of the community whose circumstances prohibit their participation in any sport attended with expense, an opportunity to relieve themselves temporarily at least of the cares and anxieties of daily life." It appears that on Boston Common, at Philadelphia's Camac's Wood, at Hoboken's Elysian Fields, and at virtually all of the early ball fields, at least a few from the lower ranks of society joined people from the middle and upper classes in watching amateur antebellum baseball.

After the Civil War promoters and clubs charged an admission fee for many of the top matches, in part because they wished to exclude many of the lower classes from these contests. Yet there is considerable evidence that baseball games continued to draw fans from a wide variety of social groups during the 1860s. In describing the huge throng that attended an 1865 contest between New York's Mutuals and Brooklyn's Atlantics, the *Clipper* noted that it was composed of all classes, with minority representation of "roughs," the "blackleg fraternity," and pickpockets. An 1867 upstate New York championship game brought out a mixed collection of "judges, lawyers, bankers, doctors, clergymen, merchants, clerks, mechanics, students, railroad men, laborers, farmers, officials, editors, printers' devils, bootblacks, and so on, all anxious to see a good game.". . .

The baseball matches that generated the most excitement and attracted the largest crowds before the Civil War were the 1858 New York City versus Brooklyn all-star series at the Fashion Race Course and the 1860 Atlantic versus Excelsior matches in Brooklyn. Most of these drew crowds of at least 5,000, with a few going well over 10,000. Many who came to the first of the Fashion Course baseball games were prosperous; they arrived in "the dainty buggy with its fast trotting single nag—the dashing wagon and pair . . . .—the gay barouche replete with crepe and crinoline—and the comfortable coach with its four inside." The spectators at the second game included "a large number of fancy characters" who took less interest in the competition than in their "peculiar interests." But apparently not all who watched the third and deciding game were fashionable, for "a large deputation of overgrown boys from Brooklyn occupied a prominent position in the Grand Stand, and they materially interfered with the pleasure of the game by their noisy and very partial comments on the decisions of the Umpire, when unfavorable to the Brooklyn Nine."

The popularity of early American baseball cannot be judged solely by the numbers who witnessed these special matches, because they were exceptional public amusements that received a great deal of newspaper publicity. A better indicator is the attendance at the regular contests among the leading and lesser clubs. In New York, Brooklyn, Philadelphia, Boston, and a few other large cities the premier baseball games regularly attracted a few thousand people, despite inconvenient travel and burning heat. The *Clipper* estimated the throng at the 1865 Mutuals—Atlantics match to be between 18,000 and 20,000. . . .

As is always true at sporting events, people attended these early games for widely different reasons, and experienced them in as many different ways. Players frequently appeared at important matches to observe the skills of their fellow athletes and future opponents. Sportswriters such as Henry Chadwick stressed the aesthetic appeal of the sport. Many stories presented a detailed critique of the quality of play, and complimented clever bowling or pitching, fine fielding, and strong batting. Journalists commonly referred to "the beautiful game of baseball." Charles King Newcomb, a Philadelphia man of letters, thought that baseball provided object lessons in art and science. . . . [Writers] lobbied for the elimination of the rule permitting an out when a ball was caught on the first bound, arguing that taking it "on the fly" was more difficult and more exciting for spectators.

A major attraction was the excitement of the competition, especially for local, state, and national championships, coupled with the uncertainty of the outcome. A surprise upset intensified interest. . . . The advent of unofficial championships and open professionalism after the Civil War drew thousands to ballparks, as the Athletics, Atlantics, Mutuals, Red Stockings, and other powerful teams fought for supremacy.

As admission fees became more common during the late 1860s, journalists began to demand that the patrons of baseball get their money's worth. Some newspapers complained about clubs that charged a price for practice or exhibition games, while others asserted that rumors of fixed games dampened enthusiasm and reduced attendance. In 1866 Philadelphia's *Sunday Dispatch* scolded the Athletics for displaying a "miserly spirit" in collecting ten cents for an intrasquad session "wherein the players are only anxious to 'keep their hands in,' and not to show their skill." The *Clipper* noted that because of doubts about the legitimacy of major matches, games that attracted 10,000 and 15,000 spectators in 1867 and 1868 did not draw one-third of the latter figure in 1869. The following year the *Spirit* explained that only 1,000 people witnessed a Chicago White Stockings victory over the Atlantics because the Brooklyn club was "getting into such bad repute, from the constantly flying rumors of 'sells' and 'thrown' games, that few people care to expend their time and money in going to witness what may turn out to be merely a 'hippodroming' exhibition."

The vicarious involvement of the spectators in the thrill of victory (or the agony of defeat) was as obvious in the 1850s and 1860s as it is today. Every team had its "club followers," who identified with their heroes and came to root them to victory. Sometimes they revealed their loyalties all too plainly. . . . Partisanship intensified after the Civil War, especially among the fans of the leading nines. . . .

Although undoubtedly there were many who flocked to these matches for the fine plays and excitement of the competition, some certainly had a more pecuniary interest in mind. Sports gambling already had a long history in America when the first baseball games were played. Not only did the public wager on these events, but so did some of the contestants. Clergymen and other leaders of public opinion continued to condemn it during the 1850s, but the many references to wagering in the daily press seem to indicate that the public had come to tolerate it. . . .

Wagering on baseball was a nearly universal practice during the sport's formative years, even though the National Association of Base Ball Players, founded in 1857, prohibited players from betting. But since that organization had no means of enforcement, and since many of the New York area clubs and the large majority from other states were not members, its rule remained a dead letter. Whenever gambling produced ugly incidents at contests, some of the prominent clubs passed resolutions against the practice. But this obviously did nothing to prevent New York's spectators from placing their bets, and many players probably continued to wager in private. . . .

After the Civil War the baseball boom fed a gambling fever, especially at championship matches. In 1867 a reporter for the *Newark Daily Advertiser* described the scene at an Athletic–Atlantic game: "a few men, with their hands full of greenbacks, were walking around the skirts of the crowd calling for takers of bets at a hundred dollars to twenty that the Athletics will beat two to one." He estimated that "over one hundred thousand dollars changed hands." The next year pools of bets were sold at a game between the Atlantics and the "Haymakers" of Troy, New York. The Troy *Budget* thought that it was "lamentable to see what an extent the betting mania reaches." It stated: "It pervades all classes. At the game played with the Mutuals on Tuesday women brought their money and bet on their favorite Haymakers to the last cent in their possession. We hear of Lansingburg sewing girls who sent down their five, ten, and twenty dollars each by male friends to bet on the Haymakers."

While the artistry of players, the excitement of the competition, and the chance to profit were all major attractions of early American team sports, many also enjoyed the spectacles that the leading events provided. As Warren Goldstein has pointed out, there were important similarities between the cultures of baseball and the theater during this era. The sportsmen played out the drama of a match on their special stage, dressed in costumes that symbolized their club affiliation. Like the world of the theater, baseball had associations with both respectable society and the less reputable life of Victorian popular amusements. People flocked to games for many of the same reasons that they came to see plays that were produced for the masses; their tastes were both highbrow and lowbrow. Some attended simply to watch an exciting contest on a beautiful day, while others anticipated a good time spiced with some liquor and wagering. . . .

The special events that drew thousands produced a carnival atmosphere, as the great crowds attracted con men, tradesmen, vendors, and thieves. At the Fashion Course series spectators arriving at the entrance encountered "thimble-riggers and card sweaters" who were trying to swindle a few dollars out of the "greenies." At the second game between the Atlantics and Excelsiors in August 1860, outside of a huge circle of onlookers there were "various itinerant tradesmen and vendors of eatables and drinkables." Under fancy colored tents the fans quenched their thirst with beer or stronger spirits, such as "Jersey lightning," which increased the business of the police force. Pickpockets plagued these contests and others. Newspapers reported their activities and warned people to be on the alert. After the war pickpockets flocked to feature events, "such a favorable opportunity seldom occurring for picking up stray pocket-books, watches, etc." At an 1867 game between the Mutuals and the Irvingtons several "Newark rowdies" staged a fight in order to give some thieves an opportunity to work the crowd.

Most sports clubs made a special effort to encourage ladies to attend their matches by providing them with tents, seats, refreshments, and other accommodations. Sportsmen believed that female spectators would enhance the respectability of their pastimes while restraining the behavior of males in the crowds. The sporting weeklies and daily press cooperated by urging women to patronize the new team sport. The *Brooklyn Daily Eagle* recommended baseball as "a rational and manly pastime, which our wives, sisters, and sweethearts can witness, and enliven us with their presence, without the fear of a word or deed that would call the blush to the cheek of the most fastidious." Frank Queen, editor of the *Clipper,* solicited the approval of the ladies for the new sports. Although he suspected that women came to sporting events primarily for social reasons, he wanted the ladies to exert their positive influence on troublemakers. He proclaimed:

> Let our American ladies visit the cricket grounds, the regattas, the baseball matches, and the most rough or rude among the spectators would acknowledge their magic sway, thus conferring a double favor upon the sports they countenance, because the members of our sporting organizations are usually gentlemen and always lovers of order, but they can no more control the bystanders than they can any other passengers along a public highway. When ladies are present . . . . no class of our population can be found so debased as not to change their external behavior immediately, and that change is always for the better.

. . . Females did appear in sizeable numbers at ballgrounds, especially for the premier interclub and all-star contests. On several occasions they showed their approbation of the new sport as moral, wholesome recreation by presenting the participants with American flags or bouquets of flowers. . . .

It seems likely that many women attended these matches primarily for social reasons, following the urging of the menfolk in their lives. Newspaper descriptions of their attire suggest that most were from the "respectable" middle and upper classes. Some probably came to ball fields out of curiosity or because of the beauty and excitement of the play. More than a few were well-posted on the fine points of the sport and were vociferous as fans. . . . Some apparently joined in the gambling, for at the second game of the 1858 Fashion Course series, "in many instances ladies were found exchanging little wagers among themselves." Whatever their motives, their appearance at ballgames proved that team sports had become respectable recreations for the American middle class. . . .

As contests between the leading baseball clubs began to attract thousands before the Civil War, crowd control became a serious problem in several cities. The presence of ladies had little impact on those spectators who liked to be active and vocal during the games. Heated rivalries generated much emotion, which led to physical and verbal interference and fighting by club followers, hecklers, gamblers, and rowdies. Baseball players and club managers were sensitive to the problem of crowd control, and attempted to cope with it by appeals to the spectators and by hiring police. Quieting an unruly group was a delicate task, even when contestants tried to calm their own supporters. Usually the players were able to preserve decorum, as for example in July 1860 when Brooklyn's Atlantics and Putnams "suppressed all outside talk, by simply requesting the spectators to cease, which they did at once.". . . Some of the Brooklyn baseball clubs owned their own grounds and hired police to maintain order and to remove objectionable persons. Brooklyn's Excelsiors enjoyed a reputation for preserving the peace at their field in South Brooklyn, while the Atlantics at Bedford did not control their grounds and therefore had more trouble with spectators. On a few occasions, such as the deciding game of the Atlantic–Excelsior series of 1860, even the police were unable to restrain disorderly spectators.

During the amateur era most of the baseball matches were played on unenclosed grounds. When thousands appeared to witness a contest, clearing the field of spectators was no easy task. Keeping them away from the players during the game could also be difficult. Generally the crowd cooperated by staying behind lines marked as bounds, but when groups of club followers got too close to the action, they could interfere with play and thus influence the outcome of the match. Outfielders often had to retrieve balls from amongst a forest of legs. Supporters of the home team could make life miserable for visitors. When Brooklyn's Excelsiors defeated New York's Gothams in 1858 at Bedford, the immense crowd surrounding the contestants interfered with the progress of the game. . . .

More common and annoying than physical interference was heckling. Prominent sportswriters blamed gamblers for causing many instances of verbal abuse by spectators, which irritated the umpire, the players, and others in the crowds. . . .

When the Excelsiors defeated the Niagaras in a Brooklyn junior contest in 1857, "some of the Niagaras' friends did not behave as gentlemen should." Whenever the Excelsiors were about to strike the ball, some in the crowd yelled "such remarks as 'shanks,' 'Shanghai,' and other words not quite as decent as the above.". . .

Fights and other disturbances among boys and men in the crowds also created problems for baseball clubs. In July 1860 a Jersey City resident reported that "spectators are seriously annoyed on the Hamilton's grounds by the misconduct and noise of rude and rowdyish boys." He urged officials "to see that good order is preserved, and that the nuisance caused by groups of yelling, hooting and wrestling boys mixing themselves with the quiet spectators, and sometimes insulting the visiting club, should be prevented.". . . . He explained: "I remember following an adherent of the Atlantics . . . . several blocks to drugstore where his wounds from [a] gunshot were treated. Near-riots were frequently the results of clashes between hucksters and drivers who on top of their vehicles in Columbia Ave. hurled remarks at each other until these ended in fistic encounters. But this was all off the field of honor." There were also a few fights between white and black spectators, including one at Charleston, South Carolina in 1869.

The intense partisanship that frequently marked baseball matches reflected a contentiousness that plagued most antebellum American cities. Urban violence and mob activity were commonplace in the divided and tumultuous world of these fast-growing centers. Baseball reporters realized that the riot which ended the At-lantic–Excelsior series was only a symptom of a much deeper problem that troubled their communities. There were elements of both nationalism and social class antagonism in that rivalry, as the Atlantics were more Irish and more working class than the gentlemen of the Excelsiors. A *Clipper* editorial identified the true cause of all urban disorder as "the *spirit of faction* . . . . in which the foreign element of our immense metropolitan population, and their native offspring, especially, delights to indulge." While noting that gambling contributed to the trouble, that periodical stated that the real evil lay in "the bitterness of party spirit and sectional strife," in fire department fights, in lower-class gangs, and in sectarian religious jealousies. "In short," it continued, "whether it is 'our country,' 'our party,' 'our company,' 'our club,' or 'our church,' the same evil spirit rules the actions and paralyzes the virtuous tendencies of all who succumb [*sic*] to its baneful influence, replacing kindly feelings with bitter hatred, and manly emulation and generous rivalry with revengeful retaliation." For the *Clipper,* the remedy lay "in the self control of contending clubs and parties, and in a strict adherence to the rules that guide the actions of a man of honor and a gentleman." All the proper conduct in the world among the contestants, however, did not guarantee peace and quiet among the spectators. When issues of social class or nationality appeared in certain matches, as they apparently did in the Atlantic–Excelsior matches of 1860, there was always the potential for problems in the crowd.

The commercialization of baseball after the Civil War did not bring any drastic changes in the behavior of audiences. Some promoters and enthusiasts thought that the coming of more enclosed grounds and admission fees ranging from 10 to 50 cents for most games would restrict spectators to a more select and well-mannered population. But this was not usually the case, in part because many from the lower classes were willing to pay to see the feature events. Also, thousands of fans congregated outside the fences and often found ways to view the sport over or through the barriers. One reporter marveled at the numbers waiting at the entrance to deposit their quarters to see a Mutuals–Athletics contest in 1867. He wrote: "One would imagine that in these times of high rents and low wages that the patronage of the base ball arena would be somewhat limited at such a high tariff as a quarter of a dollar; but the fact is a quarter is nothing for such an hour or two's exciting sport as a well contested ball match yields." Those who were unable or unwilling to pay often could still see the action (and create a disturbance). When the Athletics routed the Atlantics in 1868 at the Union Grounds at Williamsburg, Brooklyn, "several thousands managed to witness the game without disbursing the required admittance fee." The *Clipper* reported: "Owners of trucks and other vehicles drove a brisk trade by stationing their establishments close to the high fence surrounding the ground, and letting out 'standing room only' to those who preferred this method of looking on. Others secured the prominent 'peek-holes' in the fence, while others still, after the game was under way and the attention of officers was centered in the exciting contest, boldly took up their position on the fence and held them to the close."

Charging admission to enclosed fields did lead to better accommodations for ladies, the press, and the general paying public, but it did not eliminate fan interference, fights, or crowd disorders. An 1866 contest between the Athletics and the Atlantics ended in the bottom of the first inning after a fight between police and spectators and a rush of people onto the field disrupted play. Fisticuffs in the stands were commonplace. . . . People who paid 25 or 50 cents for admission also fought over good seats, and were enraged when others blocked their view or that of their lady friends.

By 1870 commercial baseball played by professional teams was a smashing success, and even amateur games often drew large and spirited audiences. The sport was popular because of the artistry, excitement, and opportunities for gambling it offered, and also because it provided colorful and respectable public amusements. Baseball had become a new form of recreation that all could enjoy. People flocked to these ballgames for all kinds of reasons, and enjoyed the action in all kinds of ways. The majority of these spectators behaved themselves reasonably well, but an unruly minority drank, cheered, heckled, gambled, and fought in the grandstands. Today, more than a century later, baseball's hold on its spectators remains powerful, even as the sport continues to suffer from many of the abuses introduced by its first fans during the era of the Civil War.

FURTHER READING

Melvin L. Adelman, *A Sporting Time: New York City and the Rise of Modern Athletics, 1820–1870* (1986)

Bruce Bennett, "The Making of Round Hill School," *Quest* 4 (April 1965), 53–64

John R. Betts, "Mind and Body in Early American Thought," *Journal of American History* 54 (1968), 787–805

John R. Betts, "Sporting Journalism in Nineteenth Century America," *American Quarterly* 5 (1953), 39–56

John R. Betts, "The Technological Revolution and the Rise of Sport, 1850–1900," *Mississippi Valley Historical Review* XL (1953), 231–56

Linda J. Borish, " 'Do Not Neglect Exercise nor Recreation': Rural New Englanders, Sport and Health Concerns," *Colby Quarterly* 32 (March 1996), 25–35

Linda Borish, "Farm Females, Fitness and the Ideology of Physical Health in Antebellum New England," *Agricultural History* 64 (Summer 1990), 17–30

Frances B. Cogan, *All-American Girl: The Idea of Real Womanhood in Mid-Nineteenth Century America* (1989)

Lawrence W. Fielding, "War and Trifles: Sport in the Shadows of Civil War Army Life," *Journal of Sport History* 4 (Summer 1977), 151–68

Stephen Freedman, "The Baseball Fad in Chicago, 1865–1870: An Exploration of the Role of Sport in the Nineteenth Century City," *Journal of Sport History* 5 (Summer 1978), 42–64

Erich Geldbach, "The Beginning of German Gymnastics in America," *Journal of Sport History* 3 (Winter 1976), 236–72

Warren Goldstein, *Playing for Keeps: A History of Early Baseball* (1989)

Harvey Green, *Fit for America: Health, Fitness, Sport, and American Society* (1986)

George B. Kirsch, *The Creation of American Team Sports: Baseball and Cricket, 1838–1872* (1989)

Peter Levine, "The Promise of Sport in Antebellum America," *Journal of American Culture* 2 (1980), 623–34

Robert Lewis, "American Croquet in the 1860s: Playing the Game and Winning," *Journal of Sport History* 18 (1991), 365–86

Roberta J. Park, "The Attitude of Leading New England Transcendentalists Toward Healthful Exercise, Active Recreation, and Proper Care of the Body: 1830–1860," *Journal of Sport History* 4 (Spring 1977), 34–50

Roberta J. Park, " 'Embodied Selves': The Rise and Development of Concern for Physical Education, Active Games and Recreation for American Women, 1776–1865," *Journal of Sport History* 5 (Summer 1978), 5–41

W.H.P. Robertson, *The History of Thoroughbred Racing in America* (1964)

Ronald Story, "The Country of the Young: The Meaning of Baseball in Early American Culture," in *Cooperstown Symposium on Baseball* (1991), 324–42

Patricia Vertinsky, "Sexual Equality and the Legacy of Catharine Beecher," *Journal of Sport History* 6 (Spring 1979), 39–49

James C. Whorton, *Crusaders for Fitness: The History of American Health Reformers* (1982)

CHAPTER
5

Sport and Higher Education in America, 1865–1910

Intercollegiate athletics provided one of the most important breeding grounds for organized sport in America. This started with inter-class competitions in the early 1800s due to the example of Oxford and Cambridge in staging intercollegiate contests that existed virtually nowhere else.

The first inter-school competition in the United States occurred in 1852 between Harvard and Yale crews, with Harvard winning. Six years later, the College Union Regatta was organized as the first intercollegiate sports league. Crew was followed as an intercollegiate sport by baseball in 1859, football in 1869, and track and field in 1873. Baseball was the principal college sport until the late 1880s, when the "big game" became the annual Thanksgiving Day football match between traditional rivals.

Why did football supplant baseball? Was it profits? By the early 1890s the Yale eleven was earning over $50,000 a year. The test of manliness? The rituals of the "big game"? Spectators saw games marked by brute strength and power—mass momentum with little deception or guile. Did the sport fulfill its promise? Faculties usually supported intercollegiate competition, which supposedly taught proper social skills, promoted manliness, advanced civilization, boosted school spirit, and advertised the institution's name. However, historians generally agree that the ideals of football and the realities of the game were far apart. How and why were the goals of amateur college sport undermined? Were they realistic goals? What was the role of the professional coach? In what ways were they role models? How did college presidents, alumni, and students contribute to subverting the ideals of amateurism?

Recruiting violations were commonplace, and it was easy to keep players eligible despite poor academic performances. By the 1890s the fervor for intercollegiate sport had spread westward, especially to growing state universities that were seeking both publicity and larger enrollments.

Around the turn of the century, football underwent a lot of external appraisals and self-criticism due to violence and the deaths of several players. This scrutiny led to the Intercollegiate Athletic Association in 1906 (renamed the National Collegiate Athletic Conference in 1910), which established nationwide playing rules and eligibility requirements. What was the relationship between developing a more wide-open game that employed the forward pass and the commercial aspects of the sport? The exciting play on the field, the development of gridiron heroes ("All-Americans"), the entertaining rituals that accompanied the game, and the ability of schools to get graduates and others to identify with the team helped make college football extremely popular. In the 1920s some of the greatest sports heroes were football players like Red Grange, who played in stadiums (increasingly publicly financed) that seated 80,000 or more spectators.

D O C U M E N T S

The first document reports on the Harvard-Oxford boat race of 1869, the first international intercollegiate competition. The second document comprises Walter Camp's recommendations to college athletes that they play with high standards of sportsmanship. Camp was a star football player at Yale from 1875 to 1882, when it fielded the dominant team in America. He subsequently coached Yale to their greatest seasons, authored twenty books on sports, was largely responsible for drawing up the game's rules, and selected the All-American teams from 1889 to 1924. The third document is a report by Richard Harding Davis, one of the foremost journalists of his day, in which he describes the social festivities surrounding the 1893 championship Thanksgiving Day football match between Yale and Princeton. In the fourth document, muckraker Henry B. Needham examines how college athletic associations subsidized star athletes who were actually professionals rather than simon-pure amateurs.

The *New York Times* Reports on an International Match: The Harvard-Oxford Boat Race, 1869

The two greatest commercial nations of the world were engaged yesterday, not in the usual pursuit of gain, but in watching an extraordinary trial of strength between eight young men. There is no race but the Anglo-Saxon with whom such a competition would have been possible. We may, without boasting, add that only Americans would have traveled three thousand miles from home in order to challenge the strongest crew ever seen upon foreign waters, under circumstances unavoidably adverse to themselves. It was impossible from the first that the conditions could be made quite equal on both sides. The Oxonians are at home on the Thames, and every man in their boat had already taken part in one or more successful struggles with a crew only second to their own. They were animated with all the confidence and buoyancy which a recent victory naturally inspires. They had nothing to learn about the river, and no changes to make in regard to the construction of their boat. Moreover, they had the sympathy of nine-tenths of the spectators with them, and in a trial which imposes the severest strain on all the powers this is an advantage

From "The Boat Race" [editorial], *New York Times*, August 28, 1869.

difficult to overestimate. . . . The American crew had little more than three weeks active training, . . . they have been obliged to change their boat twice or thrice, and to recast the crew more than once. . . .

. . . It has been superiority of physical strength quite as much as any moral qualities which has given the Anglo-Saxon race a noble supremacy in the world. A people which looks upon an athlete as a useless incumbrance upon the face of the earth, or as a paradox in nature, is not likely to hold its own for centuries together. It is often alleged that in this country we are too apt to neglect a purely physical training—the systematic and careful development of strength and muscle—in the education of our youth. If that charge were well-founded, nothing could so quickly remove all occasion for repeating it as a contest like that of yesterday. We undertake to say that boat-racing will henceforth be more popular than ever among us. Young men now beginning their college studies will be stimulated to earn the distinction which the Harvard crew so brilliantly won for themselves yesterday in the old and the new world. Emulation of this kind is of the greatest value to a people in an age when the young are thrust into the battle of life before there has been time for a full expansion of their powers. A weak, sickly, flabby race may be a pleasing spectacle to theorists who live chiefly in the clouds, but for the destiny yet lying before us we cannot have too many of the attributes which are popularly included in the word "manliness." There are situations in which "mind" can do nothing, and we are forced to base our hopes upon "matter." An international boat race between nations like the American and the English cannot, therefore, be regarded as a trivial incident. We are unable, indeed, to regard a single trial of the kind as a decisive test of the superiority either of a race and breed, or of a system of rowing. But it challenges the world to admire physical pluck, endurance, hardiness, a sound constitution, and other gifts which we were intended to cultivate and rejoice in no less than in the pretentious intellectual forces. How many men are there on either side of the Atlantic whose nerves would have enabled them even to begin the task which these young men from Harvard nearly carried to a successful issue yesterday?

. . . We honor the Harvard men for persevering against all difficulties in one of the most gallant contests ever recorded, and we hope that we shall some day have the opportunity of congratulating the Oxonians on a similar exhibition of mettle. . . .

Coach Walter Camp on Sportsmanship, 1893

"Be each, pray God, a gentleman!". . . Do you live up to it? Or are you letting it come down a little here and there; so little, perhaps, that you hardly notice it until you make comparison? A gentleman against a gentleman always plays to win. There is a tacit agreement between them that each shall do his best, and the best

From Walter Camp, "Walter Camp on Sportsmanship," in *Walter Camp's Book of College Sports* (New York: Century, 1893), 1–9.

man shall win. A gentleman does not make his living, however, from his athletic prowess. He does not earn anything by his victories except glory and satisfaction. . . . There is still no harm where the mug or trophy hangs in the room of the winner is indicative of his skill; but if the silver mug becomes a silver dollar, either at the hands of the winner or the donor, let us have the laurel back again.

A gentleman never competes for money, directly or indirectly. Make no mistake about this. No matter how winding the road may be that eventually brings the sovereign into the pocket, it is the price of what should be dearer to you than anything else,—your honor. . . .

If you are enough of a man to be a good athlete, and some one asks you to use that athletic ability upon their behalf, don't take money for it, or anything that amounts to pay. If you are on the school team or nine and go into training, don't break faith with your captain, yourself, and your fellows by surreptitious indulgencies. . . . If you are the captain and you find a man breaking training in spite of your orders, and you consider it advisable to put him off, don't be afraid to do it. Gentlemen are not cowards, mentally or physically.

If a man comes to you and endeavors to affect your choice of a college by offers of a pecuniary nature, he does not take you for a gentleman or a gentleman's son, you may be sure. Gentlemen neither offer nor take bribes.

Now, my young college friend, it is your turn. Remember it is upon you that the eyes of the preparatory school-boy are fixed, it is toward you that the younger brother looks for example, and whatever you do in your four years' course, you will see magnified by the boys who come after you. Support your class and your college in every way compatible with your position. Gentlemen are not stingy, nor are they selfish. Play it if you can and your class or college needs you. Pay if you can afford it, but do not allow a false pride to lead you into subscriptions beyond your means. Don't be ashamed of enthusiasm. A man without it is a man without a purpose.

I remember a little incident of my own college course. I was a freshman, and knew almost no one in college except a certain junior. I had entered in two events in the fall athletic games, one a quarter mile, the other a hurdle race. I had run the quarter and been beaten, although I finished second. My opponents had all been upper classmen, and I received no little encouragement from their friends. I felt very lonely and disgusted with myself and life in general when I got on the mark for the hurdle. I had but two competitors, and both had been cheered when they came to the scratch. Suddenly as we were getting on our marks I heard a voice half-way down the course call out, "You can do 'em," and I saw my junior friend waving his hat to me. It was not a classical remark, but it made me feel better. I was clumsy in getting off, and when we came to the sixth hurdle was nearly five yards behind the other two, but from that time on I could hear my friend roaring out, "Go in!" "You've got 'em yet!" "Now you're over," as I went up each flight. I *did* finish first, and I had hardly touched the tape before he was patting me on the back. I don't suppose it cost him much to yell for a poor freshman, but I know that I always thought of him as one of the best fellows I ever knew, and in after years I have remembered enough of the feeling that was in my heart toward him, to go out and try to make some others feel that even a freshman has friends.

Apropos of this, a word to non-contestants. . . . A gentleman is courteous. It is not courtesy upon a ball-field to cheer an error of the opponents. If it is upon your grounds, it is the worst kind of boorishness. Moreover, if there are remarkable plays made by your rivals you yourselves should cheer, conceal any chagrin you may feel at the loss it may be to your side, but be courteous to appreciate and applaud an exceptional play by the opponents. . . .

Finally, to non-contestants, I want to say a word regarding "celebrating." Primarily, do not, I beg of you, do anything because it looks smart. Enjoy yourselves, but do not try to "show off.". . . A little unusual hilarity, a tendency to believe that everything is expressly for the collegian, can be upon these occasions overlooked and forgiven, but be ready to appreciate the point beyond which it is carried too far; be ready to apologize quickly and instantly where offense is taken. Show that behind the jolly fun there is the instinct and cultivation of a gentleman's son. . . .

Now for the contestants. I wish I could impress indelibly upon your minds the fact that with you rests the most enduring standard for amateur sports. With no disrespect to any class or condition—with the best regard for all strong legislation in outside athletic bodies—I say that the collegian's standard of purity in his sports should be the highest. The very fact of having the leisure to devote four years to a higher education, should be taken to involve the duty of acquiring a keener perception of right and wrong in matters where right and wrong depend upon a delicacy of honor. Gentlemen do not cheat, nor do they deceive themselves as to what cheating is. If you are elected the captain of a nine, team, or crew, read over your rules, and note exactly who are allowed as contestants by those rules, not by the custom of some predecessor, nor by what you think some rival will do, but by the rules themselves. Having done that, never let a thought enter your head of making use of any man not clearly and cleanly eligible. . . .

What if, at the time, your side may be the weaker? Don't be a coward on that account. Face it like a man, and say with your whole heart that you are on the side of the men who want no chance of retreat or escape, only a fair contest and certain victory or defeat at the end of it. . . .

Be each, pray God, a gentleman!

Richard Harding Davis Scrutinizes the Rituals of the Thanksgiving Day Football Game, 1893

There is nothing more curious or more interesting in the history of New York city within the last decade than the development of the Thanksgiving-day Game. Ten years ago the game was a sporting event, and nothing more. . . . To-day the sporting character of the event has been overwhelmed by the social interest it has aroused in itself, and which has enveloped it and made it more of a spectacle than an athletic contest. But it is still the greatest sporting event and spectacle combined

From Richard Harding Davis, "The Thanksgiving Day Game," *Harper's Weekly* 37 (December 1893): 1170–71.

that this country has to show. . . . No one who does not live in New York can understand how completely it colors and lays its hold upon that city, how it upsets and overturns its thoroughfares, and disturbs its rapid routine of existence. . . .

Ten years ago Thanksgiving day in New York was an event of moment and meaning; there still clung to it the semi-religious significance that gave it its place. . . . But the game up at the polo grounds caused many desertions and annual mutinies. . . . It was not that they cared so much for football, but there was nothing better offered, and, in short became "the thing to do". . . .

Now . . . the city surrenders herself to the students and their game as she never welcomes any other event, except a Presidential election. . . . She begins to prepare for them early in November . . . with the colors of two rivals, and from Ninety-fourth Street in Harlem to lower Broadway, . . . and from the east side to the North River, the same colors in every form and texture hang on the outer walls, and the cry is that "they come." But long before they come, every other young woman you meet, and every little boy, and elderly men even, begin to parade Broadway with bows of blue stuck on their persons, or long strips of orange and black ribbon . . . which proclaim their allegiance and their hopes. . . . Service in many of the churches . . . were held one hour earlier than usual last Thanksgiving day, because the rectors found they could not get a full congregation unless the service was over in time to allow the worshipers to make an early start for Manhattan Field. . . .

Everything on four wheels and that will hold twenty men on its top . . . goes up Fifth Avenue on Thursday morning. It is like a circus procession many miles long. It begins at ten in the morning, four hours before the game, when the coaches meet in front of the Fifth Avenue and the Brunswick hotels, where a crowd has gathered to cheer them as they start. The streets are empty, for it is a holiday, and the sounds of the bugle calls and coach horns and the riflelike cheer of Yale and the hissing sky-rocket yell of Princeton break in on the Sabbath-like quiet of the streets like the advance of an army going forth triumphantly to war. There is everything, from the newest English brake to omnibuses, draped from their tops to the level of the street with cloths of yellow and blue, hung in festoons or dropped in four straight curtains from each corner and dragging in the mud and with wheels covered up entirely or decorated with ribbons around their spokes, and suggesting monster revolving pinwheels. . . . All blanketed in the true colors, . . . every coach carries twenty shouting men and exciting young women smothered in furs; and the flags, as they jerk them about, fill the air with color; and the coaches themselves toss like shops in a heavy sea, rocking from side to side, and sinking and rebounding on their springs as the men on top jump up and down in time to the rhythm of the rival cheers.

Every coach load yells for all the pretty girls on the next coach if they wear the proper colors and race scornfully past those who do not; and from the Washington Arch to the layers of flats in Harlem there are holiday-makers out along the route to see the procession pass, standing in some places three and four deep along the sidewalk. And from houses all along the course there are bits of bunting and big flags; sometimes it is only a strip of paper muslin fluttering from the eighth story window of a cheap apartment-house, and again it is a big silken banner swinging from the housefront of some important friend of one or the other of the two colleges. . . . And as the decorated horses and bedecked hansoms and brakes and coaches and omnibuses go galloping up the Avenue there are special cheers of the orange flag and the big black P in front of the Sloanes and the Alexanders and the Scribners, and for the blue banners and white Y before the homes of the Whitneys and the Vanderbilts.

Manhattan Field, where the game has been held of late years, and where it took place last week [attended by] thirty thousand. . . . When every other one . . . stood up and yelled and waved a blue or an orange and black flag, the effect was worth crossing an ocean to see. There are certain traditions of these games which are interesting, and which were observed last weekend with much enthusiasm. One of these is the singing of words expressive of the sentiments of the rival colleges to the tunes of hymns and popular songs in which the names of the "star" players are handed down to immortality. . . .

It is also interesting to the stranger to note how systematically the cheering is given, how it is timed to destroy the effect of the rival cheering, and that certain men are selected to lead and give the time for these yells, who hold a position similar to that of a leader of an orchestra. This year there was a new and an unintentionally pretty effect in the introduction of blankets by the substitutes, in the place of "sweaters." They found that it took too long to pull a jersey on and off a player while he was waiting for a comrade to revive, or for the two captains to discuss a disputed point with the referee, and that throwing a blanket around him kept him warmer. So this year the substitutes lay around the lines stretched at full length on blankets of double length, and whenever time was called, as it was at almost every fifth minute of each half, they would swarm over the field, . . . and smother the eleven men of their college. . . .

There is no change so noticeable in the Thanksgiving day game as the difference in the manner in which it is reported for the daily papers. It is no longer considered enough to cover it with two men—one to write the introduction, and [the] other to describe the play. Now each paper sends its star men, its artists, and photographers, and engages many ex-players of reputation to describe the game from the points of view of adherents of each college, and to make diagrams which show where the ball was at every minute. . . . At the last Thanksgiving day game that I helped to report for the *Evening Sun,* there were seventeen men assisting one another. . . .

Henry Beach Needham Decries the Professionalization of College Athletes, 1905

For the good of sport, a distinction is made between an amateur and a professional. This distinction does not in itself involve a moral question. It is a classification in the interest of fair play. The professional, having made something of a business of athletics, presumptively outclasses the amateur who plays only for enjoyment and

From Henry B. Needham, "The College Athlete: How Commercialism Is Making Him a Professional," *McClure's Magazine* 25 (June 1905): 115–28.

recreation. Therefore, contests in which professionals of any degree are pitted against amateurs are . . . "unequal, if the facts are known, unfair, if the facts are concealed."

[In 1898] the Conference on Intercollegiate Athletics . . . simply stated, a student becomes ineligible who accepts compensation, "direct or indirect" for his athletic services. . . .

Winning at Any Cost

The *paid* coach has to win. If he develops a winning team, his services will be retained; if his team meets with defeat, there is something radically wrong with his methods. He has not "delivered the goods". . . .

In 1899 Columbia determined to go in for football. There had been no eleven for eight years, during which time the athletic energies of the university had been devoted mainly to rowing—the cleanest of all sports. Columbia saw greater advertising possibilities in football. . . . Played in New York, the games would attract large crowds, and sufficient revenue . . . to support athletics in general. A coach was engaged at a salary which the average college professor accepts gladly. A Yale athlete, George Foster Sanford . . . knew the secrets of Yale's success, and was willing to teach them to a rival college for a proper consideration. . . . He had to have apt pupils. The game as developed required men of weight and muscle. Such men . . . he could not find matriculated at Columbia. . . . So this enterprising coach got several "stars" outside—or rather had the manager of the team hire them. He put them in Columbia uniforms, and they beat Yale. . . . His salary was raised to $5,000 per year.

. . . Thanks to the influence of the colleges, there is growing up a class of students tainted with commercialism. . . . They are resolved that their athletic ability shall put them through college, and they propose to go to the institution offering the best "opportunities". . . . Said Professor Hollis, for seven years chairman of the Harvard Athletic Committee:

"The evils of college athletics are the evils of every-day life. Commercialism is a characteristic of American life."

"Opportunities" at Prep School and College Contrasted

James J. Hogan, captain and right-tackle of the Yale eleven . . . entered Exeter, a poor boy, at the age of twenty-three. That was over eight years ago. He had been earning his own living when he set about to complete his education. . . .

Harvard joined Yale and Princeton in competition for this great prep athlete. Hogan went to Yale, which is not far from his home. . . .

The career of this athlete at the university has been one of marked success. Hogan with his room-mate . . . occupies a suite in Vanderbilt Hall—the most luxurious of the Yale dormitories. . . . He takes his meals at the University Club . . . an expensive undergraduate organization. . . . After the football season of 1903, . . . the Yale trainer . . . with Hogan, then captain elect of the Yale eleven, as a traveling companion made a ten-day trip to Cuba. The athletic association paid for the excursion, which cost . . . $25 per day for Hogan.

. . . Hogan receives $100 a year, the income of the John Bennetto Scholarship. In addition, . . . his entire tuition is abated. The baseball association gives to Hogan (and two teammates) the score-card privilege. From the sale of the cards at the intercollegiate games and from the advertising, these athletes take the entire proceeds. . . . At Yale the football and baseball score-card privileges are regarded as "sort of scholarship for athletes."

Bartering a Reputation

Hogan's income is further augmented by commissions paid him by The American Tobacco Company, whose agent he is. It is well known about the campus that, through the influence of the Yale captain, the "Egyptian Deities" and the "Turkish Mogul" cigarettes were placed on sale at "Mory's." These brands are spoken of at Yale as "Hogan's cigarettes." . . .

It is not to be argued that this employment affects Hogan's amateur standing. The "business arrangement" is important only as showing the growth of commercialism in collegiate sport. Hogan entered Yale a skillful player. College coaching made of him a "star." He was selected as captain of the varsity football team, which added greatly to his popularity, practically insuring him election to a senior society. The success of the eleven gave him a wide reputation. This reputation and popularity—largely a gift of the university—have been bartered, doubtless unconsciously on Hogan's part, for dollars and cents—money sent by sympathetic fellow students in acquiring a taste for certain brands of cigarettes.

The Tramp Athlete

[Andrew L.] Smith is the man who goes to college with the *one* idea of engaging in athletics. . . . As full-back of the eleven of Pennsylvania State College, he played a "magnificent game" against the University of Pennsylvania, October 4, 1902. The following Monday he was practising [*sic*] with the University of Pennsylvania second eleven. . . . He immediately began to attend classes. . . . The following fall he played for his new college. . . . Then it became known that, between October 4th and November 7th, 1902, when practicing with the "scrub" and attending classes at the University of Pennsylvania, he played three games . . . for *Penn State.* . . . Smith was thereupon . . . declared ineligible.

. . . Yet this man was permitted to represent Pennsylvania on the gridiron last fall (1904), and to the victory of Harvard he contributed greatly. Afterwards, in the middle of his senior year, he was dropped from college. His football days [were] over, and he was no longer a useful member of the college community. . . .

The only justification of Pennsylvania's unsportsmanlike behavior is found in Harvard's attitude toward this sister institution. . . . It was noised about that Harvard would "drop Penn" if a decisive victory was won in 1904. Pennsylvania, therefore, in order to continue in the competition of the "Big Four" *had* to produce a winning team.

An Example and a Moral

. . . William Clarence Matthews, the young colored student, who is best known to the public as short-shop on the 'varsity nine for three years, and as an end-rush in the last football game against Yale . . . has worked his way through the university, practically completing his four years' course in three years. . . .

Matthews is a product of Tuskegee, where he fitted himself for Phillips Andover. . . . At Harvard he had a Price Greenleaf Aid, paying $200 his freshman
year, but since then has had no scholarship. . . . As at Andover he has worked his
way, doing what he could during the college year. . . , and working steadily during
the summers in hotels, or on Pullman sleeping cars. This year he has taught in one
of the North Cambridge night-schools.

Here is a man who, to maintain his standing as an amateur, has repeatedly refused offers of forty dollars per week and board to play semi-professional baseball
in summer. . . .

"The trouble with accepting favors . . . to help one through college is, that in
the end you find they have *made you dependent*."

Here is the answer to those who advocate the indirect subsidizing of athletes.

"Mr. Washington taught us at Tuskegee . . . that the best help a man can get is
an opportunity to help himself."

E S S A Y S

The two essays in this section examine both the commercialization and the integrity of
sport at the college level in the United States. The first essay, by Ronald A. Smith, a
professor of physical education at Penn State University and a leading pioneer in sport
history, questions a fundamental tenet of major college sports programs: Were these
programs ever as truly amateur as their ideology asserted? Was it even possible for
them to be truly amateur? In the second essay, Robin Lester of the Francis Parker
School in Chicago (and for nearly two decades a headmaster at prestigious independent secondary schools) analyzes three of the essential aspects of big-time, highly
commercialized sport at the University of Chicago—the roles of spectators, athletes,
and the football coach. The University of Chicago was established in 1892 as a major
research university. Its president, William Rainey Harper, recruited top scholars to the
university with Rockefeller money. However, Harper knew it would take some time to
gain recognition through scholarship, so he also invested heavily in sports to quickly
gain national attention. He brought in former Yale star athlete Amos Alonzo Stagg to
coach by offering the promise of a high salary and faculty status. Stagg built the football program, as well as other sports, into a national powerhouse that brought fame
and profit to his institution.

Amateurism in Late Nineteenth-Century College Sports

RONALD A. SMITH

The rise of the professional coach was a major force in the early movement in
American intercollegiate athletics to adopt a professional model. By the late nineteenth and early twentieth century, it was clear that the professional model

From Ronald A. Smith, *Sports and Freedom: The Rise of Big-Time College Athletics* (New York: Oxford University Press, 1988), 165–74.

produced victories. Only those with idealistic blinders on, such as *Outing* editor Caspar Whitney, believed that the amateur sport model would outlast a professional one in America. Only Whitney, or someone of his ilk, could claim in 1894 that professional sport was dead in America and that true amateurism had conquered all. Men's intercollegiate sport had accepted much of the spirit of professionalism as its own. Yet college athletics expressed an amateur ideal during this period, as it did nearly a century later. One might say that Americans for well over a century have tended to profess amateurism while they have exhibited the professional spirit in most areas of "amateur" sport. This was no more apparent than in intercollegiate athletics. Why have Americans accepted the professional model, and why have they felt the need to justify their actions in the name of amateur athletics?

The historic amateur-professional dilemma in college sport required, as all dilemmas do, a choice between equally undesirable alternatives. The collegiate dilemma might be stated as follows: if a college has truly amateur sport, it will lose prestige as it loses contests; if a college acknowledges outright professional sport, the college will lose respectability as a middle-class or upper-class institution. The unsatisfactory solution to the dilemma has been to claim amateurism to the world, while in fact accepting a professional mode of operation.

The term amateur has been a charged one. Historically, since the mid-nineteenth century, the word "amateur" as used in sport has stood for positive values in relation to "professional" which has had negative worth. Amateur has meant good and elevated; professional has meant bad and degraded. The exaltation of the amateur and the debasement of the professional, as has been noted, was a function of nineteenth-century British social class elitism.

Amateurism as Defined by the British

"Ancient amateurism is a myth," classicist David Young boldly stated in his perspective *The Olympic Myth of Greek Amateur Athletics*. The heart of amateurism, he has pointed out, is social elitism, born in Victorian England by the upper classes to exclude those of the working class. Though the ancient Greeks had no concept of amateurism, the English social elite developed the myth and then passed their own amateur legislation as if they had past precedent to rely upon. In the 1870s, the elite British Amateur Rowing Association separated itself from plebeian types by passing an amateur law. In so doing it gave us one of the many negative definitions of amateurism which have plagued sport since then. The upper-class rowers ruled that no person is an amateur "who is or ever has been by trade or employment for wages a mechanic, artisan, or labourer or engaged in any menial duty." Since then, nearly every definition of an amateur in sport has been a negative one. Thus, an amateur is a person who has:

- never competed in an open competition;
- never competed for public money;
- never competed for gate money;
- never competed with a professional; and
- never taught or pursued athletics as a means of livelihood.

Amateurism has almost always been defined in terms of what it is not, rather than what it is. There appears never to have been a successful, positive, workable definition of amateurism, even as amateurism has served principally the social and economic elite since the mid-1800s. The philosopher Paul Weiss was basically right when he stated:

> A rich man does not need to become a professional player. Since he has more leisure time than most, he also has more time to devote to sport. As a consequence, he may become an amateur athlete. . . . By and large the line between amateur and professional is mainly a line between the unpaid members of a privileged class and the paid members of an underprivileged class.

Harold Harris, the late classical historian, echoed the same theme in his volume *Sport in Britain*. Harris believed that "the distinction between professional and amateur had been purely one of social class." The British amateur attitude was carried to America, but because America lacked entrenched classes, at least to the degree that Britain had them, the amateur attitude would never flourish in practice as it did in the elite-led sports in Britain.

If amateurism has not been defined in negative terms (for example, an amateur is one who has never participated for remuneration), then it has generally been defined as a state of mind determined by the motives of the athlete. The athlete participates only for the love of the sport. Amateurism, to many, has been an attitude, not a state of being. If amateurism is an attitude determined by the athlete, it leads to a perplexing problem—a dilemma of rather large dimensions. First, external judges can never prove the motives, the state of mind or attitude, of the amateur. Second, the historic claiming of positive virtues of the amateur relative to the professional is a false concept. There is simply no evidence that an amateur is more virtuous than a professional. In fact, the reverse may be true, for the amateur at the upper levels of competition often received financial advantage for participation in amateur sport—certainly a hypocritical stance. This has been the situation in collegiate sport since the 1880s, and a few cases before that.

The paradoxical or self-contradictory situation in intercollegiate athletics since the 1870s demands documentation, for there are those who believe that at one time American college athletics were purely amateur, a paragon of athletic amateur virtue. There are two problems with that belief. First, one must believe that amateur athletics equate with virtue, second, that they were once without a professional element. The first is debatable; the second is simply not true.

Professionalism in Nineteenth-Century College Athletics

. . . Eight categories have been chosen which indicate the characteristics of professionalism which existed in nineteenth-century American college sports:

1. competition for valuable, non-cash prizes;
2. competition for money prizes;
3. competition against professionals;
4. charging money at the gate;
5. costs of a training table not borne by the athlete;
6. payment of athletic tutors by others than the athlete;
7. recruitment and payment of athletes; and
8. payment of a professional coach.

While a number of the categories may not appear to be truly in the professional realm to late twentieth-century observers, it is important to note that they were considered to be so by many people in the nineteenth century. Thus, it is logical to think of professionalism in nineteenth-century not twentieth-century terms.

Whether non-cash prizes should be considered part of the professional element is debatable. More than a century ago, as today, few questioned a non-cash prize if its value were small. Early on, though, collegians were receiving very valuable prizes for victories in crew, especially, and also in track and field. In the very first intercollegiate competition between Harvard and Yale at Lake Winnipesaukee, New Hampshire, in the summer of 1852, the prize for the winning Harvard crew was a pair of expensive black walnut oars. College crews continued to row for costly prizes for the next generation, leading to the opulent 1870s when, at the fashionable intercollegiate regatta rowed on Lake Saratoga, silver goblets were offered, worth double what an average laborer might earn in a year. It is probably not surprising that the first intercollegiate track contests, held in conjunction with the intercollegiate regatta, included valuable prize trophies. A Harvard student noted that it was worth several months of intense practice to win one of the track prizes at Saratoga. Dartmouth College, which held its own track and field contests in the 1870s, offered such prizes as opera glasses, silver ink-stands, silverware, and the works of Thomas Macaulay, John Milton, and William Shakespeare. There is no question that nineteenth-century college athletes were competing for expensive prizes, often at the expense of just a love of sport.

If competing for non-cash prizes was a somewhat questionable professional practice, it was less doubtful when monetary prizes were offered. Harvard probably started it all in the 1850s when its four-oared crew, including a graduate student and future Harvard president Charles Eliot, rowed in a meet which had a $100 first prize. That was more than enough to pay for their rowing shell. By the next decade, Harvard was competing for purses as high as $500 in Boston regattas. In track and field several colleges were offering gold medals for individual track events. Yale offered money prizes until the practice was questioned by a reputable sporting journal.

Competition against professionals, like the competition for cash and non-cash prizes, was moving towards the professional model in intercollegiate sports. Again, Harvard's crew was involved, when its athletes competed against professional scullers in the 1850s. Harvard even once split the first prize with professionals after defeating their pro rivals. More than crews, college baseball teams competed against professionals. Almost as soon as professional teams were formed, colleges picked them out for good competition. Yale played 60 percent of its games against professionals from 1868–74. Harvard, in 1870, won thirty-four games and lost only nine—eight being to professional teams. Charles Eliot, who was president of Harvard by this time, eventually attempted to rid Harvard of the practice of playing professionals through inter-institutional controls. He failed. Students, who controlled college athletics, did not want to give up this aspect of the professional mode.

Charging money at the gate was also considered by some to be an agent of professionalization akin to competing against professionals. Harvard faculty believed that collecting money at its contests gave an "undesirable professional tone" to college athletics. The faculty felt so strongly about gate receipts that they banned them on the campus in the 1870s. Students were so determined to collect them that they left the campus to participate in baseball games in Boston so that they could collect money from spectators. By the 1880s and 1890s, most colleges had accepted the idea of charging spectators. And, of course, Harvard eventually succumbed to the temptation. Harvard even built the first reinforced concrete stadium in America in 1903 and could then extract tribute from 40,000 spectators for its annual football game with Yale.

One might question whether these activities were really anti-amateur in the pure sense of playing the game for love of the sport. Similarly, one might question another characteristic of professionalism, the training table. Creating the training table, which began with crew in the 1860s, was intended to produce winning teams through better food. In the 1800s, it was generally thought that amateur athletes should pay for the general cost of board and that only the additional cost of training table extras should be borne by athletic funds. Yet it was increasingly common for the entire food costs to be picked up by athletic associations, giving the athlete a "free ride."

Another way of paying athletes was to use athletic funds to provide them with tutors. To keep athletes eligible was a problem for Ivy League schools then as now. Yale, the "jock" school of America for the half-century following the 1870s, was also the richest school athletically. Until 1905, Yale was paying for athletic tutors out of a secret fund kept under Walter Camp's control. Yale, though, was only one of a number of institutions which tried to keep its athletes academically eligible using professional means.

Yet, the tutoring of students was never the concern which recruiting of students to participate in athletics and the payment of athletes were. The recruiting of athletes, however, was predated by half a century by the recruiting of sub-freshmen for college literary societies. Literary and debating societies formed around the ferment of the American Revolution and were the first organized extracurricular activities. It was important to competing literary societies to recruit preparatory students to enhance their society in the eyes of the others. Recruitment occurred early in athletics also. After the first intercollegiate baseball game in history between Williams and Amherst in 1859, Williams charged Amherst, the winner, with recruiting its pitcher from a blacksmith's shop. Some years later, Hamilton College successfully advertised in the *New York Clipper* for a pitcher and catcher for its baseball team, to the dismay of Cornell, which had to play Hamilton. By the end of the century, the William and Mary baseball team was petitioning its faculty with the following strange request: "We wish to request that, if we should secure a 'pitcher' and would provide for his support at the college hotel, you would allow him to matriculate free of charge." The faculty opposed the action because they considered it "professionalism." Recruitment for the major sports of rowing, baseball, football, and track and field were common by the twentieth century. A number of the athletes were being paid to participate. At Columbia, in 1899, five men of the football team had their tuition, board, and room paid for through illegal actions of the student manager of the team. Other colleges were taking similar actions as college sport was moving toward the professional model. Pennsylvania State College was one of the first to legalize the recruitment and payment of athletes when in 1900 the Board of Trustees sanctioned athletic scholarships to include room, board, and tuition.

While recruiting and paying athletes extended the amateur model to the extreme, it was no greater challenge than the change from amateur to professional coaches. The professional coach may have been the single most important element in intercollegiate professionalism. In the opinion of many advocates of amateurism in college sport, the pro coach was anathema. It began in crew at Yale during the Civil War, and within a generation there were professional coaches in the major sports of rowing, baseball, football, and track and field, as well as a number of minor sports.

By the early twentieth century, there was probably no college in America which was able to preserve amateurism in men's sport, as competition for money and non-money prizes, contests against professionals, collection of gate receipts, support for training tables, provision for athletic tutors, recruitment and payment of athletes, and the hiring of professional coaches pervaded the intercollegiate athletic scene. Professionalism had invaded college sports and had defeated amateurism as it was understood in the nineteenth century.

To conduct athletics in a professional mode while calling them amateur was both a self-contradiction and an hypocrisy, a pretense at virtuous character without possessing virtue. To call collegiate sport amateur was in fact playacting, the ancient Greek definition of the term hypocrisy. Intercollegiate athletics, which had many virtues according to numerous individuals, was acting the part of amateur sport while playing like professional athletics. Thus, the amateur-professional athletic dilemma developed. If a college had truly amateur sport, it would lose contests and thus prestige. If a college acknowledged outright professional sport, the college would lose respectability as a middle-class or higher class institution. Be amateur and lose athletically to those who were less amateur; be out-right professional and lose social esteem.

The solution to the dilemma, then, was to claim amateurism to the world while in fact accepting professionalism. The solution worked amazingly well, but it was not honest intellectually, thus the dilemma. Why did this occur? Why was there a need for colleges to espouse amateurism while practicing professionalism? Could amateurism ever have worked in American colleges as it did at Oxford and Cambridge? If not, what in American society precluded amateurism in intercollegiate athletics?

A Professional Model and an Ideology of Freedom and Equality

A dominating nineteenth-century American ideology, based upon freedom and equality, would not allow the British upper-class concept of amateur sport to permeate American college sport. The United States may have begun with ideas of political freedom and equality of rights, but the liberal ideology was transformed in the nineteenth century to a freedom, or equality, of opportunity. As the English historian J. R. Pole has so aptly stated, "Equality of opportunity was the chief meaning that Americans could now hope to extract from a tradition which had been handed down to them as equality of rights." Americans had rejected the British concept of a fixed status system based upon birth, wealth, and education, and it had telling implications for "amateur" intercollegiate sport.

The amateur concept involved a system of privilege and subservience that would not and could not hold up in American society. Americans repudiated an antiquated system that did not meet the criterion of freedom of opportunity to achieve excellence in college sport. To achieve excellence, the professional model proved to be far superior to the amateur model. As Americans opposed the aristocratic social system of England. . . . Americans did not accept the tenets of amateurism.

It might be argued that the pervasive ideological belief of freedom of opportunity led to a breakdown of amateurism and to a logical accent on professionalism in college sport. With a greater freedom of opportunity in America, it is likely that the American college developed differently from the system of higher education in England. One of the major differences was that until the nineteenth century, Oxford and Cambridge had a monopoly of higher education in England. Those two universities dominated the entire period of the development of intercollegiate sport. In America no two institutions, such as Harvard and Yale, could control higher education even though they might have chosen to do so. In America, there was greater freedom and opportunity to found colleges and to develop them. . . . Thus, in America great private institutions such as Harvard, Stanford, and Yale evolved as well as outstanding state-supported institutions such as California, Michigan, and Wisconsin. There was no upper-class control of higher education and no upper-class control of athletics, with its elitist concept of amateurism, as occurred at Oxford and Cambridge.

Even if America's most elite institutions had wanted to develop amateur sport based on the Oxbridge model, they could not have succeeded. There simply was no easy way to control sport in a select group of colleges, because there was no way to control the quality or quantity of institutions of higher education. Any individual, group, or level of government could found a college, and any college which wanted to raise intercollegiate athletics to a level of excellence was free to do so with a commitment of time, effort, and financial backing. Freedom of opportunity was a pervasive element in the development of the American college and its athletics. Oxford and Cambridge, for instance, had no equivalent to the American intercollegiate experience in crew in the 1870s. In America, small colleges had the freedom to develop crews as Yale and Harvard had done before them. Thus, the farmers from Massachusetts Agricultural College, or the mechanics from outback Cornell, or the Methodists from Wesleyan could produce crews and challenge the established colleges from the colonial era and garner victories at the intercollegiate regatta. The egalitarian principles were more dominant than any elitist desires that might have existed at Harvard or Yale, the closest equivalent to Oxford and Cambridge which America had to offer. Separate, dual competition between Harvard and Yale, in an attempt to keep themselves socially and athletically above the fray as Oxford and Cambridge did for generations, meant that both Harvard and Yale would eventually lose athletic esteem and prestige. Harvard and Yale could not long remain athletically superior to, and separate from, the newer and less prestigious institutions in America.

In a similar way, the upper-class amateur ideal of participating for the enjoyment of the contest and for no other motive, including financial considerations, could not easily exist in a society whose freedom of opportunity ideology allowed all to seek excellence through ability and hard work. Intercollegiate athletics fit well into that ideological model and a meritocracy based upon effort and talent resulted in college athletics from an early time. Achieved status in colleges and in athletics became the American way, rather than the ascribed status as seen in England's elitist universities and their athletics.

The English amateur system, based upon participation by the social and economic elite and rejection of those beneath them from participating, would never gain a foothold in American college athletics. There was too much competition, too strong a belief in merit over heredity, too abundant an ideology of freedom of opportunity for the amateur ideal to succeed. It may be that amateurism can never succeed in a society which has egalitarian beliefs. It may be that amateur athletics at a high level of expertise can only exist in a society dominated by upper-class elitists.

This historic amateur-professional dilemma, which existed almost from the beginning of intercollegiate athletics in American colleges, remained into the early years of the twentieth century and well beyond. American colleges practiced a type of professionalism, and yet they claimed amateurism. The dilemma resulted from the need to protect college sport from outside criticism by using acceptable amateur language while at the same time desiring the prestige and status which came from a highly professionalized model that produced excellence and winning.

The Rise of the Spectator, the Coach, and the Player at the University of Chicago, 1895–1905

ROBIN D. LESTER

Harper's University fostered the growth of football so successfully at the turn of the century that Chicago gained the leadership of intercollegiate football in the West in 1905. Maroon football had two extraordinary assets. First, located in the nation's second most populous [city], the university could count on many players and spectators. And those spectators ensured the end of the players' innocence, the cessation of play as an end in itself and the beginning of play as an instrument of larger economic and cultural values. Second, Amos Alonzo Stagg was the perfect athletic entrepreneur to match William Rainey.

The Rise of the Spectator

The most significant development during the period was the rise of the spectator—the widespread acceptance and use of the Chicago football enterprise by the students, faculty, and alumni of the university community and by the larger civic community. . . . The university became very successful in selling its athletic product and even of applying monopolistic principles, as a kind of "athletic Darwinism." Although some of its academics grew chary of the strong community interest and nascent control by 1900, most judged that the activity was useful to the university's larger purpose.

From Robin D. Lester, *Stagg's University: The Rise, Decline and Fall of Football at the University of Chicago* (Urbana: University of Illinois Press, 1995), 32–64.

... The "windy city" newspaper boosters maintained their civic reputation with unsupportable claims for the Stagg men. The journalists themselves were a prime market for the game, even as they became the chief salesmen; they soon believed and printed virtually everything that Stagg told them.

Boosterism came full circle in 1902 when the first "Gridiron Fest" was sponsored by the Chicago Press Club. Coaches, athletic managers, football officials, and players joined the propagandists in the formal unification of the press and the new intercollegiate football industry.

The university strategy in taking the game to the Chicago community was divulged by Horace Butterworth, manager of Maroon athletics. . . . He reasoned that early season victories promoted attendance and enthusiasm for the later contests; this approach accounts for the scheduling from 1896 to 1905 of teams which managed only twenty-seven points in thirty-six early season games, while Chicago scored 1,116 points. Butterworth described the Chicago marketplace as possessing two elements—the "society element" and the public. Athletic Director Stagg added a third constituency, "the college people" (he estimated 50,000), by which he meant the citizens who had attended other institutions whose loyalty might be partially transferred to the Chicago Maroons. All of these groups, including the press and the non-college "subway-alumni" were addressed carefully during the rise of the spectator.

. . . Chicago was a limited football marketplace in the early 1890s because few Chicagoans knew the game either as players or spectators. The public's interest in football picked up when the sport was introduced into the secondary schools during the 1890s, but the greatest single influence on public perception was the football enterprise that Harper and Stagg built. There was a steady supply of university contests played on the Midway from 1896–1905 (almost 90 percent of all Chicago games were played at home) and a persistent publicity which argued that the honor of the collegiate and civic community was at stake on the Maroon gridiron.

Chicago students showed a ready acceptance of the idea that the intercollegiate team was "theirs" and that the game had some validity for institutional comparisons. . . . The games became a weekly meeting place for the new and old members of the university community. . . . The campus community suffered and rejoiced communally over their team's performances. . . .

. . . Our collegiate communities have developed the football festival of the campus weekend with its attendant rituals and abnormal behavior. Certainly the outlines of Chicago student behavior toward the team were clear and fixed by 1905. Pre-game rallies, school songs, football banquets and receptions, celebrity bonfires and parades—all these spectatorial accoutrements to the Chicago football industry were begun, developed, and refined during the period to such a degree that they changed little over the next decades. . . .

The women of the university took the lead in producing cheers. Dean Marion Talbot . . . announced a prize contest for the "best gridiron lyric.". . . Talbot expected that the new compositions would be practiced weekly by the assembled students to improve their team support on Saturdays. The committee was none too sure of the quality of the entries—a scale of prizes was set up for the "best composition," $10.00 if the composition was "satisfactory," and only $5.00 for the composition "whether it is satisfactory or not."

Women were shut out of what was becoming one of the surest means to social acceptance on the American campus—intercollegiate athletic participation. The role of women in intercollegiate football and the larger society was graphically evident in 1902 as they helped lead a rally for the beaten Chicago team after their second consecutive loss to Fielding Yosts' remarkable Michigan elevens. . . . The *Tribune* ran a photo of Chicago student Agnes Wayman encircled with posies and captioned "Coed Rouses Spirit of Defeated Maroons.". . .

The football team's relations with the faculty and alumni also became more regular and formalized during the period. Faculty leaders made frequent appearances at football mass meetings and some could be counted upon for stirring rhetoric. . . . Professors who showed anything less than wide-eyed, uncritical enthusiasm for the Maroons courted swift unpopularity. . . .

The development of consistent support by alumni occurred later than the development of student and faculty support and was contemporaneous with the support of the larger civic community. Chicago was in a unique position during the 1890s, for, although it opened and functioned as a fully staffed university with a comparatively large student body, it took about a decade of graduations to produce a sufficiently large and interested alumni. By the season of 1902 a total of 1,866 degrees (70% undergraduate) had been awarded by the university. There was also a sizeable number of students who had attended the institution during the first decade without taking a degree. The Chicago alumni were joined around 1900 by other universities' alumni to provide enthusiastic backing for Stagg's teams and a collateral desire to demand victory regardless of means.

The first decade witnessed an informal interest by the alumni in the athletic fortunes of the university teams, but little organization beyond the seating of alumni in the Chicago section of the stands was accomplished. . . . The first successful concerted effort by the alumni to influence athletic policy occurred at the annual [pre-Thanksgiving Day] dinner in 1902 where some critical remarks were directed to Stagg's alleged ineptitude at recruiting top high school athletes. This alumni influence combined with the increasing sense of team ownership felt by the civic and journalistic communities was so strong that Stagg and his staff were stirred to more active recruiting and periodic reports to the alumni; in return, the alumni-civic coalition provided long-running protection for his winning program and rendered coach Stagg a campus untouchable. Harper and Stagg were more than willing to go along with the demands for victory even when the result was the bending and warping of the original stated values of their intercollegiate athletic program.

The selling of the Maroon football team went well at Harper's University. The rise of the spectator on the Midway and in the city was so marked that the Maroons did not leave the city once for their twelve matches in 1902. . . . From 1903 through 1905 Stagg scheduled twenty-eight games in Chicago, five away. Football revenue had so outgrown football expenses that the surplus was devoted to maintaining the other activities in the Department of Physical Culture; and increasingly, this dependence on football was becoming a major argument for maintaining the large commercial football enterprise at Chicago and elsewhere.

The Rise of the Coach

Amos Alonzo Stagg rose to a position of considerable power in Harper's University. . . . Stagg's rise was due to his special relationship to Harper, his dominant personality, the precedentless department which he headed, the innovative "profession" of coaching of which he was a pioneer and the enlargement of his national reputation based upon his unparalleled entrepreneurial and football genius.

President Harper and Coach Stagg grew increasingly close and mutually dependent; it was a good marriage, as each of them knew what to expect from the other and both endeavored not to let the other down. Harper was constantly vigilant about the best way to present the Maroon football show to the paying customers. In 1897, he suggested to Stagg the addition of "a bulletin board" (scoreboard) on the field so that "all can see and understand" the progress of the game and then wondered, "Should there not be a band at the Michigan game Thanksgiving day?". . .

The relationship of Harper with Stagg also had its trials. Harper showed unhappiness over his coach's management in 1895 when a university summer baseball team (one of Stagg's delights was to play in these more informal games), composed partially of non-university students, played teams the president deemed inappropriate: "We have had a series of games with negroes [sic] etc. which has brought disgrace upon us." Stagg seems to have sorted out the baseball issue by the summer of 1896, although we are left with many unanswered questions. Few African-Americans played for Stagg, but for that matter, few were enrolled at Chicago. Perhaps the most celebrated black athlete was Henry Dismond, one of Stagg's sprinters who held a world record.

The Harper-Stagg colleagueship was severely strained at times because the coach was frequently at the heart of a campus imbroglio and often was himself the focus of antagonism. His insistence upon what he considered points of "principle" frequently was seen by others as overly forceful or even tactless behavior. Stagg was a man of imperious character who frequently saw issues more simply than his faculty colleagues; he committed himself completely to a position, sometimes squelching those who were less committed or sure of a solution. His sense of personal and departmental prerogative grew with his increased reputation within and without the university. He became more bold when he dealt with his superiors and increasingly sensitive to what he considered any infringement of his preserve . . . :

> I understand that I am not to be hampered in any way in my work through this arrangement of finances; that [Comptroller] Rust is not to request *reasons why* this or that expenditure; that I am not compelled to *explain* to him for what ever purpose certain money is to be used . . . and am not to be called to account by *him* for the same.

Harper backed Stagg and it was not until the University Council and the Board of Trustees many years later investigated the special autonomy Stagg enjoyed that his department was brought into line with others.

Stagg's impatience with those who might challenge his point of view was not confined to his relations with university officials. His dealings with the representatives of other universities led to complaints that the coach had behaved imperiously toward them. The Intercollegiate Conference of Faculty Representatives, the Midwest's pioneer athletic governance organization, had been formed in 1895–96 and provided the context for such protests. President C. K. Adams of the University of Wisconsin leveled extensive charges against Stagg in 1898 to the effect that it was the duplicity of Stagg that had ruined athletic relations between Wisconsin and Chicago. A year later Adams wrote a longhand "Personal and Private" plea to President Harper regarding the "assumption of superiority" which he felt Stagg had demonstrated toward him . . . at a conference meeting. And the fact that Chicago alone was represented by an instructor in athletics rather than by Harper or one of the traditional academics at Chicago was an issue. . . .

Coach Stagg combined a successful athletic career with early physical education training at Springfield to prepare him to serve as the pioneer of a new profession, the college coach. . . . The same societal forces behind the "cult of efficiency" . . . was a part of the culture which produced the nation's football coaches. The vulnerability of the coaches to "the great strength of the business community and the business philosophy in an age of efficiency" was considerable and these influences molded their work—few were allowed to remain simply as coach-educators. The professionalization of the college coach can be seen in Stagg's career: he moved from the player-coach of the first generation of coaches into the "scientific" coach-manager and the celebrity-entrepreneur-coach stages of successive generations. . . . Many other coaches followed his model, e.g., football coaches assumed control over all other intercollegiate activities as "athletic directors" because of the dominant economic position of football on the campuses about twenty to thirty years after Stagg. Stagg even led the chosen few toward the final coaching stage— the celebrity-entrepreneurs of the twentieth-century American university who often occupied a cultural and financial niche well above their college president or state governor. . . .

Stagg was lauded by a leading Chicago newspaper in 1902 as "better known than anyone connected with the University of Chicago, Dr. W.R. Harper and John D. Rockefeller alone excepted.". . . A mystique surrounded his activities on the gridiron and extended well beyond its perimeter where his abstemious behavior was appreciated. It is not improbable that Amos Alonzo Stagg personified, for many Americans, a purer, less materialistic, lost Christian America.

Stagg's preeminence lay in the acquaintances and contacts he maintained in the East, as well in his position as a leading coach and athletic director. His co-authorship of the first avowedly "scientific" football book *A Scientific and Practical Treatise on American Football for Schools and Colleges* in 1893 had also brought considerable attention. He knew most of the eastern athletic authorities of the 1890s and the East continued its hegemony of the West in athletics during the early years of the century. In 1904, Stagg became the first non-eastern representative on the Football Rules Committee which legislated the rules of the sport for the entire nation. . . .

University of Chicago football teams became nationally known because of their precedent-setting inter-regional trips and games. . . . The 1898 game with Pennsylvania at Philadelphia's venerable Franklin Field was not only an important institutional milestone, it was the match "that put western football on the map." Penn was considered the best team in the country that year based on a twenty-four game winning streak. . . . Chicago, featuring the play of back Clarence Herschberger, led at the half and surprised the East with a new style of play that featured deception and quickness. . . . Veteran observer Caspar Whitney ranked Chicago equal to the best of the East that year. At the end of the season, Herschberger became the first non-eastern . . . player selected by Walter Camp on his All-American team. . . .

Stagg's football teams consistently played more difficult schedules than their opponents. Perhaps the profit instinct was operating here, for well known, successful opponents insured greater revenues, but Chicago regularly played two or three times the number of major opponents as the other members of its conference. For example, Chicago's 1904 schedule included seven major university teams out of eleven opponents; Michigan played two major opponents in nine games, Wisconsin two of seven . . . and Minnesota two of ten. . . .

The Rise of the Player

The most concise statement of the change in the place of football in the player's life at Harper's University came from a Maroon veteran in 1897: "I have no more fun in practice games. It isn't amusement or recreation any more. It is nothing less than hard work". . . . The status of the player changed as well as the spectator and coach, and the period 1895 to 1905 was marked by the displacement of the student-player by the player-student. . . .

The role of the football player was becoming an identifiable one; it can be described as the two-fold development of the player as a "campus commodity" and as a "campus physical elite." The young student-player who complained of the business-like manner with which he was expected to approach the sport of football in 1897 became an anachronism by 1905, for by then he was required to continue his football training year-round.

The basis for Stagg's new cult of player efficiency can be seen in his explanation of the award of the coveted "C" monograms to Chicago athletes—the Order of the C was "the first athletic-letter club ever formed," according to him. Stagg controlled these awards and he noted that they were based upon the athlete's "merit, amount of work done, and usefulness to the team and the university". . . .

An excellent supply of college level players for the university's use was . . . available locally. Chicago was in the median enrollment position among Intercollegiate Conference schools and from 1902, Stagg's earlier plaint of the lack of material was not applicable—he had excellent players for years after that. Illustratively, the Maroons of 1896 averaged 173 pounds, those of the 1905 aggregation, 186 pounds, and there was an almost yearly increase in the size and quality of the players. The player commodities were supplied by the high schools and by the Chicago Football League which sponsored a "prairie" (sandlot) game for youths. Both of these agencies, especially the former, grew rapidly from 1895 to 1905 and were similar to the sources the eastern colleges used.

The Recruitment of the Campus Commodities

Stagg and Harper developed a number of recruiting methods which enabled them to improve markedly the quality of Chicago's football teams. Shortly after the turn of the century they sought to create a special relationship with interscholastic players and officials. [In 1902] Harper himself presented an ingenious plan (hatched by Stagg) to the Board of Physical Culture and Athletics [regarding] the widespread recruitment of schoolboy athletes. . . .

. . . [The proposal] . . . established a bold experiment of using the nine "affiliated" prep schools in Illinois and Indiana as places of employment for Maroon athletes and as athletic "feeder" schools . . . [and] for using the public schools in much the same way. Recommendation number five . . . was the most cryptic and significant of the seven: "That a system be devised for obtaining information in regard to athletics in secondary schools". . . . This recommendation led to a comprehensive card file on high school athletes to whom recruitment letters were sent and followed up.

Finally, the sixth recommendation . . . legitimated an event which had already been planned and scheduled by Stagg: . . . "That interscholastic meets be held of the Academies and high schools in relationship to the University." Within eight days the "First Annual Interscholastic Track Meet" was history, as about 200 athletes from forty schools who had won state meets in Illinois, Michigan, Wisconsin, and Iowa competed at Marshall Field. . . . The visiting athletes, termed "young prospectives," were housed in university fraternity houses and were entertained in "great style" by the athletic management and by enthusiastic student groups.

The decision by the Chicago coaching staff to engage in a recruitment drive and capture beefy and/or speedy campus commodities constituted a change from their public position on the matter. Stagg had often railed against "scouting" by other universities and their alumni; in 1900 he had argued that recruiting was contrary to the "spirit of amateurism." Two unsuccessful football campaigns later, Stagg and the Board "discovered that something had to be done if Chicago expected to compete with other western universities.". . .

The Chicago coaches, the football captain, and interested faculty members met periodically to assess their recruitment progress. They reviewed past communication with the prospects, charted new letter contacts and prepared for the fall season. The prospects for the 1902 season had been poor, but the number of football aspirants grew from thirty to nearly sixty by early October. The recruitment success of 1902 was enlarged in 1903 with the prophetic, "Maroons Sound Doom of Yost's Great Eleven," due to the snaring of "one of the greatest collections of giants ever collected in the West." Earlier "unusual activity" by "several old alumni" was credited, along with the track meet, for the "very fertile" athletic prospects of the freshmen of 1903. The Chicago newspapers greeted each Midway acquisition as a civic resource and with bold headline: . . . "Hogenson Captured for the Maroon Team,". . . "Stagg gains Another Star Prep Athlete," and "Stagg Secures Star."

President Harper worked with the coaching staff to initiate the recruiting system. He led the organization of the university alumni early in 1904 . . . at his annual football dinner. . . . "We have 6000 alumni in and about Chicago. Why do not these alumni see that the university gets its fair share of the athletic material?" Harper then urged that a committee be appointed to organize the alumni into "a recruiting organization." The alumni complied within days.

The interscholastic track meet grew rapidly in its importance for the Chicago football enterprise. The second year of its existence, Stagg's meet more than doubled its size. . . . "Stagg's Interscholastic" was the premier meet in the West by 1905. . . .

A battle over the recruitment of prominent Chicago high school players erupted in 1903 between Chicago and Michigan. The scalps were difficult to count, for some of Stagg's new wards had not completed high school and it was not always easy to pry them into Chicago. Fielding Yost of Michigan also recruited his share of Chicago public high school juniors in 1903. . . .

This undignified recruiting scramble by two major universities drew some criticism, but not from the eminent academics within those institutions. The criticism came from the public press and from high school administrators and officials. . . . One respected columnist had described late in 1902 the "new and dangerous development . . . of semi-official recruiting bureaus" . . . was "most unworthy of the dignity and purposes of a great institution of learning". . . .

The most telling indictment of the player recruitment chaos came from Chicago Superintendent of Schools Edwin G. Cooley. Cooley was an alumnus of the university (Ph.B., 1896) and an acquaintance of President Harper. The Superintendent described the Chicago-Michigan approaches to Chicago school boys in 1903 as "practically stealing boys out of high school for athletic purposes before their high-school courses are completed". . . .

Vagabond players peddled their football playing abilities to the highest-bidding school at the turn of the century, and in the absence of standardized eligibility regulations, the bidders were many. Illustratively, two candidates for the 1902 Chicago team practiced one week, disappeared, and emerged at the Michigan practice field. One of the tourists returned to Chicago's team followed by the other; Wisconsin was then rumored to have captured their fancy. Finally, one went to Ann Arbor to play, the other remained at Chicago.

The most difficult recruitment for Chicago's football enterprise occurred in 1905 with the acquisition of Walter Steffen, future All-American, from a Chicago high school. His attendance at the Midway did not end the battle for his services, however, for . . . the universities of the Middle West . . . did not scruple to recruit athletes enrolled at another institutions. According to his father, Steffen had "matriculated, paid his tuition, bought his books and attended classes for a week" at Chicago when he left for Madison, Wisconsin. He was accompanied by Wisconsin coach Philip King and the Wisconsin captain who had journeyed to Chicago ostensibly to see a Chicago game with Iowa. Steffen's announced reason for the visit was an earlier promise made on one of his two previous trips "to see what they had." To that end, he attended football practice to ascertain the football future that Wisconsin, and perhaps he, could expect. Steffen returned to Chicago after a three day absence. He claimed that the journey was made "entirely against my will" and that he "was ashamed to make the trip. . . ." When the valuable young man returned to the Maroon practice field, President Harper quietly forgot his threats to require an explanation for Steffen's absence from President Van Hise of Wisconsin; Coach Stagg stated that the athletic department would take "no official notice" of Steffen's confused behavior.

The Retention of the Campus Physical Elite

Retaining players proved as difficult as recruiting them, and the elevation of players to a special status in order to retain their services produced the physical elite on the Midway. . . .

The specter of ineligibility was constant for the Chicago players. At least five of the best players on the 1900 team were found academically deficient in July of that year. One leading player was frustrated enough to charge that "he was flunked by a professor who is opposed to athletics." The charge would be difficult to prove because the Chicago faculty generally showed a benign interest in the football team. Indeed, the player who complained of the anti-football professor was given a special make-up examination by Professor O.J. Thatcher of the History Department, who was in constant attendance at team practices. The errant player was soon back on the field.

Special examinations administered by a football enthusiast were only part of the indication of faculty kindness. Another valuable player for Chicago journeyed with the team to West Point, New York, for the 1903 Army game although when he departed he was ineligible. The player's eligibility was reinstated by telegram to Stagg from Dean George Vincent after the team's arrival in New York. . . . The *Chicago Interocean* surveyed the arrangements at the Midway and concluded, "It seems safe to say that no really valuable man will be lost to the team on account of any little educational deficiency.". . .

The regular academic program consisted of three "majors" of course work each quarter for undergraduates. . . . The academic records of the 1903 football team during the fall quarter show that of the twenty-three members of the team, only three members were registered for the normal three majors of work. . . . The athletic and academic authorities exercised "careful supervision" over the athletes to limit their course work to two majors. . . . The team maintained a 2.01 grade-point average . . . as a group. . . .

Coach Stagg himself kept a watch on his players and was not above using an informal conversation with an instructor as an appeal for a player's eligibility. When his captain flunked a course after Stagg claimed he was told by the instructor the player would pass, Stagg wrote a protest to Harper. The coach stated he thought the case justified his breaking "a rule of my own not to intercede in behalf of any delinquent athlete". . . .

The rise of the football player as the physical elite on the Midway was accomplished outside the curriculum as well. Early in the century a set of chimes was installed in newly constructed Mitchell Tower on the campus. Stagg had the idea of a special playing of the carillon for the Maroon athletes, especially for those who tended to miss curfew, and gave a sizeable gift toward that end. His gift was to provide "a nightly curfew to the men in training". . . .

The special nightly ringing of the carillon for the benefit of the athletes was consistent with the new elitist status of the group. The concern for the football players' welfare led to a special diet for them at a "training table." The original training plan was to ask all football candidates to live on or near the campus to enable them to eat together. The concept was extended to their living quarters in 1896 when two flats of a private apartment house were engaged as a training center where the "candidates, coaches, and trainers" would "spend all of their time when not in the recitation-room or on the athletic field." That hope vanished by 1897 when local housing proprietors claimed that the footballers had "played such havoc" that they would not be accepted as tenants again. The university countered this refusal by putting a portion of Snell Hall at the disposal of

Stagg's men and by 1902 the newest and most luxurious residence hall was reserved for the intercollegiate athletic teams. Hitchcock Hall, termed the "millionaires' den," became the site for the training table and quarters for about thirty players. . . .

The separation of the football team from the rest of the student body was accomplished with no discussion of its effect upon student life and values. The idea of separate and unequal training facilities for the players was viewed simply as an efficient use of the physical elite. But students petitioned the faculty overseers of the Men's Commons to move the athletes and their training table to the midst of the commons so that mutual acquaintance and "school spirit" could develop properly. Their argument asked for the return to a time when student-athletes were not restricted as to the sphere of their activities and when student spectators were acquainted with the players for whom they cheered. The plea was to no avail.

If the physical man was furnished at the training table and at the training quarters, the mental and emotional man was also served. Academic advice came from the faculty members most interested in the success of the team and from Coach Stagg who watched his men's study habits carefully. President Harper inaugurated a special tutorial program for football players by requesting instructors to coach them in troublesome areas. The emotional balance of the football team was sometimes strained during the season as the pressures for winning mounted. When the Maroons suffered "Nervous Fits" in 1905, Stagg suspended practice sessions and took the team . . . to exclusive Onwentsia Golf Club in Lake Forest for a weekend of relaxation at university expense.

The University of Chicago administration and many faculty were lavish in their praise of the function which the new physical elite performed on campus. The football captain was elected at President Harper's annual dinner; he became the most revered undergraduate figure. . . .

. . . The players were given post-game theater parties, dinners, and trips to other campuses to view football games, accompanied by proud professors and paid for by the game receipts. . . . Thanksgiving dinner after the traditional Michigan game had an important place on the players' calendar, especially when select female students were included as guests of the young gladiators and themselves became an auxiliary elite.

The rise of the intercollegiate football player as a campus commodity and as campus physical elite can be illustrated in the career of Walter Eckersall, the most acclaimed intercollegiate athlete in University of Chicago history and a consensus all-time All-American quarterback. . . .

The future star was born and grew up in the Woodlawn area of Chicago, adjacent to the university. . . . At Hyde Park High School Eckersall set a ten second flat Illinois 100 yard dash record in 1903 that stood until . . . 1928. . . . One year Hyde Park played Brooklyn [Poly Prep], the best eastern school team, for the "high school national championship" and won 105–0. . . .

Coach Stagg precipitately announced in the autumn of 1902 that he had secured "Eckersall's promise to enter the Midway school" the following year. In June of 1903 . . . it was reported that "Michigan has had secret embassies calling on Eckersall," and was "stooping to the lowest practices to steal Eckersall from us". . . . The uncertain young man did not make his college decision until just prior to the opening of the two universities in 1903 and he was aided mightily by Stagg who later admitted grabbing Eckersall off the train platform before he could entrain to Ann Arbor. . . .

Walter Eckersall brought more publicity to the University of Chicago than any other student in the institution's history, with the possible exception of the kidnap-murderers, Nathan Leopold and Richard Loeb. . . . Eckersall was a figure who could not be gainsaid, even by the enemy. The Michigan enemy composed an Eckersall chant, hopefully fatal, but implicitly laudatory: ". . . Eckie, Eckie, break your neckie. . . ."

. . . Eckersall . . . compiled an atrocious academic record, but he was permitted to pursue that path until his football eligibility ended. . . . From his first quarter at Chicago as a sub-freshman (since he had not completed college preparatory work), the quarterback led his teammates off—as well as on—the field, in failing grades and in total absences from his classroom work. . . .

The reconstruction of Eckersall's eligibility began during the spring quarter of 1904 to ensure his football play that autumn. He was enrolled in two history courses for Senior College (upper division) students. His enrollment in "The Renaissance Age" would appear peculiar as the course was described as appropriate for those wishing to do graduate work in history and such students were advised to take the course in their third year at Chicago. Eckersall's registration would appear peculiar, that is, if the teacher were other than the Chicago athlete's friend, Oliver J. Thatcher. Appropriately, Eckersall was given a "C" for his work by Thatcher who did not flunk a single student in the class of sixty-seven. . . .

. . . He maintained his eligibility to participate in intercollegiate athletics, but he found that after three and two-thirds years of higher education, he was still classified in the Junior Colleges (lower division). His lack of the full secondary school preparation for his college work was partly responsible—at least eight of his courses were applied toward making up his admissions deficiencies. At the end of the autumn quarter, 1906, the All-American had earned only fourteen course majors of credit toward the thirty-six required for graduation. . . .

The last term in which . . . Eckersall was enrolled was the 1906 autumn quarter during which he completed his football eligibility. . . . A notation dated January 25, 1907, on his official transcript reads: *"Mr. Eckersall is not to be permitted to register in the Univ. again—for cause.* By Order of Acting President Judson."

The patronage of President William Rainey Harper, the spectator and player supply offered by the dynamic midwestern metropolis, and the single-minded "saintly" coach had combined to ensure that the Chicago football enterprise was hugely successful by 1905. President Harper had adopted university founder John D. Rockefeller's Darwinian *modus operandi* closely enough to recruit professors and players alike and to use them successfully in promoting the new academic creation. It was, moreover, Harper's and Stagg's keen sense of the basics of the institution and their artful collaboration in the athletics of Darwinism which promoted football within and without the university. Their institution and football were now synonymous, stable, and famous.

🏐 *F U R T H E R   R E A D I N G*

Joseph R. De Martini, "Student Culture as a Change Agent in American Higher Education: An Illustration From the Nineteenth Century," *Journal of Social History* 9 (1976), 526–41

William G. Durick, "The Gentlemen's Race: An Examination of the 1868 Harvard-Oxford Boat Race," *Journal of Sport History* 15 (1988), 41–63

Robin Dale Lester, *Stagg's University: The Rise, Decline and Fall of Football at the University of Chicago* (1995)

Guy M. Lewis, "The Beginning of Organized Collegiate Sport," *American Quarterly* 22 (1970), 222–29

Patrick B. Miller, *The Playing Fields of American Culture: Athletics and Higher Education, 1850–1945* (forthcoming 1998)

J. Hammond Moore, "Football's Ugly Decade, 1893–1913," *Smithsonian Journal of History* 2 (1967), 49–68

Michael Oriard, *Reading Football: How the Popular Press Created an American Sporting Spectacle* (1993)

David Riesman and Reuel Denney, "Football in America: A Study of Cultural Diffusion," *American Quarterly* 3 (1951), 309–25

Harold J. Savage, et al., *American College Athletics* (1929)

Ronald A. Smith, ed., *Big-Time Football at Harvard, 1905: The Diary of Coach Bill Reid* (1994)

Ronald A. Smith, *Sports and Freedom: The Rise of Big-Time College Athletics* (1988)

Murray Sperber, *Shake Down the Thunder: The Creation of Notre Dame Football* (1993)

CHAPTER
6

Sport and the Rise of the
Industrial Radial City, 1870–1920

⦿

*The coming of the modern city dramatically influenced the development and char-
acter of American sport. Antebellum American cities were "walking cities," which
were small, commercialized towns characterized by unspecialized land uses. In contrast, the new industrial radial city of the 1870s had a much larger population,
and it encompassed far more space, which was usually gained through annexation.
It had highly specialized land uses, a central business district, distinctive class-
based residential areas, and it was economically grounded in industrial production. These cities covered large areas and required innovative forms of mass transit,
which culminated in the electric powered streetcars and subways in the 1890s and
early 1900s.*

*How did the growth of cities shape our sporting heritage? The sporting options
of urbanites were directly affected by such diverse issues as changing land use patterns, local politics, ethnicity, race, wealth, and the social values of a city's dominant and subordinate groups. As cities grew, older forms of sport that required a lot
of space were displaced. The loss of traditional recreational spaces encouraged a
boom in the park movement that advocated construction of large suburban parks
on the model of New York's Central Park.*

*What was the impact on sport of overcrowded urban neighborhoods? What
kinds of sports could be played in urban slums? It was difficult to play a regular
game of baseball in the more densely populated neighborhoods, and youths would
have to initiate special ground rules if they played in narrow alleys. How successful
was the playground movement's quest for small play spaces in crowded inner city
neighborhoods?*

*Another consequence of urbanization was the great increase in potential
markets for commercialized sports. Entrepreneurs established professional sports
leagues and built ballparks, race tracks, and indoor arenas and gymnasiums to
cater to the growing demand for spectator sports. Innovative businessmen also
established a vast sporting goods industry that took advantage of a host of new
products and innovations in industrial production to manufacture cheap mass-
produced goods to satisfy growing consumer demands for athletic equipment.*

⚾ *D O C U M E N T S*

The documents in this section describe certain sporting facilities available to urbanites, the importance of those sites for the benefit of the community, and the sporting
options available to city people. The first document is comprised of two *New York
Times* editorials evaluating the status of New York's Central Park. The editorials laud
the park as an important site for receptive (nonactive) public recreation, but they also
criticize the inadequate access of the park both for people other than the well-to-do
and for its strict policy of keeping patrons off its grass. The next document reports on
the opening of New York's Jerome Park Racetrack in 1866, which signified the rebirth
of racing after the Civil War as an elite pastime.

   The third document reports in detail various aspects of the March 1879 Astley
Belt race at the old Madison Square Garden. This was a series of six-day "go-as-you-
please" races that began in London in 1878. The winning prize for each event was up
to $20,000; in addition, the winner of the series received a gold and silver belt donated
by Lord Astley. The events were enormously popular and drew capacity crowds to see
men struggling to run 500 miles and more in six days. England's defending champion,
Charles Rowell, successfully defended his title by covering 530 miles in six days, and
for the first time in history, two other competitors also bettered the 500-mile mark.
The fourth document, an 1888 *New York Times* editorial, explains how a professional
baseball team boosted a city's pride, even though the players were all out-of-towners.

   The booster mentality is also seen in another *Times* editorial at the turn of the century that urged the municipality to take over the new Madison Square Garden, which
was built in 1890. Designed by renowned architect Stanford White, it was the most famous sports arena in the United States and the second tallest structure in New York
City. The original Garden, operated by William Vanderbilt from 1879 to 1886, had already hosted many great sporting events including the Horse Show, boxing matches
starring John L. Sullivan, and long-distance running races. The sixth document, drawn
from *Harper's Weekly,* certifies the vitality of urban sportsmen and describes how
the urban milieu facilitates the sporting life by offering multitudinous athletic
opportunities.

The *New York Times* Evaluates the Accessibility and Utility of Central Park, 1873, 1875

. . . How great a boon these grounds have been to the public may be judged from
the fact that during last year nearly 11,000,000 persons visited them, the average
daily number being about 30,000, or about twenty-three per cent larger than on any
former year. On one fine Sunday, in September, the visits ran up to 109,000. Thus
far, however, these beautiful grounds are more for the recreation of the rich than
the poor, as the average number of visits made daily in carriages and on horseback
was 14,000, while the average number of pedestrians was about 9,000. This proportion will undoubtedly constantly change. Means will be contrived for carrying

From editorials, *New York Times*, March 6, 1873 and November 15, 1875.

the masses of the people from the crowded tenement-house quarters, cheaply to these charming scenes. We hope in the future for what may be called "workmen's cars," going at low rates from the poorer wards, directly to the park, on Saturday afternoons. The children, too, of the laboring people, will more and more spend their holidays there. It must be remembered that the great and valuable use of the Central Park, in the future, will be its affording a bit of quiet, rural scenery, and a breath of fresh country air to the people of the poorer and middle classes. The rich can get their pleasures anywhere, but hundreds of thousands of persons of small means are forced to find their only out-door enjoyment in this, almost our only park. In this view, it is of the utmost importance that nothing should be done for the future which should destroy its quiet, rural character. Enough space already has been given up to drives and stately promenades; enough is already occupied by, or devoted to, public buildings. What the laborers and the children of the poor and the tired business men most need are simple, pleasant country scenes, with solitary rambles and quiet walks.

. . . [T]he rules about not walking on the grass are now enforced so rigidly that sending children to the Park is rather a punishment for them than a treat. Policemen hunt them about as if they were little criminals who were "wanted" at headquarters. The children are obliged to keep on the hard, narrow paths, like prisoners in a yard. In every park in the country but our own, children are allowed to play on the grass—and certainly Central Park grass has cost enough to be good for something. Prospect Park, Brooklyn, is the delight of young and old, because of the absence of those vexatious restrictions with which the Central Park Commissioners do their best to drive the public out of their own property. Indeed, Prospect Park is now in every way a much more beautiful park than ours. Between the malaria of the lakes, and cast-iron rules, and the way in which policemen threaten and bully every little child who wanders for a minute on the grass, the Commissioners are likely soon to have the Central Park all to themselves. . . .

The *New York Clipper* on the Opening of Jerome Park Race Track and the Revitalization of the Turf, 1866

Jerome Park

This is the name of a new race track which was opened to the public for the first time on Tuesday, September 25th, under the auspices of an association called the American Jockey Club. The newspapers, for the past few weeks, have given us numerous articles laudatory of Mr. Leonard Jerome and the enterprise originated by him; we have been told that the object of the club is to improve the breed of the horse, to popularize the sport of horse racing, and all that sort of thing; we have also been informed that Mr. Jerome—who is a very wealthy gentleman—at his

From *New York Clipper* 14 (October 6, 1866): 202.

own expense and risk purchased the section of land on which the new course is located, constructed the track, and placed the project upon a sound basis before appealing to the patrons of the turf for co-operation in the enterprise, etc. Gentlemen of the highest social position, wealth, intelligence, and influence unhesitatingly became active participants in the movement, we have been given to understand. Hints were also thrown out some time ago that the public would be admitted to the course free of charge, in order that the sport should be made popular. Well, the opening of this new track took place, as we have said, on September 25th, under the most encouraging circumstances; the day was all that could be desired, being clear, cool and pleasant in every way. The attendance was very large, it being estimated that thirty thousand spectators were present, including between two and three hundred policemen, as well as many ladies. There were two races on the programme for the opening day—a dash of a mile and a quarter and a race of four-mile heats—both of which were witnessed with seeming interest by the large assemblage. And so ended the inaugural ceremonies at Jerome Park. We are willing to give due credit to the wealthy gentleman who set the ball in motion; to the influential citizens who have co-operated with him in the enterprise, and to the stewards of the meeting for the races they prepared for the entertainment of their patrons; but we are not willing to let the opportunity pass without entering our protest against certain practices which will *not* have a tendency to popularise the sport of racing as conducted by the American Jockey Club and the wealthy founder of Jerome Park. We have frequently exposed frauds practiced on the Long Island tracks, race courses which were *not* founded by Mr. Jerome, nor managed by wealthy citizens; and we shall not be backward in exposing the shortcomings of this rich combination at Fordham. In the first place, the public were led to believe, until the day before the opening ceremonies, that Asteroid, the great Western turf representative, would take part in the four mile race, and contend with Kentucky for the victory; we should not like to believe that it was known some time previous that Asteroid had gone amiss, and would not start for the prize. With Asteroid out of the race, the event was divested of all interest, for it was well known that none of the others could compete with Kentucky with the slightest chance of success. Yet his was the grand event that the masses went to see, and which attracted so many strangers to the city. To say that the disappointment was great at the non-appearance of Asteroid is to put it in a mild form. But what the public most object to is the somewhat exalted scale of prices of admission to the track and stands. Instead of the public being admitted free, a high tariff was imposed upon all who sought to enter the gates of Jerome Park. At the first gate one dollar was demanded of each person; this did not give the privilege of going upon the track; to do this, and to gain admission to the public stand, another dollar must be paid; and to pass on to the quarter stretch, five dollars is the toll. So the reader will see that, and notwithstanding the high social position of the gentlemen composing the club, the almighty dollar has not been lost sight of by Mr. Jerome and his co-operators.

To make racing popular, in this country, the public should be permitted to enjoy the privileges of our race tracks at a small charge for admission, say fifty cents. When two and five dollars are charged, very few except the wealthy classes can afford to indulge in the "luxury of horse racing." To make the track accessible to the masses, and thus popularise sports of the turf, we were given to understand, was one of the objects in forming the American Jockey Club and locating the new track. That such was not really the intention of those gentlemen is now quite evident, for the enterprise looks more like a money making speculation than a public spirited endeavor to provide amusement for the people at reasonable prices. The press has not had a word to say upon this subject; yet this is not to be wondered at when the wealth of the Jockey Club is taken into consideration. For our part, we can see no difference between Jerome Park and the race tracks on Long Island. Money is the great object of all alike, and the idea of elevating and popularising the sports of the turf is entirely lost sight of in the eager greed for gain. The new track savors of Wall Street, and its projector doubtless figured up the chances of making the concern pay a heavy per centage on the original investment when he purchased the ground and erected the buildings for Jerome Park.

The *New York Clipper* Reports on the Astley Belt Race of 1879

As we write the contestants in the fifth race for the belt presented by Sir John Astley are hard at work in Madison-square Garden, this city, having started at 1 A.M. on Monday, Sept. 22. Notwithstanding that the price of admission was placed at a dollar, the crowd present at the start was fully as great as upon the occasion of the previous contest for the same trophy at this place, the throng fully testing the capacity of the Garden. By dint of hard work, day and night, from Saturday morning, a pretty good track, composed of sifted loan and tanbark, with a light top dressing of sawdust, had been prepared. It was not as wide by three feet as before, but still it afforded plenty of room for the thirteen competitors, each one of whom had a tent to himself, furnished with everything necessary. . . . The most intense excitement prevailed among the spectators, and it was with great difficulty that they could be prevented from encroaching upon the track; but there was a strong force of police present, and, considering the immense crowd, comparatively good order was maintained. The pedestrians were started promptly at one o'clock A.M. Monday, Sep. 22, and nearly all commenced the long journey at a walk, notable exceptions being Hazael and Rowell, the former going off with an easy lope and the latter again setting to work with the dog-trot so familiar to New-Yorkers. Rowell was the favorite with the betting fraternity, the bookmakers offering 1½ to 1 against him, 2½ to 1 against Weston, 3 to 1 against Hazael, 10 to 1 against Guyon, 30 to 1 against Panehot or Ennis, 20 to 1 against Krohne or Hart, 35 to 1 against Merritt, and as much as 50 to 1 against the others. The bookmakers had their stands erected in the centre of the main floor, and drove quite a thriving business, . . . The only man who kept to a walk for any length of time after starting was Fedemeyer, whose long hair and beard and odd attire caused him to present a strange appearance. He walked steadily for several hours, and then, finding that

---

From *New York Clipper* (September 27, 1879): 210.

he was getting further and further behind, he changed his gait to a jog, which did not carry him along much faster, and he retained the last place. A great deal of interest was manifested in the colored boy Hart, who walks much better than he runs, and whose style is very much like that made familiar to New Yorkers by O'Leary. He is a tough-looking lad, and seems likely to make an excellent record during the week. . . .

While we are writing, those of the competitors who by their performance have proved themselves worthy of participating in the fifth contest for the trophy offered by Sir John Astley, and emblematic of the championship of the world in long-distance, go-as-you-please pedestrianism, are still contending for the supremacy, and nearing the end of a race which, from a sporting point of view as well as financial, has been decidedly more successful than any other similar six-day tournament ever held here or in England. In no other contest of like duration have the chances appeared so even as in this, nor the public interest been excited and sustained from first to last by the spectacle of the four or five leading men separated from one another by so short a distance, and all doing so well that the foremost man is forced to continually crowd the fastest previous record, and occasionally excel it. It had been expected by nearly everybody except Manager Hess that the placing of the price of admission at one dollar to all parts of the house was a mistake which would have the effect of limiting the attendance during the middle of the week. Had the competition proved a one-sided affair, no doubt these anticipations would have been realized; but the character of the contest increased to such an extent the interest already felt in the result that the public extended a more than liberal patronage throughout the six days. Taken as a whole, the class of people who have visited the Garden during the week have been superior to the general character of the supporters of like events, and, while we hold that the privilege of gratifying their desires should not be placed beyond the reach of the masses of the people, there can be no doubt that to this fact is attributable the excellent order which has been maintained. The arrangements for keeping the people informed of the state of the contest were about on a par with previous tournaments, the positions of the six leading competitors being indicated on a huge blackboard placed at the east end of the building, upon which the miles made by each man were placed opposite his name. The lap-scoring was done by means of dials painted on a long board fence erected at the outer edge of the inner circle and facing the north, opposite to which was the scorers' and press-stand, built up against the wall in front of the ladies gallery. The fence alluded to might have been made a little lower, as it was just high enough to prevent the spectators on the main floor and on the south side of the house from obtaining a view of the finish. The scoring was attended to by members of different athletic clubs, some of whom were experienced in the business and attentive, while others were inexperienced and seemingly careless as well, which was no recommendation to persons appointed to discharge duties of so important a nature. The track is not so wide by about three feet as before, and being made in a hurry, was rather soft at first, but has been well looked after, and the pedestrians have had little reason to complain of it since the first day. As we had from previous experience been led to anticipate, the attempt to prevent smoking even on the floor of the house (except along the edge of the track was a pronounced failure, as it always must be on such occasions, and where the lessees are anxious to sell all the poor cigars they can at high prices. . . .

The *New York Times* Lauds Baseball and Community Pride, 1888

A considerable number of intelligent and respectable citizens of New-York are daily disgusted at the evidence of the interest taken by a still more considerable number of persons whom they assume to be less intelligent and respectable in the game of baseball. They regard it as monstrous and absurd that the papers should devote so much space to chronicling the procedures of nine persons of no eminence except for their capabilities of throwing, catching, and hitting balls and of running short distances with rapidity. They deplore the effect of these chronicles upon the young, and they resent the absence from the public prints of matter more interesting to themselves which they assume is displaced to make room for the accounts of baseball matches. Those of them whose disgust has not prevented them from learning anything at all of its subject point out that it is not even a local pride that is properly involved, since the players are mercenaries who may appear this season in the green shirts and scarlet stockings and blue caps of one community, and next year in equally kaleidoscopic raiment betokening a new allegiance.

This is all true, and yet the zealots of baseball, at least in this city, have some reason on their side, though they may not be able to produce it. However illogical it may be that local pride should be aroused by the victories of one team of professional baseball players over another or touched by its defeats, yet, as a matter of fact, that feeling is enlisted on the part of a considerable fraction of the population in the varying fortunes of the so-called "New-Yorks," and we hold that anything whatsoever that can excite the local pride of New-York is so far a good thing. For local pride is much the same thing as public spirit, which at least cannot exist without it, and there is no city in the world that is more deficient in public spirit than New-York, or that ought to welcome more anything that tends to stimulate that quality.

It is in some respects a misfortune for a town to be the biggest in its country, though doubtless it is a misfortune that other towns would gladly assume. Its inhabitants are too apt to assume that its bigness puts it out of competition and that it is superfluous for it to be anything else but big. The New-Yorker who goes to Boston or to Philadelphia or to Chicago is sure to have the excellences and advantages of those towns respectively pointed out to him by the inhabitants thereof, and he is equally sure to regard the indication as "provincial," assuming that the establishment by the census that there are more "head" of New-Yorkers than of Bostonians or Philadelphians renders any other indication of its superiority unnecessary. He is only internationally sensitive. When he goes to London or Paris, or when a Londoner or Parisian is under his charge in his own city, he is apt to wish that he

From *New York Times*, September 23, 1888.

had something else to point out than the bigness in which their cities exceed his own. He would like them to admire New-York, though he is above soliciting the admiration of his countrymen. . . .

If New-York were not so big as to be out of competition in that respect it would doubtless be a better place to live in, and anything that brings it into direct competition with other cities, even in so trivial a matter as playing baseball, has wholesome elements. It is not at all municipally important that the New-Yorks should win the championship, but it is important that New-Yorkers should be anxious that their city should excel in anything. When *Iroguois* won the Derby it was plausibly said that the victory raised the United States higher in the estimation of the general mass of Englishmen than any other they had ever achieved. A cynical philosopher, replying to a person uninterested in aquatic sports, who betrayed the same impatience with the inordinate attention paid by the press and the public to the international yacht races that we are now remarking upon with reference to baseball, defended the public interest upon the ground that the *America's* Cup was really the only trophy the country had to show. Possibly a similar remark about the possession of the champion baseball pennant by New-York would be equally exaggerated, but at all events the competition proves that it does not quite suffice for all New-Yorkers that New-York is big. If this sentiment were extended in more rational directions there might actually come an irresistible public demand that New-York should become the best paved, cleaned, and policed city and the most attractive place of residence in the United States. Meanwhile, any stir of local pride is to be welcomed that makes a beginning in the direction of that distant and Utopian end.

The *New York Times* Considers Madison Square Garden as a Civic Institution, 1900

. . . The representatives of the owners of Madison Square Garden cannot be blamed for trying to sell their property to the Government for a Post Office. Such a sale would enable them to unload a burden some of them have been carrying for many years for the benefit of all the rest of us, and which they may well desire that somebody else shall now take up. Neither can the representatives of the government be blamed for dealing to acquire a site for the Post Office which is at least far more eligible than the site now occupied for that purpose. . . .

They ignore the importance of the civic and municipal functions which the amphitheater of the Madison Square Garden now fulfills, and has fulfilled since its erection. There are certain shows and celebrations which cannot be given anywhere else, and which add immensely to the attractiveness of the city, and also to the profits of the men who do business in it, that simply could not be given in the absence of a Madison Square Garden to give them in. The Horse Show is the most conspicuous of these entertainments. It cannot be rivaled or approached in any

From *New York Times*, February 28, 1900.

other American city, mainly for want of so good a place in which to hold it. It is safe to say that it is the municipal possession which is most envied of New York by citizens of the other great cities.

Why should it not be made, in name as well as in fact, a municipal possession, as other things have been, through private munificence? The proposition is by no means so startling or so anomalous as it may at the first glance seem. The city is empowered, under its charter, to acquire real estate "for any public use or purpose." Surely there is not difference in principle between acquiring land for the purpose of public entertainment and instruction and devoting to such a purpose land of which the title is already in the city. And this latter has repeatedly been done, with the general approbation. For the New York Public Library the city has given both ground and building. For the Metropolitan Museum of Art, for the Museum of Natural History, for the Zoological Garden, or the Botanical Garden, it has given the land. In all these cases it has gone into partnership with private munificence and public spirit. None of these enterprises, perhaps, could sustain itself but for the perfectly legitimate assistance it has derived from being made free of rent and taxes. Here is another public enterprise not less important, which has been demonstrated not to be self-sustaining purely as a commercial enterprise. Why should the city not lend its countenance to this also?

It is to be noted that in every one of the other cases private citizens have given earnest of public spirit and munificence before the city has been called in to aid. That condition should not be relaxed in this instance. If there is in the community enough of interest in the purposes which the Madison Square Garden subserves to induce subscribers to make a free gift to the city of the building of the Madison Square Garden, they would have made an excellent case for the city to treat them as it has treated other admirable and public-spirited enterprises, by aiding them to carry on their public work. This it could do by taking title to the land on which the building stands. As a continuous corporation the city could not lose by such an investment. In fact, it would be a good investment, since it would be provided that after a certain or an uncertain term of years, when the place should have outlived its usefulness as a unique place of public entertainment, the whole property should revert to the city, to be put to the more profitable uses of which it would have become ready. . . . The sole question is, or ought to be, whether there is public spirit enough among the rich men of New York to retain for public uses the place which has so admirably served those uses ever since it was built.

Harper's Weekly Examines New York City's Athletic Clubs, 1892

The natural conditions of rural life are the most favorable to health. But the artificial conditions are not always the best in the world. Even in our small towns the social organization is too loose-jointed and spiritless to enter heartily into schemes

From "City Athletics," *Harper's Magazine* 68 (1892): 297–305.

for the thorough education of the body; and as to farm life, there is a vast deal of balderdash talked about that Arcadian mode of existence. . . .

Careful consideration of these facts may convince the most fettered slaves of childhood's fond delusion that the male dweller in the city need not be an absolute physical wreck. There is a saving muscular grace of the town man, and it is found in what is known as "amateur athletics." But even he who has some genuine light on the subject will be surprised to learn to what an extent and how successfully the young New-Yorker seeks after this saving grace, and will receive with incredulity the statement that New York is in a fair way to become the amateur athletic capital of the world.

It does seem somewhat startling; but it is true. In the first place, Nature has given the child of Manhattan every possible facility for making his recreation literally a re-creation—a building up of new strength of body, controlled in its development by gymnastic skill. It seems almost as though the original plan of New York island and the surrounding region had been laid out with this end solely in view.

Look at the map. To the south . . . is a broad bay at the confluence of two rivers. . . . This spread of waters offers accommodations to all kinds of conditions of crafts from a canoe to a Cunarder. . . .

Two good roads lead from the city proper to the suburbs north, where the new wards in Westchester offer fairly cheap sites for ball-grounds and race-tracks. Ground may be had, likewise on Staten Island, to the south, or in Jersey, to the west, where are the best roads for bicycling this side of Boston. And the bold hunters . . . have all Long Island to themselves.

But does the young New-Yorker take advantage of his opportunities? . . . In 1868 there was one athletic club in New York. The year before there was none. . . . To-day the score of 1867 is beaten by seven. . . . These are the athletic clubs pure and simple, those that encourage all manly sports. Of clubs that make a specialty of one form of exercise there is no end. . . .

In looking over the *Herald,* or, . . . some other distinctively "popular" paper, you will see a brief paragraph stating that the employés of the Smith Manufacturing Co. defeated the Jones, Brown and Robinson Brothers Club in a boat-race or a game of base-ball. Now you will never hear of those sturdy young toilers at the spring games or the annual meetings of the New York or the Manhattan Athletic clubs; . . . but they are, in fact, the truest athletes of all. They do not seek semi-professional celebrity; the applause of their friends—especially of their young female friends— . . . represents to them all that glory and fame can give. . . .

There are such clubs as these in most of the large mercantile and manufacturing establishments, and they compete with each other in a more or less friendly spirit. There is a certain social rivalry between different houses in the same trade, often between different divisions of one house. Compositors do battle with pressmen, weavers with dyers, the hands in the wholesale department with the hands in the retail store. . . .

It is natural that men who make their living by manual labor, and earn their board literally in the sweat of their brows, should be athletes. Likewise the athletic clubs of the militia regiments may be taken as a matter of course. . . . It is surprising to see how the mania for forming associations for physical exercises has spread through all the classes of a great city. The young men of a certain neighborhood gather together and get up a loosely organized little club to play baseball or cricket; the establishment of a good bowling-alley is the signal for the appearance of a half a dozen new bowling clubs. . . .

Seeing that these gatherings of muscle-seekers have no yearnings after public notice, and that their incorporate existence rarely passes the limit of two or three years—for young men grow up and marry, bowling alleys are crowded out by local growth and appreciation of real estate. . . .

The bowling alley is, as a rule, an adjunct of . . . a beer garden. . . . The proprietor generally furnishes some small solid refreshments, and each member pays for the liquids he consumes . . . and at the end of the evening the expenses . . . consisting of hall rent and the hire of the attendant boys are divided up. . . . The fix may be fifty cents a head or thereabouts.

. . . Physical training is, in a negative way, moral exercise. The man who is in training must needs keep early hours . . . and generally lead a sober and temperate life. . . . His associates are young men of from eighteen to twenty-five, with a few old veterans. . . . These young men are clerks, lawyers, and the like; the majority of them Americans; the others principally Germans and Irish of the better sort. . . .

At the top should stand, by right of seniority, the New York Athletic Club. Organized in 1868 . . . , the N.Y.A.C. originates most of the laws which bind the National Association of Amateur Athletes of America. . . . It will cost the young man who is properly introduced ten dollars for an admission fee and twenty-five dollars for yearly dues. . . .

The Manhattan holds the championship emblem, and it does more than any other organization to keep the athletic ball rolling. It has two "grounds"—one place at Fifty-sixth Street and Eighth Avenue, and another at Eighty-sixth Street. The latter . . . will be when it is finished the largest and best of its sort. It covers a whole block, has space for base-ball, foot-ball, lacrosse and lawn tennis, a quarter-mile track for running and bicycling, and a shady, airy grand stand, where the lasses may sit at the games and watch their favored lads. . . . If you want exercise . . . or fame as a runner, a vaulter or a heaver of heavy weights, the Manhattan is your club. . . .

Do you row? And are you unwilling or unable to pay $100 or $120 for a shell wherein to paddle in selfish solitude? You can join, for twenty-five dollars admission fees and twenty dollars annual dues, the New York Rowing Club, where there are more than a hundred other young men . . . who have the freedom of a well-fitted up boat-house just above the elevated railroad bridge on the Harlem.

If this does not suit you, you may take your choice between the Nassau and the Atalanta. If you are in bondage to learning at Columbia, you will join the college boat club; if you are a budding broker . . . you may sit on the sliding seats of the Stock Exchange Rowing Club's shells.

If you wish to be a bicycler . . . if you are not afraid of being held an outcast from society because you put on neat knee-breeches and a polo cap, and straddle the wiry wheel which the "average citizen," not daring to mount, doth much deride and ridicule; if you wish to enjoy a ride where you have the combined joy in strength and speed of horse and rider; . . . if you desire wiry legs, good digestion, and should sleep o'nights—you may join the band of wheelmen who are forbidden to travel in the mazy ways of Central Park because an occasional horse has shown an antipathy to knickerbockers and rubber tires. . . .

You may hire a bicycle . . . and practice . . . till such times as you feel that you may wisely invest ninety or a hundred dollars in a "special Columbia" or from twenty to fifty more in an imported "Humber," or a native "Expert."

. . . If you would reach the wished-for goal—sound health, self-reliant spirit, well-disciplined forces . . . . there are few places where you may reach the goal more surely or more swiftly than in this good city of New York.

E S S A Y S

The two essays in this section reflect the great interest urban historians have in how urbanization has influenced the direction of sport history and how, in turn, the rise of sport has affected urban life. They look at the city not only as the site of sport but also as a part of the process of city building—the interplay of its physical structures, organizations, and values.

Drawn from his broader study of sport in Boston, *How Boston Played,* Stephen Hardy examines in detail how and why municipal parks were built in Boston in the late nineteenth century despite the varied interests of important local political blocs. He emphasizes the agency of Irish working-class people in securing the kinds of parks they wanted with space to play ball rather than the staid suburban parks advocated by the middle class. Steven A. Riess of the Department of History, Northeastern Illinois University, examines the integral role of machine politicians in the development of prize fighting, horse racing, and baseball (the three major professional sports at the turn of the century) in New York City, the national capital of professional sport. New York politics was heavily influenced by its powerful Tammany Hall machine, but in cities all across the country, local politicians were prominent sports entrepreneurs, who relied upon their clout to facilitate their sporting interests.

Parks for the People: The Rise of Public Parks in Boston, 1869–1900

STEPHEN HARDY

. . . The development of a public park system marks a significant chapter in Boston's sport history. For one, the parks represented the first major civic response to the amusement question. Indeed, parks provided much of the open space upon

From Stephen Hardy, *How Boston Played: Sport, Recreation and Community, 1865–1915* (Boston: Northeastern University Press, 1982), 65–84.

which Bostonians pursued their favorite sports. But the parks issue also embodied many of the philosophies and arguments aired in a city rudely awakened to the fact that urban growth was not all positive. Commercial and industrial success rested on top of a much denser population that included hordes of immigrants; the by-products of "progress" included an inexorable sprawl of housing, a choking pollution of the air, and the erosion of cultural homogeneity. In large part, public parks were first presented as a reform to many of these problems. But the record of park development reveals that simple solutions were not easily implemented. Urban growth was accompanied by widening divisions between social classes and interest groups within the city's boundaries. Residents in new and old neighborhoods sought to control the use of local space. New political machinery had developed to represent their divergent interests. The working of this changing social and political order complicated, challenged, and transformed the park system in Boston. Their complexity argues against simple notions about the nature and process of this important urban reform.

Most historians have viewed parks and their close relation, playgrounds, as the creation of middle- and upper-class reformers who desired to provide order for both the urban landscape and its inhabitants. As a recent article on Frederick Law Olmsted, consultant and chief architect for the Boston park system from 1875 to 1895, maintains, "Olmsted's parks seemed to offer an attractive remedy for the dangerous problem of discontent among the urban masses." . . . Olmsted and other early park advocates quickly and continually discovered that factional strife and class resentment could erupt and envenom debates on the placement, benefits, and beneficiaries of nature's blessings. In Boston, as in Worcester, the larger urban constituency—laborers and clerks, artisans and bookkeepers, natives and immigrants, men and women—expressed their interests, either directly or through their political representatives. Their pressure forced adjustments in the initial visions of genteel reformers like Olmsted and his supporters.

The park movement in Boston was part of an active, conscious search for order amid the environmental, political, social, and cultural dislocations. . . . Much of the initiative clearly lay with established middle- and upper-class groups who designed their programs for all Bostonians. But it would be wrong to think that the remainder of Boston's population sat passively as major public policy filtered down from above. On the contrary, both the form and essence of public parks developed in ways determined by interest groups representing a wide range of citizens, as one discovers by comparing the early rhetoric with the later reality.

The main story begins in 1869, when the pressures of increased growth and a heightened awareness of the Common's inadequacies resulted in a series of proposals for public park systems. Unfortunately, the fear of higher taxes, coupled with the conviction that the nearby suburbs provided ample scenery, prevented the approval of such early legislation as the Park Act of 1870. The debate over parks continued unchecked, however, and within five years Boston's citizens had swayed enough to approve the Park Act of 1875. Accordingly, the mayor appointed three commissioners (approved by the city aldermen) who were charged to entertain citizens' proposals and examine possible acquisitions "with regard to many different points such as convenience of access, original cost and betterments, probable cost of improvements, sanitary conditions and natural beauty." The commissioners retained Frederick Law Olmsted as a consultant until 1878, when he was appointed chief landscape architect for the park system.

Early park advocates claimed (convincingly enough) that the entire city benefited from and supported the movement. As one popular newspaper urged:

> A public park is now a great necessity and not an expensive luxury. It is the property of the people, rich and poor together, and the only place where all classes can daily meet one another face to face in a spirit of fraternal recreation.

Another claimed on the eve of the park referendum:

> The moment anything is done under the act it will open a new field for laborers, and at the same time enlarge the possessions in which their wives and children will have an equal inheritance with the most favored. Indeed, the great benefit of public parks is gathered by those who are not rich.

Park boosters, often among Boston's most prominent and established residents, felt their arguments represented those of all citizens, rich and poor. Their formula for reform was simple. Parks would offer both escape from and control of the traumas caused by the rapid spread of houses, factories, and people, with their congestion, noise, and pollution. Parks would provide something the much-revered small town always had offered; open space and rural scenery. Thus, while park proponents tended to revel in the prospect of a booming Boston, they also desired to brake its unchecked growth by imposing at least three qualities that the small-town community seemed to offer: fresh air and open space, healthy citizens, and pervasive morality.

It was not so much that park proponents wanted to make Boston a small town. They desired, rather, to balance urbanization with a form of ruralization. With parks the city would always retain part of what it had had in the past. Few denied the inexorable nature of the population's advance. . . . Unfortunately, the congestion of humanity threatened the existence of open space and pure air, and so endangered the lives of individual inhabitants as to threaten the life of the city itself.

During the heated debates of 1881, the critical year of parkland acquisition, one alderman emphasized the changes that had occurred in his thirty-seven years as a Bostonian. The city had been smaller, but at the same time, "the boys could go anywhere, the lands of all seemed to be public. . . . Now you will find a sign up, 'No trespassing'; 'Keep off the grass.' " He warned his colleagues that they voted not for their generation, but for "those that follow us. . . ."

Shaping the city environment by means of well-planned open space was matched in urgency by the concern for health. It was a well-circulated belief that parks were the "lungs of the city.". . . Parks would be part of a triad of services which, along with pure water and efficient sewage systems, would "make the cities in all ways healthful and beautiful. The weight of the medical profession aided the momentum for parks. Physicians cited numerous statistics and studies to show that urban areas suffered higher death and disease rates, which could in large part be traced to foul air and insufficient sunlight. Particularly alarming were the facts disclosing high rates of cholera infantum and stillbirths in cities like Boston. The haunting conclusion remained that "unless open spaces of sufficient extent are provided and properly located, we shall create and shut up in this city the conditions, of which disease, pestilence and death will be the natural offspring."

Others saw a different therapeutic value in parks. One alderman wove the sights and sounds of parks into a logical argument about the requisites of labor and wealth. Since wealth rested on labor, and labor involved expenditures of force, "it follows that without recuperation and recreation of force, the ability of each individual to labor is diminished and his power to add to the wealth of the community is lost.". . .

Physical health, or the lack of it, was delicately entwined with the issue of public morality. To those concerned with a degenerating social order, the benefit of public parks in this area was unrivaled. . . . It was, said Dr. [Edward] Crane, the "close atmosphere" of his house and street that drove the tired workman to the saloon to seek relief. If only he had a park accessible to him, the poor laborer would seek it with his family "as instinctively as a plant stretched toward the light." The park would "educate him and his family into the enjoyment of innocent amusements and open-air pleasures." Somehow, by an association with nature, the workingman and his family would experience a florescence of morality previously stifled by the choking air of city streets. Thus the parks would help resolve the nagging problem of urban amusements. . . .

. . . By 1876, as the speakers at a public park rally made clear, it was necessary for the city to provide asylums for . . . wholesome activities. The cost of parks would be far less than the cost of the jails, prisons, and police used in repressing wasteful indulgences like liquor and gambling. Parks would provide the blue sky, the gurgling brook, and the green trees that acted as immeasurable moral agents in the village. The country would elevate the minds and manners of the urban poor. If the masses could not get to the country, let the city "bring the country to them, and give them a chance, at least, to experience its humanizing and blessed influence." Since parks belonged to all the people, rich or poor, all could mingle freely in a neutral cultural asylum. Fresh air would naturally improve the temperament of working-class men and women, for they would be induced "by public orders and public favor to elevate themselves and their condition in society" by associating with their betters through the medium of nature.

Boston needed parks to preserve her environment, her health, and her morality. But she also needed parks to prove her legitimacy as a first-class American city. . . . The best public schools, art museums, conservatories of music, and schools of design could not ensure Boston's reputation as the Athens of America if she lacked the spirit by which public parks were developed. A City Council committee concluded that "if Boston cannot afford such an expenditure to secure the priceless benefit of parks, it must be because she has entered the ranks of cities like Newburyport and Salem, which have ceased to grow." Civic boosterism clearly accelerated the growing demand for public parks. Boston's top business firms favored parks as a grand advertisement of the city's commercial health, and claimed that their beauty would attract wealthy merchants from around the globe. Moreover, these plush pleasure grounds would convince the prosperous classes to retain their homes within the city's limits and eschew the flight to rural suburbs. As Oliver Wendell Holmes maintained, parks would help provide the city "with the complete equipment, . . . of a true metropolis."

The argument supporting public parks was clear. They would improve the physical environment of the city and, more important, elevate the living conditions of her inhabitants. Rich and poor alike would enjoy the benefits of nature, placed in perpetuum within the city limits. Families in the impoverished North End or in the elegant Back Bay could rest assured that fresh air would be forever available to their children and to their children's children. Finally, Boston, by displaying the spirit necessary for such a project, would reestablish her reputation as America's premier city.

There can be no doubt that a broad consensus supported the position of park advocates. By 1900, the park system surrounding Boston was, in large part, complete. . . . By means of parkways, expanses of greenery were effectively linked throughout the city. . . .

But while Bostonians agreed upon the general benefits that parks could produce, they differed over answers to several specific questions that arose during the implementation of the plan proposed by Olmsted and the commissioners. These questions and their resultant friction revolved around three interrelated concerns. First, where in the city should parks properly be located? Second, for whose benefit were the parks ultimately intended? Finally, how exactly were parks to improve the leisure, and through it the life, of all citizens? . . .

The task of locating a park or parks was not an easy one. While advocates stressed the benefits to be enjoyed by the entire city, politicians and citizens' lobbies were more concerned about the advantages or disadvantages of placing parks within their particular neighborhoods. . . . Each section of the city concluded that all would be best served by locating a park within its boundaries.

By 1881, the year in which the City Council considered the bulk of park bonds, this parochialism had become so acute as to threaten the very purpose of a park system. . . . A City Council committee pleaded that "an end be put to sectional contentions respecting park lands." Yet as the votes in the Common Council indicate, local interests rivaled general concerns. Every area of the city, from East Boston to West Roxbury, was represented by a politician who steadfastly maintained both the urgent need for a park in his district and the general benefits to be derived from placing one there.

The voting patterns on two key proposals . . . display the type of parochialism that worried Olmsted. For instance, in 1877 the first proposal to purchase land for a Back Bay park failed because of negative votes from members of the Common Council representing the congested inner wards and the outlying suburban wards. The proposal succeeded only when it was reevaluated as a necessary instrument for the improvement of the city's sewage system. Second, and more clearly, one can view the local interest pattern in the December 1881 vote on the purchase of land for the West Roxbury (Franklin) Park, the linchpin of Olmsted's system. . . . Opposition to the suburban park came from congested wards in the inner city. At the same time, councilors from wards adjacent to the park were almost unanimous in their approval of the costly ($600,000) acquisition. . . . Many citizens viewed park benefits in local, not general terms. The debates and votes on the placement of public parks thus exhibited the polarity in urban politics so well described in historical literature: centralized reform groups at odds with localized political machinery. In this case one sees Olmsted's grand vision matched against legitimate neighborhood and ward interests. The parks commissioners were forced to deal with an ever-increasing parochialism that reared its head early and often, as when many Ward 3 voters qualified their rejection of the 1875 Park Act by voting "No, unless Copps Hill is taken."

These attitudes continued even after the parks were completed. Some neighborhoods objected when "outsiders" availed themselves of local greenery. For instance, in 1892 a group of South Boston residents complained to the commissioners that Marine Park "had been an injury to South Boston on account of the rabble it had attracted there." Sunday arrests had involved far too many "Cambridge people"; they worried that the park had attracted "undesirable visitors to the neighborhood.". . .

But despite Olmsted's fears, parochial interests never seriously threatened the success of the park system. On the contrary, they may have *ensured* success, by forcing central planners to accommodate local interests. Olmsted and the parks commissioners might have had more than topographical considerations in mind when they designed a *series* of parks spread about Boston's various districts. Perhaps they realized the growing importance of neighborhood communities within the larger city boundaries. The overall park plan succeeded politically in 1881 because it offered a chain or package, with a little something for everyone. . . .

There was another side to the problem of locating parks. Most of the acreage, as originally conceived and as expanded by local pressure, was situated in less-congested wards. While land was more available and cheaper here, the anomaly raised serious questions. For whom were parks really intended? The rich or the poor? . . .

With elitist sentiment lurking under the surface of public proclamations, it was no wonder that the *Boston Daily Advertiser* worried about approval of the Park Act of 1875, noting that "in some of the northerly wards there will be formidable opposition, the laborers and others having been made to believe that in some way the act will be against their interests." Many had doubts. The councilors from inner-city wards realized that "the people" could not enjoy distant parks as easily as some believed. As one representative from Ward 7 reminded his colleagues, the poor workingman was not likely to march his family across town on a hot summer night just "to enjoy the benefits of the park which Boston, in its wisdom and philanthropy, has furnished for the laboring classes.". . .

One clearly deduces from the public record a sense of working-class frustration with the outlying parks. . . . Many continued to regard much of the system as essentially "rich man's parks," to enjoy which required either a carriage, or, later, an automobile.

But the changing political structure provided workingmen with more clout than they had previously enjoyed. Working through their local representatives in the City Council, the people of Charlestown effectively lobbied for a park in their area. During the mid-nineties, John F. Fitzgerald, the ward boss of the North End, continually pressured the commissioners for a park in his district. His unfailing energy and political savvy ensured the project's success despite the city's financial troubles. The North End park was thereafter his personal "monument." In like manner, the West End could count on strong political support to increase the capacity and facilities of its Charlesbank gymnasium. The inhabitants of the inner city did not reap the promised fruits of the outlying "emerald necklace," but they traded off support for rural parks in return for open space in their local neighborhoods.

Much of this open space would take the form of small parks and playgrounds. These breathing spaces did not fit the classic model of an Olmsted park. They offered only limited foliage or serenity. But they did offer working people something tangible, and their development represented an important accommodation in the original vision of the park system.

The final area of contention was closely related and involved the question of appropriate activities for park patrons. Park advocates claimed that properly placed enclaves of "rus in urbe" would elevate the life of all citizens. Parks would provide true recreation for Boston's collective body and soul. The practical question, however, became whether or not the masses could be educated into the "proper" use of parks. . . .

The central figure in this issue was, of course, Frederick Law Olmsted, who guided the Boston Park System until 1895. . . . Because of his national influence and, of course, his position as chief architect, his views were indelibly stamped on the policies of the Boston parks commissioners. . . .

Olmsted believed that the city was the source of civilization's great advances, but he also saw that its population density could induce a reactive alienation, a "quickness of apprehension, a peculiarly hard sort of selfishness." As an antidote to this pejorative side of urban life, Olmsted, along with other urban reformers, looked to recreative amusements. Expanding the concept of recreation, he wrote:

> All forms of recreation may, in the first place, be conveniently arranged under two general heads. One will include all of which the predominating influence is to stimulate exertion of any part or parts needing it; the other, all which cause us to receive pleasure without conscious exertion. Games chiefly of mental skill as chess, or athletic sports, as baseball, are examples of means of recreation of the first class, which may be termed that of *exertive* recreation; music and the fine arts generally of the second or *receptive* division.

Olmsted obviously fashioned his views of parks around the notion of receptive recreation. . . . To Olmsted, . . . action had little or no place in a public park. Boston's parks commissioners took Olmsted's views to heart and banned almost all active pursuits in the park system. There would be no "orations, harangues or loud outcries," no parades, drills, or processions, no individual music making. The rules allowed little legitimate activity beyond quiet picnics, meditations, and tours.

This tranquility would not last; the patrons had their own ideas about the activities that ought to occur in a park. They continually pressured for accommodation in the regulations, and, in Olmsted's view, constantly threatened the integrity of his receptive-recreation grounds. . . .

The growth of interest in athletic sports proved to be a major problem for the parks commissioners. While the wealthy could join suburban country clubs for playing space, the majority of the population looked to the new parklands for sports. The commissioners tried to suppress this appetite, particularly that of baseballers, and finally declared in 1884: "No entertainment, exercises, or athletic game or sport shall be held or performed within public parks except with the prior consent of the Park Commission." Olmsted was in full agreement, citing similar rules in Hartford, Baltimore, Chicago, Buffalo, New York, and Philadelphia. Only a corner of Franklin Park was allotted to active sports, and that for children only.

Yet by the turn of the century, the City Council and public pressure had forced the commissioners to permit virtually every popular sport within the confines of the parks. Cricket clubs battled baseball interests for exclusive privileges. By the mid-1890s, several parks were the scene of scheduled football matches; tennis courts and a golf course were laid out in Franklin Park; the parkways whirled with wheels, many in procession and in parade! At the turn of the century, "horseless carriages" began to intrude; by 1902 they had received full privileges. Although certain sports were restricted to particular places and times, and much of the sporting activity was funneled to the related playground system, the evidence in the Parks Department minutes clearly indicates that the concept of public parks in Boston was altered, by special-interest groups, to include provisions for active sports. . . .

Athletic sports were probably eventually accepted as legitimate park recreations because they represented a less severe encroachment than commercial amusements. As soon as the parks neared completion, the commissioners were inundated with license petitions from operators of hurdy-gurdy machines, merry-go-rounds, photo tents, refreshment stands, and amusement theaters, to name but a few. The operator of one theater argued that "the purpose of amusing the public is a public benefit entirely consistent with the use of the public parks." Further, the operators claimed that they desired only to satisfy an overwhelming demand for their services.

Alderman Martin Lomasney, the powerful boss of Ward 8, accurately voiced one attitude of the inner city when he opposed a rule outlawing mechanical "flying horses" or similar commercial amusements on the Sabbath:

> I don't believe we should be activated by the same spirit that prevailed in the days of the old Blue Laws, when on Sunday you would have to walk down Washington Street carrying a Bible in your hand and not speak to anybody on the street. . . . Certain people in the North End and in South Boston can reach these parks Sundays who cannot reach them any other day, and I don't believe they should be deprived of going on the flying horses if they wish to do so.

The laborer who found his relief in a nickel beer and free lunch at the saloon, or in a 25-cent seat at the Columbia Theatre, might well expect similar offerings at the parks. Olmsted's vision had to accommodate Lomasney's. Working through their connections on the City Council and even on the Parks Commission, commercial amusements operators succeeded in placing merry-go-rounds, photo tents, refreshment stands, and vending machines among the elm trees, brooks, and beaches. . . .

The development of a park system involved an active and conscious attempt by Bostonians to shape and control the physical aspects of their community. In this respect, the Parks Department can arguably be described as the city's first municipal planning board. Olmsted and his successors successfully blended the available topography to reconcile beauty and space for recreation with basic needs like adequate drainage and traffic flow. Beyond all else, the park system was a farsighted response to a prevailing belief that the city was fast gobbling up both open spaces and a way of life; it was what Olmsted called a "self-preserving instinct of civilization." The islandlike quality of these parks today is testimony to the accuracy of that instinct.

If the Boston case is at all representative, however, it cautions the historian to take special care in categorizing urban park systems as a vehicle of genteel reform or social control whereby an elite class, whatever its members' motives, could readily manipulate the behavior of inferiors. Considerable evidence suggests this as the intent of many park advocates, but its basis lies largely in the arguments of early proposals. . . . An equally compelling body of evidence, the public record, displays the active role which the "popular mass" took in altering this vision. Special interest groups—neighborhood citizens' lobbies, athletic clubs, amusement operators—all representing a wide range of social classes, continually worked directly and through their political representatives to influence major decisions in park placement and policy. These groups succeeded in getting parks where they wished them; they pursued their own choice of recreation on the park grounds. Thus, the park movement in Boston was a reform that issued from the "bottom up" as well as from the top down. Because of this, the ultimate product of reform differed from the intended product. . . .

Professional Sports and New York's Tammany Machine, 1890–1920

STEVEN A. RIESS

The close connection between commercialized sport and urban politics was probably first evident in prizefighting. As early as the 1830s and 1840s, gangs of New York youths worked actively with Tammany Hall in seeking the immigrant vote for the Democratic party. . . . The most famous was Irish-born John Morrissey, the American boxing champion from 1853 to 1858. . . . Morrissey utilized his fame to get elected to the Congress. . . . Ward leaders and public officials in this era often became boxing patrons, arranging bouts for side bets at hangouts like Harry Hill's Dance Hall, a favorite meeting place for the sporting crowd [and] rewarded favored fighters with jobs as emigrant runners, bouncers, tavern keepers, and policemen.

. . . After the Civil War, Tammanyites remained interested in boxing, but formal matches were difficult to pull off because the violent and bloody sport was illegal. Contests had to be fought in out-of-the-way sites such as barns, barges, or saloon backrooms. Some of the important exhibitions in the early 1880s were held at Madison Square Garden, . . . until 1885, when the promoters gave up after repeated police interference. . . .

Prizefighting staged a revival in the New York metropolitan area in the early 1890s, and New York regained its preeminence in the sport. The main site of bouts was Coney Island, a wide-open resort that was becoming a major sporting center. . . . The principal boxing club there was the Coney Island Athletic Club

From Steven A. Riess, "Sports and Machine Politics in New York City, 1890–1920," in *The Making of Urban America*, ed. Raymond A. Mohl (Newark, DE: Scholarly Resources, 1988), 102–18.

(CIAC), organized in May 1892 by [Boss John] McKane and various machine politicians. McKane owned the arena, provided political protection, and prevented any big bouts at Coney Island unless he had a share of the action. . . .

The CIAC was only one of several boxing clubs in the metropolitan area sponsored and protected by local politicians. These clubs operated even though professional boxing was illegal. For example, in 1895 the New Puritan Boxing Club of Long Island City held its matches at a site owned by the town's former mayor, James Gleason. His partners included Big Tim Sullivan and former Justice Dick Newton, recently released from a jail sentence for corrupt electioneering.

Tim Sullivan was first elected to the state assembly in 1886 at the age of twenty-three and moved to the Senate in 1893. He served in the U.S. Congress from 1902 to 1906, but in 1908 he returned to his power base in the state senate. . . . Sullivan was associated early in his career with such gangsters as Monk Eastman, Kid Twist, and Paul Kelly, who provided him with intimidators and repeaters at election time. In return, organized crime was allowed to flourish. Big Tim was idolized by his constituents as a friend of the poor. He provided them with patronage, relief, outings, and any other assistance. Sullivan was a great sportsman . . . [who] raced horses, gambled heavily, and, after 1895, dominated the New York poolroom business. Furthermore, by 1898 he also monopolized boxing in New York State, except in Brooklyn, where the new CIAC was protected by Democratic Boss Hugh McLaughlin.

In 1896, under Sullivan's guidance, a bill passed the legislature and was approved by the governor legalizing "sparring" matches of up to ten rounds at licensed athletic clubs. New York became the only state with legalized boxing. . . .

Tammany control of the police department further obviated fears of harassment at . . . politically connected athletic clubs. Police Chief Bill Devery rarely interfered with boxing bouts, even well-advertised matches like the heavyweight championship match in 1899 between titleholder Bob Fitzsimmons and challenger James J. Jeffries at the new CIAC, . . . Devery . . . owed his rise to the sponsorship of Boss Croker and Tim Sullivan. His career was marked by several episodes of incompetence and corruption. . . .

Legalized boxing lasted only until 1900, when the state legislature repealed the Horton Act because of the sport's brutality, the gambling menace, and the Tammany influence in boxing. Approximately 3,500 contests had been staged over five years, mainly in New York City. . . .

The repeal of the Horton Act did not completely stop boxing, since it survived surreptitiously in saloon backrooms and at club smokers. Private clubs circumvented the law by holding three-round exhibitions for the entertainment of "members," who paid a one-dollar "fee" to join the club. The most prestigious of the membership clubs was Tim Sullivan's National Athletic Club, which reputedly had 3,000 members. By 1908 fifteen clubs in New York held weekly bouts. . . .

Tammany politicians tried in vain for several years to legalize boxing again. Prospects brightened in 1911 when the Democrats gained control of both the state legislature and the governor's mansion for the first time in years. This enabled Senator James J. Frawley, a former president of the Knickerbocker Athletic Club, to pass a bill legalizing ten-round, no-decision boxing contests. The sport was placed under the supervision of an unpaid three-man State Athletic Commission responsible for licensing athletic clubs and fighters. A 5 percent tax was levied on the box office take, which came to nearly $50,000 in 1912. The Frawley Act resulted in a renewed interest in boxing, and by the end of 1912 there were eighty-nine licensed boxing clubs in the state, forty-nine in New York City. The bouts were held in small neighborhood boxing clubs and large downtown arenas like Madison Square Garden.

Prizefighting operated under the Frawley Act until 1917, when the law was repealed by a Republican administration. The prestige of the sport remained low. Its brutality, the low-life types associated with it, and incessant gambling and rumors of fixes did little to improve the standing of boxing as a sport. The Athletic Commission . . . became overtly politicized by the Republicans, who regained control of the state legislature and the governorship in 1915. . . . [Governor] Whitman called for repeal late in the session as a party measure, getting his bill approved on a strict party vote. Not one Democratic senator voted to abolish boxing. Whitman's battle against boxing was a politically astute move signifying to upstate voters that the Republican party stood for tradition and high moral values, unlike the Democrats who had supported an immoral blood sport with dubious connections to urban political machines and gangsters.

The repeal of the Frawley Act was a major blow to American prizefighting. The sport was legal in twenty-three states in 1917, but it was severely restricted, if not completely outlawed, in the major markets of New York and Chicago. Even in San Francisco, which had temporarily supplanted New York as the boxing capital after the repeal of the Horton Act, the sport was greatly curtailed by a 1914 state law limiting matches to four rounds. The outlook for boxing improved markedly during World War I, however, because the sport was used to help train soldiers for combat. Consequently, boxing's image became much better. Even the reform-minded *New York Times* became an advocate of pugilism. . . . In 1920, under the direction of Senate Minority Leader Jimmy Walker, a loyal son of Tammany, the legislature enacted a law permitting twelve-round matches, with judges empowered to choose a victor if the contest went the distance. An unpaid athletic commission was established to supervise the sport and license boxing clubs, trainers, and fighters.

The passage of the Walker Act enabled New York City to regain its position as the national center of boxing. In the 1920s local fight clubs became important sources of top-flight fighters. Most major American bouts were held at Madison Square Garden. The promoter there was Tex Rickard, probably best known for his successful work in pulling off the Jeffries-Johnson championship fight of 1910 in Reno, Nevada. . . . An out-of-towner, Rickard generated a lot of jealousy among local promoters and politicians, compelling him to provide passes, favors, and bribes to bring off . . . match[es]. By 1920, Rickard had learned his lesson and developed important connections in Tammany Hall. His backers included Governor Al Smith, who interceded on Rickard's behalf with the owners of Madison Square Garden, helping the promoter get a ten-year lease for $400,000. . . .

Politics dominated not only the "sport of pugs" but also the "sport of kings." Despite the aristocratic image of the sport, horse racing often came under severe moral scrutiny from church leaders and moral reformers because of the gambling, crooked races, and animal abuses associated with the turf. More than any other sport, racing depended upon betting for its appeal and survival. Consequently, thoroughbred racing at the turn of the century was widely forbidden. Where the sport did operate, as in New York, it was heavily influenced by machine politicians and politically active elites, such as William C. Whitney, Thomas Fortune Ryan, and August Belmont II. These men used sport to facilitate cross-class coalitions in the Democratic party to help protect their transit franchises. Streetcar executives out of necessity became intimately involved in urban politics; they needed inside information, long-term leases, and rights of way. Elite sportsmen like Ryan and Belmont owned and operated racetracks. Along with machine politicos like Croker and Tim Sullivan, they owned, bred, and raced thoroughbreds, and they wagered heavily at the track. Sullivan and other professional politicians were also prominent in the business of gambling, usually as organizers and promotors of bookmaking and offtrack poolroom, or betting parlor, syndicates. The elite and plebeian members of the sporting fraternity worked together on issues of mutual concern, such as the facilitation of racetrack operations and the legalization of ontrack betting. They were bitter enemies, however, when it came to offtrack betting.

Thoroughbred racing . . . enjoyed a boom in the 1820s and 1830s but faltered in the North after the depression of 1837. . . . The turf did not revive in the North until 1863, when John Morrissey staged races at the resort town of Saratoga Springs to attract elite vacationers. He was supported by wealthy sportsmen Leonard Jerome, William R. Travers, and John Hunter, who apparently were not adverse to working with a former Tammany shoulder hitter.

The Saratoga experiment was such a resounding success that Jerome, Chairman August Belmont of the national Democratic party, and other elite sportsmen organized the American Jockey Club (AJC) in 1866 to sponsor races in the vicinity of New York City. Jerome played a leading role in securing 230 acres in Westchester, where a racetrack was built and named Jerome Park in his honor. . . .

Not all of the 862 original members of the AJC . . . were socially elite. . . . The membership included such politicians as the notorious Tammany Boss William M. Tweed. . . .

New York horsemen needed considerable political savvy to circumvent the legal barriers to gambling, the backbone of the sport. An antipool law was passed by the state legislature in 1877 in response to the widespread wagering on the Tilden-Hayes election. Despite fears that this law would hurt track attendance, the turf continued to flourish, largely because the auction pool system of betting was replaced by bookmaking. The locus of racing moved to the Coney Island area, a forty-cent, one-hour train ride from mid-town Manhattan. Local politicians were expected to protect the tracks from rigorous enforcement of the penal codes. In June 1879, William A. Engeman, builder of the Brighton Beach Hotel and politically well connected, established a proprietary racetrack at Brighton Beach. The track was quite successful, and, by 1882, Engeman was netting $200,000 per year. Late in 1879, Jerome organized the prestigious Coney Island Jockey Club (CIJC), which included Belmont, William K. Vanderbilt, and Pierre Lorillard, Jr. . . . Finally, in 1885, the politically astute Dwyer brothers, plungers who had made their fortune as butchers, opened Gravesend as a proprietary track. These three tracks were tolerated and protected by local politicians under the direction of Boss McKane, who permitted pool-selling to flourish. . . .

In 1887 representatives of the racing interests passed the Ives Anti-Poolroom Law forbidding off-betting but permitting betting at the tracks during the May to October racing season. The state also levied a tax on the race courses to raise money. . . . The new law resulted in a boom in racing and gambling. It led directly to the formation of the Metropolitan Turf Alliance (MTA) in 1888, an association of over sixty well-connected bookmakers who sought to monopolize the bookmaking privilege at the tracks. . . . Another result was that, in 1889, John A. Morris constructed Morris Park Racetrack in Westchester to replace Jerome Park, which the city had purchased for a reservoir. Morris . . . had made his fortune operating the infamous Louisiana Lottery. He was politically influential, . . . and his Tammanyite son was the district's assemblyman. Managed by the New York Jockey Club, Morris Park had the largest grandstand and the longest track in the United States. The facility cost several hundred thousand dollars and was regarded as palatial by contemporaries. It immediately became an important resort for the social set who traveled to the track in expensive carriages. . . .

Poolroom operators learned to adapt and stay in business despite the Ives Anti-Poolroom Law. Poolrooms were mainly located in midtown or the Tenderloin. . . . Occasional raids were instigated by reformers like Anthony Comstock of the Society for the Suppression of Vice, but the poolrooms usually operated with impunity. The poolroom operators were well protected by Mayor Hugh Grant and other Tammany friends, . . . by payoffs to police and local political powers. Machine-appointed jurists were also supportive. . . .

. . . Early in the spring of 1893, the police instigated a major attack against local poolrooms, possibly at the instigation of Boss Richard Croker. The Tammany boss had recently purchased the famous Belle Meade stud and wanted New York tracks to prosper so he could race his horses there. In addition, Croker was a good friend of the Dwyers, who had often given him betting tips, and he hoped to protect their interests. With Croker's support, and despite the opposition of Tim Sullivan, the state legislature enacted the Saxton Anti-Poolroom Law making the keeping of a poolroom a felony.

The status of horse racing was seriously threatened one year later by a coalition of social reformers, clergymen, and other Tammany opponents. This group used the September 1894 state constitutional convention as a forum to ban all horse-race gambling. There was widespread sentiment against betting, particularly at illegal poolrooms. . . . Opponents were bolstered by the closing in December 1893 of New Jersey's tracks, which had been totally controlled by corrupt machine politicians. The New York State constitutional convention adopted a proposal banning horse-race betting completely. When the proposal was approved by voters in fall elections, the end of racing appeared imminent.

Racing interests waged an all-out campaign to save the sport. Calmer minds recognized that the convention might have gone too far. Even the reform-minded *New York Times* sought to save racing, which it believed helped improve the breed. The turf had powerful friends in Albany. Racing advocates flexed their muscle in the passage of the Percy-Gray Act, establishing a state racing commission to supervise the sport. . . .

Offtrack betting was also back in business, even though a new law had been passed accompanying Percy-Gray that banned such betting. The enterprise now came under the protection of Big Tim Sullivan, and, under his patronage, offtrack betting soon reached its apogee. Sullivan's operation had Croker's approval. As many as 400 poolrooms belonged to the syndicate, each paying from $60 to $300 per month for the privilege of staying in business. . . . The poolroom operations were extraordinarily successful, and in 1902 the syndicate earned $3.6 million. . . .

Thoroughbred racing's greatest crisis came in 1908, when Governor Charles Evans Hughes in his annual address to the state legislature called for the end of racetrack gambling. . . . The progressive governor believed that gambling on races was both a moral outrage and a flagrant violation of the state constitution. . . . He used his influence to get Republicans behind a bill to abolish on-site betting. . . . Hughes . . . convened a special session of the legislature, which passed the Agnew-Hart bill by a margin of one vote in the Senate. This victory was described by a Hughes biographer as his "most dramatic venture in the area of moral reform."

The new law severely hampered the racing industry, a $75-million business nationwide. The major tracks tried to remain open by allowing oral betting, which the courts ruled was legal, but attendance declined by two-thirds. In 1910 the legislature passed the Agnew-Perkins Act, making racetrack owners liable for any gambling violations at their facilities. The result was that tracks still operating immediately went out of business. In 1911 and 1912 there was no thoroughbred racing in New York. However, in 1913, Judge Townsend Scudder ruled in the *Shane* case that track managers were liable only if they had wittingly permitted bookmakers to operate. As a consequence, Belmont Park and two minor tracks, Jamaica and Aqueduct, reopened. But such historic racetracks as Gravesend and Sheepshead Bay, each worth about $2.5 million, never reopened.

. . . Baseball owners were regarded as selfless, civic-minded men who sponsored teams out of a concern for the public welfare. But in reality, owners were not drawn from the "best people." New York baseball magnates included a heavy representation of machine politicians. They used their clout to benefit their teams, which provided patronage, financial and psychic rewards, and good public relations.

Baseball in New York from its earliest days was closely tied to local politics. Tammany was an early sponsor of amateur baseball teams, the most important being the Mutuals, established in 1857. By the 1860s, when Tweed had become involved with the club, it was already one of the leading amateur nines. Players were subsidized with patronage jobs in the sanitation department and the coroner's office. In 1871, when the Mutuals joined the first professional league, the National Association of Professional Baseball Players (NA), its board of directors included the sheriff, several aldermen, two judges, and six state legislators. One of only three teams that played in all five NA campaigns, the Mutuals in 1876 joined the new National League (NL). But late in the 1876 season, after refusing to make a costly western trip, the Mutuals were expelled by the NL.

New York City was without major league baseball until 1883, when Tammanyites John B. Day and Joseph Gordon and former minor leaguer John Mutrie were awarded franchises in both the NL and the year-old American Association (AA). They devoted most of their attention to the Giants (NL). . . . The Giants played at the old Polo Grounds at 110th Street until 1889, when political pressure forced them to move north to a new site at 157th Street. A competition was established across the street in 1890 in the new Players' League, a cooperative venture of capitalists and players revolting against the reserve clause. The financial backers were prominent Republicans, who bought out the Giants in 1891 after the collapse of the Players' League. Tammany regained the Giants at the end of 1894, when Andrew Freedman, an intimate friend and business partner of Boss Croker, purchased the club for $48,000. Freedman held no elective office but wielded great influence through Croker and in his own right as a member of Tammany's powerful Finance Committee. In 1897, Freeman became treasurer of the national Democratic party. . . .

Freedman of the Giants used his clout to cower other owners, and sportswriters claimed that he then ran his team as a Tammany appendage. The object of considerable abuse from fans, the press, and fellow owners for mismanagement and encouraging rowdy baseball, and disappointed with his profits, Freedman decided to sell out after the 1902 season. Besides, he had more important matters to attend to, principally the construction of the New York subway system. He sold most of his stock for $125,000 to John T. Brush, an Indianapolis clothier. Brush had just sold his Cincinnati Reds baseball team to a local syndicate consisting of Mayor Julius Fleischmann, Republican Boss George B. Cox, and Water Commissioner August Herrmann, Cox's right-hand man. According to one journalist, Brush had been forced to sell out to the machine, which threatened to cut a street through the ballpark.

Despite the sale, the Giants remained the Tammany team. Still a minority stockholder, Freedman was more than willing to use his clout for the club. Brush died in 1912, and his heirs sold the team in 1919 for $1 million to Tammanyite Charles Stoneham, a curb-market broker of limited integrity. . . .

The Giants were enormously successful on the diamond in the early 1900s under [John] McGraw's management. They won six pennants from 1904 to 1917 and became the most profitable team in organized baseball. From 1906 to 1910 the club annually earned over $100,000, and by 1913 earnings surpassed $150,000. After World War I, baseball experienced an enormous boom in the city, largely because of the legalization of Sunday baseball. In 1920 the Giants established a league record $296,803 in profits. . . .

The Giants had Manhattan to themselves until 1903, when the rival American League (AL) secured a New York franchise. The junior circuit had failed to organize a New York team earlier because Freedman controlled virtually all the potential playing sites through his political power and real estate interests. Even after Croker was exiled to England on the heels of Seth Low's election as mayor in 1901, Freedman and his Tammany friends still had enough power to stymie any interlopers. . . .

. . . In March 1903 the AL granted a franchise to a syndicate headed by Joseph Gordon, a figurehead for the real owners—poolroom king Frank Farrell and former Police Chief William Devery. They soon constructed a field on a rock pile at 165th Street that Freedman apparently had ruled out as unsuitable for baseball. Devery and Farrell paid the local district leader $200,000 for excavation and another $75,000 to build a grandstand. . . .

The Highlanders (later known as the Yankees) failed to prosper, either on or off the field. . . . Devery and Farrell sold out in 1915 for $460,000 to brewer Jacob Ruppert, Jr., and C. Tillinghast Huston, a rich civil engineer. Ruppert was a prominent member of the sporting fraternity who bred and raced dogs and horses. A great fan of the Giants, he was a notable member of Tammany Hall, served on its Finance Committee, and had been selected personally by Croker in 1897 to run for president of the city council. . . . One year later he was chosen to run for Congress from a Republican district, was elected in an upset, and went on to serve four undistinguished terms. . . .

New York owners took advantage of their political connections to enhance their baseball operations in valuable ways. Clout was used to deter interlopers from invading the metropolitan area. Influence at city hall provided access to the best possible information about property values, land uses, and mass transit, all essential matters when teams built new ballparks. This was especially crucial once teams began constructing permanent, fire-resistant ballparks that cost in excess of $500,000. In 1911 the Giants built their new Polo Grounds in Washington Heights on the site of the old field that had burned down. . . . A decade later the Yankees moved into their own ballpark in the Bronx. . . .

Political connections facilitated various mundane but necessary business operations. Teams without such protection could find themselves vulnerable to political pressure and high license fees. Cities also provided teams with a variety of municipal services, including preseason inspections to check for structural defects in the ballparks. . . . The most important ongoing service was police protection. Officers were needed to maintain order among those waiting to get into the park, keep traffic moving, and prevent ticket scalping. Inside the grounds, police prevented gambling and kept order among unruly spectators who fought with other fans, umpires, and even players. . . . New York teams got free police protection inside the grounds until 1907 when the reform commissioner Thomas A. Bingham stopped it. . . .

The prominence of professional politicians, particularly urban bosses, as promoters and facilitators of professional sports was not limited to New York. It was a nationwide pattern common to urban areas with a citywide machine and cities where the local ward machine model prevailed. . . .

As befitted their venal reputations, the machine politicians were especially prominent in prizefighting and horse racing, sports that operated under severe moral disapproval and widespread legal restrictions. In New Orleans, . . . John Fitzgerald [was] referee of the seventy-five-round bare-knuckle championship fight in 1889 between John L. Sullivan and Jake Kilrain. Fitzgerald was elected mayor in 1892 but was later impeached. After the sport was banned in New York in 1900, San Francisco became the major site of pugilism. Its leading promoters all were affiliated with Boss Abe Ruef, who received payoffs to guarantee licenses for staging bouts.

In horse racing, it was commonplace for proprietary tracks to be affiliated with political machines. Offtrack betting operations were always closely allied to urban bosses for the necessary protection. In New Jersey, for instance, racing in the early 1890s at the state's six major tracks was controlled by machine politicians. Although horse-race gambling was nearly always illegal, notorious outlaw tracks like Guttenberg and Gloucester operated with impunity, servicing the sporting fraternity from New York and Philadelphia. Gloucester was owned by Bill Thompson, the local political boss, while Guttenberg received its protection from the notorious Hudson County machine that enabled it to operate year-round. In Chicago, the racing center of the Midwest, certain track officials were so closely allied to the local machines that the sporting press claimed its horsemen were outdoing Tammany. The most flagrant example in the early 1890s was Garfield Park, a proprietary track owned by West Side bookmakers. Their political clout emanated from Mike McDonald, reputed head of syndicate crime; Bathhouse John Coughlin, boss of the infamous Levee District; and Johnny Powers, "Prince of Boodlers" in the city council and boss of the Nineteenth Ward. These political connections were also important in Chicago's bookmaking circles, since nearly all the handbook operators were tied to local ward machines.

The national pastime was not as tightly controlled by machine politicians as either prizefighting or horse racing, but nonetheless, professional baseball was dominated by notable politicos. Historian Ted Vincent has found that politicians made up nearly half of the 1,262 officials and stockholders of the nineteenth-century ball clubs he studied. . . . The pattern established in the nineteenth century continued until 1920. Between 1900 and 1920 every American and National League team's ownership included professional politicians, traction magnates, or friends or relatives of prominent power brokers. A similar situation existed in the minor leagues. . . . All the teams welcomed political connections as a means to protect the franchise against interlopers, to secure vital inside information from city hall, and to obtain preferential treatment from the municipal government.

Baseball best exemplified the pastoral world that white Anglo-Saxon Americans sought to maintain and protect in the face of industrialization, immigration, and urbanization. The sport helped to certify the continuing relevance of traditional values. But, paradoxically, baseball was in large measure controlled by men who typified all that mainstream America detested in the immigrant-dominated cities.

FURTHER READING

Paul Boyer, *Urban Masses and Moral Order in America, 1820–1920* (1978)

Dominick Cavallo, *Muscles and Morals: Organized Playgrounds and Urban Reform, 1880–1930* (1981)

Gerald R. Gems, *Sport and Culture Formation in Chicago* (1997)

Stephen Hardy, *How Boston Played: Sport, Recreation and Community, 1865–1915* (1982)

Stephen Hardy and A.G. Ingham, "Games, Structures and Agencies: Historians and the American Play Movement," *Journal of Social History* 17 (1983), 285–301

Bruce Kuklick, *To Every Thing a Season: Shibe Park and Urban Philadelphia, 1909–1976* (1991)

John A. Lucas, "Pedestrianism and the Struggle for the Sir John Astley Belt, 1878–1879," *Research Quarterly* 39 (1968), 587–95

Gerald Marsden, "Philanthropy and the Boston Playground Movement, 1885–1907," *Social Science Review* 35 (1961), 48–58

Michael P. McCarthy, "Politics and the Parks; Chicago Businessmen and the Recreation Movement," *Journal of the Illinois Historical Society* 65 (1972), 158–72

Steven A. Riess, *City Games: The Evolution of American Urban Society and the Rise of Sports* (1989)

Roy Rosenzweig, *Eight Hours for What We Will: Workers and Leisure in an Industrial City, 1870–1910* (1983)

Roy Rosenzweig and Elizabeth Blackmar, *The Park and the People: A History of Central Park* (1992)

Dale A. Somers, *The Rise of Sports in New Orleans, 1850–1900* (1972)

Ted Vincent, *The Rise and Fall of American Sport: Mudville's Revenge* (1994)

CHAPTER
7

Sport and Class, 1870–1920

Although historians do not consider the issue of class as an essential factor in the shaping of American history compared to the European experience, they do recognize its importance as a variable. Most people in this era were manual laborers, followed by a large middle class of white-collar workers and farm owners. The upper class comprised the richest five percent of Americans who owned about a third of the total national wealth. Their standards of taste and refinement were established by a small elite of well-born white Anglo-Saxon Protestants who came from old money, married into the most distinguished families, and had access to power. What was the impact of this social structure upon American sporting practices? In particular, how did income and discretionary free time determine sporting options? How did social status influence sporting choices?

The upper class, whose members had the broadest options in selecting their favorite recreations, preferred very expensive sports that were inaccessible to people of lower social rank. They used their sporting participation to certify their high social status and separate themselves from the upper middle class. Contemporary social critic Thorstein Veblen disparagingly characterized their behavior with the term "conspicuous consumption."

The middle classes had opposed the antebellum sport of the male bachelor subculture because it was immoral, debilitating, and not recreational. However, middle-class interest in sports grew with the development of modern sports and the articulation of a sports creed that rationalized sports as a positive social force. The middle classes had sufficient discretionary income, leisure time, and access to sporting facilities to become very active in physical culture.

Lower-class Americans also participated in sports, but under significant limitations during this era. Artisans in the preindustrial era had considerable control over their pace of work and free time. What was the impact of the rise of the factory system on wages, working conditions, and leisure time? Industrialization at first had a negative impact on working-class participation as certain jobs like shoe-making were de-skilled and as all workers lost control over the workplace and the pace of work. By the late nineteenth century, 85 percent of industrial workers were semiskilled or unskilled. They earned low wages and worked extremely long hours, usually six days a week, and they lived in inner-city slums. How did these conditions affect their sporting opportunities? On the other hand, craftsmen (who worked shorter hours for higher pay) and blue-collar city employees, like *policemen, encountered relatively few hindrances in their leisure activities. After the turn of the century, hours of work declined in most industries, but it was not until the 1920s, when most workers enjoyed significantly higher standards of living, that blue-collar Americans could enjoy a full choice of sporting pleasures.*

⚾ D O C U M E N T S

The first two documents examine two aspects of upper-class sport. Caspar Whitney, a noted late nineteenth-century journalist who specialized in high-status sports, explores the nature of the exclusive country club where the rich could separate themselves from lesser groups in a convivial atmosphere. Though the country club was important for both men and women, exclusive hunting lodges were solely for rich men. Hunting in and of itself was hardly an elite activity, but as the article on hunting illustrates, the rich could make it an exclusive sport by stalking game in relatively inaccessible sites or private preserves with well-paid private guides.

The third document examines the reasons for the cycling fad, which became an enormously popular middle-class pastime in the early 1890s. Cycling had previously been a very difficult sport to master until the invention of the English safety bicycle, which had two equal-sized tires.

The final two documents examine aspects of working-class sport. Picnic games were sponsored by ethnic groups, labor unions, and political organizations. These popular working-class outings were composed of athletic competition and social activities such as dinner-dances. The fourth document is a critical report of the annual picnic games of New York's printers, whose events were usually well organized. Editor William B. Curtis of The *Spirit of the Times* had been a founder of the prestigious New York Athletic Club, and he took a snobbish view of working-class athletics. The final document is an examination of elite working-class sports clubs. It is often forgotten that there were outstanding athletic clubs like the Pullman Athletic Association that were composed largely of working-class athletes, or that several American gold medal winners in the early 1900s were policemen. The high-status athletic clubs of the late nineteenth century rarely admitted working-class athletes, regardless of their physical prowess. In the early 1900s, highly skilled blue-collar athletes, some of whom competed and won Olympic medals, formed their own sports clubs, usually under the auspices of ethnic organizations.

Caspar W. Whitney Probes the Evolution of the Country Club, 1894

. . . The history of the country club, as much as anything else, bears witness to our tendency to superlative development. From having not a single country club in the entire United States of America twenty-five years ago, we have . . . in half that period, evolved the handsomest in the world. . . . The country club has done

---

From Caspar Whitney, "Evolution of the Country Club," *Harper's New Monthly Magazine* 90 (December 1894): 16–33.

appreciable missionary work in bringing us in contact with our fellows, where another than the hard business atmosphere envelops us, and in enticing us for the time being to put aside the daily task.

. . . Country-club benefits remain so abundant as not to be easily computed. . . . It has at the same time cultivated a love of out-doors for itself, and stood as the rallying point for every sport in America in which the horse is a factor. Modern organized hunting in America began in 1877 with Queens County drag hounds . . . and immediately found support from the men who afterwards made country clubs possible; so also with polo, introduced in '76; and pony-racing, first centralized under an association in '90. Probably coaching and driving generally, however, have profited most by the country club. . . . With the creation of country clubs long drives became a possible and delightful feature of the year. . . .

Only a careful study of our country's history and its social traditions will give us a full appreciation of what the country club has done for us. It has, first of all, corrected to a large extent the American defect of not being able or at least not willing to stop work and enjoy ourselves: it has brought together groups of congenial, cultivated people. . . .

It is impossible to overestimate the blessings of the country club in adding comforts to country living that before were utterly unattainable, and in making it possible to enjoy a degree of that rural life which is one of England's greatest attractions. . . .

. . . The need of a rendezvous was . . . realized in the establishment, in 1882, of the Brookline Country Club, the first of the genus in America, albeit some of the hunting clubs had been and are to this day filling a similar sphere.

Probably the country club has rendered its greatest service in tempting us out of doors, and cultivating a taste for riding and driving that has so largely benefited both sexes. With the evolution of the country club we have been developing into a nation of sportsmen and sportswomen. Indeed, sport of one kind or another and the origin of the country club are so closely connected, it is exceedingly difficult to decide which owes its existence to the other. It may be asserted that country clubs, generally speaking, have been created by the common desire of their incorporators to make a home for amateur sport of one kind or another. Some grew directly out of sport, as, for instance, the Country Club of Westchester County, which was originally planned for a tennis club, the Rockaway, Meadow Brook, and the Buffalo clubs, that were called into existence by the polo and hunting men. Others owe their existence to a desire to establish an objective point for drives and rides, and a rendezvous within easy access of town like the Brookline and Philadelphia Country clubs. Others have been called into being as the centralizing force of a residential colony, as Tuxedo. . . .

If sport has not been the *raison d'être* of every club's establishment, it is at all events, with extremely few exceptions, the chief means of their subsistence. Practically every country club is the centre of several kinds of sport, pursued more or less vigorously as the seasons come and go. . . .

The intrusion of "fashion," so called, into some of our choicest summer resting-places has robbed them of all that charm which superb scenic surroundings and relief from society's conventionality formerly gave. One goes into the country in summer to rest and be rid of the set scene of the winter functions. Newport has long been given over to society's star performers, and to simple-minded provincials who journey thither to gape at the social menagerie. . . .

. . . The one distinguishing feature of the country club . . . is its recognition of the gentle sex, and I know of none where they are not admitted either on individual membership or on that of *paterfamilias*. . . .

It is the sporting side of the country club, however, that gives it life and provides entertainment for its members: the club and our sporting history are so closely interwoven as to be inseparable. Polo, hunting, and pony-racing owe to it their lives, and to the members we are largely indebted for the marked improvement in carriage horseflesh during the past five years. They founded the horse show, made coaching an accepted institution, and have so filled the year with games that it is hard to say whether the country-club sporting season begins with the hunting in the autumn or with tennis in the spring, for there is hardly any cessation from the opening to the closing of the calendar year.

Once upon a time the country was considered endurable only in summer, but the clubs have changed even that notion: all of them keep open house in winter, some retain a fairly large percentage of members in residence, and one or two make a feature of winter sports. Tuxedo holds a veritable carnival, with tobogganing, snow-shoeing, and skating on the pond, which in season provides the club table with trout. . . .

Spring opens with preparations for polo, lawn-tennis, and yachting. Not all country clubs have polo and yachting, but every one has courts, and several hold annual tournaments that are features of the tennis season, and where the leading players are brought together. . . .

All the clubs dabble in live-pigeon trap-shooting, which is regrettable, for it is unsportsmanlike, to say nothing of the cash prizes, professionalizing the participants. It is a miserable form of amusement and unworthy the name of sport. . . . Hunting and polo in the early days constituted the sole sport of the country club members, but the introduction of other games in the last five years has divided the interest that was once given to them entirely. . . .

Probably the most characteristic country-club scene, however, is created by the pony-race meetings given on the tracks with which several of the clubs are provided. Here there is ample opportunity for the hysterical enthusiasm so dear to the feminine soul, and plenty of time between events for them to chatter away to their hearts' content. Here, too, there is the certainty of seeing one's friends not only in the carts and on top of the coaches that line the course, and on the temporary little grand stand, erected for the near-by residents of the club colony, but frequently riding the ponies. . . .

. . . On such an occasion the social and sporting sides of the club are revealed at their best. Turn your back to the race-course and you well might fancy yourself at a huge garden party. . . .

As the eldest and one of the most picturesquely located, the Country Club of Brookline deserves precedence. It had its origin in J. Murray Forbes's idea of an objective point for rides and drives, and was organized in 1882. No other club possesses a hundred acres of such beautiful land within such easy access, for it is only five and a half miles from the State House, and can be reached from Boston without going off pavement, and, better still, in its immediate neighborhood none of the rural effects have been marred.

The club-house, originally a rambling old building, is very picturesque, and has been enlarged from time to time to meet requirements. Its piazza overlooks the race-course, in the centre of which is one of the best of polo fields. Before the organization of the club the Myopia Hunt, then in its infancy, held steeple-chase meetings on its property. . . . There is a shooting-box, where clay pigeons are used, a toboggan-slide, golf-course, and good tennis-courts, both grass and gravel. . . .

Who shall deny the country club to have been a veritable blessing, what with its sport and pleasure and health-giving properties that have brushed the cobwebs from weary brains, and given us blue sky, green grass, and restful shade in exchange for smoke-laden atmosphere, parboiled pavements, and the never-ceasing glare and racket of the city? And womankind too has partaken of country-club as she should of all blessings, in relaxation from the petty trials of house-keeping, and the parade and deceits of "society," while the hue of health has deepened in her cheeks. It has been a wholesome growth all round. Beginning life as somewhat of a novelty, the country club has become so familiar an institution that we wonder, as about the New York elevated railway, how we ever managed to get on without it.

The *Chicago Daily News* Describes a Paradise for Hunters, 1895

This is the time of year when the millionaire sportsman gets his hunting traps in shape and prepares for a month or two of sport in some wild section of the country where he can doff the habiliments of conventionality and roam at will in the wild woods searching for the kind of "game" he fancies most.

The American hunter has a big advantage over his English cousin, notwithstanding the boasted game preserve and hunting estate of the latter, which have been handed down by many generations. It costs a mint of money to support one of these estates and endless bother, with oftentimes a barren season of shooting as a result.

For a very moderate sum the sportsman here can belong to a fine hunting club and have the use of tens of thousands of acres of land, a finely appointed clubhouse to lodge in at night and many congenial spirits always on hand to while away the indoor hours. There are other clubs to which only a millionaire can afford a membership, but the sport is hardly a bit better than that to be had from the more moderate affairs.

There are hundreds of fine shooting preserves in the country to-day and the number is constantly being added to. Millions of acres are under the control of able game guardians. In the Adirondack region alone, the hunting grounds of the New

---

From "A Paradise for Hunters," *Chicago Daily News*, October 1, 1895, p. 7, cols. 1, 2.

York millionaire, there are 1,000,000 acres controlled and owned by shooting clubs.

The finest thing of the kind in the land is located at Jekyl Island, on the Georgia coast, near Brunswick. It has been estimated that the combined wealth of the members of this club reaches the stupendous sum of $1,000,000,000. The island is crescent-shaped, about twelve miles in length and two in width and holds the best game to be found anywhere on the coast. . . .

Jekyl Island is really a sportsman's paradise. The clubhouse had the appearance of a huge castle and is maintained with princely splendor. It is a four-story structure of brick, with a tower extending twenty-five feet above the roof. From this tower a view can be had of the whole island, the mainland and the ocean. There are seventy-eight rooms in the house, all gorgeously furnished. . . .

The island is full of wild turkeys, snipe, woodcock, and quail and there are large numbers of deer and wild hogs. The duck shooting there is also fine. Fishing in the surrounding waters is the easiest kind of sport. Recently many foreign varieties of birds have been placed on the island and when they become more plentiful will add to the varieties of the sport.

The easterly end of Long Island abounds with shooting preserves and the first shooting club to be organized in the country was established there. It was called the South Side Sportsmen's club and 1,600 acres near the now fashionable town of Islip were purchased.

Of recent years Long Island has almost been done to death in a hunting sense, but there are still deer to be found in the thick woodlands, while the duck and quail shooting is only fair. A well equipped fish hatchery is located near the large clubhouse and the streams are kept abundantly stocked. The trout fishing to be had there ranks with the best, and this is the favorite sport of the members. . . .

Of the individual hunting grounds, those of W. Seward Webb in the Adirondack region, comprising 75,000 acres, are about the finest in the country. Dr. Webb calls his estate Ne-Ha-Se-Ne park and during the season his fine house there is always filled to overflowing. He keeps an immense arsenal of hunting weapons always on hand for the convenience of his guests and large kennels stocked with all varieties of dogs of the chase. With the wealth of the Vanderbilts at his disposal, he conducts everything on a lavish scale and the rough guides of the Adirondacks are kept in a perpetual state of astonishment at the amount of money the New York swells spend to shoot a deer, whose market value may be $12.

. . . Austin Corbin . . . spends most of his shooting season at his own estate, called Blue Mountain Forest park near Newport, N.H. The estate comprises 26,000 acres and the owner has spent tens of thousands of dollars in stocking it. . . .

He has 500 deer . . . and 300 wild boars. There are 90 moose and 450 elk, besides vast numbers of German hares, Chinese pheasants and the game native to the region. The animals have such a vast area of country to roam over that they are wild and timid and afford splendid sport in the chase. None of the buffalo are hunted, as they are such easy marks with the long-range rifles of to-day that it would be pure slaughter to kill them; besides Mr. Corbin's sole purpose is to increase their number.

Philip G. Hubert, Jr., Reflects on the Bicycle:
The Marvel of Its Day, 1895

. . . When one begins to tell why the bicycle is one of the great inventions of the century, it is hard to begin, because there is so much to say. A bicycle is better than a horse to ninety-nine men and women out of a hundred, because it costs almost nothing to keep, and it is never tired. It will take one three times as far as a horse in the same number of days or weeks. In touring with a bicycle I can make fifty miles a day as comfortably as twenty miles on foot, and I can carry all the clothing I need, besides a camera and other traps. The exercise is as invigorating as walking, or more so, with the great advantage that you can get over uninteresting tracts of country twice as fast as on foot. In fact, as any bicyclist knows, walking seems intolerably slow after the wheel; even easy-going tourists, with women in the party, can make forty miles a day and find it play. Perhaps even greater and more important than its use as a touring machine is the bicycle as an every-day help to mechanics, factory hands, clerks, and all people who live in or near small towns. Thanks to this modern wonder, they can live several miles away from their work, thus getting cheaper rents and better surroundings for their children; they can save car-fares and get healthful exercise. For the unfortunate dwellers in cities it offers recreation after working-hours and induces thousands who would never walk to get out into the air and find out for themselves that life without out-door exercise is not living.

How tremendous has been the change in the fortunes of the nickel-plated steed within the last five or six years. . . . The bicycle was still a toy five or six years ago. Half a dozen manufacturers exhibited their wares, and the pneumatic tire, then a curiosity imported from England, was viewed with interest, but much doubt as to its practical usefulness. The wheel was still something of a curiosity as a machine for grown men, while women who braved public opinion far enough to ride one in public were looked upon with suspicion.

The high 52-inch wheel, upon which the rider perched himself at the risk of his neck, was still the only one in common use, and had the "Safety" pattern not appeared, it is pretty certain that we should see but little more of the bicycle now than we did then. When I look at the high wheel to-day I rather wonder that any one was ever reckless enough or skilful enough to ride it. It was a matter of weeks to learn to get on it at all, and of months to ride it well; many persons who tried gave it up after a few bad falls. At best the big wheels of a few years ago were fit only for athletic young men; they were out of the question for all other persons and of course for women. . . . When a wheel was offered that anyone—man, woman, or child—could learn to ride well inside of a fortnight; that exposed the rider to no dangerous falls while learning, and that possessed all the speed of the high wheel with none of its dangers, then, seemingly, every one began to talk bicycles. Now

From Philip G. Hubert, Jr., "The Bicycle: The Wheel of To-day," *Scribner's* 17 (June 1895): 692–97.

no one is too old or too young to ride a "Safety," and the woman who objects to bicycling is soon likely to be looked upon as more eccentric than her sister who skims along the road in bloomers.

While the "Safety" pattern made the bicycle possible to everyone, of course the pneumatic tire is a great invention. . . . Its purpose is not merely to act as a spring or cushion, but much more. . . . Upon a perfectly smooth board floor less power was required to propel a steel-rimmed wheel than one with a pneumatic tire. But let a few fine pebbles be sprinkled upon the track and then the power required for the steel tire had to be doubled and even tripled, while that for the pneumatic tire required only a slight increase. . . . With the pneumatic tire the pebble simply makes a dent in the soft tire, which passes over it without rising. A country road, or almost any road except a smooth floor, offers to the wheel a succession of minute obstacles. . . .

Various estimates have been made of the output of bicycles for 1895, the figures running as high as four hundred thousand. The sales of wheels last year are said to have been two hundred and fifty thousand. It is generally reported that the business has taken a sudden jump within the last six months, and almost all the manufacturers have been running their factories night and day. . . .

In one respect the bicycle show was peculiar; all classes seemed to be represented. At the horse show, for instance, or the dog show, the mechanic is never seen; at the bicycle show I noticed hundreds of men, evidently prosperous mechanics, who had come to see more of a machine that offered tham at once economy and recreation, a healthful exercise and a saving of car-fares in getting to and from their daily work. . . .

I was glad to find a manufacturer who would admit that we should some day get good machines for less than $50. Personally I am satisfied that a poor bicycle is a most costly affair. At the same time, the price asked for the best machines, although it has dropped this year from $150 to $125 for specials, and from $125 to $100 for standards, still seems out of proportion to the actual cost. It is . . . hard to see why a good bicycle cannot be sold at a fair profit for $50 or less. Probably when the supply catches up with the demand it will be. This year's cut in prices is a promise of better things to come. . . .

The *Spirit of the Times* Denigrates the Printer's Benevolent Association Games, 1887

New York City, Aug. 13. —Their annual "Picnic Games," held Saturday last, compared in every respect, very unfavorably with those of preceding years. Owing to a boycott placed upon the Empire City Colosseum by the labor unions they were unable to secure these very desirable grounds, and those they did secure were abominable. The track, twelve laps to a mile, was a caricature; it was evidently intended

From *Spirit of the Times* 114 (October 1, 1887): 342.

to represent a cinder path, for all sorts and conditions of cinders were strewed around indiscriminately, forming mountainous hillocks and undulating valleys. No attempt has been made to pack this refuse, and at one particularly bad turn the contestants actually sank to above their ankles. Of course, even fair time was out of the question on such a track, and therefore the times given herewith must be viewed with a suspicion, especially Burkhardt's time in the mile walk, during which I believe the timekeeper forgot to tally one of the minutes as they flew by, owing to an anxious state of mind. . . .

The management was on a plane with the track—"preserving the unities," as it were. It was far worse than the usual picnic order, and chaos reigned from beginning to end. Sam Austin was down on the program as referee, but having last year's experience in mind, was conspicuous by his absence. They finally induced a meek, inoffensive sort of a chap to accept the position, and then proceeded to make life weary to him. The first snag he ran against was a burly six-footer who was dissatisfied with the handicap a friend of his had received; and insisted on the referee changing it then and there. He was with difficulty convinced that wiping the ground with the referee wouldn't bring about the desired change. Then the contestants "kicked" about the track; insisted that the referee should procure a roller and pack the track. As the nearest roller was at the old New York A.C. grounds, fully a mile away, the poor fellow was somewhat justified in refusing this rather unreasonable request. Then the Pastime party fell foul of him. It seems that McNally, the Pastime's distance runner, had sent an entry for the 2 mile run, but it had come too late. The Secretary of the Association had sent back McNally's money with the information that the entries were closed. Nevertheless, McNally came up prepared to run, and the referee was besieged by the crowd, urging him to let McNally start, even under protest. Here was a man whose entry had not been accepted, and still they endeavored to bulldoze the referee into letting him start. They got him decidedly "rattled." First he decided that McNally could start; then he decided that he couldn't; then he asked the other competitors whether they would allow McNally to start, which, of course, they wouldn't. After consulting two or three dozens of people he finally came to the conclusion that McNally could not start. And this referee is a member of one of our most prominent athletic clubs! Well may *The SPIRIT* say that nine-tenths of the amateurs know nothing of athletic laws.

"Billy" Robertson was down as starter, but when he heard of all the bright and beautiful young women that were going to the Best & Co "excursion games" he basely absconded. But he sent a substitute. Now, whether this is one of the "Sparrow's" practical jokes, or whether he meant to let us see what a really good starter W.H. Robertson is in comparison with others, is not plain to me. But the substitute's sufferings were. I really never saw such an unwieldy, pugnacious pistol before. It was in a continuous struggle with the starter all day. . . .

What the timing would have been under favorable circumstances I do not know. But timing was attempted, under circumstances not at all conducive to correctness. Mr. Sullivan, President of the Pastime A.C., who officiated, or attempted to officiate, as timekeeper, is the fortunate possessor of an elegant gold stop watch, presented by the members of the Pastime A.C. as a mark of esteem to their president, and naturally he values it highly. Mr. Hemment, the amateur walker, lost a valuable gold stop watch at picnic games a short while ago, and this caused a slight uneasiness in Mr. Sullivan's mind as he noticed the circumstance. This uneasiness was intensified as he noticed half a dozen decidedly tough-looking strangers crowding him continually, asking the time on the slightest pretext and endeavoring to catch a glimpse of the watch in his hand. He only clutched the watch tighter at these questions, . . . He finally called several of his friends to his aid, among them P. O'Keefe, the champion slugger of the club, and requested them to stick to him as closely as the would-be highwaymen did. These hung on for quite a while, but finally gave it up and left him. Long before this Sullivan had passed the watch to O'Keefe and was timing the events by one of those cheap nickel watches, and, not being accustomed to it, made guesses at the time, which is, therefore, not to be depended upon. Two of the suspected parties afterward appeared in costume, giving exhibitions of broad jumping and passing the hat. Several of the spectators recognized in one the famous professional jumper, Hamilton.

There was a very poor class of amateurs in the events, mainly picnic "fiends." The prizes were exceptionally valuable and attractive. Athletes do not seem to thrive among the printers, as in their four exclusive events only nine men were entered.

Charles J. Lucas Criticizes the Commercialization of Amateur Athletics, 1906

The Amateur Athletic Union is a national organization intended to maintain and to regulate non-professional athletics throughout the country. . . . The national Amateur Athletic Union is in the hands of a board of governors representing . . . various associations. . . . The controlling interest resides in New York and, to be more particular, in the hands of the Metropolitan Union. This body in turn is largely under the control of Mr. James E. Sullivan, secretary-treasurer of the Amateur Athletic Union.

. . . The Amateur Athletic Union has done large service to the cause of amateur sport. This was particularly true when territorially athletics were limited to the cities lying east of the Alleghenies. The new prominence of western universities and athletic clubs has, however, given rise to a number of rather distressing situations. Furthermore there have been at work certain very marked tendencies making for the commercializing of the athletic club and its athletes. As a result the A.A.U. to-day is in serious need of reformation. . . . It is provincial rather than national; it can not control the action of athletic clubs belonging to the Metropolitan district; and it is becoming increasingly a creature of a business house. . . .

Fred Lorz, a member of the Mohawk Athletic Club, New York City, who tried to steal the Marathon race at the Olympic Games in St. Louis in 1904, was suspended for life by the Amateur Athletic Union. Eight months later he was reinstated through the efforts of eastern men on the ground that he was temporarily

From Charles J. Lucas, "Commercializing Amateur Athletics," *World Today* 10 (1906): 281–85.

insane. This reinstatement was in the face of affidavits by George Hench, St. Louis correspondent of the Associated Press . . . and Mrs. J.T. Beals, official photographer of the Fair, and myself. We all saw Lorz riding in an automobile and talked with him as he ran in the race after riding eleven miles. . . .

For a number of years the New York Athletic Club had dominated eastern amateur sport. Year after year the Mercury foot representatives had captured A.A.U. championships until the fall of 1903, when John Flanagan and other crack men were dropped by the New York Athletic Club. Then it was that the Greater New York Irish Athletic Club was organized with James E. Sullivan as its first president, and the now notorious Celtic Park, Long Island was selected as the home of the club. It was not long before Mr. Sullivan became tired of the position and believing in pure amateur sport resigned his position. The club went after the best men in the districts, securing Myer Prinstein, who forsook the honest Twenty-second Regiment Engineers' team for the Irish team; Martin Sheridan of the Pastime Athletic Club, one of the oldest and most honored A.A.U. Clubs, and a number of other athletes.

It was not long before the New York Athletic Club saw its boasted supremacy threatened. In 1904 the Irishmen won both the junior and senior A.A.U. championships at St. Louis. With the backing of Tammany, the Irishmen began a war on Mr. Sullivan in the hope that he would permit them to carry on match races at Celtic Park, which, from an amateur standpoint were impossible. . . .

And now will come the worst attack upon amateur sport ever witnessed. The Greater New York Irish Athletic Club has a number of sinecures in the way of government jobs at its disposal for college men, together with huge gate receipts at Celtic Park. The New York Athletic Club has a sumptuous clubhouse and beautiful Travers Island, not to mention various sinecures put at its disposal through the kindness of members who want victory at any cost. Who will win? The Irish club has already secured Hymen, formerly of Pennsylvania, who has a government job on Long Island. Amateur sport has got to such condition in and around New York that resort is made to the courts when A.A.U. officials legislate so as to displease the Tammany crowd. . . .

A decided detriment to amateur sport throughout the United States is the control of A.G. Spalding & Brothers over the Amateur Athletic Union. . . . The Spalding discus is the official discus; the Spalding basketball is the official ball . . . ; the Spalding football is the official ball for intercollegiate contests.

Last spring Garrells, of Michigan, made a world's record with a discus not of the Spalding manufacture. Mr. Sullivan promptly stated that the record would not be allowed. . . .

Mr. J.E. Sullivan is secretary-treasurer of the national Amateur Athletic Union. He is also president of the American Sports Publishing Company, by whom is published the Spalding Athletic Library, one of the most effective mediums for advertising the Spalding products. . . . He is commonly considered as being the general manager for advertising of A.G. Spalding. . . . And finally, it was Sullivan who prevented the exhibition in the Physical Building at St. Louis of any athletic and gymnastic equipment except that manufactured by A.G. Spalding & Brothers.

◉ E S S A Y S

Each of these essays examines aspects of the sporting experience of different social classes. The first, by Donald Mrozek of the Department of History, Kansas State University, discusses how ultra-rich Americans utilized their wealth to promote their particular sporting interests. They were not interested in sport to regenerate themselves but to display their wealth and status. The second essay by Steven A. Riess focuses on middle-class sport. Riess examines the process by which middle-class men began relying upon sports as a means for defining their manliness. During the nineteenth century when the middle classes shunned sport because it represented anti-Victorian values, respectable men gained their sense of manliness from hard work, marriage, and fatherhood. However, in the late nineteenth century, as they became less independent in their careers, and as sport became a positive social force, these men turned to sport to demonstrate their masculinity. The third essay, by independent scholar Ted Vincent, grew out of a sports history produced in radio station KPFA, Berkeley, California, in 1975 and 1976. Vincent, in his book *The Rise and Fall of American Sport: Mudville's Revenge* (1994), analyzes how sport has been influenced from the bottom up. In this selection Vincent examines the influence of the masses upon late nineteenth-century professional track and field. Although track and field was perceived as a highly amateur sport, enjoyed for the pure love of competition, opportunities did exist for top athletes to earn a living at sport. At that time most Americans would consider the idea of working at play (except for baseball) to be "un-American."

Sporting Life as Consumption, Fashion, and Display— The Pastimes of the Rich at the Turn of the Century

DONALD MROZEK

It has been argued that the newly emerging class of extravagantly rich Americans whose wealth was rooted in industrial capitalism came to challenge the role of social leadership and political power of the traditional American gentility. Later historians have questioned the degree of antipathy between old and new wealth. But in sport, quantities of money meant the ability to govern the games that could be played. Although ultra-rich Americans did not dictate institutionalized sport among other classes, they made possible the emergence of certain sports that required large outlays of money for facilities and their maintenance. Most important in the interplay of varying attitudes about sport in the early twentieth century, the ultra-rich—the Vanderbilts, the Harrimans, and others—embodied an alternative sensibility about sport. They conducted it as a mode of consumption and as a fashion, and what regeneration they were likely to experience through sport flowed from its social outlets. That the remnant of the gentility, such as Roosevelt and Lodge, might have harbored such sentiments at an unconscious level is possible; but that they could have pursued them deliberately is nearly inconceivable. In this

From Donald Mrozek, *Sport and American Mentality, 1880–1910* (Knoxville: University of Tennessee Press, 1983), 103–35.

difference lay the curious contribution of the ultra-rich toward attitudes about sport. . . .

. . . Democracy of nearly any description had no place in the world of the very rich. Using their sports as badges of social status, the ultra-rich generally confined themselves to pursuits whose cost put them out of reach of ordinary Americans. Yachting, polo, fox-hunting, tennis, and golf—these were the characteristic sports of the American rich. Indeed, their penchant to use sport as a means of establishing social exclusiveness and prestige showed itself not only in the activities that they favored but in their departure from various sports that they could not control. . . .

In this passion for exclusiveness, the very rich, who sought means of certifying their worth, often made the criticisms of Thorstein Veblen seem a miracle of understatement. In the words of Price Collier, they were "a widely advertised, though fortunately small, class, diligent in making themselves conspicuous, who, having been recently poor, are trying to appear anciently rich." In a 1911 volume predicting their passing, Frederick Townsend Martin called them the "idle rich.". . . It was a criterion that differed fundamentally from the standards of duty and dedication to the public interest which held such deep appeal for middle- and upper-middle-class Americans. Yet the new ultra-rich were accorded a peculiar publicity; and, while excluding those of an inferior economic class from the scenes of their sport, they nonetheless assumed a certain paradoxical visibility, through which they became the embodiment of the quest for pleasure and self-gratification.

Simultaneously a source of personal amusement and a component of an exclusionary social system, the sports of the very rich industrial magnates and financiers were thus special in kind, special in place, and special in function. The characteristic sportive activities of the rich took place in distinctive environments shaped for their pursuit—whether a country club or even a whole compound such as at Newport, Rhode Island. Sport further served as a device for governing their etiquette and signifying their status. Ironically, the rich found their own way of giving meaning to Grantland Rice's maxim that what mattered was "how you played the game"; and social manners frequently predominated over athletic prowess in determining who really won or lost. Yet, for this reason, sport itself seemed all the more real, as it was tied to the very core of one's social goals and aspirations. Sport thus gained an added constituency that perceived it to have value, fastening on it as a nonproductive amusement and an instrument of display.

The Exclusionary Sports of the Rich

By the very sporting ventures they chose, the American rich set patterns of behavior that distinguished them from the masses and even from much of the respectable middle class. Infected with a desire to set fashion and keep pace with its mercurial changes, the wealthy elite often opted for the customs of the British upper classes—a phenomenon that showed itself in the sudden vogue of tennis and golf and invited satire in the rise of fox-hunting. A key means of distinguishing fashionable sport from common amusement was the price tag. Those requiring expensive and well-maintained facilities had a special appeal for the rich, who affected a lack of interest in the cost of their undertakings while glorying in the ability to pay it. It was the attitude of J. Pierpont Morgan who, when asked how much it cost to maintain his yacht, replied that anyone who had to ask could not afford one. Thus, the difference in dollars segregated the very rich from the majority of Americans, even if temperament might not always have done so. . . .

Although many advocates of pure amateurism from varying economic backgrounds were concerned to avoid excessive attention from journalists and sports fans lest it lead to commercialism and subversion of gentlemanly values, the desire for privacy harbored among the rich was another matter entirely. The seclusion of the country club, for example, halted not the corruption of American life but the dilution of upper-class society. Yet, while seeking privacy at one level, the rich invited public attention at another, partly because their exclusionary measures provoked idle curiosity and also because the magnificence of their display could hardly have escaped notice under nearly any circumstances. The first American country club, Brookline, opened in 1882 as a center for Boston's elite in polo, racing, and the hunt. Soon it added golf links, making available to its aristocratic membership yet another sport whose expense barred it from the common citizen. The Newport Country Club, spearheaded by sugar magnate Theodore A. Havemeyer, attracted founding members from the moneyed class such as Cornelius Vanderbilt, Perry Belmont, and John Jacob Astor. Similarly, men of wealth took the spotlight when they joined in 1908 to promote tournament play through the National Golf Links of America; and the roster of promoters included the fashionable names of William K. Vanderbilt, Harry Payne Whitney, and Henry Clay Frick. . . .

Among wealthy women, the same bias against workers and the common middle class appeared as among men. Anne O'Hagan's "Athletic Girl," described in *Munsey's Magazine* for August, 1901, had little truck with the common working woman. Even for O'Hagan, some gymnasiums seemed to set unreasonably steep and exclusionary fees. . . . [One gym] cost . . . a hundred dollars a year. Other clubs whose appointments were "less Sybaritic" charged membership dues on the order of forty dollars per year. O'Hagan rather blithely noted that, "if one has the distinction of being a working woman," ten dollars would suffice to obtain gymnastic instruction. Although O'Hagan found ten dollars an inconsiderable amount of money, the working girl for whom this represented a week's pay may have thought differently. Among many Americans, bodily exercise was still essentially a private matter; and the inaccessibility of gymnasiums on economic grounds meant the exclusion of large numbers of Americans from the kinds of activities that took place there. . . . As a result, glib pronouncements about the availability of gymnasiums with pillowed couches and well-trained maids said "Let them eat cake" to people who struggled for bread. . . .

Women of upper-class instincts and means thus tended to isolate themselves from the preponderance of Americans of their sex. Welcoming greater interest in sports and games, they nonetheless used it—perhaps unconsciously—in ways that only sharpened their distinctiveness from men and from working women. . . .

. . . Suggestive of the importance of class distinction, the desirability of tennis for women evidently stemmed from its social effects as much as from its hygienic benefits. According to Elizabeth C. Barney, . . . the enjoyment of tennis revolved around the "social intercourse" at the club house. The game strengthened and unified the community by drawing together the young people who played and the matrons who watched. . . . This sporting scene served as a common ground upon which women could develop social values, much as the sporting options open to men enabled them to realize their own ideals; but the codes for women differed from those of the men. For Elizabeth Barney and others of her station, tennis served to organize polite society and to put a healthy flush in its cheeks.

The flow of fashion which illuminated the wealthy woman's sporting habits extended into the physical trappings that surrounded them, such as clothing styles and accessories. In a society that prized conspicuous consumption and wasteful dress, the realm of sport had the advantage of adding a whole new set of activities for which special costumes could be devised and socially mandated. . . . Commentators promoted the wasteful and unproductive behavior that Thorstein Veblen termed conspicuous consumption, emphasizing the value of certain sports—often marginal sports, one might add, such as croquet and fencing—in enhancing the worth of woman as an object of pecuniary display.

The conduct of sports themselves became an object of fashion, and social grace competed—successfully—against athletic ability in the design and management of tournaments. In woman's events as in men's, strict control was exerted over admission to play in ostensibly national events. Elizabeth Barney, for example, reported that upper-class women were able to contribute "beautiful form" to the mixed doubles matches in tennis . . . at the country club; and they carried the same spirit over into tournament play. The *crème de la crème,* Barney noted, made their way, in 1894, to the Ladies' National Championship at the Philadelphia Country Club, which ranked with "the foremost in tone and social standing, and every thing that it does is in the best of style." The tournament operated on rules that ensured protection of the women competitors from contact with their social inferiors. Matches were determined by invitation only, in a way that openly violated the supposedly democratic quality of modern sport, and only those of "assured social position" would think to submit their names for screening. . . .

The enthusiastic and influential physical educator Dudley A. Sargent observed, in an article published in 1901, that fashion actually accounted for the rise and fall of many sports themselves, rather than merely the costumes for their pursuit. Archery and fencing, for example, would be pursued as "fads and be rushed for a few seasons, and then become obsolete." Obedient to society's edicts, the *beau monde* took up even serious sports as "the proper thing" and dropped them with equal unintelligence when style changed. . . .

Special Places for Special Sportsmen

Although there was a strong current in America toward sharing certain sports which were national in sweep and were usually conducted in public places, the new rich bucked the trend and created a more specialized environment for sports. The country club was their most repeated form, and lavish clubhouses designed by leading architectural firms served as centers of social interchange as well as focal points of golf and tennis. . . . Separated and distinct from work, sport had become an autonomous focal point in the life of the rich. Unlike middle-class Americans who claimed that sport ingrained in players those qualities that empowered them to do life's work, the rich favored sport for its inutility. Their country clubs, then, became symbols of a quite different, pleasure-oriented ethic, which was to make a major contribution to the American notion of leisure.

The physical segregation of sporting activities in a special place for their pursuit, which was an intrinsic feature of the country club, had equivocal implications. On the one hand, it suggested the isolation of play, as ritualized in the games at the club, from work. On the other hand, it made a comprehensive and interactive, if separated, system out of the activities which were conducted there. . . . In short, the sporting life of the rich thus assumed an institutional shape, one which affirmed the viability of sport as an autonomous enterprise and one whose very comprehensiveness helped to provide foundation for the belief that a man might even pursue sport as a calling and an independent source of meaning in one's life. . . .

. . . Many of the business features that had appeared in the earlier resorts were absent at Newport. Gambling went private, and even the admission of spectators to competitions in sports such as tennis was restricted on social grounds. Although the aim was to create an isolated playground for the rich in which social distinction exceeded athletic ability in the pursuit of diversion, the effect was also to lay the groundwork for the concept of the "destination resort". . . .

. . . Eager for acceptance among the more reputable classes, [John] Morissey evidently hoped to curry their favor by catering to their desire for amusement. He built lavish facilities at Saratoga which pampered his guests while adding to his own wealth; but he soon identified a restiveness among the patrons, who seemed to crave more elaborate, exciting, and active entertainments. He succeeded in enlisting the advice of the prominent New York stockbroker William R. Travers, whose ideas contributed much to the quality of the early racing seasons.

Whatever the motives of Travers, who was to become a leading figure in the social life of Newport, Morissey's interests in sport grew principally from his growing need to keep Saratoga a commercial success; and even his desire for social acceptance could not possibly be fulfilled unless he continued to attract the rich and wellborn as guests. . . .

The enclosure and definition of space, whether public or private, give it cultural and even ceremonial meaning. In the late nineteenth century, this process exemplified the passion for discipline and order in life that pervaded middle-class society, and it enhanced the sense of importance shown toward the activities pursued within it. With the establishment of the grand compound of the rich at Newport, there came upon the American scene such a defined and enclosed space that was devoted exclusively to leisure; and, although sport was not the only entertainment or amusement pursued within its confines, it occupied a major place and thus became integrated into the concept of leisure itself. Although this latter phenomenon prevailed only within a rarified community at the time, namely the very rich, it lent credence to an interpretation of the worth and respectability of sport that was quite different from what was encouraged by the middle class and the remnant of the gentility. In such a view, sport no longer needed to be a "healthful amusement" that readied one for work; it could become an end in itself, to be sought only as a means of diversion and pleasure.

The concentration of summer houses for the rich at Newport came largely during the last third of the nineteenth century, although it continued much later. In a process that began in 1859, Newport emerged as the summer social center of the "great American families," who had previously been scattered about in resorts of their own choosing. The gravitation toward Newport suggested a certain nationalization, or centralization, of America's rich upper crust; and this, in turn, was to lend itself to a standardization of behavior and amusements among the wealthy. . . . Even then, it was a refuge from the world and its troubles, or, somewhat more exactly, a world unto itself with its own cares and concerns. In a sense, even the absorption into the social rounds that became a staple of Newport's image and self-image furthered the sense of insulation from the practical affairs of business and politics, sharpening the sense of protective enclosure. . . .

Nonetheless, the annual renewal of social ties at Newport itself became a kind of competition, in which sporting events and social occasions became devices for the definition and measurement of status, as had not been the case before, except perhaps in the colonial Tidewater. The relationship applied within the social elite and also between wealthy society as a whole and the rest of America. In the great bulk of cases, the actual performance of athletic feats was less important than the grace and style with which people performed them; and instances in which competitive excellence was prized—notably in yachting—themselves hinged partly on the purchase of expensive, specially designed vessels and on the maintenance of a substantial crew and staff. Even in yachting, however, a social note obtained; and extravagant expenditures conspired with contempt for "new money" to govern participation in competition on the waters off Newport. The dedicated British yachtsman Sir Thomas Lipton was snubbed widely at Newport since he had made his money in trade, and much too recently at that. At least a generation or two was needed to separate the glamour of wealth from the tawdriness of its sources; and so the names of Oliver Belmont, Pierre Lorillard, Cornelius Vanderbilt, and E.J. Berwind loomed high over that of a mere British baronet. As rigid as they could be with outsiders, so were the sportsmen of Newport competitive among themselves, always seeking to put forward the best image and the most stylish display as a substitute for pedigree and as a proof of wealth.

The tendency of the rich at Newport to use sport as part of a whole system of leisure showed itself in their disdain for games that needed no more than an open field and a ball. Instead, they lavished their attention on pastimes that demanded much time, special facilities, expensive equipment, and, sometimes, extensive travel. Although the enthusiasm for yachting, lawn tennis, fox-hunting, and the like was often genuine, so was their social role. As J.P. Morgan put it succinctly, "You can do business with anyone, but you can go sailing only with a gentleman." The devotion of resources to sport and other aspects of leisure thus became more than an emblem of wealth, although it was assuredly that; it also became a means of delineating leisure as an institution whose complexity invited members of the wealthiest classes to pursue it as if it were life's very purpose.

This kernel of difference helps to account for the interest of the American rich in the sporting life of the British upper class. It has been suggested that American sport was largely an imitative extension of British sport. . . . Among the very rich the imitation ascended toward parody. The wealthy Americans aped what they thought to be the sporting traditions of the British upper class in an effort to stay in international fashion and to act convincingly as an American aristocracy by recreating the behavior of a confessedly leisured society. . . . Polo ponies were kept in lavish stables, sleeping on monogrammed linen sheets. (Oliver Belmont housed his ponies on the lower level of his own house because he could not bear to treat them as if they were not members of the family.) Pink-coated riders pursued the fox across the fields of disgruntled Rhode Island farmers. . . . The passion for things British, for example, encouraged the rich to show interest in lawn tennis, although the game's survival also depended on its suitability to the needs of the American rich. First brought to New York by Mary Outerbridge after a vacation in Bermuda, where she had observed the game played by British officers, tennis soon became a fixture of Newport's summer season. Partly because it brought the well-dressed spectators together at the Casino, Tennis Week—the informal name for the National Lawn Tennis Tournament—emerged as the most estimable sporting event of the season. The very choice of a grass surface gave it an air of greater style, since it required much more careful and costly maintenance than hard-packed clay. Players in the tournament, which was initiated in 1881, came from the ranks of social fashion. . . . Clad in knickers, blazers, and caps, they competed in a mild game, paced by "the genteel pat of the ball against languid strings." Richard D. "Dicky" Sears, who won the first championship match and held the title for eight consecutive years, came from a reputable Boston family; and he held a certain charm for the spectators who gathered behind ropes on camp-stools, watching him play with his tongue lapping out of his mouth somewhat like a napping dog's. Not until 1890 was a grandstand installed, nor were invitations to compete allowed by the Casino's board of governors to players outside the Newport social set until the turn of the century. As with the rest of Newport's summer activities, tennis was as much a matter of style as one of athletics.

Yet one should not miss the fact that this sense of sport—this definition of sport in terms of style, manners, and expression—allowed it a certain space as an autonomous variable and a separately observable force within the life of the rich. Special costume, special facilities, special identity among the players, special limits among spectators—all became a part of the landscape of sport as an independent branch of leisure. In the process of seeking to use sport to define themselves as a special aristocratic class, the American rich thus also did much to confirm the institutional status of sport itself, as an enterprise with facilities, rules, demands, and, above all, purposes of its own.

The Special Role of Sport for the Ultra-Rich

Although the ultra-rich pursued sport as a fashion, it was still something that could be a calling. In this regard, they veered sharply from the gentility. . . . Traditionalists such as Roosevelt found little to approve in the antics of the ultra-rich. Roosevelt never condoned the use of sport for purely personal purposes, arguing that it was a means through which one prepared for societal tasks. Yet, among the very rich, ever more elaborate trappings were forged in service of selfish goals, seeking to use material splendor as proof of personal importance. At the same time, however, the likes of Roosevelt also objected to the implications of the physical separation of the very rich from the great majority of Americans. . . . The very process of physical exclusion that showed itself in the growth of country clubs and in the development of the wealthy colony in Newport ran afoul of the gentility and the middle class, even as it made the undiluted pursuit of a sporting life a more credible and creditable option among the rich themselves. . . . For the very rich, however, the dignity of sport inhered in the lavishness of circumstance and in the impertinence of its pursuit. Truly, the ultra-rich were pioneers of sport as a leisure activity which required no justification. Precisely this, which so alienated and disgusted the traditional gentility because it seemed to debase sport by subordinating it to motives that were trivial because they were merely personal, constituted the major contribution of the turn-of-the-century rich to the development of twentieth century attitudes toward sport.

. . . The ultra-rich came to their sport partly from the vantage of excess "spare" time. . . . In an age that equated activity with life itself, it seemed senseless and unacceptable to fall into total indolence or passivity. It was in this context of the general need for the sensation of action and the specific need for the impression of economic inutility that the very rich helped to create the American sense of leisure. Contrary to Marx's sense that it was simply uncommitted spare time or rest, the wealthy American capitalist made leisure a rather exhausting round of organized amusements and consumer activities. Transcending or even just ignoring the traditionalists' focus on duty and service, the ultra-rich thus developed a sense of leisure and leisure time that was permeated by activities and suffused with an underlying conviction of the primacy of experience. It was insufficient to have free time, unless you showed it.

Nor was leisure convincing without material expression. Even as the common sense of what constituted the sports hero came to center on the primacy of deeds over virtues, so did the more general sense of a hero of culture center on action over character. In at least one of their guises, the rich thus did much to create the concept of the "sportsman." The very rich could establish influence—other than their manifest economic power—only by accumulating objects and by establishing a record of elitist activities. The absence of usefulness in sport was more than charming, then; for it made sport a superb instrument for the creation of leisure. Ironically, the wealthy Americans' emphasis on the intertwined goals of self-gratification, identity, relief from the tedium of a stultifying structured life, and expressive display resembled the supposed preferences of the laboring class more closely than those of the economic and social middle. In this way, the very rich helped to advance notions about sport and its role in purposeless leisure which would simultaneously compete with the middle class's concentration on the work-ethic and service and encourage the working class to see sport as a part of the American Dream. Like the very rich, workers could prove their achievement of leisure only by expressing this fact through action, as deeds increasingly assumed greater eloquence than words in the formulation of American ideas. Sport had become a fixture among the idle rich; and Americans who cherished a belief in upward material mobility were prone to follow the reigning models of the culture. . . .

The very clarity of the sporting system among the rich made it possible for them to avoid the ambivalence, ambiguity, and occasional sophistry that plagued the exponents of middle class and genteel virtues. Wealth—not virtue—was its own reward; and it was association with wealth that kept a sport worthy of further interest. At the same time, wealth served to guard and insulate a sport so that it remained not only limited in clientele but rarified in its social role. . . . Whatever social benefit the very rich saw in sport was "social" only in the small sense, serving to sharpen lines of status. But the effects of sport in individual gratification, in what Veblen called a renewed "clannishness," and in activity-oriented leisure were numerous and systemic. Untroubled by issues of moral purpose, the rich thus established the prototype of the sportsman as an unrestricted consumer.

What the defenders of the older tradition criticized as "monomania" in sport, whether among the rich or among the professionals, passed as a form of virtue among the ultra-rich. The wealthy Americans luxuriated in expensive yachts, "Sybaritic" clubs, and costly holidays. Yet the middle class and the gentility proved ineffective in stamping out their influence. In part, this may have been due to self-contradiction, as when Theodore Roosevelt expressed his belief that most men lived within forty-eight hours of a wilderness area and need only choose a companion to set out for a month in the wild. His glib prescription and its presupposition that the man could afford both the trip and any attendant loss of income suggest the limits of democratic thought and opportunity among the middle class and the gentility. At least the very rich made the best of it, turning a rather vulgar instinct for display into a form of candor. Thus impervious to the internally flawed arguments of their critics, the rich stood as a significant point of gravitation within the realm of sport and so also as a constituency lending sport an aura of legitimacy. It is an enduring irony that, given their privileged and powerful position, they had a largely radical effect, which finally touched the mass of Americans just as deeply as did the self-appointed protectors of American values.

Sport and the Redefinition of American Middle-Class Masculinity, 1840–1900

STEVEN A. RIESS

At the onset of the Victorian era, middle-class American men had little interest in sport or physical culture. They were shopkeepers, professionals, agents, clerks, and farmers—hard-working, devout, future-orientated individuals who had little precious free time to take away from the serious business of earning a living. With the exception of clerks, generally young men learning the business with the expectation of a future partnership or an entrepreneurial career, middle-class men were competitive workers who were their own bosses. They frowned upon the popular mass sports of the day as a waste of time, immoral, illegal and debilitating, which should be avoided at all costs. Yet by mid-century a respectable middle-class sporting culture was beginning to evolve, and after the 1870s, it boomed. The purpose of this article is to explain how middle-class men's concerns with their masculinity contributed to make sport an integral part of their lives. Sport redefined for them their sense of manliness and provided mechanisms to achieve it.

From Steven A. Riess, "Sport and the Redefinition of American Middle-Class Masculinity," *International Journal of the History of Sport*, 8 (May 1991): 5–22.

The Rise of a Respectable Middle-Class Sporting Culture, 1840–70

. . . Athletics and physical culture had historically always been an almost exclusively male activity, and prowess in sporting competitions had always been regarded as a mark of manliness which meant the possession of such characteristics as courage, determination, strength and vigour. At the start of the Victorian era, when the United States was overwhelmingly an agrarian society, the leading sportsmen were members of a traditionally orientated male bachelor sub-culture who lived on the frontier, in the South, or in a few crowded urban centers. The sporting fraternity was comprised of urban machine politicians, artisans, seasonal workers, Irish immigrants and men from the dregs of society along with young rakes from the social elite. They participated in sports for fun, to develop camaraderie, and to display their honor and manliness. Their favorite contests were blood and gambling sports that were usually illegal and reprehensible. The social ethic expressed by the pre-modern life-style and values of the male bachelor sub-culture was totally antithetical to the bourgeois ethos of early Victorians. A manly middle-class individual in the *ante-bellum* era gained his identity through work, not leisure, earned his money through hard work, not gambling, and was a good and steady provider for his family. He was reliable, independent, and resisted temptation. The manly middle-class American did not shun domesticity for the saloon or poolroom, but rather made family and home the centerpiece of his life.

Middle-class opposition to sport and physical culture began to wane in the 1840s and 1850s at a period when the country was starting to become modernized. As the United States began to undergo the processes of urbanization, industrialization, immigration, and 'civilization,' the nature of sport underwent substantial changes and began to appeal to urban middle-class needs and sensibilities. This development was the product of the role-models of immigrant and upper-class sportsmen, the evolution of new sports that were congruent with the values and behavior of the middle class, and, most of all, the influence of a new positive sports creed. This ideology was popularized by Jacksonian reformers who believed that non-violent, clean, gambling-free, outdoor physical exercise and sport would be socially functional activities that could counter the growing urban pathology and social anomie. . . .

. . . The ideology posited that participation in clean sport would improve public health, raise moral standards and build character; that clean sport would provide a substitute for the vile practices of the sporting fraternity; and that such rational recreations would encourage the development of sport among the sedentary middle class. Supporters of this physical-fitness movement came from a wide variety of interests, and included religious leaders like the Unitarian Rev. William Ellery Channing, Utopians like Robert Dale Owen, educators like Horace Mann, transcendentalists like Ralph Waldo Emerson, scientists like Dr. Lemuel Shattuck, physicians like Dr. Oliver Wendell Holmes, Sr., and health faddists like Sylvester Graham. . . .

. . . The severest critic of middle-class lassitude was Dr. Holmes, a noted oarsman in his own right, who . . . in an article entitled 'The Autocrat of the Breakfast Table,' denounced 'the vegetative life of the American' whom he compared unfavorably with the English gentry who had been a popular role-model for the

American elite since the colonial era. Holmes rated American college students poorly in comparison with the vigorous Oxbridge athletes, and recommended they learn from their English brothers who rowed and engaged in other sports. . . . Holmes foresaw a rapid decline of the race, certain that 'such a set of black-coated, stiff-jointed, soft-muscled, paste-complexioned youth as we can boast in our American cities never before sprang from loins of Anglo-Saxon lineage'. . . .

The advocacy of improved public health and the city's need for fresh air and space to play out-of-doors led to the development of a municipal park movement, based largely on British antecedents. . . .

The American park movement, . . . was led by journalists, . . . physicians, and scientists. . . . Their primary purpose was to improve the urban public's physical and mental health by providing access to fresh air, beautiful vistas, and playing space. The municipal park movement's first major achievement was New York's Central Park, which opened in 1858. The original design by Frederick Law Olmsted and Calvert Vaux set aside space for formal gardens and wooded areas for receptive recreation and areas for playgrounds and cricket fields for more active sports. Central Park was a huge success, and became a model for suburban parks across the country after the Civil War. . . . They were all situated far from the centers of population, expensive to get to by public transport, and at first stressed receptive over active recreation. Consequently the new parks were . . . a primarily middle-class resort.

The second function the new sports creed ascribed to clean sports was an ability to teach morality and promote the social order. Middle-class urbanites were confident they could transmit their high moral standards to their children but were concerned about the more exuberant behavior of lower-class urban youth. The growing impersonality of large heterogeneous cities seemed a far cry from the close-knit communities of mythical small-town America. Rising crime rates, periodic riots and rampant hooliganism reflected growing anomie and the erosion of basic values. . . . Middle-class moral guardians promoted moral leisure activities to curtail the behavior of working-class youth who were independent of the traditional customs and social controls that regulated village life and found themselves with ample opportunities for immoral commercialized entertainments. Rational recreations like sports and physical training were expected to provide a healthy alternative to such dissipating pastimes as drinking, fornication and gambling. . . .

The third element of the new sporting ideology was the presumed character-building qualities of competitive sports which was of great concern to the middle classes. Historian Melvin L. Adelman argues that this aspect of the sports creed developed in the 1850s as an adjunct to the morality thesis but became more prominent after the Civil War when sports participation was identified as a moral equivalent of war. The key to the character-building argument was the assumption that participation in sports promoted manliness. Sport was regarded as almost inherently a male sphere, inappropriate for Victorian women, and the contemporary press described nearly all sports as manly. Advocates of the sport creed not only believed that competitive sports engendered traits that were essential to middle-class success—self-discipline, self-denial, and even courage—but also that sedentary white-collar workers could utilize sports to demonstrate manliness which was widely identified with physical labor. Real men earned their keep by the sweat of their brow and the strength of their back. Athletes were real men who had graduated from childhood and were prepared for the battles of life or death (i.e., war).

The character-building qualities of sport were widely promoted by the apostles of muscular Christianity, an English-based philosophy that sought to harmonize the mental, physical and spiritual dimensions of man. . . .

The idea that a man who was moral and devout could and should also be physically fit tied in very well with prevailing middle-class values and the new sports creed. Hale, Higginson, Holmes and Ralph W. Emerson all became leading spokesmen for muscular Christianity. . . . Muscular Christianity was such a strong justification for sporting activities that it largely eliminated all but the most conservative pietistic opposition to athletics, especially when physical culture was sponsored by the evangelical Young Men's Christian Association (YMCA). The 'Y' movement began in England in 1844 and was brought to America seven years later to assist farm youth to adjust to urban life in a moral environment. By 1860 it was supporting moral athletics and gymnastics as 'a safeguard against the allurement of objectionable places of resort'. . . . In the late nineteenth century the YMCA became one of the most important facilitators of sport and physical training for middle-class youth and young men.

Sexuality was an essential, if implicit, aspect of the character-building element of the sporting ideology. Muscular Christians and other mid-Victorians saw sport as both a sexual substitute and a check on effeminacy, concerns that became increasingly important over the course of the nineteenth century. Sports reformers wanted to create a manly Christian gentleman who 'was the athlete of continence, not coitus, continuously testing his manliness in the fires of self-denial'. The middle classes not only disdained the sexual liberties of immoral members of the male bachelor sub-culture but were also worried about a loss of sexual energy and sperm which were believed to have a finite, irreplaceable limit. Sport would provide an alternative expenditure of energy and help build manliness which would give young men the strength to resist the 'secret vice' (masturbation). Moral men could earn their manhood on the playing field instead of the bedroom.

Clean sport was viewed by contemporaries as a means to counter effeminacy. In 1859 the *New York Herald* attributed the feminization of culture in part to the absence of sports in America. . . . Through sport men would retain such physical qualities as ruggedness and hardiness instead of degenerating into foolish fops. It was manliness the nation needed, not flabby sick weaklings, if it was to fulfill its destiny.

At mid-century middle-class young men who were convinced by the new sports creed that physical culture was an excellent and useful activity had a number of options to choose for their recreation. They nearly always preferred sports, usually competitive sports, to mere exercise, because callisthenics were boring and no fun. Virtually any sport that did not rely on gambling for its appeal or brutalize other men or beasts was regarded as appropriate for respectable, forward-looking, middle-class men or individuals with middle-class aspirations. But unless the activity was 'manly', requiring a high level of dexterity, physical skill and courage, and not played by women, it could not be a character-building game. . . . Bicycle-riding was originally a manly sport, but became less so over time as the vehicle was modernized and roads were improved. In the late 1860s riding a velocipede, or 'boneshaker', could be construed as manly because it was so difficult to master and so uncomfortable to ride. Similarly, it took a 'man' to master the ordinary bicycle, the odd-shaped vehicle introduced in 1876 with a huge front wheel and tiny rear wheel, on dangerous poorly constructed roads. However, once technological innovations had produced the safety bicycle of the 1890s, which was light and easy to maneuver, riding became a popular fad among millions of Americans including middle-class women. Hence cycling was only manly under certain conditions such as when 'scorching' (speeding), or participating in strenuous 100-mile outings. . . .

. . . Hunting and fishing were popular rural sports, but the growth of cities made fields and streams more distant, and sports more expensive and time-consuming. . . . The middle classes did not rush to gymnasiums to emulate . . . manly immigrant sportsmen because exercising on apparatus was pretty dull. They preferred agonistic activities more in line with the competitive middle-class spirit. . . .

The main opportunity for middle-class sportsmen to participate in competitive organized sports in the *ante-bellum* era was in team ball-games which commentators regarded as particularly effective in indoctrinating respectable young men with Victorian ideals of masculinity. This was ironic because team games were not really congruent with the independent nature of middle-class work then. But over the course of the century, as white-collar jobs became less independent with the rise of bureaucratization, team games would fit in more and more with the character of non-manual employment.

Cricket was the first major team sport. . . . Very few contests were played in the United States until 1840 when English merchants, agents and artisans in New York formed the St. George Cricket Club. A cricket fad soon developed and it was the most popular ball game until the late 1850s. . . .

Cricket eventually lost out to baseball for several reasons; it was an English game; historic rules and regulations did not readily adapt to American needs; the game took too long for busy Americans; and it was hard to play. Americans had not yet developed a ball-playing tradition, in spite of the English example, and ball-playing was regarded at least until the 1840s as a child's or young boy's amusement. The English perception of cricket as a very manly game and appropriate recreation for young men and adults did not readily transfer to the United States. In the 1840s journalists working in the United States who covered the rise of a respectable sporting culture were generally strong supporters of cricket because they identified it as a masculine amusement . . . because it required physical and mental exertion that was beyond a child's capabilities. . . . The *New York Clipper* lauded the sport for testing mental and physical ability and strength of character. Immigrant journalist Henry Chadwick, . . . applauded cricket for teaching such virtues as sobriety, self-denial, fortitude, discipline, fair play and obedience. . . . These comments took to task the canard that ball-playing was necessarily childish (which it was not in England). Not only was playing cricket a manly activity because of the skill involved, but it also built a manly character.

The modern game of baseball was established in 1845 by the Knickerbocker Base Ball Club, middle-class men who played for outdoor exercise and amusement. . . . In the early 1850s the game began to gain popularity, at first mostly among white-collar men who were probably influenced by the new sports creed and the example of cricket. Baseball soon got more press coverage, became organized with the formation of the National Association of Base Ball Players in 1858, and was spoken of as the national pastime.

From 1857, journalists began describing baseball as a masculine game. *Beadle's Dime Base-Ball Player* (1860), edited by Henry Chadwick identified the manly attributes of the game:

> [Players] must possess the characteristics of true manhood . . . Baseball to be played thoroughly, requires the possession of muscular strength, great agility, quickness of eye, readiness of hand, and many other faculties of mind and body that mark the man of nerve.

. . . Despite these views, there was still some doubt about baseball's manliness because the level of skill required was noticeably less than cricket. Writers advocated a change in the fly rule to make the sport more difficult and less of a children's game. Instead of being allowed to catch a batted ball on the bounce, Chadwick and others recommended that it had to be on the fly. . . . The NABBP did not adopt the change until 1864 for fear it would make baseball too much like cricket and because players were afraid of getting hurt! This rule change persuaded Chadwick to turn his allegiance from cricket to baseball, a manly exercise valuable for American youth and more suited to the American character. . . .

The coming of the Civil War slowed down the rise of middle-class sport, but the necessary conditions had been established which led to an enormous boom in middle-class athletic activity soon after the war's end. The new sports creed had been so well articulated that it had become the conventional wisdom. Employers who had once criticized their workers for neglecting their duties to play baseball changed their minds. In the late 1860s, two Chicago department store moguls, John V. Farwell and Marshall Field, became so convinced that baseball taught such Victorian values as thrift, sobriety, virtue and hard work that they organized company teams and gave players time off for practice and games. A respectable, gambling-free sporting culture was evolving, based on behavior and attitudes consonant with Victorian values which stressed the functionalism of competitive athletics. Sport was no longer merely child's play or vile amusement for the bachelor sub-culture but a useful recreational activity appropriate for respectable middle-class young men who would be transformed into manly specimens, sound of body and pure of heart.

The Martial Spirit, Teamwork and Middle-Class Sport, 1870–1900

Sport in the late nineteenth century continued to shape the middle-class sense of manliness. Middle-class masculinity was still mainly based on the role of breadwinner and head of household, but . . . men were undergoing a serious identity crisis that sport could help resolve. The enormous changes under way with the rise of Big Business and the corporate state were causing a loss of individuality and self-esteem. The expansion of the federal government in the 1870s and the rise of big business in the 1880s was accompanied by the bureaucratization of the workplace which created a great demand for managers, professionals, salesmen and clerks. But these salaried workers were now subordinates, no longer independent workers or entrepreneurs, and they did not enjoy the same sense of creativity and accomplishment previously enjoyed by the old middle class. A second identity crisis was that young men questioned their own courage, having been too young to have fought in the Civil War and unsure if they could measure up to the bravery of their fathers, uncles and brothers who had worn the blue or gray. Finally, the third crisis was the feminization of American culture which had led to the over-civilization of society. American Protestantism was becoming feminized, with church pews dominated by women and stressing feminine values like humility and meekness, and was unable to reach out to young men. The eastern elite establishment and other opinion-makers were becoming frightened that the Anglo-Saxon male had become effete, was losing his sexual identity, and was becoming impotent. . . . In the 1890s concerns for manliness were epitomized by such new words as 'sissy,' 'stuffed shirt,' and 'molly-coddle.' Manliness was now less a stage of development out of childhood than the opposite of femininity.

One important response by middle-class men to this self-questioning was to turn to vigorous physical activity as a means of proving their manliness to themselves and others. They participated in a wide variety of strenuous, clean, outdoor sports to develop strength, courage and virility, and regain confidence in their masculinity. The preeminent exponent of using a 'strenuous life' to achieve and certify one's masculinity was the elite New York civic reformer and future president, Theodore Roosevelt. Roosevelt had outgrown a sickly childhood by a regimen of daily vigorous exercise and participation in such sports as boxing, riding and hunting. He promoted a cult of masculinity through widely read essays published in the early 1890s in such prestigious mainstream periodicals as *North American Review* and *Harper's Weekly.* Roosevelt did not advocate manly activities merely for the physical joy it brought, or even its sense of accomplishment, but because the qualities that strenuous recreation endowed would make men into leaders who would contribute significantly to the common weal. He believed there was 'a certain tendency to underestimate or overlook the needs of the virile, masterful qualities of the heart and mind', and tried to awaken public consciousness to those needs. In 1893 Roosevelt argued in 'The Value of an Athletic Training' that 'in a perfectly peaceful and commercial civilization such as ours there is always a danger of placing too little stress upon the more virile virtues—upon the virtues which go to make up a race of statesmen and soldiers, of pioneers and explorers.' The young reformer recommended that men remedy the situation by participating in exercise and manly out-of-door sports. He was optimistic about the future and was pleased to report a significant change for the better among well-to-do youth of the 1890s compared with their forebears at mid-century who had led effeminate and luxurious lives, a change he attributed to peer pressure.

Among the sports Roosevelt recommended were big-game hunting, boxing and football. . . . While hunting and boxing were individualistic sports that may have been excellent means of building manliness, few middle-class men followed those routes to character development, preferring instead team sports which were sociable, entertaining, sufficiently hazardous to promote manly qualities, and highly congruent with their future work options. The new game of football seemed particularly relevant to the needs of upper-middle-class and elite sons. First played on an intercollegiate basis in 1869, it became Americanized from soccer and rugby and became the most prominent sport at the elite eastern universities. Football seemed the kind of game appropriate for a nation ripe for a clean, violent, virile yet gentlemanly sport. Coming after the carnage of the Civil War in an era dominated by the social Darwinian concept of the survival of the fittest, football appeared the best sport to teach well-born young men the virtues of the martial life (subordination and co-operation, presence of mind, endurance, precision and courage) without the terror and bloodshed of war. . . .

. . . Students from all social backgrounds showed a strong preference for intercollegiate athletics over traditional extracurricular activities like debating and literary clubs because it was exciting, promoted a sense of community, and operated independently of adult supervision. Furthermore, they believed that participation in team sports would help prepare graduates for modern, bureaucratized society.

The college game was extremely violent, dangerous and at times brutal. The style of play in the 1890s emphasized mass and momentum rather than deception and wide-open offences; passing was virtually non-existent. The single most frightening play was the kick-off return when teams employed the flying wedge formation, introduced by Harvard in 1892, to burst through the defence for long gains. Players wore little protection, and the number of injuries and deaths was staggering (twelve deaths in 1902 alone). Furthermore, strategy sometimes dictated players on one squad gang up on an opposing star performer to put him out of the game. The bloodshed and such ungentlemanly behavior encouraged critics like Harvard President Charles Eliot and E.L. Godkin, mugwump editor of the *Nation,* to urge the banning of the sport.

Proponents of football turned several of the criticisms of the game's violence on their heads. Most sports journalists joined with coaches and the majority of athletic administrators in advocating the game, believing that its very violence and danger made it a manly sport and a moral equivalent of war. . . . Professor Woodrow Wilson of Princeton, a former college coach, believed that football, like other sports, developed precision, presence of mind and endurance, but particularly promoted co-operation, self-subordination and discipline. Director Eugene L. Richards of the Yale Gymnasium described football as 'the most manly and most scientific game in existence.' The Harvard coach Lorin Deland, designer of the devastating flying wedge, and Yale's renowned coach Walter Camp co-authored *Football* in 1896 in which they argued that the physical and moral courage learned on the gridiron was excellent training for life. . . .

If football seemed to many upper-class and upper-middle opinionmakers the team sport that most directly prompted manliness for their sons, baseball was the game that was probably most influential in building manly characteristics among most middle-class young men. The national pastime was the most popular sport played and watched by the middle classes. Not only was it originally more prominent on college campuses, it was the pre-eminent sandlot sport. Besides the millions who played on a recreational basis, there were thousands who played in more organized settings; by the 1880s every city usually had an amateur white-collar workers' league. Furthermore, middle-class fans had ample opportunities to observe and learn from the manly behavior of professionals because they had sufficient leisure time to attend briskly played minor league or major league games which were scheduled at convenient times at fields usually located in the vicinity of middle-class residential neighborhoods.

Baseball was not only a manly game because of the courage needed to play (standing in the batter's box against a fast pitcher; sliding hard to break up the double play), but was even identified by certain commentators with a martial spirit. . . . Far more important was that baseball was a team game highly congruent with the bureaucratic middle-class work-place, yet also offered an opportunity to exercise one's individuality that could not be done on the job. Baseball provided a milieu where traditional and contemporary values could be merged. Sedentary workers might develop a sense of team spirit and co-operation that were essential in their jobs, learning to sacrifice for the good of the team. But at the same time winning relied on nine players individually carrying their share of the load, each man doing what he did best. The result was pride and enhanced self-esteem through the *team's* success.

By the end of the Victorian era, the college athletic hero and what he represented provided an important role-model for children and adolescents. The genre of juvenile pulp-fiction portrayed young athletic heroes as manly individuals who had achieved prowess in sports, yet maintained a proper balance between mind and body. These idols were of sound character and befriended and protected those who were less gifted. The prime example was Frank Merriwell, a fictional character first introduced by Burt L. Standish (Gilbert Patten) in 1896. The series, which ran for more than twenty years, followed the exploits of Frank and his brother through Fardale School and Yale. At the height of the series' popularity, more than 500,000 copies were sold per week. Merriwell excelled at all forms of athletics, and had the uncanny knack of scoring the winning touchdown on the last play of the game, or hitting a homer in the bottom of the ninth to snatch victory from defeat. Frank was a handsome, model student whose 'look of manliness . . . stamped him as a fellow of lofty thought and ambition.' In each story Merriwell usually had to overcome a villainous and jealous schoolmate while protecting a weaker classmate. Standish's readers were taught that if they participated in athletics with sportsmanship and led a righteous life just like Frank Merriwell, they would develop all the best traits of manliness and their future success was assured.

The intercollegiate sports program also provided a model for secondary schools to emulate. The student body at high schools in the late nineteenth century were from the middle class or above, many were college-bound, and they shared the same values as collegians. They copied many college extracurricular activities, like inter-school athletic competition under the control of student organizations. Students and educators shared the conventional wisdom that athletics built character and trained values that could be readily transferred to the business world. The manly ethic of sports was most prominent, however, not at the public schools, but at the elite boarding schools, which following the lead of Groton headmaster Endicott Peabody in 1884, adopted the muscular Christianity philosophy and made athletics compulsory. In emulation of student life at elite eastern colleges and the English public schools, competitive sports were employed to build up youths physically, morally and spiritually as they learned to play by the rules, control their emotions, and carry out their responsibilities as members of disciplined teams. Sociologist Christopher Armstrong argues that 'as games became the most popular schoolboy activity, manliness tended to overshadow Godliness and good learning.' Headmasters hoped to train future leaders who would first prove themselves on the playing field and go on to 'become good Christian soldiers, as prepared for moral combat or war as properly trained football players were for the big game.' Once-pampered boys would leave Groton, St. Paul's or Exeter ready for the manly playing fields of New Haven or San Juan Hill. They left school imbued with a moral code that called for playing by the rules, always trying their best, and discipline. These sportsmen were gentlemen who could now control and channel their aggression, unlike lower-class athletes who were supposedly over-aggressive and out of control. Thus as Armstrong indicates, the boarding school youth were taught through sports a class-linked version of masculinity. Presumably many of the same lessons were also taught at Boston Latin and Brooklyn Tech.

Conclusion

Sport in the Victorian era played an important role in redefining the criterion of middle-class masculinity, moving beyond the man's relationship to his work and family to include his character and physical self. Then, once sport defined the attributes of respectable manliness, it was employed to indoctrinate proper bourgeois virtues in succeeding generations. At the onset of the Victorian period sport had been totally antithetical to middle-class behavior. Sports were violent, dangerous, immoral, prone to gambling, and occurred in exclusively male settings of dubious character. Sport had originally promoted a manly ethic congruent with the nature of life in pre-modern societies where life was harsh, hazardous, often uncivilized, and unpredictable. These values fit in well with life on the frontier, southern plantations, the open range, mining camps, and rough urban neighborhoods, but did not fit in well at all with life in settled communities or at the workplace under industrial capitalism.

The respectable urban middle class began to participate in sport at mid-century as they learned from immigrants, social critics, health faddists and other social reformers that physical culture could be enjoyed free of nefarious influences, and that participation was fun and uplifting at the same time. A new sport ideology developed that promoted team sports and other athletic pastimes that were consonant with the social values of hard-working, religious, future-orientated Victorians and promised to improve health, morality and character (that is, manliness). Sedentary students and workers who were worried about their fitness and the unmanly nature of their work were drawn to sports to improve their health and gain respect for their manliness. Sport was no mere child's play, but would create muscular Christians: rugged, disciplined manly gentlemen would be produced out of effete childlike youths. These men would be responsible, physically fit, moral adults, who continued to live within traditional middle-class norms, abstaining from pre-marital sex, living within the virtues of domesticity, and serving as good providers.

Sport boomed as a middle-class recreation in the late nineteenth century and contributed significantly to the redefinition of middle-class manliness. The rise of bureaucratization, the threat posed by the new immigrants, an uncertainty of measuring up to brave ancestors, and the feminization of culture encouraged middle-class young men to test their manliness through vigorous physical activity, especially team sports. Participation in strenuous, if not dangerous, clean outdoor sports would develop strength, courage and virility, while restoring self-confidence. Sport tested one's mettle and prepared one for adulthood. Follow-ers of the strenuous life would grow up to become self-controlled, disciplined men of action who were team players in the work-place, bearers of the white man's bur-den, who would protect the race against inferior immigrant strains and surmount the feminization of American culture.

Working-Class Runners in the Late Nineteenth Century

TED VINCENT

In large part, athletics for pay developed because of a lack of opportunity for orga-nized athletics without pay. There were no public running tracks or jumping pits; until 1887 there was not a city in the United States with a public playground. . . .

Because of the long hours and short pay that were the lot of the proletariat of that time, any chance to escape that toil was welcomed. . . . The itinerant sprinter, wandering from town to town in search of a race, was avoiding hoeing, shoveling, or some similar endeavor. The crowds that rimmed the banks and bridges of the Charles River in Boston to watch the sculling races cheered in the hope that their favorites might be the ones to take home the prize money that could mean a respite from having to work. . . .

. . . There had been a time when "work" meant workmanship, craftsmanship. The shoemaker of old had constructed entire shoes; but in the newly built shoe fac-tories the shoemaker was reduced to the bored and low-paid operator of a last-making or stitching machine. There was as much creativity and craftsmanship in becoming a good sprinter as in what was left of many traditional crafts. At the starting line for a dash, the sprinters could be seen in a remarkably creative array of upright and crouched poses. Some even faced backwards, believing a whirl-around made for the fastest start. . . .

. . . In the beginning, the prime attraction of pedestrianism [long distance run-ning] was . . . —gambling. . . . Be it baseball, track, rowing, shooting, skating, swimming, billiards, cock fighting, boxing, or wrestling, the people who showed up to watch the event generally loved to gamble. Paterson, New Jersey, was a pop-ular town for running during the early 1870s. The New York *Herald* and the *Clip-per* reported crowds of 2,000 to 3,000 turning out at Paterson for a single race. The stakes generally ran from $100 to $200 a side, and in one instance were "one hun-dred dollars and a bucket of wine." The papers reported that side betting was heavy at Paterson, although the reported total sums were in the $1,500 to $3,000 range, far below the wagering for a good horse race, which seems to suggest that there were not all that many well-to-do pedestrian fans.

In those forms of pedestrianism conducted along the lines of boxing and wrestling matches, the athletes were among those frequently "taken" by the gam-

From Ted Vincent, *The Rise and Fall of American Sport: Mudville's Revenge* (Lincoln, NE: University of Nebraska Press, 1994), 40–66.

blers and the other shysters of that particular sporting crowd. The announcement that the noted sprinter Henry Crandall was going to run against McNally in Buffalo for $500 a side didn't mean that one of the two would emerge $500 richer. In stakes races, the pedestrians were generally underpaid hired athletes, employed by "sporting gentlemen" who put up the wager and gave the pedestrian a cut of the winnings. . . . When the backers in track had a real income, it was usually from something like a saloon. For example, Madame Anderson, the leading lady pedestrian, was backed by the proprietor of a Brooklyn billiard hall.

In any of the sports connected with gambling there could be found athletes going under the title "the Unknown." A sporting patron could hardly find a better way to show daring than to risk putting up his athlete against an unknown, the questionable party often turning out to be a ringer of marked ability. One has to believe that there was a distinct air of insecurity at the reported match of two professional women wrestlers in which each was an "unknown.". . . Until the 1880s, when the amusement parks and sponsors of cub picnics started offering substantial prizes, the professional runners were pressed to rely upon private backers. If the runner was mediocre, backers were few, and if the runner was superior, the opposition would demand a sizable head start as a condition of the contract. . . .

The gambling input contributed to the very shady reputation of professional track. Fixed races, or "throw-offs," as they were called, were common enough to keep sprint running relegated to outlying areas during the 1870s. In lieu of races in New York City the crowds went to Paterson, to the old vice den of Hoboken, or to the newly created vice den of Coney Island. In time the sporting public would decide it was safer to bet on the horses than on the match races of pro sprinters. . . .

From the mid-1870s on, there was a gradual decline in pro sprint match racing, but not in the number of sprinters. Great numbers of them were available when the amusement parks began holding sprint contests for prizes, and when the sponsors of picnic meets found they could get substantial press coverage if they invited in top pros. . . .

In the United States the excitement over sprinting came to be focused at the amusement parks. The 1880s were a decade for the construction of such facilities, and visitors were given the opportunity to try for prizes, not only at the baseball toss and sledgehammer but also on the running track. The typical amusement park built in this period was a collection of concessions, and an enclosed track stadium was a common concession, particularly for the park located along the eastern seaboard. All-comers meets were held on a weekly basis from late spring through the fall months. D. E. Rose's "Roman Amphitheatre" at Coney Island featured long-distance pedestrianism as well as sprints, but the other tracks went mostly for the sprints, the better known of the track stadiums being located in Boston, Providence, New Britain, Hartford, New York, Brooklyn, Newark, Paterson, Philadelphia, Harrisburg, Hoboken, and Reading. Some track stadiums added an inner ring for roller skating and bicycle races, and Acton & Taylor's Pastime Park in Philadelphia also had races for dogs.

These entrepreneurial track stadiums built their popularity on having a great volume of runners rather than subsisting upon the star appeal that might be held by the few of high quality. . . . The promoters found no problem enticing young people to dish out their hard-earned nickels and dimes to pay the fee to get into organized competitive running. The large volume of runners helped the promoters drag in paying spectators, typically for 25 cents' admission. Friends and neighbors of a kid who had the previous week outrun the cop on the beat in a street chase could now come to the track stadium to see what the youngster could do with his speed in a more constructive setting. Neighborhood businesses and politicians got into the act by adding prize money.

Contestants at the all-comers meets had to pay their way into the stadium and then pay race entrance fees ranging from a dime to a dollar. But there was no shortage of contestants. Races started at 3:00 P.M. and continued until dark, but even this proved inadequate time for the running of the necessary heats in the feature races that offered $75 to $100 for first place . . .

Amusement-park track was decidedly working-class sport. Proper society had traditionally shunned such places. Fanny Kemble, for instance, had been struck by the absence of members of her own class at Hoboken's Elysian Fields amusement park, which she found crowded with "journeymen, labourers, handicraftsmen, tradespeople, with their families, bearing all in their dress and looks evident signs of well-being and contentment.". . .

In that portion of the sporting press catering to the laboring classes, amusement-park track was considered an important addition to pedestrianism. In 1881 the *Police Gazette* applauded D. E. Rose for construction of his amphitheater near the Iron Pier at Coney Island, where "a large amount in prizes to both male and female pedestrians" would be given out "during the coming season.". . .

The "dignitaries" who provided the purse for feature races were not that wealthy. The Sam Allen 140-yard handicap at Pastime Park, for example, was sponsored by a saloon keeper who dabbled in sports and GOP politics. This particular race was for a $75 first prize, a $15 second prize, and a $10 third. It needed thirteen preliminary heats just to start the process of elimination. The contestants in this handicap ranged in age from fourteen years to twenty-six, with nearly half of them being under twenty. Each of them paid a 50-cent race entrance fee. . . . To attract the stars Pastime Park upped the purse for some of its feature races to $350, and Schuetzen Park in New Britain went to $400. It was not only a bid for the topnotch pros, but also an attempt to increase the small but steady flow of ex-collegiate sprinters who were turning pro.

Bigger purses required higher admission prices and race entry fees. To have lined up "all the best sprinters," as claimed in an ad for an 1884 Pastime Park meet, required a substantially different financial outlay than did the usual all-comers weekend affair. Professional sprinting had arrived at the point at which continued growth hinged upon an appeal to a higher class of spectator. But the genteel of that Victorian age had their prejudices against sports of the masses, especially one like pro track. . . .

While amusement-park sprint races presented a commercialized version of participatory track, the six-day walking marathons in indoor arenas offered a grand, if rather gauche, commercialized spectator show. These exhausting endurance tests helped to launch many an indoor facility into the sporting limelight.

The six-day marathons were the creation of promoters eager to capture the public interest for cross-country walks and channel it through the turnstiles of a stadium or arena. In the first efforts along these lines, horse tracks had been rented for individual attempts to cover 1,000 miles in 1,000 hours or perform similar feats. But these shows hadn't drawn enough spectators to keep the walkers from claiming more than they had actually done. . . .

The six-day marathon proved to be a lucrative capitalization upon public hero worship of cross-country walking stars. Marathoning was launched into the sporting limelight in the United States in contests featuring two of these folk heroes, E. P. Weston and Daniel O'Leary, the latter an Irish immigrant who had begun walking competitively in the early 1870s in his adopted hometown of Chicago. After handing Weston a series of defeats, O'Leary was able to use the savings from his winner's shares to finance the inaugural marathons in a number of cities. . . .

By the 1880s O'Leary had turned his attention to promotion of younger marathoners who soon stretched the six-day record to 568 miles, and by 1890 to 619 miles. O'Leary became the marathon promoter at Madison Square Garden, which had first featured marathons in 1878, when he was a contestant. At that time the promotion was in the hands of Joseph J. Doyle, owner of a gambling den, close personal friend of Tammany Hall boss John Kelly, and later a founder of the Brooklyn Dodgers baseball team.

It was marathoning which first established Madison Square Garden as the premier spot for indoor track. The racing oval had been laid out in 1874 by P. T. Barnum when he refurbished the old abandoned railroad station at Madison Square. Barnum used the track for chariot racing, a fitting addition to the attractions in the place he called the Great Roman Hippodrome. Barnum held the lease to the Hippodrome for only a year before turning it over to a local bandleader, who rented the place out to a wide variety of users, few of whom were involved in sports.

For marathons at the Garden spectators were charged 25 cents' admission, and if they desired they could stay the whole time, sleeping on the boards of the bleachers. A special section in the stands was set aside for women and children, where no unaccompanied "gentleman" was allowed. . . .

A description of Madison Square Garden on marathon days tells of the track being covered with loam and sawdust to ease the footing of the contestants. At the east end of the building the walkers were provided small wooden houses for use during their rest periods—they had to be on the track a minimum of twelve hours a day. Behind a picket fence on the infield of the track was a small army of officials. They were volunteers from the sporting world, and often politicians looking for a little public exposure. Among the officials were sheet scorers who made notations, as the lapmen in charge of sets of dials recorded the miles being covered. Another official recorded the progress of the individual runners on a large blackboard.

To the casual observer the marathon walks could appear little more than sadomasochistic exhibitions. Attendance was particularly high on the last day, when spectators had their best chance of seeing at least one walker collapse in agony and exhaustion. . . . The aficionados who brought their blankets and/or wine bottles and took advantage of the privilege of their quarter's admission to stay the entire six days certainly got to know the contestants in a rather personal manner. The true fan enjoyed knowing when the hero on the track was merely feigning fatigue in order to set up the opposition for the demoralizing sight of a fresh burst of energy. . . .

When the six-day event at the Garden had proved profitable, the owners of the premises saw fit to up the rent. In 1881 O'Leary was charged the then enormous sum of $10,000 to rent the Garden for six days. The admission price had to be doubled to 50 cents, and at this price some gimmicks were needed to draw in sufficient numbers of spectators. To encourage attendance during the first days of the race, special prizes were offered to the runner leading at the halfway point, or at the end of the first 200 miles. The promoters in various sports of the 1880s were beginning to see the commercial value of making a fuss over statistical records, and at the marathons a distinct world record time was designated for each mile covered. . . .

. . . Ideally, the promoters wanted the walkers to put out 100 percent effort 100 percent of the time. The athletes on the track, however, were in it strictly for the money, and it gradually became clear that the way to win was to save one's energy for the finish, even if that meant the pack was slowed to a virtual crawl. And winning meant avoiding the fan-pleasing style of alternating fast and slow laps. The promoters and paying spectators wanted more than a final sprint, so a new rule was put in, stipulating that contestants had to cover a set number of miles or there would be no prize. Four hundred and eighty miles was a common cutoff distance, below which even the first-place finisher wouldn't realize a dime. There were occasions when the athletes refused to get on the track until the cutoff distance had been lowered; and one such strike caused the cancellation of a professional bicycle marathon in Minneapolis.

The higher admission prices, and the new breed of walker who plodded along "with no style," caused a waning of interest in the marathon. Promoters now began going for six-day bicycle and roller skating races. . . . The six-day "go as you please" marathon walks were still held once or twice a year at the Garden on into the 1890s, and then they faded from the sports scene. . . .

Marathoning had been the one form of pro track to develop a substantial cash flow, and it was relatively free from gambling scandal, but it was bound to fail. It was all too obviously a sport for the coarse and unrefined segments of society. . . .

One form of mixed pro and amateur track which developed immense popularity was the track meet of the ethnic and occupational clubs. Such a meet was variously known as the club's "games," "picnic and games," or "athletic meet." The distinguishing feature of picnic track, as opposed to a mere picnic, was that the competitors at top picnic meets included the very best world class record-holding athletes; sometimes it was the best amateurs, other times the best pros. There were assorted running and jumping contests and "vaulting with pole"; "putting the heavy stone"; "putting the light stone" (16-lb. shot); dance contests; pitching quoits or horseshoes; a tug-of-war; and at some meets, baseball-tossing or throwing the caber (the trunk of a young tree). As a measure of their popularity, it may be noted that picnic meets were often held before capacity crowds at rented ball parks of major-league baseball teams. Far and away the best-used facility for picnic track in Brooklyn was the grass track at the ball park of the team later known as the Dodgers. Running lanes were marked by ropes rather than chalk, so as not to mar the grass. . . .

Around 1880, in addition to more press coverage, there appears to have been a great proliferation in the number of clubs and organizations sponsoring track and field programs. . . . There were those sponsored by Irish, Scottish, and German immigrant groups; the Printer's Union games in New York; military regiment meets; [and] sprint meets at amusement parks. . . . The social organizations putting on track meets might be newly formed, or they might be older groups conducting a membership drive, but all could see the publicity value of a paragraph or two in the local sporting papers.

There were a variety of ways to elevate one's picnic and games in importance. To earn prestige organizations most closely connected to the working class tried to attract many thousands of people to their picnics. The crowds came not only to watch but to participate in events ranging from footraces and other athletic contests to the dances, penny pitching, and pie tossing, and such incidentals as an "award for the best dressed gentleman," or lady. On the athletic field there were opportunities for both sexes and for many different age-groups to become winners, much as in the popular distance runs today, which have many categories of participants and winners.

To better the chances of press coverage, efforts were made to attract some star performers. . . . There was not only appearance money but often such valuable merchandise prizes as pianos and grandfather clocks, and on many occasions there were outright cash prizes. Occasionally, a top pro agreed to appear at the picnic and merely give exhibitions, allowing the locals to seek the prizes. Duncan C. Ross, the noted wrestler, and world record holder in hammer throwing and weight tossing, made an agreement of this kind with the San Francisco Caledonian Club in 1885; he agreed to participate in three events at the Club's annual "picnic and games," and agreed to give any prizes he might win to the man finishing behind him. The appearance of Ross and a turnout of 6,000 people helped the Caledonians get national press coverage. Among the thirty-eight events mentioned in the *National Police Gazette* report there were races for men over forty-five, men over fifty-five, boys under sixteen (two races), girls under sixteen, "members' daughters under fifteen," and "married ladies," plus a sack race and a number of runs open to all comers. There was also field-event competition divided by age-group, and there were numerous dance contests. Almost all races were handicapped.

The sporting scribes had difficulty deciding whether picnic meets were pro or amateur sport. Some sporting papers reported the picnics under the heading "pedestrianism," which was commonly used for pro track, while others ran picnic results with the college-meet reports in the general section for amateur sports, usually titled "athletics." The typical picnic had one or more events designated "professional," while others were described in the words "amateurs only," or "for members only.". . .

* * * *

The sport at the picnic meets, which was pleasantly reported upon at length in the mass circulation journals such as *Police Gazette* and *Sporting Life,* was sarcastically criticized when [William] Curtis deigned to discuss it in the *Spirit [of the Times]*. He blasted the annual New York Clan Na-Gael picnic in 1881 for unruly spectators who "made themselves, in every way possible, thorough nuisances," while the "special policemen and other badge-wearers . . . made no attempt to preserve order, or keep the inner ring clear. About half the assembly amused themselves with eating, drinking and dancing, while the remainder swarmed all over the field." In other reports, Curtis criticized the Caledonian Society games for their noisy bagpipers and crowds of wild dancers, and he put down the games of a British immigrant society with the comment: "Many members of the society didn't bother to show up until the evening ushered in the music and dancing.". . .

The picnic meets of the late nineteenth century provided an opening for working-class sports participation by handling the funding problem in a manner befitting the age of Phineas T. Barnum and torchlight parades. The track event was spiced with dance music, raffles, and cash or merchandise prizes for winning athletes. Big-name professional peds were invited to add stature to the meet and to the competition of a group the sponsors considered "amateur"—that is, the club members and friends who ran and jumped for a prize at the games of Caledonian Societies, Irish clubs, trade unions, benevolent societies, and businesses which sponsored annual picnics for employees. An example of the latter is the McCreery dry goods company's annual picnic in New York, which by the mid-1880s had become a gigantic extravaganza open to the running and jumping enthusiasts employed in any dry-goods store in the city.

The picnic sponsors generally interpreted the amateur question in the manner then applied to the sport of baseball. In the national game the accepted definition of a professional in the 1870s was a player who worked at baseball for a salary or attempted to live off the gate receipts of games. All other players were free to consider themselves amateur, even if they competed in tournaments granting substantial cash prizes to winning teams. . . .

◗ *F U R T H E R   R E A D I N G*

E. Digby Baltzell, *Sporting Gentlemen: Men's Tennis from the Age of Honor to the Cult of the Superstar* (1995)

John R. Betts, *America's Sporting Heritage, 1850–1950* (1974)

John Cumming, *Runners and Walkers: A Nineteenth-Century Chronicle* (1981)

Steven M. Gelber, "Working at Playing: The Culture of the Workplace and the Rise of Baseball," *Journal of Social History* 16 (June 1983), 3–20

Richard Harmond, "Progress and Flight: An Interpretation of the American Cycling Craze of the 1890s," *Journal of Social History* 5 (1971), 235–57

J. Thomas Jable, "Cricket Clubs and Class in Philadelphia, 1850–1880," *Journal of Sport History* 18 (1991), 205–23

Guy Lewis, "World War I and the Emergence of Sport for the Masses," *Maryland Historian* 4 (1973), 109–22

Donald Mrozek, *Sport and American Mentality, 1880–1910* (1983)

Wilma J. Pesavento, "Sport and Recreation in the Pullman Experiment, 1880–1900," *Journal of Sport History* 9 (Summer 1982), 38–62

Steven W. Pope, *Patriotic Games: Sporting Traditions in the American Imagination, 1876–1926* (1997)

Benjamin G. Rader, "Quest for Subcommunities and the Rise of American Sport," *American Quarterly* 29 (1977), 355–69

Steven A. Riess, *City Games: The Evolution of American Urban Society and the Rise of Sports* (1989)

Gary Tobin, "The Bicycle Boom of the 1890s: The Development of Private Transportation and the Birth of the Modern Tourist," *Journal of Popular Culture* 7 (Spring 1974), 838–49

Glenn Uminowicz, "Sport in a Middle-Class Utopia: Asbury Park, New Jersey, 1871–1895," *Journal of Sport History* 11 (1984), 51–73

Ted Vincent, *The Rise and Fall of American Sport: Mudville's Revenge* (1994)

Joseph D. Willis and Richard G. Wettan, "Social Stratification in New York City Athletic Clubs, 1865–1915," *Journal of Sport History* 3 (Spring 1976), 45–63

The Commercialization and Professionalization of Sports, 1870–1920

There were limited opportunities to make money from sport in the United States prior to the late nineteenth century. The first sports entrepreneurs were innkeepers who sponsored animal-baiting contests and hunting matches. Athletes during the period (antebellum) competed for prizes in boxing, pedestrianism (long-distance running), and horse racing. However, these events were haphazardly organized and staged only on an irregular basis. Then a big sporting boom occurred in the late nineteenth century. How have historians explained this development? What were the roles of the modernization of sports, the rapid growth of urban populations, changing standards of living, and the emergence of ambitious entrepreneurs poised to exploit potential new markets? What was the relationship between these entrepreneurs and the professional athletes employed to draw in the crowds?

Unlike amateurs, who played at sport, professionals worked at playing excellently. Cycling, football, and basketball joined the list of minor professional sports like track and field and rowing; nonetheless, the major sports remained prize fighting, thoroughbred racing, and baseball. Pugilism was still shunned by respectable folk for reasons of violence and gambling, and major fights had to be held in secret because boxing was banned everywhere until the 1890s. Thereafter prize fighting was only briefly permitted in various towns until 1920, when it was permanently allowed in New York. Thoroughbred racing, the "sport of kings," was revived by elite horsemen during the 1860s, and elite and proprietary tracks were established in major cities. However, the turf was widely forbidden around the turn of the century because of gambling, crooked races, and animal abuse. Thoroughbred racing enjoyed an enormous revival in the 1920s, supported by working-class urbanites who enjoyed gambling, state legislators seeking new sources of revenue, and machine politicians (financed by organized crime) who were seeking to rejuvenate gambling.

The preeminent professional sport was baseball, whose first professional league, the National Association of Professional Base Ball Players, was organized in 1871. It was supplanted five years later by the National League. Major league baseball became a profitable business by the 1880s, attracting competing major leagues, and encouraging the organization of minor leagues (forty-six in 1912). The American League was the sport's most successful interloper, gaining full recognition from the NL in 1903.

The commercialization of sports also resulted in the rise of a sporting goods industry. Technological innovations and extreme division of labor and separation of parts in factories made possible the mass production of cheap sporting goods like gloves, bats, and balls. Inventors developed new types of equipment like the safety bicycle. Sporting goods companies were established to efficiently manufacture and distribute sporting goods, and to become important suppliers for outlets such as department stores and mail-order catalogues.

⚾ D O C U M E N T S

The first document examines the corruption of prize fighting and describes an 1896 fight between heavyweight contenders Bob Fitzsimmons and Sailor Tom Sharkey. The latter won the fight on a controversial eighth-round disqualification just as he was about to be knocked out. The referee was the noted gunfighter Wyatt Earp (who had been disarmed by the police before entering the ring!), whose integrity was widely impugned, both before and after the fight. The second document examines the daily operations of thoroughbred racing in the early 1900s, and the third, the problem of illegal off-track gambling by bookmakers and poolroom operators.

The remaining documents examine various aspects of professional baseball. Document four describes the new Chicago ballpark of 1883, considered the finest of its day. The playing field was extremely small by modern standards—left field was just 180 feet, right field 196, and center field 300. This enabled Ned Williamson to set a major league record with twenty-seven homers in 1884. The social composition of late-nineteenth-century baseball crowds is described in the next document. Document six is a critical analysis of employee-employer relations by John Montgomery Ward, the star shortstop of the New York Giants. Ward, a lawyer by profession, founded the Brotherhood of Professional Baseball Players in 1885, the first athletic labor union, which organized its own major league in 1890. The seventh document by H. Addington Bruce is a classical statement of the positive functions that baseball was said to play during the Progressive Era. The eighth document summarizes Supreme Court Justice Oliver Wendell Holmes, Jr.'s landmark 1922 decision that exempted major league baseball from federal anti-trust laws. At the end of the section, advertisements for sporting equipment that appeared in the semiannual Sears, Roebuck catalogue are reproduced. Note the affordable prices of the bats, gloves, and balls!

The *National Police Gazette* Indicts Wyatt Earp as Crooked Referee, 1896

When Bob Fitzsimmons made the positive declaration that the results of his late battle with Tom Sharkey was a prearranged affair and that he would bring into court evidence calculated to prove the truth of his allegation, nobody regarded it as anything but the argument of a man who, angered at the unexpected turn of affairs, was prepared to say or do anything that would have a tendency to overcome the belief that he had committed the alleged foul which brought the contest to a culminating point. Recent developments, however, tend to show that there was more truth than fiction in his words, and evidence taken in court under oath is sufficiently corroborative to prove collusion and conspiracy between Referee Wyatt Earp, Sharkey, Lynch, his manager, Groom and Gibbs, who control the National Club, under whose auspices the affair was held.

The injunction case to restrain the Anglo-California Bank from paying over to Sharkey the purse of $10,000 . . . was begun in San Francisco on Dec. 3, and furnished a bona-fide sensation. It had been rumored about that Australian Billy Smith and George Allen, who helped to train Sharkey, had made confessions to Fitzsimmons's attorney implicating Sharkey and several others in a plot to win the recent fight by fraud. The story was not generally believed, however, until Colonel Kowalsky, attorney for Fitzsimmons, entered Judge Sanderson's court. . . .

Kowalsky called Smith to the stand. . . . Smith's evidence was as follows:

My name is William G. Smith; I am a blacksmith by trade. I sometimes box and train other boxers for a living. I have only known Wyatt Earp since last Wednesday. I trained Sharkey for his recent fight. I have had several conversations with him. Our first conversation about three weeks before the fight. . . . He asked me to name some men able at the position of referee. I nominated Hiram Cook. Sharkey spoke to Lynch about Hiram Cook, and Lynch referred to me again. He asked me if I knew Cook well enough to talk business with him. I said no. Lynch then said he would call on Cook, who holds some position at the City Hall. When Lynch returned he said, "Hiram Cook won't do." Sharkey told me subsequently why Lynch didn't like Hiram Cook for referee. He said Lynch had put a case to Cook as follows: Supposing your brother and a Chinaman were to fight and the Chinaman was getting the best of it, how would you decide it? Cook replied, "If the Chinaman had the best of it, I would decide in his favor." Lynch told Sharkey he didn't want any of Cook's kind of refereeing. On another occasion Sharkey told me that the National Club consisted of Lynch, Gibbs, Groom and Sharkey, and that Lynch and Sharkey were to get 20 percent of the gate receipts after the $10,000 purse had been taken out. He said that Gibbs, Groom and Lynch were all broke, and that he, personally, had to put up $2,500 apiece by himself, and Fitzsimmons's appearance money. . . . At another time he said Lynch knew a race-horse man

From "Wyatt Earp as Crooked Referee," *National Police Gazette*, 26 December 1896, p. 10, col. 1.

named Wyatt Earp and that if he could be got for referee it would be all right. He said the job would be worth $1,500 to the referee, and that the plan decided upon by Lynch and himself was to object to every man named for referee until the time came for the club to step in and make the selection; then the club would select the man Sharkey and Lynch wanted.

I had a conversation with Sharkey at 10 o'clock on the day of the fight. He said "We have the referee we want. It is Earp and he will suit. I am to win on a foul in the first round, and the referee is to decide in my favor. I am to watch for the first body punch that Fitz gives me, then Needham will jump in and claim the foul. . . ."

When the end of the eighth round came I did not see the blow, but I thought Sharkey was knocked out. I ran over, and picked Sharkey up and took him to his corner. Lynch came over to us shortly after. He said: "Now Tom, keep your hands down low and pretend to be in great pain." Tom said, "all right." Lynch then told us to take Sharkey to his dressing room in the pavilion. He carried him there bodily. Lynch said to us, "Don't let a soul see him, and above all, no reporters or doctors. Don't let anyone examine him until we get to the hotel, and don't take anything off him."

. . . The trainer's story was corroborated by George Allen, who was also an aide in Sharkey's camp and one of the latter's handlers in the ring on the eventful night of the fight. Allen's story was a confirmation in almost every detail of what Smith had testified.

He did not declare, however, that Sharkey was awarded the decision and the $10,000 check as a result of a conspiracy entered in before the fight. Of this alleged plot, he knew nothing, not being in the confidence of the sailor and his managers.

"Did you see the blow that felled Sharkey?"

"I did. In the eighth round, just at the close Fitzsimmons feinted a couple of times, and then Sharkey seemed to try to land a blow, but fell short. Just then Fitz came down on Sharkey with what we call a 'left shift.' Sharkey commenced to fall and as he did so Fitz swung his left and gave him an uppercut. . . ."

René Bache Computes the Cost of a Day at the Races, 1906

. . . Beneath the main grand stand more than a hundred bookmakers cater to the eager demand of the people for an opportunity to risk their money, each of them surrounded by a struggling, pushing, elbowing crowd. In his right hand each bookmaker holds up a small rectangular board, the left side of which is occupied by a slate ruled in vertical columns, with the figures one, two, three at the top; while on the other side is fastened with clamps a strip of programme giving the names of the horses. From time to time he chalks down, rubs out and chalks again the odds he is offering against the various equine participants in the race about to be run. . . .

From René Bache, "What an Average Day's Horse Racing Costs," *Outing* 48 (July 1906): 412–18.

Beneath the field stand, which is in a separate inclosure, a similar scene is being enacted simultaneously. But it is a much cheaper crowd, composed largely of clerks and other relatively humble folks from the near-by city, who prefer a seat at one dollar to the comparative luxury of a place on the main grand stand at three dollars. Rarely do their bets exceed five dollars, and as a rule their wagers are only one dollar or two dollars. For these are the "pikers"—the small-fry patrons of the racing game, whose money is nearly always lost, because, unlike the great plungers, they venture it not upon any basis of accurate information or knowledge, but merely on a guess. . . .

The club has its own private grand stand—a broad piazza at an adequate elevation, on which the members, with their families and guests, including many beautifully costumed women, repose themselves in easy chairs, amusing themselves during the intervals between races with conversation, the consumption of mint juleps or other beverages fetched from the bar below, and the incidental placing of wagers, which are sent into the ring through their own messengers. . . .

If it be reckoned that a quarter of a million of dollars is spent on racing in this country every week-day during the season, the estimate in all probability will not be excessive. The figures that follow apply to an average day, of course:

Three thousand grand-stand tickets at $3	$9,000
Four thousand field-stand tickets at $1	4,000
Expenses of 200 bookmakers, at $50 each	10,000
Profits of 200 bookmakers at $50 each	10,000
Fifteen thousand programmes at ten cents	1,500
One hundred Pinkertons	500
Pay of starter and assistants	100
Pay of two judges	100
Pay of other officials	100
Upkeep of the track and park	5,000
Interest on investment in track and park	5,000
Expenses of stable owners	5,000
Maintenance of 1,000 pool rooms	200,000
Total	$250,300

. . . Expenses, . . . are very large. A park such as that at Sheepshead Bay represents an original outlay of about three million dollars, including grand stands and other buildings. To maintain it costs a good deal of money—perhaps seven hundred dollars a day for labor alone, with five to six hundred dollars added on each racing day for the employment of Pinkerton men as extra police. . . .

There is an expensive corps of officials, who, though appointed by the Jockey Club, are paid by the track association. The starter, at fifty dollars a day, has five assistants at ten dollars a day each. Five thousand dollars a year is paid to the handicapper, a very important functionary, who allots the weights to be carried. There are two judges, at fifty dollars a day each; a timer, at ten dollars a day, and a starting judge at ten dollars. . . .

The most important single item of expenditure by far, however, is for purses; the track association sometimes contributing as much as thirty-five thousand dollars to render the stakes attractive for special occasions, while on an ordinary day it may put up seven or eight thousand dollars. In this way the owners of the park at Sheepshead Bay give away something like one hundred and fifty thousand dollars during the two brief meetings of a season. . . .

Great sums of money are spent in maintaining the racing stables. Probably it does not cost James R. Keene less than one hundred and twenty-five thousand dollars a year to keep the forty horses which he now has in training. Sydney Paget has an equal number stabled at the Sheepshead Bay track. . . .

If you are a millionaire, and are seized with an ambition for the turf, it will cost you anywhere from fifty to two hundred thousand dollars to make a start in the racing business. Supposing that you want a string of about twenty horses, you go into the market and buy yearlings on speculation, unless you prefer to acquire at fancy prices animals with records already made. For the yearlings you may pay from one hundred to ten thousand dollars apiece, according to "looks" and pedigree. They are always a gamble, inasmuch as nobody can tell how they will turn out. . . .

To the telegraph companies racing is a vast source of income, and until recently (when the law made certain drastic reforms) they were obliged to pay large sums to the track associations for their privilege. The amount of matter sent out over the wires from the tracks to the pool rooms and to other places all over the country is in the aggregate enormous, the dispatches flowing in a continuous stream, and reporting not only results, but each race in all the stages of its progress from start to finish. This, indeed, is only a part of the electric correspondence transmitted; and it appears that wireless telegraphy has now entered the field, the new floating pool room on Lake Michigan—a steamer specially constructed for gambling, and equipped for the accommodation of one thousand persons—being provided with the necessary apparatus.

A few years ago, enterprising racing men in St. Louis started in to improve the game by running horses at night under electric light. . . . The law stepped in, and the gambling fraternity, to its profound disgust and indignation, has since been compelled to restrict its racing activities to the daytime. . . .

. . . The business of the bookmakers at the tracks is, from a legal point of view, on exactly the same basis as the selling of lottery tickets. But the restrictions imposed by the statutes are evaded by the simple expedient of placing all gambling transactions of the kind on a basis of "honor," as it might be termed, instead of contract. Nowadays, if you make a bet with a bookmaker at any of the New York tracks, you place yourself entirely at his mercy in the matter. . . .

In the last ten years the total gross receipts of the racing associations doing business under license in the state of New York have risen from about five hundred thousand dollars annually to nearly four millions of dollars. This gives a notion of the increase in the popularity of racing. Out of these receipts something like one million five hundred thousand dollars is paid out in the shape of purses to winners. In addition, five per cent, (amounting to nearly two hundred thousand dollars for 1905) is taken by the state and paid over to the agricultural societies—county and town fair associations. This tax, it should be explained, was originally levied as a license fee for betting privileges at the tracks—a source from which the track owners under the old régime derived immense revenue.

Racing furnishes the only satisfactory test for the selection of stallions and brood mares. It gives incitement to breeders of superior horses by making prices for such animals high. Hence its undeniable usefulness to growers of equine stock—a relation in which it assumes an importance distinctively agricultural. To the state of New York it brings largest profit because here prizes are greatest and competition keenest. It is possible here for horses of merit to earn more money than anywhere else in the world. . . .

Racing, considered as a sport, is healthful. It takes hundreds of thousands of people out-of-doors, furnishes them with recreation, and distracts their minds from the cares and worries of every-day life. In a spectacular sense the sport is delightful. But on the present basis it is primarily a gambling game, and on this side lies its chief interest for the public at large. That it does an immense deal of harm is undeniable. . . .

Josiah Flynt Delineates the Evils of Off-Track Poolrooms, 1907

The pool room as it exists in New York city is more or less of a distinct type. Before [District Attorney] Jerome seriously got after the pool-rooms I have been told that there were not less than two thousand . . . in the metropolis. . . .

I was talking with a friend at Forty-third Street and Broadway . . . and I said, "I want to get down a bet. Where shall we go?"

"Come along with me," he replied.

We walked up Broadway two blocks . . . and stopped at No. 146. . . . To all appearances it was vacant. . . . We went . . . to the basement door, where my friend knocked. His knock was answered without delay, and the door swung upon a few inches. A man about twenty-five years old, well-dressed, Jewish in type, looked through the opening. The look that he and my friend exchanged was sufficient to make good for our entrance into that particular spider's den. . . .

We climbed some stairs leading to the parlor floor. . . . On reaching the first landing we met a second guard. . . . This fellow was heavy, red-faced, and brutal looking, . . . but he knew my friend by sight, and nodded. . . .

There were about a hundred men in the room. Nearly all of them were smoking and the place was stiflingly close. . . .

. . . Nothing less than five dollars was accepted as a bet. On that day I had invested fifty cents in a paper which declared that it gave all the selections of the best handicappers in New York. . . .

I noticed that the original prices did not appear against the horses after the card had been hung up. I found out, also, that it was a common practice to "shave" the

From Josiah Flynt, "The Pool-Room Spider and the Gambling Fly," *Cosmopolitan* 42 (March 1907): 513–21, and "The Men Behind the Poolrooms," (April 1907): 639–48.

prices from the time they reached the pool-room. . . . Most of the shaving was done in the "place" and "show" prices. . . .

As soon as the card on the first . . . race had been hung up, the money began to be pushed through one of the small windows. . . . Each better wrote on a slip of paper the name of the horse he wished to play, that amount he wished to bet, and the position. . . . This slip with the money, was handed in at one of the windows.

In the total of two thousand pool-rooms in New York city, fifty were for women exclusively. In these rooms social caste was unknown. The betting fever has no favorites. The woman of wealth and social standing mingles with women of the half-world and with shop-girls. . . . Inside the pool-room there is an intimacy among these women, born of a common passion for gambling. These rooms were often conducted under a "stall," or a pretense of legitimate business. They were "button-factories," "millinery-shops" . . . but in reality pool-rooms.

. . . In the West the word "pool-room" means many things. At Hot Springs [AR] it means a magnificently appointed hall resembling the office of a stock-broker. . . . In other cities west of New York, the pool-room may be located in a store-building in the heart of the city. Usually it is in the rear of a saloon. In Chicago, however, there are no pool-rooms of the kind familiar to the New Yorker. Instead Chicago has the handbook. . . .

"Handbook" is used to describe those books made without the apparatus necessary in the pool-room proper. A pencil, a pad of paper, and the memory of the Bookmaker are all that is required. The handbook, in the beginning, was a child of necessity. When the police raid the wide-open pool-room, betters and Bookies are driven into the street. . . . Suckers . . . are willing to make their bets on the curb-stone, in saloons, in cigar-stores, or in any other makeshift place where there is a man with a book. In New York, where the handbook has not been such a necessity to the betting public as in Chicago, there has been so much "welching" as to bring it onto disrepute. In most cities the handbook is a distinct gambling institution; it is the walking pool-room. . . . The most popular pool-room and handbook man in Chicago is "Mont" Tennes. . . . In one year he made ninety thousand dollars in the handbook business. His place at 123 Clark Street has been raided oftener than any other betting place in America. . . . The determination with which Tennes has defied the police and the care he has taken to provide immediate release for customers arrested in his place have endeared him to the Suckers. . . .

So rapid has been the growth of the pool-room evil in late years, in response to the horse-racing madness of the people that there are comparatively few pool-rooms or handbooks backed and controlled by one individual. No matter where you find them, pool-rooms or handbooks are controlled by a syndicate—a close combination with police attachment. In one city there may be one syndicate, or there may be several. In New York there are sub-syndicates operating in different parts of the city. They are all dependent for their existence, also for friendship, on one man—"Big Tim" Sullivan. Of course there are also the systems known as the Sullivan, the Peter DeLacey, and the "Jere" Mahoney syndicates.

Each one of these syndicates has a clearing house and information headquarters. The first is a place where the managers of the several books attached to that particular syndicate settle with the syndicate managers on the play of the day before. When police conditions are mixed it is found more convenient to send an agent of the syndicate around to the different books to make the settlement. The syndicate tries to back the books connected with it. Each book, however, has its individual manager . . . a man familiar with the betting trade in a certain district. . . .

The Chicago pool-room crowd is next in importance to the one in New York. Its political machinations and its police attachments are of the same character. . . . It came into existence . . . as the result of more or less similar conditions. There was a growing sentiment against the wide-open gambling-house of Western style and the police raids on that class of institution. . . . There was the complacent public that tolerated one of the most pernicious systems for wrecking men that ever infested the country. There was the false cry of the track-owner that a healthy sport was being carried on and should not be interfered with because a few meanly inclined individuals were criminal enough to turn "the sport of kings" into a gambling device.

The meanest man, because he is the biggest, of the Chicago pool-room crowd is James O'Leary. . . . The genial Jim brought to his new business the reputation of being a "good fellow." . . . Nicholas Hunt . . . , [who was] the inspector of the Hyde Park police district . . . , and O'Leary were friends. Hunt directed the appointment of the police captain at the stock-yards. . . . The stock-yards police showed a wholesome respect for . . . O'Leary. But with the passing of the old-fashioned forms of gambling and the growth of playing the ponies, O'Leary did away with faro, roulette, "stud" poker, and craps, and equipped his place as a pool-room. He became the biggest individual operator in Chicago. . . . He anticipated the coming of the day when public sentiment would suppress the pool-room. . . . So he built a shack outside of the city, and equipped it with telegraph and telephone wires . . . He advertised his place far and wide. . . . At one time he went so far as to employ a press-agent. . . .

Whether in New York, Chicago, or elsewhere, the type of the big pool-room man—the man higher up—is about the same. He is either a politician or the friend of politicians. To be precise, he is "in right."

Harper's Weekly Describes the New Chicago Baseball Grounds, 1883

The grounds of the Chicago Ball Club, indisputably the finest in the world in respect of seating accommodations and conveniences, are located on what is known as the Lake Front property, the title to which is in the city of Chicago. The

From "The Chicago Base-ball Grounds," *Harper's Weekly* 27 (12 May 1883): 200.

inclosure begins at Randolph Street on the north, and extends along the east line of Michigan Avenue southward to a point about midway between Washington and Madison streets. On the east are the tracks and switch yards of the Illinois Central Railroad Company, which has for several years past made a standing offer of $800,000 (not one-half its value) for the property; but as the city has been enjoined either from selling the tract or from permitting its use for permanent buildings, the ball club has continued to enjoy the rare privilege of grounds situated within a two minutes' walk of State Street, the chief retail thoroughfare of Chicago. Partly on account of the convenient location of the grounds, but more by reason of the exceptional management of the Chicago ball team, and its success in winning the National League championship for three successive seasons, beginning with 1881, the game of base-ball is extremely popular in Chicago, and the average attendance at League championship games is considerably greater there than in any other city in the United States. During the season of 1882 the attendance at the forty-five League games played in Chicago was upward of 130,000 or an average of 3000 persons to a game. With this fine patronage, made up in good part of the better classes of the community, the Chicago Club is amply able to maintain its costly team of players, and to equip its grounds and fixtures in a manner that by comparison with the usual style of base-ball appurtenances might be termed palatial. At an outlay of $10,000 since the close of the playing season of 1882 the Chicago Club, under the direction of President SPALDING, has completely remodelled its seating arrangements. Every exposed surface is painted, so as to admit of thorough cleansing from dust, the item of paint alone amounting to $1800. The grand stand seats 2000 people, and the uncovered seats will accommodate 6000 more, so that with the standing room the total capacity is fully 10,000, and this without invading the playing field. A fence six feet high encircles the field in front of all the seats, which are elevated so as to command the best view of the play. Overlooking the main entrance is a handsomely ornamented pagoda, built for a band stand, and to be occupied by the First Cavalry Band throughout the season. Surmounting the grand stand is a row of eighteen private boxes, cozily draped with curtains to keep out wind and sun, and furnished with comfortable arm-chairs. By the use of the telephone and gong President SPALDING can conduct all the preliminary details of the game without leaving his private box. Besides club officers and players, the services of forty-one persons are required at each game to attend to the grounds and seating arrangements, viz., seven ushers, six policemen, four ticket-sellers, four gate-keepers, three field-men, three cushion-renters, six refreshment boys, and eight musicians. Aside from players' salaries, ground rent, and including advertising, the cost per game on the Chicago grounds is $200; add to this the salaries of players, rent of grounds, travelling and hotel expenses, and $10,000 expended this year on improvements, and the total outlay for the season is $60,000, so that the Chicago Club must average $525 for each of the ninety-six League championship games to be played during 1883. But the patronage attracted by the famous champion team both at home and in other cities may be depended upon to make good this large sum, and possibly leave something besides for stockholders. The fact that so large an outlay can be safely made tells its own story of the popularity of base-ball.

The *New York Sun*'s Portrayal of a Typical Baseball Crowd, 1884

The first thing that impresses one on a visit to the Polo Grounds on any day of the week is the number of spectators. It makes no difference what day it is or which clubs are to compete, there are always crowds on hand to witness a match. On Fridays and Saturdays there are more persons than on other days. But a match between two of the more prominent nines of the League will call out 7,000 or 8,000 persons, no matter what the day may be. The wonder to a man who works for his living is how so many people can spare the time for the sport. They are obliged to leave their offices down town at 2 or 3 o'clock in order to get to the Polo Grounds in time, and very many of them are constant attendants on the field. The next thing that impresses the visitor is the absolute and perfect knowledge of base-ball which every visitor at the grounds possesses. Nearly every boy and man keeps his own score, registering base hits, runs and errors as the game goes along, and the slightest hint of unfairness on the part of the umpire will bring a yell from thousands of throats instantaneously. The third notable characteristic . . . is the good nature, affability, and friendliness of the crowd. The slim schoolboy ten years of age, and the fat, lager-beer saloon proprietor of fifty talk gracefully about the game as it progresses as though they had known each other for years. Men exchange opinions freely about the game with persons they never saw before and everybody seems good-natured and happy.

The Majority of the Men

are intensely interested in the game. Most of them come well provided with their own cigars, and sedulously evade the eye of the man who peddles "sody-water, sarss-a-parilla lemonade, pea-nuts and seegars." There is little drinking of any sort and much smoking. . . . At times when the umpire renders a decision that does not meet with popular approval, there will be a terrific outbreak, and for the next ten minutes the offending one is guyed unmercifully. Every decision he renders is received with jeers, and sarcastic comments are made upon the play. The good sense of the crowd gets the better of this boyishness, however, and unless the umpire is decidedly biased, which rarely occurs, the crowd soon settles back into its accustomed condition of contentment.

Perhaps the most enthusiastic and expert spectators at the Polo Grounds are the stockily built young Irishmen. They may be bartenders, light porters, expressmen, clerks, loungers, policemen off duty, or merchants out on a holiday. One of them is a type of a thousand others. He is usually square shouldered and well built. Probably he has had a taste of athletics himself and plays. . . .

It has often been remarked that there are at the Polo Grounds every day AN EXTRAORDINARY NUMBER OF FAT MEN. No one can tell why this is. It is

---

From *New York Sun,* June 16, 1884.

said that men of extraordinary avoirdupois who find it impractical, inelegant, and more or less sensational to throw hand-springs, steal base, and run swiftly at 250 pounds weight, enjoy the spectacle of the cat-like and rapid movements of the athletes on the field. . . .

A good many gray heads and gray beards are to be seen on the grand stand. They belong to men who have been base-ball enthusiasts from boyhood up. They enjoy the sport more than they would any play, horse or boat race, and they are full of reminiscences of the game. Scattered in among them are bright-face boys, who are well dressed, well mannered and intelligent. They are looked upon by the men as of enough importance to warrant sober treatment, and their opinions are as gravely accepted as those of men. Another pronounced type is the young business man. Hundreds of spruce, well-dressed and wide-awake young men who are apparently clerks, brokers or business men from downtown are to be seen about the grounds. They talk balls and strike, but principally ball. They do not know as much about it as . . . the solid young Irishmen, but they make up in enthusiasm what they lack in knowledge. Their interest in the game consists largely in the money have on it. They always bet freely among themselves, and return home happy or crestfallen, according to their winnings.

There are among the ladies who attend ball matches a few, perhaps a dozen in all, who thoroughly understand the game and are actually and warmly interested in the sport. Most of them, however have such a superficial knowledge of the game that they grow tired before the ninth inning is reached, and conceal their weariness when they leave early, by expressing a desire to avoid the crowd.

John Montgomery Ward Asks, "Is the Base-ball Player a Chattel?"

. . . The first reserve agreement was entered into by the club members of the National League September 30, 1879. By that compact each club was conceded the privilege of reserving for the season of 1880 five of its players of the season of 1879. . . . The five men so chosen . . . were . . . forced either to sign with the club reserving them at its own terms or withdraw. . . . The club thus appropriated to itself an absolute control over the labor of five of its men, and this number has since been enlarged to eleven, so that now the club controls practically its entire team. . . .

In order to justify this extraordinary measure and distract public attention from the real causes making it necessary, the clubs tried to shift the blame to the players. They declared that players were demanding extortionate salaries, and that the rule was needed as a protection against these. They attempted to conceal entirely that the real trouble lay in the extravagant and unbusiness-like methods of certain managers and in the lack of good faith between the clubs themselves. . . .

From John Montgomery Ward, "Is the Base-ball Player a Chattel?" *Lippincott Magazine* 40 (May 1887): 310–19.

And was it really against the players or against themselves that the clubs were obliged to combine for protection? The history of base-ball deals between different clubs is full of instances of broken faith, and in most such cases where a player was involved the favorite procedure has been to whitewash the clubs and black-list the player. . . .

In the enactment of the reserve-rule the clubs were probably influenced by three considerations: they wished to make the business of base-ball more permanent, they meant to reduce salaries, and they sought to secure a monopoly of the game.

At the close of each season there was always a scramble for players for the following year. . . . There was no assurance to the stockholders of a continuing fixed value to their stock, for the defection of a few important players might render it almost worthless. But with the right of retaining the pick of its players the club was assured of a good team, and the stock held its value.

Again, in this annual competition for players, clubs often paid extravagant salaries to certain very desirable men, and the effect was to enlarge the average scale so that it was assuming undue proportions. But with the privilege of retaining its best men at its own figures, the average salary would be forced down. . . .

The third consideration, was the desire to create a monopoly. It was just beginning to be seen that base-ball properly managed might be made a lucrative business. . . . With all the picked players reserved to it and the prestige thus given, it was thought that the League might easily retain the control of the business. . . .

The effect of this was that a player reserved was forced to sign with the club reserving him, or quit playing ball altogether. . . . As new leagues have sprung up, they have been either frozen out or forced into this agreement for their own protection, and the all-embracing nature of the reserve-rule has been maintained. There is now no escape for the player. . . . Like a fugitive-slave law, the reserve-rule denies him a harbor or a livelihood, and carries him back, bound and shackled, to the club from which he attempted to escape. We have, then, the curious result of a contract which on its face is for seven months being binding for life. . . .

On the other hand, what reciprocal claim has the player? Absolutely none! . . . The club reserves the right to release the player at any time, "at its option," by ten days' notice, and that its liabilities under the contract shall thereupon cease and determine. That is to say, the club may hold the player as long as it pleases, and may release him at any time, with or without cause, by a simple ten days' notice; while the player is bound for life, and, no matter what his interests or wishes may be, cannot terminate the contract, even by ten years' notice.

. . . The reserve-rule . . . inaugurated a species of serfdom which gave one set of men a life-estate in the labor of another, and withheld from the latter any corresponding claim. . . . Its justification, if any, lay only in its expediency. It was a protective measure which gave stability to the game by preserving the playing strength of the teams, and it acted as a check on the increase of salaries. . . .

. . . The rule itself was an inherent wrong, for by it one set of men seized absolute control over the labor of another, and in its development it has . . . grown so intolerable as to threaten the present organization of the game. Clubs have seemed to think that players had no rights, and the black list was waiting for the man who dared assert the contrary. Players were cowed into submission. . . .

. . . The reserve rule . . . is . . . being used not as a means of *retaining* the services of a player, but for increasing his value for the purpose of sale. . . . The clubs claimed that the right to retain the services of a valuable player was necessary for the conservation of the game, and with that understanding the players tacitly acquiesced in the seizure. They never received any consideration for the concession. . . .

These are, in part, the relations which exist between base-ball players and the associations by which they are employed. Is there a base-ball official who will claim them to be governed by any semblance of equity? Is it surprising that players begin to protest, and think it necessary to combine for mutual protection?

Encouraged by the apparent inactivity of the players, the clubs have gone on from one usurpation to another until in the eye of the base-ball "magnate" the player has become a mere chattel. He goes where he is sent, takes what is given him, and thanks the Lord for life. The demand exceeding the supply, the growth and cultivation of young players has become an important branch of the business. They are signed in large numbers, and, if they turn out well, are disposed of as a valuable commodity to the highest bidder. If they fail, they are simply released. . . .

. . . The whole thing is a conspiracy, pure and simple, on the part of the clubs, by which they are making money rightfully belonging to the players. Even were we to admit, for the sake of argument, that the reserve-rule does give a right to sell, we naturally ask, What consideration did the club ever advance to the player for this right? What did the Chicago Club ever give Kelly in return for the right to control his future services? Absolutely nothing; and yet that club sells that right, so cheaply acquired, for ten thousand dollars! . . . Any such claim by one set of men of a right of property in another is as unnatural to-day as it was a quarter of a century ago. . . .

. . . The interests of the national game are too great to be longer trifled with in such a manner, and if the clubs cannot find a way out of these difficulties the players will try to do it for them. The tangled web of legislation which now hampers the game must be cut away, and the business of base-ball made to rest on the ordinary business basis. . . . The players will catch the spirit of the new order; base-ball, to them, will be more of a business and less of a pastime; contract-breaking will be impossible, and dissipation will disappear; the profession of ball-playing will be looked upon as a perfectly honorable calling, and the national game be more than ever the greatest of out-door sports. . . .

H. Addington Bruce Analyzes Baseball and the National Life, 1913

. . . Veritably baseball is something more than the great American game—it is an American institution having a significant place in the life of the people, and consequently worthy of close and careful analysis.

From H. Addington Bruce, "Baseball and the National Life," *Outlook* 104 (May 1913): 104–7.

Fully to grasp its significance, however, it is necessary to study it, in the first place, as merely a game, and seek to determine wherein lie its peculiar qualities of fascination. As a game, as something that is "playable," it of course must serve the ordinary ends of play. These, according to the best authorities on the physiology and psychology of play, are threefold: the expenditure of surplus nervous energy in a way that will not be harmful to the organism, but, on the contrary, will give needed exercise to growing muscles; the development of traits and abilities that will afterwards aid the player in the serious business of life; and the attainment of mental rest through pleasurable occupation. . . .

. . . Success and progress depend chiefly on the presence of certain personal characteristics. Physical fitness, courage, honesty, patience, the spirit of initiative combined with due respect for lawful authority, soundness and quickness of judgment, self-confidence, self-control, cheeriness, fair-mindedness, and appreciation of the importance of social solidarity, of "team play"—these are traits requisite as never before for success in the life of an individual and of a nation. . . . But it is safe to say that no other game—not even excepting football—develops them as does baseball.

One need attend only a few games, whether played by untrained school-boys or by the most expert professionals, to appreciate the great value of base-ball as a developmental agent. Habits of sobriety and self-control are established in the players if only from the necessity of keeping in good condition in order to acquit one's self creditably and hold a place on the team. Patience, dogged persistence, the pluck that refuses to acknowledge either weariness or defeat, are essential to the mastery of the fine points of batting, fielding, or pitching—a mastery which in turn brings with it a feeling of self-confidence that eventually will go far in helping its possessor to achieve success off as well as on the "diamond."

So, too, courage, and plenty of it, is needed at the bat—courage not simply to face the swiftly moving ball, but to "crowd" the "plate" so as to handicap the pitcher in his efforts to perform successfully and expeditiously the work of elimination. . . . The courage of the batsman . . . had no small share in winning for the "Giants" the National League honors in 1911 and again last year.

As an agent in the development of the "team spirit" baseball is no less notable. The term "sacrifice hit" eloquently expresses one phase of the game which must leave on all playing it an indelible impression of the importance in all affairs of life of unselfish co-operation. . . .

. . . Baseball is also a splendid mind-builder. The ability to think, and to think quickly, is fostered by the duties of its every position as well as by the complicated problems that are constantly arising in its swiftly changing course of events. Time and again games have been won, or the way has been cleared to victory, by the quickness of a player or a manager in appreciating the possibilities of a critical situation and planning a definite plan of campaign to meet the emergency. . . .

So incessant and so varied are the demands made on the ball-player's intelligence that any one who really knows the game will be inclined to indorse unreservedly the published declaration of that most successful baseball-player and most successful business man, Mr. Albert G. Spalding:

"I never struck anything in business that did not seem a simple matter when compared with complications I have faced on the baseball field. A young man playing baseball gets into the habit of quick thinking in most adverse circumstances and under the most merciless criticism in the world—the criticism from the 'bleachers.' . . ."

. . . With the passage of time the technique of the game has been improved to an extent that makes it more of a developmental agent than it was even ten years ago. Lacking the strength, skill, and experience of the professional player, the schoolboy whose efforts are confined to the "diamond" of the vacant lot or public park plays the game under precisely the same rules as the professional, and with no less zest and earnestness, and profits correspondingly. To be sure, in playing it he does not dream for an instant that he is thereby helping to prepare himself for the important struggles of maturity. He plays it merely because he finds it "good fun"—merely because, in its variety and rapidity of action, in the comparative ease with which its fundamental principles may be learned, and in its essentially co-operative yet competitive character, it affords an intensely pleasurable occupation. It is, in truth, a game which makes an irresistible appeal to the instincts of youth precisely because it so admirably meets the principal objects of play—mental rest through enjoyment, exercise for the muscles, the healthy expenditure of surplus nervous energy, and practice and preparation for life's work. . . .

. . . An instinctive resort to sport [is] a method of gaining momentary relief from the strain of an intolerable burden, and at the same time finding a harmless outlet for pent-up emotions which, unless thus gaining expression, might discharge themselves in a dangerous way. . . . It is no mere coincidence that the great sport-loving peoples of the world—the Americans, the English, the Canadians, and the Australians—have been pre-eminent in the art of achieving progress by peaceful and orderly reform. . . .

Baseball, then, from the spectator's standpoint, is to be regarded as a means of catharsis, or, perhaps better, as a safety-valve. And it performs this service the more readily because of the appeal it makes to the basic instincts, with resultant removal of the inhibitions that ordinarily cause tenseness and restraint. For exactly the same reason it has a democratizing value no less important to the welfare of society than is its value as a developmental and tension-relieving agent. The spectator at a ball game is no longer a statesman, lawyer, broker, doctor, merchant, or artisan, but just a plain every-day man, with a heart full of fraternity and good will to all his fellow-men—except perhaps the umpire. The oftener he sits in grand stand or "bleachers," the broader, kindlier, better man and citizen he must tend to become.

Finally, it is to be observed that the mere watching of a game of baseball, as of football, lacrosse, hockey, or any other game of swift action, has a certain beneficial physical effect. It is a psychological commonplace that pleasurable emotions, especially if they find expression in laughter, shouts, cheers, and other muscle-expanding noises, have a tonic value to the whole bodily system. So that it is quite possible to get exercise vicariously, as it were; and the more stimulating the spectacle that excites feelings of happiness and enjoyment, the greater will be the resultant good. Most decidedly baseball is a game well designed to render this excellent service. . . .

Supreme Court Justice Oliver Wendell Holmes, Jr., Explains Why Baseball Is Not Subject to Antitrust Laws, 1922

MR. JUSTICE HOLMES delivered the opinion of the court.

. . . The plaintiff is a base ball club incorporated in Maryland, and with seven other corporations was a member of the Federal League of Professional Base Ball Clubs, . . . that attempted to compete with the combined defendants. It alleges that the defendants destroyed the Federal League by buying up some of the constituent clubs and in one way or another inducing all those clubs except the plaintiff to leave their League, and that the three persons connected with the Federal League and named as defendants, one of them being the President of the League, took part in the conspiracy. Great damage to the plaintiff is alleged. The plaintiff obtained a verdict for $80,000 in the Supreme Court and a judgment for treble the amount was entered, but the Court of Appeals, after an elaborate discussion, held that the defendants were not within the Sherman Act. . . .

The clubs composing the Leagues are in different cities and for the most part in different States. The end of the elaborate organizations and sub-organizations that are described in the pleadings and evidence is that these clubs shall play against one another in public exhibitions for money, one or the other club crossing a state line in order to make the meeting possible. . . . Of course the scheme requires constantly repeated travelling on the part of the clubs, which is provided for, controlled and disciplined by the organizations, and this it is said means commerce among the States. . . .

The business is giving exhibitions of base ball, which are purely state affairs. It is true that, in order to attain for these exhibitions the great popularity that they have achieved, competitions must be arranged between clubs from different cities and States. But the fact that in order to give the exhibitions the Leagues must induce free persons to cross state lines and must arrange and pay for their doing so is not enough to change the character of the business. . . . The transport is a mere incident, not the essential thing. That to which it is incident, the exhibition, although made for money would not be called trade or commerce in the commonly accepted use of those words. As it is put by the defendants, personal effort, not related to production, is not a subject of commerce. . . . To repeat the illustrations given by the Court below, a firm of lawyers sending out a member to argue a case, or the Chautauqua lecture bureau sending out lecturers, does not engage in such commerce because the lawyer or lecturer goes to another State.

If we are right the plaintiff's business is to be described in the same way and the restrictions by contract that prevented the plaintiff from getting players to break their bargains and the other conduct charged against the defendants were not an interference with commerce among the States.

From *Federal Club v. National League*, 259 U.S. 200 (1922).

1897 advertisements from the Sears, Roebuck catalogue. By the late nineteenth century Americans could purchase cheap mass-produced sporting equipment from department stores, small retailers, specialty shops, and mail-order companies. Note the prices and also the simplicity of the equipment, especially the gloves. (Courtesy of Sears, Roebuck and Co.)

⚾ *E S S A Y S*

The two essays in this section examine how two professional sports initially became organized. The first essay was written by the late Harold Seymour, a pioneer sport historian. One of the major themes in his classic *Baseball: The Early Years* (1960), the first of a trilogy on baseball history, was that the baseball business was run in the same ruthless and highly integrated manner as other contemporary big businesses. In the selection that follows, Seymour examines in depth the organization of the National League in 1876 and focuses on the leadership role of Chicago White Stockings President William Hulbert. In the second essay, John L. Sullivan's biographer, Michael Isenberg of the U.S. Naval Academy, examines how boxing clubs got into the business of promoting prize fights. Until the early 1890s matches were made directly by managers meeting in a bar or through the good offices of Richard K. Fox, editor of the *National Police Gazette*. How did the Olympic Club of New Orleans change this system? For years thereafter, politically connected boxing clubs arranged most professional bouts. Few independent entrepreneurs were able to break in until the advent of Tex Rickard, best known for his promotion of the Jack Johnson–Jim Jeffries heavyweight championship fight in 1910.

The Creation of the National League in 1876

HAROLD SEYMOUR

Baseball entered . . . [a new] period in 1876. The time was opportune for change. The National Association of Professional Baseball Players was reeling. Its weak organization could not cope successfully with the cancerous evils of gambling, revolving, and hippodroming. As these became more flagrant, spectators began to stay away, and the clamor for reform grew louder.

While it is true that the Association made some effort to correct the situation by fining some players and reportedly pressuring others to resign, results were negligible. Critics insisted that unless crooked players were expelled, they were not really being punished at all, and the press continued to fire questions at the Association: What are you going to do about it? Do you really intend to act? How can the public have faith?

The heavy mortality among Association clubs has already been mentioned. Some clubs caused their own downfall by assuming heavier salary obligations than their resources warranted—like the Forest Citys of Cleveland, who upped salaries in 1872 to hold their players, only to go into receivership in mid-season after losing 15 out of 21 games. Rich clubs raided weaker rivals for players, thus adding to the number of club casualties. This short-sighted policy was detrimental to those

From Harold Seymour, *Baseball: The Early Years* (New York: Oxford University Press, 1960), 75–85.

who indulged in it as well, because as a result clubs often had trouble finding teams strong enough to give them a battle and bring in the fans.

Gravitation of the best players toward one team meant one-sided competition. For example, the Boston Red Sox, four-time pennant winners, won 71 and lost only 8 games in 1875. Their closest rivals, the Athletics, might just as well have been in another league for all the threat they offered, because they won only 53 and lost 20. The Atlantics, who finished last, were hopelessly outclassed, losing 42 games out of 44. The gap between winner and also-rans was even greater in other years. This disparity in playing strength cooled spectator interest, with the result that even the winners could lose money, as the Red Sox did in 1872. As long as these uncertain and unstable conditions obtained, it was highly unlikely that backers would risk money in baseball ventures.

At the same time these weaknesses of the Association were becoming acute, profound economic and social changes were taking place in America, changes which created an environment congenial to the new direction in which baseball was to move. In just the brief span of time from the close of the war to 1878, America's modest railroad system became the finest in the world. Her industrial investment practically doubled, and except for periodic depressions, each decade saw the pace accelerated so furiously that "a new vocabulary and almost a new arithmetic" were required to describe it. The transformation of America from a rural to an urban society was accomplished as native and immigrant alike crowded into the urban industrial centers, particularly in the Northeast. The twin forces of industrialism and urbanism were, as one scholar said, "more fundamentally responsible for the changes and developments in sport during the next generation than any other."

Long hours of drudgery at factory machines understandably created a craving among the city masses for diversion and excitement. Their traditional pattern of recreation was broken because they necessarily had to forsake the yeoman sports of an earlier period. On the other hand, cities had not yet assumed any responsibility for the leisure-time activities of citizens, and the recreation movement aimed at supplying these needs was still to come. People therefore turned to the cheap, the passive, the commercial, and the sensational. Typical attractions were the saloon, dance hall, and minstrel show. People also turned to the excitement of spectator sports, where they could experience vicariously the thrills and satisfactions heretofore enjoyed at first hand. Sitting in ball parks passively watching others perform was perhaps not the best form of recreation—there is a whole literature criticizing "spectatoritis"—but at least it was much better than some far less wholesome activities that might have been pursued.

It was no accident that professional baseball reached its highest development in the urban centers which offered a permanent stage and an ever-ready audience. There were entrepreneurs quick to capitalize on the situation. In this buoyant era of confidence and opportunity, men with drive, organizing ability, and an eye for the main chance could climb to the top. Oil had its Rockefeller, flour its Pillsbury, meat its Armour and Swift, railroads their Vanderbilt and Gould. . . . Baseball, too, was to have its business leaders, although they performed on a smaller scale. Men like Cammeyer and Wright had already sensed the possibilities of converting baseball into a paying entertainment business. Others now emerged with the ability and vision to benefit by the Association's experience and to organize professional ball on a real business basis.

Foremost among them was William A. Hulbert. He was born in a small town in Otsego County, New York, not far from Cooperstown, but grew up in Chicago. After attending Beloit College, he entered business and was for fifteen years a member of the Chicago Board of Trade. In 1875 he became an officer of the Chicago Baseball Club. Hulbert was a strong leader who applied his business experience to professional baseball. He was one of those convinced that it could be made a paying business if properly managed. He was largely responsible for bringing about a new regime in baseball, and it was under his guidance that the present National League survived during its first crucial years. Unfortunately, Hulbert died prematurely in 1882 before he could realize the full fruits of his efforts. . . .

Hulbert quickly saw the disastrous financial effects of inflated salaries, caused by the scramble for players, and he understood the National Association's need for a "new and better rule" to curb this competition for men. In October 1875, the Chicago *Tribune* printed a lengthy article analyzing baseball's difficulties under the Association and offering a set of proposals to remedy them. According to the *Tribune,* too many good clubs were losing money playing second-raters that could not draw well at the gate—"fun for the little fellows" but "death" for the leading clubs, as it was called. For the Chicago Club to cover costs, pay good salaries, and maybe realize a "modest" dividend, it would have to limit its schedule to games with the more solid teams. The Chicago management was afraid, therefore, that if the "whole gang be let in" the Association again in 1876, half the clubs would not make expenses. The *Tribune* called upon the Association to institute reforms; otherwise it would be the "plain duty" of its leading clubs to withdraw from the Association and form an organization of their own—"a closed corporation, too."

Significantly, the reforms advocated by the *Tribune* were among those soon adopted by Hulbert for the new National League. Because of this, Lewis Meacham, sports editor of the *Tribune* and writer of the article, has been credited with originating the organizational plan of the National League. However, it is more likely that he was acting as Hulbert's mouthpiece. The wording of the article sounded suspiciously like Hulbert, who was probably launching a trial balloon to test the scheme he had in mind. . . .

Hulbert's first overt act was to strengthen his own club by the bald expedient of raiding the Boston Red Sox, the standout club of the Association. Much as he might deplore the practice in principle, he did not shrink from pirating players of other clubs when it suited his purpose. While the season of 1875 was in progress, he approached Al Spalding, still under contract to the Red Sox, and induced him to join Chicago for the following season. Then, with Spalding's help, he signed three more Boston stars, Cal McVey, James "Deacon" White, and Ross Barnes. He also enticed Adrian C. "Cap" Anson of the Philadelphia Athletics, destined to be one of the greatest players of the era, and Ezra B. Sutton, although the latter changed his mind and remained in Philadelphia.

This buccaneering was, of course, in bold defiance of the Association's rule that, if a player signed with any club other than the one he was with before the season was over, he was liable to expulsion. Spalding and his fellow contract-jumpers took the gamble on Hulbert's assurance that "you boys are bigger than the

Association," backed by his promise to pay their salaries even if they were expelled. The Hulbert-Spalding deal becomes all the more telling in view of their
later repeated castigations of players who broke their agreements.

Hulbert was now ready for his next move, a mixture of idealism and materialism. He had already shown his lack of respect for the Association and felt quite
sure he could flout it; but what if the Eastern clubs, angry over his player raids,
ganged up and had him expelled? After all, he must have realized that the Eastern
clubs held the balance of power in the Association. Better to anticipate such a
reprisal and move first. Another motive may have been Hulbert's wish to retali-
ate against the Association, which he "never forgave" for awarding a disputed
player, Davy Force, to the Philadelphia Athletics instead of his own Chicago
club.

Hulbert's aim was nothing less than the displacement of the Association with a
strong new organization, composed of selected clubs only, East and West, with all
others arbitrarily excluded. He hoped that such an organization would check the
evils that were reducing attendance, and that better gate receipts would come from
exploiting intersectional rivalry with a better balance between Eastern and Western
clubs. First, he traveled to St. Louis in the fall of 1875 to confer with Charles
Fowle, owner of the local Association club, and Campbell Orrick Bishop, an attorney who had played with the St. Louis Unions in the 1860's and then became Vice
President of the Association and a member of its Judiciary Committee. Bishop
drew up a constitution for a new league based upon a draft submitted to him by
Hulbert. Next Hulbert and Fowle met secretly in Louisville on December 17, 1875,
with representatives of the Cincinnati and Louisville clubs, strong independent
teams. . . .

. . . At Louisville, Hulbert and Fowle were appointed a committee with full
power to act for the four Western clubs and given the job of going east to negotiate
with the Eastern teams they wanted to include. Louisville, therefore, was the real
birthplace of the National League, not New York City. Four Eastern clubs—Hartford, Boston, New York, and the Philadelphia Athletics, all Association members—were invited to send representatives armed with authority to act for their
clubs to a meeting on "matters of interest to the game at large," especially "reforms
of existing abuses" and the formation of a "new association." Boston and Philadelphia of course were victims of Hulbert's recent player raids. . . .

The Eastern clubs accepted, and the delegates met February 2, 1876, at the
Central Hotel, New York City. Results were massive for baseball history. This
small group proceeded to spring a *coup d'état,* by-passing the Association and setting up a new organization vastly different in character. . . .

The name chosen by the group for the new organization—the National League
of Professional Baseball Clubs—was highly significant. Up until then, all baseball
organizations, amateur or professional, were player associations. Now the players
were relegated to a secondary position. The clubs would be dominant. The specialization increasingly characteristic of American life, and especially of American industry, was becoming ever more noticeable in the baseball business. The managing
end of the game was to be separate and distinct from the playing end, thus allowing
the players to concentrate on performance and leave business affairs and promotion to the owners. . . .

The rest of the proceedings at the meeting were faithfully recorded by Harry Wright, secretary *pro tem.* The constitution readied in advance by Hulbert and Bishop was adopted after a session which lasted all day and throughout the evening, except for a recess for supper. The new document listed as its broad objectives a desire to elevate baseball and make ball playing "respectable and honorable" by enacting and enforcing "proper rules" for the conduct of the game. The founders also expressed the desire to protect and promote the "mutual interests" of clubs and players and to establish and regulate the baseball championship of the United States. They were aware of the need for improving the operation of the business, and there is no doubt that in the years to come the National League did much to put the game on a more respectable plane. However, as time passed and the League became more institutionalized, the idealistic objectives of its founders were emphasized and their other motives subordinated or forgotten. . . . The men of the National League, particularly when under attack by rival organizations or their own dissatisfied players, conveniently forgot their less worthy motives, such as establishing a monopoly and improving their financial position by dropping the weaker clubs. Instead they preferred to recite the lofty objectives voiced in 1876. The constant refrain was, "The National League was organized in 1876 as a necessity, to rescue the game from its slough of corruption and disgrace." As for the League organizers' statement about "the mutual interests" of players and clubs, it should be remembered that before this, the two were essentially one and the same. Now Hulbert and the others first made a distinction between them and then paid their respects to "mutual interests."

The provisions of the constitution concerning regulation of member clubs made plain the monopolistic intent of the League. Like so many tycoons of the time, they gave lip service to competition while working overtime to eliminate it. Restrictive measures controlling consumer markets were introduced immediately. These so-called "territorial rights" have been maintained by the baseball business ever since. Each League club was given exclusive control of its own city and the surrounding area within a radius of five miles. No League club could play an outside team in another League city, even if the local League club consented. The boon of territorial rights was particularly apparent in the case of the Philadelphia Athletics, still smarting under the loss of Anson to Chicago. The A's had been competing with two other clubs in Philadelphia, to the financial detriment of all three. Now they were to have the field to themselves.

Theoretically, other clubs could join the League. Practically, they had little chance of doing so. Since the constitution allowed but one club to a city, and the owners had no intention of having more than eight clubs in the circuit, a member club had to leave before a new one could enter. To ensure gate receipts, a new club must represent a city of not less than 75,000 unless given special exemption by unanimous vote of the incumbent members. Two blackballs were enough to block admission of a new club. Members were required to pay $100 annual dues—ten times those of the Association.

Each club was to play ten games with every other club between March 15 and November 15. Five of the ten games might be played on the club's home grounds. The team finishing with the greatest number of victories was to be proclaimed champion and awarded an appropriate pennant costing not less than $100. In the event of a tie in total number of victories, the club with the smallest number of losses would receive the title. If a club used an ineligible player or failed to put in an appearance (unless unavoidably prevented by accident or traveling conditions) it forfeited the game. Each club was to furnish sufficient police to preserve order, and after each game the complete score and particulars were to be sent to the League secretary.

Another group of restrictive measures was applied to the employees, the players. They were regarded as members of the League, to the extent of being "amenable to the provisions of the constitution and its privileges." Each club had the right to contract with its players and to discipline them, so long as it did nothing contrary to the constitution. Ever since 1879 professional baseball has required all clubs to use a uniform players' contract, but during the first three years—1876 to 1879—no formal wording was necessary. Each club had to inform the League secretary as soon as a player was signed. By making the secretary's office a clearinghouse for registration of all player contracts, the danger of revolving would be greatly reduced.

No club was prevented from engaging a player, even though he was under contract with another League club, provided his services were not to begin until after completion of his first obligation. A player released by one League club was free to contract with another League club after a lapse of twenty days—if he had an "honorable discharge" from his former club. Otherwise, he was presumed to have been expelled.

The League constitution also provided for a favorite weapon of employers in those days—the blacklist. Players who tried to avoid discipline by the simple trick of jumping to another club found their escape choked off, because no other League club was allowed to employ any man guilty of violating the constitution or playing rules of the League, or one who had been discharged, dismissed, or expelled from any League club. A club that did employ such a disqualified player would itself be expelled and boycotted by the League.

The League was to be governed by a five-man board of directors serving one-year terms. One of its members was to be chosen president of the League. The board was the "sole determinant of violations of the Constitution" when differences arose between clubs. Should a board member's own club be involved, however, he could not "sit on trial." The board was also "sole tribunal" for players appealing dismissal, expulsion, or discipline. Its findings were final in squabbles between clubs or pleas by players. The board was obliged to elect as secretary of the League "a gentleman of intelligence, honesty and good repute, versed in Base-Ball but not connected with the press and not a member of any professional club." His job was to look after League records and funds—all for a salary of not less than $300 nor more than $500 per year plus traveling expenses.

Recalcitrant clubs were to be judged by their peers. A two-thirds vote of member clubs could expel a fellow club for: (1) disbanding or failing to appear for games; (2) failing to obey a lawful rule of the board; (3) violating the constitution; and (4) breaking contractual agreements with players (when the latter were not at fault), either by failing to engage them after agreeing to do so or by not paying their salaries. As far as the players were concerned, however, democracy was conspicuously absent in the League constitution. The players had no franchise, no

elected representatives, no voice in the conduct of affairs. They could not get justice through trial by their peers but, as in feudal days, must depend for it on the
court of their overlords. And, as time passed, their rights and freedoms were further restricted.

The undemocratic character of Organized Baseball's governmental structure,
which exists to the present day, contradicts the repeated attempts of the owners and
their spokesmen to equate the business with democracy, or at least to make it a
symbol of democracy. One of the earliest of such attempts was made by Al Spalding, who asserted that "The genius of our institutions is democratic; Base Ball is a
democratic game.". . .

To the end of the League constitution the owners attached a flowery statement,
obviously for propaganda purposes, lamenting the abuses which had crept into the
National Game, blaming the Association for the unpleasant differences which had
arisen among them, announcing their withdrawal from the Association and the formation of the National League, and repeating their purpose to elevate "our national
sport" and protect the interests of "our players." But Hulbert and Fowle expressed
themselves more forthrightly to the New York correspondent of the Chicago *Tribune.* Too many weak semi-pro teams (they were reported as saying) were placing
themselves on a par with the genuinely professional clubs by simply joining the
Association. The "instinct of self-preservation" required the seceding clubs to better their financial condition by banding together and shutting out the weak sisters.
Their new regime would have the added advantage of making it possible to eliminate dishonest players.

The president and board were selected by a drawing: the names of the
clubs were written on identical cards, and the first five drawn received the
honors. It was agreed that the presidency would go to the club whose name came
up first in the drawing. Hartford's card was the first drawn, so to Morgan G. Bulkeley fell the honor of being the National League's first president. Bulkeley served
only one term, then hastened to resume his insurance business and political activities, eventually becoming director of numerous banks and corporations, Governor
of Connecticut, and United States Senator. Despite Bulkeley's slight contribution
to baseball, he was one of the first selected for the Cooperstown Hall of Fame. After the League's first year, Hulbert, its real leader, was formally named president
and served until his death. The first secretary-treasurer of the League was Nicholas
E. Young, long connected with the Washington Club and for several years secretary of the old Professional Association.

As Spalding acknowledged, the new National League was "born in rebellion."
It proceeded to grow through trial and error. Policies and measures introduced on
this basis became sanctified by time and usage; now they are regarded as essential
to the successful operation of the business.

The formation of the National League was one of the most important events
in the development of baseball. It provided for a new order, ingeniously designed
to be nourished on both monopoly and competition. Under its aegis, member
clubs were to compete with each other for renown and receipts, but only within
the confines of a prescribed pattern. In the years to come, the League would
bring to professional baseball both stability and the disruption of bitter trade wars.
It would bring both a superior brand of ball playing and trouble with ball players.

It would build up public confidence in baseball, yet at times create public disillusionment. . . .

The Sullivan-Corbett Championship Fight of 1892 and the Modernization of Ring Promotion

MICHAEL ISENBERG

I

The New Orleans Olympic Club, . . . founded in 1883 as an athletic association for the young men of the city's Third District, . . . rapidly made an impact on the Crescent City's sporting life. It began to stage financially successful boxing matches in 1890, holding them in a leased cotton press yard on Royal Street under the novel electric lights. The club reached the pinnacle the following year, when it successfully staged a middleweight title fight between the champion, Jack ("The Nonpareil") Dempsey, and Bob Fitzsimmons; the Australian challenger won in thirteen gruesome rounds. More importantly, the club's members successfully tested the Louisiana law that allowed gloved contests but prohibited prizefights. After winning this case, in September 1891, the members were free to develop the business of prizefighting.

. . . The club's president, Charles Noel, at first attempted to get Sullivan and Mitchell together, but this effort was quickly dropped once Corbett's friends got to work. Sullivan's challenge, coupled with Corbett's surprising ability to raise ten thousand dollars so rapidly, had quick results. On March 15, 1892, the representatives of the two men met in the *New York World* offices and signed fight articles on Sullivan's terms. The fight would be with five-ounce gloves under the Marquis of Queensberry Rules. (Corbett had never fought a bareknuckle bout, and he felt that the use of gloves could only dilute Sullivan's punching power.) The size of the purse immediately caught the attention of sporting America. Sullivan's huge demands had been met, and if the champion was bluffing, he had been called. The two men would fight for a purse of $25,000 and a side bet of $10,000 apiece, a total of $45,000—winner-take-all! John L. insisted on the last part. Members of the Olympic Club agreed to pony up the $25,000 purse; with Corbett's $10,000, this left only the champion's $10,000. Old-time fans rejoiced that their hero would enter the ring again, . . .

With Corbett and Sullivan signed, the Olympic Club went further. It scheduled what was billed as a "Triple Event," a three-day boxing festival that would culminate on September 7 with the battle for the heavyweight championship. On September 5 the lightweight title would be contested between Jack McAuliffe and Billy Myer, and the following day would see a featherweight championship bout featuring Jack Skelly and George ("Little Chocolate") Dixon, the only black

From Michael Isenberg, *John L. Sullivan and His America* (Urbana: University of Illinois Press, 1988), 307–23.

among the six pugilists. That John L. was returning to the ring was news enough, but the extravaganza of the Triple Event immediately created a wildfire of excitement in the sporting world, which the Olympic Club was happy to stoke throughout the summer of 1892.

At the end of his theatrical tour in May, John L. got a medical checkup before commencing training. It was the first thorough physical examination of his life. The doctor, George F. Schrady of New York City, found him in perfect health "except for superfluous flesh around the middle.". . . . John L. left the doctor's office convinced that he would be, with training, as good as he had ever been. . . . People visiting the Canoe Place Inn were treated more than once to Sullivan's old boast that a shave and shampoo were all the training he needed to beat any man living.

For his part, Corbett was working feverishly for the chance of a lifetime. The industrious Brady booked him for a tour throughout the country, and Jim made headlines with his offer to give one hundred dollars to anyone who could last four rounds with him. For weeks Jim plowed his way through the theaters and halls of the nation's cities, sparring himself into peak condition. He was being trained by Billy Delaney, a friend from Oakland, who had sold his business for the opportunity to work with the challenger. On the tour Corbett impressed many with his stamina and rapidly developing ring craft, but he was reminded often that he would be stepping into the ring with a national idol. . . .

. . . He set up training camp at Asbury Park, New Jersey, and surrounded himself with some of the toughest pugs in the fight game in order to learn the rougher tricks of the trade. . . . To reporters he seemed surprisingly relaxed and in control of himself. He often took an afternoon off to bet on the horses at nearby Monmouth Park, and most evenings he could be seen gobbling plates of ice cream at the local parlor. But he always returned to the punching bag, the rope, and his sparring partners. By early September he had pared himself to 178 pounds and had to add weights to his pockets to deceive his backers into believing that he would enter the ring at close to 200.

Young Stephen Crane, then reworking *Maggie: A Girl of the Streets,* was in Asbury Park that summer. . . . Crane marked especially Jim's "gentlemanly bearing and quiet manners." It was obvious the challenger was serious about his mission. In Sullivan's camp, close observers were not so sure about the champion. Visitors noted his graying hair and the deep furrows that now seamed his face. During his light workouts with Ashton, they could also see that he was breathing heavily and that the fold of fat around his midsection did not seem to be vanishing. Casey was doing the best he could; John L. was allowed to eat only food carefully prepared by Phil's sister. But the champion's heart was not really in it. Late in August he even began rehearsing his new play, *The Man from Boston,* at a Brooklyn theater.

Also in August, he put the finishing touches on his autobiography. . . . He presented an image of calm nervelessness: "I can sleep till within a minute of the time to enter. I never lost a pound worrying over anything; I guess all my nerves are in my muscles." He sensed the kind of fight that was ahead of him, saying that a boxer must be ready to change his plan of campaign at the last minute. "A man fights as much with his head as with his hands, especially with such a 'shifty' boxer as Mr. Corbett is reputed to be.". . . .

On August 16 John L. went up to Cambridge to get one last thorough physical, from Dr. Dudley A. Sargent, director of the Harvard College Gymnasium. Sargent's report was the most detailed ever done on the champion, and Sullivan thought so much of it that he had it reproduced as an appendix to the autobiography, complete with photographs. Sargent noted that John L. had lost 20 pounds (actually 30) and was at 216. For a man of 5 feet 10½ inches "this weight is considerably in excess of what it should be for a man in good condition, of this stature, and is surpassed by less than one per cent of the persons on my tables." All the girth measurements were "unusually large," from head to calf. Sargent felt (correctly) that John L.'s power came from his exceptionally thick trunk, hips, and thighs. The doctor was surprised at his subject's lung capacity, bettered by only 5 percent of his other patients. What made Sullivan a phenomenon, he said, was that John L. could operate his arms and legs with the "vital machinery" of rapidity usually found in much smaller men. Still, Sargent could easily see the warning signs: "I cannot help thinking that Sullivan's respiratory apparatus is his weak point vitally. . . ." Even so, he remained impressed. Sullivan, he concluded, was an excellent example of "the brawn and sinew that conquers both opponents and environments and sustains the race." . . .

. . . He had said, several times before, that his next fight would be his last; this time he meant it. He was tired, not of the crowds and the praise, but of the physical price that had to be paid. His training, he knew, had been at best only half-successful; he was still a good fifteen pounds over his best fighting weight and short-winded to boot. Yet, as the Triple Event grew nearer, the old roaring confidence returned. The Dude was inexperienced, callow, lighter by a good twenty pounds. Once more, then—one more time, winner-take-all!

II

New Orleans was in a complete dither over the Triple Event. The city now found itself the national center of boxing, to the great pride of the Olympic Club and its sundry supporters, to the considerable distress of the better sort. The local papers denounced the coming festivities, arguing that these would do little to reduce the community's reputation as a "city of sin." Brothel-keepers, whores, gamblers, and hoteliers were eagerly anticipating the influx of well-heeled fight fans. Merchants redoubled their advertising space in the press, and one railroad reported selling three thousand tickets to excursionists. City fathers estimated that over twelve thousand people would be coming from out of town, a commercial bonanza. Street-corner hawkers offered photographs of all the fighters. Thoroughfares were suddenly filled with the sartorial dazzle of the fight crowd. Bystanders saw parades of pink-and-blue shirts, festooned with both polka dots and stripes, along with neckties and scarfs "so gaudy that the very horses in the street shy at them." The Olympic Club had done its part; for forty thousand dollars a spanking new arena, lit by electricity and holding ten thousand people, had been erected to stage the extravaganza.

The "Sullivan Special" left New York on September 1 on the West Shore Railroad. . . . The trip south was a celebration. All along the route hundreds came to the depot to catch a glimpse of their hero. They were there in Utica, Syracuse, Rochester, Buffalo, and Erie. They continued to come as the Special rolled through

Cleveland, Ashtabula, and Dayton. In Springfield, Ohio, a town that had refused John L. a permit to perform during the Grand Tour, over three hundred people crowded the platform, cheering and yelling. Sullivan walked to the back of the train and acknowledged his fans by raising a yachting cap. The cheers redoubled. The crowd could see that his head was close-cropped once again, that he "meant business.". . .

. . . By September 4 they had reached New Orleans. John L. immediately weighed himself; even at this late date he was at 217 pounds. He plunged immediately into a daily routine of exercise, skipping rope and punching a bag. One trainer who had watched him prepare for Kilrain three years before thought Sullivan was 50 percent better than he had been in 1889. . . .

The betting was running as high as four to one on Sullivan. A local pool room offered $2,000 to $1,200 that John L. would beat Corbett, but got no takers. A few high rollers, looking to an upset, formed betting combinations and backed the San Franciscan. Peter Jackson was in town, billed as the "black heavyweight champion." His sentiments, unsurprisingly, were with Corbett, for if Jim won, then Jackson might get a shot at the crown. Bat Masterson was there, too, still smarting from his financial losses in the Kilrain fight. Now he claimed that Sullivan had met only inferior fighters and that Corbett would win—Bat wagered every dime he had on Gentleman Jim.

The Triple Event kicked off on September 5, with the *Daily Picayune* solemnly asserting that the bouts would be held "as quietly as a theatrical performance"; the police would be on hand to keep order. Many leading newspapers had sent reporters. A writer for the *National Police Gazette* claimed that the "whole civilized world" was anxiously awaiting the results of the great pugilistic carnival. Benjamin Harrison and Grover Cleveland, currently waging a lackluster campaign for the presidency enlivened only by the hell-for-leather oratory of the new Populist party, had for the moment been exiled to the back pages. Telegraphic bulletins by the hour kept the nation informed of the happenings in New Orleans. Even as McAuliffe and Myer stepped into the ring to begin the extravaganza, the *New York Herald* had been forced to observe that "the odium which rested upon the prize ring and the majority of its exponents a decade or two ago, because of the disgraceful occurrences connected with it, have [*sic*] in a measure been removed, until now the events on hand are of national and international importance." It was true, and it was John L. Sullivan who had made the difference.

Jack McAuliffe had claimed the lightweight title since 1884, when The Nonpareil had moved up into the middleweight class. He and Billy Myer had met before, in 1889, when McAuliffe, fighting with a broken right arm for the last fifty-six rounds, had battled "the Streator Cyclone" to a sixty-four-round draw. Now, before a crowd of sixty-four hundred in the Olympic Club's new arena, McAuliffe showed his skills with a pair of pea-green gloves, laced with red tape. For fourteen rounds he sliced Myer's face with short, sharp blows before finally knocking him out in the fifteenth. The lightweights were great crowd pleasers, and the news was quickly telegraphed to the nation that "the greatest fighter in his class that the world ever saw" was still champion.

The following evening belonged to a new division, the feather-weights. Boston's George Dixon had already proved that he was one of the finest small fighters who ever lived. He had won the title the year before (the lighter divisions were never as race-conscious as Sullivan had made the heavyweights) and was so good that his following numbered many whites as well as blacks. To their credit, the members of the Olympic Club were determined to pull off a title match free of race baiting, and this they did, aided by New Orleans's relatively tolerant history of racial intermixture. For the first time, the club admitted black fans to see their Little Chocolate, although it seated them in a special section.

Jack Skelly, on the other hand, was a journeyman, probably the least talented of the six fighters mustered for the Triple Event. For eight rounds Little Chocolate carved him up, battering the Irishman's face until it was no longer recognizable. It got so bad that Dixon's blood-soaked gloves would make a squishing sound as they struck the features of his hapless opponent. A few whites visibly winced. "A darky is all right in his place here," wrote one ringsider, "but the idea of sitting quietly by and seeing a colored boy pummel a white lad grates on Southerners." As a result of the bout, there was much editorial comment, mostly negative, on the propriety of mixing the races in the prize ring. Yet when Skelly was finally able to struggle to his feet after being knocked out in the eighth, the crowd gave Dixon a great ovation. Little Chocolate retired to his dressing room, where he puffed on a cigar and downed two glasses of beer. He would hold his crown for seven more years before finally losing it to Terry McGovern.

The betting pools had parlayed McAuliffe, Dixon, and Sullivan. Two of the champions had won decisively. Now it was the turn of the third, the greatest of them all. All day on the seventh, intense excitement coursed through the streets of the Crescent City. Every public place, from saloon to pool hall to barbershop, was jammed. Visitors of all classes—lawyers, politicians, merchants, gamblers— rubbed elbows and endlessly propounded their particular brand of fight wisdom. Admission prices were scaled from five to fifteen dollars, and every ticket was taken, around ten thousand in all. Sullivan and Corbett would be watched by the largest crowd that had ever gathered to see a prizefight. . . .

III

The Dude's calm had its source in his own ring experience and in the fact that he had worked for weeks with Mike Donovan at the New York Athletic Club. Donovan, since his years in the ring, had developed into a highly respected teacher of boxing. Patiently he taught Corbett defenses against John L.'s three basic blows: a chopping left to beat down his opponent's guard; a right jab, delivered with tremendous power; and a right cross that usually whistled in on the neck or just behind the ear. His pupil was a fast learner. By the end of their sparring sessions the smaller, quicker Donovan was unable to land a blow on Corbett's constantly bobbing and weaving head. Mike was confident enough in the Dude's skills to have backed him with one thousand dollars of his own money.

Donovan also told Corbett what else to expect when the two fighters met in the ring—John L.'s ferocious, intimidating scowl. On reaching the arena, the Dude tried some gamesmanship. Word came from Sullivan's backers that the champion wanted to toss for corners. Corbett responded flippantly that John L. could take any corner he liked because he, Corbett, was entering the ring last— a violation of the champion's prerogative. This contretemps was solved when

Brady won a coin flip. After balking somewhat, Sullivan entered the ring first, to the expected tremendous ovation. Corbett followed shortly, and at last the two men were face to face. . . . Around them the Olympic Club seats rose up, tier after tier, into the wooden rafters, where they merged with a rat's nest of electrical wiring. Corbett noticed an oddity: the ring was not raised, and its floor was turf rather than boards. He skipped around to check his footing and found it solid. . . .

The referee, John Duffy, called the pair to the center of the ring for their final instructions. John L. stood with arms folded, staring straight at Corbett, bounding up and down on his toes. . . . John L. was beyond his usual self-induced rage at the apparent indifference of his opponent. More than ever, he was convinced he was facing a glib young coxcomb who needed to be taken down a peg. When Duffy called "time!" he hurtled across the ring at the Dude, eagerly slapping his left hand against his thigh. As Donovan had predicted, he chopped with his left and followed with a right cross. Corbett easily slipped away. He was wary of being backed into a corner. Again the rush, with the same results. Sullivan was having trouble even landing a punch, and so it continued for the first two rounds, as the crowd roared in continuous frenzy. . . .

In the third, the Dude delivered his first solid shot, a left to John L.'s nose as the champion rushed by him. Blood spurted immediately, the crowd noise redoubled in volume, and Corbett continued to work over Sullivan's nose and jaw for the rest of the round. When John L. at last retired to his corner, his face, arms, and chest were smeared with blood, more than he had lost in all his previous fights together. His nose was broken.

He continued to bleed profusely for the next few rounds, but he also began to recover somewhat. . . . At the start of the seventh Corbett simply beat Sullivan to the punch, sinking rights and lefts into John L.'s stomach, doubling the champion up into a jackknife of agony. But again the Dude did not press in for the kill, backing off, feinting warily, and looking for openings. More and more of his quick hooks were striking home.

By now the crowd could sense an upset in the works. John L.'s lack of conditioning was beginning to tell. He came out for the eighth round puffing hard. . . . The combination of loss of blood, his inability to hit Corbett, and the Dude's swift counterpunches were all taking their toll. He could barely lift his arms to defend himself, but like Kilrain three years before he was not about to quit. The lighter man danced around him, landing punch after punch over John L.'s lowered guard. . . . The Dude had considerable punching power, and his timing was excellent. By the fourteenth Corbett was landing straight shots to Sullivan's battered nose without a return.

John L. was disintegrating as a fighter, before the entire nation. . . . John L.'s face and jaws were repeated targets now, and the amazed fans began to anticipate the kill. In the sixteenth the champion made a desperate rush for Corbett, but the Dude skipped away like a dancing master, making Sullivan's futile efforts look like a game of tag. Maddened even further, John L. ran at Corbett, trying to strike him with his body, his arms so tired he could no longer lift them. Over and over he banged into the ring ropes as Corbett nimbly dodged aside. . . . Half conscious, eyes glazed and almost closed, he swept the handlers away and stood for a moment, swaying from side to side. . . . Slowly, he stumbled to the ropes, groping with his left hand until he found a grip on a ring post. He held up his right hand; the cheering and applauding stopped instantly. In a low, halting voice, thickened by dehydration and weakened from the pounding he had taken, he spoke:

> Gentlemen—gentlemen, I have nothing at all to say. All I have to say is that I came into the ring once too often—and if I had to get licked I'm glad I was licked by an American. I remain your warm and personal friend, John L. Sullivan.

It was his finest moment in the prize ring. Nothing became him more during his years of dominance in his chosen profession than his manner of leaving it. The simple speech anchored him in the hearts of his admirers once and for all. Many in the crowd were weeping openly. Donovan was convinced he was seeing a man "head and shoulders above all the rest." In defeat as in triumph, John L. Sullivan was "always on the level.". . .

IV

For the moment, money fell in golden heaps on Corbett, Brady, and the city of New Orleans. The new champion immediately wired $10,000 to his father to pay off the mortgage on the house and livery stable. Later, he and Brady went off on tour in a play, *Gentleman Jack,* written expressly for him. The project netted the partners $150,000 during the 1892–93 theatrical season. The Olympic Club, for its part, made more than $50,000. Over half a million dollars changed hands as a result of the Triple Event; it was a gamblers' paradise. In the upshot, however, it was Corbett's particular tragedy to have dethroned an idol. Despite his youth, good looks, and undoubted boxing skills, he was never a popular champion, certainly not close to Sullivan's stature. Thus his time in the spotlight was clouded by bitterness and some confusion over what his role should be. . . .

V

In the years that followed it became common to mark the Sullivan-Corbett fight as a cultural event of significance, a kind of way station along the route of American progress. Skill and balance, it was held, came to dominate over sheer brute strength. . . .

The usual argument has been that Sullivan was "caught in a period of transition," that Corbett was a new breed of fighter. . . . Before 1892 there was Sullivan—ill-trained, self-taught, pure flaming instinct in the prize ring. After 1892 there was Corbett—educated in ring "science," cool, calculating, an "intelligent" fighter. With their bout as a watershed, John L. and the Dude have taken their place as milestones in the maturation of American culture.

These analyses, which are still common in sporting and cultural histories, are vastly overblown and unfair to both boxers. In Corbett's case, they overlook the Dude's considerable strength and punching power and also ignore the fact that he did something John L. had longed to do and never accomplished: in 1894 Corbett kayoed Mitchell in three rounds. Also, when Corbett himself was further along in ring years, he was knocked out twice (1900 and 1903) by another plodding fighter of exceptional strength, Jim Jeffries.

In Sullivan's case, the charge that his style was primitive, relying on bull-like rushes and sheer physical force, was true. But there would be other champions with the same qualities well after Sullivan—Jeffries, Jess Willard, Primo Carnera (to name three), and, at least in part, Jack Dempsey. Indeed, the heavyweight division has always featured boxers with the qualities of both Sullivan and Corbett. The men who combine the two—like Joe Louis and Muhammad Ali—have been, in their prime, unstoppable. Moreover, Sullivan preferred gloved fights, fought most of his bouts with gloves, and saw nothing wrong with gloves in the Corbett match. To see him as the last of the bare-knuckle breed and Corbett as the harbinger of a new era of "scientific" boxing simply overstates the argument.

John L. Sullivan was beaten because boxing, beyond almost all other athletic endeavors, is a sport for young men in the very prime of physical condition. With Corbett, John L. gave away eight years and countless boxing lessons. He gave away speed, conditioning, and the real desire to win. Nobody knows how much he gave away with his riotous life-style. The amazing aspect of his fight with Corbett is not that the Dude won. It is that a prematurely aged, overweight, short-winded man, who had been out of the prize ring for three years, stood in for one solid hour of battle with a man in his physical prime. If there was ever such a thing as "fighting heart," John L. had it in spades in New Orleans. . . .

⚾ *F U R T H E R   R E A D I N G*

Charles C. Alexander, *John J. McGraw* (1988)
Richard Crepeau, *Baseball: America's Diamond Mind* (1980)
Michael Gershman, *Diamonds: The Evolution of the Ballpark* (1993)
Stephen Hardy, " 'Adopted by All the Leading Clubs': Sporting Goods and the Shaping of Leisure," in Richard Butch, ed., *For Fun and Profit* (1990), 71–92
Stephen Hardy, "Entrepreneurs, Organization and the Sport Marketplace," *Journal of Sport History* 13 (1984), 14–33
Stephen Hardy, "Entrepreneurs, Structures, and the Sportgeist: Old Tensions in Modern Industry," in Donald G. Kyle and Gary Stark, eds., *Essays on Sport History and Mythology* (1990), 83–117
J. Thomas Jable, "The Birth of Professional Football: Pittsburgh Athletic Clubs Ring in Professionals in 1902," *Western Pennsylvania Historical Magazine* 62 (1979), 136–47
Peter Levine, *A. G. Spalding and the Rise of Baseball: The Promise of American Sport* (1985)
Lee Lowenfish, *The Imperfect Diamond: A History of Baseball's Labor Wars*, rev. ed. (1992)
Marc Maltby, "The Origin and Early Development of Professional Football, 1890–1920," Ph.D. diss., Ohio University (1987)
Henry A. March, *Pro Football* (1934)
Leo N. Miletich, *Dan Stuart's Fistic Carnival* (1994)
Eugene C. Murdock, *Ban Johnson: Czar of Baseball* (1982)
Carl Nardinelli, "Judge Kenesaw Mountain Landis and the Art of Cartel Enforcement," in Peter Levine, ed., *Baseball History* III (1991)
Robert W. Peterson, *Cage to Jump Shots: Pro Basketball's Early Years* (1990)
Benjamin G. Rader, *Baseball: A History of America's National Game* (1992)

Steven A. Riess, "In the Ring and Out: Professional Boxing in New York, 1896–1920," in Donald Spivey, ed., *Sport in America* (1985), 95–128

Steven A. Riess, *Touching Base: Professional Baseball and American Culture in the Progressive Era* (1980)

Lawrence Ritter, *The Glory of Their Times* (1966)

W. H. P. Robertson, *The History of Thoroughbred Racing in America* (1964)

Harold Seymour, *Baseball: The Early Years* (1960)

Harold Seymour, *Baseball: The Golden Years* (1971)

Leverett T. Smith, *The American Dream and the National Game* (1975)

Dean A. Sullivan, ed., *Early Innings: A Documentary History of Baseball, 1825–1908* (1995)

David Q. Voigt, *American Baseball: From Gentleman's Sport to the Commissioner System* (1966)

David Q. Voigt, *American Baseball: From the Commissioners to Continental Expansion* (1970)

Uniforming Sportswomen

One of the most remarkable recent developments in American sport has been the boom in women's athletics. The photographs in this section illustrate that this was a slow process. At the turn of the century, sport was barely considered an appropriate activity for women, and those who did participate were constrained by traditional clothing that made free, rapid movement uncomfortable and difficult. Upper- and middle-class young women had more opportunities than others to engage in high-status sports such as golf and tennis and more strenuous college contests such as baseball and rowing. Often idealized as the "Gibson girl"—attractive, slim, and physically fit—the woman athlete of this period wore a shirtwaist and long skirt that provided greater freedom than most contemporary apparel. However, female physical educators led a fight against competitive sport for women because they believed it was manly, immodest (as it involved wearing bloomers and playing in front of men), debilitating, and corrupting. From the 1920s until the early 1970s, women athletes had few outlets other than sports that were considered suitably feminine, such as figure skating, tennis, and golf.

As recently as 1972, when Title IX of the Education Act became law and made gender-based discrimination illegal at all institutions receiving federal aid, only about 4 percent of American girls participated in athletics, compared to 50 percent of American boys. In that year women composed only about one-seventh of the American Olympic team. Since then there has been a revolution in women's athletics. More women have become serious competitors, and they have successfully challenged barriers in such sports as the marathon. By 1996 about one-third of American girls participated in school sports, nearly half of college varsity players were women, and women made up nearly three-sevenths of the Olympic squad.

Chicago golfers, c. 1900. Golf was expensive, elitist, sociable, and nonstrenuous, and it did not require exposing one's body. (H. C. Rew/Chicago Historical Society)

Chicago tennis players, c. 1910. Tennis was less exclusive than golf. Most women tennis players wore restrictive clothing, but the better, more active players began wearing looser apparel. (John Becker/Chicago Historical Society)

A 1920s basketball squad from the Jewish People's Institute, a settlement house on Chicago's West Side. This team was one of the best in the United States. The JPI provided a rare opportunity for young working-class women to participate in sports. (Chicago Historical Society)

Dorothy Herrick leaping over a hurdle, Boston College of Secretarial Science athletic meet, 1921. This athlete's uniform made hurdling difficult. In 1928, there were just five women's track events in the Olympics, and no hurdling races. (Underwood & Underwood/Chicago Historical Society)

Dorothy Griesheber and Wilma Bieber striking a fencing pose, Chicago, 1930. Fencing was one of the first sports advocated for women in the early 1900s, especially in Europe, because of the sport's aristocratic associations. Although it required aggressiveness, fencing was considered to be graceful and cerebral, and it became an Olympic event in 1924. (*Herald and Examiner*/Chicago Historical Society)

Archery meet, Chicago, 1930. For centuries aristocratic women enjoyed archery. The sport required little physical exertion and no special clothing. At the 1904 Olympics, archery was the only sport for women. Participants then belonged to exclusive women's clubs. (*Chicago Daily News*/Chicago Historical Society)

All-American Girls' Softball League players practicing batting at Wrigley Field, 1944. This league was renamed the All-American Girls' Baseball League in 1945. Team owners encouraged players to appear as feminine as possible—they even hired instructors to teach them proper grooming techniques. The women originally played in skirts. (*Chicago Tribune* photo)

Florence Griffith Joyner at the 1988 Olympics in Seoul. The world record holder in the 100-meter dash (10.49 seconds), Joyner won three Olympic gold medals in 1988, wearing an aerodynamic, skin-tight uniform. Joyner's athleticism, glamour, and charisma brought her enormous international publicity. (Reuters/Bettmann)

Gender and Sport in Modern America, 1870–1920

For most of American history, people assumed that sport was a manly activity. Why was sport a gendered activity? Sport was identified as exertive activities that required ruggedness, strength, courage, and vigor. The male bachelor subculture identified prowess in sport, as well as the ability to drink and seduce women, as excellent indicators of manliness. Muscular Christians, who came from an entirely different perspective—sport for them promoted sound morals—also regarded the playing fields as a first-rate site for young men to certify their manliness. Manliness in the mid-nineteenth century had meant the end of boyhood. In the late nineteenth century, people continued to consider athletic prowess as a manly activity through which men could demonstrate how far removed they were from any feminized influences such as religion, education, and culture. This was especially important for upper-class and middle-class men who had not served in the military, engaged in "manly" (physical) labor, or socialized at private men's clubs. Sport provided a venue for them to test their mettle and to prove they were not sissies or "mollycoddles," but rather robust, energetic, and vital.

If sport was considered manly, what place was there for women in athletics? Middle-class women participated in sociable coed sports like ice skating and croquet, but vigorous athletics were inappropriate for women. The conventional wisdom was that Victorian women had little need for physical fitness and that active sports were unfeminine. True believers in the cult of domesticity saw a woman's role as being in the home raising children and establishing a moral environment for her family. Women were warned against sport because they were too weak, could learn such bad (male) values as pride and aggressiveness, could have such good (female) qualities as self-control and modesty undermined, and would become masculine and unprepared for domesticity. What woman would dare participate in sports?

The first sportswomen were mainly from the upper and upper-middle classes wherein their social status protected them from ridicule. They participated in physical activities such as cycling and sports that were sociable, feminine, and not too strenuous. They would play tennis and golf—often at their fathers' country clubs. They briefly engaged in competitive intercollegiate sports under modified rules. The

*participation by such "new women" in sport reflected their increasingly active roles
in society. However, female physical educators successfully resisted intercollegiate
competition because it promoted masculine values ("win at all costs"). They preferred sport for sport's sake in intramurals and play days that largely supplanted
inter-school contests. Sport remained inappropriate for most American women,
especially young working-class women who had limited free time, had few
opportunities to learn to play sports, and had been pressured by parents
and friends to conform to conventionally defined norms of femininity and
respectability.*

⚾ D O C U M E N T S

In the first document, Professor Woodrow Wilson of Princeton University, a fanatic
football fan, explains how football promoted manliness. In the next document,
Theodore Roosevelt discusses how American boys become men by playing sports.
No American spoke as forcefully as Theodore Roosevelt, the leading advocate of the
strenuous life theory, about the manly qualities of sport.

The other documents focus on sport as it relates to women. Document three describes the rise of the Berkeley Ladies' Athletic Club in New York City during the late
1880s. This is followed by Anne O'Hagan's description of women's growing participation in sports and her detailed analysis of sport's positive features for women's
health and clothing. The fifth document is an essay by Senda Berenson, director of
Physical Education at Smith College, describing the positive values of women playing
a form of basketball that was adapted from the men's game to fit women's particular
skills and values. In the sixth document, Dr. Dudley A. Sargent, perhaps the leading
professor of physical education in America, with forty years' experience at Harvard,
answers the widespread fears that sports were making girls masculine. The final document is comprised of the lyrics of one of the all-time popular songs "Take Me Out to
the Ball Game," with lyrics by Jack Norworth and music by Albert Von Tilzer—neither of whom had previously attended a major league game. The song was first publicly sung by Nora Bayes, Norworth's wife, who was a leading vocalist of the day.
"Take Me Out to the Ball Game" is not about a child asking to go to a ball game, but
rather a young lady's plea to her boyfriend to take her to the ballpark for their date.
The song indicated that young women enjoyed baseball games and were very familiar
with the rituals at the ballpark.

Woodrow Wilson Supports Football and Its Promotion of Manliness, 1894

Prof. Woodrow Wilson of Princeton . . . discussed the question, "Ought Football to
be Encouraged?" recently before the Art Club of Philadelphia. . . .

From *New York Times*, February 18, 1894.

"The question has two sides to it," said Prof. Wilson. "Are we going to encourage the game for the sake of others, or are we going to encourage it for the sake of the game itself? It seems to me unquestioned that anything which the colleges can control they should continue to control in the future for the sake of the athletics of this country, because you will observe that it is only by a leadership of gentlemen that this thing can be kept manly and clean. Notwithstanding the fact that the game of cricket has become popular in England, it is, nevertheless, a gentleman's game. They set the standard. The question therefore is, Are manly influences and gentlemanly influences to control football and preside over it? I think I can show you that college men can play ball better than others, and, therefore, they can maintain their leadership, and it will win, as it has in the past, in the leadership of the most manly crowd."

Then, taking up the other side of the question, Shall the game be encouraged for the sake of the game itself? he said: "I must give a most unhesitating affirmative, because I believe it develops more moral qualities than any other game of athletics. Ordinary athletics produce valuable qualities—precision, decision, presence of mind, and endurance. No man can be a successful athlete without these four qualities.

"This game produces two other qualities not common to all athletics, that of co-operation, or action with others, and self-subordination. These are things to be encouraged, and they unquestionably come from the game of football. In football I have been close enough to it to understand all its developments.

"Why is it that Harvard don't win in football? President Eliot says they don't play well because of the elective system of studies, and I think he is practically right. The elective man is never subject to discipline. Let me assure you that the years in which Princeton was defeated were the years when she had not sense enough to win—or, in other words, the men organizing didn't have the qualities of generalship. . . . Prof. Wilson held that football contests should be played only in the large cities. He had heard the game called a "prize fight" and a "bull fight," but it was because the men who played were in their athletic suits. The only reason they did not appear in evening dress was because it was inconvenient, and, as to the large gate receipts, the players did not share in them, as the money was devoted to keeping grounds in order, maintaining an organization, &c. . . .

Theodore Roosevelt Examines How Sport Makes
Boys into Men, 1900

. . . During the last few decades there certainly have been some notable changes for good in boy life. The great growth in the love of athletic sports, for instance, while fraught with danger if it becomes one-sided and unhealthy, has beyond all question had an excellent effect in increased manliness. Forty or fifty years ago the

From "The American Boy," in Theodore Roosevelt, *The Strenuous Life: Essays and Addresses* (New York: Century, 1900), 155–57.

writer on American morals was sure to deplore the effeminacy and luxury of young Americans who were born of rich parents. The boy who was well off then, especially in the big Eastern cities, lived too luxuriously, took to billiards as his chief innocent recreation, and felt small shame in his inability to take part in rough pastimes and field-sports. Nowadays, whatever other faults the son of rich parents may tend to develop, he is at least forced by the opinion of all his associates of his own age to bear himself well in manly exercises and to develop his body—and therefore, to a certain extent, his character—in the rough sports which call for pluck, endurance, and physical address.

Of course boys who live under such fortunate conditions that they have to do either a good deal of outdoor work or a good deal of what might be called natural outdoor play do not need this athletic development. In the Civil War the soldiers who came from the prairie and the backwoods and the rugged farms where stumps still dotted the clearings, and who had learned to ride in their infancy, to shoot as soon as they could handle a rifle, and to camp out whenever they got the chance, were better fitted for military work than any set of mere school or college athletes could possibly be. Moreover, to mis-estimate athletics is equally bad whether their importance is magnified or minimized. The Greeks were famous athletes, and as long as their athletic training had a normal place in their lives, it was a good thing. But it was a very bad thing when they kept up their athletic games while letting the stern qualities of soldiership and statesmanship sink into disuse . . . In short, in life, as in a foot-ball game, the principle to follow is:

Hit the line hard; don't foul and don't shirk, but hit the line hard! . . .

Eleanor Waddle Reports on the Rise of the Berkeley Ladies' Athletic Club, 1889

Physical grace, in its relation to feminine perfection, has not until recently been sufficiently considered as an accumulative quality, capable of growth and augmentation. American women, for the most part, have, hitherto regarded it only as a natural gift or attribute. . . . [However] judicious physical culture will . . . vastly improve upon the natural framework of a woman's figure as to successfully eliminate original blemishes.

Perhaps no enterprise bearing upon this question of athletics for women has awakened so universal an interest in New York, latterly, as the classes organized in connection with the Berkeley Lyceum—now known as the Berkeley Ladies' Athletic Club, and about to pass into its second year. . . . This association now numbers 212 members, with an average increase of thirty-five per month, there being no noticeable diminution during the summer season when half the world is out of town, but, on the contrary, a perceptible addition, thus numbering at the present time almost half of the absolute limit of members (500) . . .

From Eleanor Waddle, "The Berkeley Ladies' Athletic Club," *Outing* 15 (October 1889): 57–63.

The object, primarily, of this private institution has been to afford women the benefit of such gymnastic exercises as are available to men, and, indeed, the result has justified the expectations of the projectors in every way—so much so, in fact, as to warrant Dr. John S. White (the originator of this scheme . . .), in erecting a beautiful club house adjoining the Berkeley Lyceum on Forty-fourth street, West, which has been made ready for occupancy this fall. . . . The ground floor . . . is planned for a reception room and parlor, while in the rear . . . is located a spacious library. In the basement . . . is the swimming pool, lined with white marble, in which the fair athletes may . . . learn their strokes. . . . Cowardice in the water is a well-known characteristic of woman's nature. . . . The remainder of the basement space is utilized by three bowling alleys, overlaid with patent felting, in order to deaden the noise. . . . The entire upper half of the building is . . . left free for the gymnasium, which in point of size and construction is certainly unrivaled in this country. . . .

. . . We are familiar, of course, with the idea of sporadic gymnastics for womankind: individual attempts to overcome existing defects . . . but a permanent organization of this sort, composed of young women of the best representative families of New York—conservative and refined—indicates an arousing of general interest in the subject, which only needed Dr. White's executive ability to project. . . .

The ladies' classes at the Berkeley were taught last winter between the hours of 10 and 4 on Mondays and Fridays, so as not to interfere with the men. Apropos, girls are found to be such enthusiasts when once they have undertaken gymnastics that it is quite necessary to restrain them. Indeed, they resemble squirrels in their ambition and ability, nor will they rest satisfied unless permitted to do everything their brothers are doing at college, and they even try to excel them. . . .

Miss M. Augusta Requa, whose position as instructress won such deserved encomiums of praise during the initial year . . . is a graduate of the Brooklyn Normal School for Physical Culture . . . and is, therefore a thorough mistress of the art. . . . She is not at all the typical athlete, with specimen biceps and iron integuments, . . . but a thoroughly womanly and refined personality rather under the medium size. . . . To see her swing Indian clubs, . . . is not only a surprise, but a privilege. . . . Medical instruction was not included in Miss Requa's course of studies—such knowledge being now deemed requisite for one in that position at the Berkeley Ladies' Club.

. . . Dr. Mary Bissell has been appointed in her stead. . . . Dr. Bissell is well known . . . as being admirably equipped to fill such a position, not only in her professional capacity, but from her practical knowledge of athletics as well—there being in the rear of her office on Fifth avenue, a model gymnastic retreat, thoroughly appointed for the testing of every part of the human anatomy and repairing the condition of every known muscle. . . .

* * * *

By the way, it is not such an easy matter to become a member of this institution as might perhaps be imagined. A mere application and the ability to pay the fee must be surrounded by a modest amount of red tape. Any member of the club may propose a name, but it must be seconded by the club before admission is assured, and if one does not happen to be acquainted with a member an appeal must then be made to the secretary of the commission on admission with at least two references.

This appeal is thereafter submitted and passed upon by the so-called governors — a baker's dozen of well-known social leaders.

* * * *

The costume . . . consisted of a dark, blue cashmere blouse and divided skirt. The latter is simply a very full skirt, gathered into an elastic band at the waist, divided at the bottom into two equal parts. . . . These two parts are then each gathered into an elastic at the knees, Turkish fashion, and the effect obtained is extremely good, granting all the necessary freedom to the legs and presenting, at the same time, a graceful and modest garment. . . . Black hose and black gymnastic shoes complete this equipment. . . . Underneath this woolen uniform was usually worn . . . either a linen garment or one of Egyptian cotton, lisle thread or silk˙. . . but no corsets or bones . . . to hamper the free play of the muscles. . . .

The costume for use in the swimming pool will naturally be of fundamental simplicity, known in theatrical parlance as "tights," made of jersey webbing, woven in a single piece without sleeves or foot covering, and very snug to the figure.

. . . The tyro's first attempts are limited to freehand exercises, followed by the use of the wooden dumb bells usually not over one-half pound or a pound in weight; Indian clubs never over two pounds, although the young ladies have not as yet become very expert in swinging them. . . . Chest weights are greatly used for the general building up of the muscular system, but not with heavy leverage . . . and the rowing machines with sliding seat and pulley weight attachment are also efficacious for certain faults in physique.

The ladies do not practice much on the horizontal bar nor at vaulting, but use the rope ladders, and the inclined ladders for under climbing, while those whose muscles and endurance are not yet equal to this sort of exercise may exploit with the rope-climbing machine—a novel device with wooden pulleys which accurately balances one's weight and offers all of the advantage of climbing without lifting the feet from the ground.

These superb indoor privileges, available to all of the club members at all hours, are charmingly supplemented by the freedom of the Berkeley Oval at Morris Dock, on the Harlem River. . . . One fee covers the use of the gymnasium bowling alleys, swimming pool, parlors and rooms for games recreation and rest in the Ladies' Club House . . . as well as the extraordinary advantages of these suburban grounds with tennis courts, archery range, areas of quoit pitching and croquet, the liberty of boats from the boat house and a private locker at both the grounds and the town gymnasium.

The Ladies' Club House at Morris Dock is a picturesque old stone mansion, with ample acreage and numerous trees of sturdy growth, which has been purchased and refitted in a tasteful and appropriate manner. The site is unrivaled. . . .

. . . After an exhaustive review of these exceptional opportunities it becomes a matter of surprise that the request for admission to membership . . . does not far exceed the capacity of their club houses. At any rate, if New York girls do not shortly awake to the privileges of physical gain and growth which lie within their reach it will not be because an enthusiast has not endeavored to put before them a conscientious statement of facts.

Anne O'Hagan Describes the Athletic American Girl, 1901

To whomsoever the athletic woman owes her existence, to him or her the whole world of women owes a debt incomparably great. Absolutely no other social achievement in the behalf of women is so important and so far reaching in its results. . . . With the single exception of the improvement in the legal status of women, their entrance into the realm of sports is the most cheering thing that has happened to them in the century just past.

The Benefit to Body and Mind.

In the first place, there is the question of health. The general adoption of athletic sports by women meant the gradual disappearance of the swooning damsel of old romance, and of that very real creature, the lady who delighted, a decade or so ago, to describe herself as "high strung," which, being properly interpreted, meant uncontrolled and difficult to live with. Women who didn't like athletics were forced to take them up in self defense; and exercise meant firmer muscles, better circulation, a more equable temper, and the dethronement of the "nervous headache" from its high place in feminine regard.

The revolution meant as much psychologically as it did physically. . . . In dress, . . . no boon has been granted to woman so great as the privilege of wearing shirt waists and short skirts. When the tennis players of ten or fifteen years ago first popularized that boneless, free chested, loose armed bodice they struck a blow for feminine freedom. . . . The woman who plays golf has made it possible for the woman who cannot distinguish between a cleek and a broom handle to go about her marketing in a short skirt; she has given the working girl, who never saw a golf course, freedom from the tyranny of braids and bindings. . . .

To have improved half the race in health, disposition, and dress would seem almost enough for one movement to have accomplished. But athletics have done more than this. They have robbed old age of some of its terrors for women, and they promise to rob it of more. . . .

When "Play" Was "Wisely Banished."

Twenty five years ago a woman so fortunate as to live in the country probably rode on horseback—primarily as a means of locomotion, however. She could also play croquet. The city woman might walk, and she too might play croquet, if she had a large enough lawn; but that was about the sum of the sports permitted.

The change began with the gradual introduction of physical training into the schools. Today there is not a girls' school of any standing that does not include in its curriculum a course in gymnastics, and encourage or insist upon some sort of outdoor exercise. . . . Boards of education require that the newer school buildings shall be properly equipped with gymnasiums. . . .

From Anne O'Hagan, "The Athletic Girl," *Munsey's Magazine* 25 (August 1901): 729–38.

The Growth of College Sports.

From being the chief factor in the athletic life of the women's colleges, the gymnasiums have grown to be distinctly subsidiary. They supplement the outdoor exercises which the location of most of the institutions for higher education makes so natural and attractive. Each has its specialty in the line of sport, and the young woman who wins a championship in rowing, swimming, track events, basket ball, bicycling, or whatever it may be, is a lionized creature who tastes for once the sweets of the cup of utter adulation.

At Wellesley, where the distinctive sport is rowing, Float Day is the banner festival of the year. No girl is allowed to row upon the crews who is not able to swim, but, . . . the only contest permitted is in rowing form, not in speed. Bryn Mawr has by far the most complete and elaborate of the gymnasiums connected with the women's colleges, and its basket ball is famous wherever college women, past, present, or to be, are gathered together. . . .

There are many reasons why college athletics for women are the most important of all. In the first place, a girl who, while struggling for a degree, develops a taste for outdoor sports, never loses it. The chances are ten to one that as a grandmother, she will be an active pedestrian or mountain climber. . . . Moreover, it is college athletics that have the greatest effect upon the physique of women. Once they have attained their full growth, exercise may keep them well, or make them stout or thin, but it will not have the marked effect upon their bodily development that it has upon that of a growing girl.

Physical Culture in the Cities.

Once upon a time the young woman who came out of college was somewhat at a loss how to expend her energy and to keep up her sports. Bicycles, golf, and the country clubs have altered that. Moreover, . . . there are, in the large cities at any rate, excellent gymnasiums. In New York, for instance, apart from the gymnasiums in all the schools, in the working girls' clubs, and in the various branches of the Young Women's Christian Association, there are at least six well known private gymnasiums where women may pursue physical culture to their hearts' content and the good of their bodies. . . .

Between three and four hundred women are enrolled as pupils of the Savage Gymnasium, which, both in attendance and equipment, is the largest in New York. There are classes and there is individual work. Fencing and boxing, both of which have many ardent disciples, are taught privately. Girls of five and women of fifty and sixty are among the patrons. . . .

The cost of being a gymnast in New York varies. There is one gymnasium with pillowed couches about the room, soft, lovely lights, and walls that rest weary eyes; where a crisp capped maid brings the exerciser a cup of milk during her rest upon the divan, where her boots are laced or buttoned by deft fingers other than her own. For these privileges and the ordinary ones of gymnastic training the charge is a hundred dollars a year.

Forty dollars covers the cost in less Sybaritic circles, and if one has the distinction of being a working woman, ten dollars will pay for gymnastic instruction and privileges. The gymnasiums connected with the Christian Associations, the working girls' clubs, the settlements, and the like are even less expensive.

What New York offers women in gymnastic opportunities, all the other large cities duplicate. Chicago, indeed, is in advance of the metropolis, for it has a woman's athletic club, the only large and successful one now in operation in this country. It was started more than a year ago through the efforts of Mrs. Pauline H. Lyon, who interested Mrs. Philip Armour, Mrs. Potter Palmer, . . . and other wealthy women in the project. A business building was remodeled to fit the needs of the club, the cost being about sixty thousand dollars. In addition to the gymnasium proper, a swimming tank . . . has been constructed. . . . A Swedish teacher of swimming was engaged, and the gymnasium instructor is also a graduate in the Swedish methods. There are bowling alleys, rooms for fencing, a Turkish bath, parlors, library, a tea room, diningroom, and everything that such a club could possibly require. . . .

Women on the Golf Links.

With the gradual athletic development of women, the tendency of men to regard their gymnasiums and country clubs as close corporations from which women must be barred at any cost, is disappearing. Of all the twelve hundred golf clubs which dot the United States . . . only one was instituted upon the monastic principle of excluding women. . . .

There are, however, many courses where women are not allowed to play on Sundays and holidays. There is excellent and almost universal masculine testimony to the fact that on crowded days nothing so discourages a man as women playing before him on the golf links. . . .

. . . The best drive of the champion women players is equal in distance to the average drive of the average man. Miss Beatrix Hoyt, . . . three times the national woman's champion, has a drive of from a hundred and twenty to a hundred and sixty yards. A good average drive for a man is a hundred and fifty yards. . . .

. . . In the rest of the game the well trained woman has an equal chance with a man. . . . At Shinnecock Hills there is a separate course for women known as the "red" course. It is of nine holes, but the distances are not short. Until a woman has played this course at least three times in a certain minimum number of strokes, she is not allowed to play upon the "white," or eighteen hole course. . . .

In some places women have been more enterprising than men in the matter of forming clubs. The Morris Country Club, of Morristown, New Jersey, was started and managed by women alone. In the associations of golf clubs there are both women's and men's. There is a Women's Metropolitan Association, under whose direction the women's championship matches have been played. There is a women's association of the clubs around Boston, though there is not yet a men's. . . .

. . . The aim of athletics among women has been the establishment and maintenance of a high general standard of health and vigor, rather than some single brilliant achievement.

So far, with a few notorious exceptions, . . . women have made freedom and fun their objects in athletics; and there are certain indications that this temperate view of the subject is gaining ground even in the ranks of the record breaking sex itself.

Senda Berenson Asserts the Value of Adapted Women's Basketball, 1901

Within the last few years athletic games for women have made such wonderful strides in popularity that there are few directors of physical training who do not value them as an important part of their work. They have become popular, too, not as the outcome of a "fad" but because educators everywhere see the great value games may have in any scheme of education. Gymnastics and games for women are meeting less and less opposition, and gaining larger numbers of warm supporters because our younger generation of women are already showing the good results that may be obtained from them in better physiques and greater strength and endurance.

Now that the woman's sphere of usefulness is constantly widening, now that she is proving that her work in certain fields of labor is equal to man's work and hence should have equal reward, now that all fields of labor and all professions are opening their doors to her, she needs more than ever the physical strength to meet these ever increasing demands. And not only does she need a strong physique, but physical and moral courage as well.

Games are invaluable for women in that they bring out as nothing else just these elements that women find necessary today in their enlarged field of activities. Basket ball is the game above all others that has proved of the greatest value to them. . . .

It is said that one of woman's weaknesses is her inability to leave the personal element out of thought or action. If this is so—and there is some ground for such a supposition—a competitive game like basket ball does much to do away with it. Success in this game can be brought about only by good team-play. A team with a number of brilliant individual players lacking team-work will be beaten always by a team of conscientious players who play for each other. This develops traits of character which organization brings; fair play, impersonal interest, earnestness of purpose, the ability to give one's best not for one's own glorification but for the good of the team—the cause.

. . . Just as basket ball may be made an influence for good so may it be made a strong influence for evil. The gravest objection to the game is the rough element it contains. Since athletics for women are still in their infancy, it is well to bring up the large and significant question: shall women blindly imitate the athletics of men without reference to their different organizations and purpose in life; or shall their athletics be such as shall develop those physical and moral elements that are particularly necessary for them? We can profit by the experience of our brothers and therefore save ourselves from allowing those objectionable features to creep into our athletics that many men are seriously working to eliminate from theirs. . . . It is a well known fact that women

From Senda Berenson, "Significance of Basketball for Women," in *Line Basketball for Women,* ed. Senda Berenson (New York: A. G. Spalding, 1901), 20–27.

abandon themselves more readily to an impulse than men. . . . This shows us that unless we guard our athletics carefully in the beginning many objectionable elements will quickly come in. It also shows us that unless a game as exciting as basket ball is carefully guided by such rules as will eliminate roughness, the great desire to win and the excitement of the game will make our women do sadly unwomanly things. . . .

The modifications in the rules contained in this pamphlet were carefully considered and are entirely the fruit of experience. The two important changes are the division of the playing field and the prohibiting of snatching or batting the ball from the hands of another player.

The division of the gymnasium or field into three equal parts, and the prohibiting of the players of one division from running into the domain of another seems an advantage for many reasons. It does away almost entirely with "star" playing, hence equalizes the importance of the players, and so encourages team work. This also encourages combination plays, for when a girl knows she cannot go over the division line to follow the ball, she is more careful to play as well as possible with the girls near her when the ball comes to her territory. The larger the gymnasium the greater is the tax on individual players when the game is played without lines. It has been found that a number of girls who play without division lines have developed hypertrophy of the heart. The lines prevent the players from running all over the gymnasium, thus doing away with unnecessary running, and also giving the heart moments of rest. On the other hand, the lines do not keep the players almost stationary, as some believe. A player has the right to run anywhere she may please in her own third of the gymnasium.

The divisions, then, concentrate energy, encourage combination plays, equalize team work and do away with undue physical exertion.

Allowing snatching or batting the ball from another person's hand seems the greatest element toward encouraging rough play in the game. It is apt to encourage personal contact; it has an intrinsic quality that goes against one's better nature; it has an element of insult in it. When a player gets the ball it should be hers by the laws of victory, ownership, courtesy, fair play. To prevent this rule, however, from making the game slow and spiritless, a rule was made that a player should not be allowed to hold the ball longer than three seconds under penalty of a foul. Preventing snatching or batting the ball has also developed superb jumping; for a player knows that since she cannot snatch the ball away from her opponent, by jumping in the air as high as possible she may catch the ball before it gets to her opponent.

When the game was first started many saw the danger of "dribbling." The objectionable element was done away with by not allowing the players to bounce the ball more than three consecutive times or lower than the knee. Since then the Y.M.C.A. rules have done away with dribbling together. It seems a good rule to eliminate it when the game is played without division lines—where a player by dribbling can easily get from one basket to the other—but that necessity is overcome with division lines. To allow a player to bounce the ball three times gives an opportunity for having possession of the ball longer than three seconds when she wishes to use a signal or combination play. On the other hand, by demanding that the ball shall be bounced higher than the knee gives a quick opponent a fair opportunity to bat the ball away when it is between the floor and the player's hands. . . .

The original rules allow only five on a team. We have changed the rules to allow any number from five to ten players on a team. My own conviction is that the smallest number of players should be six instead of five, for when the game is played with division lines the work in the centre is much too hard for one player. Some of the strongest and quickest work is done in the centre. The size of the gymnasium should decide the number of players on a team. . . .

Should people imagine that these modifications take the fire and spirit out of the game, they can either try it with their own teams "without prejudice," or witness a game where such modifications are adopted to be convinced of their mistake. Perhaps it may not be out of place to quote some passages from an account which appeared in one of our leading newspapers with reference to a game played with modified rules at one of our colleges for women: "the playing was very rapid and extremely vigorous. From the time the ball went into play until a goal was tossed there was no respite. The playing could not properly be called rough. There was not an instance of slugging, but the ball was followed by the players with rushes, much the way it is on the gridiron. One who supposes it is a simple or weak game would be surprised to see the dash and vigor with which it is entered into. It is a whirl of excitement from start to finish, and yet, with all the desperate earnestness and determination with which the game is played, there is excellent control and much dexterity shown. There is splendid temper and true sportswomanlike spirit in the game. The services of a referee to end a dispute are seldom needed, and there are no delays on account of kicking. The amount of physical strength and endurance which is cultivated is readily apparent. One might suppose that it would be a namby pamby exhibition with much show, many hysterical shrieks and nothing of an athletic contest; but nothing could be more contrary to facts. True, there is no slugging or exhibition of roughness, but the play is extremely vigorous and spirited, and is characterized by a whirl and dash that is surprising to the uninitiated. The possession of self-control, both of temper and physical action, was clearly in evidence yesterday, even during the most exciting stages of the game."

Dr. Dudley A. Sargent Asks,
"Are Athletics Making Girls Masculine?", 1912

. . . Heretofore women have been more creatures of the kitchen and fireside than of the great outdoors, and the present generation of young women who will become the mothers of the next generation have more muscle and more lung capacity than their own mothers. The growth of athletics for girls is largely responsible for this. Colleges for women have more or less grudgingly made room in their

From Dudley A. Sargent, "Are Athletics Making Girls Masculine? A Practical Answer to a Question Every Girl Asks," *Ladies' Home Journal* 29 (March 1912): 11, 71–73.

curricula for gymnastics and athletics, and the non-collegiate world has followed suit and made athletic sports accessible to women. . . .

Many persons honestly believe that athletics are making girls bold, masculine and overassertive; that they are destroying the beautiful lines and curves of her figure, and are robbing her of that charm and elusiveness that has so long characterized the female sex. . . .

Do Women Need as Much Exercise as Men?

From a physiological point of view woman needs physical exercise as much as man. She has the same kind of brain, heart, lungs, stomach and tissues, and these organs in her are just as responsive to exercise as in men. Fundamentally both sexes have the same bones and muscles. They are much larger, however, in the average male than in the average female.

The average male weighs about one hundred and thirty-five pounds without clothes and is about five feet seven inches in height, while the female weighs about one hundred and fifteen pounds and is about five feet two inches in height. The male has broad, square shoulders, the female narrow, sloping ones. The male has a large, muscular chest, broad waist, narrow hips and long and muscular legs, while the female has little muscle in the chest, a constricted waist, broad hips, short legs and thighs frequently weighted with adipose tissue. . . . In point of strength the female is only about one-half as strong as the male. . . .

No Athletic Sport Prohibitive to Women

I have no hesitation in saying that there is no athletic sport or game in which some women cannot enter, not only without fear of injury but also with great prospects of success. In nearly every instance, however, it will be found that the women who are able to excel in the rougher and more masculine sports have either inherited or acquired masculine characteristics. This must necessarily be so, since it is only by taking on masculine attributes that success in certain forms of athletics can be won. For instance, . . . [s]he could not hope to succeed in rowing or in handling heavy weights without broadening the waist and shoulders and strengthening the muscles of the back and abdomen. . . .

. . . Nor do the limitations which I have mentioned apply to young girls from ten to fifteen years of age, who, if properly trained, will often surpass boys of the same age in any kind of game or athletic performance. But it is at these ages that girls have neat, trim and boyish figures. If girls received the same kind of physical training as boys throughout their growing and developing period they could make a much more creditable showing as athletes when they become adult women. The interesting question is, Would such girls become more womanly women, and the boys more manly men? . . .

The Best Sports for Girls

There are no sports that tend to make women masculine in an objectionable sense except boxing, baseball, wrestling, basket-ball, ice hockey, water polo and Rugby football. These sports are thought better adapted to men than to women, because they are so rough and strenuous. . . .

These Make Women More Masculine

Physically all forms of athletic sports and most physical exercises tend to make women's figures more masculine, inasmuch as they tend to broaden the shoulders, deepen the chest, narrow the hips, and develop the muscles of the arms, back and legs, which are masculine characteristics. Some exercises, like bowling, tennis, fencing, hurdling and swimming, tend to broaden the hips, which is a feminine characteristic. . . .

Just how all-round athletics tend to modify woman's form may be judged by comparing the conventional with the athletic type of woman. The conventional woman has a narrow waist, broad and massive hips and large thighs. In the athletic type of woman sex characteristics are less accentuated, and there is a suggestion of reserve power in both trunk and limbs. Even the mental and moral qualities that accompany the development of such a figure are largely masculine, . . .

Sports Should Be Adapted to Women

. . . While there is some danger that women who try to excel in men's sports may take on more marked masculine characteristics . . . this danger is greatly lessened if the sports are modified so as to meet their peculiar qualifications. . . . All the apparatus used and the weights lifted, as well as the height and distance to be attained in running, jumping, etc., should be modified to meet her limitations. Considering also the peculiar constitution of her nervous system and the great emotional disturbances to which she is subject, changes should be made in many of the rules and regulations governing the sports and games for men, to adapt them to the requirements of women.

Modify Men's Athletics for Women

. . . Women as a class cannot stand a prolonged mental or physical strain as well as men. . . . Give women frequent intervals of rest and relaxation and they will often accomplish as much in twenty-four hours as men accomplish. . . . I have arranged the schedule of work at both the winter and summer Normal Schools at Cambridge so that periods of mental and physical activity follow each other alternately, and both are interspersed with frequent intervals of rest.

The modifications that I would suggest in men's athletics so as to adapt them to women are as follows: Reduce the time of playing in all games and lengthen the periods of rest between the halves. Reduce the heights of high and low hurdles and lessen the distance between them. Lessen the weight of the shot and hammer and all other heavy-weight appliances. In heavy gymnastics have bars, horses, swings, ladders, etc., adjustable so that they may be easily adapted to the requirements of women. In basket-ball, a favorite game with women and girls, divide the field of play into three equal parts by lines, and insist upon the players confining themselves to the space prescribed for them. This insures that everyone shall be in the game, and prevents some players from exhausting themselves. . . .

I am often asked; "Are girls overdoing athletics at school and college?" I have no hesitation in saying that in many of the schools where basket-ball is being played according to rules for boys many girls are injuring themselves in playing this game.

The numerous reports of these girls breaking down with heart trouble or a nervous collapse are mostly too well founded. . . . These instances generally occur in schools or colleges where efforts are made to arouse interest in athletics by arranging matches between rival teams, clubs and institutions, and appealing to school pride. . . . The individual is not only forced to do her best, but to do even better than her best, though she breaks down in her efforts to surpass her previous records.

There will be little honor or glory in winning a race, playing a game, or doing a "stunt" which every other girl could do. It is in the attempt to win distinction by doing something that others cannot do that the girl who is over-zealous or too ambitious is likely to do herself an injury. For this reason girls who are ambitious to enter athletic contests should be carefully examined and selected by a physician or trained woman expert. . . .

A Female Fan Tells Her Beau, "Take Me Out to the Ball Game" (1908)

Katie Casey was baseball mad,
Had the fever and had it bad;
Just to root for the home town crew,
ev'ry sou Katie blew
On a Saturday, her young beau
called to see if she'd like to go,
To see a show but Miss Katie said "no,
I'll tell you what you can do":

(Chorus:)
Take me out to the ball game,
Take me out with the crowd.
Buy me some peanuts and Cracker Jacks,
I don't care if I never get back.
Let me root, root, root for the home team.
If they don't win it's a shame,
for it's one, two, three strikes, you're out,
at the old ball game.

Katie Casey saw all the games
Knew the players by their first names;
Told the umpire he was wrong,
all along, good and strong
When the score was just two to two,
Katie Casey knew what to do,
Just to cheer up the boys she knew,
She made the gang sing this song:

(Chorus:)

From Jack Norworth and Albert Von Tilzer, "Take Me Out to the Ball Game" (1908).

⚾ *E S S A Y S*

The two essays in this section explore how sports defined appropriate parameters for gendered behavior and how, in turn, being male or female established stark parameters around an individual's sporting options. In the first essay, drawn from *The Manly Art: Bare-Knuckle Prize Fighting in America* (1986), one of the outstanding books in sport history, Elliott J. Gorn analyzes how the art of self-defense helped define for men the penultimate qualities of a manly individual. In the mid-nineteenth century, boxing demarcated several qualities of manliness for the male bachelor subculture, which included courage, self-discipline, and self-control. In the late nineteenth century, the potential to gain such traits through sparring made the sport popular with certain segments of the upper and middle classes who were worried about their own manliness and ability to measure up to their brave and virile ancestors. The second article, by Roberta J. Park, a prolific sport historian at the University of California, Berkeley, focuses on the opportunities that middle-class women around the turn of the century had to participate in the male-defined world of sports. Park is particularly interested in the British influence on American women's athleticism. This selection is drawn from a broader monograph on sport and gender that also considers the relationship between sport and manliness in Victorian culture.

Manliness in the Squared Circle

ELLIOTT J. GORN

Within the magic circle of the ring, not only were concepts of wealth altered, but gender too became inverted. With the breakdown of the household-based artisan economy, sexual identity grew increasingly bifurcated. Moreover, men and women were encouraged to moderate their passions and keep them from interfering with the goal of economic success. In the bourgeois canon, masculinity meant, above all, taking responsibility, controlling one's impulses, and working hard in order to support a family. Being a good provider was the touchstone of being a man, so probity, dependability, and resistance to temptation defined a middle-class male ideal. The very word manly was usually conjoined with "independence" or "self-reliance," thus linking the bourgeois concept of masculinity with autonomy and self-possession, key elements of Victorian character which flowed from diligent labor. Not all Victorian men fulfilled the role; many slid back into less morally rigid ways. The sporting underworld could stir the envy of those who felt themselves deprived of the freedom and openness they perceived in working-class culture. Despite these deep feelings of ambivalence, however, the bourgeois male ideal remained compelling, and it was reinforced by a new female role. For middle-class women, the home became a separate sphere, not a place of production but a haven where their superior morality refined men, nurtured children, and inculcated tender emotions. This domestic ideal placed women at the center of moral

From Elliott J. Gorn, *The Manly Art: Bare-Knuckle Prize Fighting in America* (Ithaca, NY: Cornell University Press, 1986), 140–202.

life, freeing men to go out into the corrupting world, then return to a purifying sanctuary.

If the fundamental test of masculinity was, by Victorian lights, being a good breadwinner, if work was a man's primary source of self-definition, the measure of his worth, and proof of his manhood, then many working-class men in industrializing cities were doomed to failure. Of course, those who performed heavy or dangerous tasks could take pride in their strength and stamina. But fathers now had diminishing legacies of wealth or skill to pass on to sons, and for most men, earnings were small and opportunities limited. Put simply, daily labor undermined rather than buttressed masculinity. It made sense, then, that many workers turned to a more elemental concept of manhood, one they could demonstrate during leisure hours. Toughness, ferocity, prowess, honor, these became the touchstones of maleness, and boxing along with other sports upheld this alternative definition of manhood. The *manly* art defined masculinity not by how responsible or upright an individual was but by his sensitivity to insult, his coolness in the face of danger, and his ability to give and take punishment.

Sociologists have talked of a "bachelor subculture" to capture a phenomenon so common to nineteenth- and early twentieth-century cities: large numbers of unmarried males finding their primary human contact in one another's company. In some large cities unweddedness was so common that at mid-century, 40 percent of the men between twenty-five and thirty-five years of age were single. Irish immigrants contributed to this tendency, bringing a tradition of late marriage and high rates of bachelorhood to America, but even among the native-born, working men in the nineteenth century tended not to marry until their late twenties. The bachelor subculture, however, included betrothed men as well as unattached ones. Sullivan, Hyer, and Morrissey, for example, were all married, but their wives seemed almost tangential to their lives as the champions passed their nights drinking and carousing among friends. With the breakdown of the household economy, men and women spent diminishing amounts of their work time together, and many chose to take their leisure too in gender-segregated realms. In saloons, pool halls, and lodges as well as in gangs, firehouses, and political clubs, men gathered to seek companionship, garner one another's esteem, and compete for status.

Here, implicitly, was a rejection of the cult of domesticity so characteristic of bourgeois Victorian life. Members of the bachelor subculture expected women to be submissive; they also tended to view them as either pure and virginal or exciting and whorish. Women were both exploitable and less than central to men's affective lives. Rather than spend their nonworking hours within the confines of the family circle—where women's allegedly superior moral nature and "instinctive" sense of self-sacrifice tamed men and elevated children—members of the sporting fraternity chose to seek rough male companionship. It was not only men, however, who felt stifled by the domestic ideal. The Victorian home emotionally suffocated many middle-class women as well, and to compensate for the deprivations caused by their gender-based role, they sought one another's company. The homoerotic tone of letters women wrote to each other and the sensual descriptions of their meetings at spas where they went for physical and emotional therapy had less to do with simple homosexuality (though no doubt homosexual acts and relationships occurred) than with women reaching out for the warmth, love, and emotional contact that homelife denied.

There was a parallel in the bachelor subculture that supported the ring. Of course heterosexual prowess was an important element of masculinity; fathering a family, picking up unattached women, and frequenting prostitutes all demonstrated virility. But maleness seemed most emphatically confirmed in the company not of women, but of other men. The loving descriptions of boxers' bodies so common in antebellum fight reports grew less from narrowly defined homosexuality than from a common male aesthetic. Men perceived men as creatures of beauty because they focused so much emotional attention on one another. In the saloon, the firehouse, or the gang, many working-class males found their deepest sense of companionship and human connectedness. The boxer's physique was a palpable expression of such masculine values as strength, power, and stamina. With his body alone the prize fighter attained financial autonomy. Conversely, women were associated with those family responsibilities made so onerous by low pay and lack of economic opportunity. Rather than accept domesticity as the highest good—and domesticity, after all, was a bourgeois luxury; working-class women often toiled in factories or as laundresses or maids—many laboring men sought refuge from the family in all-male peer groups where heroic prize fighters symbolized independence through physical prowess.

Here the concept of male honor helps us understand the culture of the ring. Honor, as historians have recently applied the term, is distinct from the more modern ideals of conscience and dignity. The Victorian man of character possessed a particularly well-developed conscience (an internalized sense of morality stressing strict self-control) and a profound belief in human dignity (especially faith in the fundamental equality of all men). Thus each Christian faced God alone, businessmen were responsible for the fulfillment of their contracts, and good citizens acted on inviolable principles to perfect society. Although the approbation of others was gratifying for such men, good deeds brought their own internal satisfactions and immoral acts evoked a sense of guilt.

But honor more than conscience or dignity depended on external ratification. It was conferred when men acknowledged one another as peers, often in symbolic acts such as buying drinks, spending money lavishly, or toasting one another's accomplishments. Honor had no existence outside group life, for only reputation and the esteem of others conferred it. Honorific societies have tended to be tightly knit and nonbureaucratic, placing special emphasis not on inward virtues but on outward signs that must be approved or rejected by one's status equals. The objects of honor have varied across time and cultures. They have included the protection of the chastity of wives and daughters, grand displays of hospitality, and tests of male prowess. But regardless of the specifics, an individual had honor only when his kin or his fellows said he did. Honor was denied him when his peers refused to acknowledge his status as an equal, and no amount of arguing could restore it. Only acts of valor, especially violent retribution, expunged the sense of shame, proved one's mettle, and reasserted one's claim to honor.

The fights between boxers and the collectivities they belonged to—fire brigades, gangs, political factions, saloon cliques, militia companies, and so forth—were often animated by a sense of lost honor, of having had one's status impugned. Stake money for fighters, turf between gangs, and elected office for political parties, these were tangible objects to contend over, but the real battle was for peer recognition, for a sense of distinction that made a man first among equals in the small male cliques of working-class society. Saloons were so central to the culture of the ring in part because here, with alcohol lowering inhibitions, men affirmed their right to drink together or, alternatively, to cast aspersions that only blood could redeem. The ethic of honor had roots in the Old World, but it continued to thrive where individuals were concerned less with morality or piety, more with flaunting their status among peers through acts of masculine prowess. In mid-nineteenth-century America, then, character, conscience, and dignity were hallmarks of middle-class culture, while honor remained central to the lives of the poor and marginal, the acid test of personal worth in the male peer society.

The Rites of Violence

Perhaps most important, the bloodiness displayed in the ring was symptomatic of the violence endemic to urban working-class life. Unemployment and poverty were constant threats, and a cycle of alternating depression and inflation made the antebellum years particularly unstable. New York City's per capita wages fell by roughly 25 percent in the decade before mid-century. Moreover, the *New York Times* estimated in the middle of the 1850s that a family of four needed a minimum yearly income of six hundred dollars, double the salary of many laborers and well over what the majority of working-class men earned. In the impersonal market economy, lack of job security and inequalities of wealth and power were becoming intractable problems. . . . Staggering numbers of men were killed or maimed on the job. Indeed, by 1860 there were four Irishwomen for every three Irishmen in New York City, partly because of desertions, partly because of breadwinners' need to travel in search of work, but also as a result of brutally high job-related mortality rates. In addition, poor diet, overcrowding, and lack of modern sanitation contributed to waves of deadly epidemics. Between 1840 and 1855 the city's mortality rates rose from one in forty to one in twenty-seven, and nearly half of all New York children died before reaching age six.

The death sounds of livestock slaughtered in public markets, the smell of open sewers, the feverish cries of children during cholera season, the sight of countless men maimed on the job, all were part of day-to-day street life. The poor lived as their ancestors had, in a world that did little to shield them from pain. Men tolerated violence—created violence—because high death rates, horrible accidents, and senseless acts of brutality were a psychological burden that only stoicism or bravado helped lighten.

This context makes sense of the ring's violence. Boxing, as well as cockfighting, bullbaiting, and ratting, did not just reflect the bloodiness of life. Rather, these and similar sports shaped violence into art, pared away its maddening arbitrariness, and thereby gave it order and meaning. Here, ideally, was true equality of opportunity, a pure meritocracy free of favoritism and special influence. At their best, the ring and the pit rendered mayhem rule-bound instead of anarchic, voluntary rather than random. Boxers, like fighting cocks and trained bulldogs, made bloodshed comprehensible and thus offered models of honorable conduct. They taught men to face danger with courage, to be impervious to pain, and to return violence rather than passively accept it.

As members of male peer societies steeped in the conflicts of their day, prize fighters embodied community values, giving them concentrated symbolic expression. Often harsh and brutal, working-class life required a dramatic form to express its reality. Boxing acknowledged, rather than denied life's cruelty, even celebrated it. In the midst of nagging hatreds and festering rivalries, often unleashed by flowing alcohol and blustering attacks on masculine honor, the cool restraint needed to sign articles, train, organize excursions, and bring off matches made bloodletting comprehensible. A properly carried out fight was a performance, a pageant, a ritual, that momentarily imposed meaning on the savage irrationalities of life. Out of chaos the ring created an aesthetic of violence based on bodily development, fighting skills, and controlled brutality.

This is not to argue that boxing and similar sports supplanted real with vicarious brutality. On the contrary, as recent research reveals, symbolic displays of violence tend to promote further violence. Even as pugilism brought order to bloodiness, made it comprehensible by confining it to two men who represented larger collectivities and fought by rules, the ring also upheld, indeed gloried in the fact that brutishness was part of man's fate. Not the pious homilies of evangelicals, the sentimental humanitarianism of reformers, nor the optimistic progressivism of the middle class, prize fighting as a metaphor declared that there was limited good in this world, that every man's victory implied another's loss, that the way was harsh and bloody for all, and that hardship, even death, were the soulmates of life. The ring thus expressed an outlook in which pain and defeat were ineluctable parts of living, a notion almost heretical in this rationalistic age.

Despite the divisions among sportingmen, then, all were united by disruptive change in their patterns of work, alienation from bourgeois or evangelical ways, and shared attitudes toward wealth, labor, leisure, masculinity, and honor. Working-class men adopted their own forms of expressive culture, and prize fighting symbolically affirmed their distinct ethos. If not a political threat to new alignments of social and economic power, the ring at least offered cultural opposition; if not a challenge to evangelical or bourgeois authority, here at least was a denial of the values that undergirded oppressive social relationships.

Above all, the manly art gave men a way to get a symbolic grip on the contradictions in their lives, to see these conflicts neatly arranged and played out. It offered an alternative to the Victorian vision of an ever-improving world, stressing instead a constant balance between victory and defeat. As drama, the prize fight depicted pain as the portion for both winner and loser, violence as a necessary means to human ends, and loyalty to one's communal group along with honor in defending one's good name as the very highest human ideals. The ring celebrated the high-stakes gamble, the outrageous boast, the love of strife. Prize fighting made Old World virtues such as prowess, courage, and virility the essence of manhood, while loving descriptions of muscles and sinews gave palpable expression to naked physical beauty as a source of masculine pride.

Of course the culture of the ring had an ugly, disturbing side. Bare-knuckle fighting attracted some social misfits who reveled in brutality. Boxing could become an outlet for bully boys who enjoyed inflicting pain, sociopaths who responded only to their own pleasure at others' suffering. The special order of the ring moreover, sometimes broke down under the tensions it symbolically reconciled, unleashing further violence. Prize fighting also defined masculinity in a narrow way that encouraged male exploitation of women and alienated men from a whole range of softer emotions within themselves. But at its best the ring dramatized a world of victory for the socially downtrodden, realistically counterposed to defeat and bloodshed. It offered colorful, satisfying rituals that emobodied the most profound human strivings but always presented them in mercilessly unsentimental terms. Boxers responded to a violent world by embracing violence, by accepting brutality and returning it with interest, by being as tough and savage as life itself.

In all of these ways bare-knuckle prize fighting was woven into the texture of working-class culture during the antebellum era. A plethora of urban street institutions supported the ring, as boxing helped crystallize the ethos of laboring men. Pugilism gave controlled expression to the schisms of working-class life, not in order to drain away violent passions but to make those divisions comprehensible and thereby transform chaos into meaning. Divided by neighborhood, ethnic, and workplace tensions, large segments of the lower classes were nonetheless united in opposition to key Victorian values, values on which an onerous new social system was built. Every bout inverted bourgeois and evangelical assumptions about such fundamental social phenomena as money, gender, and violence. More, the prize ring conveyed its own alternative outlook. Pugilism was an autonomous expressive form that symbolically opposed the drift of modern society. In crucial ways, then, boxing during the age of heroes captured the values, the ethos, the distinct culture of countless working men who felt dispossessed amidst the Victorian era's heady optimism.

. . . By late in the century countless American men of good families were personally familiar with boxing. The small numbers who had attended sparring classes given by the old professors of pugilism before the Civil War now became a multitude. Young men from the wealthiest backgrounds, such as Theodore Roosevelt at Harvard and William C. Whitney at Yale, fought with gloves in college during the 1870s. By the 1880s cabinet secretaries such as James G. Blaine and Zackary Chandler, former governor Flower and ex-senator Conklin of New York, all took sparring lessons. Exclusive athletic clubs hired boxing coaches, YMCAs offered instruction, and self-defense manuals proliferated. The New York Athletic Club even sponsored the first national amateur boxing championship, in 1878. *Frank Leslie's Magazine* acknowledged pugilism's recent popularity when it bewailed the worship of brute force which filled New York City sparring rooms and urged that "prize-fighters be once more regarded as outlaws and not as public entertainers."

Quite the opposite occurred, for amateur sparring's newfound popularity helped redeem professional ring fighting. The New York Athletic Club, for example, retained middleweight champion Mike Donovan to teach "gentlemen eminent in science, literature, art, social and commercial life." Unlike his professional ancestor, William Fuller, Donovan did not hesitate to assist at and arrange regular prize battles, apparently offending none of his elite clientele. Other cities followed New York's lead. The gentlemen of San Francisco's Olympic Club were so pleased with their sparring master, prize fighter James J. Corbett, that they paid him $2,500 per year. Boston elites also learned the fistic arts in their own private institutions. The Cribb Club, for example, where ring fighter Jake Kilrain gave lessons, had over one hundred enrollees by the mid-eighties, among them businessmen, lawyers, physicians, and journalists. Nomination by two members and the approval of an election committee were required for admission. Similarly, the Commercial Athletic Club charged an initiation fee and monthly dues to discourage all "unruly and turbulent spirits."

Even an occasional Christian voice now spoke up for the prize ring. Reverend Brobst of Chicago's Westminster Presbyterian Church believed the Sullivan-Kilrain fight in 1889 contained important lessons for the faithful. Before going into training, the principals were "drinkers, sensual, beastly" men. But once articles had been signed, Brobst noted, the opponents resisted all temptation: "Talk about taking up your cross, Christians! You ought to be ashamed of yourselves. Take a lesson in hardship and denial from these pugilists!" The ends of prize fighting might be corrupt, but the means were divine, for hard training brought boxers to physical and mental perfection. Here was an important change from earlier decades. Although a few writers had praised the abstemiousness of boxers in training, no minister in the era of Heenan, Hyer, and Morrissey would have dared refer to prize fighters as paragons of Christian virtue. But Brobst argued that men in the ring offered models of will power, fortitude, and endurance to the faithful. Boxing was a metaphor for a grim world of stern competition, where toughness was both a religious and a secular duty. "Take a lesson," Brobst admonished his congregation, and no doubt many did, seeking spiritual enlightenment at the next convenient bout.

In one form or another, then, boxing became familiar to men of solid social standing. Courage and confidence, self-command and graceful bearing, vigor and decisiveness, pugilism fostered all of these traits. The animal world, psychologist G. Stanley Hall declared, was filled with the struggle for survival. Man's aggressive "instinct" sometimes embroiled him in senseless combat, yet anger was a valuable trait and real men rejoiced in noble strife. Hall—who championed the concept of a distinct adolescent stage of life, with its own psychology—believed that boys must learn to fight, lest they grow up to be unmanly and craven milksops. Boxing lessons were the perfect means to channel aggression, tempering adolescent violence yet engendering courage, force of will, and self-assertion.

Soon respectable journals advocated pugilism. Daniel L. Dawson, writing in *Lippincott's Monthly,* argued that sparring was among the very best forms of exercise, encouraging not only muscular development but also courage, temperance, and quickness of thought. *Outing,* which claimed to be *the* gentleman's magazine of sport, travel, and outdoor life, became a repository of information for genteel boxers. Essays not only discussed leverage, mechanics, and physiology; they upheld the moral worth of pugilism. Amateur bouts, A. Austin declared in "The Theory and Practice of Boxing," were tests of character, forcing men to confront their moral strengths and weaknesses.

Some writers now called for the reform of prize fighting. Charles E. Clay, who wrote about yachting and exotic travel for *Outing,* did a series of articles based on his personal boxing experiences. The gentlemanly fighter, like Eakins's men in the ring, was beautiful: "His shoulders are broad, but graceful and sloping, and from them the arms, with full and rounded biceps, fall so easily and naturally to their proper position at the sides! . . . The chest expansive, and well filled out, shows plenty of room for the lungs to work. The deltoid and shoulder muscles are all thoroughly developed, and go to form a strong and shapely back." But the benefits were more than merely physical, for boxing taught pluck and endurance. Those who entered the ring developed the resourcefulness, the confidence, and the command to overcome life's daily obstacles and become leaders among men. However, Clay added, only the rules of glove fighting made boxing so excellent for moral and physical training; the old bare-knuckle ways must go.

Duffield Osborn concurred. His "Defense of Pugilism," published in the *North American Review* in 1888, argued that as civilization grew overrefined, it degenerated into "mere womanishness." The rigorous self-denial of boxers in training, their unflinching courage in the face of pain and fatigue, helped counter these pernicious tendencies. Those who valued "high manly qualities" ought therefore to array themselves against the "mawkish sentimentality" that threatened to transform Americans into "a race of eminently respectable female saints." Boxing, Osborn concluded, must be reformed and supported.

John Boyle O'Reilly, poet, editor of the *Boston Pilot,* and an acknowledged leader of the Irish-American middle class, became the ring's most articulate champion. Prize fighting was too valuable to be sullied by gangsters and criminals. "Let it stand alone," O'Reilly argued, "an athletic practice, on the same footing as boating or football." Sparring was the perfect recreation for businessmen whose nerves were frayed by competition and energies depleted by the frenetic pace of life. No other sport exercised the trunk, limbs, eyes, and mind so well. The intensity of sparring made it ideal training for the young: "The boxer in action has not a loose muscle or a sleepy brain cell. His mind is quicker and more watchful than a chess player's. He has to gather his impulses and hurl them, straight and purposeful, with every moment and motion." Watching honest professionals fight with gloves also taught valuable lessons in manly fortitude and confidence. "Where else in one compressed hour," O'Reilly asked, "can be witnessed the supreme test and tension of such precious living qualities as courage, temper, endurance, bodily strength, clear-mindedness in excited action, and above all, that heroic spirit that puts aside the cloak of defeat though it fall anew a hundred and a thousand times, and in the end, reaches out and grasps the silver mantle of success?" Ideal training for all citizens, boxing must be rescued from gamblers and thugs and restored to gentlemanly luster.

Pugilism, then, was filled with meaning for turn-of-the-century America. Bloodletting, merciless competition, and stern self-testing in the ring addressed the newly perceived need of middle- and upper-class men for more active life. Alive in every nerve, the boxer was in complete control of his body, negating by example the pervasive fears of overcivilization, nervous breakdowns, and neurasthenia. The ring countered effeminizing tendencies, preparing men for the life of strife.

The physical and mental acuteness of two fighters in combat offered an intriguing symbol for a society extolling "manly competition" in the market place and a culture beginning to substitute a cult of personal experience for tight self-control. Pugilists were models of poise and courage for an old upper-class that felt threatened from above by new industrial wealth and below by immigrant hordes and labor radicals. Prize fighting upheld fantasies of untrammeled masculinity for a new white-collar class locked into distinctly unvirile, corporate jobs. As a spectator sport, boxing symbolically reconciled contradictory cultural imperatives. Pugilists were models of aggressiveness but also of self-discipline and self-control. Moreover, the fans, by passively imbibing images of ultramasculine action, by sitting back and watching others bleed, could have it both ways, extolling prowess while filling the role of consumer.

And here was the problem. Upper- and middle-class men were enthralled by the drama, the violence, the pageantry of the ring, but few were willing to accept prize fighting because of its associations with gangs, criminality, and the urban underworld. Change was needed, to purge the sport of its rowdy, even criminal elements yet retain the old vibrancy. For such men as Roosevelt and O'Reilly, the solution was to assimilate professional boxing to amateur rules. . . .

Sport, Gender, and Society in the Late Nineteenth Century

ROBERTA J. PARK

This chapter attempts to cast some further light on nineteenth- and early twentieth-century concepts of sport and gender, specifically in a transatlantic Anglo-American perspective. The focus is upon 'middle class' constructs and the involvement of women. Considerable attention is also given to men and sport, as modern sport has been defined and dominated by the male model. Moreover, the notion of gender makes little sense in human societies unless 'male' and 'female' are compared and contrasted. . . .

The forms which sporting and recreative activities took helped to define and reinforce prevailing concepts of *gender*. In fact, in the decades following the American Civil War, . . . organized sport and various forms of vigorous physical activity became major vehicles for defining and acting out male gender roles. This was true whether one participated, watched, discussed, read about or wrote about sport. On both sides of the Atlantic, nineteenth-century sport came to be forcefully and graphically depicted as the 'natural' province of males; hence, sport contributed substantially to establishing and maintaining ideologies about the proper sphere of women. . . .

During the nineteenth century American concepts of manliness changed. So, too, did the concept of the ideal woman. Anthony Rotundo has recently described this major shift in middle-class ideals of manhood from a standard '. . . rooted in the life of the community and qualities of a man's soul to a standard of manhood based on individual achievement and the male body'. These new values could be seen, in part, in the rapid rise of interest in intercollegiate athletics, the out-of-doors movement, and the anthropometry craze of the 1880s and 1890s. They could

From Roberta J. Park, "Sport, Gender and Society in a Transatlantic Victorian Perspective," in *From "Fair Sex" to Feminism: Sport and the Socialization of Women in the Industrial and Post-Industrial Eras,* ed. Roberta Park and J. A. Mangan (London: Frank Cass, 1987), 58–87.

also be seen in growing anxieties about masturbation, impotence, illness, and a feebleness in the American (read middle-class Anglo-Saxon American) race.

. . . Ideas about woman's proper sphere had begun to change in the early 1800s. Her range of activity and influence was increasingly confined to the home at the same time that her body was encased in whalebone corsets and layers of clothing which covered her from throat to floor. Her physiology, dominated by the reproduction function, confined her to an entirely 'separate sphere'. By the middle years of the nineteenth century the tradition that women had useful work to per-form had given way to newer ideals of grace and ornament, at least for those fami-lies which could afford such life styles. The leisured woman, unsullied by toil, well but modestly dressed, became a visual symbol of the success of the household, giv-ing status to its male head.

I

Middle-class Americans were . . . familiar with much of the Victorian British health reform literature, drawing upon it for many of their pamphlets and manuals. They also expressed their own concerns in a wide assortment of journals and periodicals. Vegetarians, Grahamites, hydropathists, phrenologists, and advocates of exercise systems bombarded the public with their ideas. An anxiety that Ameri-cans were physically inferior to their English contemporaries, apparent in literary, educational, religious, and popular journals before the Civil War, became even more evident in the 1870s. By the 1890s, however, Americans were asserting that they were the world's foremost nation, and that they were physically and techno-logically, if not intellectually and morally, superior to everyone. Sport—that is, male sport—was frequently used in an effort to establish and give weight to this presumption of superiority. . . .

No American in the middle decades of the nineteenth century was as constant and impassioned a spokesman for the cause of 'manly exercise' as was Thomas Wentworth Higginson, aptly called America's prophet of 'muscular Christianity'. Higginson also believed in greater opportunities for women, and in 1862 he dis-cussed the relative poor health of American girls and the benefits they might derive from gymnastic exercises, concluding that England '. . . furnish[ed] the represen-tative types of vigorous womanhood'. Catharine Beecher's extremely popular *Physiology and Calisthenics for Schools and Families* (1856), a work which had a considerable impact on education for women as well as on ideas regarding physi-cal education, informed its readers: 'In this nation it is rare to see a married woman of thirty or forty, especially in the more wealthy classes, who retains the fullness of person and the freshness of complexion that mark good health. But in England, al-most all women are in full perfection of womanhood at that period of life'. . . . Many Americans *believed* that British men and women were healthier, more phys-ically active, more prone to take out-of-door exercise, and, it was usually feared, superior beings. . . .

Before the 1860s, organized sport was embryonic in the United States. . . . Even . . . rudimentary forms of sport for women would have been unthinkable, given prevailing Victorian standards. Calisthenic exercise and simple recreations, however, were another matter. Sara Josepha Hale, who edited *Godey's Lady's Book* for nearly 40 years, advocated somewhat increased participation in physical activity for girls, using the authority of contemporary physicians to legitimize her claims. A spate of periodicals, of which the *Journal of Health and Longevity* was one example, urged dietary reform, callisthenic exercises, the 'water cure', out-door amusements and physical education for girls and women, as well as for boys and men. . . . On the eve of the Civil War Dioclesian Lewis opened his New Gym-nasium for Ladies, Gentlemen and Children and began publication of his *Boston Journal of Physical Culture.* Lewis gave considerable attention to the physical training of females, and in 1861 established a Normal Institute for Physical Educa-tion which sought to train both 'ladies and gentlemen' to teach gymnastics. The benefits of healthful exercise in the formation of proper female virtue, and as preparation for the important duties of motherhood were frequently stressed. . . . A few early women's rights advocates, however, saw in physical education a means to emancipation and self-fulfilment. . . .

. . . Of all the pre-Civil War female women's rights advocates, Stanton was most convinced that vigorous physical activity and a stronger and healthier body were vital to the advancement of women. Writing for *The Lily,* a newspaper founded by Amelia Bloomer and dedicated to women's issues, Stanton rejected 'man's claims to physical superiority', stating: 'We cannot say what the woman might be physically, if the girl were allowed all the freedom of the boy, in romping, swimming, climbing and playing ball. . . .' Such hoydenish activities could help women to become intelligent and self-reliant. It was for this reason, far more than because healthy women would be better mothers, that Stanton continually insisted that girls and women should have improved physical education. . . .

II

. . . Attitudes regarding what constituted the *ideal* man changed, as did attitudes concerning the *ideal* woman. By the 1890s, among the better educated, in par-ticular, Victorian womanly virtues were being challenged by those of 'the New Woman': there was much ambivalence, however, even among those who sub-scribed to more equity for women. Characteristics which this 'New Woman' em-bodied included independent spirit and athletic zeal: 'She rode a bicycle, played tennis or golf, showed six inches of stocking beneath her skirts, and loosened her corsets'. . . .

. . . By the last decades of the century Americans . . . had taken to athletic sports with a vengeance, converting most of them into models which were highly visible, businesslike, professional and thoroughly infused with pragmatic Yankee values. This tendency was criticized in the British press and also by numerous Americans who preferred what might be called an idealized interpretation of 'mus-cular Christianity' and English schoolboy sport. The conflict between the two views became intense in the 1890s and early 1900s, especially in intercollegiate athletics and with regard to programmes like many of those conducted by the Amateur Athletic Union. . . .

III

In late April 1898 the United States had declared war on Spain over the issue of Cuban independence. The 'Splendid Little War' was over all too soon for those who, like Theodore Roosevelt, revelled in the cult of the 'strenuous life'. What war could not provide, perhaps sports could. The litany of strenuosity issued from the pages of an astonishing assortment of journals and periodicals on the eve of the twentieth century. Of all the sports, football became the most martial, and within the college ranks, the most popular. It was touted as the game which exemplified all the qualities of the best of American manhood. It was also the game which most encapsulated, in multiple layers of performative frames, the salient values of American society. . . .

Increasingly varsity athletes were depicted as men who possessed those qualities which the American nation most needed: leadership; executive power; perseverance; determination; courage; virility. Arms akimbo, in the battledress of sport, they were living portrayals of captains of industry or of Commodore Dewey in Manila Harbor. At the same time, however, athletes were expected to develop 'a faithful obedience to authority'. In December 1892 the Chicago *Graphic* declared: 'Football is typical of all that is heroic in American sport'. The *Saturday Evening Post,* three months after the short-lived Spanish–American War, asserted: 'The capacity to take hard knocks which belongs to a successful football player is usually associated with the qualities that would enable a man to lead a charge up San Juan Hill . . .'. The jingoism was unmistakable. While a Rough Rider was not identical to a member of the immortal 'Light Brigade', each was infused with physical stamina, virile masculinity, and manly courage—or so the ideology proclaimed. Each soldier was doing good work for his country, just as the athlete was doing 'good work' for his school. Young, strong, courageous, competent, the athlete was the idealized hope of the future: imperialistically, economically, socially *and* biologically. In an age which believed in the possibility of the inheritance of *acquired* characteristics, the athlete was the image of the ideal sire. It is more than chance that many who advocated vigorous athletics were also active in early twentieth-century eugenics movements. . . .

No American physical educator in the late 1800s was as ardent an anthropometrist as Dudley Allen Sargent, M.D., Director of the Hemenway Gymnasium at Harvard University. Between 1887 and 1889 Sargent published a three-part series in *Scribner's Magazine* on the physical development of the 'typical man', 'women', and 'the athlete'. The anthropometric movement was preoccupied with ideal *forms,* statistical abstractions derived from scores of measurements of the length and girth of various body segments of thousands of individuals. Based on these, individual measurements were judged to be deficient in certain attributes, and students were required to engage in gymnastic programmes devised to correct whatever measurements were deemed inferior. Male athletes constituted a separate—and elevated—group, with special subcategories rapidly developed for each of the various sports. A man was now defined not only by what he accomplished; he was also given identity and status on the basis of his morphology. Similar measurements were also applied to female students, and few American college women and men in the decades between 1890 and the First World War were not subjected to various batteries of anatomical measurements. Dr. Delphine Hanna compiled anthropometric tables from the measurements of 1600 women students at Oberlin College in 1893, and Dr. Claes Enebuske's intensive study of the strength, endurance, and skill improvements of

26 female students at the Boston Normal School of Gymnastics was published in the 1892 *Proceedings* of the American Association for the Advancement of Physical Education. Reflecting nineteenth-century reasoning, Enebuske argued that '. . . a sound, healthy, and shapely body . . .' benefited a woman's posterity, and maintained that schoolgirls needed to develop sufficient strength to support their 'brain-work'.

Strenuousness, vigour, action and similar concepts were used by many Americans to define 'maleness' in the last decades of the nineteenth century. So was bodily form which was also used to define 'female'. . . . A host of strength manuals, of which William Blakie's popular *How to Get Strong and How to Stay So* (1879) was a popular example, extolled the virtues of muscular power and a well-proportioned male body. . . . Blakie's book urged American girls and women, as well as American males, to engage in vigorous exercise as did their British and European counterparts. In an effort to assuage any concerns about the development of '. . . hard and knotted muscles' among women, Blakie pointed out that Venus and Juno had taken exercise but retained the classical beauty of female form.

IV

Higher education and athletic sport were both instrumental in the transformation of American concepts regarding the feminine ideal in the late 1800s. Traditional notions associated with the 'Cult of True Womanhood' continued to exist alongside the emerging model of the 'New Woman', and tensions between the two sets of values were often quite apparent. The belief that women and men were entirely dissimilar—a belief which had gained ascendancy in Victorian Britain and America—began to be slowly challenged by discoveries in physiology which disclosed that women might be quite like men in all save the reproductive function. Increasingly after 1890 the debate focused upon *where* the division between gender should be made, not whether or not there should be any division. . . .

Oberlin College in Oberlin, Ohio, had admitted 30 women students in 1833, but it was not until 1865 when Vassar College in Poughkeepsie, New York, opened that higher education began to be accessible to numbers of American women. From the beginning Vassar students were required to engage in callisthenic exercises. By 1877 they were permitted to substitute boating, gardening, walking or croquet, a diversion which had been imported from Britain in the 1860s and had enjoyed a flurry of interest among young middle-class Americans. When Henry Durant opened Wellesley College near Boston in 1874, callisthenics and sports were a required part of the curriculum. . . . Wellesley . . . served as a model for many of the other small elite eastern women's colleges which were founded in the late 1800s. Wellesley College also became America's most influential and prestigious institution for training women college directors and instructors of physical education after 1909 when it merged with the Boston Normal School of Gymnastics. When women began to enter higher education a great deal of concern was expressed that intellectual study would result in breaking down their physical health. The required programmes of callisthenic exercises and simple forms of recreational activities were intended to enable them to become strong enough to withstand the rigours of 'brain work'. Many American men, and not a few women, were convinced that higher education would masculinize females and make them unfit mothers, thereby threatening the well-being of the nation. . . .

In the late 1800s most Americans, even most feminists, accepted the evolutionists' belief that men and women differed in their physiology and psychology. . . . It would be necessary, . . . for women to demonstrate that academic work did not either break their health or make them unfit mothers before Victorian assumptions would begin to be modified. And changes, when they did come, reflected the tensions of the older and the newer concepts of woman. . . .

The state universities of the Mid- and Far-West and several private institutions, such as for example the University of Chicago, admitted women quite early, largely in order to bolster enrollments. Those women who were admitted soon demonstrated that they could do very well in academic work and that study did not cause their health to break down. . . . Colleges and universities rapidly developed departments of physical education and engaged medical doctors and gymnasium assistants to oversee the health of their students and provide for them programmes of callisthenic and gymnastic exercises. Initially sports were student-initiated extracurricular activities, but by the 1890s these were increasingly brought under the control of the faculty. Whereas before 1900 most directors of physical culture or physical training . . . at the coeducational universities were men—quite frequently medical doctors—by the early 1900s many of these institutions had established separate departments of physical education for women, often engaging a woman physician to examine female students and serve as the director of physical training for women. . . .

. . . Goucher College enrolled its first class in September 1888. When Daniel Coit Gilman, president of neighbouring Johns Hopkins University, delivered the inaugural address to Goucher's young women, he declared that the first of the seven things to be secured by a liberal education was '. . . sound, healthy, active bodies'. Considerable attention was devoted to the health and physical well-being of Goucher students. A Department of Hygiene and Physical Training was established in 1891, headed by a woman physician who held the rank of full professor. The required programme was modelled on that of Stockholm's Royal Central Gymnastic Institute, but a variety of games rapidly became an important part of the total programme of physical activities. The first Professor of Physical Training, Lecturer in Human Anatomy and Physiology, and Director of the Gymnasium, Dr. Alice T. Hall, had graduated from Wellesley College and the Women's Medical College of Pennsylvania. . . .

. . . Sports soon became quite popular at Goucher. In their *History of Goucher College,* Knapp and Thomas state:

> In the fall of 1897, with the coming of a graduate . . . of an English athletic school as gymnasium instructor, hockey and golf were introduced. The call for hockey players brought so many volunteers—over eighty—that instead of one club which had been planned, there were three. The advent in 1899 of Miss Hillyard . . . as the new assistant in 'physical culture', whose special work it was to develop an interest in English out-of-door games, intensified the zest for hockey.

The Boston Normal School of Gymnastics (BNSG), which became the Department of Hygiene and Physical Education, Wellesley College, in 1909, is the prototype for American women's college physical education and sport. The BNSG was founded in 1889 through the benefaction of Mary Hemenway, a Boston philanthropist, and the persistent efforts of Amy Morris Homans, who had directed Hemenway's projects since 1877. Its programme was modelled on that of Stockholm's Royal Central Institute of Gymnastics. At the time of its founding only four Normal (teacher-training) Schools of Physical Education existed in the United States. . . . Homans served as director of the BNSG/Department of Hygiene and Physical Education, Wellesley College, for 40 years. Early in her career she embarked on a successful mission of placing her graduates in positions as directors of programmes in colleges and universities across the United States, thereby ensuring the dissemination and perpetuation of the BNSG/Wellesley College ideology. . . . Swedish gymnastics formed the core of the activity curriculum, but by the 1890s swimming, games, dancing, basketball, boating, tennis and athletics were also included. Field hockey was added in the early 1900s. On the walls of the Wellesley gymnasium were placards inscribed with the words: 'Her voice was ever soft, gentle and low: an Excellent thing in woman'. These lines from *King Lear* admirably convey Homans' philosophy. Although her graduates might be accomplished in gymnastic activities and sports, sound businesswomen and able administrators, they were never to forget that they were first and foremost *ladies*.

American female collegiate physical education directors present an interesting and still not well-explored group. In order to succeed, they had to possess the same types of attributes as successful businessmen. Their stock in trade was games and callisthenics, the former, in particular, deemed to be substantially the province of males in the late nineteenth and early twentieth centuries. They were often among the few women on a college or university faculty which might include many men who were hostile to the idea of higher education for women. How were they able to succeed? In part, because they invoked either the Victorian feminine ideal or the Image of the New Woman, whichever the situation called for—and they learned to do this with consummate skill. Additionally, they endlessly insisted that only women, creatures who shared the same physiology, could know what was best for college girls. In coeducational institutions, the women's physical education department was a bastion which males were not encouraged to enter: an enclave within the broader campus much as the Victorian home had been a sheltered refuge in a competitive and male-dominated society. In the smaller sex-segregated women's colleges and within these separate departments of physical education, female directors usually ruled with iron, but not unkindly, fortitude. . . .

V

During the 1880s, as wealthy and 'comfortable' Americans sought ways to define and legitimize their elevated status in society, they created a variety of social clubs which were equipped with facilities for various sports, especially tennis and golf. Membership in an elite 'country club' was seen to be a visible symbol of achieved success. An article which appeared in *The Fortnightly Review* in 1894 entitled 'The American Sportswoman' conveyed with some accuracy the nature and extent of country club and athletic club sport for women which existed in the United States. Most country clubs, hunt clubs, tennis clubs and other sporting clubs had a ladies' department or affiliated memberships. Beginning in 1887, a Ladies' National Tennis Championship was held each year at Philadelphia. According to one commentator, lawn tennis had been the only 'game' available to American women in 1889, although propriety also permitted them to ride, walk, row or 'play at mask and foil'. Discussing the emergence of tennis as a game for women at such places as the Philadelphia Cricket Club and the Staten Island Cricket and Baseball Club, the author noted: 'To enumerate and describe all of the clubs in the neighborhood of New York City which gladly welcome ladies to membership would be an almost endless task. . . .'. None the less, he believed that '. . . the English girl plays lawn tennis much better than the American simply because she is physically her superior, and can more easily handle a racquet of adequate weight . . .'. Marion Jones, who lost the 1898 Ladies' tournament to Juliette Atkinson, spent part of 1900 in England, returning with renewed enthusiasm for the game thanks to her experiences with British women's tennis. Riding, in Hunt Clubs emulating the best English clubs, was considered *de rigueur* 'among girls of the highest circles'. . . . Golf was taken up by the fashionable set at Newport in the 1890s. In 1895 the first women's championship was held at the Meadowbrook Hunt Club under the auspices of the United States Golf Association. Books on the subject soon began to appear. . . . *The Book of Sport,* published in 1901 as a tribute to upper-class American sportsmen and sportswomen, contained numerous references to upper-class English sport and was patterned on similar British publications.

Introduced into the United States from Britain in the early 1870s, bicycling had become a craze for all who could afford a machine by the 1890s. Many women joined clubs, and in some instances formed their own. When cycling became one of the principal types of outing for the middle classes—shopkeepers, tradesmen, mechanics and clerks—those upper-class women who cycled tended not to do so in public. As with so many of the physical activities in which women might engage in the 1890s and early 1900s, commentators attributed varied and sometimes conflicting benefits and dangers to exercise taken on the bicycle. The author of an article which appeared in *Physical Education,* the monthly journal of the International YMCA Training School, argued that cycling was an ideal form of exercise for women. The American college girl 'with a very highly organized nervous system . . . cannot work for any great length of time . . .'; cycling, however, would help by strengthening the participant. As cycling necessitated the use of large muscle groups (the legs), deep breathing, vigorous circulation and an erect posture, it was deemed an especially effective means of developing strength. Married women, it was held, might also benefit from the bicycle because it offered both exercise and a respite from the ceaseless toil of caring for their children.

The bicycle required women to wear special clothing so that the skirt would not catch in the gears or wheels. Much has been said by historians about the roles which both sporting attire and games have performed in the emancipation of women from traditional Victorian constraints. This was also the feeling of contemporaries. In 1896 Sophia Foster Richardson, a graduate of Vassar College, addressed the Association of Collegiate Alumnae on 'Tendencies in Athletics for Girls in Colleges and Universities'. College women, Richardson pointed out, were now boating, doing gymnasium work, and playing tennis and basketball, all to their physical, intellectual and moral betterment. American women had finally begun to learn the advantages of those outdoor games which had traditionally been part of the English girl's education. . . .

Although it is clear that field hockey was played at Goucher College before 1900, Miss Constance M.K. Applebee is credited with introducing the game to the United States at the 1901 Harvard Summer School for Teachers, using ice hockey sticks and an indoor baseball for equipment. It was largely through her dedicated efforts that the game spread to women's colleges and women's physical education departments in co-educational institutions. For seven decades 'the Apple' was the revered, and feared, patroness of field hockey in America. It soon became a popular autumn sport in elite eastern women's colleges and at those institutions which engaged women physical educators who had studied at these colleges. In 1905 *Outing Magazine* reported on women's hockey, declaring: 'Certainly there is no game to test endurance, wind and agility of womankind, that can be compared with hockey as they play it in England. . . . Because it was perceived to be an elite British schoolgirl sport, field hockey was frequently considered an acceptable, even desirable, albeit vigorous women's sport. It was, for example, quite permissible for a woman to run nearly an hour in a hockey match while it might be totally unacceptable for her to run in a track meet. Female hockey players might traverse the length of the 100 yard field but be confined to half or less of an 80 foot basketball court.

The reasons why hockey retained its respectability as a game for women while track, and even basketball, began to fall into disfavour with many women physical educators in the 1920s, have not yet been fully explored, but part of the explanation must be sought in the elite English origins which Americans associated with field hockey. Additionally, in America the game was confined almost exclusively to women. In her excellent study of games in late Victorian British girls' public schools, Kathleen McCrone has argued that at schools like Roedean and St. Leonards 'the introduction of new sports, like hockey, netball, and lacrosse, that did not carry the stigma of overt masculinity'. . . .' fostered the notion that at least some team games could be acceptable for girls and young women. Such sports, contemporaries claimed, did not require '. . . physical contact, awkward positions, endurance and great strength'. The same non-strenuous qualities in women's sports were also deemed extremely desirable by Americans. . . . The ideology was reinforced by the incessant proclamations of those women physical educators who established and supported professional organizations like the Committee on Women's Athletics of the American Physical Education Association and its various successor organizations, as well as by the images of women portrayed in the popular press. . . .

There is some evidence that in women's colleges—and in some American high schools, especially in rural areas—the matches of distaff 'first teams' could be of consequence in developing the desired *esprit de corps*. Janice Beran has argued persuasively, for example, that girls' basketball in rural Iowa in the late

1800s/early 1900s was held in esteem by school administrators as well as by students and townspeople. It would be a gross exaggeration, however, to imply that girls' and women's games attained a level of significance anywhere near that of boys' and men's games. . . . None the less, by the early twentieth century American college women were playing many of the games that male students were playing; and the intensity with which the women approached their sports could be fully equal to that of their male contemporaries.

Although James Naismith had created basketball as a winter game for young men, its appeal among college women was almost instantaneous. In October 1901 the Spalding's Athletic Library series published *Basket Ball for Women,* edited by Senda Berenson of Smith College in Northampton, Massachusetts. In her opening editorial, Berenson declared: '. . . directors of gymnasia for women saw at once that it was, perhaps, the game they were eagerly seeking', as it was interesting and had the potential to develop strength and physical endurance. Women graduates of physical training schools rapidly adopted and spread the game, and by 1901 it was referred as '. . . the most popular game that women play. . . . This emphasis on teamwork and at least some physical ability reflects many of the changes which were associated with the New Woman at the turn of the century. Dr. Luther Gulick, an early president of the American Association for the Advancement of Physical Education, observed that this was '. . . a time of great unrest in regard to the status of women', for they were beginning to enter '. . . many lines of work that hitherto have been carried on entirely by men'. If they were to succeed in these new endeavours, Gulick and others held, they would need both physical stamina and the type of teamwork and loyalty which it was assumed came naturally to men. Basketball was deemed an admirable game for teaching such qualities.

With few exceptions, however, women played their sports away from the prying eyes of the public. Whereas the male sports model was intentionally a very public cultural performance, women's sporting events remained largely cloistered. . . . An article which appeared in the *Cosmopolitan Magazine* in 1901 entitled 'A Girl's College Life' aptly reflects the collegiate experience of many early twentieth-century American women. College women, it was asserted, were serious (perhaps more serious) than college men because the majority of them were in college to prepare themselves to earn a livelihood. While it was not acceptable for these young women to engage in riotous behavior over an athletic victory, as the men often did, '. . . the triumph of their class and colors [was] just as dear to them'. Within their own precincts these young women could be, and often were, extremely enthusiastic about their sports. It became customary in the early 1900s for each college to hold a 'Field Day'—later a 'Field Week'—to culminate the year's athletic work. On this *special* occasion a public display of athletic accomplishment was permitted. It was also permissible at these well-defined times to 'break previous records' and exalt and fête winners. Once a year the newly emerging mould in which the New Woman and the Victorian Angel in the House were still bound together could be broken. But in athletic sport, one of the few remaining male bastions in twentieth-century America, it would not be until the 1970s that anything even beginning to resemble equality for the two sexes would become available.

FURTHER READING

David L. Chapman, *Sandow the Magnificent: Eugene Sandow and the Beginnings of Body-building* (1994)

Joseph Ernst, *Weakness Is a Crime: The Life of Bernarr McFadden* (1991)

Elliott Gorn, *The Manly Art: Bare-Knuckle Prize Fighting in America* (1986)

Harvey Green, *Fit for America; Health, Sport, Fitness and American Society* (1986)

Cindy L. Himes, "The Female Athlete in American Society, 1860–1940," Ph.D. diss., University of Pennsylvania (1986)

Michael Isenberg, *John L. Sullivan and His America* (1988)

J. A. Mangan and Roberta Park, eds., *From "Fair Sex" to Feminism: Sport and the Socialization of Women in the Industrial and Post-Industrial Eras* (1987)

Patricia Marks, *Bicycles, Bangs, and Bloomers: The New Woman in the Popular Press* (1990)

Donald Mrozek, *Sport and American Mentality, 1880–1910* (1983)

John F. Reiger, *American Sportsmen and the Origins of Conservation* (1975)

Gerald F. Roberts, "The Strenuous Life: The Cult of Manliness in the Era of Theodore Roosevelt," Ph.D. diss., Michigan State University (1970)

Debra S. Shattuck, "Bats, Balls and Books: Baseball and Higher Education for Women at Three Eastern Women's Colleges, 1866–1900," *Journal of Sport History* 19 (1992), 91–109

Ronald A. Smith, "The Rise of Basketball for Women in Colleges," *Canadian Journal of History of Sport and Physical Education* 1 (1970), 1–21

Martha Verbrugge, *Able Bodied Womanhood: Personal Health and Social Change in Nineteenth-Century Boston* (1988)

Patricia Vertinsky, *The Eternally Wounded Woman: Women, Doctors and Exercise in the Late Nineteenth Century* (1990)

James Whorton, *Crusaders for Fitness: The History of American Health Reformers* (1982)

Race and Ethnicity in American Sport, 1890–1940

Ethnic and racial factors played an enormous role in the development of sport. The original immigrants who came from Western Europe between 1840 and 1880 brought a vital athletic tradition that they sought to maintain in the United States. How did their experience compare to that of the millions of new immigrants from Eastern and Southern Europe who arrived in the period 1882–1914 from premodern cultures where sport was largely unknown?

Though these newcomers found American sports to be a waste of time, their American-bred children became very interested in sports. Were the athletic experiences of second-generation Jews, Italians, and Poles similar to those of second-generation Germans and Irish? Second-generation Americans idolized leading athletic heroes, followed their favorite teams in the penny newspapers, and played sports themselves. However, their options were limited by poverty and by parental disapproval. These young men looked to sport as a means to gain respect, prove they were not greenhorns, and even make money. They were most successful in those sports that fit in with their environment, like boxing and basketball. How did their sporting experiences compare to those of American-born people of color? Native Americans produced several prominent major-league ballplayers, and the Carlisle Indian School fielded powerful football teams that competed with distinction against the top collegiate elevens. African-Americans also participated in high level sports, but they encountered more discrimination than any other group. In the late nineteenth century many leading jockeys were African-Americans, and there were excellent professional African-American baseball players and prize fighters. However, prejudice forced them out of organized baseball and most other sports by the turn of the century. African-Americans were only allowed to remain in the low-status sport of boxing, and following Jack Johnson's tenure (1908–1915) as heavyweight champion, none received an opportunity to fight for that prestigious title until Joe Louis in 1937.

❂ D O C U M E N T S

The documents in this section emphasize how the host society was prejudiced against ethnic and racial groups, and they also point out the importance of sports in promoting community pride. The first document describes the quadrennial meeting of the national German turnverein society (an association of gymnasts) in Milwaukee, a major center of
German-American culture. It was a glorious moment for the largest immigrant group in
the United States. The second document, drawn from the pink pages of the *National Police Gazette,* a popular weekly among members of the male bachelor subculture found in
most barber shops and billiard parlors in America, indicates how strongly ethnicity influenced prize fighting. It presents a negative stereotype of Italian immigrants and suggests
how sports will "improve" those people. The next two documents examine the American
Indian athletic experience. In one, Captain Richard Henry Pratt, founder of Carlisle, directed his players to be good sportsmen because of the positive impact it would have
upon prevailing racial prejudice of white Americans toward the Indian. Then in the next
document, *Outing* magazine analyzes the significance of track and field star Jim Thorpe's
confession to having been a professional athlete. Thorpe had played in organized baseball
prior to the 1912 Olympics, where he won both the decathlon and the pentathlon, gaining
recognition as the world's greatest athlete. The final three documents focus on the trials
and tribulations of African-American athletes. The first is a St. Louis *Post-Dispatch* article (reprinted in the black *New York Age*) that tried to rationalize the apparent superiority
of African-American ballplayers. This is followed by Hall of Famer James "Cool Papa"
Bell's memories about his days in black baseball. Reputedly the fastest man who ever
played professional baseball (he was so quick that he supposedly could turn off the lights
and jump back into bed before the lights went out), Bell was an outstanding center fielder
who played professionally for twenty-nine years (1922–1950). He batted .391 in fifty-
four games against barnstorming major leaguers, and in one season in the Mexican
League hit .437. The final item, drawn from the report of the Chicago Commission on
Race Relations that analyzed the causes of the 1919 Chicago Race Riot, provides evidence of the discrimination African-Americans encountered at public sporting facilities.

The *Chicago Daily News* Describes the Quadrennial National Turner Festival, 1893

Milwaukee is the center of German-American life, and the 20,000 strangers who are
to-day crowding its streets and participating in its festivities represent the German-
speaking population of every city in the country. The North American Turner Bund at
present comprises 230 societies with a membership of 50,000 men. . . .

The reception this evening will be preceded by a torchlight parade from the depot through the principal streets to the banquet ball. Dr. Henry Brann, president of
the Turner Bund, will deliver an oration, after which Mayor Koch will welcome the
visiting turners. . . . After the inaugural festivities the men will proceed to the

---

From "Big Day for the Turners," *Chicago Daily News,* July 21, 1893, p. 6, col. 1.

encampment at the athletic park and fair grounds, where they will be quartered during the four days of the tournament. The number of active turners who will participate in the gymnastic exercises will exceed 3,000, and the other turners and visitors who will come are expected to swell the crowd to about 50,000. The turners believed that physical exercise is as important for women as for men, and the reports . . . show that more than 200 women are already entered in the gymnastic contests.

. . . The representation of the various turn districts . . . will be as follows: New York, 132, Indiana, 100, St. Louis, 235; New England, 90; Wisconsin, 198; Chicago, 408; Philadelphia, 200; New Jersey, 140; . . . .

The North American Turner Bund was founded in Washington, D.C., in 1864, on the day that Richmond fell . . . Before that time the turners . . . were separated into two distinct bodies. . . . The first turnfest of the present national organization was held in Cincinnati from Sept. 2 to 6, 1865, when about 2,000 turners participated, of whom only 200 competed for prizes. Since that time, however, the membership of the bund shows a wonderful increase in numbers and each successive quadrennial fest has a greater attendance.

To-morrow evening there will also be competitive singing and declamatory exercises in the Exposition Building. On Sunday the turners will prepare for the performance to be given by them on the following Wednesday at the World's Fair. About 100 classes, formed into three groups will go through a large number of movements with dumb-bells and wands. In the afternoon the exercises will be accompanied by songs by a chorus of 300 voices. . . . On Monday the individual turners will compete for prizes. In the evening 150 of the best turners in the city will form pyramids on twelve ladders. The effect will be heightened by a flood for calcium lights. Prize-winning exercises will take place at Bohn's swimming school. . . .

In the afternoon all the turners who will perform at the World's Fair . . . will give a grand gymnastic exhibition in Athletic park. . . . On Tuesday the pioneer turners will hold a reunion. . . . On Wednesday morning, . . . the visitor will leave for Chicago on early morning trains in order to arrive on time in Jackson park, where they will give evidence of their accomplishments in the arena reserved for that purpose on the World's-Fair grounds.

Probably one of the strongest teams entered to compete . . . is the one from the New York Turnverein. They expect to eclipse the record of the famous Rochester team of 1887, which, with thirty-five men captured thirty-seven individual prizes, almost making a clean sweep.

The *National Police Gazette* Supports the Rise of Italian Boxing, 1905

The Irish race is not losing its fighting propensities if we were to judge by the familiar Celtic names which appear in present day ring statistics, but personal investigation bears out the assertion that there are but few men of Irish birth or descent in the game

From *National Police Gazette,* September 30, 1905, p. 10, col. 4.

to-day. Nearly all the early pugilists in this country, Heenan, Morrissey, McCloskey and the older Sullivan, were either Irishmen or the sons of Irishmen, and it has come to be accepted as a rule that prize fighters and boxers should bear Irish names. Of the pugilists of the present time, however, the great majority of them are young Italian-Americans, who, for convenience or other reasons, have taken Celtic names.

Immigrants from Italy coming into New York have had the name of being inclined to use knives when they fought, instead of their fists. This was true of the Italian immigrants, but it does not apply to the second generation of Italians, born and reared in the city of New York.

Unlike the older Italians, they have developed here a strong partiality for American athletics, and the number of amateur boxers and professional fighters among the children of Italian parents residing here is very large. It is increasing, too, so much so that a special designation for them has become current.

In the same way that there has been a change in the fighting proclivities of Italians, the stiletto of one generation being succeeded by the hard knuckles of the next, the Russian Jews who came to this country as immigrants and who are known as peaceable and inoffensive, have in some parts of town been succeeded by a generation of turbulent young men from whose ranks have been graduated a number of professional pugilists and boxers. Note the number who are making ring history and then ask yourself, where are the Irish?

Richard Henry Pratt Encourages Indian Sportsmanship, c. 1894

First, that you will never, under any circumstances, slug. That you will play fair straight through, and if the other fellows slug you will in no case return it. Can't you see that if you slug people who are looking on will say, "There, that's the Indian of it. Just see them. They are savages and you can't get it out of them." Our white fellows may do a lot of slugging and it causes little or no remark, but you have to make a record for your race. If the other fellows slug and you do not return it, very soon you will be the most famous football team in the country. If you can set an example of that kind for the white race, you will do a work on the highest interests of your people.

The *Outlook*'s Dismay with Indian Sportsman Jim Thorpe and the Forfeiture of His Olympic Medals, 1913

When an American Indian, who had won the championship as the best all-round athlete in America, established his right in the Olympic Games at Stockholm last

---

From Richard Henry Pratt, *Battlefield and Classroom: Four Decades with the American Indian, 1867–1894,* ed. Robert M. Utley (New Haven: Yale University Press, 1964), 317.

From "The Amateur," *Outlook* 103 (February 8, 1913): 293–95.

July to be regarded as the greatest amateur athlete in the world, and was so declared by the King of Sweden, there was widespread gratification in America. Now that that great Indian athlete, James Thorpe, has been stripped of his honors because, by his own confession, he had received money for playing baseball, and therefore was not an amateur but a professional and had no right to enter into competition with amateur athletes, the humiliation is not confined to him; it extends to all who value their country's reputation for fairness in sport as in all other matters.

Every such incident lends aid and comfort to those who are constantly looking for proof of their assertions that Americans are constitutionally devoted to the doctrine that nothing should stand in the way of winning. This incident in particular will afford an opportunity to those unfriendly to this country to declare again their opinion that the ideals of the gentleman are beyond the comprehension of American athletes, and that American sport is thoroughly commercialized. The fact that these aspersions are unjust and ill founded only makes it the more humiliating for such an incident as this to occur. . . .

James Thorpe is a student at the Carlisle Indian School. He is of the Sac and Fox tribe, and, like many other Indians, has sufficient property to afford him support. The Carlisle School is well known for its athletes and its athletic teams. In particular, the Carlisle football team has established a reputation for a peculiar skill and brilliance. Thorpe has been the best-known football player at the School and one of the greatest football players in the country. He is almost as well known as a player of baseball. "In the summer of 1909 and 1910" (this is his own phrase) he played baseball in North Carolina, and for this received money. In the fall of 1911 he was readmitted to the Carlisle Indian School. He took part not only in the sports of the School but also in the athletic meets of the Amateur Athletic Union. Last summer he went with the rest of the American team to Stockholm and competed in the Olympic Games. His achievements there astonished the whole world of athletes. In particular, he took part in two great series of athletic events. One, known as the Pentathlon, is a series of five athletic events; the other, the Decathlon, is a series of ten athletic events. In the first series, out of a possible five firsts he won four; in the Decathlon he registered 8,412 points as against the 7,724 of his nearest competitor, a Swede. . . .

. . . American public opinion should cordially support the officials of the Amateur Athletic Union, whose action was so prompt and sure in this matter that the repudiation of Thorpe as an amateur was officially made simultaneously with the news of the discovery of his offenses. There was a chance for the representatives of organized amateur sport in America to make clear to the world that their standards of amateur sport were inexorable; and they used that chance to the best advantage. They might have allowed a very legitimate sympathy for this Indian student, and their recognition that he had done only what others had done with impunity, to cloud their judgment and to obscure their sense of duty toward the cause of pure athletics. This they did not do. Like everybody else who thinks about this, they must from the first have seen that there was a large element of individual injustice to Thorpe himself in the consequences that followed his acts as a boy. For a young man to be humiliated before the whole world simply because he played baseball one summer and thoughtlessly accepted money for his playing, as others were doing and as a great many professional players do without any disgrace whatever, seems to be an extraordinarily disproportionate punishment. It might be said that his punishment came from the fact that he concealed his having received money, but the fact that he played for the fun of it and not for the sake of the money may well have led him to believe thoroughly in his own amateur spirit and standing. He was mistaken; but the consequence to him is a very severe penalty for such a mistake. . . . Humiliating . . . as the experience is in one respect, it is emphatically encouraging in another, for it has afforded evidence to the whole world that organized amateur athletics in this country will not countenance disregard of amateur standards.

. . . In the course of his letter . . . acknowledging that he had received money for baseball-playing, Thorpe writes:

> On the same teams I played with were several college men from the North who were earning money by ball-playing during their vacations and who were regarded as amateurs at home. I did not play for the money there was in it, because my property brings me in enough money to live on, but because I liked to play ball. I was not very wise to the ways of the world and did not realize that this was wrong and it would make me a professional in track sports, although I learned from the other players that it would be better for me not to let any one know that I was playing, and for that reason I never told any one at the School about it until to-day. . . . I never realized until now what a big mistake I made by keeping it a secret about my ball-playing, and I am sorry I did so. I hope I will be partly excused by the fact that I was simply an Indian school-boy and did not know all about such things. In fact, I did not know that I was doing wrong because I was doing what I knew several other college men had done: except that they did not use their own names. . . .

Prejudice Against African-American Ballplayers in the St. Louis *Post-Dispatch*, 1911

There is some doubt if baseball, after all, is the great American game. We play it, to be sure, but the colored people play it so much better that the time is apparently coming when it shall be known as the great African game.

The St. Louis Giants, a black baseball team, have easily beaten everything in town but the Browns and the Cardinals, and neither of these latter will play them. The Chicago Giants, all alligator bait, have done the same thing in that city, and there are no end of people up there willing to wager that they can beat either the White Sox or the Cubs.

Your Negro is not a bad athlete. Peter Jackson only missed being heavyweight champion of the world because the holders of that title through the years of his prime would not fight him, and Jack Johnson, more fortunate, bestrides the

As quoted in *New York Age,* September 28, 1911, p. 6, col. 5.

earth to-day like a black Collossus. The greatest bicycle racer America ever produced was Major Taylor, a Negro. Forced off on the other side of the track by the
white conspiracy against him, he rode yards and hundreds of yards further than
anyone else in the race, and still usually won it. Subsequently the best riders of
Europe sat up on their machines and watched the sunlight flash on his black
heels.

But it is in baseball that the descendant of Ham is at his athletic best. Less removed from the anthropoid ape, he gets down on ground balls better, springs
higher for liners, has a much stronger and surer grip, and can get in and out of a
base on all fours in a way that makes the higher product of evolution look like a
bush leaguer.

It requires some courage to predict that colored baseball, like colored pugilism,
is to supersede the white brand, but someone has to think ahead and indicate whither
we drift, and we therefore wish to go upon record as having said that it will. . . .

James "Cool Papa" Bell Remembers Negro League Baseball in the 1920s and 1930s

Of course, most of the time nobody kept any records, so I don't know what my
lifetime batting average is. Nobody knows. If I had to guess, I'd say around .340 or
.350. I batted .437 one year, in the Mexican League. I batted .407 in 1944, .411 in
1946. I played twenty-nine years of baseball, and the lowest I ever batted was
.308, in 1945. Other than that it was .340 on up to .400. That's twenty-nine seasons, 1922 through 1950. Plus twenty-one winter seasons. That makes a total of
fifty seasons. That's the way you have to count it, by seasons.

I was born in Starkville, Mississippi, in 1903; . . . I had five brothers, all good
athletes. When I got to St. Louis, four of them were playing with a semipro team,
the Compton Hill Cubs. I joined up with them, as a left-hand pitcher. . . .

. . . I was with the Cubs about a year and a half, playing Sundays and holidays
and during the week working in the packinghouse.

Then one day I pitched a good game against the St. Louis Stars, a professional
team with a lot of first-rate ballplayers. A few nights later my brother, who owned
a restaurant, said to me, "The manager of the St. Louis Stars was over here. Wants
you to play ball.". . .

So I went with the Stars and pitched for them for two years, making $90 a
month. Then they switched me to the outfield. . . . We played five days a week in
what they called the Western League, and we played against Chicago, Indianapolis, Detroit, Kansas City, Cleveland, Dayton, and Toledo. . . . In 1928 or '29 we installed lights, years before the major leagues did. We drew crowds of 3,000 to
5,000, and more than that once we got the lights. . . .

From James "Cool Papa" Bell interview, in Donald Honig, *Baseball When the Grass Was Real* (Lincoln, NE: University of Nebraska Press, 1975), 164–75.

I was with the Stars from 1922 through 1931. Then the league broke up and I went with the Homestead Grays in Pittsburgh. I played with them in part of 1932, but then they stopped paying us. That was the worst of the Depression then, 1932. So I moved from there to the Kansas City Monarchs and finished the season with them. No salary there either. We were on percentage, barnstorming around. We wound up playing in Mexico City that winter, but still hardly making any money. . . .

In the Negro Leagues the audience was mixed but mostly colored. Even down South there were some white people at the games. When we played the Birmingham Black Barons in their park, there were always lots of whites in the crowd, but they were separated by a rope. You could be sitting right next to a white man, but that rope was always there. . . .

In 1933 I joined the Pittsburgh Crawfords and stayed with them four years. Left there in 1937 to go to the Dominican Republic. Remember Trujillo, the dictator? He was killed a few years ago, you know. Well, they were fixin' to do that back in 1937. But they like baseball down there and they were having championship games, and they said if he would win, they would keep him in office.

So Trujillo got a lot of boys from the States, as well as from Cuba and Panama and Puerto Rico. Mostly he wanted Satchel Paige. They showed him a lot of money, offered him a big salary, and he jumped. . . .

But even with Satchel they needed some more ballplayers, because they were losing. So they asked him to send back and get some players from the Negro Leagues. He called Pittsburgh, where I was with the Crawfords. Now, I never did jump nowhere unless something was going bad, and that year it was going bad. The owner of the Crawfords was losing money, and he was giving us ballplayers a tough time, not paying us. Matter of fact, the whole league was going bad at that time. So I was *looking* for somewhere to go when Satchel called. . . .

Satchel put the head man on the phone, and he said okay, he'd give us each $1,000.

. . . We went to San Pedro de Macorís—about 40 miles from Santo Domingo—which is the little town they kept the ball club in. . . . They kept us under guard at a private club. Had a head man there with us all the time, with a .45 pistol. We were allowed out on only two days of the week. They said they were going to kill Trujillo if we didn't win. . . . We won the championship. We won it the last day of the season. I guess we saved Trujillo's life. . . .

Then from 1938 through 1941 I played in Mexico, first with Tampico, then with Torreón. In 1942 I came back to the United States and played with the Chicago American Giants. . . . We always had contracts, but they didn't mean much. They wouldn't pay you your money, and that was that. You'd just go somewhere else.

In those days, the thirties, after the big-league season was over, the major leaguers would go barnstorming. We played against all of them. In 1931 Max Carey brought a team to St. Louis to play us. . . .

Here's the thing. In a short series we could beat those guys. In a whole summer, with the team we had, we couldn't. We only had fourteen or fifteen men to a team. We'd play about 130 league games, and *another* 130 exhibition games. Anywhere from 250 to 300 games a season.

Later on there were those famous games where Satchel pitched against Dizzy Dean. I was in center field most all of those games. Dean was a good pitcher, no mistake about that. The feature for those games was always Paige and Dean. Nobody else got any publicity.

Dean beat us a game in New York broke our heart. We had beaten them four in a row, and we went to New York, and everybody said we couldn't do it again. Dean shut us out, 3–0, at Yankee Stadium.

There was a play that day I still remember. I was on second, and Josh Gibson was up. He hit one on a line way back in deep center field. Jimmy Ripple caught it, and I tagged up and rounded third and came all the way home. The ball came in to the catcher . . . the same time I did, but high, and I slid in under it before he came down with the tag. And the umpire said, "Out!" I said I was safe, but the umpire laughed, and said, "I'm not gonna let you do that on major leaguers. Maybe you can do that in *your* league, but not against major leaguers."

Heck, I often scored from second on a long outfield fly. . . .

It was rough barnstorming. We traveled by bus, you see. You'd be surprised at the conditions we played under. We would frequently play two and three games a day. We'd play a twilight game, ride 40 miles, and play another game, under the lights. This was in the 1940's. On Sundays you'd play three games—a doubleheader in one town and a single night game in another. Or three single games in three different towns. One game would start about one o'clock, a second about four, and a third at about eight. Three different towns, mind you. Same uniform all day, too. We'd change socks and sweat shirts, but that's about all. When you got to the town, they'd be waiting for you, and all you'd have time to do would be to warm your pitcher up. Many a time I put on my uniform at eight o'clock in the morning and wouldn't take it off till three or four the next morning.

Every night they'd have to find us places to stay if we weren't in a big city up North. Some of the towns had hotels where they'd take us. Colored hotels. Never a mixed hotel. In New York we'd stay at the Theresa, in Harlem, or the Woodside. In the larger cities in the South we'd stay at colored hotels. In smaller towns we'd stay at rooming houses or with private families, some of us in each house.

You could stay better in small towns in the South than you could in the North, because in a small town in the North you most of the time don't find many colored people living there. And those that are there have no extra rooms. But in a small town in the South there are enough colored people living there so you can find room in their homes. . . .

We went into a lot of small towns where they'd never seen a colored person. In some of those places we couldn't find anyplace to sleep, so we slept on the bus. If we had to, we could convert the seats into beds. We'd just pull over to the side of the road, in a cornfield or someplace, and sleep until the break of day, and then we'd go on into the next town, hoping we'd find a restaurant that would be willing to serve colored people.

All those things we experienced, today people wouldn't believe it.

The Chicago Commission on Race Relations Examines Racial Contacts in Recreation in the Late 1910s

Representatives of each park commission said that they had no rules or regulations of any kind discriminating against Negroes, and that all races were treated in exactly the same way. The only case in which this rule appeared to be violated was in connection with Negro golf players at Jackson Park. Two Negroes participated in the Amateur Golf Tournament at Jackson Park in the summer of 1918 and made good records. The only requirement for entrance into the tournament at that time was residence in the city for one year. In 1919 the requirements were increased, entries being limited to the lowest sixty-four scores, and membership in a "regularly organized golf club" being required. Since Negroes are not accepted in established golf clubs, the Negro golf players met this qualification by organizing a new club, "The Windy City Golf Association." In 1920 the restriction was added that contestants must belong to a regularly organized golf club affiliated with the Western Golf Association. As it was impossible for Negro clubs to secure such affiliation, it is impossible for Negroes to compete in the tournament.

Unofficial discrimination, however, frequently creeps in. According to the representative of the Municipal Bureau, "the person in charge of the park is largely influenced by the attitude of the people outside the park. We had trouble at Beutner Playground because of the tendency on the part of the director, who was a white man, to be influenced by the attitude of the white people in the neighborhood, and either consciously or unconsciously showed by his actions to the colored people that they were not fully accepted." Beutner Playground later became an example of unofficial discrimination in favor of the Negroes, for the Municipal Bureau decided to "turn over the playground particularly to Negroes" and instructed the director "to give them more use of the facilities than the whites." But this was found to be impossible as long as a white director was employed, because he was influenced by the feeling of the whites in the neighborhood who did not want the playground turned over to the Negroes. The desired result was finally obtained by employing a Negro director. "Then the switch suddenly came," said the park representative, "and the playground was turned over to the Negroes almost exclusively."

A similar method was employed with reference to the Twenty-sixth Street Beach, according to the head of the Municipal Bureau, who said: "As the colored population gradually got heavier and more demand came for the use of that beach it gradually developed into a beach that was used almost exclusively by Negroes. And we did as we did in the Beutner case: we employed a Negro director when the preponderance was Negro.". . .

Clashes—Clashes between Negroes and whites at various places of recreation are reported as far back as 1913. These clashes in the main have been initiated by

---

From Chicago Commission on Race Relations, *The Negro in Chicago: A Study of Race Relations and a Race Riot* (Chicago: University of Chicago Press, 1922), 277, 288–89, 296–97.

gangs of white boys. In 1913, for example, the secretary of boys' work at the Wabash Avenue Y.M.C.A. (for Negroes) conducted a party of nineteen Negro boys from the Douglas Center Boys' Club to Armour Square. They had no difficulty in entering the park and carrying out their program of athletics. The party then took shower baths in the field house. The Y.M.C.A. secretary had noticed the increasing crowds of white boys near-by but had no misgivings until the party left the park. Then they were assailed with sandbags, tripped, walked over, and some of them badly bruised. They were obliged to take refuge in neighboring saloons and houses in Thirty-third Street west of Shields Avenue. For fully half an hour their way home was blocked, until a detachment of city police, called by the park police, scattered the white gang.

That same year the Y.M.C.A. secretary had found it impossible to proceed east through Thirty-first Street to the lake with groups of Negro boys. When this was tried they inevitably met gangs of white boys, and fights ensued with any missiles procurable. Attempts to overcome this antagonism by continuing to demonstrate that the Negro boys had a right to use these streets were unavailing for the next two years.

In 1915 similar conflicts occurred. That winter Father Bishop, of St. Thomas Episcopal Church, took a group of the Negro Y.M.C.A. boys to Armour Square to play basket-ball. The party, including Father Bishop, was beaten up by white boys, their sweaters were taken from them, and they were otherwise maltreated. The Y.M.C.A. staff then decided not to attempt to use the park or field house during the evenings. . . .

An altercation between white and Negro boys in Washington Park is on record as early as the summer of 1913. These boys were sixteen or seventeen years of age. During the spring and summer of 1919, numerous outbreaks occurred because of the use of the baseball diamonds in Washington Park by Negro players. White gangs from the neighborhood of Fifty-ninth Street and Wentworth Avenue, not far from the park, also came there to play baseball, among them some of "Ragen's Colts." Gang fights frequently followed the games. Park policemen usually succeeded in scattering the combatants. The same season gangs of white boys from sixteen to twenty years of age frequently annoyed Negro couples on the benches on this park. When the Negroes showed fight, minor clashes often resulted.

In Ogden Park, as far back as 1914, there were similar instances of race antipathy, expressed by hoodlums who were more or less organized. A Negro playground director said that if Negro boys attended band concerts in that park, white gangs would wait for them outside the park, and the Negroes were slugged. The white gangs also tried to keep Negro boys from using the shower baths at the park. . . .

Though the Negro areas are as well supplied with ordinary playgrounds as the rest of the city, they are noticeably lacking in more complete recreation centers with indoor facilities for the use of older children and adults. Several of these recreation centers . . . border on Negro areas but are not used to any great extent by Negroes because the Negroes feel that the whites object to their presence. Though

there are three publicly maintained beaches within the main Negro area the Negroes feel free to use only the Twenty-sixth Street Beach, though many of them
live as far south as Sixty-sixth Street. Where Negroes do not use nearby facilities
to any great extent they have usually either been given to understand, through unofficial discrimination, that they are not desired, or they have been terrorized by
gangs of white boys. Few attempts to encourage Negro attendance have been
made. . . .

Voluntary racial groupings and serious clashes are found mainly at the places
of recreation patronized by older children and adults—the large parks, beaches,
and recreation centers. Trouble is usually started by gangs of white boys, organized and unorganized. The members of so-called "athletic clubs," whose rooms
usually border on the park, are the worst offenders in this respect. If they do not
reflect the community feeling they are at least tolerated by it, as nothing is done to
suppress them. Some park authorities that have made sincere efforts to have these
hoodlums punished are discouraged because they get no co-operation from the
courts, and the policeman who takes the boy to court gets a reprimand, while the
boy is dismissed. . . .

The most important remedies suggested to the Commission for the betterment
of relations between Negroes and whites at the various places of recreation were:
(1) additional facilities in Negro areas, particularly recreation centers which can be
used by adults; (2) an awakened public opinion which will refuse longer to tolerate
the hoodlum and will insist that the courts properly punish such offenders; (3) selection of directors for parks in neighborhoods where there is a critical situation
who will have a sympathetic understanding of the problem and will not tolerate actions by park police officers and other subordinate officials tending to discourage
Negro attendance; and (4) efforts by such directors to repress and remove any
racial antagonism that may arise in the neighborhood about the park.

E S S A Y S

The essays in this section examine two of the most important ways in which race
and ethnicity influenced American sport. In the first, biographer Randy Roberts of
Purdue University examines one of the most important prize fights of the twentieth
century, the heavyweight championship bout of July 4, 1910, between titlist Jack
Johnson, and the "Great White Hope," Jim Jeffries, a former champion. The fight
represented the efforts of the white race to protect its preeminence over other races
by demonstrating superiority inside the ring. Roberts also examines the riotous impact of the Johnson victory upon the public. The other essay, written by historian Peter Levine of Michigan State University, offers a microcosmic view of how sport influenced the behavior of second-generation Eastern European Jews, an ethnic group
characterized as undersized, physically unfit, and unmanly. Levine offers an in-
depth examination of the basketball experiences of Jewish youth during the 1920s
and 1930s at a time when these young men had little money for alternative activities.
In an account based heavily on oral testimony, Levine recreates the Jewish world of
Brooklyn during the inter-war era and shows how sport promoted community and
individual self-esteem.

The 1910 Jeffries-Johnson Fight and Its Impact

RANDY ROBERTS

Few if any fights in history generated as much interest as the 1910 Johnson-Jeffries match. . . . From the very first, it was advertised as a match of civilization and virtue against savagery and baseness. As early as April 1909 the *Chicago Tribune* realized what was at stake. It printed a picture of a cute young blond girl pointing a finger at the reader; underneath was the caption: "Please, Mr. Jeffries, are you going to fight Mr. Johnson?". . . Humanity needed Jeffries. He had inherited the White Man's Burden and he could not plead retirement to cloak his weariness. . . .

The money, the success, the fame, the smile, the body—women now more than ever were attracted to Johnson. In New York he met Etta Terry Duryea, whom he would eventually marry. She was a sporting lady, though technically not a prostitute. Born in Hempstead, Long Island, and brought up in a fashionable section of Brooklyn, Etta had married Charles C. Duryea, an Eastern horse-racing patron. The marriage did not last long, but even after the two separated Etta continued to attend the races. One afternoon at the Coney Island track she met Johnson, and shortly thereafter the two began living together, Etta taking the unofficial title "Mrs. Jack Johnson." About her there was a certain sense of sadness. Her beauty was of a haunting sort—cold, distant, aloof. Her hair and eyes were dark, her chin pointed and dimpled. She had a beautifully shaped mouth, but one that appeared unused to smiling. In pictures her lips are always locked in a perpetual pout. But it was her eyes that registered the real sadness. They seemed to stare without seeing, as if they knew all too well that sight was not worth the effort of focus. It is difficult to look at pictures of Etta and still be surprised that she committed suicide.

When Johnson left New York for Philadelphia, Etta went along. So too did Belle and Hattie. The two prostitutes were used to the arrangement, but Etta was not. There were several scenes, but nothing Johnson could not handle. The three stayed in separate hotels and waited for Johnson. That was his normal procedure when traveling with more than one woman. At any time in the day or night he might make a brief appearance for the purpose of intercourse, but he usually left after a short stay. Belle and Hattie, as prostitutes, were accustomed to such behavior. He treated Etta differently. She stayed at the hotel where he stayed. She was, it soon became clear, the number one Mrs. Jack Johnson. . . .

. . . The Ketchel fight had dramatically enhanced his reputation and he was sought after by several vaudeville agencies. In December 1909, while in New York, he signed for a tour with Barney Gerard's "Atlantic Carnival" show. For the tour, which was due to start in early 1910, Johnson was guaranteed $1,300 per week. It was a star's salary, and initially Johnson seemed satisfied. As he left to begin the tour, a reporter for the *Chicago Tribune* noted that Johnson was "his usual happy self." He was expected only to be himself, or what whites per-

From Randy Roberts, *Papa Jack: Jack Johnson and the Era of White Hopes* (New York: Free Press, 1983), 85–111.

ceived was his true nature. He was told to dance about the stage, shadow box, sing a bit, and tell a few amusing stories.

He was also supposed to accept the indignities that came with being a black performer. Even the top black vaudevillians were treated shamelessly. Bert Williams, one of vaudeville's greatest stars, . . . was never supposed to mix socially with the white members of the tour, and a clause in his contract specified "that at no time would he be on the stage with any of the female members of the company.". . .

Johnson was also expected to live with the inconveniences. Frank Calder, a stage manager, recalled working with Johnson at the Cleveland Star Theatre and the Indianapolis Empire Theater. Even though it was bitter cold, Johnson was not allowed in the heated dressing room that the other performers used. Rather he was forced to change clothes in the cellar. Unlike Williams, Johnson rebelled against such treatment. At the Fairland Theatre in Terre Haute, he refused to perform. It was too cold, he said, to go on stage in just boxing tights and gloves. An argument with the management followed, and Johnson angrily left town. . . .

Money was no longer an immediate problem. Ahead of Johnson was a rainbow, and beyond it the pot of gold. The rainbow was Jeffries, the pot of gold their proposed match. Toward the end of 1909 Jeffries succumbed to the pressures of race and dollars. Hundreds of letters were sent to Jeffries with a single theme: it was incumbent upon him as a white man to shut Johnson's smiling mouth once and for all. White Americans doubted not that Jeffries was up to the task. They believed the Jeffries mythology—that he cured himself of pneumonia by drinking a case of whisky in two days, that with a broken leg he was still able to knock out a leading heavyweight contender, that upon inspection a physician told him that he was simply not human. Across America white bartenders told customers that if Jeffries fought Johnson, he would "probably kill the Negro." After more than a year of such stories Americans—and, more important, Jeffries—believed that he probably *would* kill Johnson.

It was left to the business managers to work out the details. Sam Berger negotiated for Jeffries, George Little and Sig Hart for Johnson. They told reporters that the fight was open for bids and that the person who offered the most money could stage it. The leading promoters in America handed in their bids, which were supposed to be opened in public at the Hotel Albany in New York City. However, both boxing and the promotion of boxing matches were illegal in New York, and at the last minute the scene for the opening of the bids was shifted across the Hudson River to Meyer's Hotel in Hoboken, New Jersey. . . .

The bids were opened. They were all attractive, but George L. "Tex" Rickard's was the best. He guaranteed the fighters $101,000 and two-thirds of the movie rights. In addition, he promised a cash bonus of $10,000 for each fighter upon signing. It was money unheard of in the boxing world, but it was not just talk. Rickard was backed by Thomas F. Cole, a Minnesota millionaire who owned silver and gold mines across the United States and Alaska.

In an age when a laborer still might earn only a dollar a day, the amount Jeffries and Johnson stood to make struck some observers as disgraceful. Not only would the winner get 75 percent of the $101,000 guarantee, and the loser, 25 percent, but additional revenues would be gained through their percentages of the film rights and vaudeville contracts. Edward R. Moss, sports editor for the *New York Evening Sun,* estimated that if Jeffries won, the white fighter would make $667,750 and Johnson would earn $358,250. If Johnson was victorious, the film rights would be worth less and he would make only $360,750 to Jeffries's $158,000. . . .

Behind the new era and manipulating the million dollar match were Tex Rickard and Jack Gleason, who was brought in on the promotion to please Jeffries. Rickard was a new sort of promoter. He did not know much about boxing, and in 1910 he had few connections in the pugilistic world. . . . As a teenager he moved to Texas and worked as a horse wrangler and later a frontier marshal. In 1895 his wife and baby died and he left Texas, drifting north to Alaska. It was a time for making money and getting rich, and Rickard panned for gold, tended bar, and gambled. He managed the Northern Saloon in Nome but lost everything he earned at the poker and roulette tables. Tired of Alaska, he drifted south, this time ending up in the gold fields of South Africa. Back in the United States, he opened the famous Northern Saloon in Goldfield, Nevada, where another gold rush was under way. There in the hot, dirty-rich town of Goldfield Rickard tried his hand at promoting boxing matches. He did it not for the love of boxing or even the love of money, but to draw the nation's attention to Goldfield. He matched Joe Gans, the magnificent black lightweight champion from Baltimore, against the rugged Battling Nelson, and for forty-two rounds the two men butted and kicked, sweated and bled, and occasionally punched until Nelson sank a left hook in Gans's groin and lost on a foul. But the scheme worked. Overnight Goldfield became famous and Rickard became a success as both a promoter and an advertiser. . . .

In Johnson and prizefighting [rural-based] reformers saw the incarnation of everything they opposed, feared, and hated. They embraced traditional, rural, puritanical values, the values that at least in popular theory had accounted for everything pure and great about America. The world of prizefighting, they argued, was as alien to those values as an illiterate Jewish immigrant from Russia. Professional boxing was viewed as an immigrant sport that attracted Irish and Polish Catholics, Russian Jews, and other undesirable sorts. . . . It was also quite correctly seen as having close ties with saloon keepers and Democratic urban machine politics. And the epitome of the evil of the prizefighting world was Jack Johnson. He drank, supported prostitutes, and threatened the very social and racial order of America. He was not the type of man rural Anglo-Saxon Protestants felt comfortable with. Instead he was a constant reminder of the powerful threat to the traditional American order.

When the site of the Johnson-Jeffries fight was announced as San Francisco, reformers strapped on their swords. It was an affront to civilization, they said. In Cincinnati a million post cards were distributed among the faithful for signing and posting. They were addressed to the governor of California and contained the simple message: "STOP THE FIGHT. THIS IS THE 20TH CENTURY." Other protests were staged in California. Fifty ministers formed a prayer session on the capitol's steps in Sacramento. They prayed for Governor J. N. Gillett to see the light of civilization and reason. . . .

Up until then Gillett had steadfastly supported the match, claiming that it in no way conflicted with the laws of California. The potential obstruction of the

Panama-Pacific Exposition, however, made him reread the statutes. After some soul-searching he concluded that the Johnson-Jeffries contest would not be a boxing exhibition, which California law permitted, but a prizefight, which state statutes forbade. In an open letter to the attorney general of California Gillett claimed, "The whole business is demoralizing to the youth of our state, corrupts public morals, is offensive to the senses of the great majority of our citizens, and should be abated, as a public nuisance, and the offenders punished."

Moral outrage and economic pressure had won for the reformers. Although Mayor Pat McCarthy opposed the governor's decision, the fight was pushed out of San Francisco. . . .

To Rickard fell the task of finding another city to stage the fight. He had already sold $133,000 worth of tickets and had invested between $30,000 and $50,000 in the stadium, licenses, and various political payoffs. Now he had only two weeks to find another city, build a stadium, and complete the many other arrangements. He received offers from Reno, Goldfield, and Salt Lake City. He chose Reno because of its superior railroad facilities and because the mayor of the town assured him that a 20,000-seat stadium could be constructed there within the two-week deadline. Further incentives were offered by Governor Denver S. Dickerson. He told the promoter that no reform movement had any power in Nevada and no amount of protest could force him to cancel the fight. Thus guaranteed, Rickard, Jeffries, Johnson, and everyone else involved in the match boarded a train for Reno. . . .

For American reformers, however, the site was important. They wanted to prevent the match from being staged anywhere in the United States. . . . Across the nation protest was intense, and in the end useless. Dickerson refused to budge. For many godfearing Americans, Reno became a national disgrace. . . .

This strident tone of the reformers' protests revealed their true objectives. To be sure, they opposed boxing matches in the past and would do so again. But their opposition had never been so angry and forceful. The difference between the Johnson-Jeffries match and the other prizefights they opposed was the problem of race. The Reno fight was not simply another brutal and demoralizing prizefight; it was a battle that was widely perceived as a struggle for racial supremacy. . . .

. . . Just to allow the fight to take place was to admit a sort of equality. It implied that blacks had an equal chance to excel in at least one arena of American life. . . . White reformers, therefore, considered the fight a no-win proposition. Win or lose, if the fight took place Johnson would achieve a symbolic victory for his race.

And in that victory whites saw disturbing possibilities. They were sure that if Johnson won, the result would be race war. "If the black man wins," a *New York Times* editorialist noted, "thousands and thousands of his ignorant brothers will misinterpret his victory as justifying claims to much more than mere physical equality with their white neighbors.". . . This prediction was echoed throughout the United States, especially in the South. Southern congressmen "talked freely of the danger of the negroes having their heads turned" by a Johnson victory. . . . Southerners believed a Johnson victory would increase the possibility of physical contact between young, proud blacks and white women. This haunting specter led naturally to thoughts of racial warfare.

Whites were not alone in predicting that the fight would beget violence. Conservative blacks feared the same possibility. Black admirers of Booker T. Washington had never felt comfortable about the implications of Jack Johnson. . . . They feared that Johnson challenged an order they wished to placate and that his emancipated life-style eventually would cause a violent white reaction. . . .

For many Americans Reno was a moral as well as a physical desert. They assumed that most of the town's population of 15,000 was to some degree associated with vice and sin. There was the gambling—not normal secretive gambling, conducted behind locked doors and pulled blinds, but illuminated, unabashed gambling. In Reno gambling was legal. . . . And there was the drinking. In a four- or five-block area there were more than fifty saloons. . . . Most notoriously of all, there were the divorcees. Reno even then was the divorce capital of America. . . .

According to most observers the more than 20,000 people who traveled to Reno for the fight did nothing to upgrade the town's reputation. It was a sporting crowd—boxers, ex-boxers, prostitutes, saloon owners, gamblers, pickpockets, hoboes, profligate sons of the wealthy, and high rollers of every kind. They came to drink, spin the roulette wheel, and talk about the upcoming fight. They talked and dressed loud. Bright plaid vests, thick black cigars, and large diamond rings were the order of the day. There were sporting men from England, France, Germany, Italy, Australia, and all over the United States. There were black sports as well as white sports. It was an atmosphere rife with tall tales, hard luck stories, big dreams, and grandiose plans.

Perhaps at no time before had so many reporters descended upon so small a town. Upwards of 500 correspondents were present to report the town's celebrations. Every day in the week before the fight between 100,000 and 150,000 words about the fight—enough for two popular novels—were sent out from Reno. Some of the reporters were leading writers. Jack London, Rex Beach, and Alfred Henry Lewis, three of the leading writers *cum* Sports, detailed the activities. But far more famous were the boxers and wrestlers *cum* reporters. Covering the fight for various newspapers were John L. Sullivan, James J. Corbett, Robert Fitzsimmons, Abe Attell, Battling Nelson, Tommy Burns, Frank Gotch, William Muldoon, and a host of others. . . .

Another faction well represented in Reno was the criminal class. Thieves of all types roamed about the town's streets, and "if a hand was not dipped into your pocket sooner or later it was almost a sign of disrespect. . . . Nor were all the criminals there to work. Some of the more famous and prosperous had come just to watch the fight and wager a few thousand dollars. . . . Even the notorious Sundance Kid was reported to be on his way to Reno. . . .

By the Fourth of July the entire nation was a bit nervous. Henry Wales of the *Chicago Tribune,* reviewing his long career as a reporter and an editor, said that no event so captured the public mind until the Lindberg flight seventeen years later. It was fitting that the fight was scheduled for the national holiday, for the celebration and the excitement were intense. Never had so illustrious a group of Sports gathered in one spot. . . .

And everyone had an opinion about who would win. The betting was ten to six or seven on Jeffries, but as Arthur Ruhl wrote, the talk was 1,000 to 1 in favor of the white fighter: "You couldn't hurt him—Fitzsimmons had landed enough times to kill an ordinary man in the first few rounds, and Jeffries had only shaken his head like a bull and bored in. The negro might be a clever boxer, but he has never been up against a real fighter before. He has a yellow streak, there was nothing to it, and anyway, 'let's hope he kills the coon.'. . . .

Most boxers and intellectuals also predicted a Jeffries victory. John L. Sullivan, James J. Corbett, Robert Fitzsimmons, Tommy Burns, Abe Attell, Battling Nelson—the list is extensive. They all favored Jeffries. Even black boxers like Sam Langford and Joe Jeannette picked the white. Perhaps Jeannette, who had fought Johnson more than any other man, spoke for them all: "Why, Jeffries can lose half of his strength, have his endurance cut in two, carry a ton of extra weight and still whip Johnson. He has the 'head' and the 'heart' to do it." The head and the heart: it was a common theme among intellectuals too. A psychologist writing for the London *Lancet* remarked that Jeffries's brain should be the deciding factor. . . .

Even America's churches were not immune to the excitement. In Hutchinson, Kansas, the Colored Holiness Church announced that it would hold special services during the fight to pray for Johnson. To counterbalance this plea for divine help a Midwestern white minister said he would pray for Jeffries. . . . Although some ministers disagreed with such statements, most did agree that there was something much greater at stake in Reno than a championship belt.

On the Fourth of July the nation was ready. Every section of the country was connected electrically with Reno. . . . Outside newspaper buildings in every major city crowds gathered to follow the progress of the fight. At Tuskegee Institute Booker T. Washington, who declined to cover the bout as a reporter, set aside a special assembly room to receive telegraphic reports from Reno. If the fight was a racial Armageddon as everywhere it was advertised, then the results would be known to everyone as soon as it concluded.

"The day dawned spotlessly clear, one of those still crystalline mornings which come in the thin dry air of the mountain desert country." Because of the shabbiness of the event that was to follow, reporters in Reno remembered the beauty of the morning. They recalled the order with which the drunken mob, 15,000 to 20,000 strong, moved toward the stadium on the outskirts of Reno and checked their firearms at the gate; how they poured in through the four tunnel-like entrances into the huge eight-sided arena; how their voices rose strong and clear into the hot afternoon air; how a brass band climbed into the ring and played "All Coons Look Alike to Me" and other "patriotic" selections. . . .

Johnson was the first into the ring, wearing a gray silk robe and blue trunks with an American flag for his belt. A litany of racial slurs greeted him, but as always he seemed not to notice. Beach watched for some sign of fear, but Johnson merely "grinned and clapped his hands like a boy." Jeffries was greeted like an emperor. He looked nervous, chewing gum rapidly and glaring across the ring at Johnson. . . .

Jeffries looked big but also old and tired. A few days before Jeffries had told reporters, "I realize full well just what depends on me, and I am not going to disappoint the public. That portion of the white race that has been looking to me to defend its athletic superiority may feel assured that I am fit to do my very best.". . .

Tex Rickard, who had named himself as referee, also felt the "vast concentration of thought," and he feared it might erupt into violence. In order to cool the heated racial feeling, Rickard called on William Muldoon to give a speech. Muldoon, the once great wrestler, was a pompous, humorless man who genuinely believed in such notions as honor and fair play. In a forceful voice he told the spectators so. It was necessary, he said, not to judge Johnson too harshly just because he was black, and regardless who won, the verdict must be accepted in a sense of fair play. Muldoon's speech and the lemonade, which was the only beverage served in the arena, seemed to sober the crowd.

During the preliminary activities not all of the tradition of the prize ring was observed. Certainly all the ex-champions were introduced. . . . However, by pre-arranged agreement Johnson and Jeffries did not shake hands before the fight. No detail more clearly illustrated the symbolic importance of the match. Not to observe such a fundamental ritual, the very expression of sportsmanship and fair play, indicated that this was not simply another championship fight.

No fight could do justice to such an extended buildup. This one did not even come close. "It was not a great battle after all, save in its setting and significance," wrote Jack London. Johnson established the tempo of the fight in the first round—slow and painful. He waited for Jeffries to lead, then threw straight right and left counters. . . . For all the talk of Jeffries's grizzly strength, Johnson was by far the stronger of the two men. He tossed Jeffries around with alarming ease. . . .

In the second round Johnson started talking to Jeffries. "Don't rush, Jim," he said as he pushed Jeffries across the ring. "I can go on like this all afternoon," he exclaimed as he hit the challenger with a solid right hand lead. Jeffries's famous crouching, rushing, wild-swinging style was useless against the grace and economy of Johnson's defense. . . . During the clinches Johnson would talk to Jeffries or to the challenger's corner. . . .

Most of the reporters believed that Johnson could have ended the fight in an early round. They said he did not because he was a good businessman and a vengeful person. Financially a quick fight would have been disastrous. It would have destroyed the potential of the film as a revenue source. But beyond the money question, reporters believed Johnson enjoyed watching Jeffries suffer. By round twelve Jeffries's mouth was cut inside and out; his nose was broken and bleeding; his face and eyes were bruised and smeared with blood. Even Johnson's chest and back were covered with Jeffries's blood. There was no reason for the fight to go on. But it did. . . .

In the fifteenth Jeffries's face was bleeding and swollen, and his movements were languid. But he continued to move toward Johnson. The round-by-round report accurately, if unemotionally, reflects the horror of the scene: "He shambled after the elusive negro, sometimes crouching low . . . and sometimes standing erect. Stooping or erect, he was a mark for Johnson's accurately driven blows. Johnson simply waited for the big white man to come in and chopped his face to pieces." Finally a combination of rights and lefts forced Jeffries onto the ropes. There Johnson landed fifteen or twenty punches to Jeffries's head and face. Jeffries fell to the canvas for the first time in his career. He was dazed, and Johnson stood over him until Rickard made the champion move back. At the count of nine Jeffries struggled to his feet. Johnson charged and landed another combination of punches. Again Jeffries fell to his knees. At the count of nine he once more arose. At this stage ringsiders shouted, "Stop it, stop it. Don't let him be knocked out."

But the fight continued. Jeffries was helpless. A left-right-left combination knocked Jeffries into the ropes. He sprawled over the lower rope, hanging half outside the ring. Rickard picked up the timekeeper's count. At seven one of Jeffries's handlers rushed into the ring, and Rickard stopped the fight. The "fight of the century" was over.

Silence. Insults and cheers were few. The spectators accepted the end as they might the conclusion of a horse race where the favorite broke a leg and had to be destroyed. Johnson was clearly superior, so there was nothing to argue about. Jeffries was old and tired and should never have attempted a comeback. More than talking or yelling, the sad boxing fan wanted to leave the arena as quickly as possible and find a bar that served something stronger than lemonade. Across the nation thousands of other men who crowded around newspaper offices for news of the fight experienced similar reactions. And so they went to the saloons, and when they finished drinking and brooding about the fight they expressed their displeasure in spontaneous outbursts of violence. The emotions exposed by the Johnson-Jeffries fight were quite sincere and, once uncovered, were deadly.

In Greenwood, South Carolina, close to the border of Georgia, Benjamin E. Mays was almost 2,500 miles from Reno. Only fourteen in 1910, the future educator remembered clearly how white men in his town reacted to the news of Johnson's victory. They could not accept the outcome. Because a black boxer defeated a white boxer in faraway Nevada, whites in Greenwood beat up several blacks. Fear swept through the black population, and in the presence of whites they dared not discuss the fight. The match, which prompted random violence and brutal deaths, touched every section of the country. Compared with many cities, Mays's Greenwood was tame. . . .

. . . The rioting claimed other casualties. In Houston, Charles Williams openly celebrated Johnson's triumph, and a white man "slashed his throat from ear to ear"; in Little Rock, two blacks were killed by a group of whites after an argument about the fight on a streetcar; in Roanoke, Virginia, six blacks were critically beaten by a white mob; . . . Other murders or injuries were reported in New Orleans, Baltimore, Cincinnati, . . . and many other smaller cities and towns. The number of deaths and injuries is unknown. . . .

Many of the riots followed a similar pattern. They were started by blacks who, inspired by Johnson's example, refused to shuffle and briefly lifted their heads and raised their voices in pride. In New York City, Nelson Turner, a black, was almost lynched for yelling to a crowd of whites, "We blacks put one over on you whites, and we're going to do more." . . .

Participants in the riots also displayed similar traits. Most striking was the class element. The rioting largely saw lower-class whites attacking lower-class blacks, although occasionally a middle-class black might also be assaulted. Often white sailors or soldiers were to blame. . . . Just as common were attacks by white laborers on black laborers. . . . In larger cities organized gangs caused the most harm. In New York City "roving bands of white hoodlums" like the Pearl Button Gang and the Hounds of Hell roamed through the city beating every black they could catch. In the districts known as the Black and Tan Belt and San Juan Hill, tenement houses inhabited by blacks were set ablaze and attempts were made to lock the tenants inside. The match, then, not only initiated widespread race warfare but also caused racially motivated class conflict. . . .

It was this theme—disorder—that was stressed by most commentators on the match. Editors warned that the result of the fight would disrupt traditional race relations: "In spite of occasional lynchings in the South, the social adjustment between the white and the black races was coming to a better status than ever before when along came the Jeffries and Johnson prize fight and put the conditions back at least forty years." Translated, such comments meant that race relations were most stable when blacks remained in their clearly defined, circumscribed place and when there was no nonsense about equality. Johnson's victory proved that in at least one arena blacks were not inferior. . . . Nowhere is the effect of Johnson's accomplishment on the psyche of the black community better expressed than in the folk ballad that was written after the match:

> Amaze an' Grace, how sweet it sounds,
> Jack Johnson knocked Jim Jeffries down.
> Jim Jeffries jumped up an' hit Jack on the chin.
> An' then Jack knocked him down agin.
>
> The Yankees hold the play,
> The White man pull the trigger;
> But it makes no difference what the white man say;
> The world champion's still a nigger.

For whites, the fact that the world champion was black made a great deal of difference. It challenged the old notion of the blacks as an inferior race and raised once more the specter of black rebellion. A cartoon in *Life* magazine graphically portrayed white fears. In the middle of the page stands a large, apelike Johnson. He is smiling, and a halo circles his head. Beneath his right foot is Jeffries's head; he is pushing the white fighter's face into the dirt. No longer the respectful darky asking, hat in hand, for massa's permission, Johnson was seen as the prototype of the independent black who acted as he pleased and accepted no bar to his conduct. As such, Johnson was transformed into a racial symbol that threatened America's social order. . . .

Disorder, sensationalism, shabbiness—such were the terms white observers used to describe the title bout. They doubted not what had taken place. But what was to be done? The most obvious solution was to prevent a repetition of the sordid affair. Their effort to do so, an attack on Johnson's world, was launched on two fronts. First, there was a widespread feeling that boxing should be abolished. Prominent magazines like *The Nation* denounced the "disgusting exhibition" and suggested that hereafter newspapers should refuse to cover such an uncivilized sport. This by itself was not unusual: genteel and reform journals had long been opposed to prizefighting. For the first time, however, they found support in surprising places. Ardent defenders of boxing like Theodore Roosevelt turned against the sport. In a classic Progressive appeal Roosevelt wrote, "I sincerely trust that public sentiment will be so aroused, and will make itself felt so effectively, as to guarantee that this is the last prize fight to take place in the United States. . . .

Basketball and the Jewish-American Community, 1920s–1930s

PETER LEVINE

I

While hardly all Jews embraced basketball as valid enterprise, by the late 1930s, certainly sportswriters identified it as the "Jewish" game. Paul Gallico, longtime sports editor for the New York *Daily News,* explained the intimate connection between Jews and basketball. "Curiously . . . above all others," Gallico wrote, "the game appeal[s] to the temperament of the Jews." While "a good Jewish football player is a rarity . . . Jews flock to basketball by the thousands," he insisted, because it placed "a premium on an alert, scheming mind . . . flashy trickiness, artful dodging and general smart aleckness," traits naturally appealing to "the Hebrew with his Oriental background." One year earlier, in 1936, Stanley Frank, former varsity trackman and campus sports editor at the City College of New York (CCNY), offered his own version of Jewish attachment. Rejecting the implicit anti-Semitism of Gallico's remarks, nevertheless Frank insisted that no other sport so required "the characteristics inherent in the Jew . . . mental agility, perception . . . imagination and subtlety. . . . If the Jew had set out deliberately to invent a game which incorporates those traits indigenous in him . . . he could not have had a happier inspiration than basketball." Describing Jewish domination, Frank concluded, "ever since Dr. James A. Naismith came up with a soccer ball, two peach baskets and a bright idea . . . basketball players have been chasing Jewish athletes and never quite catching up with them."

Providing slightly different spins on the same biological deterministic ball, Frank and Gallico offer no more satisfactory explanations of Jewish involvement in basketball half a century ago than similar arguments sometimes offered to explain black domination of the game today. But they were right in one respect. Although you didn't have to be Jewish to play basketball, especially in large eastern and midwestern cities containing substantial numbers of first-generation East European immigrant Jews, Jewish children flocked to the sport, making it a significant part of everyday community life and ultimately earning some of them local and national reputations for their exploits in the cage and on the court.

Not surprisingly, in urban, ethnic working-class neighborhoods, a game open to improvisation and requiring little space or equipment proved attractive to children. As early as the turn of the century, in the streets and on the school yards, at

From Peter Levine, *Ellis Island to Ebbets Field: Sport and the American Jewish Experience* (New York: Oxford University Press, 1992), 27–36, 38–40, 46.

settlement houses and YMHAs, their imagination and control of their own turf along with more structured opportunities for sport shaped their introduction to the game.

Certainly that's how Nat Krinsky and Harry "Jammy" Moskowitz, my high-school gym teachers, remember it. Harry was born in 1904 and Nat in 1901 in Brownsville to Russian immigrant parents. They went to local high schools and attended respectively the Savage School for Physical Education and CCNY. Later, they became good friends and neighbors as well as colleagues at Brooklyn's James Madison High School, where for some forty years "Jammy" coached basketball and Nat track and field. They were also competitors, teammates, and stars of amateur, college, and professional basketball teams in the New York City area.

"Jammy" . . . first played basketball on Bristol Street when he was nine years old. As both he and Nat recall, ashcans placed on brownstone stoops served as baskets, roughly simulating the more formal game where backboards did not exist in any form and baskets were freestanding. A bunch of rolled-up rags, an old stocking stuffed with them, or a woolen stocking cap sufficed as balls. Neither running nor dribbling were allowed; instead playmates tapped the ball to each other. . . .

Three years apart in age, Krinsky and Moskowitz moved their street skills to the gym and school yard of P.S. 84 where they played on class teams and also on clubs like the Mercurys, the Beavers, and the Invincibles—teams defined by age and weight that represented the local evening recreation center. Enthusiastically recalling his boyhood at the age of 83, Jammy remembers watching Nat play for the senior Invincible team which matched its skills against opponents from the Educational Alliance, the College Settlement House, and even professional teams; all at a time when the professional game was in its unorganized infancy and when little distinction was made between professional and amateur. Jammy himself starred for the Invincible Cubs, a team composed of high-school freshmen who weighed no more than 140 pounds. The Cubs . . . made their own schedule and dominated similar teams throughout the city as newspapers like the *Brooklyn Citizen* carried news of their triumphs in its sports pages.

Barney Sedran and Max "Marty" Friedman, among the first Jewish basketball players elected to the Basketball Hall of Fame, recall similar childhood experiences. Born two years apart on the New York's Lower East Side, they first became teammates in their early teens when they played in 1903 for the "midget" team of the University Settlement House located on Eldridge and Rivington streets. Coached by Harry Baum, a Jewish settlement house worker who migrated from Austria in 1883, their team, "the busy Izzies," won settlement house and metropolitan American Amateur Union (AAU) championships. Fondly, they remember the importance of their settlement house days. Growing up in a neighborhood which simply had no space for baseball diamonds, Sedran, who learned the game at University Settlement and in Hamilton Fish Park, recalls that basketball was "the only sport I could play with little trouble." Marty Friedman, who bypassed college and became a professional ballplayer at the age of sixteen, remembers that when his friends joined him as professionals, the newspapers nicknamed them the "Clark University alumni,". . . because they had "graduated" from the Clark and University settlement houses.

... Nat Holman, without question one of the most celebrated and well-known basketball players of all time, a member of the Basketball Hall of Fame, head basketball coach at CCNY for 36 years, ... grew up on the Lower East Side and attended P.S. 72, P.S. 62, Commerce High School, and the Savage School of Physical Education. He learned the sport that made him the best-known professional basketball player of his generation in the streets, school yards, and settlement houses of his youth. Commenting on his early basketball days, Holman credits the "inspirational qualities" of his elementary-school physical education teacher for attracting him to the game. Also critical were the games he and his friends played at settlement houses and Ys scattered throughout New York. As he put it, "there is no question in my mind that the settlement houses were instrumental in popularizing the game of basketball as well as developing some of the most outstanding players in the history of the sport. . . . Basketball was THE GAME on the Lower East Side and every youngster tried to excel at it.". . .

Not surprisingly, social reformers concerned with using such settings as agencies of assimilation emphasized the positive role of basketball in turning immigrant youth into solid American citizens. Consistent with his position as a senior physical education instructor at the Brooklyn YMHA where basketball was the most popular sport, Nat Krinsky, writing in 1923, made the connections quite clearly. Writing for the Y's newspaper, he emphasized that "the gymnasium and the athletic field are ideal places to develop . . . the qualities of courage, respect for authority, co-operation, unselfishness, and a desire to play cleanly and in a sportsmanlike manner." Such rhetoric served as code words for organized play advocates, settlement house workers, and YMHA enthusiasts who hoped that the ability to inculcate these traits into the children of immigrants would ease their entrance into the American mainstream.

Whether or nor Krinsky's remarks reflect his own childhood experiences at settlement houses and in evening recreation programs, other men who first became involved in basketball in similar ways certainly remember their power and persuasion. Red Sarachek was born in the Bronx in 1912, and raised in the Williamsburgh section of Brooklyn. Workmen's Circle coach and also mentor in the American Basketball League as well as coach and athletic director at Yeshiva University for 39 years, he clearly recalls efforts to use sports as a means of acculturating the children of immigrants. As he put it, "they expected it to grow on them and it did grow on them. After all, they gave them a home, a place . . . the incentive to do something would carry over."

... More impressive for . . . the many . . . who joined Ys, settlement houses, the Educational Alliance, and evening recreation programs was their own part in determining their participation. Joining because of their enthusiasm for sport or, . . . to get free milk and cookies, even within these organized programs they often maintained control of their own activities. On their own but within the framework of Jewish family and community, they learned more about "American" values and survival skills than what they absorbed from the actions and words of social workers and physical education teachers. Though not without conflict between themselves and their parents, their early basketball experiences illuminate the role of sport as middle ground in all its many versions.

Certainly that's how Sammy Kaplan remembers the Dux. The Dux took shape in the summer of 1925 when a bunch of high-school freshmen and sophomores in Sammy's Brownsville neighborhood got together and won a basketball tournament at a summer recreational program in the school yard of P.S. 184. Veterans of punchball, stickball, hide and seek, kick the can, and Johnny on the pony, . . . they decided to form a club in order to play basketball at their school's evening recreation center. As Kaplan recalls, they chose the name "Dux" because it meant leader in Latin and for the more practical reason that it only contained three letters, making it cheaper to sew the name on uniform shirts and jackets.

Recreation center rules required the club to hold weekly meetings, collect dues, and keep minutes, all in the spirit of a philosophy well articulated by youth organizations at this time which insisted that such practices would teach good citizenship and respect for authority. The Dux dutifully followed procedures, independently turning the experience to their own ends. Establishing ten-cent weekly dues, they used the money to promote their basketball. One member acted as a booking agent, arranging games with other clubs around the city. Visiting teams received as much as $2 for participating. Occasionally, the Dux even rented out the main school gym for $5 to host their opponents, money recouped by charging five-cent admissions to the games and by betting club dues on the outcome.

Sammy joined the club in 1926 at the age of fourteen, on the recommendation of his life-long friend Dudie Lynn that he was a good punchball player. . . . A growth spurt during the summer of 1927, which made Kaplan the tallest member of the club, moved him into the Dux starting lineup. The team relied on Sammy to win the center jumps held each time someone scored.

In 1928 the Dux represented P.S. 184 in a city-wide evening recreational basketball league and won the city championship, defeating P.S. 171 of Manhattan by a score of 33–15. To celebrate their success, the club put out a single issue of its own newspaper. Appropriately called *The Leader,* it proclaimed the Dux as city champions and detailed the exploits of the team, giving due credit not only to its young Jewish stars but also to Alvin Borten, who ran the center and coached the team. Edited by Kaplan and Lynn, the paper also included accounts of other center activities, taking great care to mention as many participants as possible by name. . . . The inclusion of so many names assured that neighborhood children and their parents would buy the paper at its five-cent price and turn a profit for the club. . . .

. . . Much as David Nasaw describes the street and work life of turn-of-the-century immigrant children in cities throughout the United States, the Dux's control over their own fortunes, both literally and figuratively, gave them a sense of independence, optimism, and a taste of success that made them more comfortable and accepting of a new American environment than many of their parents. In love with a city that offered all kinds of possibilities for fun and adventure, Kaplan remembers the freedom and opportunity involvement in basketball gave him and his friends. As he put it, "the street, the school yard and the candy store was [*sic*] our second home. . . .

Collecting dues, booking games, betting on the outcome, and selling their own celebratory announcements gave them a sense of independence and taught them first hand about American capitalism and the pleasures of success within it.

Building on their growing reputation, after 1928 the Dux left the evening recreation league and moved over to Hopkinson Avenue to represent the Hebrew Educational Society (HES), primarily because it had a bigger gym. Although Meyer Landesman, its head, tried to get the boys interested in the society's religious, educational, and social activities, basketball remained their focus. After two years the club broke its affiliation and freelanced throughout the city, playing college and professional teams as well as fives in established leagues. As Kaplan remembers, the "city was teeming with YMHA's, YMCA's, settlement houses, temples, Educational Alliances, Boys club, Harlem Hebrew Institute. . . . All the institutions were trying to get the immigrant children and their parents into the American mainstream and off the streets. They had all kinds of athletic programs, arts and crafts, drama, night classes which taught English and trades. And the immigrants seeking only a chance, grasped these opportunities with both hands. . . . We played them all. We played three or four times a week and demanded more expense money. . . .

By 1930 the Dux played throughout New York's five boroughs and also in upstate New York, New Jersey, and Pennsylvania. Successful on the court and at the gate, they "were even able to shower more than once a week," a mark, for Kaplan, of their separation from their immigrant parents. Occasionally, when they traveled outside the city limits, the boys would hire a bus and charge their friends $1.50 for the opportunity to accompany them. Charged by their love of the game and "their own incentive to do well," Kaplan asserts the Dux took responsibility for their own lives and never wanted "somebody to give us a handout or do something" for them.

Basketball provided the Dux and other clubs like them opportunities for learning American ways. Whether playing in their own neighborhood or representing other Jewish communities, their games also became an integral part of the social life of Jewish neighborhoods, especially for other second-generation friends and neighbors. Cheering their own to victory, they chose to be caught up in a web of assimilating experiences, both by deciding as American consumers how and where to spend their leisure time and by vicariously identifying with modern values of competition and meritocracy that victory on the court demanded.

So intense were basketball rivalries and fan loyalties among New York's Jewish communities that, during the 1933–34 season, the Staten Island Jewish Community Center hired the Brooklyn Dux to represent them in the YMHA league. Led by Sammy Kaplan, the Dux by this time were already established as one of the best independent clubs in the New York area. As the JCC Dux, they played a schedule that included other Y and Jewish center teams, local college teams such as NYU and CCNY, and a host of professional clubs including the New York Jewels, the Jersey City Reds, and the Chicago Studebakers. The schedule also included games with independent barnstorming teams that took on Jewish names to heighten crowd appeal. The Hebrew Cyclones, the House of David, and the Jersey City Hebrews, a team of former college and professional ballplayers that included Hank Greenberg, . . . all did battle with the Dux.

The Dux were unabashedly billed as the Brooklyn club. Nevertheless, the Staten Island *Advance* praised the boys as their own. In graphic prose the paper described a March 1934 victory over a previously undefeated Holman-coached City College club, noting how the "Dux went beserk in the final two periods as their passing attack . . . suddenly began to click on all cylinders—a quickening tempo that hypnotized" the jam-packed crowd of over 600 "into taut silence for a while and then into a wildly exuberant mob as shots repeatedly went in." Despite the fact that the Dux were clearly earning expenses and appearance money, the paper billed them as the "city's best amateur team" and emphasized the "tremendous local interest" they generated. In part this was due to a 17-game home-court win streak which ended when the JCC Dux lost to eventual national collegiate champions NYU by a 32–24 score before 500 fans. The same issue of the *Advance* that reported this despairing news to the Staten Island faithful also offered a column headlined "Jewish Centers Click on Court" which ranked the Dux among the top of the current crop of New York Y teams. Commenting that the teams were generally composed of ex-college stars and younger players of "college timber," the *Advance* suggested that "never before in the history of Jewish centre basketball has the interest been widespread and attendances so good.". . .

People who watched the 92nd Street Y varsity and the Dux came to enjoy good basketball, cheer their friends and neighbors, and also to see each other, catch up on local gossip, and socialize. Invariably, the price of admission also included refreshments and dancing to live music after the game. Fans attending a basketball carnival at the Port Richmond Community Center on Staten Island in December 1933 to raise money to supply Christmas food baskets to Staten Island's needy could see two games, one featuring the Dux, and danced afterward to midnight to Charles Bischof's Brownies eight-piece orchestra, all for 50 cents. Over in Paterson, New Jersey, anyone attending a 1934 game between the Dux and the local Y team could also count on dancing to the music of Natey Platt's orchestra, regardless of whether their local heroes triumphed on the court. . . .

Although not all stories are as well documented as that of the Dux or the 92nd Street Y, in Jewish communities large and small, scattered throughout the United States, the children of East European Jewish immigrants, as players and as spectators, took up this American game and made it their own. Twenty years before the Dux began, Joseph Weiner and a handful of New Haven Jewish boys, after learning the sport at the local boys club, formed their own organization, the Atlas Club. Holding weekly meetings, collecting dues, even publishing a club newspaper, over the next quarter-century this Jewish social athletic club participated in a wide variety of sports but excelled most prominently in basketball. In the early 1920s, its varsity team not only won city, state, and regional amateur championships but also played for pay against professional teams scattered throughout Connecticut and nearby states. During the 1919–20 season, for instance, the team, often referred to as "the Jewish boys" by the New Haven press, went undefeated over a 24-game schedule that included games with YMHA teams from Bridgeport and Waterbury as well as contests with the New York Collegiates and the Invincible Deaf Mutes of Lexington, New York.

Even though many of its members came from orthodox Jewish homes . . . basketball games often were scheduled for Friday nights. As one member recalls, that evening turned out to be the most profitable, attracting large numbers of youthful Jewish supporters interested both in basketball and the dance at the Music Hall that followed. Violation of Sabbath observance, however much [as] it might have upset their parents, did not diminish the club's own sense of Jewish purpose. Playing in cities which had never seen a Jewish athlete, Joseph Weiner recalls that club members "looked upon ourselves not simply as another team of players but as a group of goodwill representatives on behalf of the Jewish community. We were shattering the stereotype of the nebbich Jew.". . .

No doubt their athletic success also made other Jews both proud and hopeful of their own chances for success in America. Certainly the club's victory over the Yale varsity basketball team in a 1922 exhibition game which raised $2100 for the Jewish Relief Fund encouraged such sentiments. Playing before 2800 spectators at the Meadow Street Armory, the largest crowd ever to see a basketball game in New Haven up until that time, the Atlas, led by "Mickey" Botwinik and George Greenberg, crushed the Elis by 42–22. So too did the fact that many of the boys who played for the Atlas Club over the years went on to Yale or other colleges and then to careers in business and the professions. . . .

Basketball, then, all within the setting of Jewish community, provided second-generation participants and spectators opportunity to experience dominance and success in an American enterprise. In community centers and gymnasiums, neighborhood people also participated as American consumers by purchasing a ticket and choosing to root for whomever they pleased. They became fans of an American invention and more "American" in turn, by watching their own kind transform it into a Jewish majority sport. These Americanizing experiences unfolded in ways that encouraged ethnic pride and identification. Although this dynamic was to receive far greater publicity with the success of Jewish boxers and major league baseball players, the achievements of local boys in local settings carried a most immediate, palpable sense of American possibility for all Jews.

Witnessing friends excel in American sport while socializing in settings distinctly Jewish even provided opportunities for maintaining Jewish tradition. Whether raising money to buy Passover matzoh for poor Brownsville residents or for the Jewish Relief Fund in New Haven, or using basketball revenues, as the 92nd Street Y did, to send children to summer camps or to supplement its Keren Ami Fund which raised money for a host of Jewish charities, those who participated in basketball both as players and as spectators also expressed collective concern for community welfare consistent with the long-standing Jewish tradition of tzedakah—God's directive to help others less fortunate than yourself. Engaging sport as a middle ground, participants in this world of basketball and Jewish community acquired American ways while absorbing Jewish sensibilities, even as they moved inexorably away from the Jewish world of their immigrant parents.

II

Not everyone was happy about this transformation. Harry Glantz, who glowingly reported on the success of Los Angeles Jewish community basketball teams for his *B'nai B'rith Messenger* readers, chastised the local B'nai B'rith lodge for sponsoring league games on Friday nights. Players certainly have the chance to be home for the "Shabbus feast." But as soon as the meal is over, he lamented, "they bundle their athletic trunks and shoes in their grips and they're away as fast as they can— to uphold the fair name of a Jewish club on a basketball court," in violation of the true meaning of "our most important holy day."

Fathers and mothers also voiced disapproval. Even those eager to see their children make their mark as successful Americans were often appalled by their children's passion for basketball and other sports. Talking about his boyhood Brownsville street life, William Poster, a poet and writer, remembers parents "who assured us as we came streaking in from a punchball game covered with sweat and grime" before rush[ing] off to one of a hundred feverish nocturnal activities that we were all bums, gangsters, boolvans and paskudnyaks." Poet and teacher Milton Klonsky, who also grew up in the late 1920s and early 1930s a little further south in the Jewish neighborhood surrounding Brooklyn's Brighton Beach, recalls similar memories. Proudly he remembers his loyalty to his club, the Trogans, and their inventive use of streets and sidewalks in their all-consuming love and interest in sport. "We played hard with a will to win so strong it willed itself," he remembers. "Sometimes we became so engrossed by a punchball or a stickball game that night would fall without anyone's being aware of it." Their passion, however, was not shared "by mothers who complained because they had to complain and even more by the old ones, those zaidas with embroidered yamelkas and their white beards worn like orders upon their chests. They wondered whether we were Jews or a new kind of shagitz. . . . They painted a picture of our decline and fall stage by stage . . . until someday we would be eating pig and pulling beards on the streets of New York.". . .

Parents, they remember, caught up in their own struggle between new American desires and traditional East European ethnic ways, often expressed displeasure with their sons' love of sport. More important, however, they were too preoccupied with making ends meet to devote time and energy to the daily direction of their children's lives. When they did raise objections, it had little to do with fears that children were abandoning any sense of traditional Jewish life but rather that they were squandering opportunities for education and economic opportunity offered by a new American world. For some parents, over time, their children's accomplishments in this American game softened their disappointment, even serving as a common ground between generations both caught up in learning how to be American.

When asked if his parents objected to his playing basketball, Harry Litwack recalls that they were too busy trying to survive to worry about how he spent his time. Although not orthodox, his Polish parents kept kosher, observed the high holidays, and spoke only Yiddish in the home. Noting the difficulties they experienced in coming to terms with America, he mentions that his mother never learned English and that his father struggled with it. Harry's father repaired shoes, putting in hours from 6 a.m. until his day's work was done. Only on Sunday afternoons did he take time off from his labors, when after a tub bath he went out to buy his supplies for the following week. In such a setting, there was no time for outside interests or for worrying about his son's participation in athletics. Not once, through his playing days at Philadelphia's Southern High School, Temple University, or even with the renowned Philadelphia SPHAs, did his parents come to see him. "All the parents in the ghetto," Harry remembers, had no interest in sport. "All they understood were books, books, books, knowledge, knowledge, knowledge." His parents' only concern, as Harry recalls it, was that "I came home at night."

Left to his own devices, basketball provided Litwack with a ticket to college, a sense of empowerment and independence as an adolescent, and ultimately a highly successful career in basketball, all unfolding in the Jewish world of South Philadelphia. Several thousand miles away and almost a generation later, Harry Glickman offers a somewhat different version of family and community. Born in Portland, Oregon, to immigrant parents from Russia and Poland in 1924, he grew up in Portland's small East European Jewish neighborhood that he remembers as distinctly "Jewish." His parents divorced when he was five and Harry was raised in an orthodox, kosher home by his mother, who worked as a finisher in the garment trade to make ends meet. Although not an outstanding basketball player, his childhood memories remain dominated by his days spent at the local Jewish community center where he played basketball with his Jewish friends—friends he still sees regularly today. His mother, he recalls, encouraged his interest, worrying only that he might be injured. . . .

Clearly it would be unfair to suggest that these stories about basketball and Jewish life, offered by exceptionally talented athletes, were typical of the experience of all other men of their generation. Well-marked Jewish enclaves like Brooklyn's Brownsville, Chicago's Maxwell Street, or Philadelphia's south side, where everyone and everything seemed "Jewish," did not describe the situations of Jews growing up in places like El Paso, Texas, or Montgomery, Alabama. Moreover, neither in Brownsville nor on Maxwell Street did all young boys find basketball and sport their all-consuming passions.

Still, in neighborhoods located in eastern and midwestern cities where most Jews lived, for those who played the game and for friends who offered their support, basketball provided a large segment of second-generation Jewish youth from urban East European working-class backgrounds opportunities to relish what was most exciting about being an American. Social reformers and religious leaders certainly tried to impose their own definitions of propriety and citizenship on them, even using sport as one means of cutting their own versions of Americans out of immigrant cloth. But through basketball, these children of immigrants became active participants in the process of deciding what it was to be an American and what it was to be Jewish. For them, it was never a choice between remaining part of some idealized version of European immigrant culture or blending into an American Gentile world. Rather, in the context of their own ethnic world, they shaped their own sense of Americanism, one that ultimately fused what they considered to be ethnic and mainstream values. In short, these people recognized an incredible feature of American life totally alien to their parents' European beginnings. Here, public definitions of community, of Americanism, of Jewishness, and of the place of sport in it all were not dictated by secular or religious authorities. Even in the face of opposing views from within and without their own communities, they were free to determine what assimilation meant for themselves.

❿ *F U R T H E R   R E A D I N G*

Arthur Ashe, *A Hard Road to Glory: A History of the African-American Athlete, 1619–1986*, 3 vols. (1988)
William J. Baker, *Jesse Owens: An American Life* (1986)

Gwendolyn Captain, "Enter Ladies and Gentlemen of Color: Gender, Sport and the Ideal of American Manhood and Womanhood During the Late Nineteenth and Early Twentieth Century," *Journal of Sport History* 18 (1991), 81–102

John M. Carroll, *Fritz Pollard: Pioneer in Racial Advancement* (1992)

Gerald Gems, *Windy City Wars: Labor, Leisure and Sport in the Making of Chicago* (1997)

Hank Greenberg, in Ira Berkow, ed., *Hank Greenberg: The Story of My Life* (1988)

Stephen Hardy, *How Boston Played: Sport, Recreation, and Community, 1865–1915* (1982)

Neil Lanctot, *Fair Dealing and Clean Playing: The Hilldale Club and the Development of Professional Baseball, 1910–1932* (1994)

Peter Levine, *Ellis Island to Ebbets Field: Sport and the American Jewish Experience* (1992)

Gary Ross Mormino, "The Playing Fields of St. Louis: Italian Immigrants and Sports, 1925–1941," *Journal of Sport History* 9 (Summer 1982), 5–19

Roberta J. Park, "German Associational and Sporting Life in the Greater San Francisco Area, 1850–1900," *Journal of the West* 26 (1987), 47–64

Robert Peterson, *Only the Ball Was White* (1970)

Samuel O. Regalado, "Sport and Community in California's Japanese American Yamato Colony, 1930–1945," *Journal of Sport History* 19 (1992), 130–43

Mark Ribowsky, *A Complete History of the Negro Leagues, 1884 to 1955* (1995)

Steven A. Riess, "A Fighting Chance: The Jewish-American Boxing Experience, 1890–1940," *American Jewish History* 74 (March 1985), 223–54

Andrew Ritchie, *Major Taylor: The Extraordinary Career of a Champion Bicycle Racer* (1988)

Randy Roberts, *Papa Jack: Jack Johnson and the Era of White Hopes* (1983)

Donn Rogosin, *Invisible Men: Life in Baseball's Negro Leagues* (1983)

Rob Ruck, *Sandlot Seasons: Sport in Black Pittsburgh* (1987)

David K. Wiggins, "Isaac Murphy: Black Hero in Nineteenth Century American Sport, 1861–1896," *Canadian Journal of History of Sport and Physical Education* 19 (1979), 15–32

David Zang, *Moses Fleetwood Walker's Divided Heart: The Life of Baseball's First Black Major Leaguer* (1995)

CHAPTER
11

Sports Heroes and American Culture, 1890–1940

Why was sport such an important source of heroes in the early twentieth century? Although there were a few earlier sports idols like pugilist John L. Sullivan, by the 1920s it seemed that every major sport had its own hero or heroine: baseball had Babe Ruth; boxing had Jack Dempsey; football had Red Grange; swimming had Gertrude Ederle; tennis had Bill Tilden; and golf had Bobby Jones. There were not only heroes for the broader society but also certain idols for ethnic subcommunities like boxer Benny Leonard for Jews and baseball star Tony Lazzeri for Italians.

What made certain athletes heroic? Why was there such a great need for heroes at this time? Sociologist Janet Harris in Athletes and the American Hero Dilemma (1994) states that heroes "provide active displays of prominent human characteristics and social relationships. . . . They are thought to help define individual and collective identity, compensate for qualities perceived to be missing in individuals or society, display ideal behaviors that people strive to emulate, and provide avenues for temporary escape from the rigors of daily life." How did sportsmen and women become identified as heroes? A sports hero was recognized for athletic accomplishments that were readily measurable, usually gained over a long period, earned, according to historian David Voigt, through "hard work, clean living, and battling obstacles." A hero was more than a celebrity, who was famous simply for his/her athletic accomplishments. Society expected heroes to be morally and socially responsible and to serve as role models. Heroes were thought to be very important for youngsters to emulate (particularly when American society was undergoing many major changes because of industrialization, urbanization, bureaucratization, and immigration). They exemplified stability and direction, certified that traditional values like rugged individualism, self-reliance, and courage still counted, and occasionally also epitomized the relevance of newer traits like teamwork and cooperation.

◉ D O C U M E N T S

The first document in this chapter is a fictional account of the athletic exploits of Dick Merriwell at Yale College. It is drawn from *Dick Merriwell's Power,* one example of the 208 novels that comprised Burt Standish's [Gilbert Patten's] Merriwell series, which dominated the juvenile sport literature market at the turn of the century. In this particular story Dick Merriwell is frightfully ill and is kept out of the football game against Brown on the orders of his doctor. But with Yale losing, he comes off the bench late in the contest, disregarding his own welfare, to win the big game for his teammates and his school. Standish's principal hero was Dick's older brother, Frank, whose athletic deeds and off-the-field exploits provided exciting reading for American boys. Dick followed in Frank's footsteps, duplicating all of his brother's outstanding athletic skills and character traits.

Juvenile sports fiction, according to Michael Oriard, "defines exactly who the representative American hero is." Oriard considers Frank Merriwell the epitome of a sports hero. He was a self-made muscular Christian who had great athletic skill, and exemplified such traditional values as hard work, honesty, bravery, loyalty, modesty, and self-sacrifice. American boys who read the Merriwell stories were encouraged by them to emulate the behavior and character of the Merriwell brothers.

The second document is a memorial written to honor Christy Matthewson, the athlete generally considered the closest anyone was in real life to the fictional Merriwell boys. Matthewson was a tall, blond, college-educated pitcher, who won 373 games for the New York Giants—the most ever in National League history. "Matty" was an outstanding moral hero who taught Sunday School and often spoke to youth organizations on clean living and sportsmanship. He served overseas as an officer during World War I, and took some poison gas while inspecting German trenches. His weakened condition left him vulnerable to tuberculosis, from which he died prematurely in 1925.

The third document focuses on the Black Sox Scandal in which eight players on the Chicago White Sox were thrown out of baseball because of their presumed involvement in fixing the World Series of 1919. This document consists of excerpts from the confession of star outfielder "Shoeless" Joe Jackson, who did not play to lose, batting .375 in the Series. However, he knew of the fix and received a portion of the payoff. Jackson was uneducated and unsophisticated, and he was inadequately represented by attorney Alfred Austrian when he signed the confession. Austrian had ulterior motives because as the White Sox's lawyer, his agenda was to protect the interests of team owner Charles Comiskey. When the case went to trial, Jackson's confession and those of pitchers Lefty Williams and Eddie Cicotte were reported lost, and the eight indicted players were acquitted. The jurors carried them out, having certified the integrity of their heroes. However, Judge Kenesaw Mountain Landis, the newly appointed commissioner of baseball, expelled them anyhow. When Jackson sued the Sox in 1924 for back pay, the confessions suddenly materialized in Comiskey's office, and Jackson lost his suit.

The fourth and fifth documents are drawn from the columns of Grantland Rice, the preeminent sports journalist of the 1920s, who was renowned for his ability to turn a phrase and to praise great athletes. In one selection he compares the ability of heroes like John L. Sullivan and Babe Ruth to attract huge audiences to see them perform. Ruth was not a traditional hero because he was a natural player who exemplified brawn over brain (the opposite of Ty Cobb), and his culinary and sexual excesses flaunted traditional morality, epitomizing the free spirit of the 1920s. Rice's other article describes the heroic qualities of two amateur athletes, the stoic golfer Bobby Jones and imperturbable tennis star Helen Wills.

The final document, a eulogy given by Congressman Louis Stokes, honors Jesse Owens, who was perhaps the greatest track and field star in the history of the Olympics. Stokes had grown up in Cleveland, Owens's home town, and had idolized Owens, a world record–holding sprinter and long jumper who earned four gold medals at the 1936 Olympics in Berlin—a feat that momentarily set back the racist Nazi propaganda machine.

Burt Standish's Dick Merriwell Saves the Game, 1909

By the game with Brown, Dick Merriwell developed an attack of malaria. That, not withstanding his perfect physical condition, completely knocked him out. Although Dick insisted that he was suffering only from a slight cold, the doctor urged Coach Fullerton to give the boy a lay-off, unless it was absolutely necessary to put him into the game.

So on the day of the game, Sharon was sent on to the field to fill Merriwell's place, and Dick was sent to the side lines.

Brown had a fine team and it fought hard. Yale's touchdown and goal in the first half was made through a fluke, and old Bill Fullerton employed his opportunity between halves to make a few scathing remarks to the Elis. . . .

Brown opened the second half with a substitute fullback, a giant, who weighed at least 230 pounds. This man Perkins, soon showed that he was more formidable than the fellow who had been discarded from the back-field. He was also fearless and surprisingly fast on his feet. Whenever the forwards tore a hole in Yale's line, and Perkins plunged into that hole, there was sure to be a tremendous shake up. He battered and beat men down before him, and left them stretched like dying soldiers on the field. In less than five minutes he had injured three of four forwards, and sent them from the field.

. . . The team showed no signs of wavering, not a symptom of fear. And yet, if this slaughter kept up Perkins would make such cripples of the Elis that, with a lead of only six points, the blue might go down in defeat.

. . . A few of them took note of what was occurring on the side lines. They saw old Bill Fullerton kneeling on one knee, send out substitute after substitute. They saw Dick Merriwell approach him thrice and appeal to him. They saw Fullerton shake his head, although they were not near enough to hear him say, "Doc says no, you can't go in." Suddenly there was a pause. Still another Yale man lay stretched on the damp sod.

It was Sharon. The half-back who had been filling Dick Merriwell's regular position. "Let me in coach—let me in!" pleaded Merriwell's voice in Fullerton's

From Burt Standish, *Dick Merriwell's Power, or Hold 'Em Yale* (New York: Street & Smith, 1909).

ear. "Somebody must stop that man Perkins. If he isn't stopped they will win this game. Let me in."

"Go ahead," cried old Bill suddenly: "If anybody can stop him, you're the man."

. . . They thrilled as Merriwell came running out from the side line. The Yale crowd cheered madly as it always cheered Dick.

Again Brown's forwards made a hole in the line through which Perkins plunged. But the new right half-back was there to meet him. He flung himself headlong, squeezed the giant's knees, held him tight, and stopped him there. When the snarled mess of men untangled, Merriwell rose promptly for the next clash.

Twice it was Dick who checked the giant's charges in that manner. Then Perkins was sent round the end with two interferers to look after him.

Buckhardt took care of one of those; Kirk Chambers got at the other. Dick Merriwell slammed Perkins to the ground with such fury that it seemed as if the earth must quiver from the shock.

Then both the giant and Merriwell were sent stretched silent and motionless side by side.

Although Merriwell had been stunned by the shock, the effect of the collision was not nearly as severe upon him as upon Perkins. The giant's left arm was wholly out of commission, and his right leg was twisted so that he could scarcely bear his weight upon it. He insisted on playing some more, but after two more scrimmages, he was taken out.

With the stop of Perkins the tide turned. From that time forward Yale has her own way, even though Brown fought stubbornly to the last ditch.

Commonweal Memorializes Christy Matthewson, a Real-Life Merriwell, 1925

. . . During these days we have all injected curves and lusty smashes into our vista of world news, showing thus how firm a nucleus for our thoughts and emotions is afforded by the national game. And yet there came also the sudden, saddening, report that one of the supreme gentlemen of sport had died, leaving to the world a fine memory and at least a momentary heartache. Christy Matthewson was, of course, a wonderful pitcher—no other man probably has ever brought a President of the United States half way across the continent to a seat at a crucial game; and certainly no other pitcher ever loomed so majestically in young minds, quite over-shadowing George Washington and his cherry tree or even that transcendent model of boyhood, Frank Merriwell. Yet "Big-Six" was very much more than an illustration of diamond craft.

With straightforward, manly character he entered the lists of sport a gentle-man, and came out a deserving hero. There was about him no flash, no scandal, no cheap clamor for notoriety. One had a securely comfortable feeling that Matthew-

---

From editorial, *Commonweal* 2 (October 21, 1925): 288.

son would not betray the trust of his position and uncover flaws over which the cheap journals could grin and sentimentalize. During the years following his war experience, when it became more and more evident that gas had weakened his constitution beyond recovery, there was no attempt to capitalize upon his record, but merely a simple resignation to the circumstances and a brave battle with death. Such men have a very real value above and beyond the achievements of brawn and sporting skill. They realize and typify, in a fashion, the ideal of sport—clean power in the hands of a clean and vigorous personality, a courage that has been earned in combat, and a sense of honor which metes out justice to opponents and spurns those victories that have not been earned.

The Black Sox Scandal and the Fallen Hero: The Confession of Joe Jackson, 1920

Q: Did anybody pay you any money to help throw that series in favor of Cincinnati?

A: They did.

Q: How much did they pay?

A: They promised me $20,000, and paid me five.

Q: Who promised you the twenty thousand?

A: "Chick" Gandil. . . .

Q: Who paid you the $5,000?

A: Lefty Williams brought it in my room and threw it down.

Q: Who was in the room at the time?

A: Lefty and myself, I was in there, and he came in.

Q: Where was Mrs. Jackson?

A: Mrs. Jackson—let me see—I think she was in the bathroom. . . .

Q: Does she know that you got $5,000 for helping throw these games?

A: She did that night, yes.

Q: You say that you told Mrs. Jackson that evening?

A: Did, yes.

Q: What did she say about it?

A: She said she thought it was an awful thing to do.

Q: When was it that this money was brought to your room and that you talked to Mrs. Jackson?

A: It was the second trip to Cincinnati. That night we were leaving.

Q: That was after the fourth game?

A: I believe it was, yes. . . .

Q: Were you at a conference of these men, these players on the Sox team, at the Warner Hotel sometime previous to this?

A: No, sir, I was not present, but I knew they had the meeting, so I was told.

From Joe Jackson, confession before the Grand Jury of Cook County, September 28, 1920 (copy in author's possession). Jackson's confession has been published in several books, including David Gropman, *Say It Ain't So, Joe! The True Story of Shoeless Joe Jackson* (New York: Citadel Press, 1992).

Q: Who told you?

A: Williams. . . .

Q: What did he tell you?

A: He told me about this meeting in particular, he said the gang was there, and this fellow Attell, Abe Attell, I believe, and Bill Burns is the man that give him the double crossing, so Gandil told me.

Q: You say Abe Attell and Bill Burns are the two people that Claude Williams told you gave you the double cross?

A: Chick Gandil told me that.

Q: Then you talked to Chick Gandil and Claude Williams both about this?

A: Talked to Claude Williams about it, yes, and Gandil more so, because he is the man that promised me this stuff.

Q: How much did he promise you?

A: $20,000 if I would take part.

Q: And you said you would?

A: Yes, sir.

Q: When did he promise you the $20,000?

A: It was to be paid after each game.

Q: How much?

A: Split it up some way, I don't know just how much it amounts to, but during the Series it would amount to $20,000. Finally Williams brought me this $5,000, threw it down.

Q: What did you say to Williams when he threw down the $5,000?

A: I asked him what the hell had come off here.

Q: What did he say?

A: He said Gandil said we all got a screw through Abe Attell. Gandil said that we got double crossed through Abe Attell, he got the money and refused to turn it over to him. I don't think Gandil was crossed as much as he crossed us.

Q: You think Gandil may have gotten the money and held it from you, is that right?

A: That's what I think, I think he kept the majority of it.

Q: What did you do then?

A: I went to him and asked him what was the matter. He said Abe Attell gave him the jazzing. He said, "Take that or let it alone.". . .

Q: And you were to be paid $5,000 after each game, is that right?

A: Well, Attell was supposed to give the $100,000. It was to be split up, paid to him, I believe, and $15,000 a day or something like that, after each game.

Q: That is to Gandil?

A: Yes.

Q: At the end of the first game you didn't get any money, did you?

A: No, I did not, no, sir.

Q: What did you do then?

A: I asked Gandil what is the trouble? He says, "Everything is all right" he had it.

Q: Then you went ahead and threw the second game, thinking you would get it then, is that right?

A: We went ahead and threw the second game, we went after him again. I said to him, "What are you going to do?" "Everything is all right," he says, "What the hell is the matter?"

Q: After the third game what did you say to him?

A: After the third game I says, "Somebody is getting a nice little jazz, everybody is crossed." He said, "Well, Abe Attell and Bill Burns had crossed him," that is what he said to me.

Q: He said Abe Attell and Bill Burns had crossed him?

A: Yes, sir. . . .

Q: Who do you think was the man they approached?

A: Why, Gandil.

Q: What makes you think Gandil?

A: Well, he was the whole works of it, the instigator of it, the fellow that mentioned it to me. He told me that I could take it or let it go, they were going through with it.

Q: Didn't you think it was the right thing for you to go and tell Comiskey about it?

A: I did tell them once, "I am not going to be in it." I will just get out of that altogether.

Q: Who did you tell that to?

A: Chick Gandil.

Q: What did he say?

A: He said I was into it already and I might as well stay in. I said, "I can go to the boss and have every damn one of you pulled out of the limelight." He said, "It wouldn't be well for me if I did that.". . .

Q: Do you recall the fourth game that Cicotte pitched?

A: Yes, sir.

Q: Did you see any fake plays made by yourself or anybody on (sic) that game, that would help throw the game?

A: Only the wildness of Cicotte.

Q: What was that?

A: Hitting the batter, that is the only thing that told me they were going through with it.

Q: Did you make any intentional errors yourself that day?

A: No, sir, not during the whole series.

Q: Did you bat to win?

A: Yes.

Q: And run the bases to win?

A: Yes, sir.

Q: And field the balls at the outfield to win?

A: I did. . . .

Q: The fourth game Cicotte pitched again? It was played out here in Chicago and Chicago lost it 2 to nothing? Do you remember that?

A: Yes, sir.

Q: Did you see anything wrong about that game that would lead you to believe there was an intentional fixing?

A: The only thing that I was sore about that game, the throw I made to the plate, Cicotte tried to intercept it. . . .

Q: Did you do anything to throw those games?

A: No, sir.

Q: Any game in the series?

A: Not a one. I didn't have an error or make no misplay. . . .

Q: To keep on with these games, the fifth game, did you see anything wrong with that or any of the games, did you see any plays that you would say might have been made to throw that particular game?

A: Well, I only saw one play in the whole series, I don't remember what game it was in, either, it was in Cincinnati.

Q: Who made it?

A: Charlie Risburg.

Q: What was that?

A: It looked like a perfect double play. And he only gets one, gets the ball and runs over to the bag with it in place of throwing it in front of the bag. . . .

Q: When did Eddie Cicotte tell you he got $10,000?

A: The next morning after the meeting we had in his room.

Q: Did you tell him how much you got?

A: I did.

Q: What did you tell him?

A: I told him I got five thousand.

Q: What did he say?

A: He said I was a God damn fool for not getting it in my hands like he did.

Q: What did he mean by that?

A: I don't know, that he wouldn't trust anybody, I guess.

Q: What did he mean, that's what he meant by it?

A: Why, he meant he would not trust them, they had to pay him before he did anything.

Q: He meant then that you ought to have got your money before you played, is that it?

A: Yes, that's it.

Q: Did you have a talk with any of the other players about how much they got?

A: I understand McMullin got five and Risburg five thousand, that's the way I understand. . . .

Q: Weren't you in on the inner circle?

A: No, I never was with them, no, sir. It was mentioned to me in Boston. As I told you before, they asked me what would I consider, $10,000? and I said no, then they offered me twenty.

Q: Who mentioned it first to you?

A: Gandil.

Q: Who was with you?

A: We were all alone.

Q: What did he say?

A: He asked me would I consider $10,000 to frame up something and I asked him frame what? and he told me and I said no.

Q: What did he say?

A: Just walked away from me, and when I returned here to Chicago he told me that he would give me twenty and I said no again, and on the bridge where you go into the club house he told me I could either take it or let it alone, they were going through.

Q: What did they say?

A: They said,"You might as well say yes or say no and play ball or anything you want." I told them I would take their word. . . .

THE FOREMAN: Q: What makes you think that Gandil was double crossing you, rather than Attell and Burns?

A: What made me think it was Gandil going out on the coast, so I was told, I was surmising what I heard, they came back and told me he had a summer home, big automobile, doesn't do a lick of work; I know I can't do that way.

MR. REPLOGLE: Q: In other words, if he double crossed you fellows he couldn't come back and face them, and he had plenty of money to stay out there. It wasn't at the time that you thought Gandil was double crossing you, you thought Gandil was telling the truth, is that right?

A: No, I told Williams after the first day it was a crooked deal all the way through, Gandil was not on the square with us. . . .

Q: Do you have any suspicion about the White Sox, any of the players throw any of the games this summer?

A: Well, there have been some funny looking games, runs, I could have just my own belief about it, I wouldn't accuse the men.

Q: Where at?

A: A couple in New York, this last Eastern trip, looked bad, but I couldn't come out and open and bold and accuse anybody of throwing those games. . . .

Grantland Rice on John L. Sullivan and Babe Ruth as Prowess Heroes, 1925

Who have been the two greatest drawing cards, the two most popular figures in the history of sport? . . .

. . . For drawing-card value and personal appeal the two names that head the cast must be John L. Sullivan and Babe Ruth. Their glory began in Boston. John L. was born there and Babe Ruth began his major league career in the same city.

The study of crowd-drawing psychology is interesting. Sullivan and Ruth, great in their respective lines, did not appeal to the millions for this reason alone. They live, in action or in memory, as something more than great competitors. Each had an appeal to great multitudes far beyond his abilities with fist or bat.

Jeffries was as great a fighter as Sullivan. Possibly an even greater one, with greater bulk and greater strength. Yet Jeffries' popularity could never be mentioned as faintly rivaling Sullivan's. Ty Cobb, George Sisler and Rogers Hornsby are not

From Grantland Rice, "What Draws the Crowds," *Collier's* 75 (June 20, 1925): 10, 44.

to be rated below Ruth in the way of baseball brilliancy. Yet all three together could never draw the gate that Babe alone can draw, or could draw when he was riding the crest. . . .

The personalities of John L. and the Babe have surged beyond the ring and the playing field into the arena and the stands, beyond the arena and the stands into the outside nation, and then on beyond the seas into other lands that knew them only by reputation. . . .

There is something more to consider. Most champions are forgotten in defeat. When the count of ten is finished over their battered forms the cheering multitudes melt quickly away, to follow the new king. Yet twenty years after he was beaten by Jim Corbett, Sullivan appearing on the streets of a big city would still draw a greater gathering than any champion of that day or this could pull together. Twenty years after defeat John L. made it a point to ride in the larger cities rather than walk because the crowds—bless 'em—gathered with such bulk and swiftness that he found it impossible to make any headway.

Babe Ruth in the last five years has drawn at least $1,500,000 into various ball parks, . . . We recall one season when Connie Mack's Athletics were not drawing 500 a day. . . . Yet when Babe Ruth came to Philadelphia with the Yankees the reserves had to be called out three days in succession to handle the mobs which stormed the ball park. . . .

What are the attributes that made these two men the greatest drawing cards ever known to sport?

Both were big, bluff, boisterous or in a fashion roistering types. Neither was the world's strictest adherer to training or discipline. The language of neither was ever intended for the fashionable chit-chat of a ballroom. They will be remembered as given to straight talk, without compromise or diplomacy. They will both be remembered as models in the raw, rather than as smooth and polished specimens. Neither made any attempt to conceal rough edges, to cover up such edges with a cloak of any polite sort.

But their names have always carried a thrill, dating back to the time that each came to his glory.

In the first they were both, at their heights, Apostles of the Punch. They were wallopers—each a record maker of prodigious punching power—and the multitudes have always esteemed the roar or thud of the wallop as the sweetest of all melodies. . . .

Both looked their parts as perfectly as Forbes Robertson or Barrymore ever looked Hamlet. In physical form and manner they were perfectly cast. No little man could have ever loomed so against the sporting horizon. . . .

And from each there has always been that indescribable personal magnetism that pervades the field and the streets, wherever each might have elected to be. Both have had grace and speed and rhythm as well as power. There was no lumbering, ungainly motion to the actions of either. . . .

And that, once more, isn't all. For each loved his game beyond any other passion. The ring was John L.'s home. A fight to him was the greatest pleasure he could know. In less than one season he knocked out over a hundred and fifty opponents, meeting all comers from coast to coast. He loved to fight and the crowd knew it. He took pride in his profession, and the crowd knew this too. Fighting was his business, his recreation, his soul's desire.

The same has always been true of Babe Ruth. He has made a fortune at baseball, but the crowd could see that he was playing the game for fun above all else. . . .

Both John L. and Ruth violated all the common-sense rules of economy and thrift, and this also added a few sprigs to their laurel wreaths, possibly as being further proof that money to them was unimportant, that it was only the game and the glory of the game that counted.

Each one had in his day of top fame the capacity to thrill crowds, and neither ever withheld from any crowds the thrills expected. And there was in Sullivan, as there was and is in Ruth, a great love for all kids. And it was all real. Sullivan was supposed to be a terror in the ring, one who battered all opponents to unconsciousness as soon as he could. Yet one day when a youngster fell and cut his face badly Sullivan, with tears running down his face, picked him up in his arms and hurried to the nearest doctor. He might beat up a cop, but any kid could have anything John L. Sullivan had.

The same has always been true of Ruth, who still in spirit is only a kid of fourteen or fifteen. You might think the kids would stand aside in awe of the home-run kid. But once let upon the field they are all over him, climbing his vast body, pulling him down to play with him as if he were some big pet, sent there for a frolic and a romp. And Ruth in the meanwhile has spent innumerable hours going out of his way to help youngsters singly and in groups, to take them autographed baseballs, to help pay their doctors' bills, to prove that he is still one of them in every manner of life.

Above all else, both were on the level in this sense: each gave to his game all he had, at every start, with a deep appreciation of the great public that brought him fame and fortune. The usual method of the champion is to despise this public. Few champions have liked crowds. To John L. Sullivan and to Babe Ruth these crowds stood as sponsors of their greatness, as makers of their greatness, audiences entitled to the finest work of the artist at every move. Neither ever faked, neither ever shirked, and with all their crudities both, in addition to being skilled artisans at their trade, were dramatists of high degree with peculiar qualities of crowd attraction that no one else in the game has known. They were the architects of personal destinies that no mere skill alone could ever hope to reach.

Grantland Rice Describes the Heroic Qualities of Bobby Jones and Helen Wills, 1928

There are many stars and a few super-stars in sport. There are champions who bag a coronet now and then, and there are others who dominate some game year after year. In other words there are Bobby Jones and Helen Wills.

From Grantland Rice, "Making of the Mighty," *Collier's* 82 (November 3, 1928): 17.

Bobby Jones is twenty-six years old. At this age he has won eight national titles at match and medal play. He has won four of the last five amateur gold championships of the United States. . . . At medal play he has won the British Open twice and the U.S. Open twice. . . .

Helen Wills is twenty-four years old. At this age she has won her last five starts in the women's national tennis championship of the United States and she has overwhelmed every European opponent since Suzanne Lenglen left the amateur ranks.

Bobby Jones and Helen Wills not only keep winning, but they leave so wide a winning margin that no one else seems to be second or third. Their victories are not mere victories. They are routs. . . .

What has Bobby Jones to show that lifts him so far above the amateurs at match play and so far above the professionals in the medal-play test of the open?

Jones happened to start golf at the age of seven, and at that plastic age copied a model who had a sound, compact swing. The model was Steward Maiden—at the East Lake Club. So Bobby got the right start and the instincts of correct swinging planted in his system before he had a chance to develop any faults. At the age of ten he had about as good a swing as you will see on any golf course today.

At the age of fourteen Jones was almost as good a shot-maker as he is today. He had a strong pair of hands and a pair of powerful wrists. He had a strong body and stout legs. I saw him then march around a championship course in 70. I saw him finish with a 4 for a 31 on the last nine at Merion against Frank Dyer—all at the age of fourteen.

Why was it, then, that Jones had to wait eight years—until 1924—before winning his first amateur championship?

There were two reasons. In the first place, in his earlier campaigns, most of his opponents—the known stars and the unknowns—had the habit of playing their golfing heads off against the young Georgian. Dave Herron at Oakmont in 1919 was 3 under 4's in the final round; Francis Ouimet at the Engineers in 1920 was around in 70. Willie Hunter at St. Louis in 1921 was traveling at a 70 clip. Jones had a 71 with a 7 on one hole. Jess Sweetser handed him a 67 at Brookline to feed on and Max Marston handed him a 70 at Flossmoor.

In addition to these hostile killing blasts, Jones' early golf temperament was far from perfect. His tournament conduct at this time was beyond reproach but he was high-strung, over-keen, boiling inwardly at his own mistakes. He had never had the capacity for the relaxed mental state of Walter Hagen.

With all the physical qualifications, Jones had an unusually fine brain and unusual determination and courage. But he had always had the high-strung temperament that goes better in football and tennis than it goes in golf—the yearning for action rather than the feeling of restraint and nerve control.

Those seven years of defeat in one match or another were like white flame applied to iron ore. They were making steel. Those defeats were teaching him lessons more valuable at that time than victories could have done.

He won his first open at Inwood in 1923, and his amateur championship at Merion in 1924. From that point on he was set. At the age of twenty-two he had won an open and an amateur championship. He had all the physical qualifications—big, strong hands, strong wrists, a strong body, and a great pair of legs. The hands and legs tire first in golf and when they do there are storms ahead.

Jones had stamina, courage, determination, and a keen, analytical mind. He had been a great shot-maker for eight or ten years. Now, at twenty-two, he had, in addition, experience under heavy and withering fire, valuable lessons in nerve control, sounder judgment—and all this was his with his youth intact and the years still ahead. . . .

I think Jones became a great and a winning golfer the moment he added a fine putting touch to his long game. For five years he has been one of the greatest putters in all golf. . . .

Why is Helen Wills so far above all competition in her field? Lenglen ruled first with a finer all-round game, carrying far greater foot speed and better technique. When she retired, Miss Wills was set to take her place. Where Bobby Jones had very few weaknesses of any sort to fight, Helen Wills had to make up for her lack of foot speed, which limited both her attack and defense. It gave her no chance for the footwork of a Lenglen or a Tilden. To offset this she had to fall back upon power and control of power. The wonder is that she could achieve the control she has shown for the last two years.

There have been few people in competitive sport blessed with a finer temperament for match play. She outclassed Mlle. Lenglen in this respect. Nothing upsets her mental poise. Nothing seems to affect her serene confidence and determination. She staked her chance upon a smashing drive game that she could handle ably at all times.

I saw her in a number of matches this season hitting the ball, from back court, as hard as most men can hit it, and placing it time after time within a few inches of where she wanted it to go. It required a combination of tennis genius and amazing patience and long, hard practice to get this result.

No woman player today would have even the slightest chance against her. For no woman player could come close to matching her power and control.

Any good male player would have trouble beating Miss Wills from back court—as several have testified. As none of the women has a first-class net game they are all forced to meet her where she is strongest and almost invincible, where she has all the excess in both power and control of power. So the result is usually as expected.

Bobby Jones and Helen Wills had the knack for their games and they established this knack at early ages. They were experienced campaigners before they were twenty—campaigners under heavy fire against the best in their game. Both happened to be equipped with physical power. And, which is even more important, both happened to be rigged out with the type of iron determination that is often known as "the will to win."

They have outclassed their fields—especially the amateur fields—because they have had the skill, the experience, the stamina, the physical power, and the unbreakable determination to carve their way through.

Congressman Louis Stokes Eulogizes His Hero,
Jesse Owens, 1980

Mr. Stokes. Mr. Speaker, thank you for giving me the opportunity to participate in this special order in the U.S. House of Representatives honoring this country's greatest athlete—Mr. Jesse Owens. The son of an Alabama sharecropper, James Cleveland Owens, popularly known as Jesse Owens, died of lung cancer on Monday, March 31, 1980, at the age of 66. . . .

Jesse Owens was the symbol of athletic excellence in this country. Moreover, he was the beacon of hope and inspiration for those who had to compete in the sometimes turbulent races that life presents. . . .

I have always felt a special closeness to Jesse Owens. We have been friends through the years. He grew up in Cleveland where he began his illustrious track career on the sidewalks of East 107th Street. His track career progressed through his student days at Fairmount Junior High School and East Tech High School in Cleveland. Finally, he entered Ohio State University as a world track contender.

From these beginnings, Jesse Owens went on to dominate the world of track in the 1930's. He won the Big Ten championships in Ann Arbor, Mich. in 1935 setting world records in the broad jump, the 220-yard dash, the 220-yard low hurdles and tying the world record in the 100-yard dash. Jesse's performance in this competition proved only to be an overture to his phenomenal performance in the 1936 Berlin Olympics.

Jesse Owens was one of only 10 black members of the U.S. 1936 Olympic team. The late Congressman Ralph Metcalfe was also a member of that team. During the Olympics, Jesse Owens became the first man ever to win four gold medals by winning the 100-meter dash, the 200-meter dash, the broad jump, and the relay. He set a world record in the 200-meter dash in Berlin. His performance was so stunning that one sports writer commented: "His German rival couldn't have equaled his performance even if he had been fired from a cannon."

In 1936, I was 11 years old. When Jesse Owens came back to Cleveland, there was a great parade staged in his honor. My family and I then lived on East 69th Street between Cedar and Central Avenues. I can recall joining our entire neighborhood to watch the parade come down Central Avenue. As Jesse passed us in a Lincoln convertible, my heart swelled with pride to see this great Cleveland athlete. Needless to say, most of the black youth in Cleveland, including myself, thought we too would grow up someday and become great track stars like Jesse Owens.

There were also many newspaper articles about his achievement. The most memorable one for me was the one in which Jesse recanted his feelings before one of the races in Berlin. He said:

> You think about the number of years you have worked to the point where you are able to stand on that day to represent your Nation. It's a nervous, terrible feeling. You feel as you stand there, as if your legs can't carry the weight of your body. Your stomach isn't there and your mouth is dry, and your hands are wet with perspiration. And

From *Congressional Record,* April 17, 1980, p. 8327.

you begin to think in terms of all of those years that you have worked. In my case, the 100 meters, as you look down the field, 109 yards 2 feet away, and recognizing that after 8 years of hard work that this is the point that I have reached and that all was going to be over in 10 seconds. Those are great moments in the lives of individuals.

But, his four gold medals, which was not surpassed until the 1972 Olympics, proved to be more than an athletic victory. It also served to set the record straight on Hitler's Aryan racial superiority philosophy. The world seemingly embraced this lesson as people of all nationalities and from all walks of life rallied to become eternal fans of Jesse Owens. For many, he was the sports hero of the world. . . .

. . . When Jesse Owens returned to this country from Berlin, there were no grand receptions at the White House. But rather, he was only honored in small gatherings like the parade in Cleveland that I witnessed. He was an athletic hero. But, in his native land, he was discriminated against like other blacks. He never let this destroy his love for his country.

Jesse Owens was more than just a premiere athlete and devoted American. He was a humble and kind man who possessed an uncanny ability to motivate others. He especially loved working with young people. He once said:

> We all have dreams, but in order to turn dreams into reality, it takes an awful lot of determination, dedication and self-discipline and effort. These things apply to everyday life. You learn not only sports but things like respect of others, ethics in life, how you are going to live and how you are going to treat your fellow man.

⚾ E S S A Y S

Cultural historian Roderick Nash of the University of California, Santa Barbara, examines the significance of sports heroes for Americans during the 1920s in a tightly written essay. The United States had become a primarily urban nation; each sport seemed to have a great hero. According to Nash, this was not by chance. Nash argues that the "nervous generation" of the 1920s was worried about their society's future in light of a number of events: the end of World War I, when we won the war but lost the peace by failing to approve the League of Nations; the Red Scare (the perceived spreading menace of Bolshevism); growing labor unrest, including a general strike in Seattle and a police strike in Boston; and the Black Sox Scandal in 1920. Sports heroes reassured Americans that all was well with the world and that traditional values still counted.

In the second document, attorney Chris Meade examines how Joe Louis became a hero to the African-American community during his quest for the heavyweight championship of the world. African-Americans were barred from many athletic endeavors, but not the low-status sport of prize fighting. However, because of racism, no blacks since Jack Johnson could get a shot at the prestigious heavyweight championship, which denoted the toughest man in the world. In the mid-1930s the young contender Joe Louis seemed to be the man to break that barrier. Well before he became a national hero, Louis was *the* hero in his own community. In 1937 Louis got his championship match against Jim Braddock and won the title, which he kept for a record twelve years.

Sports Heroes of the 1920s

RODERICK NASH

Heroes abounded in the American 1920s. Their names, especially in sports, have been ticked off so frequently they have become clichés. Less often have commentators paused to probe for explanations. Why were the twenties ripe for heroism? And why did the heroics follow a predictable pattern? Such questions lead to an understanding of the mood of the people, because heroism concerns the public as well as the individual. It depends on achievement but even more on recognition. In the final analysis the hopes and fears of everyday Americans create national heroes.

The nervousness of the post-World War I generation provided fertile soil for the growth of a particular kind of heroism. Many Americans felt uneasy as they experienced the transforming effects of population growth, urbanization, and economic change. On the one hand, these developments were welcome as steps in the direction of progress. Yet they also raised vague fears about the passing of frontier conditions, the loss of national vigor, and the eclipse of the individual in a mass society. Frederick Jackson Turner and Theodore Roosevelt, among others, had pointed to the liabilities of the transformation at the turn of the century. World War I underscored the misgivings and doubts. By the 1920s the sense of change had penetrated to the roots of popular thought. Scarcely an American was unaware that the frontier had vanished and that pioneering, in the traditional sense, was a thing of the past. Physical changes in the nation were undeniable. They occurred faster, however, than intellectual adjustment. Although Americans, in general, lived in a densely populated, urban-industrial civilization, a large part of their values remained rooted in the frontier, farm, and village. Exposure of this discrepancy only served to increase the tightness with which insecure people clung to the old certainties. Old-style pioneering was impossible, but Americans proved ingenious in finding equivalents. The upshot in the twenties saw the cult of the hero—the man who provided living testimony of the power of courage, strength, and honor and of the efficacy of the self-reliant, rugged individual who seemed on the verge of becoming as irrelevant as the covered wagon.

Sports and the star athlete were the immediate beneficiaries of this frame of mind. The American sports fan regarded the playing field as a surrogate frontier; the athletic hero was the twentieth-century equivalent of the pathfinder or pioneer. In athletic competition, as on the frontier, people believed, men confronted tangible obstacles and overcame them with talent and determination. The action in each case was clean and direct; the goals, whether clearing forests or clearing the bases, easily perceived and immensely satisfying. Victory was the result of superior ability. The sports arena like the frontier was pregnant with opportunity for the individual. The start was equal and the best man won. Merit was rewarded. True or not, such a credo was almost instinctive with Americans. They packed the stadiums of the 1920s in a salute to time-honored virtues. With so much else about America

From Roderick Nash, *The Nervous Generation: American Thought, 1917–1930* (Chicago: Rand McNally, 1970), 126–32, 135–36.

changing rapidly, it was comforting to find in sports a ritualistic celebration of the major components of the national faith.

Writing in the *North American Review* for October 1929, A. A. Brill, a leading American psychologist of the Freudian school, took a closer look at the meaning of athletics. Why, he wondered, do men play and why do they select the particular kinds of play they do? Brill was also interested in the reasons spectators came to games. His main point was that sports were not idle diversions but intensely serious endeavors rooted in the values and traditions of a civilization. "The ancestry of sport," Brill declared, "is written very plainly in the fact that the first games among all nations were simple imitations of the typical acts of warriors and huntsmen." The primary motivation of play, according to Brill, was the "mastery impulse"—an inherent aggressiveness in man stemming from the Darwinian struggle for existence. Modern man had largely transcended direct physical struggle, but the need for it persisted in the human psyche. Sports were contrived as substitutes for actual fighting, mock struggles that satisfied the urge to conquer. Brill did not suggest a relationship between American sports and the American frontier, but his argument suggested one. So did the fact that the rise of mass spectator sports and the decline of the frontier were simultaneous in the United States.

By the 1920s the nation went sports crazy. It seemed to many that a golden age of sport had arrived in America. Football received a large portion of the limelight. As they had in the declining days of Rome, fans thronged the stadiums to witness contact, violence, bloodshed, man pitted against man, strength against strength. The vicarious element was invariably present. For a brief, glorious moment the nobody in the bleachers *was* the halfback crashing into the end zone with the winning touchdown. For a moment he shared the thrill of individual success and fought off the specter of being swallowed up in mass society.

Big-time professional football began on September 17, 1920, when the American Football Association was organized with the great Indian athlete Jim Thorpe as its first president. When the Green Bay Packers joined the Association in 1921, the saga of pro football was solidly launched. Attendance rose dramatically. On November 21, 1925, the presence on the playing field of the fabled Harold "Red" Grange helped draw 36,000 spectators to a game. A week later 68,000 jammed the Polo Grounds in New York to watch Grange in action. The names of the pro teams were suggestive. As on the frontier of old, it was cowboys versus Indians, or giants versus bears—with the names of cities prefixed.

The twenties was also the time of the emergence of college football on an unprecedented scale. Heroes appeared in good supply: Red Grange at Illinois, Knute Rockne's "Four Horsemen" at Notre Dame in 1924, Harold "Brick" Muller who began a dynasty at California that extended through fifty consecutive victories in the seasons 1919 through 1925. Hundreds of thousands attended the Saturday games, an estimated twenty million during the season. Millions more followed the action over their radios and made a Sunday morning ritual of devouring the newspaper accounts of the games of the previous day. To accommodate the crowds colleges and universities built huge new stadiums. Yale's and California's seated eighty thousand; Illinois, Ohio State, and Michigan were not far behind. The number of Americans who attended games doubled between 1921 and 1930. A *Harper's* writer caught the spirit of college football in 1928: "it is at present a religion, sometimes it seems to be almost our national religion." So, once, had been westward expansion.

Despite its popularity, football tended to obscure the heroic individual. It was, after all, a team sport. Even Red Grange received an occasional block on his long runs. But in sports pitting man against man or against the clock the heroism latent in competition achieved its purest expression. Americans in the 1920s had a glittering array of well-publicized individuals from which to choose their idol. In golf Robert T. "Bobby" Jones, Walter Hagen, and Gene Sarazen were the dominant figures. Tennis had "Big" Bill Tilden and "Little" Bill Johnson whose epic duels on the center court at Forest Hills filled the stands. The competition was even more direct in boxing with its "knock out," the symbol of complete conquest. During the twenties promoters like Tex Rickard built boxing into a big business. Jack Dempsey and Gene Tunney proved so attractive to the sporting public that a ticket sale of a million dollars for a single fight became a reality. By the end of the decade the figure was two million. Fifty bouts in the twenties had gates of more than $100,000. More than 100,000 fans came to Soldier's Field in Chicago on September 22, 1927, to see the second Dempsey-Tunney fight with its controversial "long count" that helped Tunney retain the championship and earn $990,000 for thirty minutes of work. In a nation not oblivious to the approach of middle age, it was comforting to count the heavyweight champion of the world among the citizenry. Here was evidence, many reasoned, that the nation remained strong, young, and fit to survive in a Darwinian universe. Record-breaking served the same purpose, and in Johnny Weismuller, premier swimmer, and Paavo Nurmi, Finnish-born track star, the United States had athletes who set world marks almost every time they competed. Gertrude Ederle chose a longer course when she swam the English Channel in 1926, but she too set a record and was treated to one of New York's legendary ticker-tape parades.

And there was the Babe. No sports hero of the twenties and few of any decade had the reputation of George Herman Ruth. Baseball was generally acknowledged to be the national game, and Ruth played with a superb supporting cast of New York Yankees, but when he faced a pitcher Babe Ruth stood as an individual. His home runs (particularly the 59 in 1921 and the 60 in 1927) gave him a heroic stature comparable to that of legendary demigods like Odysseus, Beowulf, or Daniel Boone. Ruth's unsavory background and boorish personal habits were nicely overlooked by talented sportswriters anxious to give the twenties the kind of hero it craved. The payoff was public adulation of the Babe and of baseball.

The twenties also saw the public exposure of corruption in baseball and confronted Americans with the necessity of reviewing their entire hero complex. On September 28, 1920, three members of the Chicago White Sox appeared before a grand jury to confess that they and five other players had agreed to throw the 1919 World Series to Cincinnati for a financial consideration. Gradually the unhappy story of the "Black Sox" unfolded. Big-time gamblers had persuaded selected players to make sure that a bet on the underdog Cincinnati team would pay off. Some of the greatest names in the game were involved, preeminently that of "Shoeless" Joe Jackson. An illiterate farm boy from South Carolina, Jackson's natural batting eye helped him compile a .356 average in ten seasons as a major leaguer. In the process he became one of the most idolized players in baseball. It was

Jackson's exit from the grand jury chamber on September 28 that allegedly precipitated the agonized plea from a group of boys: "Say it ain't so, Joe!" According to the newspapers, Jackson, shuffling, head down, replied, "Yes, boys, I'm afraid it is."

Reaction to the Black Sox testified to the importance baseball had for many Americans. One school of thought condemned the "fix" in the strongest terms and agitated for the restoration of integrity to the game. It was a serious matter. The Philadelphia *Bulletin* compared the eight players with "the soldier or sailor who would sell out his country and its flag in time of war." Suggesting the link between sports and the national character, the *New York Times* declared that bribing a ballplayer was an offense "which strikes at the very heart of this nation." If baseball fell from grace, what could be honest in America? The question haunted journalists and cartoonists. *Outlook* for October 13, 1920, carried a drawing of a crumpled statue of a ballplayer whose torn side revealed a stuffing of dollar bills. The statue bore the inscription "The National Game." A small boy wept in the foreground; the caption to the cartoon read "His Idol."

Baseball officials and club owners were similarly dismayed at the revelation of corruption and determined to clean up the game. Charles A. Comiskey, owner of the Chicago White Sox, led the way with a public statement that no man involved in the fix would ever wear the uniform of his club again. Other owners followed suit until all organized baseball, even the minor leagues, was closed to the Black Sox. On November 12, 1920, Kenesaw Mountain Landis, a former federal judge, was appointed commissioner of baseball with full control over the game and a charge to safeguard its integrity.

The everyday fan's response to the fix differed sharply from that of the sportswriters and owners. Many Americans seemed determined to deny the entire affair; more precisely, they didn't *want* to believe anything could be wrong with something as close to the national ideal as baseball. Like the boys of the "say it ain't so" episode, they begged for evidence that the old standards and values still applied. Especially in 1920 in the United States sports heroes were needed as evidence of the virtues of competition, fair play, and the self-reliant individual. Consequently, when confronted with the scandal, the average American simply closed his eyes and pretended nothing was wrong. The heroes remained heroes. When the Black Sox formed an exhibition team, it received enthusiastic support. Petitions were circulated in the major league cities to reinstate the players in organized baseball. But the most remarkable demonstration of the public's feeling came at the conclusion of the Black Sox trial on August 2, 1921. After deliberating two hours and forty-seven minutes, the jury returned a verdict of *not* guilty. According to the *New York Times* reporter at the scene, the packed courtroom rose as one man at the good news, cheering wildly. Hats sailed and papers were thrown about in the delirium. Men shouted "hooray for the clean sox." The bailiffs pounded for order until, as the *Times* reported, they "finally noticed Judge Friend's smiles, and then joined in the whistling and cheering." Finally the jury picked up the acquitted ballplayers and carried them out of the courtroom on their shoulders!

Baseball officials and journalists regarded the acquittal of the Black Sox as a technical verdict secured by the lenient interpretation of the Illinois statute involved. The fans in the courtroom, however, and, presumably, many elsewhere were on the side of the players regardless, and viewed the verdict as a vindication. They were not prepared to believe that baseball or its heroes could become tarnished. The game was too important to the national ego. Following baseball gave Americans an opportunity to pay tribute to what many believed was the best part of their heritage. The game was a sacred rite undertaken not merely to determine the winner of league championships but to celebrate the values of a civilization. As one newspaper account of the scandal put it, to learn that "Shoeless" Joe Jackson had sold out the world series was like discovering that "Daniel Boone had been bought by the Indians to lose his fights in Kentucky.". . .

In the late 1920s the Boy Scout *Handbook* featured an unusual drawing. In the foreground was a clean-cut Scout, eyes fixed on adventure. Behind him, signifying the heritage from which he sprang, were the figures of Daniel Boone, Abraham Lincoln, and Theodore Roosevelt, men who were staples in the annals of American heroism. But there was also a new face, that of Charles A. Lindbergh of Minnesota. At the age of just twenty-five Lindbergh rose to the status of an American demigod by virtue of a single feat. On May 20, 1927, he took off in a tiny single-engine airplane from New York City and thirty-three hours later landed in Paris. The nonstop, solo run across the Atlantic catapulted the average American into a paroxysm of pride and joy. Overnight Lindbergh became the greatest hero of the decade. There was but little exaggeration in the contention of one journalist that Lindbergh received "the greatest ovation in history." Certainly his return from Paris to the United States generated a reception extraordinary even for an age that specialized in ballyhoo. The *New York Times* devoted more space to Lindbergh's return than it had to the Armistice ending World War I. A virtual national religion took shape around Lindbergh's person. A 1928 poll of schoolboys in a typical American town on the question of whom they most wanted to be like produced the following results: Gene Tunney, 13 votes; John Pershing, 14; Alfred E. Smith, 16; Thomas A. Edison, 27; Henry Ford, 66; Calvin Coolidge, 110; Charles A. Lindbergh, 363. If the amount of national adulation is meaningful, adults everywhere would likely have responded in similar proportions.

The explanation of Lindbergh's popularity lies less in his feat (pilots had flown across the Atlantic before) and more in the mood of the people at the time it occurred. The typical American in 1927 was nervous. The values by which he ordered his life seemed in jeopardy of being swept away by the force of growth and change and complexity. Lindbergh came as a restorative tonic. He reasserted the image of the confident, quietly courageous, and self-reliant individual. He proved to a generation anxious for proof that Americans were still capable of pioneering. Even in an age of machines the frontier was not dead—a new one had been found in the air.

The reaction to Lindbergh's flight in the national press stressed these ideas. "Lindbergh served as a metaphor," wrote one commentator in *Century*. "We felt that in him we, too, had conquered something and regained lost ground." A writer in *Outlook* made the point more explicitly: "Charles Lindbergh is the heir of all that we like to think is best in America. He is the stuff out of which have been made the pioneers that opened up the wilderness first on the Atlantic coast, and then in our great West." A newspaper cartoon showed a covered wagon leaving for California in 1849 and next to it Lindbergh's plane taking off for Paris in 1927. Colonel Theodore Roosevelt, the son of the President, remarked that Lindbergh "personifies the daring of youth. Daniel Boone, David Crockett, and men of that type played a lone hand and made America. Lindbergh is their lineal descendant." Calvin Coolidge, who personally welcomed Lindbergh home, simply said that he was "a boy representing the best traditions of this country."

For one journalist the most significant part of the Lindbergh phenomenon was not the flight but the character of the man: "his courage, his modesty, his self-control, his sanity, his thoughtfulness of others, his fine sense of proportion, his loyalty, his unswerving adherence to the course that seemed right." His unassuming manner fit the traditional hero's mold. Many observers of the postflight celebration noted how the hero refused to capitalize financially on his popularity. It was telling evidence as an essayist put it, that the American people "are *not* rotten at the core, but morally sound and sweet and good!" The generalization from the individual to society was easily acceptable because Americans in 1927 desperately wanted to keep the old creed alive. Lindbergh's flight was popularly interpreted as a flight of faith—in the American experience and in the American people.

Joe Louis as Emerging Race Hero in the 1930s

CHRIS MEADE

Black papers covered Louis well before any white papers did. The *Chicago Defender* published a full-page cartoon tribute to him when he won the AAU light-heavyweight title in St. Louis as an amateur. In December 1934 the *Defender* warned then-champion Max Baer, "Look out Maxie—Louis is threatening." Other black papers printed accounts of Louis's life story six months before white papers paid any attention to Louis and quoted Max Baer saying he wouldn't draw the color line.

Thanks to the black press, by late 1934 Louis was becoming a familiar figure in black America. Louis remembered in his autobiography:

> I started noticing some things I thought were strange. A lot of black people would come to me and want to kiss me, pump my hand. I thought they were congratulating me for my fighting skills. Now they started saying things like, "Joe, you're our savior," and "Show them whites!" and sometimes they'd just shout, "Brown Bomber, Brown Bomber!" I didn't understand, then.

As a leading heavyweight contender, Louis had already made more progress in the white world than any but a handful of blacks. And when Louis got his big break and went to New York for his fight with Primo Carnera, he immediately became the most prominent black in America. Louis took Harlem by storm. Before he went into training for Carnera, Roxborough and Black booked him into the Harlem

From Chris Meade, *Champion—Joe Louis* (New York: Charles Scribner's Sons, 1985), 189–206.

Opera House. Louis filled the place four times a day for a brief show; he climaxed his performance by punching a speed bag into the audience while a band played *Anchors Aweigh.* Louis soon left Harlem for Pompton Lakes, and the crowds followed him. Thousands of blacks flocked to Louis's training camp on weekends. Roxborough and Black charged admission and profited from a thriving concessions business.

Louis stepped into the ring against Carnera on June 25, 1935, as the new but unproved hero of blacks all over America. There was no live broadcast of the fight; Mike Jacobs thought radio would hurt the gate. When Louis's victory was finally announced on the radio, blacks in every major northern city joined in an astounding spontaneous celebration. Thousands of blacks poured into the streets to dance, form impromptu parades, and commandeer streetcars. They brought traffic to a standstill, weaving in front of and around cars, and made fun of any whites they saw.

In Harlem 20,000 blacks, at seventy-five cents a head, jammed the Savoy ballroom for the celebration and the promise of an appearance by Louis himself. The crowd cheered Louis's victory but soon grew impatient waiting for Louis to show up. Understandably tired after the fight, Louis wanted to go to bed, and even Bill Robinson, the famous black tap dancer, could not convince him to make an appearance. Finally, someone told Louis that he had to show up to prevent a riot. Louis reluctantly arrived at the Savoy at 2:30 A.M. and spoke a few words into a dead microphone. The crowd was making so much noise that the words would have been lost anyway, but Louis's appearance mollified his fans, and the crowd broke up.

In Detroit a crowd gathered around the house Louis had bought for his mother and called for her to come out, cheering when she finally opened the door and waved.

Similar demonstrations followed every Louis victory for over a decade. Louis's fights became major social events for most blacks. The black press printed the names of upper-class blacks in the ringside seats at Louis's fights; it was a sort of social register. Most blacks could not afford to see Louis fight in person, so they listened to the fights on the radio and looked forward to celebrating in the streets afterward. In the midst of the Great Depression, with no other signs of improvement in race relations, blacks had precious little to celebrate, and Louis assumed a special significance. He became a symbol of success for all blacks, just as his success earned him symbolic status among whites.

In the South celebrations had to be more restrained, but blacks there felt the symbolism of Louis's fights just as strongly. Maya Angelou, in her account of life in the southern black belt, *I Know Why the Caged Bird Sings,* described rural blacks crowding into her uncle's village store to listen to the radio broadcast of a Louis fight:

> The last inch of space was filled, yet people continued to wedge themselves along the walls of the Store. Uncle Willie had turned the radio up to its last notch so that youngsters on the porch wouldn't miss a word. . . .
> "They're in a clinch, Louis is trying to fight his way out."
> Some bitter comedian on the porch said, "That white man don't mind hugging that niggah now, I betcha.". . .

"He's got Louis against the ropes and now it's a left to the body and a right to the ribs. . . . It's another to the body, and it looks like Louis is going down."

My race groaned. It was our people falling. It was another lynching, yet another Black man hanging on a tree. One more woman ambushed and raped. A Black boy whipped and maimed. It was hounds on the trail of a man running through slimy swamps. It was a white woman slapping her maid for being forgetful. . . .

This might be the end of the world. If Joe lost we were back in slavery and beyond help. It would all be true, the accusations that we were lower types of human beings. . . .

"And now it looks like Joe is mad. . . . Louis is penetrating every block. The referee is moving in . . ."

Champion of the world. A Black boy. Some Black mother's son. He was the strongest man in the world. People drank Coca-Colas like ambrosia and ate candy bars like Christmas. Some of the men went behind the store and poured white lightning in their soft-drink bottles. . . .

It would take an hour or more before the people would leave the Store and head for home. Those who lived too far had made arrangements to stay in town. It wouldn't do for a Black man and his family to be caught on a lonely country road on a night when Joe Louis had proved that we were the strongest people in the world.

The black press celebrated Louis's importance by devoting more attention to him than to any other black from 1935 through 1941. Sociologists St. Clair Drake and Horace Clayton, in their study of black Chicago, noted, "Joe Louis, between 1933–1938 received more front page exposure in the *Chicago Defender* than any other Negro.". . . The *Defender* and other black papers published special editions on the nights of important Louis fights. Louis's picture popped up everywhere and anywhere in black papers, accounts of his fights occupied whole pages, and Louis appeared often in advertisements. He endorsed Murray's Superior Hair Pomade:

Besides being a great fighter, Joe Louis is one of the best dressed men in America. He says, "I always try to be well-groomed and the last thing I do before I go into the ring before any fight is to see that MURRAY'S POMADE has my hair smooth and perfectly in place."

A mail-order house sold Joe Louis ashtrays, "an exercise in self-respect," for one dollar. The black press's obsessive interest in Louis carried over to his wife Marva, who became the first lady of black America. Black papers printed pictures of Marva in her splendid outfits, and Mrs. Louis even wrote a fashion column for the *Chicago Defender.*

The black press avoided some of the worst stereotypes that characterized white coverage of Louis, but Louis generally had the same public image in the black press as in the white. Black reporters called him the Brown Bomber and the Dark Destroyer, and they often referred to him as a killer. They didn't go in for the jungle imagery and the references to Louis's primitivism that so delighted white reporters, however. The black press . . . avoided the darkie image of Louis that appeared in the white press. Black papers did not call Louis lazy, they described him accurately as an enthusiastic and hardworking fighter. And the black press studiously avoided quoting Louis in dialect. They quoted him in overwrought English or in sportswriting clichés.

The black press followed the white press closely when it came to promoting Louis's official image as a well-behaved, clean-living fighter. Black reporters were aware that Roxborough, Black, and Louis were trying to sell a good image to whites, and they did all they could to aid the process. They even criticized Louis and his managers when they strayed off the path of virtue. . . .

From a modern perspective, Louis's exaggerated decorum and catering to white sensibilities might be considered "tomming" and would probably draw disgust, not admiration, from the black masses. But in the 1930s, when Louis was the only black consistently winning in white America, and when most blacks understood the implacable racism of their society, Louis's official image did not diminish his popularity among blacks. The official image could not hide the nature of Louis's victories: he wasn't just defeating whites; he was beating them up in the process. As . . . [historian] Lawrence W. Levine wrote in 1977:

> However quietly and with whatever degree of humility he did it, Joe Louis, like Jack Johnson before him, stood as a black man in the midst of a white society and beat representatives of the dominant group to their knees. In this sense no degree of respectability could prevent Louis from becoming a breaker of stereotypes and a destroyer of norms. He literally did allow his fists to talk for him, and they spoke so eloquently that no other contemporary member of the group was celebrated more fully and identified with more intensely by the black folk. . . .

Sociologist E. Franklin Frazier wrote in 1940: "Joe Louis enables many lower class youths (in fact many Negro youths and adults in all classes) to inflict vicariously the aggression which they would like to carry out against whites for the discriminations and insults which they have suffered."

This vicarious thrill appeared in folk songs about Louis. Many of the songs contained images of white fighters on their knees before Louis. Black kids in Harlem sang this song after Louis defeated Bob Pastor for the second time in the fall of 1939:

> Bob Pastor was on his knees
> Said, "Joe
> Don't hit me please,
> Just go trucking out of the ring."

Black dock workers in Fernandina, Florida, sang:

> Joe Louis hit him so hard he turn roun and roun,
> He thought he was Alabama bound. Ah, Ah,
> He made an effort to rise agin,
> But Joe Louis's right cut him on the chin, Ah, Ah,
> Weak on his knees and tried to rise,
> Went down crying to the crowd's surprise, Ah, Ah.

During the 1930s, blues singers celebrated Joe Louis over and over, more than any other black figure from the period. Blues scholar Paul Oliver has noted the special appeal Joe Louis had for the blues singers:

> There are no blues devoted to the achievements of Paul Robeson, George Washington Carver . . . or Ralph Bunche. . . . For the blues singer, Joe Louis was the singular inspi-

ration of a man who had within his achievements all the drama, the appeal and the invincibility of the traditional Negro ballad hero. . . .

Louis's victories over Carnera and Baer in 1935 inspired a host of songs. Though the black artists were blues singers, the songs differed from traditional blues in subject matter and mood. The early songs about Louis were exultant and happy, and in their portrayal of Louis as a heroic figure they resembled old Negro ballads. Memphis Minnie McCoy, with Black Bob on the piano, recorded "He's in the Ring (Doin' the Same Old Thing)," and she also did the "Joe Louis Strut." Ike Smith recorded "Fighting Joe Louis,". . . and Lil Johnson did "Winner Joe (the Knock-Out King)." All these songs came out within a year after Louis broke into the big time with his knockout of Carnera in 1935. Billy Hicks and the Sizzling Six did "Joe the Bomber" after he won the heavyweight championship in 1937, and Bill Gaither recorded a song about Louis's victory over Max Schmeling in their 1938 rematch.

The impression Joe Louis made on black music and oral culture only begins to suggest the depth of Louis's penetration into black consciousness during the 1930s. Swedish sociologist Gunnar Myrdal found a one-room black school in Georgia where the children had received no education and had so little contact with the outside world that they could not name the president of the United States. Nor could they identify the NAACP or black leaders W.E.B. DuBois or Walter White. But they knew who Joe Louis was.

Martin Luther King, Jr., remembered another example of the powerful meaning Joe Louis had for blacks:

More than twenty-five years ago, one of the southern states adopted a new method of capital punishment. Poison gas supplanted the gallows. In its earliest stages, a microphone was placed inside the sealed death chamber so that scientific observers might hear the words of the dying prisoner to judge how the human reacted in this novel situation. The first victim was a young Negro. As the pellet dropped into the container, and gas curled upward, through the microphone came these words: "Save me, Joe Louis. Save me, Joe Louis. Save me, Joe Louis. . . ."

Louis's powerful image touched all blacks. To them he was hope, and pride. For Richard Wright, author of *Black Boy,* Louis was

the concentrated essence of black triumph over white. . . . From the symbol of Joe Louis's strength Negroes took strength, and in that moment all fear, all obstacles were wiped out, drowned. They stepped out of the mire of hesitation and irresolution and were free! Invincible! A merciless victor over a fallen foe! Yes, they had felt all that. . . .

Louis was not only a symbol, he was a role model. Malcolm X remembered, "Every Negro boy old enough to walk wanted to be the next Brown Bomber." Malcolm himself took up boxing at the age of thirteen, but two quick defeats ended his ring career. Malcolm was not alone. After Louis beat Carnera, poor black kids filled boxing gyms all over the country. . . .

Louis's meaning to blacks struck home the night of June 19, 1936, when Louis lost to Max Schmeling. Lena Horne was singing with Noble Sissle's band in Cincinnati's Moonlight Gardens that night. She remembered:

Until that night I had no idea of the strength of my identification with Joe Louis.

We had the radio on behind the grandstand and during the breaks we crowded around it to hear the fight. I was near hysteria toward the end of the fight when he was being so badly beaten and some of the men in the band were crying. . . . Joe was the one invincible Negro, the one who stood up to the white man and beat him down with his fists. He in a sense carried so many of our hopes, maybe even dreams of vengeance. But this night he was just another Negro getting beaten by a white man. . . . My mother was furious with me for getting hysterical. "How dare you?" she screamed. "You have a performance. The show must go on. Why, you don't even know this man."

"I don't care, I don't care," I yelled back. "He belongs to all of us.". . .

After Louis's defeat, the black press commented on the hope and pride he had given blacks and described the depression in black neighborhoods. The depression was even deeper because the loss followed close on the heels of Italy's conquest of Ethiopia and the fall of Haile Selassie, who had become a hero to American blacks. Adam Clayton Powell, Jr., then just emerging as a black leader in New York, wrote in the *New York Amsterdam News:*

. . . along came the Brown Bomber, Death in the Evening, and our racial morale took a sky high leap that broke every record from Portland to Pasadena. Surely the new day was just around the corner. . . .

Then along came the sudden fall of Addis Ababa and the Yankee Stadium fiasco and something died. Gone today is the jauntiness, the careless abandon, the spring in our stride—we're just shufflin' along. . . .

Black identification with Louis was so great that there was a desperate need to explain or forget. Black papers ran headlines for weeks voicing wild rumors that Louis had been doped before he went into the ring. On June 27, the *Baltimore Afro-American* replaced the large picture of Louis that had dominated the front page the week before with a front-page picture of Jesse Owens. At the time blacks needed symbols to break the myth of inferiority, an uphill battle that could tolerate no losers.

But Louis, of course, came back, and as he did, he lifted the spirits of blacks to new heights. His championship fight with James J. Braddock was an event of signal importance. Even after Louis broke into the big time, and even as he seemed to be winning white acceptance, blacks remained deeply skeptical about Louis's chances of getting a title bout. After Louis beat Baer in September 1935, Al Monroe of the *Chicago Defender* suggested the Baer's loss to Braddock earlier that year had been intentional. According to this theory, Baer wanted to fight Louis because he knew the fight would make a lot of money, but he didn't want the title to fall into black hands. So, in effect, he loaned the title to Braddock. The theory . . . reflected the depth of black pessimism. . . .

As the date of the championship fight approached, the black press underlined its importance by trying to downplay its meaning, just as many white papers underlined the importance of Louis's fights by downplaying them. The *New York Amsterdam News* ran a front-page editorial the week before the fight with the headline "Win or Lose, Let's Be Sane" and said, "By all means, let us accept the fight in its true light: a great sports event and nothing else.". . .

. . . The black press reflected the ambivalence of middle-class blacks toward Joe Louis. On the one hand, middle-class blacks were just as thrilled by Louis's victories as any other blacks. Louis was their avenger and hero, too. Like them, Louis was trying to project an image of middle-class respectability, and they could only applaud Louis's intentions. On the other hand, Louis was uneducated, and he was "just" a boxer. . . .

Educated blacks often tried to separate themselves from other, less fortunate blacks when they downplayed Louis's importance. The *Chicago Defender* said in an editorial before the Louis–Braddock fight:

> Joe Louis as a prizefighter represents the same sum total to the intelligent black people of America as James Braddock represents to the intelligent white people of America. It is assumed that white America does not regard Mr. Braddock as a leader in the social, economic, and political life in the great scheme of their existence.
>
> In the same sense black America desires to be seen in like light. In other words intelligent black people regard Mr. Louis in no different manner than intelligent white people regard Mr. Braddock.

Not only did middle-class blacks disassociate themselves from poorer blacks; they also lectured poorer blacks for their overenthusiastic celebrations following Louis's victories. Al Monroe of the *Chicago Defender* wrote after the Louis-Baer fight:

> The powers of boxing are afraid to trust the heavyweight crown in the hands of the black race and the Race folk of New York and Chicago are responsible for this fear. They have, by their thoughtless demonstrations, caused politicians and city officials to consider the risk too great to give one of their own the topmost rung in boxing, a position Joe Louis should not be thrown into. . . .

For some educated blacks, however, Louis was not an embarrassment at all. . . . To men like Richard Wright and Paul Robeson, Joe Louis was a bond to black people everywhere. Wright had written several moving novels on the black experience, and Robeson used his gifts as a singer to revive Negro spirituals. In 1940 the two men joined with Count Basie, the black jazzman and band leader, to record a song called "King Joe (Joe Louis Blues)." Wright wrote the lyrics, Basie wrote the music, and Robeson sang. "King Joe" was a tribute to traditional black culture.

> Black eye peas ask corn bread,
> What make you so strong?
> Corn bread says I come from
> Where Joe Louis was born.
>
> Rabbit say to the bee
> What make you sting so deep?
> He say I sting like Joe
> An' rock 'em all to sleep.

No matter their personal feelings about Louis, black leaders used him as a rallying point, and they used his image and popularity to appeal to whites. When the Daughters of the American Revolution (DAR) caused a national incident by refusing to let black contralto Marian Anderson sing at Constitution Hall in Washington,

D.C., in the fall of 1939, Anderson immediately visited Joe Louis's training camp. Louis and Miss Anderson posed for pictures, and Louis invited her to sing the national anthem before one of his fights. On March 30, 1941, the National Urban League sponsored a radio program over the ABC network, a national appeal to let blacks participate in the rapidly growing defense industry. Joe Louis dominated the program. . . . Louis made a carefully worded appeal to whites on behalf of his fellow blacks. "We can defend this country if everyone has a job to do. . . . I know America believes in fair play and I feel that America will give Negroes a chance to work.". . .

In what was probably the most perceptive article written along these lines, Theophilus Lewis, a black writer for the *New York Amsterdam News,* predicted the impact Louis would have on white attitudes. On October 5, 1935, Lewis wrote:

> His place in the limelight makes Joe Louis the world's most conspicuous Negro. . . . Hundreds of stage shows and thousands of newspaper stories have associated the word "Negro" with crime and irresponsibility. In the mind of the average white man, the personal qualities of the most conspicuous Negro are merely an enlargement of the racial traits of all Negroes. . . . Give [whites] the impression that Negro is a synonym for Joe Louis and race relations will change for the better.

Confronted with a black fighter widely conceded to be an admirable person, white writers downplayed the racial aspects in Louis's fights. Joe Williams, a white reporter for the *New York World-Telegram,* wrote before the Louis-Kingfish Levinsky fight in 1935:

> It is probably just as well that nobody, not even in the interest of ballyhoo, has attempted to interject the matter of racial supremacy into the Joe Louis-Kingfish Levinsky fight. Such interjections are usually sponsored by the Caucasians. In this instance the jury might find it necessary to render an embarrassing verdict.

Jim Jeffries, the man who had come out of retirement to fight Jack Johnson "for the honor of the white race," in 1910, said in an article for the *Saturday Evening Post* in 1935:

> I'm not handing out that kind of hokum now. The races of mankind don't have to defend their honor by throwing a couple of prizefighters into the ring, and there never was a time when I thought they did. . . . Right now if a black fighter wins the title fair and square I'm for him, and I hope he behaves himself and keeps his nose clean while he's up there.

Whites were aware of Louis's symbolic significance to blacks. Every white sports page that carried an account of a Louis victory also carried an obligatory column or two under a headline like "Harlem Celebrates Louis Victory." Sometimes the stories were patronizing, evoking the old southern stereotype of blacks as children, but more often the stories had the ring of dispatches from a foreign country, as though blacks were strange and exotic people. . . . A Universal Newsreel feature on Harlem's reaction to Louis's victory over Max Baer made it sound as if blacks were observing some pagan rite. As pictures of blacks crowding toward the camera, smiling and waving, played across movie screens all over the country, a narrator said:

New York's great Negro quarter and its hot spots turn into a frenzied, howling, cele-brating mass of dark-skinned hysteria, when Joe Louis's gloves lay Max Baer low. . . . A people gone wild with enthusiasm, chanting the praise of the Detroit Bomber, Joe Louis, the bronze idol of his race.

Whites understood the excitement in black neighborhoods and approved of the black reaction to Joe Louis. Many white reporters wrote that Louis was a good ex-ample, that he would have a positive influence on his fellow blacks. Because Louis was taking care not to offend whites, because he was quiet and "well behaved" and undemanding and he made no waves, whites hoped other blacks would imitate Louis.

Perhaps whites would not have been so sanguine had they realized the depth of the impression Louis was making on blacks. Louis was a hero of revolutionary proportions—a black man who beat whites in direct competition before a national audience. The mood in black America was changing. As Lawrence W. Levine wrote: "For the young Malcolm X and his peers the career of Joe Louis was a testa-ment to the fact that defeat at the hands of the white man was no longer to be taken for granted."

FURTHER READING

Charles C. Alexander, *Ty Cobb* (1984)

William J. Baker, *Jesse Owens: An American Life* (1986)

Dominick J. Capeci, Jr., and Martha Wilkerson, "Multifarious Hero: Joe Louis, American Society and Race Relations During World Crisis, 1935–1945," *Journal of Sport History* 10 (1979), 5–27

Robert Creamer, *Babe: The Legend Comes to Life* (1974)

J. L. Cutler, *Gilbert Patten and His Frank Merriwell Saga* (1934)

Mark Dyreson, "The Emergence of Consumer Culture and the Transformation of Physical Culture: American Sports in the 1920s," *Journal of Sport History* 61 (Winter 1989), 261–81

Larry Englemann, *The Goddess and the American Girl* (1988)

Elliott J. Gorn, "The Manassa Mauler and the Fighting Marine: An Interpretation of the Dempsey-Tunney Fights," *Journal of American Studies* 19 (1983), 27–47

Donald Gropman, *"Say it Ain't So, Joe!": The True Story of Shoeless Joe Jackson* (1992)

Robert Lipsyte and Peter Levine, *Idols of the Game: A Sport History of the American Century* (1995)

Christian K. Messenger, *Sport and the Spirit of Play in American Fiction* (1981)

Gerard O'Connor, "Where Have You Gone, Joe DiMaggio?" in Ray B. Browne et al., eds., *Heroes in Popular Culture* (1972), 87–99

Michael Oriard, *Dreaming of Heroes: American Sports Fiction, 1869–1980* (1982)

Benjamin G. Rader, "Compensatory Sport Heroes: Ruth, Grange, and Dempsey," *Journal of Popular Culture* 16 (1983), 11–22

Steven A. Riess, "Sport and Social Mobility: American Myth or Reality," in Donald G. Kyle and Gary Stark, eds., *Essays on Sport History* (1990), 83–117

Randy Roberts, *Jack Dempsey, The Manassa Mauler* (1979)

Leverett T. Smith, *The American Dream and the American Game* (1975)

Henry W. Thomas, *Walter Johnson: Baseball's Big Train* (1995)

John W. Ward, "The Meaning of Lindbergh's Flight," *American Quarterly* 10 (Spring 1958), 3–16

Robert W. Wheeler, *Jim Thorpe: World's Greatest Athlete* (1979)

Sport and American Women

Since 1930

⚾

A significant development in post–World War II American sport has been the recent great increase in women's participation, though this took a very long time to
occur. How do historians explain this? Were American women successful at "feminine" sports? Historians have recently become aware of the expansion of working
class women's sports in the 1920s, which were sponsored by industrial welfare programs that sought to advertise a firm's name and to bolster employee loyalty. How
did this affect participatory sports like softball and bowling as well as high-level
individual and team competitions? What was the historical significance of Babe
Didrikson, a product of industrial sports programs, who became the track and field
star of the 1932 Los Angeles Olympics?

What did it take for women to go beyond sports like tennis, gymnastics, and figure skating that stressed "feminine" qualities and to make team sports and "unfeminine" sports acceptable activities for women? The de-emphasis of competitive sports
was reflected by the poor showing of white American women in international track
and field competition. The one group of women who excelled in that sport were students at black colleges, who used sport to gain status and respect. Given this background, how did team sports and strenuous athletics gain acceptability in the late
1960s and 1970s? Most scholars attribute the boom to the women's right movement
and to influential role models, especially Billie Jean King. Scholars also agree that
fresh attention to sport was furthered by the passage of Title IX of the Education Act
of 1972, which sought equal treatment for women in all aspects of higher education.
Prior to Title IX, funding for women had comprised less than 1 percent of intercollegiate budgets. Though Title IX resulted in more funds, historians and other scholars
still argue about how effective the program has actually been.

⚾ DOCUMENTS

The first document, "The *Saturday Evening Post* Examines Women's Softball in
World War II America," a 1942 article by Robert Yoder, analyzed the popularity of the

new International Girls' Major League. Softball was a cheap game that did not require much space or equipment, and was the most popular women's participatory sport during the Depression. It was also enjoyed by spectators, and more people watched softball than baseball. One year later, Philip K. Wrigley organized the All-American Girls' Baseball League that endured until 1954 and achieved lasting fame in the movie *A League of Their Own* (1992).

The second document is drawn from the autobiography of Billie Jean King, who was probably the most important female athlete since Babe Didrikson. King was the finest tennis player of her era during a career highlighted by a sweep of the Wimbledon championships in 1967. King helped popularize women's tennis by her personality and style of play and led the fight for women's pro tennis. She helped to organize the Virginia Slims Tour in 1971 and led the struggle to gain purses comparable to those of men at major championships (women originally got only 10 percent of the amount of men's prizes). King also defeated Bobby Riggs in "the Battle of the Sexes" in 1973.

The third document is drawn from an interview conducted by Terry Todd, Ph.D., a nationally renowned expert on body building, with Tammy Thompson, a former power lifter. Thompson used anabolic steroids to build up her strength, but their use resulted in her becoming very sick and developing secondary male characteristics. The next two documents focus on the contemporary debate over Title IX of the Education Act of 1972 that required gender equity in the funding and support of intercollegiate sports programs. The first of these is Baylor University Athletic Director Grant Teaff's statement in 1993 to a congressional committee supporting the progress achieved under the act. Teaff, a former football coach and a member of the NCAA Task Force on Gender Equality, argued that football deserved special consideration in any discussion on gender equity. A different position was offered by Ellen J. Vargyas, Senior Counsel for Education and Employment at the National Women's Law Center. She told Congress that Title IX had made insufficient headway toward equality and that the Office for Civil Rights was actually holding back progress.

The *Saturday Evening Post* Examines Women's Softball in World War II America

Such girls as Nina Korgan . . . typify a new set of career girls—the closest thing to professional ballplayers the female sex has yet produced.

It would be ungallant to call them professionals, for their athletic purity is watched over every minute by the Amateur Softball Association. But it would be equally ungallant to say the girls dally around like amateurs, for they live and play like professionals. Although this is the first year they have had a league, the individual clubs have been going strong for some time. Last year they did so well that thirty-two of the more ambitious teams formed the new circuit. Frequently they draw bigger crowds than the National or American league teams. Four of the top Chicago girls' teams played to 234,000 cash customers last year.

From Robert M. Yoder, "Miss Casey at the Bat," *Saturday Evening Post* 215 (August 22, 1942): 16–17, 49–50.

Why thousands will pay good money to see girls play softball is a question that fills conservative baseball fans with hopeless disgust. The best theory is simply that the girls are getting extremely good and that they are wonderfully erratic. They have learned every trick and every mannerism of masculine big leaguers, on top of which they have mastered every error. . . .

. . . Miss Korgan . . . is a lofty, twenty-six-year-old right-hander generally hailed as the best pitcher in the business. She has . . . an upshoot that gives the girls fits. It comes in low about the garters, and leaps right up toward the batter's swan-like throat. . . . Says Heard Ragas, her manager . . . "What makes Nina hard to hit is the fact that she pitches the ball the same way. Nobody can ever tell what's coming. She's got speed, sure, but her long suit is deception."

Although softball pitching is underhand, the girls are allowed to employ an overhand wind-up if they want to . . . Miss Korgan scorns all this falderal. She uses no wind-up at all. . . . She swings her right arm back as if bowling and sends the ball on its way with a sweep of the arm that starts only an inch or so from the ground. . . .

Softball, with a few ventures into baseball is Nina's career. In her high-school days at Council Bluffs, Iowa, Miss Korgan was the best girl athlete in town. She was especially good at the baseball far throw. . . . One day the manager of a local men's team invited Nina to pitch for him. She would lose, of course, but he figured that a girl pitcher would be an irresistible novelty. The novelty won the game and four more pitching overhand, like a man. That brought her to the attention of a doctor in Syracuse, Nebraska, who ran a girl's softball circle as a hobby. Nina spent three years as the doc's receptionist and star pitcher, growing so good she would winter in California, pitching for a girls' team in Riverside. From Syracuse she moved to a small town in Missouri, where she hurled for the Pony Express girls, and was next invited to Tulsa. Tulsa goes in for girls' softball in a big way, and signing with Tulsa meant getting into the big time. Last year Miss Korgan pitched Tulsa to the national championship . . . in Detroit, as part of the A.S.A. tournament which 200,000 softball teams, men and women, regard as the true world series. The New Orleans team, tired of trying to hit Miss Korgan, hired her.

The Bob Feller of the ladies' league stands five feet eleven inches tall and . . . , is 180 pounds of solid girl. The league is full of six-footers, although height isn't as characteristic as durability and tensile strength. . . . Not all the girls are Amazons . . . averaging for the stars around 135. . . .

All the girls have to be durable, for the big teams will play as many as 100 to 125 games a season, and the squad is only fifteen, meaning that most of the girls play four or five nights a week. Pitchers work especially hard. Miss Korgan pitched fifty games one season, winning forty-nine. . . .

The girls . . . do a good deal of moving around, but can't switch during the season. In private life they hold all manners of jobs, and sometimes none. Miss Korgan does office work—typing, filing, and so on. In winter she works like any other steno. In the summer she gets off at 2:30 in the afternoon if she is playing that night, and she is out of town a lot, taking five to ten day trips with the ball club. She is still technically an amateur, because her regular salary is all she receives. There is one exception—the girls are allowed a small fee for every game they play—two dollars and expenses.

Most of the top teams . . . are sponsored by factories or breweries. Nina . . . play[s for] the Jax Beer Company. . . . On the scale the girls are operating these days, it costs a lot of money to maintain them, and the Jax are reputed to cost their sponsor from $15,000 to $20,000 a year. On the other hand, a team that can draw fifty to ninety thousand paid admissions . . . as some of the Chicago teams do, goes quite a way toward being self-supporting.

Most of the girls have jobs with the sponsoring company, which can offer them work without putting any smirch on the girls' amateur standing, and it is reasonable to suppose that the stars find very good jobs indeed. . . . There is no rule saying that a pitcher can't get more money for typing than an ordinary typist does. The stars probably can count on forty to sixty dollars a week. . . . They do all sorts of work, some as factory hands, . . . secretaries . . . , telephone girls, and so on. . . . Two of the New Orleans flashes are housewives, and several of the stars are not only wives but mothers. . . .

The girls play nine innings and use a team of ten players, standard in softball. The extra player is a shortfielder, or spare shortstop, who works wherever she is needed, usually in short right or short left field. Their coaches are usually old-time baseball players—a fact which helps explain where the girls get so much style. The diamond is in miniature, less than half the size of a baseball layout. Men play softball with sixty feet between bases, but the girls' diamond is a full size smaller than that—just forty feet from base to base. The pitcher stands only thirty-five feet from homeplate, as against forty-three feet in masculine softball. . . .

The girls play in regular baseball pants, sometimes wool, sometimes satin, but usually wear a satin blouse over the regular jersey. . . . There are teams that wear shorts, but not the top teams. They play too strenuous a game for bare legs. The A.S.A. frowns on shorts, anyway, lest sex rear its pretty head and convert this vigorous outdoor exercise into a leg show. . . .

. . . Most of the games are over pretty fast—some in less than an hour. An hour and a half is average, and that is one reason the girls' games are popular. The show starts at nine o'clock, is over by 10:30, and most of the fans can be home by eleven. Then, too, the games are cheap. Twenty-five cents will get you in, and fifty cents will buy the best seat. . . . The tire situation is another helpful factor. Many a fan who hesitates to drive to a big-league park will walk a few blocks to see a game in his own neighborhood.

Another thing that helps the girls' teams is . . . that many of the best masculine softball players are off to the wars. . . . Nor do the girls have to be as good as men, for they enjoy the fine old novelty of being girls. Every time the girls make a good play, it is greeted with pleased surprise.

Fans inevitably register surprise at the throwing. Pitching must be underhand, but the rest of the time the girls throw overhand. . . . Olympia Savona, for instance, sends the ball to second base like a rifle shot. . . . While warming up, to please the crowd, Frieda [Savona] would throw from deep center field to the top rows of the grandstand. She could throw 300 feet. . . .

. . . Hitting is the girls' weakest department. . . . Their own explanation . . . is that the league's pitching is too good.

What interests the customers is . . . that the girls play as women are expected to. You can see all kinds of ball playing, even in the same inning, even from the same girl. They are good, they are very good, and when they are bad, it's murder. . . .

They may occasionally play like men, and occasionally even look like men, but beneath that satin perspiration shirt there beats a feminine heart.

Billie Jean King Remembers Life as an Outsider in the 1950s and 1960s

In many respects, I like being different. I also like being successful. I somehow always knew that I would succeed. I had a great sense of destiny from the time I was very young. I remember one incident so vividly. When I was only about five or six years old, I was standing with my mother in the kitchen at home in Long Beach. I told her flat out that when I grew up I was going to be the best at something. She just smiled and kept peeling potatoes or doing whatever it was she was doing. She said, "Yes, dear; yes, of course, dear," as if I had simply said that I was going to my room or going to eat an apple, or whatever. . . .

Of course, much of the reason why I've always felt that I was out of place was because of sports. First, a girl who wanted to excel in athletics was considered to be strange. In the second place, it was all a hopeless dream, anyhow. I think I began to appreciate this when I was only eight or nine, when my father took me to see the old Los Angeles Angels play the Hollywood Stars in the Triple-A Pacific Coast League at Wrigley Field in L.A. . . .

Right away, I loved it, but it was unfair of me to love it, I understood soon enough, because there was no place for an American girl to go in the *national* pastime. This all came back to me when I saw a commercial on television recently and a whole bunch of kids, boys and girls alike, are all climbing out of a station wagon or getting hamburgers or doing something fun together, and they're all dressed up in baseball uniforms. I'm sure that most people who watch this commercial think how forward it is, how progressive, showing girls on the team, girls in uniform just like the boys. And I have such mixed emotions about that commercial. It's great that they include girls, but at the same time it's cruel because all it can possibly do is make some little girl somewhere wrongly think that she can be a baseball player, too. And of course she can't. There is no life for girls in team sports past Little League.

I got into tennis when I realized this, and because I thought golf would be too slow for me, and I was too scared to swim. What else could a little girl do if she wasn't afraid to sweat? But as good as I was, and as much as I loved tennis right from the start, I found myself out of place there, too, because it was a country-club game then, and I came from a working-class family. My father was a fireman, and we didn't have any money for rackets, much less for proper tennis dresses. The

From Billie Jean King with Frank Deford, *Billie Jean* (New York: Viking, 1982), 11–19.

first time I was supposed to be in a group photograph was at the Los Angeles Tennis Club during the Southern California Junior Championships. They wouldn't let me pose because I was only able to wear a blouse and a pair of shorts that my mother had made for me. All the other players were photographed.

I had some physical defects also. I had bad eyes—20/400—in a sport where nobody wore glasses. And, even as quick and as fast as I've been, I've been fat all over at times, with chubby little legs, and there are railroad tracks on both my knees from a number of knee operations. All that has been very apparent, but perhaps what has made it even more difficult for me as an athlete is my breathing problem. I inherited sinus trouble from my mother and chest problems from my father. The worst times of all for me have been in England, where I've played my very best and set all those records. I don't think there was one year at Wimbledon when I was entirely well. I always had a problem breathing there. I guess I am nearly a physical wreck. You see, nothing about me is quite what it seems.

People mischaracterized me even before the affair [with Marilyn Barnett]. I am supposed to be tough, loud, brash, and insensitive. In fact, Larry says I am very shy, and I really dislike being in the company of more than five or six people. I'm really a one-on-one person. So many people thought I was scared and crumbling under the pressure before the Bobby Riggs match. There happened to be a regular women's tournament in Houston that same week, and I was forced to play in it if I played Riggs—can you imagine the best players today getting that treatment?—and so, one day, without warning, I showed up in the locker room, and almost every player there was scrambling to bet against me. Rosie Casals was the only one backing me. That really hurt, that they didn't have any faith in me.

I had warned Margaret Court when she first told me that she had signed to play Riggs (for $10,000—she thought that was big money) that she was going to have to deal with a whole *season*—not just a day's match. So I knew the buildup would be even greater for Bobby's and my match; we were working off the Court–Riggs momentum. We signed on July 11 for the September 20 showdown, and the hype never really stopped. If it started to slow down, Bobby would whip it back up again.

So all along, my main strategy was not to get swept along in the promotion. Just because I was half of the show on court didn't mean I had to be part of the warm-up act, too. As much as possible, and right up to curtain time, I tried to stay out of the hoopla. After all, it wasn't as if I was needed to sell tickets and hustle the television. We drew 30,472 to the Astrodome and 40,000,000 American TV viewers—plus millions more abroad—so it did well enough without my becoming another carnival barker. Bobby was quite good enough at that.

Nothing he did surprised me. The reception was very much what I expected, and it didn't faze me. I'd played arenas before, and the circus atmosphere Bobby created just made it all of a piece. The only fear I did have was when they brought me in on the litter like Cleopatra. I don't like heights and I was afraid that they were going to drop me. But even my gift of the pig to Bobby and his gift of the big Sugar Daddy to me passed immediately out of my mind. I was really concentrating on my strategy.

The thing that I thought was especially important going in was to volley well. Obviously, I wanted to hit every shot well, and I planned in practice to play an all-court game, sometimes at the net, sometimes back. But I knew Bobby felt that women were poor players at the net, and when I had seen the tape of the Court match, it was apparent that she had reinforced this opinion by playing so badly at net—on those rare occasions when she could get up there. So, to me, it would be psychologically telling if Riggs suddenly realized that this woman could volley.

And I did, too. Five of the first six times he tried to pass me with his backhand, I volleyed away winners. He had me down a service break at 3–2, but by then I knew I could take the net at will, and when I broke right back, that pretty much told the tale. Oh sure, almost right to the end there were all those people who thought Bobby fell behind only to get better odds on his courtside bets, but as far as I was concerned, almost from the first I was amazed at how weak an opponent he really was. All I ever feared was the unknown, and soon enough he was a known quantity for me.

That match was such madness. How often in this world can you suddenly have something which is altogether original and yet wonderfully classic? And what could be more classic than the battle of the sexes? The only problem for me is that I think everybody else in the world—Bobby included—had more fun with that match than I did. Men's tennis would not suffer if Bobby lost, so he had nothing to lose.

Perhaps people would have known how much it all mattered to me if they could have seen an incident a few days before.

I was practicing down in South Carolina, and I came in for a snack. Dick Butera, my friend, the owner of the Philadelphia Freedoms of World Team Tennis and the husband of Julie Anthony, another friend, was lying on the floor, watching a college football game. It was halftime, and the Stanford band was entertaining, and suddenly, as I watched, the band began playing "I Am Woman," and then I realized that they had formed my initials, BJK, on the field, and Dick looked up to share this moment with me, and we both had tears in our eyes. I think that was the happiest the Riggs match ever made me.

But it was never the match itself that upset me. It was all the people clamoring after me. My whole life, I wanted to have mobs of people cheer for tennis, but I really become quite frightened when everybody pushes around me and wants to touch me. I hate it when strangers touch me, even though I understand it is almost always for love, and that they don't mean anything harmful. Still, at the time, when it happens, it scares me.

I have often been asked whether I am a woman or an athlete. The question is absurd. Men are not asked that. I am an athlete. I am a woman. I want all other women to have their rights, because above all else, I'm for individual freedom, but there is very much about the goals and methods of the women's movement that I disagree with. That is the refusal to recognize that both men and women view each other through sexual bias. Oh, I know this is going to get me in trouble, but I'm going to mention it anyway. I've got a male friend in business, and he told me once that he'd really rather have a good-looking, well-built blonde who can barely manage as his secretary than some old lady who is a secretarial whiz. That's his privilege, I think. And if the blonde takes the job knowing that she's going to get leered at and chased around the desk, fair enough.

I'm still not even absolutely convinced that we need the Equal Rights Amendment. If it means the end of discrimination on the basis of gender, than I want it. But I don't believe you can legislate people's minds. I believe that it is persuasion you need, not force. Just because you legislate does not mean that people will change. . . .

Sometimes the women's movement reminds me too much of some organized religion, which I can't stand. I was very (quote) religious (unquote) as a kid. Also, I was much less tolerant then. That seems to me to be the trouble with movements, be they Women's Liberation or the Moral Majority or whatever. Then you always have to be against somebody on every issue, and I'm not very good at that. I don't like confrontations. But, of course, I always performed my best when the confrontation was most heightened, in the clutch—the most well-known example being the Riggs match. Nothing ever really fits for me.

I was a virgin when I was supposed to be, and I got married to the right cute boy the way I was supposed to at the time I was supposed to, but then we only had a "normal" marriage for a couple years—or, anyway, what most Americans presume a normal marriage to be, even if that ideal barely exists anymore. I never feel comfortable with a lot of so-called "normal" married people because they seem threatened by the way Larry and I live—and this was the case even long before people knew about my affair with Marilyn and could say "I told you so" instead of just "I'll bet she's queer." So I've never really felt at home in that huge world of married people, but I've also never felt at all comfortable when I've been associated with the gay world. Maybe it's mostly that everybody wants reinforcement of their kind of life, and I don't provide that for anybody.

I guess I'm just very much a loner. Except for one thing: I really can't stand to be alone for long. Sometimes I ask myself, Billie Jean, where do you belong? Do you fit in anywhere? Maybe all my life I've just been trying to change things so there would be someplace right for me. . . .

Any woman born around 1943 has had to endure so many changes—in her educational experience, in her working life, in sex, in her roles, her expectations. But with me, it always seemed that I was also on the cutting edge of that change. Any woman about my age—or, for that matter, any person who has had to deal with women, which is just about everybody—has been a part of a great social transition, and just to survive that intact has been an accomplishment for me. I was brought up in a very structured universe—in my family, in school, in tennis, in every part of my world. Then, all of a sudden, the rules all started to change, and it seemed there weren't any rules left. I tried to go with the flow, but always seemed to find myself out in front and on the line.

When I married Larry in 1965, we were going to have babies—lots of them, as far as I was concerned—and I was going to give up tennis, which is the way it was supposed to be. In fact, only two weeks after we were married, I thought I was pregnant. And I was delighted. But even when I found out I wasn't having a baby, I was happy enough just spending so much time with Larry. I'd cook him two meals at home every day and take him his lunch—even when he was on the night shift—to the factory where he worked making ice cream cartons.

As for tennis, it hardly mattered. There certainly wasn't any career for me there. It was just fun, and in those days, before professionals were accepted in the main tournaments, there was no money to speak of. We amateurs—"shamateurs" was the accepted term—took what we could in the way of "expenses" under the table, and if it wasn't much, it was still like found money to a young couple, and it helped Larry through law school.

I won Wimbledon three years running, and outside the little tennis community, very few people knew. In 1967 I won all three titles at Wimbledon—singles, doubles, and mixed—and I came back to my country, and there was no one there to meet me, no one at all. And barely six years later, there I was, in the Houston Astrodome, playing prime time to the world in what amounted to the Roman Colosseum, with everyone in civilization chanting my name, hating me or loving me. And everyone wanted—needed—part of me, for tennis or movements or friendship or politics or just for the hell of it—Wouldja, couldja, canya, Billie Jean?—and people were throwing money at me or grabbing at me or calling me a symbol or a leader or a radical feminist. I didn't know where I was. It was so complicated, and one morning I woke up, and where was I? I was in another woman's bed.

So now I know a lot of people will call me a homosexual, but to me that's just another label. As I said, I cannot stand categorization. I'm not concerned for me. I just don't want Larry and my parents and my brother and the other people who love me hurt. And maybe now I can spend some time carving out a place for me in the world around me instead of only in the record books.

Powerlifter Tammy Thompson Identifies the Dangers of Steroids, 1987

I remember after my first powerlifting meet thinking, "I can't believe I finished sixth out of the nine women in my weight class. I know I'm stronger than they are." And so, instead of training harder or going to better techniques, I figured they were taking drugs and I would too. I'd catch up. "And besides," I told myself, "if I decide this is a bad thing, I can simply stop."

The dealer was steering me. He told me, "Stay away from Dianabol and testosterone, they're not good for women." And, of course, that was tantalizing to me. I thought, "What is this? This is chauvinistic. Why can the men take these stronger drugs and not me?"

I started on Anavar and decided it didn't work, so I switched to injections of Equipoise—you know, the new veterinary steroid everyone's using—and decadurabolin. Then I added some Dianabol on top—generally five to six a day, and then, when I was about five weeks out from the U.S. Women's Nationals I started a cycle of testosterone, too. I started off with one half cc a week, then one cc the next week, then to one and one-half, then two cc's, and finally, the week before the meet, I took three cc's. I was pretty well tanked.

From Tammy Thompson interview, in Terry Todd, "Anabolic Steroids: The Gremlins of Sport," *Journal of Sport History* 14 (Spring 1987): 88.

And then three days before the meet I started taking shots of aqueous testosterone—the real nasty stuff that hurts when it goes in. I mean you put that thing in your hip and it feels like it's dripping all down the back of your hamstring. It makes the hamstrings cramp really bad. I took one cc in the morning and one cc at night for the first two days, then the day before the meet one cc in the morning and two cc's at night and the morning of the meet I took two more cc's, and then three more right before the meet started. And during the meet I took some of those sublingual testosterones—I don't remember how many—and right before the deadlifts I took an injection of adrenalin backstage—about one-half cc, I guess.

How did I feel? Like I was on top of the world. Not high, just a very super feeling. I thought I could do anything. . . .

Unwanted side effects? I didn't really notice anything the first cycle. So I figured, "OK, we're safe, this isn't going to do anything to me." And it didn't, not the first time. But the second cycle, my voice started getting lower, and I noticed these strange hairs showing up. I thought, "Well, that's no big deal. A hair here, a hair there. Big deal. I can live with it." Some of it was on my face, some on my chest. And the next cycle it got worse. But by then, I figured the damage had already been done, and I went ahead with the full cycle of steroids because I had a meet coming up. It's hard to explain to people that once you're on the drugs you lose sight of everything but winning. That's one thing they don't understand. I mean, I could look at myself, back then, and I could sort of see what was happening, but I didn't care. I don't feel that way now. I've been off the drugs for almost two years now, but I still have to shave every day.

Baylor University Athletic Director Grant Teaff Criticizes the Impact of Title IX on Intercollegiate Football, 1993

Madam Chairwoman, . . . You first ask whether "full implementation of Title IX" would automatically require severe cuts in football programs. This question is difficult to answer in general terms, because Title IX compliance is fact specific and depends on the situation from campus to campus. If an institution is out of compliance with Title IX, it has latitude to determine how to come into compliance. Whether those steps would include substantial cuts in football would depend on a variety of factors, including the institution's financial condition and its ability to invest additional funds into intercollegiate athletics, the possibility of cutting other men's sports, and the profitability of the football program. . . .

. . . I understand Title IX to require equality of athletic opportunity and effective accommodation of student interests and abilities, and not necessarily precise equality.

These concerns aside, football by its nature is a resource-intensive sport, requiring more players, more coaches, and more protective equipment than other

---

From Grant Teaff, "Statement," in "Title IX Impact on Women's Participation in Intercollegiate Athletics and Gender Equity," in U.S. Congress, House Committee on Energy and Commerce, *Intercollegiate Sports: Hearings Before the Subcommittee on Commerce, Consumer Protection, and Competitiveness* (Washington, D.C.: Government Printing Office, 1993), 16–17.

sports. The disproportionate funding needed to operate a football program makes football the prime target for efforts to identify additional resources for women's athletics or for other funding needs. An offsetting, but equally important factor, particularly at the Division I level, is that football generates revenue and often provides resources for the entire intercollegiate athletics program. Certainly, this is the case at Baylor. . . .

Your second question asks whether I agree with the statement made at the April 1992 gender equity hearing that "spending for football, for which there is no comparable women's sport and in which there is comparatively very large average squad size, contributed greatly to the spending disparities.". . . Although I cannot state positively that football, in fact, accounts for all spending disparities, I do agree that the resources required to conduct a football program are disproportionate to those required to operate other intercollegiate sports programs, so that football probably is largely, although not exclusively, responsible for the spending disparities.

In some cases, the resources acquired for use in the football program can be used on a broader basis for the benefit of women's sports or the overall athletic program. For example, when I became director of athletics last year, I centralized access to video equipment, which previously had been used exclusively for the football team, and made it available for use in all sports. While not all personnel and equipment can be used in this manner, institutions need to consider how and if some of their personnel or equipment, initially acquired for one sport, may be used to benefit the entire intercollegiate athletics program.

Your last question asks for my reaction to the statement by Ellen Vargyas that the university athletic community will not meaningfully address sex discrimination unless it is forced to do so, because special interests want to maintain intercollegiate athletics as "the boys club". I disagree.

First, the statement suggests that the intercollegiate athletic community has not taken steps to eliminate sex discrimination in athletics. Such a suggestion is wrong. The establishment of the NCAA gender equity task force and its work to date represents a true effort of the college community to address gender equity in a serious and practical manner. The statement also fails to recognize the efforts underway at many institutions to improve and strengthen the women's sports program. At Baylor, I have hired a strength coach and conditioning coach who works with all sports, men's and women's. We have two strength and conditioning facilities that are used by all of our student-athletes, male and female. Although my professional life, heretofore, has focused on football, my current goal as director of athletics is to strengthen and improve women's intercollegiate sports at Baylor. I want our women's teams to be competitive and successful, on the field and in the minds of our student body and local community, so that we increase attendance, public interest, and media coverage. I think it is imperative to emphasize promotion and fund raising in women's sports.

Second, while I agree that the college athletic community will not meaningfully address sex discrimination unless it is forced to do so, the statement fails to acknowledge the many external "forces" that are making colleges and universities address Title IX and gender equity. One of the key factors that is "forcing" change at many institutions is simply the public scrutiny and debate over gender equity and opportunities for women. The creation of the NCAA gender equity task force and the emphasis on practical ideas for promoting Title IX compliance are making members of the college community think about the nature of the intercollegiate athletics program on their campus and ways in which opportunities for women can be enhanced, without eliminating existing opportunities for men.

In addition, student interests and demands, congressional oversight, agency enforcement of Title IX, and court orders all operate to "force" colleges and universities to address ways in which to improve the quality and offerings of their women's intercollegiate athletic programs.

Moreover, I think it is overly simplistic to say that colleges and universities will not take action on their own to address Title IX and gender equity because they want to "maintain intercollegiate athletics as a boys' club". On the contrary, I already have commented on the efforts of the intercollegiate athletic community to address gender equity and to expand opportunities for female student-athletes. Whatever it once may have been, college athletics no longer is a "boys' club". Shrinking financial resources and increasing operating costs, not some effort to maintain intercollegiate athletics as an entrenched boys' club, constitute the greatest single obstacle to achieving gender equity.

In summary, we cannot change the nature of football. But that does not mean that we cannot achieve compliance with Title IX and work toward building strong women's intercollegiate athletic programs. That is the goal of the NCAA gender equity task force, and certainly is my mission at Baylor. . . .

Attorney Ellen J. Vargyas Analyzes the Inadequacies of Title IX, 1992

It is abundantly clear that 20 years after title IX's enactment, post-secondary competitive athletics, the subject of this hearing, are still characterized by persistent and pervasive discrimination against women and girls. To be sure, in certain respects women and girls have made substantial progress. Of course, given the virtual exclusion of women and girls from athletic opportunities prior to 1972 almost any improvement would be substantial. In other respects, principally in the very important area of employment opportunities, women have actually lost considerable ground over this same time period. In any event, the bottom line is the same. Women and girls are systematically denied anything even resembling equal opportunity or equal treatment in post-secondary competitive athletics. . . .

Advocates for sex equity in athletics have long known that female athletes are relegated to an unfairly and disproportionately reduced portion of the participation opportunities, scholarships, and operating support which flow to competitive post-secondary athletics. The nationally-based NCAA Gender-Equity Survey performs a significant service by adding important, nationally-based details to the analysis. The information it contains enables us, for the first time, to fully understand the

From Ellen J. Vargyas, "Statement," in "Title IX Impact on Women's Participation in Intercollegiate Athletics and Gender Equity," in U.S. Congress, House Committee on Energy and Commerce, *Intercollegiate Sports: Hearings Before the Subcommittee on Commerce, Consumer Protection, and Competitiveness*, pt. 2 (Washington, D.C.: Government Printing Office, 1992), 91–95.

depth and breadth of gender-based inequities in higher education athletics. Let me take a moment to review the key findings.

To begin with, the NCAA study confirms that women are only 30 percent of college athletes. . . . This number has held constant for approximately 15 years. The most competitive colleges and universities—those in Division I-A—have the worst female participation rates, at 28.6 percent.

The distribution of the tens of millions of dollars of athletic financial aid which is allocated annually to college and university athletes is similarly inequitable. While the NCAA does not provide information regarding total scholarship expenditures, it does conclusively demonstrate that female athletes get less than one in three athletic scholarship dollars. This is true in both the most competitive programs, and the less competitive Division II programs.

The allocation of non-scholarship resources is even less equitable. The NCAA confirms that Division I programs provide barely over one in five operating dollars to their female athletes and only 17 percent of recruiting dollars. The most competitive programs—those in Division I-A—are again the most inequitable . . . parities in expenditures in recruiting and scholarship dollars and the 30 percent female participation rate is particularly telling. With an equitable allocation of resources in recruiting and scholarships, female participation would easily reach a level commensurate with female undergraduate enrollment.

. . . Our extensive experience in working with female athletes, their coaches and advocates over the years enables us to provide these details and demonstrate just what the NCAA numbers mean to female athletes. The following is a brief summary of what I hear from female athletes and their coaches on an almost daily basis, pegged to the categories in the title IX athletic regulations:

—Many young women who want to—and have demonstrated the ability to—participate in varsity athletics are denied any opportunity at all to compete or are relegated to club programs which receive little or no institutional support. This is nearly always in the face of athletics programs which persist in maintaining twice as many varsity athletics opportunities for their male students as their female students. Recently, post-secondary institutions have refused to create varsity teams in, for example, women's ice hockey, basketball and gymnastics, despite demonstrated interest and disproportionate opportunities for male students.

—The young women who are denied the opportunity to participate are also denied access to extremely valuable athletic scholarship dollars, accounting for the discriminatorily depressed 30 percent female scholarship rate.

—Female athletes too often receive inferior equipment and supplies. In addition to disparities in actual athletic equipment, this includes uniforms which are replaced on a much slower schedule than those of their male classmates, fewer pairs of free sneakers, and the more frequent expectation that they will launder their own athletic clothing.

—Female athletes often receive less favorable competition and practice times and are assigned to the less desirable competitive and practice facilities including locker rooms. A common problem is that women's competitions are often scheduled as the "warm-up" event for the "more serious" men's competitions which are held at the most desirable times.

—Female athletes often are allocated less desirable modes of travel and travel accommodations. There are still reports of situations where a male team flies to a certain destination while a female team from the same school takes a bus. Or, the male team arrives the night before an event so that its members can rest and be in prime shape for the competition while their female classmates arrive and go straight into the competition. Female athletes are still told that because their male classmates are bigger than they are, it is only fair that the young men get more money to spend on food and are assigned fewer to a hotel room.

—Coaches of women's teams are paid less than coaches of men's teams, see discussion below, and have significantly fewer assistant coaches than their counterparts who coach men's teams. While there are many extraordinarily dedicated and capable women and men coaching female athletes, overall female athletes do not receive the level of coaching of their male classmates because their institutions simply will not pay for it.

—Female athletes still encounter trainers who will tend to their needs, if at all, only after the men are taken care of. There are still too many systems in place which allocate trainers to men's teams at a much higher rate than to women's teams regardless of the injury rates in the respective sports. Moreover, although it is now widely recognized that weight training is an important component of their training, female athletes are typically denied equal access to weight training facilities and competent coaching.

—Colleges and universities spend only a small fraction on their women's teams of what they spend on their men's teams in terms of publicity and marketing. Citing lower spectator interest in women's sports, they ignore the obvious and important role of publicity and marketing in promoting such interest. One of the most memorable figures to emerge from the Haffer litigation was that over a 3 year period, Temple spent 0.5 percent of its publicity expenditures on its women's teams. It was obvious why hardly anyone went to the women's competitions. Nobody knew about them.

In short, in 1992—20 years after the enactment of title IX—female athletes still suffer from discrimination in virtually every aspect of intercollegiate athletics.

The record is similarly clear regarding the very serious problems facing women in employment across-the-board in post-secondary athletics. Women have been forced out of many athletic related jobs, female employees are paid less than males, and coaches of women's teams are paid less than coaches of men's teams. Moreover, while there have been improvements in the situation of female athletes since title IX was passed, women who want to work in post-secondary athletics are actually in a worse situation than they were 20 years ago.

Carpenter and Acosta, two respected researchers from Brooklyn College, have found the following:

—While in 1972 women were over 90 percent of all coaches for women's teams, by 1990 they were less than half. Unchanged was the fact that in both years, less than 1 percent of coaches of men's teams were women.

—The situation in sports administration is even worse. In 1972, over 90 percent of women's programs were run by women. By 1990 that figure dropped to 16 percent. Moreover by 1990, only 32 percent of all administrative jobs in women's programs were held by women and no women at all were involved in the administration of 30 percent of women's programs. The administrators of men's programs were and are overwhelmingly male. Less than 1 percent of men's programs have ever been run by women.

The recently published ACE Factbook on Women in Higher Education . . . adds concrete numbers to show the nature of the problems facing women in athletic administration. ACE found the following for academic year 1987–1988:

In 1,410 post-secondary institutions surveyed, including both public and private and 4 and 2 year institutions:

—There were 807 male and 75 female athletic directors. The men's median salary was $42,181 and the women's was $30,120.

—There were 404 male and 26 female sports information directors. The men's median salary was $23,738 and the women's was $19,000. . . .

The 1992 NCAA survey . . . demonstrates the depth of the salary disparities facing the coaches of women's teams. . . . For example, although it is virtually the same game, Division I coaches of men's basketball teams are paid an average base salary of $71,511 while coaches of women's teams receive $39,177. Even leaving aside that these are only base figures and do not include a substantial part of the compensation packages received by coaches of men's basketball teams, women's coaches receive only 54.7 as much as the men's coaches. Yet, these are the best paid women's head coaches.

There is nothing on the women's side to compare to the average $81,574 base pay paid to Division I football coaches or even the $43,569 paid to men's ice hockey coaches.

The disparities are not only in the high visibility sports. Baseball head coaches (men's teams) receive an average salary of $34,126 while softball head coaches (women's teams) are paid $21,169. Looking at other comparable teams, men's head coaches receive more than their counterparts coaching women's teams in cross country, fencing, lacrosse, rifle, soccer, swimming, tennis, indoor/outdoor track, and volleyball. Only the coaches of women's golf, gymnastics, and skiing are paid more than coaches of comparable men's teams and the differences in compensation are quite small. . . .

It is beyond dispute that female athletes, coaches, and administrators are systematically subjected to second class treatment in college and university athletics programs. The next question is why has this situation been permitted to continue to date and what can be done?

The problems I have just set out are not caused by the failure of Federal law to prohibit discrimination against girls and women in education related athletics or by the lack of availability of enforcement mechanisms. Title IX forbids nearly all of the practices described above and with the 1988 passage of the Civil Rights Restoration Act reversing the Supreme Court's 1984 decision in Grove City College v. Ball, title IX's applicability to athletics discrimination is well established. A Federal Agency, the Department of Education's Office for Civil Rights, is charged with the administrative enforcement of title IX. . . . Why, then, has this discrimination persisted?

In my view, the answer stems from a failure of leadership in the university community which has been exacerbated by the Office for Civil Rights' abandonment of a strong enforcement role and the practical difficulties inherent in bringing private litigation. The university community has not meaningfully addressed sex discrimination in competitive athletics because it has not been forced to and because it has not found the will to resist the powerful special interests seeking to maintain intercollegiate athletics as the boys' club it has historically been. . . .

After title IX's enactment, there was an explosion in the athletic opportunities offered to girls and women in both high schools and colleges. However, by 1980 the progress had come to an end. At the same time, OCR retreated from its previous active enforcement presence and became almost invisible on questions of title IX enforcement. Following the Supreme Court's decision in Grove City College in 1984, and until the passage of the Civil Rights Restoration Act in 1988, OCR opted out of any role whatsoever in addressing athletics discrimination.

OCR has slowly reentered the field after the passage of the Restoration Act, even declaring athletics discrimination a priority in 1991. Nonetheless, serious problems remain which keep OCR from being a serious player in the effort to end the pervasive discrimination in post-secondary athletics. For example, in the spring of 1990, it distributed a manual for its investigators to use in athletics investigations which failed to address many of the major problems confronting women in athletics. . . . The title IX regulation requires that the female scholarship rate be proportionate to the female participation rate. OCR takes the view that an institution is out of compliance only if the percentage of scholarships allocated to female athletes differs in a statistically significant fashion from the female participation rate. This analysis permits post-secondary institutions to spend tens of thousands of dollars less on their female athletes than true proportionality would dictate, simply because of the nature of statistical analysis. Moreover, OCR does not even acknowledge the far more fundamental problems inherent in using a discriminatorily reduced participation rate as the basis for evaluating scholarship compliance. This is in spite of the fact that the one court to have addressed this issue concluded that schools may not rely on discriminatorily reduced female participation rates to justify similarly reduced scholarship rates. . . . OCR's disregard of scholarship discrimination against female athletes is particularly ironic in light of the major emphasis it has currently placed on eliminating limited scholarship programs targeted to minorities which are narrowly tailored to redress effects of longstanding race discrimination in this country. . . .

OCR's problems go beyond the failure to articulate appropriate policy and very much include the resolution of complaints. A case in point is the recent disposition of a major complaint regarding the athletic program of Brooklyn College of the City University of New York. The problems began during the investigation, when OCR failed to cooperate meaningfully with the complaining parties, appearing to work very closely instead with the institution which was the subject of the complaint. . . .

While OCR did ultimately find a number of violations in Brooklyn College's program, it found . . . that although Brooklyn College had violated title IX by not giving female athletes equal participation opportunities, there was no violation in the allocation of scholarships because it was proportionate to the discriminatorily reduced participation rate. As such it put its imprimatur on a system which unfairly denied women many thousands of dollars of scholarship assistance.

In resolving the Brooklyn College complaint, OCR accepted assurances from Brooklyn that it would come into compliance with title IX in certain respects. Based on those assurances OCR actually found that there was no violation of the statute although it had found many specific violations during the course of the inquiry. . . . There is no mechanism in place to guarantee that even these assurances will actually be complied with. . . .

✦ E S S A Y S

The first essay by Susan E. Cayleff of San Diego State University, author of an outstanding new biography entitled *Babe: The Life and Legend of Babe Didrikson Zaharias* (1995), examines the athletic accomplishments, personal life, and legend of the all-time greatest American female athlete. Babe was extremely versatile, first starring at basketball, and then single-handedly winning the Amateur Athletic Union championship for her company team and setting four world records. She won two gold medals and a silver at the 1932 Olympics; she was limited to three medals only because no woman was permitted to compete in more events. Babe then learned golf and became an outstanding professional.

In the second document Susan Cahn, State University of New York, Buffalo, examines the process by which women since Didrikson's time sought to compete in athletics. Cahn argues that female athletes refused to identify sport as a male bastion, regardless of the particular activity involved, the competitiveness required, and the perspiration expended. They saw sport as an activity fully in concert with their own self-definitions of femininity. In Cahn's larger study, *Coming on Strong: Gender and Sexuality in Twentieth-Century Women's Sport* (1994), she relied heavily on oral history to recover the lost memories of certain notable women's athletic programs like the All-American Baseball Conference (1943–1954). Did the emphasis in the 1950s on domesticity and femininity encourage a collective loss of memory about such presumably unladylike activities as running, sliding, hitting balls, and pitching?

Babe Didrikson Zaharias: The "Texas Tomboy"

SUSAN E. CAYLEFF

In the early 1930s, an unsuspecting New York newspaper reporter approached Mildred Ella "Babe" Didrikson. She was already, at the young age of nineteen, nationally known as a championship basketball player and double gold and silver medalist in track and field at the 1932 Los Angeles Olympics. The reporter said, "I'm told you also swim, shoot, ride, row, box, and play tennis, golf, basketball, foot-

---

From Susan E. Cayleff, "The 'Texas Tomboy': The Life and Legend of Babe Didrikson Zaharias," Organization of American Historians, *Magazine of History* 7 (Summer 1992): 28–33.

ball, polo and billiards. Is there anything at all you don't play?" "Yeah," the East Texan replied, "dolls."

A life study of Babe Didrikson (1911–1956) presents the women's and sport historian with numerous challenges and possibilities. She was unarguably the most multi-talented athlete of the twentieth century, male or female. She played semi-professional basketball, softball, enjoyed a short stint as a successful harmonica-playing stage entertainer, and when she turned her will and talent to golf in the thirties, forties, and fifties, she won an unprecedented thirteen consecutive tournaments. Ironically, "Didrikson's versatility probably had its roots in the lack of opportunities for women in sports. Male athletes specialized in one sport with aspirations of turning professional in it." But Babe, proficient in two sports that had no pro ranks for women, "moved from sport to sport as opportunities presented themselves to her" and "plied her trade by taking limited engagements in everything".

In addition to her world records and dominance in the high jump, eighty-meter hurdles, javelin toss and softball throw, she was an atypical American hero. Her ethnic Norwegian background, working-class ways, poor Southern origins, and gender posturing made her an unlikely character to capture the nation's imagination. Sports were her entree into front page headlines, but her clever manipulation of the press and unceasing hustling of gigs and opportunities made her a consummate self-promoter. She told tales of mythic proportion about herself which included scuttling her birth date to make her Olympic victories occur at age fifteen, not nineteen; the wrestling of a bull in downtown Beaumont, Texas; slugging it out with Baby Stribling, then middleweight boxing champion (in fact this was a staged photo session); scaling the outside walls of a multi-story Olympic dormitory to swipe a souvenir flag; typing 186 words per minute at her secretarial position at Employer's Casualty Insurance Company for whom she played sports in Dallas (her scant correspondence reveals rank typing skills and significant grammatical shortcomings); the false claim that she won seventeen, not thirteen consecutive golf tournaments (this "fact" appeared at her Memorial Museum in Beaumont); and her favorite sleight of hand—literally creating larger-than-life size myths about herself. She was, in fact, average in stature—five feet five inches and one hundred forty pounds—but would unabashedly exaggerate her height, weight, and strength. For Babe, the impact of a story justified any hyperbole. She learned story-telling skills from her seafaring father, and regaled her schoolyard buddies, teachers, athletic peers, and sportswriters with dazzling and barely believable feats.

As a personality she was charismatic and willful to the point of abrasiveness: few felt neutrally towards her. Women on the Ladies' Professional Golf Association tour which she helped co-found in 1948 were horrified—and intimidated—by her locker-room antics. She would enter and bellow, "What'd y'all show up for? See who's gonna finish second?" She knew how to psychologically immobilize her opponents and steal their limelight. Not surprisingly, her habit of monopolizing radio interviews with several athletes by belting out a tune on her harmonica did not endear her to many. Her uncanny ability to boast and make good on her predictions of her own accomplishments further infuriated her competitors. She warned the starting forward of the soon-to-be national champion Golden Cyclones women's basketball team (1930–32) that she would usurp her position within weeks. She did just that. She would predict the route of a golf ball's travel, or a final round's score, and delight the press and depress her opponents when her bravado proved true. All of these tactics gave her a competitive edge. In essence, she proclaimed, "I am the greatest!" decades before Mu-hammad Ali emerged as the king of self-congratulatory behavior.

That she was female, androgynous to the point of boyish-looking as a youth, coarsely spoken and physically brash made her fame and popularity all the more unique. In the years immediately following the Olympics, there was a double-edged reciprocity between Didrikson and the press. Her "deficient femininity" and "disturbing masculinity" sparked constant fears of lesbianism, or worse yet, the existence of a "third sex" in women's sports. Babe played a fascinating role in all of this. She revelled in the (early) persona of the boyish, brazen, unbeatable rene-gade, but cringed at the innuendos of abnormality. She was the consummate tomboy—beating boys at their own games. In fact, "boyishness" was tolerable and even engaging: "mannishness," on the other hand, insinuated a confirmed condi-tion out of which she would not grow. The latter charge was the greater of the two insults and confirmed her abnormality. One Associated Press release comforted the reader that "she is not a freakish looking character . . . (but) a normal, healthy, boy-ish looking girl." Babe was keenly aware of how these portrayals cast her outside of the female gender. Poisonous stories flowed from journalists' pens, likening her to Amazonian creatures. These renditions were so vitriolic that they evoked moth-ers' warnings that they would "not let their daughters grow up to be like Babe Didrikson."

Yet throughout the condemnation and ridicule, Babe persevered in her attempt to earn a living at sport in an era when it was virtually impossible for a woman to do so. Thus she participated in one-on-one demonstrations that at times had al-most carnival-like aspects. She pitched spring training for the St. Louis Cardinals; put on golf ball driving exhibitions with male golf-great Gene Sarazen; played donkey-softball with an all-male, all-bearded touring softball team, prompting the *New York Evening Post* to crow with the headline, "Famous Woman Athlete Pitches for Whisker Team;" sang and ran on a treadmill in a wildly successful al-beit short-lived stint in a one-woman vaudeville-type show and even challenged the winning horse of the Kentucky Derby to a foot race.

For these reasons, and her infinitely quotable one-liners, which shocked as much as they entertained (when asked how she drove the golf ball so hard Babe replied, "I just loosen my girdle and let 'er fly!"), Didrikson was a favorite with the press. As her brother, Bubba Didrikson, said when interviewed about his deceased sister, "They called her a sportswriter's dream because she always had time for them. . . . She never rejected anyone who wanted to interview her. She was wise. She knew that they could make her or break her . . . she knew that, and she liked it."

This symbiotic relationship debilitated Babe at times. Labelled a "muscle moll" by *Vanity Fair* in 1932, Babe perpetually battled the image of a creature not-quite-female. As she matured, and cultural tolerance for her tomboyishness waned (as it eventually does for young women who excel in male physical endeavors), she deliberately sought to deconstruct her inappropriate past and construct a non-threatening, normal heterosexual, feminine life script.

In this context, Babe experienced the difficulty of being a woman who defied the acceptable parameters of femininity. Middle-class cultural ideals of her era dictated sacrificial devotion to husband, children and home, attention to physical beautification, and a self-effacing demeanor. She consciously set about perfecting the more tolerable aspects of this ideal feminine role. According to Bertha Bowen, a friend and protector who shepherded Babe through the upper-class waters of Texas golf, they began a campaign to feminize her replete with a clothing overhaul, make-up applications, and other accoutrements of femininity such as hairdos, hosiery, and silk slips. Bowen even chased Babe through the former's Texas home with a girdle admonishing her that no decent woman would step outside without wearing one.

Babe realized that further success depended upon recasting herself to conform to acceptable notions of femininity. Women athletes in particular lived with conflicting ideals. A "youthful appearance became fashionable . . . and an 'athletic' image . . . made action itself a sort of fashion." For women athletes this meant facing the contradiction between developing the body in what was seen as an "unfeminine" fashion versus being a "real" (culturally-constructed) woman. The public attitude, therefore, was ambivalent toward women athletes, not universally approving as many historians claim. If the woman athlete was shapely but not muscular, sporting but not overly competitive, heterosexual, and participating in a "beautiful" sport (defined by sportswriters as swimming, golf, tennis or ice-skating), then and only then did she fulfill the ideal. Babe, like so many other athletes of her era, either adopted an apologetic attitude offering "proofs" of her femininity or struggled with her identity as the criticism and innuendo mounted. In her as-told-to autobiography *This Life I've Led* (1955), Babe offered numerous examples of dating boys, marriage proposals and successes at housekeeping, and sewing and cooking to prove her normality. Much of this was grossly exaggerated or fictitious.

In 1938, Babe's meeting of and marriage to George Zaharias cemented her transition to appropriate womanhood. Their meeting and courtship represented the stuff reporters dream of for they were both media hounds. Zaharias, wealthy and well-known by his wrestling tag-name, "The Crying Greek from Cripple Creek," was also a sports promoter of renown. The credentials he gained as a world-class wrestler from 1932 to 1938 were impressive enough to have him inducted into the Athletic Hellenic Hall of Fame for Greek Athletes in 1982. Significantly, George abandoned his own lucrative career in the ring in order to manage Babe's career. Thus she was the primary wage-earner, although interviews revealed she controlled none of her own monies. So it was that two of sports' most adept hustlers merged their considerable talents. The media idealized their relationship throughout their life together, some resorting to unabashedly sappy prose. The significance of this increases as their marital harmony decreases. Ample evidence exists that Babe's "Greek God" had, in her own words, become "a God Damned Greek." Yet Babe continued to nurture the image of herself as the happily married lady despite increasing periods of wanderlust on George's part, as well as discord and alienation. Babe's wish to present a happy front was most likely due to her desire to keep the ugly innuendos of years past from reemerging.

Her conscious self-transformation was two-fold: stereotypically defined femininity replaced uncouth roughness and golf became her new passion and career focus. This traditionally elite sport promised ascendancy from her gritty and impoverished working-class roots, although prior to her participation, it hardly guaranteed a financial living. Women's golf was in need of a superstar player and personality in 1943 when Babe finally regained her amateur status after an agonizing series of legal stalemates aimed at barring "her ilk" from the game. And while Babe's style provided ample interest, it was often not the kind that golf's higher-ups sought. Yet despite the sport elites' ambivalence toward her, Babe revolutionized women's golf. In 1947, when Pete Martin of the *Saturday Evening Post* interviewed Babe, he wrote of her, "Not much has been made of the undeniable fact that the Babe has revolutionized the feminine approach to golf." Other sportswriters said of her, "Babe Zaharias created big-time women's golf . . . her booming power game lowered scores and forced others to imitate her." Pushed by her manager/husband and her own high standards well beyond the comfort level, Babe's practice sessions were deservedly legendary. According to Zaharias in a 1957 *Look* magazine interview, in order to win, Babe drove balls with taped, bloodied and sore hands and complied with his grueling schedules. As Babe herself often said, "I've always been a fighter. Ever since I was a kid, I've scrapped for everything. I want to win every time. If a game is worth playing, it's worth playing to win." Babe devoted herself to perfecting her golf game with the same ferocity that she brought to the Olympic high hurdles and javelin toss. She was equally dominant in her newly chosen arena.

As Babe's powerful golf game and trans-Atlantic victories (in 1947 she became the first American woman to win the British Open) gained coverage in the national press, her outlets for competition grew extremely meager. Few professional tournaments existed for women and so Babe and several other women golfers set about establishing the Ladies' Professional Golf Association (LPGA) to introduce more paying tournaments. Sponsored by monies from sporting goods companies, the fledgling women's tour steadily increased its purses, credibility, and consequently, the number of women able to eke out a living in golf. Babe held office in the LPGA's hierarchy during the first several years of its operation and consistently ranked among the top money winners.

In 1953, her athletic career ground to a halt as she battled colon cancer in what would become a recurring struggle. Didrikson utilized sports metaphors to help her cope with her ailment. She conceptualized the disease as "a hurdle she could leap," "a hole she could birdie," and "the toughest competition of my life." By surrounding herself with familiar and successful life strategies, she coped with her ailment admirably. Unfortunately, her public visibility as a cancer self-help role model—in an era when this was virtually unheard of—was based on misinformation. Her husband and closest female friend Betty Dodd, a promising golf protegee from San Antonio who was twenty years Babe's junior, joined with physicians at the University of Texas Medical Branch at Galveston (where she was repeatedly hospitalized for cancer) in not telling her of the extent of her malignancy. Thus, falsely believing herself cured, Babe played a vital educational function for the American public who cheered her posturing as one who could "beat the beast of cancer." She devoted herself to fund raising for and consciousness raising about the disease while staging a dramatic and successful comeback as a championship golfer mere weeks after her operation. Her phoenix-like rise back to the top of the sports world endeared her to a new audience. She was honored by President Eisenhower at the White House, fêted by the Texas state legislature and the American Cancer Society, and given numerous medical humanitarian awards.

Throughout her illness, which recurred in 1955 and claimed her life prematurely in 1956, Didrikson was inseparable from her "other mate," Betty Dodd. Intimates interviewed readily acknowledge the friendship and care-taking that transpired between the two women. It clearly replaced the emotional intimacy that had waned so dramatically between Zaharias and Babe. In fact, Dodd lived with the couple for the last six years of Babe's life. They were constant travel companions on the tour, music-making buddies, and a persistent source of infuriation and friction to George who had quite literally been replaced in Babe's affections. While this relationship was never admittedly lesbian, it was undeniably the emotional and physical mainstay of Babe's later life. What is so striking is Didrikson's silence about this bond. She does not mention Dodd until the last pages of her 1955 autobiography. Only accounts from hospital and newspaper records revealed the "devoted friend" who slept on a cot beside Babe's hospital bed. Dodd, interviewed repeatedly throughout the late 1980s, openly professed her love for Babe. Theirs is a classic example of a relationship between women that was life-sustaining, yet culturally minimized due to homophobic fears.

Didrikson's life presents numerous challenges to historians and students alike. Discovering a hero with flaws, who was previously portrayed as unblemished, necessitates a new construction of her life story. Her fierce competitiveness, which served her so well on the playing field, was self-serving and at times damaged personal relationships. Her life has always been told as a series of unimpeded successful quests, much like narratives of conquering male heroes in the epic genre. But when gender, homophobia, cultural beliefs about women athletes, and sex-role expectations for women in the era from 1920 to 1960 are analyzed, a far more conflictual and complex life story emerges. Didrikson furthered opportunities for others in women's sports, although not because she was gender conscious and sought to improve opportunities for others that followed after her. She co-founded the LPGA to increase her own opportunities. But she served as a path-breaking role model by virtue of her accomplishments despite her lack of self-conscious effort to do so. Her work with medical humanitarianism was more deliberately altruistic. Thus she leaves a dual legacy: as an athlete and as a public figure who endured scrutiny to help others.

Her shrine-like gravestone in Beaumont, Texas, which fittingly dominates the family burial plot, misleadingly declares the time-worn cliché: "It's not whether you win or lose, it's how you play the game." Ironically, this epitaph embodies the legend of Didrikson as she chose to mythologize herself. It contrasts sharply with the life and values she actually lived. Hers was a life of struggle, disharmony, cultural conflict and unapproved-of intimacy; this amidst much non-introspective fun-seeking. That she worked so hard in her death-bed autobiography to portray her life as harmonious, non-conflictual and ideally bonded to husband and sports peers, speaks to her savvy desire to construct a culturally acceptable life story. Babe's life as she actually lived it allows the historian and student of history a unique chance to unravel the palpable opportunities open to—and extreme limitations encountered by—women athletes and atypical women in general during this era. Babe Didrikson's life is an invaluable window through which larger issues in women's and sport history can emerge, crystallize, and gain meaning.

Women Competing/Gender Contested, 1930s–1950s

SUSAN CAHN

Decades of controversy over female competition, masculinization, and the sexual reputation of women athletes point to an enduring opposition between sport and womanhood. In 1960, after a half-century of women's active involvement in sport, the *New York Times* published a Sunday magazine essay claiming that the great majority of women athletes did not possess "the Image." The "Image," according to author William Furlong, was simply an updated version of what 1930s sportswriter Paul Gallico had called "S.A.," or sex appeal. Furlong approved of sports that enhanced women's "decorative" appeal but condemned any sports that turned women into muscular, unbecoming athletes he called "unwomanly." He was joined by a chorus of others in the media. While journalists praised several 1960 Olympians for their "good looks and charming ways," they ridiculed the "overdeveloped muscles and underdeveloped glands" of competitors who refused the dictum to be "athletes second, girls first."

Why, despite decades of female participation, did the disparaging image of the "mannish" athlete still hold sway in the popular imagination? And why did observers, especially the fraternity of male sportswriters, find it so disturbing when a small group of women placed athletic goals ahead of standard notions of "feminine beauty"? The answer rests in the deeper-seated anxiety that underlay charges of mannishness and ugliness. The presence of powerful women athletes struck at the roots of male dominance in American society—the seemingly natural physical superiority of men. When women "surrendered their sex" to take up masculine sport, might they also be assuming the prerogatives and power of males, threatening what one sportswriter wistfully referred to as "the old male supremacy"?

The resulting sense of gender disorder precipitated a wide array of responses, ranging from those who endorsed women athletes' assertion of power to those who vehemently resisted any change in the status quo. But whether they reacted with amazement, approval, horror, or disdain, twentieth-century observers paid an almost obsessive attention to two issues: the presence or absence of femininity among female athletes, and the comparative capabilities of men and women in sport. In their frequent attempts to address these questions, journalists, educators, sport officials, and social commentators tried to reconcile sport and womanhood and to resolve the nagging question of power that lurked beneath the surface of debate.

From Susan Cahn, *Coming on Strong: Gender and Sexuality in Twentieth-Century Women's Sport* (New York: Free Press, 1994), 207–14, 216, 218–25, 228, 231–32, 234–35.

Women athletes faced an even more complicated task. In addition to enduring second-class athletic status and finding themselves the focal point of gender controversies, women in sport had to bridge the gulf between societal images of "mannish" athletes and their own positive experience of sport and its compatibility with womanhood. The masculine stigma sometimes hurt, discouraged, or constrained them. Yet they continued to play, relying on athletic peers and supportive families, close friends, or their local communities for reassurance. Most of all, athletes found strength in the actual experience of sport—in the pleasure, knowledge, and opportunities gained through athletic involvement.

Athletes had little control over athletic policies and philosophies that reinforced conventional concepts of masculinity and femininity, weaving these distinctions into the very fabric of sport. Yet they were not powerless to effect changes in their own minds and immediate surroundings. As they played, women athletes developed a kind of double consciousness; while comprehending the cultural interdiction against "mannish" athletic women, they drew on their shared experience as female athletes to generate an expansive definition of womanhood that eliminated, or at least eased, the dissonance between athleticism and femininity.

A sense of threatened manhood lay just beneath the surface of many media portrayals of women's sport. Although nearly all female athletic competition took place in women-only events, male journalists frequently described such events as a contest between women and men. For instance, even in Grantland Rice's laudatory . . . articles like "Is There a Weaker Sex?" and "The Slightly Weaker Sex," Rice could not help but compare women's marvelous athletic accomplishments to men's, wondering whether women might someday equal or exceed men's athletic feats. . . .

In the 1920s observers tended to raise these questions in a bemused tone. There was a kind of carnivalesque fascination with women's athletic feats as a symbol of the changing gender order of American society. In its most fantastic form, the image of the female athlete signaled a total inversion of established gender relations. . . .

The fascination with competition faded in the 1930s, probably because both the attention and the opportunities available to women athletes diminished during a decade of financial cutbacks and renewed skepticism toward independent women in traditionally masculine pursuits. . . .

In the few cases in which women directly challenged and defeated men in competition, the threat to male supremacy appeared even more imminent. A 1938 article titled "Foils and Foibles" recounted the story of Helene Mayer's two-day claim to the national fencing title after she unexpectedly defeated the men's champion. The U.S. fencing organization hurriedly imposed a ban on competition between men and women and revoked Mayer's number one status "for chivalry's sake.". . .

The Cold War years sparked a recurrence of the symbolism of gender inversion. Fearing that the superiority of women athletes in the Eastern bloc might ruin American chances to win the over-all Olympic medal count, the press ridiculed the combination of "strong Red ladies" and "frail Red males.". . .

Journalists revealed a similar uncertainty as they struggled to apply concepts of masculinity and femininity to successful female athletes whose skills seemed to blur these very distinctions. The surprising abilities exhibited by women athletes induced sportswriters to try to reconcile the "masculine" nature of women's accomplishments with the femininity the public (and they themselves) wanted to see. In describing female athletes' bodies, playing styles, and personalities, the media went to great—sometimes comic—lengths to attribute gender to the anomalous athlete.

To account for women's "masculine" abilities, reporters often described the bodies of female athletes in terms usually reserved for men. For example, "big, splendid, deep-chested" swimmer Gertrude Ederle was a "strapping" girl with a "column-like throat" and "muscles of steel." Yet writers also searched for feminine physical traits that would distinguish the manly female athlete from her male counterpart . . . to find evidence of physical femininity in a seventeen-year-old athlete whose astounding ten world records signaled masculine physical ability.

Often journalists paired words that suggested masculinity and femininity simultaneously. . . . Helen Wills was described as a "vision of white and pink," with a "chiseled beauty" and arms like "pistoning-columns of white muscle.". . .

There was less ambiguity about successful athletes' skill, which journalists invariably described as masculine. . . . Tennis players were said to stroke the ball with "machine-like precision" and exhibit "cold, tense, machine-like qualities." In addition to masculine, technological metaphors, journalists depicted female athletic power through sexually evocative images of male aggression. Helen Wills played "without even a pretense of mercy. It was almost as though a man with a rapier were sending home his vital thrusts against a foeman unarmed." Sexual metaphors point to the less conscious connection between sport and male virility, suggesting as well the implicit threat that active, skilled women posed to men's sense of sexual potency.

Losers, by virtue of their lesser skill, were described in more feminine terms. . . . By reserving the attributes most associated with attractive femininity—those represented by soft, smiling, pretty, slender white womanhood—for unsuccessful athletes, the media conveyed a powerful message. Femininity presupposed lesser athletic ability, and athletic success in turn signaled masculine power and failed femininity.

Yet reporters also sought to restore femininity to the successful athlete, searching for any evidence of feminine activity and interest that might offset her "masculine" sporting achievements and stature. Early coverage of Babe Didrikson invariably juxtaposed her Olympic medals to the blue ribbon she had earned for sewing or baking (reporters differed on the specifics) at the Texas State Fair. . . .

. . . Journalists and sport promoters resolved the incongruity of a female Mars by positing an idealized image of the feminine athlete as beauty queen, mermaid, or fashion model. . . . Thus the "Amazonian" female athlete shed the character of Mars and became Venus.

. . . Coverage of women athletes typically conformed to one of two stories, both of which sought to resolve the tension between athleticism and femininity. In one version the girl or woman athlete assumes a masculine persona while she competes, but after the event drops her "mask" and becomes her true feminine self, illustrated by her overtly feminine demeanor and, in some instances, the search for male love. . . . In a second version a tomboy girl athlete grows up into a champion by honing her "masculine" skills, but along the way trades in her boyish ways for feminine charms.

... The *Saturday Evening Post* cast [Althea] Gibson's remarkable achievements as a black Pygmalion story, describing her transformation from a "street-smart tomboy" to "a little lady.". . . .

The media presented athletes like Didrikson as heroines in a popular success story. But unlike such male heroes as Horatio Alger or Babe Ruth, whose accomplishments in their chosen endeavors enhanced their manhood, women athletes could only achieve a precarious heroic status. It balanced on the tension between "masculine" sporting ability and compensatory efforts to prove their femininity. The tenuous nature of women's athletic heroism found expression in the twin narratives . . . suggested that women's athletic identity was by nature temporary. In this way each scenario admitted women's athleticism without conceding the masculinity of sport or the superiority of men.

In far more subtle ways the everyday practice of sport mirrored the rhetoric of sport journalism. As particular games, styles of play, and concepts of skill were designated as masculine or feminine, gender differences were woven into the very fabric of sport. The gendered structure of athletics worked to reinforce and naturalize the cultural division between "genuine" male sport and a less legitimate female brand of athleticism.

Women have participated at some point and to some degree in all American sports. Whether a sport became popular among girls and women or attracted a primarily male constituency depended on timing, sponsorship, the interest a sport sparked, and the traditions it developed. However, over time certain sports have been seen as appropriate for one sex only. Currently football and boxing are sports that continue to be viewed as male-only sports, while water ballet and rhythmic gymnastics remain exclusively female. . . .

What differentiated ordinary "masculine" athletics from "truly feminine" sport? The masculine image of sport cohered around attributes of strength, size, rigorous training, and aggressive competition, which together made up an ideal of athletic virility. The sports onlookers and officials labeled as too masculine for women were usually sports that emphasized these qualities in the extreme. Rugby, ice hockey, and boxing—rough games involving extensive physical contact and aggression—connoted pure masculinity. Sports that demanded sheer strength or arduous training regimens, like shot-putting or long-distance running, also appeared incommensurate with femininity. In addition rugged team sports with a working-class male profile—like baseball and, by the mid-twentieth century, football—evoked a special aura rooted in the popular conception of working-class men as representatives of raw masculinity.

On the other hand, sports that emphasized the aesthetic side of athletics most often received feminine designations. . . . Sports like diving and gymnastics were understood as more feminine, by virtue of their association with beauty. . . . The camaraderie, playful roughhousing, and physical intimacy of team play projected a manly image, one jealously guarded by male athletes.

A sport's gender theoretically indicated the sex of its main participants. But social class also played an important role in determining the gender reputation of any given sport and of the athletes who played it. The development of bowling illustrates how changes in the class constituency of a sport could also alter its gender designation. The game first gained popularity in the 1890s and early 1900s. . . . Bowling's early links to working-class pool halls, taverns, and gamblers gave it a shady reputation that made it even less respectable for women than for men.

During the depression bowling broadened its appeal, especially among women. . . . The "femininity" of bowling remained in doubt, pulled between contrasting images of matronly middle-class refinement and uncouth working-class rowdiness.

. . . When the popularity of bowling soared in the 1940s and 1950s, *Newsweek* attributed the boom to the fact "that Mama has accepted it as a wholesome recreation not only for her husband but for herself and her whole family." Estimates of one million women bowlers in 1936 . . . reached six to eight million in the 1950s. As ambitious suburban developers built new bowling alleys to meet the recreational needs of young couples and families living outside the city, efforts to tailor the sport toward women grew more and more elaborate. Bowling establishments built coffee shops, beauty parlors, nurseries, and plush lounges, all designed to attract women customers during the daytime hours, when the regular male clientele was at work. . . .

Through such efforts bowling shed both its disreputable working-class image and its purely masculine reputation. It retained its blue-collar appeal but at the same time gained acceptance as a "feminine" sport by successfully associating itself with notions of middle-class feminine respectability and heterosexual leisure. . . .

. . . Cross-sex participation typically led to more extensive gender differentiation within a given sport. In softball, tennis, basketball, track, gymnastics, and other sports, athletic administrators devised gender-specific rules to mark women's activities as different from, and usually "less than," men's.

Regulations on the use of space and time in women's sport acted to limit female activity and to create an impression of lesser physical capacity. For example, to compensate for women softball players' presumed lack of arm strength and accuracy, . . . the pitching distance was shorter for women than for men. In basketball women played for shorter time periods and on a divided court. In tennis, while the court dimensions were the same for men and women, men played five sets and women three [sets]. . . .

Physical touch as well as unrestricted movement acquired masculine associations in sport. Early prohibitions on touch were designed out of concern for female frailty, sexual modesty, and mental health. . . . While "women's rules" minimized physical contact in basketball, "no-slide" rules . . . in women's softball leagues effected the same result. These restrictions contained women's athletic exertion and aggressiveness, at the same time making touch among teammates and between opponents a right (and rite) of manhood.

Along with time, space, and touch, athletic clothing also marked gender differences in sport. Often consciously designed to avert accusations of mannishness, most women's athletic dress accented feminine beauty and preserved feminine modesty. Twentieth-century tennis players eventually shed their long skirts but continued to display their femininity and purity in white, wide-skirted, ruffled dresses. Sports in which male and female uniforms differed the least—track and field and softball—were also the least reputable for women, sometimes prompting compensatory strategies like the AAGBL's use of pastel-skirted baseball uniforms. . . . Where sponsors sought to cash in on the sexual appeal of female athletes, they employed short shorts, sleeveless tops, and bright and shiny colors. . . .

Through athletic policies . . . masculinity and femininity were designated as separate but not equal. Femininity was typically constituted around the edges of sport through references to female beauty and sex appeal. Within sporting activity femininity was defined as "lesser than" (shorter distances, time periods), "different from" (women's rules, special equipment), or "derivative of" ("kitten ball" and "captain ball" as derivatives of baseball and basketball) men's sport. The primary status of male sport found expression in common language, too. Women's presence was signaled with reference to "women's basketball" or the "ladies golf tour," while the unmodified "basketball" or "golf" presumed the presence of men. Similarly, by itself the supposedly neutral noun "athlete" was in common usage a male term. . . .

The gendered rhetoric and everyday practice of sport reinforced sexual divisions and inequalities in the athletic world. More important, these arrangements shaped the contours of gender relations in the wider society, contributing to notions of "natural" male superiority, immutable sexual differences, and normative concepts of manhood and womanhood. . . .

. . . When women's sport is limited to aesthetically pleasing "feminine" activities, it perpetuates the deceptive emphasis on femininity as beauty, masking its ties to female subordination. For instance, the idea that women should compete primarily in "beauty-producing" sports like swimming, gymnastics, and ice-skating (even through they, in fact, also demand strength and competitive intensity) simply reinforces the belief that muscles, aggressiveness, and competitiveness are neither feminine nor beautiful in a woman. And by barring women from strength-building contact sports like wrestling or football, the sports world reaffirms the expectation of female passivity, submissiveness, and frailty—the demeaning aspects of femininity that underlie the aesthetic.

Cultural characterizations of masculine skill, feminine weakness, and natural male superiority . . . have had the power to influence lives, particularly by generating normative and stigmatized conceptions of manhood and womanhood. When boys and men participate in athletics, they are steeped in a culture of masculinity. . . . But those men who do not like (or excel in) sports are excluded from this path to masculine achievement. . . .

The process has worked in reverse for women's sport, in which the concept of masculinity has fostered a stigmatizing rather than a normative image of the female athlete. For this reason the majority of women have steered clear of competitive sport and the cultural traits associated with it. . . .

Early childhood experiences of sport as positive and permissible provided an initial resource against the unflattering image of the "mannish" female athlete. Successful women athletes who came of age in mid-twentieth-century America often grew up in working-class or rural enclaves where to be a "tomboy" or "outdoor girl" made one distinctive but not unacceptable. . . . Although occasionally teased by peers or discouraged by family members, young athletes on their way up were generally given a certain amount of freedom and encouragement. . . . This support instilled confidence in childhood athletes and nurtured their sense that sport was both natural and good. . . .

The liberties of girlhood did not survive the transitions to adolescence and adulthood, however. Young women who continued to compete past puberty eventually encountered the harsher image of the "mannish athlete." They realized, as Mary Pratt explained, that there was "some kind of stigma, that if you were too competitive it was wrong."

The belief that women who excelled in sport did so at the expense of their femininity was a source of irritation, anger, and concern among athletes. Yet, few stopped playing sports or dramatically altered their behavior upon realizing that their athletic ability could mark them as deviant. The tensions athletes felt were mitigated by the personal satisfaction and social possibilities they found in sport. Travel, public recognition, and a sense of belonging made athletics a worthwhile endeavor. The opportunities and the affirmation that accompanied their athletic involvement nurtured feelings of confidence and self-worth. These advantages far outweighed any fears they might have harbored about the public image of women in sport. They also provided a resource for women attempting to counter the female athlete's mannish reputation with positive images derived from their own experience.

Growing up on farms, in small towns, or in insular urban neighborhoods, most women athletes had traveled little prior to their involvement in competitive sports. While fondly recalling first train rides, fine hotels, and the wonder of venturing into new worlds, athletes also put their travel experience in a broader framework, explaining that it opened social, economic, and cultural doors that might have remained closed without sports. Phyllis Koehn spoke of baseball as a well-paid, exciting job that allowed her to escape the low-wage, monotonous clerical jobs held by many of her peers. . . . With or without financial compensation, athletic involvement heightened women's sense of independence and expanded their options. . . .

For committed female athletes sport had everything to do not only with what they did, but with who they were. In recalling the physical pleasures and social benefits of sport, many athletes explained that their social worlds and personal identities had become integrally bound up with athletic activity. This kind of personal identification with athletics created a foundation from which to challenge those who doubted their femininity or condemned their athleticism.

[They] found a sense of belonging at the playground, in high school GAAs, in college P.E. departments, and on industrial teams. They gravitated toward sport as a place where they felt accepted and appreciated in the company of like-minded peers. . . .

For those athletes who as children were teased or rebuked for tomboy behavior, the satisfaction of sport became a crucial part of identities forged in rebellion against restrictive gender conventions. . . . Grounded in their own positive experience of sport and bolstered by its social rewards, women involved in high-level competition eventually had to come to terms with the stereotype of the mannish female athlete. From the moment that personal identities and public images clashed, athletes searched for ways to reconcile their positive experiences with the idea "that it wasn't really the feminine thing to do to play [sports], . . . that maybe you had to be a little bit masculine."

Some athletes simply acknowledged that there were competing interpretations, matter-of-factly noting and accepting the discrepancy between disparaging messages from the wider culture and more positive attitudes rooted closer to home. Chicago ballplayer Irene Kotowicz summarized commonly held views of her day: "This is what people think—only men play sports. And if a woman likes sports, there's something wrong with her." Yet in an apparently contradictory statement, she also insisted that in her own community women athletes were completely accepted, so much so that she never thought twice about her intense involvement in sport. "We just did it," she stated, "because gals played ball then. They played softball and everything else, so it wasn't anything." Athletes like [Irene] Kotowicz developed a double awareness that allowed them to move skillfully between conflicting systems of meaning. . . .

Other women were more troubled by the stereotype of the mannish athlete and tried to resolve the difference between this negative portrait and their own understanding of female athletes as "normal" women. For these athletes maintaining a feminine image carried great importance. They argued in favor of dress codes, public relations stunts like beauty contests, and the suppression of any mention of lesbianism, real or imagined, in sport. Yet in doing so they did not necessarily accept the wider culture's definition of feminine and masculine traits. Instead they subtly reinterpreted femininity, expanding its borders to include the very athletic qualities that many perceived as masculine.

One common approach was for athletes to acknowledge that there were mannish athletic types and to agree that they deserved to be criticized but then insist that they themselves and the women with whom they played were certainly not among them. . . . Women who curled their hair, wore lipstick, "primped," or, most important, were known to be "nice" or "decent" individuals qualified as feminine even if they happened to be aggressive, rough, or very muscular. . . .

Hirst, Jordan, Futch, and Gleaves accepted the basic premise of natural gender distinctions to which, in principle, men and women should conform. Yet they also rejected the equation of athleticism with masculinity, employing an elastic definition of femininity based on personal reputation and on compliance with the often more flexible gender standards of local neighborhoods, rural communities, and peer groups. Femininity, by this standard, was an assumed rather than a proven trait, jeopardized only by an exceptionally "mannish" style. . . .

. . . Women athletes created standards of judgment that balanced received cultural messages with more familiar understandings rooted in personal experience and local cultures. This allowed them to articulate nuanced, complex definitions of womanhood—concepts that went beyond a simple acceptance of the status quo to expand the parameters of womanhood significantly. . . .

In contrast to those who tried to stretch prevailing concepts of gender, some athletes simply ridiculed and rejected imposed standards of femininity. They might adhere to dress and conduct codes rather than lose the opportunity to play, but this in no way implied agreement. Forced to attend the AAGBL's spring charm school, . . . [Josephine] D'Angelo recalled: "They had some professional ladies come in and give us makeup lessons, and how to walk and how to dress and how to talk and how to use a fork and knife and spoon and all that. . . . We thought it was hilarious.". . .

Rather than untangle the labyrinth of attitudes and values behind this insinuation, many athletes simply claimed that masculinity and femininity were irrelevant to sport. . . . A number of women dismissed cultural disputes over gender by insisting on the essential goodness, naturalness, or nongendered character of sport. . . .

. . . Recognizing the fact that "there are some women who are more competitive, more aggressive, [and] better skilled," [Ann] Maguire commented, "we've always assigned the term 'masculine' [to them], and I don't think that's the appropriate term." She expressed her personal belief that sport had no natural gender, but at the same time theorized that sport had become so important in some women's lives precisely because it enabled them to express feelings or interests that *others* labeled boyish, mannish, or deviant. . . .

All women in sport had to reckon with the power of the surrounding culture to stigmatize skilled female athletes. Images of mannishness, lesbianism, ugliness, and biological abnormality circulated through society, posing barriers to female athletic participation and placing an especially heavy burden on women whose very excellence evoked the nastiest kinds of accusations. However, this ideology was not monolithic. The majority of women athletes understood that their athletic ability made their femininity suspect. But in various ways they rejected or embraced only selectively the gender norms of mid-twentieth-century America.

This refusal almost never took the form of political action or critique, however. Given public hostility toward aggressive, mannish athletes, many women in sport accommodated, sometimes willingly, to pressures that they demonstrate their femininity and conform to gender conventions inside and outside of sport. Almost none saw themselves as feminist or working-class dissenters in revolt against the tyranny of middle-class gender and sexual codes. Most women simply enjoyed sports and, feeling lucky to have the opportunity to play, spent little time developing a public stance against gender inequality in sport or society.

Yet women athletes demonstrated an independence of thought and action that belied consent. As a group they lacked the social authority to topple the barriers to full female participation in sport or to resolve the cultural contradiction between sport and femininity. But their persistence, their passions, and their skills spoke to the belief that sport and womanhood were not opposed and that sport itself had no necessary gender. . . .

. . . Between 1900 and the 1960s women's presence and skill in a masculine domain had become integral to the process of making and managing gender in American society. The unsettling effects of women's athletic endeavors revealed the instability of gender and sexual arrangements many people preferred to view as natural and fixed. Women's persistent claims to "masculine" skills and games suggested that gender divisions were malleable cultural constructs and, furthermore, were matters for social and political debate. . . .

. . . Sport advocates who maintained their commitment to increasing women's athletic opportunities and by women athletes who asserted . . . their right to define sport and womanhood on their own terms, . . . forged a female athletic tradition that granted at least some women the chance to develop skills and confidence while enjoying the pleasures of physical play. Within this tradition women found space for expressions of female community and identity that stretched beyond restrictive concepts of femininity. It was women's bold insistence on the right to play and their willingness to create and model expansive definitions of womanhood that formed the thread between the early and middle decades of the twentieth century and the dramatic changes of recent years.

FURTHER READING

Adrienne Blue, *Faster, Higher, Further: Women's Triumphs and Disasters at the Olympics* (1988)

Lois Browne, *Girls of Summer* (1992)

Mariah Nelson Burton, *Are We Winning Yet? How Women Are Changing Sports and Sports Are Changing Women* (1991)

Susan K. Cahn, *Coming on Strong: Gender and Sexuality in Twentieth-Century Women's Sport* (1994)

Linda Jean Carpenter, "The Impact of Title IX on Women's Intercollegiate Sports," in Arthur T. Johnson and James H. Frey, eds., *Government and Sport* (1985)

Susan Cayleff, *Babe: The Life and Legend of Babe Didrikson Zaharias* (1995)

Mary Jo Festle, "Politics and Apologies: Women's Sports in the U.S., 1950–1985," Ph.D. diss., University of North Carolina (1985)

Merrie A. Fiddler, "The All-American Girls' Baseball League, 1943–1954," in *Her Story in Sport,* ed. Reet Howell (1982)

Barbara Gregorich, *Women at Play* (1993)

Allen Guttmann, *Women's Sport: A History* (1991)

Reet Howell, ed., *Her Story in Sport* (1982)

Joan Hult, "The Philosophical Differences in Men's and Women's Collegiate Athletics," *Quest* 32 (1980), 77–94

Joan Hult, "Women's Struggle for Governance in U.S. Amateur Sports," *International Review for Sociology of Sport* 24 (1989), 249–63

Susan E. Johnson, *When Women Played Hardball* (1994)

Mary Lou LeCompte, *Cowgirls of the Rodeo: Pioneer Professional Athletes* (1993)

Benjamin G. Rader, "The Quest for Self-Sufficiency and the New Strenuosity," *Journal of Sport History* 18 (1991), 255–67

CHAPTER
13

Sport and Race in America Since 1945

✖

Race was an important factor in American sport prior to World War II, and, if anything, it has become an even more prominent variable since then. Before the war Americans had begun to recognize the abilities of African-American athletes, most notably Jesse Owens and Joe Louis. Then during the war, when African-American soldiers were dying for their country, there were growing demands by civil rights leaders and liberal politicians for racial equality, which included integration of the playing fields.

Jackie Robinson broke color lines in 1946 when he played with the Montreal Royals, the top farm club of the Brooklyn Dodgers, and the professional football leagues followed suit when they hired their first African-American players in twelve years. One year later Robinson joined the Dodgers. Why is Jackie Robinson one of the most important men of the twentieth century? Why have historians considered his becoming a Dodger a pivotal event in modern American history?

Integration actually took place at a slow pace—it was twelve years before the last major league team, the Boston Red Sox, became integrated. Furthermore, blacks were "stacked" into certain less central positions like outfielder or cornerback rather than catcher or quarterback, and informal quotas limited the number of African-Americans that a team might keep on its roster or play at the same time. On the collegiate level, certain southern schools would not play football or basketball teams having African-Americans as late as the early 1960s, and some southern schools fielded white-only teams until the late 1960s. It was then that the Black Athletic Revolt emerged to fight racism, mainly on college campuses, but wherever it existed, most notably the apartheid in South Africa. The movement raised the consciousness of college athletes and their supporters; between 1967 and 1971 there were protests against racism at thirty-seven schools. What emboldened African-American student-athletes to fight prejudice in sports?

Historians point to factors such as the civil rights movement, the Black Power movement, and role models—most notably heavyweight champion Muhammad Ali. Ali defied conventional norms by his outspokenness, his conversion to the Muslim religion, and his refusal, on religious grounds, to serve in the military. He paid for that decision by having his title taken from him. By the 1980s, when 80 percent

370

of the NBA was black, and most NFL players were black, the most glaring elements of racism had been eliminated, particularly in salaries and stacking. However, African-American athletes were still limited when they sought to gain substantial long-term benefits from sport. They disproportionately failed out of college, and these young people remained very underrepresented in athletic leadership positions, both on and off the field.

⚾ D O C U M E N T S

The first document is a private report to the American League by Yankees president Larry McPhail in 1946 on the issue of integrated baseball. It had been strongly pushed by Bill Veeck, a minor league owner who had tried to buy the Philadelphia Phillies in 1943 and stock them with Negro League stars. However, Baseball Commissioner Kenesaw Mountain Landis had blocked Veeck's bid. McPhail, like most of the leaders in organized baseball, opposed integration, and in this presentation he argued that integration would be bad for African-Americans. However, the integration of baseball went on despite his criticisms, and Dodgers president Branch Rickey signed Jackie Robinson to a minor league contract.

Robinson was not a star in the Negro Leagues, but he had been an all-around superstar athlete at UCLA and an All-American in football. He had grown up in an integrated world in Los Angeles, was a former army officer, and was married to a sophisticated African-American woman. The second document examines his first spring training in 1946. What problems did he encounter in his initial experience with white baseball?

The third document consists of various statements made by Muhammad Ali during the late 1960s when he was barred from fighting for refusing induction into the Army.

In the fourth document, sociologist Harry Edwards of the University of California, Berkeley, reviews the origins of the Black Athletic Revolt he began in 1967 by organizing students at San Jose State to fight racism both at the college and in its athletic program.

The final document examines the attitude of the late Arthur Ashe toward the issue of Proposition 48. The NCAA adopted this edict in 1983 to promote higher educational achievement by prospective student-athletes. It required them to achieve a 700 on the SAT tests and commensurate grades before they could be granted an athletic scholarship. Many African-Americans objected to this as racist because most of the athletes affected were African-Americans. Ashe, along with certain authorities like Dr. Edwards, courageously spoke out against the majority because he recognized the ephemeral value of sport as a means of social mobility, especially when compared with educational achievement.

Yankees President Larry McPhail's Plan to Discourage Integration of Baseball, 1946

The appeal of baseball is not limited to any racial group. The Negro takes great interest in baseball and is, and always has been, among the most loyal supporters of professional baseball. . . .

From Larry McPhail, "Plan to American League on Discouraging Integration of Baseball," in U.S. Congress, Committee on the Judiciary, *Organized Baseball* (Washington, D.C.: Government Printing Office, 1952), 483–85.

The American people are primarily concerned with the excellence and performance in sport rather than the color, race, or creed of the performer. . . .

Baseball will jeopardize its leadership in professional sport if it fails to give full appreciation to the fact that the Negro fan and the Negro player are part and parcel of the game. Certain groups in this country, including political and social-minded drumbeaters, are conducting pressure campaigns in an attempt to force major league clubs to sign Negro players. Members of these groups are not primarily interested in professional baseball. They are not campaigning to provide better opportunity for thousands of Negro boys who want to play baseball. They are not even particularly interested in improving the lot of Negro players who are already employed. They know little about baseball—and nothing about the business end of its operation. They single out professional baseball for attack because it offers a good publicity medium.

These people who charge that baseball is flying a Jim Crow flag at its masthead—or that racial discrimination is the basic reason for failure of the major leagues to give employment to Negroes—are simply talking through their individual or collective hats. Professional baseball is a private business enterprise. It has to depend on profits for its existence, just like any other business. It is a business in which Negroes, as well as whites, have substantial investments in parks, franchises, and player contracts. Professional baseball, both Negro and white, has grown and prospered over a period of many years on the basis of separate leagues. The employment of a Negro on one AAA League club in 1946 resulted in a tremendous increase in Negro attendance at all games in which the player appeared. The percentage of Negro attendance at some games at Newark and Baltimore was in excess of 50 percent. The situation might be presented, if Negroes participate in major-league games, in which the preponderance of Negro attendance in parks such as the Yankee Stadium, the Polo Grounds, and Comiskey Park could conceivably threaten the value of the major league franchises owned by these clubs.

The thousands of Negro boys of ability who aspire to careers in professional baseball should have a better opportunity. . . . Signing a few Negro players for the major leagues would be a gesture—but it would contribute little or nothing toward a solution of the real problem. Let's look at the facts:

(1) A major-league baseball player must have something besides great natural ability. He must possess the technique, the coordination, the competitive attitude, and the discipline which is usually acquired only after years of training in the minor leagues. The minor-league experience of players on the major-league rosters, for instance, averages 7 years. The young Negro player never has had a good chance in baseball. Comparatively few good young Negro players are being developed. This is the reason that there are not more players who meet major-league standards in the big Negro leagues. Sam Lacey, sports editor of the Afro-American newspapers, says, "I am reluctant to say that we haven't a single man in the ranks of colored baseball who could step into the major league uniform and disport himself after the fashion of a big leaguer. . . . Mr. Lacey's opinions are shared by almost everyone, Negro or white, competent to appraise the qualifications of Negro players.

(2) About 400 Negro professionals are under contract to the 24 clubs in four Negro leagues. Negro leagues have made substantial progress in recent years. Negro baseball is now a $2,000,000 business. One club, the Kansas City Monarchs, drew over 300,000 people to its home and road games in 1944 and 1945. Over

50,000 people paid $72,000 to witness the east-west game at the White Sox Stadium in Chicago. A Negro-league game established the all-time attendance record for Griffith Stadium in Washington. The average attendance at Negro games in the Yankee Stadium is over 10,000 per game.

These Negro leagues cannot exist without good players. If they cannot field good teams, they will not continue to attract the fans who click the turnstiles. . . . If the major leagues and the big minors of professional baseball raid these leagues and take their best players—the Negro leagues will eventually fold up . . . a lot of professional Negro players will lose their jobs. The Negroes who own and operate these clubs do not want to part with their outstanding players—no one accuses them of racial discrimination.

(3) The Negro leagues rent their parks in many cities from clubs in organized baseball. Many major and minor league clubs derive substantial revenue from these rentals. (The Yankee organization, for instance, nets nearly $100,000 a year from rentals and concessions.) . . . Club owners in the major leagues are reluctant to give up revenues amounting to hundreds of thousands of dollars every year. They naturally want the Negro leagues to continue. They do not sign, and cannot properly sign, players under contract to Negro clubs. This is not racial discrimination. It's simply respecting the contractual relationship between the Negro leagues and their players. . . .

There are many factors in this problem and many difficulties which will have to be solved before any generally satisfactory solution can be worked out. The individual action of any club may exert tremendous pressure upon the whole structure of professional baseball and could conceivably result in lessening the value of several major league franchises. . . .

Jackie Robinson on the Struggles of His First Spring Training, 1946

We had a tough time getting to Daytona Beach. At one point we had to give up our seats because the Army still had priority on planes. So we took a train to Jacksonville, and when we got there we found we'd have to go the rest of the way by bus. We didn't like the bus, and we particularly didn't like the back seat when there were empty seats near the center. Florida law designates where Negroes are to ride in public conveyances. The law says: "Back seat." We rode there.

When we arrived in Daytona Beach we were met at the bus station by Wendell Smith, sports editor of *The Pittsburgh Courier,* and Billy Rowe, a photographer for the same paper. They had been there about four days and had arranged housing accommodations and other necessities. With them was Johnny Wright, a good friend of mine and a pitcher for the Homestead Grays of the Negro National League. Mr. Rickey had signed Johnny to a Montreal contract not long after he had signed me.

From Jack R. Robinson and Wendell Smith, *Jackie Robinson: My Own Story* (New York: Greenberg, 1948), 65–68, 70–75, 79–80.

Johnny had come up with a good record in the Negro National League and had been a star pitcher for a Navy team in 1945.

They took us to the home of a prominent Negro family. The rest of the team usually stayed at a big hotel on the ocean front, but this particular time they were quartered at Sanford, Florida, where the Dodger organization was looking over at least two hundred players.

As a result of our transportation difficulties, I was two days late. I learned from Smith and Rowe that Mr. Rickey was a bit upset about my late arrival; so we decided to get up early next morning and drive to Sanford, which is some twenty miles south of Daytona Beach.

We arrived in Sanford the next morning about ten o'clock, but instead of going to the ball park, we decided to go to the home of Mr. Brock, a well-to-do Negro citizen of the town and call Mr. Rickey. We had to feel our way in this entire matter. We didn't want to cause a commotion or upset anything by walking into the park and surprising everyone. It was no secret that Johnny and I were going to be there, but we felt it best to remain as inconspicuous as possible.

Smith called Mr. Rickey at his hotel and he told us we should get over to the park as soon as possible. We took our shoes and gloves and hurried over. Clyde Sukeforth met us. We shook hands. "Go right into the dressing room and get your uniforms," he said. "Babe Hamburger, our clubhouse man, is in there. He'll see that you get fixed up."

I glanced at the players on the field. They had come from every section of the country—two hundred men out there, all hoping some day to become members of the Brooklyn Dodgers. Some were tossing balls to each other; others were hitting fungoes to the outfielders; still others were running around the field conditioning their legs. Suddenly I felt uncomfortably conspicuous standing there. Every single man on the field seemed to be staring at Johnny Wright and me. . . .

We ducked into the clubhouse. It was empty save for one man, a big, fat fellow. I felt a bit tense and I'm sure Johnny did, too. We were ill at ease and didn't know exactly what to do next. The man saw us then and came right over and introduced himself. "Hiya, fellows," he said with a big, broad smile on his face. "I'm Babe Hamburger. . . . Robinson and Wright, eh? Well, that's swell. Which one is Robinson?"

I put out my hand and he gave it a hearty shake. "This is Johnny Wright," I said. Johnny shook Babe's big, soft mitt.

"Well, fellows," he said, "I'm not exactly what you'd call a part of this great experiment, but I'm gonna give you some advice anyway. Just go out there and do your best. Don't get tense. Just be yourselves."

Be ourselves? Here in the heart of the race-conscious South? . . . Johnny and I both realized that this was hostile territory—that anything could happen any time to a Negro who thought he could play ball with white men on an equal basis. It was going to be difficult to relax and behave naturally. But we assured Babe we'd try. . . .

We finally got dressed and headed for the field. Waiting for us was a group of reporters from New York, Pittsburgh, Baltimore, Montreal, and Brooklyn. They surrounded us and started firing questions:

"What are you going to do if the pitchers start throwing at you?" one of them asked.

"The same thing everyone else does," I answered, smiling. "Duck!"

The next morning we were up bright and early. We went out to the park in a taxi and this time dressed with the rest of the players. Practice that day was a bit long, but not at all strenuous.

When we got back to Brock's, Johnny and I found Wendell Smith and Billy Rowe, our newspaper friends from Pittsburgh, waiting for us. Usually, they joked and kidded with us a lot; but that night they were both exceptionally quiet and sober. We all ate together. The conversation dragged until I began to feel uncomfortable. . . .

Rowe got up from the table suddenly and said to Smith, "I'm going to fill up with gas." He had a red Pontiac that he used to cover his assignments.

"We should be able to get out of here in fifteen or twenty minutes," Smith said. "Daytona isn't far, either."

"You guys leaving us?" I asked curiously.

"No," Smith said. "We're all going to Daytona.". . .

"What about practice in the morning?" I asked. "After all, we came here to make the Montreal Club."

I was angry. What was this all about, anyway? No one had told us to move on to Daytona. . . . After all, things had been going beautifully. The first two days of practice had passed without a single incident. Surely we weren't being rejected after only a two-day trial! We were just beginning to loosen up a bit. The tenseness was going away. I was beginning to feel free and good inside.

As I sat there getting sorer by the minute, I heard Smith talking on the telephone: "Yes, Mr. Rickey," he said, "I'm with them now. We're pulling out for Daytona in about twenty minutes. Just as soon as they get their bags packed." I heard Rowe's car pull up in the driveway. . . .

We piled into the car and started for Daytona. Rowe was driving and Smith was sitting beside him. Johnny was in the back with me. None of us said a word. We stopped at the main intersection of the town for a traffic light. A group of men were standing on the street corner in their shirt sleeves. It looked like a typical small-town bull session.

I suddenly decided that Sanford wasn't a bad town at all. The people had been friendly to us. Apparently they liked ball players. The men on the corner turned to look at us. Easy-going guys, curious over where we were going—certainly not hostile, I thought. I smiled at them. I actually felt like waving.

Rowe broke the silence for the first time as the light changed and we picked up speed. "How can people like that call themselves Americans!" he said bitterly. . . .

"Now just a minute," I said "They haven't done anything to us. They're nice people as far as I'm concerned.". . .

"Yeah," Smith said, swinging around and looking us in the face. His eyes were blazing with anger. "Sure, they liked you. They were in love with you. . . . That's why we're leaving."

"What do you mean?" I asked.

"I don't get it," chimed in Johnny.

"You will," Rowe said. "You will."

"Look," Smith said, "we didn't want to tell you guys because we didn't want to upset you. We want you to make this ball club. But . . . we're leaving this town because we've been told to get out. They won't stand for Negro ball players on the same field with whites!". . .

The expulsion from Sanford was a humiliating experience. I found myself wishing I had never gotten mixed up in the whole business. When the club moved into Daytona, our permanent training base, what hope was there that I would not be kicked out of town just as I had been in Sanford? I was sure that as soon as I walked out on the field, an objection would be raised. I didn't want to go through that all over again. What could I do? Quit? . . . I wanted to; but I just didn't have the nerve to walk out on all the people who were counting on me—my family and close friends, Mr. Rickey, the fourteen million Negroes from coast to coast, the legion of understanding white people. Dejected as I was, I just had to stick it out.

The rest of the team was quartered in a big hotel overlooking the Atlantic Ocean. I stayed in the home of a private family in the Negro section of the town. When we finished practice, I'd go home and play cards with Smith, Rowe, and my wife. Once in a while we'd go to a movie. There was only one Negro movie in town and the picture ran for three days. Consequently we'd see two pictures a week. Often there was absolutely nothing to do. Our life was so restricted and monotonous that sometimes we would go to see the same movie twice.

Now and then some of the local Negroes would invite us to dinner or for a game of cards. There was also a USO Club near-by and some evenings I'd go there to play table tennis or pinochle. But no matter how I tried I couldn't find a sufficient diversion to preoccupy me. I found myself stewing over the problems which I knew were bound to confront me sooner or later. . . .

We were scheduled to play an exhibition game with the Jersey City Giants in Jacksonville. We made the trip by bus, and when we arrived at the park there was a big crowd waiting outside. We climbed out and went over to the players' gate leading onto the field. It was locked. We couldn't get in; nor, apparently, could the waiting fans.

"What's wrong here?" [Montreal manager] Hopper asked a man standing near-by.

"The game's been called off," the man said. "The Bureau of Recreation won't let the game be played because you've got colored guys on your club."

Mel Jones got hold of Charley Stoneham, the Jersey City business manager, and found that the man's report was correct. George Robinson, executive secretary of the Bureau of Recreation, had informed the Jersey City club that he would not allow the game to be played. There was nothing for us to do but drive back to Daytona. . . .

The Thoughts of Muhammad Ali in Exile, c. 1967

"I never thought of myself as great when I refused to go into the Army. All I did was stand up for what I believed. There were people who thought the war in Viet-

From Thomas Hauser, *Muhammad Ali: His Life and Times* (New York: Simon and Schuster, 1991), 171–72, 187–89.

nam was right. And those people, if they went to war, acted just as brave as I did. There were people who tried to put me in jail. Some of them were hypocrites, but others did what they thought was proper and I can't condemn them for following their conscience either. People say I made a sacrifice, risking jail and my whole career. But God told Abraham to kill his son and Abraham was willing to do it, so why shouldn't I follow what I believed? Standing up for my religion made me happy; it wasn't a sacrifice. When people got drafted and sent to Vietnam and didn't understand what the killing was about and came home with one leg and couldn't get jobs, that was a sacrifice. But I believed in what I was doing, so no matter what the government did to me, it wasn't a loss.

"Some people thought I was a hero. Some people said that what I did was wrong. But everything I did was according to my conscience. I wasn't trying to be a leader. I just wanted to be free. And I made a stand all people, not just black people, should have thought about making, because it wasn't just black people being drafted. The government had a system where the rich man's son went to college, and the poor man's son went to war. Then, after the rich man's son got out of college, he did other things to keep him out of the Army until he was too old to be drafted. So what I did was for me, but it was the kind of decision everyone has to make. Freedom means being able to follow your religion, but it also means carrying the responsibility to choose between right and wrong. So when the time came for me to make up my mind about going in the Army, I knew people were dying in Vietnam for nothing and I should live by what I thought was right. I wanted America to be America. And now the whole world knows that, so far as my own beliefs are concerned, I did what was right for me."

Time and again on college campuses, Ali sounded themes important to him:

On the war in Vietnam: "I'm expected to go overseas to help free people in South Vietnam, and at the same time my people here are being brutalized and mistreated, and this is really the same thing that's happening over in Vietnam. So I'm going to fight it legally, and if I lose, I'm just going to jail. Whatever the punishment, whatever the persecution is for standing up for my beliefs, even if it means facing machine-gun fire that day, I'll face it before denouncing Elijah Muhammad and the religion of Islam."

On being stripped of his title and denied the right to fight: "The power structure seems to want to starve me out. The punishment, five years in jail, ten-thousand-dollar fine, ain't enough. They want to stop me from working, not only in this country but out of it. Not even a license to fight an exhibition for charity, and that's in this twentieth century. You read about these things in the dictatorship countries, where a man don't go along with this or that and he is completely not allowed to work or to earn a decent living."

On the financial hardship he was enduring: "What do I need money for? I don't spend no money. Don't drink, don't smoke, don't go nowhere, don't go running with women. I take my wife out and we eat ice cream. . . .

On lack of black pride: "We've been brainwashed. Everything good is supposed to be white. We look at Jesus, and we see a white with blond hair and blue eyes. We look at all the angels; we see white with blond hair and blue eyes. Now, I'm sure there's a heaven in the sky and colored folks die and go to heaven. Where are the colored angels? They must be in the kitchen preparing milk and honey. We look at Miss America, we see white. We look at Miss World, we see white. We look at Miss Universe, we see white. Even Tarzan, the king of the jungle in black Africa, he's white. White Owl Cigars. White Swan soap, White Cloud tissue paper, White Rain hair rinse, White Tornado floor wax. All the good cowboys ride the white horses and wear white hats. Angel food cake is the white cake, but the devils food cake is chocolate. When are we going to wake up as a people and end the lie that white is better than black?"

On hate: "I don't hate nobody and I ain't lynched nobody. We Muslims don't hate the white man. It's like we don't hate a tiger; but we know that a tiger's nature is not compatible with people's nature since tigers love to eat people. So we don't want to live with tigers. It's the same with the white man. The white race attacks black people. They don't ask what's our religion, what's our belief? They just start whupping heads. They don't ask you, are you Catholic, are you a Baptist, are you a Black Muslim, are you a Martin Luther King follower, are you with Whitney Young? They just go whop, whop, whop! So we don't want to live with the white man; that's all."

Harry Edwards Reviews the Making of the Black Athletic Revolt, 1967

. . . Early rumblings of revolt revolved around the issues of segregation and social discrimination. For instance, in the late fifties and middle sixties, there were numerous cases where black athletes refused to participate due to discrimination in spectator seating at athletic events or because of discriminatory practices encountered by the athletes themselves. A firm indication that a revolt was brewing appeared in 1965 when the black athletes chosen to play in the American Football League's East-West All-Star game banned together and refused to play in New Orleans, Louisiana, because several of the Afro-American stars had been refused entrance to some of the city's social clubs. As a result of the athletes' threat to boycott the event, Joe Foss, then commissioner of the league, had the game moved to another city. This incident marked the first time in modern athletic history that a sporting event had actually been changed to another site because of discrimination against Afro-American participants. And the threat succeeded largely because of the unity among the black athletes involved, a unity forged from their firm conviction that they were men and that they in fact were going to be treated as such. . . .

After the 1964 games, black athletes got together and talked about the possibility of a black boycott of the 1968 Olympics to be held in Mexico. They discussed the justifications for the move and also the possible ramifications.

Then in the fall of 1967, two events occurred that brought all the talk and discussion to a head. First, Tommie Smith, in Tokyo for the University Games, casually commented that some black athletes would perhaps boycott the 1968

From Harry Edwards, *The Revolt of the Black Athlete* (New York: Free Press, 1969), 40–47.

Olympics. . . . A Japanese sports reporter had asked, "Do I understand correctly that there is talk in America about the possibility that black American athletes may boycott the 1968 Olympic games at Mexico?" Smith answered, "Yes, this is true. Some black athletes have been discussing the possibility of boycotting the games to protest racial injustice in America.". . . The major American wire services and most of the country's sports pages carried the story, proclaiming that Tommie Smith had stated that there was considerable sentiment among black athletes favoring a boycott of the Olympic games in order to protest racial injustice. . . .

The second event was a revolt of black students and athletes at San Jose State College in California, . . . the institution at which Tommie Smith and a number of other "world-class" athletes were matriculating. The significance of this event was that sixty of the seventy-two Afro-American students on campus (out of a college enrollment of 24,000) had banded together and for the first time in history utilized collegiate athletics as a lever to bring about social, academic, and political changes at an educational institution. The whole plan for the revolt originated from a discussion between me and Kenneth Noel, then a master's degree candidate. . . . He, like most of the black males on the campus, was a former athlete. Most of the Afro-American males on San Jose State College's campus were former athletes who no longer had any college athletic eligibility left but who had not yet graduated. . . . It suddenly dawned on us that the same social and racial injustices and discrimination that had dogged our footsteps as freshmen at San Jose were still rampant on campus—racism in the fraternities and sororities, racism in housing, racism and out-and-out mistreatment in athletics, and a general lack of understanding of the problems of Afro-Americans by the college administration.

Our first move was to approach the administration. We were promptly referred to the Dean of Students, Stanley Benz. It did not take him long to make it crystal clear that, where the interest and desires of the majority whites were concerned, the necessities of black students were inconsequential. At this point, we felt that we had no alternative but to move into the public arena. So we called a rally to commence at noon on the opening day of classes for the fall, 1967, semester . . . [for] the elimination of racism at San Jose State College. We invited all faculty members and administration officials.

We outlined a list of demands and stated publicly what our strategy would be if our demands were not met. We, in effect, declared that we would prevent the opening football game of the season from being played by any means necessary. Most observers felt that this was an inconsistent and self-defeating strategy. Why stop the football game? Why attack the only area that had granted black people full equality?

Our strategy was basically a simple one. First of all, we recognized something that perhaps the casual observer did not—that athletics was, in fact, as racist as any of the other areas of college life. Second, we felt that we had to utilize a power lever that would bring the community and student body as well as the administration of the college into the pressure situation. We had seen, all too often, the spectacle of black people demonstrating and picketing groups, organizations, and institutions of limited concern to people in positions of power. We therefore decided to use something more central to the concerns of the entire local community structure—athletics. What activity is of more relevance to a student body than the first football game of the season? What activity is of more relevance to a college town after a long and economically drought-stricken summer than the first big game? And what is of more immediate importance to a college administration than the threat of stopping a game that had been contracted for under a $12,000 breach of contract clause and the cancellation of all future competition commitments if the game were not played? The faculty also was deeply involved in the affair, particularly the faculty of the Department of Men's Physical Education and Intercollegiate Athletics. For some of the black athletes had threatened to boycott the game if the black students were forced to try to stop it.

The rally was a success and immediately afterward an organization was formed, the United Black Students for Action. It was composed chiefly of Afro-American students. . . . Our demands were as follows:

U.B.S.A. Demands

We the affiliates of United Black Students for Action, hereby put forth the following *DEMANDS:*

Public deliberation of *all* problems and proposed solutions relevant to the situation of minority groups at SJS.

Publicly announced pledges from the SJS Administration that housing—*approved, unapproved, fraternities,* and *sororities* not open to ALL SJS students will not be open to *any* student. . . .

That the highest authority . . . of *any* and *all* social and political organizations be required to stipulate *in writing* before November 1, 1967, that its particular organizational branch on the SJS campus is open to *all* students. . . .

That the Dept. of Intercollegiate Athletics organize and put into operation *immediately* an effective program that provides the same treatment and handling for all athletes including visiting prospective athletes.

That the Dept. of Intercollegiate Athletics make a public statement denouncing the racist principles upon which the present fraternity system functions and secondly, that they publicly dissociate themselves and their dept. from this system.

That the college administration either work to expand the 2% rule to bring underprivileged minority group members to SJS as students at least in proportion to their representation in the general population of California. . . .

That a permanent commission be set up to administer and operate a "tutorial" type program aimed at the recruitment of minority group members. . . .

The end result of the confrontation was that the college administration moved to meet our demands, but not before tension had reached such a pitch that the game had to be called off. . . .

So we had carried the confrontation. But more than this, we had learned the use of power—the power to be gained from exploiting the white man's economic and almost religious involvement in athletics.

Arthur Ashe on Propositions 42 and 48, c. 1980s

. . . "Prop 48" sought to raise the high-school academic requirements for students entering college who wished to compete in intercollegiate athletics. Incoming freshmen who did not meet these academic requirements could be given scholarships but could not play for their schools during their first year. "Prop 42," passed later, sought to deny athletic scholarships to such students. Behind the proposals were not only a spate of recent scandals in which former college athletes with degrees proved to be semi-literate but also a deepening sense that many athletic departments had subverted the true mission of their colleges and universities in the name of athletic success. The issue became charged with racial tones because a disproportionately high percentage of college athletes in the major American sports—football, basketball, baseball, and track—are black.

The black presence in many colleges and universities is close to a sham. In 1983, an article by sociologist Harry Edwards in the *Atlantic Monthly* documented the sorry situation. Although entrance requirements were often pathetically low, 25 to 35 percent of young black high-school athletes could not meet them. In college, as many as 65 to 75 percent of blacks with athletic scholarships never graduated. Of those who graduated, perhaps 75 percent did so with degrees in physical education or some other major or concentration designed to reflect their athletic prowess but with limited use after school. (In 1993, ten years after Edwards's article, a report revealed that one school, North Carolina State University, long famous as a power in collegiate basketball, had not graduated a single basketball player since 1985.)

Prop 48 allowed a freshman to play for one of the 277 Division I or top athletic schools only if the student had made a 2.0 grade point average (a C average) in high school and only if his or her courses included English, mathematics, the social sciences, and the physical sciences. It also required the athlete to have a combined score of 700 (out of a possible 1600) on the Scholastic Aptitude Test (SAT) or 15 (out of a possible 36) on the rival American College Test (ACT). The SAT and ACT tests are mandatory steps at most American colleges. Previously, students required only a C average, without regard to the courses taken, and many of the courses were scandalously devoid of intellectual content.

These new requirements should present no challenge whatsoever even to the average student. In recent years, however, fewer than 50 percent of black students taking the SAT had scored as high as 700; on the ACT, only 28 percent reached 15. Meanwhile, more than 75 percent of whites achieved 700 or 15 on the tests. . . .

Although these proposals would affect athletes of all races, some black college presidents, charging racism, led the opposition to them and threatened to withdraw their schools from the NCAA. Among white institutions, presidents were generally for the changes, while athletic directors generally were not; in black schools, however, opposition was often led by presidents. The president of

From Arthur Ashe and Arnold Rampersad, *Days of Grace: A Memoir* (New York: Knopf, 1993), 147–51.

Southern University in Louisiana, for example, called the proposal "patently racist." The proposal was caused, he said, by the fact that "the black athlete has been too good. If it is followed to its logical conclusion, we say to our youngsters, 'Let the white boy win once in a while.' This has set the black athlete back twenty-five or thirty years. The message is that white schools no longer want black athletes." Another official pointed out, without embarrassment, that the new entrance standards for athletes would be higher than the general entrance standards for most black colleges and even some white schools. The National Association for the Advancement of Colored People (NAACP), Jesse Jackson through his Operation PUSH group, the National Baptist Convention, and other black organizations also opposed the change.

I was one hundred percent behind the proposed higher standards. Lobbying behind the scenes, I also wrote at least one letter to the *New York Times* calling for college presidents to stand up for education; the *Times* also published my essay, "Coddling Black Athletes," in which I urged that "we should either get serious about academic standards or cut out the hypocrisy and pay college athletes as professionals." I published another essay in *Ebony* in which I talked about having visited black high schools where "the obsession with sports borders on pathology." I agreed completely with what the respected football coach Joe Paterno of Pennsylvania State University said in his provocative declaration of the 1983 NCAA convention: "For fifteen years we have had a race problem. We have raped a generation and a half of young black athletes. We have taken kids and sold them on bouncing a ball and running with a football and that being able to do certain things athletically was going to be an end in itself. We cannot afford to do that to another generation."

I found myself opposing two nationally known black basketball coaches: John Chaney of Temple University and John Thompson of perennially ranked Georgetown University. Chaney called the NCAA "that racist organization." As a highly publicized protest against the attempted passage of Prop 42, Thompson left the coach's bench during at least two basketball games involving his team. Both of these men are genuinely interested in education, but the positions they took seemed on the wrong side of all the key issues involved in the devaluation of education among blacks in the United States. In a long, sometimes acerbic telephone conversation, Thompson explained to me in detail his objections. First, whatever the benefits to our society in general, blacks would suffer from the changes because fewer would meet the requirements and be allowed into college. Once again, he argued, when America decided on some rise in standards, blacks paid the lion's share of the price for this change.

Thompson's second objection was that the proposition endorsed standardized tests (SAT and ACT) that were culturally biased; in addition, they are hardly infallible at predicting later success, including academic success. "Cultural bias" is the phrase of choice for nationalistic blacks when their philosophy collides with the basic demands of education. If whites do better, then the tests must be culturally biased. No one raises this question when the children of poor immigrants from Southeast Asia outclass native-born Americans in scholastics. My own position is different from Thompson's. Can one attribute a low test score to socioeconomic bias? Perhaps. Can one invoke cultural bias to explain a 700 SAT score? Ridiculous!

To Thompson's first objection, that black athletes would be barred by the new standards, I asserted my belief that any loss in numbers would be short-term. In response to the new standards, black youngsters would simply rise to the challenge and meet them. To the objection of cultural bias, I responded that Thompson could hardly come up with a credible alternative set of requirements that would yield a higher number of qualified entering black students. Did he really want an essay test, instead of the multiple-choice format of the SAT and ACT tests? Then, I told him—only half in jest—*no* black kid would get in, since the quality of writing among black students in general had become notoriously poor. As for John Chaney's mantra that black kids "deserve a chance"—of course they do, I responded. Everyone deserves a chance. What Chaney's plaintive cry reflects, however, is the obsession with entitlement that is rampant among young blacks. The idea that society owes them special favors for average efforts has taken root with a vengeance.

In my essay "Coddling Black Athletes," I wrote:

> We need to address the deep-seated cynicism of coddled, black public-school athletes, many of whom are carried through school with inflated grades and peer group status that borders on deification. High school coaches need to be held accountable for the academic preparation of their would-be Michael Jordans.
>
> The critics of Proposition 42 seriously underestimate the psychic value that black athletes place on their athletic success and how that could be used to motivate them academically. The screening process for superior athletes starts earlier—when they are 11 or 12—and is more efficacious than for any other group of Americans. Social status is conferred at once. And they learn early that they don't get the idolatry, attention, and, ultimately, Division I scholarships for their intellectual promise.
>
> Proposition 42—or something like it—would motivate high school coaches and their best players to take education seriously. Most important, that dedication to academic concerns among athletes would set a tone in the schools that would very likely inspire nonathletes to study harder.

ESSAYS

The first essay by Jules Tygiel of San Francisco State University examines the demanding rookie year of Jackie Robinson, the first African-American to join the major leagues since the long-forgotten Moses Fleetwood Walker who played for Toledo (American Association) in 1884. Robinson had a banner year in Montreal in 1946, winning the MVP, and he moved up to the Dodgers in 1947. What kinds of problems did he encounter on and off the field? How did he win over his teammates, his opponents, and the fans?

The second essay by Michael Oriard, a literary scholar at Oregon State University, examines the public images of Muhammad Ali, the most famous athlete in the world over the past fifty years, and the power those impressions had in the 1960s and 1970s. Ali played a major role in determining those conceptions, which radically changed the traditional athlete's self-presentation. He first came to national attention when, as Cassius Clay, he won a gold medal at the 1960 Olympics. An unusually handsome, gregarious boxer, Clay brashly predicted the outcome of his fights. After defeating the fear-inspiring Sonny Liston in a stunning upset in 1964, he announced his conversion to the Muslim faith and changed his name to Muhammad Ali. Mainstream Americans were shocked by such unconventional behavior, and they were further taken aback when Ali refused to step forward for the draft in 1966 on religious grounds. Yet, instead of becoming a pariah, Ali became a hero for standing up for his beliefs and against the Vietnam War. In 1971 the Supreme Court overturned his conviction for draft evasion and Ali resumed his boxing career, going on to regain the heavyweight championship.

A Lone Negro in the Game:
Jackie Robinson's Rookie Season

JULES TYGIEL

For Jackie Robinson, relative tranquility characterized the initial week of the 1947 season. In the first two contests, facing the Boston Braves, the rookie first baseman eked out one bunt single. "He seemed frantic with eagerness, restless as a can of worms," observed a Boston correspondent. On April 18 the Dodgers crossed the East River to play the New York Giants. Over 37,000 people flocked to the Polo Grounds to witness Robinson's first appearance outside of Brooklyn. Robinson responded with his first major league home run. The following day the largest Saturday afternoon crowd in National League history, more than 52,000 spectators, jammed into the Giants' ball park. Robinson stroked three hits in four at-bats in a losing cause. Rain postponed a two-game set in Boston, and on April 22 Robinson and the Dodgers returned to Brooklyn, where a swirl of events abruptly shattered the brief honeymoon. The next three weeks thrust Robinson, his family, his teammates, and baseball into a period of unrelenting crises and tension.

The Dodgers' first opponents on the homestand were the Philadelphia Phillies, managed by Alabaman Ben Chapman. While playing for the Yankees in the 1930s Chapman had gained a measure of notoriety for his anti-Semitic shouting jousts with spectators. Now he ordered his players to challenge Robinson with a stream of verbal racial taunts "to see if he can take it." From the moment the two clubs took the field for their first contest, the Phillies, led by Chapman, unleashed a torrent of insults at the black athlete. "At no time in my life have I heard racial venom and dugout abuse to match the abuse that Ben sprayed on Robinson that night," writes Harold Parrott. "Chapman mentioned everything from thick lips to the supposedly extra-thick Negro skull . . . [and] the repulsive sores and diseases he said Robinson's teammates would become infected with if they touched the towels or the combs he used." The onslaught continued throughout the series. . . .

The Phillies' verbal assault on Robinson in 1947 exceeded even baseball's broadly defined sense of propriety. Fans seated near the Phillies dugout wrote letters of protest to Commissioner Chandler, and newsman Walter Winchell attacked Chapman on his national Sunday night radio broadcast. Chandler notified

From Jules Tygiel, *Baseball's Great Experiment: Jackie Robinson and His Legacy* (New York: Oxford, 1983), 181–96, 200–2, 205–8.

Philadelphia owner Robert Carpenter that the harassment of Robinson must cease or he would be forced to invoke punitive measures.

Chapman, while accepting Chandler's edict, defended his actions. "We will treat Robinson the same as we do Hank Greenberg of the Pirates, Clint Hartung of the Giants, Joe Garagiola of the Cardinals, Connie Ryan of the Braves, or any other man who is likely to step to the plate and beat us," said Chapman, listing some regular targets of ethnic insults. "There is not a man who has come to the big leagues since baseball has been played who has not been ridden.". . .

The general consensus, however, judged the Phillies' behavior unacceptable. Robinson's Dodger teammates led the protest. By the second day of the series they lashed back at Chapman demanding that he cease baiting Robinson. Chapman's fellow Alabamans marched in the forefront of Robinson's defenders. Eddie Stanky called him a "coward" and challenged him to "pick on somebody who can fight back." Even Dixie Walker reprimanded Chapman, a close personal friend. Rickey later claimed that this incident, more than any other, cemented Dodger support for Robinson. "When [Chapman] poured out that string of unconscionable abuse he solidified and unified thirty men, not one of whom was willing to sit by and see someone kick around a man who had his hands tied behind his back," asserted Rickey.

Robinson publicly downplayed the incident. In his "Jackie Robinson Says" column which appeared in the Pittsburgh *Courier,* the Dodger first baseman wrote, "Some of the Phillies' bench jockeys tried to get me upset last week, but it didn't really bother me.". . . In later years he revealed his true emotions as he withstood the barrage of insults. "I have to admit that this day of all the unpleasant days of my life brought me nearer to cracking up than I have ever been," he wrote in 1972. "For one wild and rage crazed minute I thought, 'To hell with Mr. Rickey's "noble experiment.' " The ordeal tempted Robinson to "stride over to that Phillies dugout, grab one of those white sons of bitches and smash his teeth with my despised black fist."

The daily flood of mail included not only congratulatory messages, but threats of violence. In early May, the Dodgers turned several of these notes over to the police. The letters, according to Robinson, advised "that 'somebody' was going to get hurt if I didn't get out of baseball," and "promised to kill any n——s who interfered with me." In the aftermath of the threats and in light of the burden that answering the mail placed on the Robinsons, Rickey requested that they allow the Dodgers to open and answer all correspondence. In addition, Robinson agreed to refuse all invitations to speak or be honored as well as opportunities for commercial endorsements.

The Dodgers released details of the threatening letters to the press on May 9. On that same day Robinson faced other unpublicized challenges in Philadelphia, the initial stop on the club's first extended road trip. Rickey had been forewarned that Robinson would not get a warm reception in Philadelphia. Herb Pennock, the former major league pitcher who served as the Phillies general manager, had called Rickey demanding that Robinson remain in Brooklyn. "[You] just can't bring that nigger here with the rest of your team, Branch. We're just not ready for that sort of thing yet," exhorted Pennock, according to Parrott who listened on the line. Pennock threatened that the Phillies would boycott the game. . . .

When the Dodgers arrived in Philadelphia on May 9, the Benjamin Franklin Hotel, where the club had lodged for several years, refused to accept Robinson. Team officials had anticipated problems in St. Louis and Cincinnati, but not in the City of Brotherly Love. . . . Rather than force a confrontation, Robinson arranged for alternative quarters. On subsequent trips, the Dodgers transferred their Philadelphia headquarters to the more expensive Warwick hotel. . . .

A third, more ominous development, which also surfaced on May 9, overshadowed these incidents. New York *Herald Tribune* sports editor Stanley Woodward unveiled an alleged plot by National League players, led by the St. Louis Cardinals, to strike against Robinson. Woodward charged that the Cardinals, at the urgings of a Dodger player, had planned a strike during the first Dodger-Cardinal confrontation three days earlier. . . .

Rumors of the impending mutiny reached Breadon in St. Louis and on May 1 he flew to New York where the Cardinals were playing the Giants. Breadon informed National League President Frick of the strike rumors. Frick, in less eloquent terms than attributed to him by Woodward, advised Breadon to warn the Cardinals that the National League would defend Robinson's right to play and that a refusal to take the field would lead to their suspensions. Breadon conferred with player representatives Moore and Marion, both of whom denied the rumors. According to Frick, Breadon reported back, "It was just a tempest in a teapot. A few of the players were upset and popping off a bit. They didn't really mean it." If an uprising indeed had been brewing, it ended with these discussions. On May 6 the Cardinals appeared as scheduled at Ebbets Field and lost to Robinson and the Dodgers. . . .

. . . Woodward's allegations, exaggerated or not, marked a significant turning point. The account of Frick's steadfast renunciation of all efforts to displace the black athlete, following so closely after Chandler's warning to Chapman, placed the baseball hierarchy openly in support of Robinson. In addition, the uproar created by the Woodward story dashed any lingering hopes among dissident players that public opinion, at least as reflected in the press, endorsed their opinions. . . .

May 9, 1947, marked perhaps the worst day of Jackie Robinson's baseball career. Threats on his life, torment from opposing players, discrimination at the team hotel, and rumors of a player strike simultaneously engulfed the black athlete. The following day, Jimmy Cannon, describing Robinson's relations with his teammates, reported, "He is the loneliest man I have ever seen in sports.". . .

Amidst the swirl of controversy that followed the Dodgers on their first major road trip, the national interest in Jackie Robinson grew apparent. On Sunday, May 11, the Dodgers faced the Phillies in a doubleheader before the largest crowd in Philadelphia baseball history. Scalpers sold $2 tickets for $6, "just like the World Series." Two days later in Cincinnati 27,164 fans turned out despite an all-day rain "to size up Jackie Robinson." Bad weather diminished the crowds for two games in Pittsburgh, but when the skies cleared, 34,814 fans appeared at Forbes Field for the May 18 series finale. The following day the Dodgers met the Cubs in Chicago. Two hours before game time Wrigley Field had almost filled. A total of 46,572 fans crammed into the ball park, the largest attendance in stadium history. The tour concluded in St. Louis where the Dodgers and Cardinals played before the biggest weekday crowd of the National League season.

"Jackie's nimble/Jackie's quick/Jackie's making the turnstiles click," crowed Wendell Smith. Jimmy Cannon hailed him as "the most lucrative draw since Babe Ruth." By May 23 when the Dodgers returned to Brooklyn, Robinson had emerged as a national phenomenon. . . .

Robinson had also erased all doubts about his playing abilities. . . . By June, Robinson had convinced even the most hardened opponents of integration of his exceptional talents. . . . Starting on June 14, Robinson hit safely in twenty-one consecutive games. At the end of June, he was batting .315, leading the league in stolen bases, and ranked second in runs scored. . . .

Robinson's impressive statistics revealed only a portion of the tale. "Never have records meant so little in discussing a player's value as they do in the case of Jackie Robinson," wrote Tom Meany. "His presence alone was enough to light a fire under his own team and unsettle his opponents." Sportswriter John Crosby asserts, "He was the greatest opportunist on any kind of playing field, seeing openings before they opened, pulling off plays lesser players can't even imagine." Robinson's intense competitiveness provided the crucial ingredient. A seasoned athlete, even in his rookie year, Robinson seemed to thrive on challenges and flourished before large audiences. . . . Robinson's drive not only inspired his own dramatic performances but intimidated and demoralized enemy players. . . .

At the plate and in the field, Robinson radiated dynamic intensity, but his true genius materialized on the base paths. . . .

"He brought a new dimension into baseball," says Al Campanis. "He brought stealing back to the days of the twenties whereas up until that time baseball had become a long-ball hitting game." But the phenomenon went beyond base stealing. Robinson's twenty-nine steals in 1947 were actually less than the league leader of the preceding year. The style of play and the design of his baserunning antics better measure the magnitude of Robinson's achievement. He revolutionized major league baseball by injecting an element of "tricky baseball," so common in the Negro Leagues. In an age in which managers bemoaned the lost art of bunting, Robinson, in forty-six bunt attempts, registered fourteen hits and twenty-eight sacrifices, a phenomenal .913 success rate. His tactics often went against the time-worn conventional wisdom of baseball. . . .

Nor did Robinson's effectiveness require the stolen base. "He dances and prances off base keeping the enemy infield upset and off balance, and worrying the pitcher," reported *Time*. . . .

In spring training Rickey had advised Robinson, "I want you to win the friendship of people everywhere. You must be personable, you must smile, and even if they are worrying you to death, make the public think you don't mind being bothered." Robinson created precisely this image. He publicly thanked opposing players, like Hank Greenberg and Frank Gustine, who welcomed him into the league. . . .

Among northern teammates, playing alongside Robinson posed few problems. For southerners, on the other hand, it often required a significant adjustment. Several players feared repercussions at home for their involuntary role in baseball integration. "I didn't know if they would spit on me or not," recalled Dixie Walker of his Alabama neighbors. "It was no secret that I was worried about my business. I had a hardware and sporting goods store back home." Pee Wee Reese later said that in family discussions, "The subject always gets around to the fact that I'm a little southern boy playing shortstop next to a Negro second baseman and in danger of being contaminated.". . .

During the course of the 1947 season and subsequent campaigns, Robinson developed his closest friendship with Pee Wee Reese, the shortstop from Kentucky. The alliance emerged out of mutual respect and Reese's unaffected acceptance of Robinson as a teammate. Two incidents typified the Robinson-Reese rapport. In June the Dodgers stopped in Danville, Illinois, to play an exhibition game with one of their farm teams. Reese joined a golf foursome with pitcher Rex Barney, Harold Parrott, and reporter Roscoe McGowan. Robinson and Wendell Smith played behind them. At the fourth hole, Reese halted the game and invited the two blacks to merge with his foursome. As the three teammates joked and kidded each other, wrote one observer, "Reese and Barney showed, without knowing it, during the golf game that they like Robinson and he is one of them." Early in the following season in Boston, Brave bench jockeys rode Reese mercilessly for playing alongside a black man. Reese strode over to Robinson, placed his arm around his teammate's shoulder, and prepared to discuss the upcoming game. The gesture silenced the Boston bench. . . .

Robinson's acceptance by the Dodger players occurred with surprising rapidity, even more so than at Montreal. Within six weeks, says Bragan, the barriers had fallen. Eating, talking, and playing cards with Robinson seemed natural. . . .

The evolution of Dodger attitudes toward Robinson reflected a process occurring throughout the nation. Robinson's aggressive play, his innate sense of dignity, and his outward composure under extreme duress captivated the American people. Only Joe Louis, among black celebrities, had aroused the public imagination as Robinson did in the summer of 1947. Robinson's charismatic personality inspired not merely sympathy and acceptance, but sincere adulation from both whites and blacks alike.

To black America, Jackie Robinson appeared as a savior, a Moses leading his people out of the wilderness. . . . Thousands of blacks thronged to the ball parks wherever he appeared. At games in the National League's southernmost cities blacks swelled attendance. Many traveled hundreds of miles to see their hero in action. The Philadelphia *Afro-American* reported that orders by blacks for tickets for the first Dodger-Phillies series had "poured in" from Baltimore, Washington, and other cities along the eastern seaboard. For games in Cincinnati, a "Jackie Robinson special" train ran from Norfolk, Virginia, stopping en route to pick up black fans. . . .

As a boy, white columnist Mike Royko attended Robinson's first game at Wrigley Field in Chicago. Twenty-five years later he described the event:

In 1947, few blacks were seen in downtown Chicago, much less up on the white North side at a Cub game.

That day they came by the thousands, pouring off the north-bound ELS and out of their cars.

. . . The whites tried to look as if nothing unusual was happening, while the blacks tried to look casual and dignified. So everybody looked ill at ease.

For the most part it was probably the first time they had been so close to each other in such large numbers. . . .

Robinson's correspondence reflected the changes in racial attitudes that he inspired. His dynamic presence instilled a sense of pride in black Americans and led many whites to reassess their own feelings. The affection for Robinson grew so widespread that at the year's end voters in an annual public opinion poll named him the second most popular man in America. Only Bing Crosby registered more votes. . . .

. . . Despite his growing acceptance, Robinson remained an oddity in organized baseball. Throughout the season, even after he had established himself as a bona fide major league player, Robinson confronted difficulties and challenges unknown to other athletes. The burdens of racial pioneering and the restrictions imposed on his behavior still rested heavily on his shoulders.

On the road, hotel accommodations remained problematical. Throughout the Jim Crow era the issue of housing black players had loomed as a major objection to integration. Even in many northern cities, the better hotels did not allow blacks. In border cities like St. Louis and Cincinnati segregation remained the rule. Rickey and his advisers had determined that the Dodgers would not challenge local customs. . . .

In Boston, Pittsburgh, and Chicago, Robinson had no problems. In Philadelphia and St. Louis, officials barred him and he stayed at Negro hotels. The Dodgers anticipated that Robinson would not be allowed to stay with the team in Cincinnati, but the Netherlands-Plaza Hotel accepted him under the provision that he eat his meals in his room so as not to offend other guests.

The Dodgers dared not tamper with one taboo—the prohibition on interracial roommates. . . . In 1947 Robinson usually roomed with Wendell Smith, who traveled with the team as both a reporter and a Dodger employee. . . .

Robinson also received numerous money-making propositions for the winter and fall. He signed up for a theatrical tour of New York, Washington, and Chicago, traveling with three vaudeville acts. For each of his appearances Robinson would receive a minimum of $2,500. The articulate athlete became a popular radio guest and signed contracts to co-author an autobiography and to star in a Hollywood movie. Sources estimated that despite his low salary, Robinson's income for 1947 exceeded that of all major leaguers with the exception of Bob Feller and Hank Greenberg. . . .

Throughout most of the season Robinson maintained his batting average over .300, but a late season slump after the Dodgers had clinched the pennant dropped him to .297. He finished second in the league in runs scored and first in stolen bases. Robinson also led the Dodgers in home runs with 12. Despite his reputation for being injury prone, Robinson appeared in 151 of the 154 contests, more games than anyone else on the club.

Robinson's performance also benefited other National League teams. Throughout the season fans continued to watch him in record numbers. . . . By the season's end Robinson had established new attendance marks in every city except Cincinnati. Thanks to Robinson, National League attendance in 1947 increased by more than three quarters of a million people above the all-time record set in 1946. Five teams set new season records, including the Dodgers, who attracted over 1.8 million fans for the first, and last, time in the club's Brooklyn history. . . .

The saga of Robinson's first season has become a part of American mythology—sacrosanct in its memory, magnificent in its retelling. It remains a drama which thrills and fascinates, combining the central themes of the illusive Great American Novel: the undertones of Horatio Alger, the inter-racial comradery of nineteenth-century fiction, the sage advisor and his youthful apprentice, and the rugged and righteous individual confronting the angry mob. It is a tale of courage, heroics, and triumph. Epic in its proportions, the Robinson legend has persevered—and will continue to do so—because the myth, which rarely deviates from reality, fits our national perceptions of fair play and social progress. The emotional impact of Robinson's challenge requires no elaboration or enhancement. Few works of fiction could impart its power.

Indeed, so total was Robinson's triumph, so dominant his personality, that few people have questioned the strategies and values that underpinned Branch Rickey's "noble experiment." Rickey based his blueprint for integration both on his assessment of the racial realities of postwar America and his flair for the dramatic. He believed that the United States was ready for integrated baseball, but the balance remained so precarious that the breakthrough had to be carefully planned and cautiously advanced. Americans—both black and white, players and fans—needed time to accommodate themselves to the idea of blacks in baseball. The slightest false step, Rickey concluded, would delay the entry of nonwhites into the national pastime indefinitely. Rickey felt that the primary burden of this undertaking had to rest on the shoulders of a lone standard-bearer, upon whose success or failure the fate of the entire venture would be determined. The fact that this gradual process accrued publicity and added to the drama was never central to Rickey's thinking, but rather a natural component of his personality, Rickey conceived of schemes on the grand scale and enacted them accordingly. . . .

The Rickey blueprint placed tremendous pressure upon Robinson, his standard-bearer. Robinson's response to this challenge inspired a legend. His playing skills, intelligence, and competitive flair made Robinson the perfect path breaker. Still, did others exist who could have duplicated his feat? Unquestionably, many black athletes possessed major league talent, but could they have performed adequately under the intense pressure and retained their composure amidst insults? . . .

. . . In Robinson, Rickey had uncovered not only an outstanding baseball player, but a figure of charisma and leadership. For blacks, Robinson became a symbol of pride and dignity; to whites, he represented a type of black man far removed from prevailing stereotypes, whom they could not help but respect. He would not fade into obscurity after retirement as most athletes do. Robinson remained an active advocate of civil rights causes and Afro-American interests. . . .

Muhammad Ali: The Hero in the Age of Mass Media

MICHAEL ORIARD

. . . I'm not concerned here with Muhammad Ali the man, but with Ali as cultural representation. To find the "real" Ali is a quest for biographers; as a student of

From Michael Oriard, "Muhammad Ali: The Hero in the Age of Mass Media," in *Muhammad Ali: The People's Champion*, ed. Elliott Gorn (Urbana: University of Illinois Press, 1995), 5, 8–22.

American culture, I'm interested in the public images of Ali, and in the power they had in the 1960s and 1970s. Those of us who came of age during the Ali era share certain memories of Ali, however we might have differed, or differ now, in our responses to him. We can all hear Ali's voice, declaiming, "I am the greatest!" We can still hear him predicting the round in which an opponent would fall; we can hear him chant, "Float like a butterfly, sting like a bee"; if we don't remember the precise words, we nonetheless retain impressions of his poetry and his taunts at weigh-ins and even in the ring, and his seemingly hysterical tirades before and after fights. For all their familiarity, however, we should not forget how we first encountered these outpourings from the Louisville Lip, as he was called early on (a less charming later nickname termed him The Mouth). We need to remember that in his first dawning on public awareness, Ali radically changed the self-presentation of the American athlete.

The hero's boast has a long ancestry: from Achilles before the walls of Troy through the latter-day "flyting" of ring-tailed roarers on the American frontier, nearly into the age of modern sport with John L. Sullivan and his fellow bare-knuckle brawlers. But the lineage of our sporting etiquette looks more to the tradition of Castiglione's courtier and his spiritual offspring on pubic-school playing fields in Britain. America's sportsmen through the first half of the twentieth century were not uniformly "sportsmen" in this honorific sense, but officially they subscribed to the aw-shucks code of Frank Merriwell.

Those born after 1960 or so might accept as commonplace something that perhaps thrilled, perhaps offended, but in all cases startled us when we first heard a maniacally exuberant young Cassius Clay declare, "I am the greatest!"—shattering a century-old image of the sportsman. The Merriwell code still hovered over American sport before Ali's emergence. During televised games, players studiously looked away when they sensed a television camera pointed in their direction. They kept their game faces on and their mouths shut; they left the voting on #1 to pollsters and waited until after the game to say "Hi" to their mothers.

After Ali, we heard Joe Namath outrageously predict that his Jets would beat the Colts in the 1969 Super Bowl. Not quite two years later, the Kansas City Chiefs' Elmo Wright, a rookie wide receiver, introduced the first end-zone dance to the NFL—a simple two-step considerably less artful than the Ali Shuffle. . . .

These details of sporting manners reflect a major cultural transformation in post-1950s America. Surely Muhammad Ali is one of the emblems of self-assertion and self-regard in an era whose cultural mainstream has become preoccupied—obsessed—with the self. This is not to say that Muhammad Ali represented the values now associated with "me decade" narcissism and Reagan-era greed, with Yuppie self-indulgence and Donald Trump. When Cassius Clay first declared, "I am the greatest!" this was an original and radical act. It defied the spirit of gray flannel suits and social accommodation; it shattered the mask of humble silence and nonassertion demanded of blacks in America, particularly of blacks in the South. It was also full of risk: proclaiming himself the greatest, Clay/Ali challenged opponents to beat him into a liar. Moreover, at least initially, he risked the outrage of the audience on which his livelihood depended. Anachronistic or not, Merriwellian modesty was the guise that athletes were expected to adopt if they were to be accepted as popular heroes. In this matter of self-presentation Clay/Ali represented something genuinely radical. . . .

Ali was not only the greatest, he was also, as he constantly reminded us, the prettiest; in a sport, and in a division, associated with strength and violence, Muhammad Ali made us think about beauty. Ali's sculpted body and "pretty" face, together with his gentleness with children, undoubtedly accounted for much of his appeal to women of all ages, who were not typically drawn to prizefighters. This was most conspicuously the "feminine" aspect of Ali, the physical incarnation of those elements of his boxing style (his dancing, his speed and quickness—as opposed to his power) and of his poetry that American culture defines as feminine. I can think of no one in our time who so successfully embodied cross-gender wholeness. As a professor of American literature, I am more accustomed to looking at this matter from the other direction: at the dilemma of the American male artist who feels driven to assert his masculinity because art and literature have been culturally defined as feminine. Probably only the heavyweight champion of the world could declare "I am the prettiest" and not diminish his aura of physical prowess. Certainly it hasn't worked the other way: writers such as Hemingway or Mailer, for instance, insisting they are the toughest sonsabitches around, have been considerably less convincing.

Ali was the prettiest and the greatest; he was fighter and dancer, loudmouth and poet, exuberant child and heavyweight champion of the world. In describing Ali as a sum of many parts, I have been circling around one of the principal claims I want to make in this essay. *Our* Muhammad Ali is the one we know through television, radio, newspapers, magazines such as *Sports Illustrated,* and closed-circuit screenings of his fights—the collection of images transmitted through those media. The crucial fact about those images is their extraordinary range. Various images of Muhammad Ali might be assigned to different stages in his career. One might reasonably identify an early brash, youthful, and exuberant Cassius Clay, who changed with the changing of his name after winning the title from Sonny Liston in 1964. This new Muhammad Ali grew increasingly militant as a spokesman for black separatism; then another new Ali, the political martyr, emerged with his defiance of the draft board and his three-and-a-half-year exile from boxing; then yet another Ali appeared with his return to boxing in 1970, an older, more mature figure of physical and mental courage in the Norton, Frazier, and Foreman fights. Finally, Ali became the aging champion who fought too long, who not only lost bouts to Leon Spinks, Larry Holmes, and Trevor Berbick, but who also lost his physical health and verbal agility to the sport he had transformed.

Certainly there is much truth in this account of the changes over the course of Ali's career, but it is also essential to recognize that at every stage of his career there was not a single Ali but many Alis in the public consciousness. The brash Cassius Clay could seem either braggart or free spirit; the dancing Ali could seem an artist or a coward; the Muslim Ali could seem a religious or a political man; the conscientious objector could seem a con man, a pacifist, a traitor, or a martyr. To the late-1960s white counterculture, Ali surely was identified more with the antiwar movement than with black separatism; to blacks during this same period he surely represented chiefly racial pride.

All of us—young and old, black and white, poor and privileged—knew these various Alis through the media. The media did not construct a single Ali but the multiple Alis we have been considering. The anthropologist Clifford Geertz has taught scholars to approach cultural expressions as "texts" in which we can read the larger culture that produces them. In reading the texts of a complex modern culture such as ours, it is essential to acknowledge that no single interpretation is likely to be possible. Students of American culture who attempt to interpret the texts of our past confront an overwhelming challenge to discover how ordinary people interpreted them. Students of sport have this advantage: the sports journalism that has always accompanied organized sport virtually from the beginning offers, not direct access to the minds and hearts of its readers, but at least closer access to them than is usually possible. Sportswriters are themselves individual interpreters of the events they describe; at the same time, they mediate between these events and those who read their accounts. What one finds in the reporting on Ali over the years is, first, an awareness among sportswriters that Ali was a "text" that could be read in competing ways and, second, a record of the ways he was read.

To approach Ali as a "cultural text" I read through the coverage of his career in *Sports Illustrated,* and I discovered, among other things, that journalists understood Muhammad Ali in just this way, without recourse to Clifford Geertz or any other theorist. Ali fascinated some of our most respected journalists—Norman Mailer, George Plimpton, and Wilfred Sheed come most quickly to mind—but I was particularly struck by the writing of *SI*'s Mark Kram, a much less famous sportswriter. Ali's own artistry in and out of the ring clearly challenged sportswriters to create a commensurate art of their own. Kram chiefly covered Ali's second career, beginning with his return from exile to fight Jerry Quarry in 1970. In welcoming Ali back to boxing, Kram described him as a "clever dramatist" who "was creating a new theme for his fight with Quarry." Kram identified Ali's scripts for his earlier bouts: "brashness versus malevolence" for Sonny Liston; "holy wars" with Ernie Terrell and Floyd Patterson; and "the black prince on the lam" for his European fights with Karl Mildenberger, Henry Cooper, and Brian London. Now, with Quarry, Ali had cast himself as "Rimbrindt back from exile."

The specific scripts are less important here than Kram's explicit recognition that boxing matches can function as cultural dramas or texts. The following spring Kram returned to this idea before Ali's first fight with Joe Frazier. In describing the roles that Ali and Frazier would be playing in the ring, Kram stood back to look at the history of boxing from this perspective:

> Americans are the most curious in their reaction to a heavyweight title bout, especially one of this scope. To some, the styles and personalities of the fighters seem to provide the paraphernalia of a forum; the issue becomes a sieve through which they feel compelled to pour all of their fears and prejudices. Still others find it a convenient opportunity to dispense instant good and evil, right and wrong. The process is as old as boxing: the repelling bluff and bluster of John L. against the suavity and decorum of Gentleman Jim; the insidious malevolence of Johnson vs. the solidity of Jeffries; the evil incarnate Liston against the vulnerable Patterson. It is a fluid script, crossing over religion, war, politics, race and much of what is so terribly human in all of us.

Heavyweight championship fights have always been culturally scripted; equally important, as Kram noted, is the fact that these scripts are read differently by different observers. Kram went on to describe some of the most prominent "read-ings" of the upcoming fight:

> The disputation of the New Left comes at Frazier with its spongy thinking and push-button passion and seeks to color him white, to denounce him as a capitalist dupe and a Fifth Columnist to the black cause. Those on the other fringe, just as blindly rancorous, see in Ali all that is unhealthy in this country, which in essence means all they will not accept from a black man. For still others, numbed by the shock of a sharply evolving society, he means confusion; he was one of the first to start pouring their lemonade world down the drain.
>
> Among the blacks there is only a whisper of feeling for Frazier, who is deeply cut by their reaction. He is pinned under the most powerful influence on black thought in the country. The militants view Ali as the Mahdi, the one man who has circumvented what they believe to be an international white conspiracy. To the young he is identity, an incomparable hero of almost mythological dimension.

And so on. Black and white, conservative and liberal, young and old read the cultural text of Muhammad Ali in different ways. . . . It's important to keep in mind both Ali's uniqueness *and* his typicality. Among the champions of our time Ali was uniquely enigmatic—a puzzle, a mass of paradoxes; this is how sports-writers repeatedly described him, as they obsessively attempted to unravel his mystery. Their own varied, conflicting interpretations were thus to some degree a consequence of Ali's resistance to simple explanation. In this range of interpreta-tions, of course, Ali can also be considered typical: because of our diversity we Americans do not read *any* of our important cultural texts in identical ways. This may seem an obvious point, but its implications are important: no simple "domi-nant" ideology is imposed upon an unresisting public by the mass media. Sport in general, and perhaps Muhammad Ali in particular, can teach us how the media reach their diverse audience through multiple narratives.

The coverage of Ali's career in *Sports Illustrated* reveals an Ali who never fit a single role. Through the earliest years he was repeatedly termed a child: bragging, careless or casual about training, absurdly confident; a *willful* child with a short at-tention span, as unpredictable to his own managers as he was to the public. But against this sense of Clay as child stood the "remarkably calm and composed Clay" who entered the ring with the monster Sonny Liston in 1964, whose strategy had been "carefully rehearsed and meticulously perfected," who was driven by a deep sense of purpose, whose performance was remarkable for "the completeness of his ring wisdom." Tex Maule, the *SI* reporter whose words I've just quoted, commented that "the boasting and *calculated* gibes . . . had *seemed* the overween-ing confidence of a child" (my emphasis). Was Cassius Clay some kind of won-drous child of the gods or a canny ring technician whose childlike antics were meant to build interest in his fights and doubts in opponents' minds? Boxing fans answered that question in different ways and at stake were beliefs about race, about what it takes to succeed in America, even about the relative importance of biology and self-determination in human lives.

By the morning after the Liston fight, Cassius Clay was Muhammad Ali, a Black Muslim, forever altering the terms by which he would be considered, but not altering the conflicts among terms. Ali as vain self-promoter now competed with Ali as spokesman for black America; Ali as "that marvelous, whimsical, overween-ing and—when he turns the volume down—charming young man," with Ali as "black racist." Ali's Muslim connection was initially interpreted in terms of race, not religion; one writer dismissed his religious rantings as "the Allah routine." But the fighter—whether "a genius in his chosen craft" or simply a natural who did things in the ring that "no longer have any roots in intellection"—began to talk about dreams, about his sense of having been chosen for a purpose, about "divine things." The physical and the metaphysical, the natural and the supernatural, contended for reporters' and the public's attention. Following Ali's fight with Floyd Patterson in November 1965—in which the playful child had seemed cruelly contemptuous of his opponent, and of the audience as well—*SI*'s Gilbert Rogin mused: "What strange times we live in. What a strange, uncommon man is Clay. Who can fathom him? We can only watch in wonder as he performs and ponder whether, despite his truly affecting ways, he doesn't scorn us and the world he is champion of." Playful or merely cruel, pug or prophet, an already puzzling Ali was becoming a more profound riddle.

In a five-part series in spring 1966, following Ali's challenge to his draft board, *Sports Illustrated* and Jack Olsen confronted the "enigma" of Muhammad Ali head-on: the incongruous mix of "bombast and doggerel," "hardheaded bigot[ry]," and "the conscience of a genuine objector." The most accessible champion in memory, to whom children flocked constantly, was also "the most hated figure in sport." His buffoonery too often crossed the boundary into nastiness. "His life is a symphony of paradoxes," Olsen wrote in the first installment of the series. In the third, an inquiry into the seeming hysteria of Ali's prefight and postfight rantings—temporary lunacy? an act? a psychological ploy? simple fear?—Olsen compiled a long list of the images that had become attached to Ali:

> Figuring out who or what is the *real* Cassius Clay is a parlor game that has not proved rewarding even for experts. Clay's personality is like a jigsaw puzzle whose pieces were cut by a drunken carpenter, a jumbled collection of moods and attitudes that do not seem to interlock. Sometimes he sounds like a religious lunatic, his voice singsong and chanting, and all at once he will turn into a calm, reasoning, if sometimes confused, student of the Scriptures. He is a loudmouthed windbag and at the same time a remarkably sincere and dedicated athlete. He can be a kindly benefactor of the neighborhood children and a vicious bully in the ring, a prissy Puritan, totally intolerant of drinkers and smokers, and a foul-mouthed teller of dirty jokes.

Notice here—in 1966, two years after Ali changed his name—that Olsen still called him "Clay." The two names, Cassius Clay or Muhammad Ali, themselves conjured up conflicting interpretations of the heavyweight champion. Following his list, Olsen quoted Ali's physician, Dr. Ferdie Pacheco, who had heard it said that "there's 15 sides to Clay" but had decided that the fighter was "just a thoroughly confused person." Pacheco did not solve the riddle, of course, but only added a sixteenth possibility.

The hero and villain of the late sixties became more thoroughly heroic in the seventies, yet without being reduced to a single dominant image. Following his world travels and campus lectures in the United States during his exile from boxing, Ali returned to the ring in 1970 as a spokesman "for 22 million black people," as "a symbol of black nationalism and antiwar sentiment," as a man fighting "not

just . . . one man" but "a lot of men." Ali, who was once an "indefatigable consumer," now seemed to have turned ascetic. He had become a "patriarch," a
"Prophet," a tool to be used however Allah wills—a serious man, driven by a sense
of "divine destiny." But he was also a ring artist, "the ultimate action poet," and, in
certain writers' more skeptical moods, still a fame junkie, con man, and nonstop
showman.

A sense of transcendent destiny runs through much of the writing on Ali from
1970 to 1975, the nature of the drama shifting from Broadway and Tin Pan Alley to
Greek tragedy: Ali, the hero returned from banishment, fighting not just mortal opponents but mortality itself; Ali, once the golden child of the early sixties, after his
defeat by Joe Frazier in 1971 now a man of suffering, of pain, of vulnerability; Ali
the hero in the Underworld, in Sisyphean struggle against the Jimmy Ellises, the
Buster Mathises, the Bob Fosters, the Floyd Pattersons (yet again—Ali doomed to
clear obstacles once thought forever cleared), in his uphill quest to reclaim the
championship that had once been his. In these fights Ali shows his old skills but
seems too compassionate, seems to have lost his "will to kill." He is then shock-
ingly defeated by Ken Norton, after which comes a further testing (by fate? by Allah?): Norton in a rematch; Frazier in a rematch but now not for the championship
because Frazier has lost to a seemingly invincible George Foreman, the highest
mountain yet up which Ali must roll his boulder. Ali seems blessed by the gods, by
Allah, with his astonishing victory over Foreman in Africa, followed by the awe-
some *Götterdämmerung* of the third Frazier fight, the one in the Philippines. The
fighter who danced and jabbed, and about whom cynics wondered whether he
could truly punch and take a punch, became a fighter of stunning power and an almost frightening courage to withstand the most brutal blows ever thrown in the
heavyweight ring.

The question uppermost in writers' minds during this epic struggle to reclaim
his stolen championship was What drove Ali? Clearly he was driven, but was it by
a simple lust for fame or by a truly transcendent destiny? Writers on the boxing
beat, unaccustomed to metaphysical speculations, now became serious philosophical inquirers. And while Ali's popularity grew more general, the responses he
evoked continued to vary. The opposing possibilities of mortality and transcen-
dence defined the extreme limits of Ali's images in this period, culminating in a
paradoxical kind of transcendent mortality in Mark Kram's lyrical account of the
third Frazier fight: "Once, so long ago, he had been a splendidly plumed bird who
wrote on the wind a singular kind of poetry of the body, but now he was down to
earth, brought down by the changing shape of his body, by a sense of his vulnerability, and by the years of excess. Dancing was for a ballroom; the ugly hunt was
on." If Ali no longer danced and soared, in the ugly hunt he was a dauntless
hunter. . . . More prosaically, when *Sports Illustrated* named Ali sportsman of the
year in 1974, George Plimpton proposed yet more ways to read the fighter, attempting to explain how the triumph of so controversial a figure could be so popular: "I think it was the sort of joyous reaction that comes with seeing something
that suggests all things are possible: the triumph of the underdog, the comeback
from hard times and exile, the victory of an outspoken nature over a sullen disposition, the prevailing of intelligence over raw power, the success of physical grace,
the ascendance of age over youth, and especially the confounding of the experts.

Moreover, the victory assuaged the guilt feelings of those who remembered the theft of Ali's career." Th final phase of Ali's career— the precipitous decline from triumph over Joe Frazier in Manila in 1975 to defeat by Leon Spinks, Larry Holmes, and Trevor Berbick in 1978, 1980, and 1981—was played out at times as farce (the bizarre match with a sumo wrestler in Tokyo in 1976) or embarrassment, toward the end more often as tragedy: Ali, a man who "suffers wonderfully from *hubris,*" as Plimpton put it in 1974, now paying heavily for his pride and courage. . . .

. . . If [Michael] Jordan is like Ali in this status as cultural text, Ali differed— and was perhaps unique—in two important ways. First, against the crush of media attention, Ali managed to maintain an amazing degree of control over the ways he was interpreted. *He* remained the principal author of his own cultural text. When *Sports Illustrated*'s Mark Kram reviewed Ali's "one-act play of infinite variations" (the occasion was his second fight with Floyd Patterson, in 1972), he described Ali as the producer of his own show; in the ring Ali seemed like a "drama coach" feeding Patterson his lines. And it wasn't just the general public for whom Ali wrote his own scripts and enacted the dramas of his own creation. He also dictated to reporters, a group considerably less susceptible to illusions and delusions. He played for reporters the various roles that *he* wanted them to consider; he presented himself as an enigma that reporters became obsessed with figuring out, while never allowing them access to his essential mystery. Collectively, the reporters came to understand, as George Plimpton put it, that "so much of what Ali does is a game, a put-on," but both collectively and individually they never were exactly sure which part was put-on, which part serious. In one of Howard Cosell's many interviews with Ali—one act in the vaudeville show they staged over most of Ali's career— Cosell and Ali bantered over who had created whom. The answer seems obvious: Ali was not a media creation but a self-creation who used the media brilliantly. In our world of sound bites and handlers, sports itself is resistant to mere manipulation. At the heart of sport, unlike most kinds of entertainment, lies something *real:* what the athletes themselves bring to the field or the ring. As Mark Kram wrote, in anticipation of Ali's third fight with Joe Frazier, "There is nothing contrived here. This is not an electronic toy conceived in network boardrooms and then sent out and made to look like a dramatic sporting conflict." Within the world of sport, Muhammad Ali more successfully than anyone within memory resisted manipulation by others. . . . Ali was the author of his own narratives, and, moreover, he transcended all attempts to explain him.

The second way I think Ali is different from other sports heroes lies in the kind of hero he was, and is. Having circled around it, I've arrived at the issue announced in the title of this essay: the question of Ali as a "hero" in an age in which the electronic media are capable of reaching billions of people everywhere in the world, but whose images are so overwhelmingly numerous and so dependent on novelty that the lifespan of even the most powerful images seems that of the firefly. I think that David Halberstam is correct in recognizing a new kind of fame: fame potentially of unprecedented reach, due to the transmission of images via satellite into every corner of the globe, but also fame of unprecedented brevity. That this fame will emanate from the United States, chiefly through commercials and images on consumer goods, also seems clear. . . .

. . . The progression from oral to print to electronic cultures has meant the progressive shortening of the hero's endurance in popular consciousness. Muhammad Ali . . . had enormous fame, although he did not (could not?) market himself through product endorsements (if Michael Jordan is the first "new age athlete," perhaps Muhammad Ali is the last sport hero of the preceding era in which marketing was an adjunct of fame, not its principal form). It is worth noting that Ali remains a major hero in the developing countries of Asia and Africa, where Michael Jordan is virtually unknown. Where oral tradition remains strong, fame endures; heroes are passed on from generation to generation. Whether Ali's fame will transcend generations in the United States is uncertain, but for his own generation at least, Ali's fame has lasted, as has no other athlete's.

Where Ali chiefly differs from other sports heroes, however, is in something more fundamental: the very kind of heroism, he represents. Halberstam's equation of heroism with fame runs counter to a definition of the hero that we associate with fame runs counter to a definition of the hero that we associate with ages before the advent of the mass media—heroism as something more than celebrity, the hero as someone who embodies qualities we admire and wish to emulate, who ultimately represents his people in their highest aspiration. On these terms we might say that Jordan, too, is not just famous but also heroic; he embodies the dazzling grace, beauty, creativity, and competitiveness that feed the fantasies of children and inspire awe in adults. But Ali embodied that and more: the astonishing drama/melodrama/tragedy of his career gave his popular representations a kind of depth and resonance that the visual images of the electronic media cannot capture. Halberstam claims that Ali's religion and politics limited his fame. Certainly they made him a villain for many in the late sixties and early seventies, as they made him a hero to others; but they also gave moral substance to the image that emerged from the desperate fights of his comeback—the ones with Frazier and Foreman—during a politically more quiescent time, when history seemed to have proven him right in refusing induction into the army. The apparent moral courage of the draft resister and his identification with the underprivileged throughout the world deepened and enlarged the physical and psychological courage of the man who slugged it out with Joe Frazier for fourteen brutal rounds in Manila. If Ali's principles angered many in the 1960s, by the 1970s he could be admired for at least having principles. To think of Muhammad Ali in this way makes him seem an anachronism, a kind of hero perhaps no longer possible in the age of the spectacle.

Or—another possibility. Perhaps Muhammad Ali, as "cultural text," can represent a model for American culture as a whole for which we are desperately searching today. Through the 1960s, Ali was a hero to the young more than the old, to intellectuals more than blue-collar workers, to blacks more than whites, to militant blacks more than moderate and Christian blacks. By the mid-seventies, after the Foreman and Frazier fights, when Ali became almost universally admired, he continued to mean different things to different people. Mark Kram pondered the diversity of Ali's audience in the months following the third Frazier fight: "His followers cut across all class lines. There are the masses of poor, who see him as a symbol of escape from their own miseries, as an enemy of tyrannous governments. There are the moneyed, who must always be near success. There is the white middle class, that huge engine of society that once so rejected him but now jockeys for position with miniature cameras and ballpoint pens.". . .

. . . Muhammad Ali came to be a true "multicultural text," in which for over a decade we Americans, in all our diversity, were able to find important values. For most of Ali's boxing career his public images were inextricably tied to his race, and for part of that time they were bound to his racialist rhetoric. But at some point in the mid-seventies, this changed. Ali remained utterly racial yet simultaneously beyond race.

The world of sport regularly raises up a handful of heroes, who for a short time represent the fastest, the strongest, the most graceful, the most courageous, but who then yield their pedestals to the next set of heroes. The culture as a whole benefits, while the discarded heroes often become victims of their own fame, players in our modern version of an ancient tragedy. But in addition, on rare occasions, from the world of sport arises a Muhammad Ali, who not only is the prettiest, the loudest, and the greatest, but who reminds us of the deeper and broader possibilities of commitment and achievement, while still entertaining us and letting us dream.

✸ F U R T H E R   R E A D I N G

Arthur Ashe, *A Hard Road to Glory: A History of the African-American Athlete, 1619–1986*, 3 vols. (1988)

Dana Brooks and Ronald Althouse, eds., *Racism in College Athletics: The African-American Athlete's Experience* (1993)

Michael Eric Dyson, "Be Like Mike? Michael Jordan and the Pedagogy of Desire," in *Reflecting Black: African-American Cultural Criticism* (1993), 64–74

Gerald Early, *The Culture of Bruising: Essays on Prizefighting, Literature and Modern American Culture* (1994)

Nelson George, *Elevating the Game* (1992)

Elliott Gorn, ed., *Muhammad Ali: The People's Champion* (1996)

Ronald E. Marcello, "The Integration of Intercollegiate Athletics in Texas: North Texas State College as a Test Case, 1956," *Journal of Sport History* 14 (Winter 1987), 286–316

Joseph T. Moore, *Pride Against Prejudice—The Biography of Larry Doby* (1988)

Richard Pennington, *Breaking the Ice: The Racial Integration of Southwest Conference Football* (1987)

Jeffrey Sammons, *Beyond the Ring: The Role of Boxing in American Society* (1988)

Thomas G. Smith, "Civil Rights on the Gridiron: The Kennedy Administration and the Washington Redskins," *Journal of Sport History* 14 (Summer 1987), 189–208

Thomas G. Smith, "Outside the Pale: The Exclusion of Blacks From Organized Professional Football, 1934–1946," *Journal of Sport History* 15 (Winter 1988), 255–81

Jules Tygiel, *Baseball's Great Experiment: Jackie Robinson and His Legacy* (1983)

David K. Wiggins, *Sport, Race, and American Culture: African-American Athletes in a White World* (1997)

CHAPTER
14

The Business of Sport, 1945–1990

The business of sport has changed dramatically since World War II, when the only truly national spectator sports were boxing, thoroughbred racing, and professional baseball (although there was no major league team west of the Mississippi), and it is now truly a "big business." The national population rose from 140 million in 1940 to 249 million in 1990, with most of this growth occurring in suburbs and the sunbelt—some at the expense of declining industrial cities in the East and Midwest. How did these demographic shifts enhance opportunities for sports entrepreneurs? They took advantage of the emerging new markets by shifting established franchises to unexploited growing cities, creating new teams, and organizing new leagues. They were typically super-rich men who utilized their wealth to invest in sporting enterprises to make money, to take advantage of tax loopholes, and to become celebrities.

How did the rise of television affect professional sports? Boxing was the first big TV sport (discounting wrestling "exhibitions"). It was perfect for the video camera because of its restricted space, and during the late 1940s, fights were televised virtually nightly. However, by the late 1950s interest in boxing was curtailed by its oversaturation on TV, domination by organized crime, monopolistic ventures like the International Boxing Club, the absence of top white American fighters, and the dearth of charismatic champions. Horse racing enjoyed great success in this era, drawing the largest audiences of any sport from the early 1950s until the early 1990s, when it was supplanted by baseball as a spectator sport. Major-league baseball remained popular due to local coverage, although regionally televised games nearly destroyed the minor leagues in the early 1950s. Declining profits in smaller media markets led to the first major league franchise shifts in fifty years, beginning in 1953, when the Boston Braves moved to Milwaukee. Soon teams in major cities were on the move, like the Giants and the highly profitable Dodgers, who moved to the West Coast in 1958.

Though lagging behind baseball in popularity, professional football moved to the West Coast in 1946, a decade ahead of major-league baseball. The National Football League (NFL) gained significant fan support in the late 1950s, and it boomed in the 1960s due to the excitement of the sport, outstanding players and teams, and the game's compatibility with television. The NFL benefited greatly from a national TV contract that was equally divided up among its members. By the 1970s, NFL crowds averaged 90 percent capacity, and it appeared that football would surpass baseball as the national pastime.

How did players benefit from the boom in professional sports? Players received relatively little of the profits because reserve clauses in their contracts limited their negotiating power until the 1960s. Then events started moving in their favor because of court decisions that made all sports, except baseball, liable to antitrust law as well as the growing militancy of players' unions. Salaries began to edge up, especially following player strikes and the achievement of arbitration. Baseball wages rose nearly 250 percent from 1967 to 1975, and basketball by 500 percent, where players averaged over $100,000. Following the introduction of free agency, major-league baseball and NBA salaries shot up even more, and both surpassed one million dollars on average in 1993. Nonetheless, sports franchises became increasingly valuable because of multimillion-dollar TV contracts, lucrative licensing agreements, and increased attendance. By 1993, the New York Yankees and Dallas Cowboys were each worth around $200 million, making sports a truly big business.

⚾ D O C U M E N T S

The first document is drawn from the 1960 Senate Judiciary's Subcommittee on Anti-Trust and Monopoly investigation of professional boxing, which publicized the strong influence of organized crime in boxing. In this document former lightweight champion Ike Williams testifies about his financial relationship with his manager Blinky Palermo, a known underworld figure. The second document consists of former Los Angeles Major Norris Poulson's reminiscences about his dealings in the 1950s with Brooklyn Dodgers owner Walter O'Malley and his efforts to bring the team to Los Angeles. The Dodgers then were one of the most profitable franchises in baseball, but O'Malley felt that Brooklyn was in a decline, and he had his eyes on potentially huge profits on the West Coast and in pay-TV. The third document is Supreme Court Justice Thurgood Marshall's dissent in the case of *Flood v. Kuhn*. St. Louis Cardinals star center fielder Curt Flood, a twelve-year major-league veteran, had sought free-agent status in 1970 after he was traded to the Philadelphia Phillies. When his request was denied, he sued organized baseball, claiming its reserve clause violated the antitrust laws. In the fourth document, Marvin Miller, a labor attorney who became the executive director of the Major League Baseball Players' Association in 1966 and led the players to major successes against management, reviews the successful fight by pitchers Andy Messersmith and Dave McNally to secure free agency in 1975. The final document consists of Oakland, California, Mayor Lionel Wilson's analysis of why cities need professional sports franchises and are willing to go to nearly any length to keep their teams.

Ike Williams Testifies on the Corruption of Boxing in the Late 1940s

MR. BONOMI [B.]. How much money, Mr. Williams, do you estimate that you made during your ring career?

From Ike Williams, "Testimony," in U.S. Congress, Senate Judiciary Committee, *Professional Boxing: Hearings Before Subcommittee on Antitrust and Monopoly,* 86th Cong., 2d sess., pursuant to S. Res. 238, December 5–14, 1960 (Washington, D.C., Government Printing Office, 1961), 664–71.

MR. IKE WILLIAMS [*I.W.*]. Give or take a few thousand, I made a million dollars. . . .

B. Was there a period when you tried to manage yourself?

I.W. Yes, for several months [1946], but I was unsuccessful in getting a fight. At the time I had 24 fights in Philadelphia, but for some reason or another, the guild was after me, and I couldn't get a fight anywhere in the country.

B. In other words, when you tried to manage yourself, you were boycotted?

I.W. That is right. . . . I could not even get a sparring partner.

B. In fact, when you tried to manage yourself, isn't it true that Jimmy White, who was a member of the managers guild, made a public statement saying that you would be boycotted unless you got a guild member to be your manager?

I.W. Yes; he said I was a wise guy and I was putting ideas into the other fighters' heads and he said they were going to show the people just how powerful they were.

B. You were putting ideas into the other fighters' heads that they might become independent, too; isn't that right?

I.W. That is correct.

B. Did there come a time when you came into contact with a man known as Frank "Blinky" Palermo?

I.W. During the interim, when I could not get a fight around 1946 and 1947, I was laying around training camp staying in condition, and Palermo at that time managed Billy Fox.

He approached me and said he would like to manage me and he would get me straightened out with the guild, so it sounded like a pretty good idea, because I could not get a fight, so I agreed to go with him.

B. When he did become your manager, then you began to get fights again, isn't that right?

I.W. That is right.

B. Let me ask you this, Mr. Williams:

Palermo continued as your manager, did he not, from about 1946 until the time you lost the championship?

I.W. From 1947—we signed a contract in January of 1947—and he continued managing me through 1952.

B. When you lost the championship, you lost Palermo as your manager, isn't that right?

I.W. I lost the championship—actually, I was injured and after I lost the title, I had a couple of fights.

I lost those, so I retired for 6 or 7 months to get my shoulder back in shape and I had a couple of fights, and I did so-so, just so-so, and I guess he saw where my championship days were over so—

B. He dumped you?

I.W. That is one way of putting it. . . .

B. Do you recall that you fought Jesse Flores in Yankee Stadium, New York, on September 23, of 1948?

I.W. Yes, I do.

B. That was a world's lightweight title bout, was it not?

I.W. Yes.

B. What was the amount of your purse from that particular bout?

I.W. $32,500. . . .

B. Did you see one red cent of that $32,000?

I.W. No, I have not, not until today, I have not.

B. The whole $32,500 disappeared, is that right?

I.W. The entire purse.

B. Did you ever speak to Mr. Palermo about the location of the money or where it went?

I.W. Yes.

Well, he told me. Actually, I had left the money with the IBC because in 1948, that was my best year, and I made over $200,000 that year, so trying to ease the tax condition, I said I would collect the money in 1949, but I was buying some properties and I was buying an apartment house and I found I needed my end of the purse, so I told Palermo, I said, "I am going to"—you know—"collect my end of the purse."

So that is when he said, "Ike, I have been up against so and so," and so forth, and so forth.

He said, "That has been spent."

B. Palermo said things were tough for him and he had gone out and spent your purse?

I.W. He said he collected and spent it. . . .

B. Do you recall, Mr. Williams, whether the money was turned over to the manager at the time of the fight and then split with you, or whether you received the money?

I.W. The money was always turned over to the manager. . . .

B. . . . In this particular case, in the Flores bout, you asked the promoter to hold on to the money, did you not?

I.W. Until 1949, that is right.

B. Then when you went to Palermo and asked him where was your end of the purse, he said that he had run up against tough times and had spent your money, is that right?

I.W. That is right, Mr. Bonomi. . . .

B. Mr. Williams, do you recall in that same year on July 12 of 1948, you fought Beau Jack in Shibe Park, Philadelphia? . . .

I.W. That is correct, Mr. Bonomi.

B. Was Frank Palermo your manager at that time?

I.W. Yes, he was.

B. What was the amount of your purse in that particular bout?

I.W. For that fight, I received $32,400. . . .

B. Did you receive any of that purse of $32,400?

I.W. No, not 5 cents.

B. Not 5 cents.

Did you speak to Palermo about it?

I.W. Yes, I did.

B. What did he say?

I.W. I got the same story. He was up against it, and he had spent the purse.

B. So that in these two bouts during 1948, you received a total of about $65,000 in purses and you did not see 1 cent of that money, is that right?

I.W. That is right, Mr. Bonomi.

Senator KEFAUVER. Mr. Bonomi, will you clear this up? Was that $65,000 all supposed to be Mr. Williams' or was it supposed to be divided in some manner with Mr. Palermo?

I.W. Two-thirds was supposed to be mine.

B. You were supposed to receive two-thirds of each of those purses?

I.W. Two-thirds, less expenses. . . .

B. And Mr. Palermo was to receive one-third of each of those purses, is that correct?

I.W. After the expenses, that is right.

B. After the expenses.

So that your end in those two bouts amounted to about $65,000 and you did not see 1 red cent, is that right?

I.W. No, I did not. . . .

Mr. DIXON. Mr. Williams, who paid the taxes on that?

I.W. I paid the taxes, Mr. Dixon.

Mr. DIXON. You paid the taxes on money you never received?

I.W. Yes; I did.

Senator KEFAUVER. Did Palermo advise you to do that?

I.W. No; he did not.

Senator KEFAUVER. You just knew that the money was supposed to be yours and you paid taxes on it, thinking you would get it and never got it?

I.W. That is right, Senator. . . .

B. Mr. Williams, you fought Freddy Dawson in a championship bout in Philadelphia on December 5 of 1949; did you not? . . .

I.W. Yes.

B. Let me ask you this with regard to that bout: Did you receive a $30,000 bribe offer in order to dump that bout or lose to Freddy Dawson?

I.W. It was put before me, Mr. Bonomi. . . .

B. Will you relate to the subcommittee, Mr. Williams, under what circumstances you received that $30,000 bribe offer? . . .

B. Was that $30,000 bribe offer made to you through this man, Frank "Blinky" Palermo?

I.W. Yes; it was.

B. Under what circumstances was that made? What happened at that time? . . .

I.W. Well, Mr. Bonomi, I vetoed it like I did all the rest of them.

Senator KEFAUVER. You vetoed it like all the rest of them?

I.W. Yes; I did.

Senator KEFAUVER. There have been other offers from time to time?

I.W. Yes, Senator. I received several bribes. All fighters receive bribes. I will say even the biggest fighters that ever lived. I will say Joe Louis and Jack Dempsey, I will say some guy, some nut, would come to them, even with Dempsey. . . .

B. When did Palermo make this $30,000 bribe offer in connection with your bout with Freddy Dawson? . . .

I.W. I imagine it was 3 or 4 weeks before the fight.

B. What did Mr. Palermo say to you on that occasion?

I.W. That I have told you, Mr. Bonomi; that he told me that someone had offered him $30,000 for me to lose the fight to Dawson, but he said if it was me, he says, I would not take it.

I told you before that he said he told the guy to go and drop dead or something, or words to that effect.

B. You say that Mr. Palermo said that you could make $30,000, if you lost the bout to Freddy Dawson, but then he told you, "Please don't take it"? . . .

I.W. Mr. Bonomi, quote me on this. I will tell you verbatim what the man [Palermo] said.

He said, "Ike, I was approached by a fellow." Whom the fellow was I do not know. But he said—he didn't call any names—he said: "A fellow offered me $30,000 for you to lose the fight." He said, "I told the fellow to go and drop dead." And he said, "If it is me," he said, "I wouldn't take it." He said, "Use your own judgment about it."

B. But he went ahead and told you that you could make $30,000 if you lost the bout to Freddy Dawson; is that right?

I.W. He did not put it in those words. He said he was offered that.

B. But he went ahead and informed you of this, did he not?

I.W. Yes. He told me about it. He also told me if it was him, he wouldn't take it.

B. He said to use your own judgment?

I.W. That is right. . . .

B. Do you recall an incident in your dressing room on the date of the title fight, December 5, 1949?

I.W. Yes, I do.

B. What happened at that time?

I.W. I recall it vividly as if it happened this morning.

Approximately 10 minutes before the fight, I was going to defend the title against a very powerful contender, Freddy Dawson, of Chicago, whom I had fought twice before, and approximately 10 minutes, about 10 minutes to 10, a good friend of mine, Bill Keller, William Keller, of Trenton, he came in.

Well, he is an elderly man. He is 76 years of age now and he was in a high state of excitement and he said, "Ike," he said, "they are going to take the fight from you."

B. He said, "They are going to take the fight from you"?

I.W. They were his exact words.

B. What did you do at this point?

I.W. Well, Mr. Bonomi, in a condition like that, I called my trainer, Jesse Goss, who put the first pair of gloves on me, and Calvin Taylor. . . .

I was going to defend my title, the lightweight title, and I think it was the second biggest sports—I think it is the second biggest title in sports, exceeded only by the heavyweight title.

I told Calvin Taylor, I said, "Go down and get the sportswriters."

So in 2 or 3 minutes later he went down and he came back with Red Smith, John Webster, and Jack Sarnas, and all of the leading sportswriters at the fight, and I told the fellows, I said, "After I fight tonight, come back, I have a story for you."

This, you can check in the papers.

So after the fight—I won the fight, I received the decision—and they came back, they said, "Ike, what do you have to tell us?"

So I told them what the fellow told me, what Bill Keller told me.

He said if the fight went 15 rounds, I was going to lose it. But evidently the man had given me false information. . . .

B. You won by a decision, is that correct?

I.W. Decision. I won by decision, 15 rounds.

B. Did you win by a large margin, do you recall?

I.W. I remember the *New York Times,* they gave me nine rounds and gave Dawson five—nine, five, and one even.

B. So apparently if the officials had any idea of taking the bout away from you, they were scared by your conference with the newspapermen, is that right?

I.W. Probably so.

B. As a result of your conference before the bout with the newspapermen, were you called before the Pennsylvania State Athletic Commission?

I.W. I most certainly was. . . .

B. Mr. Williams, tell us what happened before the State athletic commission the day after the Dawson bout?

I.W. I was called in and I was fined $500.

B. You were fined $500?

I.W. That is right. Commissioner Raines said for inciting—I don't know—for stirring up, you know, accusing. I don't know, I don't remember verbatim what the man said, but words to that effect of accusing the officials of dishonesty or something. . . .

B. You mean you were fined $500 because you reflected on the integrity of the boxing officials in the State of Pennsylvania; is that right?

I.W. That is right, Mr. Bonomi.

B. Do you recall that you fought Kid Gavilan on January 28 of 1949 in Madison Square Garden?

I.W. That is right.

B. At that time did you receive a $100,000 bribe offer to lose that bout through Frank "Blinky" Palermo?

I.W. Yes; I do remember that. . . .

B. You say on this occasion, too, he said, "Use your own judgment"?

I.W. That is what he said, Mr. Bonomi. He said, "If it was me, I wouldn't take it."

He said, "You are doing all right. You don't need the money," but, of course, at the time I was behind with taxes, as we all are, and actually I am sorry I did not take it, Mr. Bonomi. I didn't, but I am sorry I didn't take it.

B. You are sorry you didn't take the $100,000?

I.W. I am sorry I didn't take it.

B. Why? You lost the fight anyway; is that it?

I.W. I lost the fight anyway, although I thought I won it. Most of the New York papers gave me the fight.

Dan Parker said he thought I won it, also Bill Corum. Well, most of the papers gave me the fight, but the officials, they called it against me, and that is their business, so I guess they know more about it than I do. . . .

B. Do you recall that you lost the world's lightweight title in a bout with Jimmy Carter on May 25 of 1951?

I.W. Yes, I do.

B. That bout was held in Madison Square Garden, . . .

The bout was promoted by the International Boxing Club?

I.W. That is right.

B. By the way, the manager of Jimmy Carter at that time was Willie Ketchum?

I.W. That is right. . . .

B. . . . The testimony before the subcommittee is that Mr. Ketchum was partners with Frank Carbo in the management of Jimmy Carter. . . .

Did you receive a $50,000 bribe offer through Palermo in your championship bout with Jimmy Carter, which was promoted by the I.B.C.?

I.W. I did not receive a bribe offer from him, but I was told that he was approached. He told me someone approached him.

B. Mr. Palermo said that somebody would put up $50,000 for you and Mr. Palermo, if you lost the bout?

I.W. That is right, Mr. Bonomi.

B. So on three occasions you received substantial bribe offers, on one occasion $30,000, the next occasion $100,000 and on this occasion $50,000; is that correct?

I.W. That is correct, Mr. Bonomi.

B. In all of those bouts the world's championship was at stake; is that right?

I.W. No, no, it wasn't.

B. The Gavilan bout, wasn't that a championship bout?

I.W. Gavilan outweighed me 10 or 12 pounds. I couldn't have fought him.

B. That was an over-the-weight bout?

I.W. That is right, Mr. Bonomi.

B. The third bout, however, with Jimmy Carter was a world's lightweight championship bout, is that right?

I.W. Yes, it was. . . .

B. You lost the bout to Jimmy Carter, did you not?

I.W. Yes, I did.

B. You lost your championship at that time?

I.W. I lost the championship.

B. So that when you rejected the bribe offer of $50,000, you actually lost an awful lot of money anyway, didn't you?

I.W. I lost the greatest thing I ever had in my life when I lost the lightweight title, Mr. Bonomi.

B. Did you feel the same way after the bout with Jimmy Carter as you felt after the Gavilan bout: That you lost the bout anyway; you should have taken the bribe?

I.W. No, I felt differently. I'll tell you, Mr. Bonomi, I was injured very seriously before the Carter fight, and, speaking for myself, I should have taken the money, but I didn't take it.

I should have taken it, because I said—I was due to fight, Art Aragon in Los Angeles 18 days after the Carter fight, and speaking for myself, I said even if I beat Carter, I would not be able to beat Aragon in California. So I said actually I should take the money, you know. I should take it.

But I didn't, and I lost the fight anyway. . . .

Senator KEFAUVER. You feel better that you didn't take it, though, don't you?

I.W. I do not, Senator; believe me, I don't.

Senator KEFAUVER. You feel what?

I.W. I do not.

Mr. KITTRIE. Why didn't you take it?

I.W. Why? Because the lightweight title meant too much to me and I had a lot of people, loyal friends, that I would never let down.

They have bet their hard-earned money on me and I wouldn't doublecross them. But as things went on and things got tough, I found out how loyal they were. . . .

Norris Poulson Reveals How Los Angeles Got the Brooklyn Dodgers in 1958

. . . When in February, 1957, O'Malley bought the Los Angeles Angels of the Pacific Coast League and the local ball park, Wrigley Field, he sent word confidentially through a friend that he would like to see me. He was then at the Dodger spring-training camp in Vero Beach, Florida. I flew there with a group of our city and county officials.

The meeting was primarily a sparring match. One of our officials promised O'Malley the moon, and Walter asked for more. You couldn't blame him. He had a valuable package in the Dodgers and he knew it. I assured him we wanted desperately to get the team, but made it clear we would have to come up with a plan that wouldn't get all of us run out of the city. . . .

O'Malley gave us no promises at Vero Beach, but did say that if he were to consider our city at all, he would expect us to build a ball park. Land didn't interest him in the least. . . .

O'Malley managed subtly in his conversations with us to point out what other cities would do for him. He wasn't however, unreasonable, now that he was certain we were serious. He indicated that the "Milwaukee Formula" might be acceptable to him. For the use of County Stadium, Milwaukee, the Braves at the time were giving the city five percent of receipts and fifteen percent of concessions. . . .

. . . I appointed a citizens committee to study ways and means of developing Chavez Ravine.

When I took office in 1953, some 183 acres of Chavez Ravine belonged to the Los Angeles Housing Authority, which had acquired the land from the Federal Government for public housing. However, estimates for grading the jagged terrain were so high that the idea of building there was growing less feasible.

Secretly, we got Howard Hughes to advance $5000 for a cursory survey, with the promise he would be repaid if at all possible. He never got his money back, nor did he ask for it.

The survey showed that the cost of building a baseball stadium and parking lot in the hills of Chavez would be exorbitant. Engineers estimated no less than $10,000,000 and even as much as $15,000,000. . . .

From Norris Poulson interview, "The Dodgers and Chavez Ravine," UCLA Oral History Collection, 1966.

In late May, I went to Brooklyn to see O'Malley. I explained that we couldn't raise the money to build a ball park, but suggested that we would try to get him the land at Chavez Ravine for a nominal cost, and he could build his own stadium. He hit the ceiling. "I already have one ball park there!" he exclaimed. "What am I going to do with two?"

He hastened to add that no one had built a ball park with private capital in more than thirty years, and, besides, he would have to lay out cash for indemnification to the Pacific Coast League.

Since O'Malley needed us much less than we needed him, he obviously held the trump cards. In the course of our discussion, he asked if maybe he could sell Wrigley Field to the city. I knew in my heart that the only plausible solution was a trade of Wrigley Field for Chavez Ravine, but I also knew that in dealing loosely with city property, I was getting in over my head and playing with political dynamite. . . .

When I returned to Los Angeles, I huddled privately with a small group of our leading citizens. [Frank Payne, publisher of the Los Angeles *Examiner,* and Norman Chandler, publisher of the *Times.*] . . .

. . . They suggested that I get as my representative some top-notch negotiator who understood real estate values and who could hold his own in a bargaining match with the wily O'Malley.

I followed their advice and enlisted the services of Harold C. McClellan, a highly successful business leader who had just returned from a tour of duty as Assistant Secretary of Commerce. McClellan met with City Attorney Roger Arnebergh and Chief City Administrator Samuel Leask to work out some sort of deal to offer the Dodgers. Casually, I suggested the possibility of a trade of Wrigley Field for Chavez Ravine, and the boys took it from there.

These men aren't fools. They realized that baseball would be expensive. But they also knew that the investment was sound. Local business would benefit enormously. The youth of the county would benefit. Hundreds of thousands of sports fans would derive pleasure from major league ball, and the prestige that would come to the city from having a quality team like the Dodgers would be invaluable.

The negotiations were a delicate and complicated matter. . . .

We would give the Dodgers our 185 acres in Chavez Ravine, would buy them an additional 115 acres at a price not to exceed $7,000 an acre, and would contribute $2,000,000 toward grading. With money it received from the State Gasoline Tax Fund, the Country would make available about $2,700,000 for building access roads.

In turn, the Dodgers would hand over Wrigley Field, valued at $2,275,000 for city recreational purposes in a much-needed area. The Dodgers also would set aside forty acres in Chavez Ravine for a recreational area on which they would spend $500,000 for development. For a minimum of twenty years, they would spend $60,000 a year to maintain the area. And they would pay taxes on their property, probably amounting to $350,000 annually.

O'Malley finally agreed to the contract, but not without misgivings. He still would have preferred the City's building the stadium.

I discovered early in my dealings with Walter that he does not run a philanthropic society. He is cool and clever and has the patience required of a good horse-trader. But the man, in truth, was maligned unjustly by many. He didn't make a land grab at Chavez Ravine. The property was more or less thrust upon him by circumstances. As the saying goes, he backed into it. And even though the acreage today is worth a fortune . . . it wouldn't have been if he hadn't risked the money to develop it.

Now that he had decided to move to Los Angeles, O'Malley felt that it would be advantageous both to the Dodgers and the league if a franchise could be established in San Francisco. He was reasonably certain that Horace Stoneham was ready to shift the Giants from New York—very likely to Minneapolis–St. Paul where a ball park already had been built. O'Malley asked me if I knew George Christopher, the mayor of San Francisco. Told that I did, he asked if I would set up a private meeting among the three of us. I did—at the Beverly-Hilton Hotel in Beverly Hills. O'Malley invited a fourth party, Matty Fox, president of a pay-TV firm called Skistron. At about 9 o'clock, which was midnight in New York, O'Malley placed a long distance call for Stoneham. He told the Giants president that his team would do much better in California than in Minnesota and assured him that Fox would help finance the San Francisco project in return for subscription television privileges at a future date.

. . . A few days later, Christopher flew to New York and locked up the Giants for San Francisco. As agreed, Fox began making payments to the club in 1958, but when pay TV never came into focus, Stoneham released him from the contract.

. . . All that seemed to remain to consummate the deal between the City and O'Malley was the blessing of the City Council. It was then that the revolution began. Political enemies of mine, O'Malley haters, baseball haters, crackpots, intelligent people feeling the city was being slickered, and groups with selfish motives seemed to emerge from the alcoves all at once.

They were backed by two media which seized upon the issue to further or protect their own interests. One was a large segment of community newspapers in Los Angeles and Orange counties. The other was television. The metropolitan dailies in Los Angeles favored baseball. To discredit these publications and make a grab for circulation and advertising, the community papers used Chavez Ravine as the stick with which to beat the drum. They screamed that the mayor, encouraged by the LA dailies, was giving away the people's land.

They were joined by local television, which took an immediate dislike to O'Malley. He was an outspoken advocate of pay TV. . . .

Well, the intrigue now began. To ratify the Chavez Ravine contract, we needed ten of the fifteen votes in the City Council. I was sure of eight. Four were against, one was out of town, and two were on the fence. The issue was debated at great length in the Council Chamber and the vote was delayed repeatedly, making O'Malley understandably nervous. National League President Warren Giles then got into the picture. He warned Los Angeles that unless it ratified the contract before the start of the National League meeting on October 1, the league would look unfavorably upon our city as a place to move a franchise.

I was up against it. On September 30, the Council was still arguing over the contract and not yet ready to vote. My leaders in the Council were Roz Wyman and John Gibson, who carried the discussion late into the night. All the while, I was seated in my office in another section of the City Hall, listening to the arguments over the intercom. Uneasily, I kept looking at my watch. . . .

. . . Short two votes, I decided to get help from outside forces. Quietly, I visited some labor unions and asked them to use persuasive charm with one of the fence-sitting councilmen. To put the pressure on the other, I called on downtown businessmen. . . .

On October 7, . . . our team turned up with ten votes. We cheered loudly. The battle, at last, was won—or so we thought. . . .

The resourceful enemy circulated a referendary petition for which 53,000 valid signatures were obtained, enough to bring the Chavez Ravine issue to the ballot. . . . A poll showed that seventy percent of the citizens favored the Chavez Ravine contract. . . .

To counter this competition, I suggested a scare campaign that would strike home with the low-income people who didn't belong to country clubs and social groups and who wanted big league baseball for entertainment. The referendum, we led them to believe, was unalterably a yes-or-no vote for baseball. By this time, the Dodgers had started playing in the Coliseum, and the fans loved them. The prospect of losing them wasn't appealing.

On June 3, 1958, the citizens went to the polls. The battle was touch and go, but we beat the referendum by some 23,000 votes, not too many considering the population of Los Angeles. . . .

Justice Thurgood Marshall Dissents in the Curt Flood Case, 1972

Petitioner was a major league baseball player from 1956, when he signed a contract with the Cincinnati Reds, until 1969, when his 12-year career with the St. Louis Cardinals, which had obtained him from the Reds, ended and he was traded to the Philadelphia Phillies. He had no notice that the Cardinals were contemplating a trade, no opportunity to indicate the teams with which he would prefer playing, and no desire to go to Philadelphia. After receiving formal notification of the trade, petitioner wrote to the Commissioner of Baseball protesting that he was not "a piece of property to be bought and sold irrespective of my wishes," and urging that he had the right to consider offers from other teams than the Phillies. He requested that the Commissioner inform all of the major league teams that he was available for the 1970 season. His request was denied, and petitioner was informed that he had no choice but to play for Philadelphia or not to play at all.

To non-athletes it might appear that petitioner was virtually enslaved by the owners of major league baseball clubs who bartered among themselves for his services. But, athletes know that it was not servitude that bound petitioner to the club owners; it was the reserve system. The essence of that system is that a player is bound to the club with which he first signs a contract for the rest of his playing

From *Flood v. Kuhn* 407 U.S. 258 (1972).

days. He cannot escape from the club except by retiring, and he cannot prevent the club from assigning his contract to any other club.

Petitioner . . . alleged, among other things, that the reserve system was an unreasonable restraint of trade. . . .

Americans love baseball as they love all sports. Perhaps we become so enamored of athletics that we assume that they are foremost in the minds of legislators as well as fans. We must not forget, however, that there are only some 600 major league baseball players. Whatever muscle they might have been able to muster by combining forces with other athletes has been greatly impaired by the manner in which this Court has isolated them. It is this Court that has made them impotent, and this Court should correct its error.

We do not lightly overrule our prior constructions of federal statutes, but when our errors deny substantial federal rights, like the right to compete freely and effectively to the best of one's ability as guaranteed by the antitrust laws, we must admit our error and correct it. We have done so before and we should do so again here. . . .

To the extent that there is concern over any reliance interests that club owners may assert, they can be satisfied by making our decision prospective only. Baseball should be covered by the antitrust laws beginning with this case and henceforth, unless Congress decides otherwise.

Accordingly, I would overrule *Federal Baseball Club* and *Toolson* and reverse the decision of the Court of Appeals.

This is a difficult case because we are torn between the principle of *stare decisis* and the knowledge that the decisions in *Federal Baseball Club* v. *National League,* 259 U. S. 200 (1922), and *Toolson* v. *New York Yankees, Inc.,* 346 U. S. 356 (1953), are totally at odds with more recent and better reasoned cases. . . .

In his answer to petitioner's complaint, the Commissioner of Baseball "admits that under present concepts of interstate commerce defendants are engaged therein.". . . There can be no doubt that the admission is warranted by today's reality. Since baseball is interstate commerce, if we re-examine baseball's antitrust exemption, the Court's decisions in . . . *United States* v. *International Boxing Club,* 348 U. S. 236 (1955), and *Radovich* v. *National Football League,* 352 U. S. 445 (1957), require that we bring baseball within the coverage of the antitrust laws. . . .

Marvin Miller Analyzes the Achievement of Free Agency, 1975

Andy Messersmith['s] and Dave McNally['s]. . . willingness to challenge the reserve clause . . .—led to the most important arbitration decision in the history of professional sports.

I had never made a secret of my contention from the beginning that Paragraph 10(a) in the Uniform Player's Contract clearly stated that the owners had a right to

From Marvin Miller, *A Whole Different Ball Game: The Sport and Business of Baseball* (New York: Birch Lane, 1991), 238–47.

renew an unsigned player *for one year, and one year only.* Management had always said that if a team and a player couldn't agree on salary, the club could review the player's last contract for one additional year *without* his signature and that this right of renewal had no limit. Simply stated, the claim was that a club had the right to renew a player's contract *forever.* The only alternative a player had to complying with the rule was to quit playing baseball for a living. . . .

. . . The Players Association, in not pressing for a *negotiated* settlement of the reserve clause issue in 1970 . . . was by no means surrendering its right to do so. We had made a tactical decision: We would fight the reserve clause in court rather than at the bargaining table so as not to divide our energies and resources. But when the Supreme Court in *Flood* again upheld its fifty-year-old decision . . . exempting baseball from antitrust laws, we were back to square one.

Square one, that is, on paper. For I could sense that the pressure we had put on the owners would cause them to yield somewhere down the line. The judges, after all, had not said that our desire to reform the reserve rules was wrong; they had just said that reform should be accomplished through collective bargaining. . . .

With impartial arbitration in effect, we could argue the meaning and interpretation of a contract provision. It was only a matter of time, I felt, before we could test whether a club's right of renewal of a contract lasted forever or existed only for one additional year. . . .

. . . The clubs, in spite of what they said, didn't believe an unsigned contract could be renewed more than once. Before too long, a player would find it in his own best interest to finish a season under a renewed contract and then assert that he was a free agent on the grounds that he had no contractual connection with any club.

Enter Andy Messersmith, . . . the best pitcher in the National League in 1974. Before going to the Dodgers, Andy had enjoyed five productive seasons with the Angels, and he had been shocked when he was dealt to the Dodgers. In 1974, he signed a one-year, $90,000 contract and led the league in wins (20) and winning percentage (.769). In 1975, the Dodgers and Messersmith were apart on salary, and he asked for a no-trade provision, or at least the right to approve any trade involving him. Walter O'Malley refused, and the club renewed Messersmith's 1974 contract with a modest salary increase. Andy did not sign. . . .

Messersmith was having another terrific season in 1975. When he pressed for the no-trade provision, O'Malley countered by saying, "Can't do it. The league wouldn't approve the contract."

"Bull," I said, when Messersmith told me of O'Malley's reply. "Absolute bull! There's no such regulation.". . .

Despite his policy of nixing no-trade contracts, my guess was that O'Malley would sign Messersmith. First off, he was the ace of the Dodgers' staff. He had won 19 games in 1975 with a 2.29 ERA. Secondly, though management professed they would win should the case go to arbitration, they certainly preferred to postpone a grievance as long as possible. After all, if the decision didn't go their way, they were in danger of losing it all.

. . . I found that the only other unsigned player during the 1975 season was former Orioles pitcher Dave McNally. McNally had pitched thirteen seasons for the Orioles, including four straight twenty-win seasons. After the 1974 season,

Baltimore traded him to the Expos. After starting the 1975 season there, McNally decided to leave baseball. . . .

McNally was the perfect player to challenge the reserve rule. He was a good union man; he had once been player rep in Baltimore. And having no intention of pursuing a career in baseball, he was immune to retaliation. Messersmith could sign with the Dodgers and we would still have a test case.

I told McNally, "I'd like to add your name to the grievance as insurance if Andy decides to sign a new Dodger contract."

"If you need me," he said, "I'm willing to help.". . . Once we had McNally as a reserve test case, O'Malley no longer had any reason to offer Messersmith a no-trade clause. . . .

. . . My guess is that other prominent owners were opposed to the loss of control implicit in a player's being able to veto a trade and, having been erroneously informed by Kuhn and the lawyers that the arbitrator would rule against the Association, urged O'Malley to stand firm. Besides, the challenge to the reserve rule could no longer be sidetracked by signing Messersmith. Dave McNally was waiting in the wings—a fact Kuhn conveniently forgets.

We filed two grievances on the last day of the 1975 season. Predictably, management screamed that the sky was falling. National League president Chub Feeney said that if owners bid for players' services, it would be so disastrous that "we might not have a World Series." Dodger manager Walter Alston predicted graver consequences: "If Messersmith is declared a free agent, then baseball is dead." I half expected him to claim that Los Angeles would fall into the Pacific. . . .

Peter Seitz, the arbitrator who had ruled against Charles Finley in the Catfish Hunter case, set the hearing date for November 21. An experienced lawyer, Seitz had been a full-time artibrator for twenty years. He had a reputation as a professional, intelligent arbitrator, but I didn't consider him to be prounion. . . .

Some of his more recent opinions and awards had impressed me with their objectivity. While reviewing his record, however, I found something that seemed significant. As an arbitrator for the National Basketball Association and the NBA Players Association, Seitz had noted in an opinion the 1969 California Court of Appeals ruling which gave NBA star Rick Barry the right to sign with the Oakland Oaks of the rival American Basketball Association after playing out his option year with the San Francisco Warriors. That court found that the standard basketball contract permitted a club to renew a player's contract for one year only. The wording of the renewal clause in the NBA's Uniform Player's Contract was almost identical to ours—in fact, it was copied from baseball's. Given the similarities, Seitz's opinion containing that reference to the California court ruling caught my eye. It seemed significant to me. . . .

Once the hearing started, the first matter to be considered was management's argument that the grievance was outside an arbitrator's jurisdiction. After each side had presented its case, the hearing recessed for a week. Seitz reviewed the transcript and ruled that the grievance was arbitrable. . . .

The arbitration panel consisted of John Gaherin, Peter Seitz, and me. . . . The transcript of the hearings and the correspondence between Seitz and the principals shows that Seitz did all in his power to get the parties to take the case from him by negotiating a settlement. . . . A settlement would be much wiser than risking the whole ball game.

Mayor Lionel J. Wilson Explains Why Oakland Needs the Raiders, 1984

. . . I want to describe why we feel so strongly about the Raiders staying in Oakland. . . . The Raiders and the NFL are a major civic asset in the Oakland area; they have made Oakland a big league town. . . .

To the City of Oakland and to the millions of Oakland Raiders supporters throughout Northern California, the Raiders are far more than simply a football team. They are a key part of the local economy. The Raiders' modern football stadium, called the "Oakland-Alameda County Coliseum," was built especially for the team. Financed by a public bond issue, the City and County acquired many acres of land to provide for this football stadium and attendant parking and other necessary facilities. Located entirely within the City, the stadium's present replacement value is in the range of $65 to $70 million.

From an economic standpoint, the presence of the Raiders in Oakland regularly attracts thousands of people from outside the city, and results in people within the city spending on local businesses that would not exist without the draw of a professional football team. One Oakland business community estimate is that direct spending in this connection amounts to $36 million annually, with the indirect benefits totalling $180 million. In addition, the Coliseum sports complex has served to catapult Oakland's image as a "major league" city, thus enabling the City to attract numerous and substantial outside investors for many of its projects, both public and private. So in pure economic terms, the Raiders have given us an image and a status that communities such as ours strongly need.

But the Raiders have a more important value to us than simply an economic one—they are a creative and vital part of our community. A professional football team, and especially one as successful as the Raiders, can be a tremendous unifying force to a community. People of all ages, races, and income levels are able to share a highly rewarding common interest and experience. Sports teams represent and often mirror their communities and, in turn, the communities become a part of their team. . . . As Gene Upshaw, the captain of the Raiders put it, "The Raiders and Oakland have given each other"—and I emphasize that—"given each other a sense of pride and identity.". . .

Oakland needs the pride and identity it gets from the Raiders and, in return, we have taken the team into our hearts. It is difficult for me to convey the sense of abandonment, of loss, and yes, of outrage with which East Bay residents greeted the Raiders' announcement that they were leaving Oakland for Southern California merely because a larger California community had offered them a candy store of

From Mayor Lionel J. Wilson, Oakland, Calif., "Statement," in U.S. Congress, House Committee on the Judiciary, *Oversight Hearings: Antitrust Policy and Professional Sports* (Washington, D.C.: Government Printing Office, 1984), 416–18.

supposed financial goodies. . . . The AFL chose Oakland because the East Bay area offered certain advantages to the League and to its other clubs. . . . And Joe Foss, Commissioner of the AFL, came to Oakland . . . promising our citizens that if the Raiders were consistently supported, then the team would remain in Oakland.

. . . The community of Oakland took the AFL at its word and supported the Raiders in every possible way. We built—at taxpayers expense—two stadiums, first, Frank Youell Field, and then the Oakland Coliseum, a modern stadium that is the equal of most facilities in the nation. . . .

But without the Oakland Raiders, our Oakland-Alameda Coliseum would never have been built. It was the clear intention of both the City and the then-owners of the Raiders that the Raiders, in recognition of this outpouring of public support and funds, would be located in Oakland so long as the team was well supported. In short, the Raiders franchise has been continuously integrated with the stadium. . . .

The twins grew and prospered, nurtured by intense and tremendous public support. The Oakland community responded by giving the Raiders more than ten consecutive seasons of sellout crowds—often at high ticket prices. The number of persons wishing to buy season tickets greatly exceeded the available tickets; people had to wait years to obtain season tickets. This is a record of support virtually unmatched in professional sports. . . . The Oakland community thus deserves better than what we have received from Al Davis and the Oakland Raiders in the past two years.

Our fans have made the Raiders one of the most financially successful franchises in professional football. Yet suddenly, in early 1980, the Raiders' controlling partner, Al Davis, announced the team's removal. . . .

When the Raiders announced this "move," they did not give the City or County authorities any financial information to justify their action. We felt the club was financially sound but we were kept in the dark by the Raiders. Later, from NFL records in court, we learned that in the year before the "move," 1979, the Raiders ticket receipts exceeded those of all but two of the NFL's 28 teams. We also learned that throughout the 1970s, the Raiders were a profitable and financially sound franchise; and in the later years of the decade, their operating revenues exceeded average NFL club revenues by as much as $1 million or more, and also substantially exceeded the average revenues for both the most profitable clubs and the most successful clubs on the playing field. This is not a struggling team—it is a team that is healthy, vibrant, vital to our community and far too well supported to simply turn its back and leave.

We obviously regard the Raiders as central to our community, its well-being, its image and national stature. . . .

✦ E S S A Y S

In the first essay Randy Roberts of Purdue and James Olson of Sam Houston State examine television's influence upon sport by studying the career of Roone Arledge, the long-time director of ABC Sports. Arledge was responsible for the innovative and long-lived "Wide World of Sports," produced Olympic telecasts, and introduced "Monday Night Football."

Arledge emphasized the entertainment value of sports shows by utilizing the latest technological innovations and creative programming to involve audiences in the "thrill of victory, the agony of defeat." Arledge's work helped ABC to rise from third to first place among the major television networks.

The second essay by political scientist Charles C. Euchner of Holy Cross examines how the municipality of Baltimore worked to prevent the Orioles from leaving, especially after the Colts left the city for Indianapolis "in the middle of the night." Ballparks and arenas were historically almost always privately owned and operated. In 1950, for instance, the Cleveland Indians was the only major-league team to play at a publicly owned ballpark. By 1991, twenty-one of twenty-six (86 percent) major-league teams played at publicly owned facilities. The proportion of publicly operated NFL fields rose in the same period from 36 to 93 percent. Cities whose big-league teams threatened to leave for greener pastures were coerced into subsidizing local clubs, whereas cities without big-league clubs would do nearly anything to secure a major sports franchise. Expenditures of hundreds of millions of dollars to build stadiums and arenas were justified on the grounds of economic development and hometown pride.

The Impact of Roone Arledge on Televised Sports

RANDY ROBERTS AND JAMES OLSON

. . . [Roone] Arledge not only changed the manner in which athletic events were watched and understood, but he also dramatically increased interest in sports. In a complex society, divided along economic, social, and racial lines and often sadly impersonal, sports became a currency which all races and classes dealt in. Rich and poor, black and white, young and old—if they could communicate on no other level, they could always talk about sports. They all had television sets, they watched the same sporting events, they were familiar with the same sports heroes, and they all had opinions about what they saw and what they liked. . . .

In 1960 Roone Pinckney Arledge did not look like a revolutionary. Slightly pudgy, heavily freckled, and red-haired, Arledge resembled an Irish version of the Pillsbury doughboy. Nor did his earlier career denote a revolutionary nature. Born in Forest Hills, raised in upper-middle-class affluence on Long Island, and educated at Columbia University, Arledge's background prepared him for the New York business world. During the late 1950s he produced Shari Lewis' puppet show "Hi, Mom." He won an Emmy Award for his work, and his future with NBC seemed bright. In 1960 the 29-year-old Arledge moved to ABC. About a month before the 1960–61 football season, he gave Tom Moore and Ed Sherick, the network's programming and sports directors, a revolutionary document. It contained a bold new plan for covering football games. He recommended the use of

From Randy Roberts and James Olson, *Winning Is the Only Thing: Sports in American Society Since 1945* (Baltimore: Johns Hopkins University Press, 1989), 114–31.

directional and remote microphones, the use of hand-held and "isolated" cameras, the employment of split screen, and other technical innovations. In addition, he called for a more dynamic halftime show, replacing marching-band performances with in-depth analysis and highlights from the first two quarters. In essence, Arledge wanted to bring the sporting experience into America's living rooms. He believed sports and athletes should be examined "up close and personal." The Roone Revolution had begun.

Impressed by Arledge's plan, Moore and Sherick made Roone producer of ABC's college football programs, thereby giving him an electronic pulpit from which he could preach his new philosophy. Behind his every move rested a central belief: the marriage of sports and innovative entertainment techniques would produce higher ratings. Arledge was convinced that he could use sports to entertain people who were not really sports fans. Through hype and technology he could create a large new audience for ABC's sports programming. . . .

Arledge's first task was to improve televised college football. As Arledge saw it, his job became "taking the fan to the game, not the game to the fan." The idea was simple and revolutionary, and to execute it Arledge and his staff employed sophisticated technology. He wanted the viewer sitting in his living room to see, hear, and experience the game as if he were actually in the football stadium. Before Arledge, television executives had been content simply to bring the viewer the game. Using three or four situated cameras they were able to document the game. For those who loved football, it was enough, but it was not very attractive for the casual viewer.

Arledge, of course, coveted that casual viewer, the person with one eye on the screen and one hand on the dial. Discussing his philosophy in 1966, Arledge wrote: "What we set out to do was to get the audience involved emotionally. If they didn't give a damn about the game, they still might enjoy the program." To do this Arledge used more cameras. He put cameras on cranes and blimps and helicopters to provide a better view of the stadium, the campus, and the town. His technicians developed hand-held cameras for close-ups. In the stadium he employed seven cameras, three just for capturing the environment. "We asked ourselves: If you were sitting in the stadium, what would you be looking at? The coach on the sideline, the substitute quarterback warming up, the pretty girl in the next section. So our cameras wandered as your eyes would." Often what Arledge decided would interest his mostly male viewers were young and beautiful women. . . . The game was only one part of the sporting experience.

Arledge also brought the sounds of football to the television viewer. Before Arledge, producers would hang a mike out the window to get the sound of the crowd. . . . Arledge's technicians developed the rifle-mike to pinpoint sound. Now the viewer could hear the clash of shoulder pads and helmets, the bark of a quarterback calling signals, and the thump of a well-struck punt.

Analysis and play-by-play announcing were not immune to the genius of Arledge and his technicians. The instant replay was one of Arledge's innovations. In 1960 he asked ABC engineer Bob Trachinger "if it would be possible to replay something in slow motion so you could tell if a guy was safe or out or stepped out of bounds." Trachinger designed the device. Arledge remembered using the instant replay during the 1960 Boston College-Syracuse game: "That was a terrific game and, at one point, Jack Concannon, a sophomore quarterback, was trapped in the pocket but ended up running 70 yards for a touchdown. Six or eight people had a shot of him and we replayed the whole thing in slow motion with Paul Christman analyzing the entire play as it unfolded. Nobody had ever seen anything like that before and the impact was unbelievable. That moment changed television sports forever."

From the very beginning Arledge's approach to sports was successful. As he suspected, he could satisfy sports fans and still entertain casual viewers. His college football broadcasts featured heretofore unseen angles both of football players and cheerleaders. For ABC, which in 1960 was running a distant third in the ratings race, Arledge's innovations meant better ratings, higher rates for advertising, and corporate growth. Before long ABC replaced NBC as the leader in sports programming. By the 1970s ABC was the top-rated network. Arledge played a considerable role in ABC's rise, and between 1960 and 1975 his salary rose from $10,000 to approximately $1 million a year.

For Arledge, college football was only the beginning. If sports programming was to have a significant impact on the television industry, he needed important events to televise twelve months a year. Aggressively, sometimes ruthlessly, Arledge went after the television rights for major sports events. "When it comes to acquiring rights," an executive at another network remarked, "the man is totally unscrupulous. A jackal. He'd rip my heart out for a shot at the World Series.". . . In addition to college and professional football and professional baseball, Arledge and ABC have acquired the rights for major golf tournaments, horse races, summer and winter Olympics, All-Star games, and a host of other events.

Arledge's impact upon American sports and entertainment can be seen in several of the sports shows he launched. "Wide World of Sports" was an idea he inherited from Ed Scherick but gave his own distinctive stamp. He oversaw every aspect of its production and even wrote "the thrill of victory, the agony of defeat" opening. In April 1961, after a difficult search for sponsors, "Wide World of Sports" made its debut. It fit perfectly into Arledge's definition of sports as entertainment. The program allowed ABC film crews to roam around the world and televise what they thought was interesting, even if it were only tangentially involved in athletics. The production emphasis was concerned as much with the location and personalities as with the sporting event.

Most importantly "Wide World of Sports" allowed Arledge to control time, the crucial element for programming. The shows did not have to be televised live and were not contained by seasonal schedules. It realized Arledge's vision of "a year-around sports show that could fill the void [between sports seasons] and not have to worry about blackouts." In addition, prerecorded shows could be edited to increase suspense and eliminate dead time. A three-hour downhill skiing event could be edited into two 8-minute segments; an all-day mountain climb could be fit into a half-hour slot. "Wide World of Sports" was, in short, tailored to the average viewer's attention span. "In sports they aren't that familiar with, or in events that aren't important," Arledge noted, "people do enjoy the knowledge that something different will be coming every ten minutes."

To keep "something different coming" continually, "Wide World of Sports" used the broadest possible definition of what constituted sporting activity.

Between 1960 and 1966 Arledge presented eighty-seven different sports, ranging from international track and field meets and world championship boxing contests to demolition derbies and an Eiffel Tower climb. And he used sophisticated technology to make each event as interesting—as entertaining—as possible.

. . . Sports purists claimed that "sports" was the least important word in the "Wide World of Sports" title. Programs containing the demolition derby contests particularly drew hostile comments. Again, however, the critics misunderstood Arledge's job. He was in a commercial entertainment business. His duty was to produce shows that attracted high audience ratings, not rave critical reviews. By the 1970s the demolition derby drew up to 25 million viewers to "Wide World of Sports.". . .

As far as Arledge was concerned, if an event was visually exciting and had colorful personalities it would "work" on "Wide World of Sports." And if a little creative editing could improve the excitement and color, so much the better. For example, during the Le Mans automobile race there was a major accident in a section of the course where ABC had no cameras to record the wreck. Viewing and editing the film footage back in New York, producer Robert Riger sensed that the "missing crash robbed the story of some of its excitement and drama." To correct this problem, he put several miniature cars into a flowerpot, set them on fire, and filmed the result. He then edited the footage into his Le Mans coverage. . . .

As a good business executive, Arledge gave the people what they wanted, or at least what they would have wanted if they knew it existed. Arledge used the same business acumen to find and to acquire broadcast rights for little-known events. "Wide World of Sports," for example, introduced the Acapulco cliff divers to the American audiences. Arledge negotiated personally with the head of the Acapulco divers' union. . . .

Just as "Wide World of Sports" broadened the definition of sport, it also created sports heroes out of marginally athletic individuals. A case in point was the "athletic career" of Robert Craig "Evel" Knievel. Beginning in 1967, he appeared sixteen times on "Wide World of Sports." His motorcycle stunts became sports pseudo-events. Millions of people watched Knievel not to witness the "thrill of victory" but on the chance of seeing the ultimate "agony of defeat." Knievel didn't die for ratings, but he came close on several occasions. In 1967 he broke his back and his pelvis when he attempted to jump the fountains in front of Caesar's Palace in Las Vegas. It was a spectacular crash, and "Wide World of Sports" showed it and other Knievel failures repeatedly in painful slow motion. Knievel might have been bad sports, but he was great television, and as such an Arledge success.

"Wide World of Sports" is the longest-running sports show ever televised, and like most successful series, it has produced a number of spinoffs. Oftentimes the spinoffs have had less to do with sports than the parent show. "The American Sportsman" teamed announcer Curt Gowdy with a series of celebrity "sportsmen." Together they went after wild animals and untamed fish. . . .

A second successful spinoff of "Wide World of Sports" was "The Superstars." Again, Arledge employed the same formula. Major athletic personalities were pitted against each other in such events as tennis, bowling, swimming, rowing, running, golf, bicycling, and an obstacle course race. . . . True it was a "trash sport," an ersatz sport created and packaged by television, but it was also success-ful television programming. . . .

By 1970 Arledge was ready for his next bold move. Encouraged by the com-missioner of the National Football League, Pete Rozelle, Arledge decided to in-vade prime time with "Monday Night Football." If it was not an entirely new game, success would certainly be measured by different standards. On Sunday af-ternoon, any NFL game that attracted 20 million viewers gave cause for network celebration. The same number during prime time would lead to cancellation. Suc-cess during prime time entailed an audience of between 40 to 50 million. To reach that level, Arledge had to attract a wide variety of viewers. The casual viewer sud-denly became far more important than the dedicated football fan. And sport took a back seat to entertainment.

How to attract the new viewers? One way was to use more and better technol-ogy. Arledge employed a two-unit production team. Chet Forte coordinated play-by-play, and Don Ohlmeyer handled isolated coverage. ABC used more cameras, more technicians, and more videotape than had ever been used before in a football game. The result was tantamount to a perfectly filmed and produced documentary. Every aspect of the game was filmed, and the best footage was rerun, discussed, and analyzed. The result was to make the game larger than life, to give each con-test an epic quality. The use of sophisticated technology made even an average game seem exciting.

Technology, however, had always been a staple of an Arledge telecast. The team of announcers he chose for "Monday Night Football" made the show. His casting was designed to create an entertaining balance of humor, controversy, and tension. Instead of two men in the broadcast booth, Arledge employed three. He chose Keith Jackson to do the play-by-play. . . .

Arledge picked Don Meredith for his country charm and humor. A former Dallas Cowboy quarterback, Meredith knew the game and looked good on camera. This was his advantage, for Arledge intended Meredith to be the darling of Middle America. Meredith was, in short, cast to play the untutored hayseed from Mount Vernon, Texas, come to the big city to talk on TV.

Howard Cosell rounded out the team. Cosell had been with ABC since 1956, when his radio show "Sports Focus" became the summer replacement for "Kukla, Fran, and Ollie." In 1961 he was put on the ABC-TV New York nightly news. The show that brought national attention to Cosell, however, was "Wide World of Sports." Cosell regularly covered boxing for the show, and his outspoken support of Muhammad Ali drew strong critical reactions. . . . Cosell's brash, conceited, ob-noxious style bothered viewers, but it did not make them turn the dial to another station. In fact, "Wide World of Sports" telecasts featuring Cosell scored high rat-ings. Cosell was and would remain for several decades "good TV."

For "Monday Night Football" Arledge cast Cosell as the man America loves to hate. Cosell was supposed to irritate, to get under people's skin, to arouse con-troversy. ABC research predicted that the majority of viewers of "Monday Night Football" would come from the young-adult population. . . .

Reactions to the show were predictably strong. Cosell's performance drew hate mail and death threats. On several occasions, FBI agents filled the broadcast booth. . . . Meredith's irreverent humor also attracted attention and viewers. . . . To

Arledge Football was entertainment, not a religion. And successful entertainment was a matter of good casting.

Arledge altered the cast for the second season. He replaced Keith Jackson with former New York Giant star Frank Gifford. Like Meredith, Gifford was a handsome, articulate ex-player who was popular with Middle America. Even more important, ABC research indicated that Gifford was the most popular sportscaster in New York City, the nation's largest market. . . . Gifford was given more freedom than Jackson had enjoyed. Now Arledge had a near-perfect cast—Cosell, Meredith, and Gifford. Ratings shot up. By the time Cosell left the show in 1983, "Monday Night Football" had become the longest-running prime-time hit on television, . . .

Just as Arledge "created" prime-time football, he changed the way Americans saw the Olympic Games. Before ABC acquired the rights to televise the Games in 1968, no major network had attempted any sort of comprehensive coverage of the Olympics. . . .

Arledge rightly saw the entertainment possibilities of the Olympics. And he knew how to negotiate for the rights. He promised the host city what it wanted—publicity and exposure. As "Wide World of Sports" had demonstrated, part of Arledge's formula was extensive coverage of the exotic places where sports were played. ABC's coverage of alpine skiing had provided great tourist publicity for such towns as Garmisch, St. Moritz, and Innsbruck. Arledge used this approach to win the rights to televise the 1968 Winter Olympics in Grenoble, France. . . .

Heroic technology and extended coverage best describes ABC and Arledge's approach to the televising of the Olympic Games. Arledge sent a 250-man crew to cover the Grenoble Games, and he beamed the result home via the Early Bird satellite. Over the years the numbers of Arledge's army steadily escalated. At the 1972 summer Games in Munich, Arledge's team exceeded 330 men and women. As the number of technicians increased, so did the hours of coverage. ABC squeezed 27 hours of television from the Grenoble Games. Eight years later, in Innsbruck, ABC extended its coverage to 43½ hours. The increased technology and coverage returned handsome dividends. The reviews and ratings were tremendous. Both winter and summer Games became prime-time successes.

By the mid-1970s ABC executives had found a way to capitalize on their Olympic telecasts. . . . While the other networks were televising summer reruns, ABC ran over a hundred hours of Olympic coverage from Montreal. In addition, the network devoted hundreds of commercial minutes to their forthcoming fall lineup of shows. As a result, in the fall of 1976 ABC passed CBS in the Nielsen ratings for all shows. . . .

ABC's spectacular rise forced the other networks to reevaluate their coverage of sports. Ousted by ABC from its first place in the Nielsen ratings, CBS was particularly swift to respond. Head of CBS Sports Robert Wussler and CBS chairman of the board William Paley decided that they had to beat ABC at their own game—Olympic coverage. Although CBS had long taken a cavalier attitude toward sports coverage, its chief executives were now determined to win the rights to televise the 1980 Moscow Games. . . .

The Russian negotiators adapted well to the free enterprise mode of television. ABC, CBS, and late-arriving NBC bid against each other. In the end, NBC won the battle, agreeing to pay the Soviet Union $85 million for television rights to the

Olympics. Of course, the eventual United States boycott of the Moscow Games cost NBC dearly.

The Moscow Olympic battle was the first engagement of an eight-year war between the three major networks over the control of television sports. NBC and CBS had taken note of ABC's spectacular rise. Clearly, network executives reasoned, outstanding sports programming was essential to their corporate growth. Not only did sports programming please the affiliates, but it also provided a solid platform for launching the network's fall season. Good sports promoted good ratings, and the sum total of both equalled increased corporate profits.

Such reasoning inevitably created a highly competitive atmosphere. The big-time sports industry became a sellers market, a fact that the men who controlled that industry quickly realized. Giving little consideration to the future problem of overexposure, they sold television executives all the programming the networks desired. Of course, the price was high. Pete Rozelle, commissioner of the NFL, was probably the best—and the greediest—negotiator. After becoming commissioner in 1960, this former public relations man demonstrated his ability to negotiate with network executives. In 1964 CBS agreed to pay $14 million a year for the rights to televise professional football. At the time, owners considered that amount to be staggering. In 1966 CBS raised its annual payments to $18.5 million. By the 1970s such numbers would provide only laughter at the negotiating table. Starting in 1970 Rozelle allowed all three networks to televise professional games. In 1977 the networks agreed to pay the NFL $656 million over a four-year period. In 1982 the networks upped the amount to $2 billion over five years. In 1985 each team in the NFL received $65 million from the television package. . . .

College football and professional baseball and basketball similarly profited from the networks' increased interest in sports. In 1970 the National Basketball Association received $1 million from television revenues; by 1986 that amount had been raised to over $40 million. During roughly the same period (1970–85) professional baseball's annual television revenues rose from under $20 million to $160 million. Finally, college football's revenues made the phrase "amateur sport" seem somehow empty. In 1977 the NCAA signed a four-year deal with ABC for $120 million. In 1981 the NCAA agreed to allow CBS and the Turner Broadcasting System as well as ABC to televise games. The new price was $74.3 million per year.

By the late 1970s and the early 1980s the networks seemed sports mad. With the exception of hockey, all the major professional and amateur sports profited. Behind Sugar Ray Leonard, its new hero, boxing made a strong comeback on television. Ruled by two separate organizations—the World Boxing Association and World Boxing Council—the sport offered television networks almost weekly championship fights. Television coverage of tennis and college basketball also increased dramatically. Aided by new cable stations and such all-sports networks as Entertainment and Sports Programming Network (ESPN), Americans watched more sports on television than ever before.

The major networks even turned to trash sports to augment their sports programming. Once again Arledge and ABC led the way. In 1973 "The Superstars" made its debut. The show was rooted more in vindictiveness than in imaginative programming, but it captured considerable viewer interest. In part, the NBA was responsible for the show. Between 1965 and 1973 ABC televised NBA games on Sundays. Although the ratings were never great, it captured enough of an audience to satisfy Arledge. Then in what Arledge considered a breach of faith, the NBA dumped ABC for CBS. Arguing unsuccessfully against the switch, Boston Celtics coach Red Auerbach warned, "You don't really think a man like Roone Arledge is going to take this lying down, do you?" Arledge didn't. Furious and feeling betrayed, he moved to destroy the NBA on television. He put a Sunday version of "Wide World of Sports" opposite the NBA games, publicizing the show as if it were the jewel of ABC Sports. The show was a great success. Its ratings quickly moved past those of professional basketball. During that season, Arledge filled one Sunday show with a program called "The Superstars." It was so successful that Arledge expanded the single program into a series of programs the following year. Roone had his revenge and television had a new concept in sports. . . .

Mercifully, by the early 1980s the Golden Age of trash sports had passed. More important, by that time there were signs that the Golden Age of television sports might also be ending. The industry was changing in fundamental ways. Communication satellites and the end of the legal restriction on cable television allowed local "superstations" and cable networks to compete head-to-head with the major networks. Ted Turner's WTBS in Atlanta epitomized the aggressive mood of the superstations. WTBS televised professional baseball and basketball and college basketball, and it charged its sponsors less than the major networks did for similar programming. ESPN and USA, the two major sports cable networks, similarly offered sponsors outstanding sports programming for less money. By the mid-1980s the three major networks faced a real crisis.

Increasingly traditional sports sponsors began moving their advertising dollars into other areas. For years Madison Avenue had talked about the sports package, which included sponsors from the beer, shaving cream, life insurance, and automobile industries. Advertising experts believed that most of the selling done on prime time was to women. They regarded sports programming as the last place where advertisers could reach men, and they believed that the male still decided what kind of beer he would drink, shaving cream he would use, car he would drive, and life insurance he would purchase. Since ultimately the advertisers paid most of the bills for televised sports, any change in their thinking and spending would send shock waves throughout the television and sports industries.

The first tremors were felt in the late 1970s. In December 1979, General Motors decided to pull out of CBS's NBA package. The decision—based largely on poor ratings for the NBA and the desire to move into college basketball, which attracted a younger, more affluent viewer—staggered CBS Sports and the NBA. . . .

By the mid-1980s the tremors were registering high on the Richter scale. They affected every major sport. In part, it was a result of a change in family purchasing patterns. Car-buying decisions, for example, are made more and more by women. Thus advertisers can reach their target audiences more efficiently on "Murder, She Wrote" or "Dallas." In addition, beer-drinking men can be reached much more cheaply on such cable networks as MTV. In 1980 the Miller Brewing Company spent 95 percent of its advertising dollars on televised sports; by 1985 that figure had dropped to 70 percent. A Miller spokesman noted: "Sports programming used to be a bargain compared with prime-time. Now it's as expensive or more. With that, other types of programming become just as important. We are using MTV, late-night shows like David Letterman, and some comedy programming to reach our target audience."

Television networks found themselves caught between rising costs for television rights and falling advertising prices. In 1985 the major networks lost $45 million on the NFL. Although all three networks have been hurt, ABC has suffered the most. In 1984 Olympic coverage helped ABC Sports to achieve a record $70 million profit. In 1985 ABC Sports lost between $30 and $50 million. . . .

Although the full effect of the earthquake is not yet known, the major networks are starting to assess the damages and beginning their clean-up. ABC has made the most dramatic move. In 1985 Capital City Communications, a media conglomerate, bought ABC for $3.7 billion. . . . One of Cap City's first major moves after the takeover was to replace Roone Arledge in Sports with Dennis Swanson, a no-nonsense, bottom-line ex-Marine. Swanson immediately let it be known that ABC Sports' free-spending days had ended. . . .

Less subtly, NBC and CBS have moved along the same path as the new ABC. Undoubtedly in the future, professional and college sports executives will not be able to extract as much money from the networks for sports rights. . . . CBS dropped its coverage of the Belmont Stakes, and ABC decided not to renew its contract with the Gator Bowl. The end result might well mean less sports for less money on the major networks.

Perhaps the free-spending era ended with ABC's acquisition of the 1988 Winter Olympics in Calgary, Canada. After a brutal bidding war, ABC "won" the rights at a cost of $309 million, an increase of $217.5 million, or 337 percent, over the cost of the 1984 Winter Olympics in Sarajevo, Yugoslavia. From the first, ABC realized that they had bid too high, that pride or vanity or competitiveness had overcome common sense. . . .

The Roone Revolution, then, is nearing its end, or at least network competition for sports is slackening. But sports will never be the same as they were before Arledge. Nor will television's coverage of sports return to the flat days before Arledge took over ABC Sports. More than any other person, Arledge changed the economic and aesthetic foundations of sports.

The Making of Baltimore's Camden Yards Stadium

CHARLES C. EUCHNER

. . . In 1980 Baltimore ranked fifth among fifty-eight cities on a composite measure for urban distress that includes poverty rates, decline in per capita income, and unemployment. Some 25 percent of the city's 780,000 residents in 1980 lived

From Charles C. Euchner, *Playing the Field: Why Sports Teams Move and Cities Fight to Keep Them* (Baltimore: Johns Hopkins University Press, 1993), 104–23, 126, 130.

below the federal poverty line. . . . Housing affordability, once a great Baltimore virtue, was declining: because of a shrinking capital base, property taxes increased as much as five-fold in some middle-class neighborhoods between 1980 and 1990, and the tax rates averaged twice those of neighboring Washington, D.C. The city lost 13 percent of its population during the 1970s. More than 50,000 jobs disappeared during the same period, and another 20,000 between 1980 and 1983. . . .

The political institutions of Maryland and Baltimore appeared powerless to address the city's major problems. The mayor, the Board of Estimates and City Council, the bureaucracy, the schools, political parties, and philanthropies all reacted to problems rather than confronting them in any fundamental or comprehensive way.

Reflecting the city's mixed fortunes were the fates of its two major league sports franchises. The Colts of the National Football League, once an emblem of blue-collar pride, left in 1984. Owner Robert Irsay moved the team to Indianapolis after protracted bickering and negotiating in Maryland and romancing and negotiating in Indiana and elsewhere. After the Colts' departure, Maryland approved construction of a new stadium to keep the Orioles baseball team in town. The construction project promised a glittering addition to the city's downtown but did little if anything to help the city address its basic problems.

The sports franchises had the advantage in talks with the city because they could initiate action whenever and wherever they wanted in the long process of negotiations. Even under the leadership of its most powerful mayor in the century, Baltimore had limited negotiating leverage. The city's most important tool, the power of eminent domain, was not only questionable legally but also risked pushing the team out of the city.

The Manipulation of a City

When the Colts were still playing in Baltimore, Mayor Schaefer and others rejected the idea of building a new stadium, insisting that Memorial Stadium was one of the best in sports. Schaefer wanted to avoid the expensive debt service that other cities had incurred with new stadiums. . . . [T]he Colts and Orioles refused to sign leases longer than two years, and the city's concessions to the two teams escalated. Increasingly, new facilities appeared to be the only way to keep the teams in Baltimore.

The city's relations with Robert Irsay typify the fragmented, step-by-step progression of controversies between sports franchises and cities. When Irsay acknowledged that he had met with representatives of Indianapolis and Phoenix in 1976, Baltimore officials scrambled to meet the immediate threat at the expense of coherent, long-term planning. . . .

Baltimore's public and private leaders did not always present a united front. When the Colts demanded restructuring of a loan Irsay had received in 1972 to buy the Colts, Indianapolis quickly offered a loan at 3 percent below the 1984 prime lending rate. Baltimore did not match the offer. Major Schaefer expressed frustration at the failure of local financiers to help keep the Colts. . . . In addition, local media expressed reservations about the mayor's bidding war for the team, while the Indianapolis media and public almost unanimously supported that city's efforts.

Ironically, as the Colts case shows, teams with poor management can be tougher negotiating partners. The Colts—once the envy of the NFL, with fifty-one consecutive sellouts at the 60,714-seat Memorial Stadium—suffered from a series of questionable front-office decisions. Irsay, for example, fired General Manager Joe Thomas, who had assembled a young squad that won three straight playoff berths. Irsay also let go one of the league's most dynamic young quarterbacks, John Elway. In addition, Irsay committed a number of public relations blunders, such as ignominiously benching Johnny Unitas, a local hero. It was no accident that Irsay first demanded improvements in the Memorial Stadium lease in 1979 when the team was starting to perform poorly on the field.

Since the Colts controlled the pace of negotiations, the city had to exercise care in dealing with Irsay's mercurial personal moods. . . . [In January 1984] Irsay said he and Mayor Schaefer were close to terms on a new lease and "I have not any intention to move the goddamn team." Days later, however, Irsay began final talks with Indianapolis.

The city was buffeted by a protracted game of "me-tooism" by the Colts and Orioles. The process began in 1973 when the Orioles owner, Jerold Hoffberger, put the team on the market but found no buyers; immediately afterward, he demanded and got a more favorable lease. The Colts responded by demanding a new lease based on dollar parity with the Orioles. They got the new lease, in which the Colts paid the same rent as the Orioles, in 1977, and it was made retroactive to 1975. When the 1980–81 lease talks came along, the Colts management again complained about its level of payments vis-à-vis the Orioles, and refused to sign. This time the Colts argued that they and the Orioles should not pay equal rent because the Orioles used the stadium for more games. The Colts asked for rent based on a formula rather than preset dollar amounts. The city agreed and the Colts promised to stay in Baltimore at least until 1984. . . .

In February 1983, Mayor Schaefer attempted to end the game of me-tooism by conducting separate negotiations with the Colts and the Orioles. He asked the general assembly to approve $15 million for renovation of Memorial Stadium—$7.5 million to address complaints of each of the teams. The legislature approved the measure that spring, after intense lobbying by Schaefer. Following difficult negotiations, the city and the Orioles signed a three-year lease in January 1984. The "decoupling" of Orioles and Colts negotiations was a crucial moment in Baltimore sports history, because it tacitly acknowledged that the Colts would probably leave. Schaefer's objective was to do what he could to hold on to at least one major league franchise. The Colts, now isolated, were ripe for the picking by Indianapolis. . . .

Irsay's most frustrating tactic could be termed "plausible deniability." He could take a step that seemed ominous for Baltimore, then plausibly deny intending any harm. For example, in February 1984, Irsay halted the mailing of the Colts season tickets. It was speculated that he was holding back tickets to gain leverage in stadium negotiations, but he said the delay was due to indecision on ticket prices. . . . Irsay would turn the focus first to reports of negotiations with Phoenix and Indianapolis, then to complaints about Memorial Stadium, then to comparisons with the Orioles' lease, keeping city officials off balance.

Schaefer had concentrated on wooing rather than confronting Irsay, but in 1984 aides to the mayor started to consider a more aggressive approach. Mayoral aide Mark Wasserman proposed seizing control of the Colts through eminent domain. . . .

After the Colts moved, one political ally of Mayor Schaefer suggested suing both the Colts and the National Football League—the only time the city considered addressing the real root of the problem, professional football's monopoly status. Noting that the NFL bylaws require consent of team owners for franchise shifts, attorney George W. Baker suggested, in a confidential memorandum dated March 30, that the city attack the league for failing to honor its own rules. The league, Baker suggested, might have an obligation to the city and authority over the Colts by dint of the league's definition of a franchise as the right "to operate a professional football club in a designated city.". . .

Interestingly, Baltimore won the rights to the Colts franchise in 1952 as the result of a lawsuit against the NFL. The litigation strategy might have had a chance in 1984; the mere threat of a suit against the NFL or Irsay might have induced them to seriously consider leaving the team in Baltimore. But, in the end, Schaefer decided to cooperate with, rather than challenge, the NFL. Schaefer wrote to Commissioner Pete Rozelle after the Colts move, informing him that Baltimore had formed a committee to seek a new franchise. . . .

The Eminent Domain Suit

Employing the city's greatest power—eminent domain authority—required great delicacy, since the mere mention of that power would undoubtedly unsettle Irsay and hasten his flight from Baltimore. Ultimately, the city's attempt to seize the franchise failed. . . .

For more than a year after the Colts' move, Baltimore fought Irsay in the courts. The case turned on whether Irsay had moved the franchise before Baltimore initiated condemnation procedures. At issue was whether the state still had jurisdiction over the franchise, or whether such a claim could be made by other involved states. . . .

Federal Judge Walter E. Black, Jr., dismissed Baltimore's suit in December 1984. Judge Black ruled that Baltimore did not have jurisdiction over the club when the case was filed. . . . Rather than appeal the case, which had already cost the city $500,000 in legal fees, Mayor Schaefer began a campaign to attract a new football club and to build a new stadium to keep the Orioles. The city was signaling its willingness to play sports politics by league rules. . . .

"It was a dark and stormy night"

On the night of March 12, 1984, moving vans arrived unannounced at the Baltimore Colts' training complex at Owings Mills, Maryland, to remove the club's property. . . . By morning, all the team's possessions—helmets, shoulder pads, weights, video equipment—were in a caravan of eleven moving vans headed west on Interstate 70.

Mayor Schaefer heard about the move on the radio news. He called an emergency session of the city council to consider action. . . . Public reaction was fast and angry. Hundreds of telephone calls deluged City Hall in the days after the move, and the city began preparations for a lawsuit to bring the Colts back.

The scene at the Owings Mills complex became more vivid in the public mind as time passed, and it was an important influence in the city's eventual decision to build a new stadium. The image of the departing moving vans became the symbol of the Robert Irsay's underhanded and cowardly ways. . . . Irsay's action was dubbed the "midnight move" and "midnight raid," conjuring up images of furtiveness and deceit. Irsay was reviled as a coward, a carpetbagger; his physical attributes were the source of bitter local parody. Bumper stickers condensed the long and sorry episode: "Will Rogers Never Met Bob Irsay."

As is often the case in sports discourse, the situation was reduced to a simple opposition: Baltimore versus Irsay. Ignoring the larger question of how the structure of major league sports makes franchise shifts a constant possibility undermined Baltimore's ability to take a well-rounded, rational view of the problem at hand and of professional sports in general. By focusing on Irsay's personality, the city eventually wasted millions of dollars, antagonized the NFL, and failed to confront the real meaning of the loss. . . .

As Edelman observes, "enmity is a bond as well as a divider." After a certain point Baltimore was helpless to do anything about the Colts, but its leadership became single-minded in its efforts to keep the Orioles in the city and to attract another football team. The obsession with landing a team would prevent the city and state from developing an imaginative response to the sports industry—and from dealing with the city's more entrenched problems.

With its demonizing of Irsay, Baltimore set itself up to be manipulated again—the next time by the NFL, which set rigid standards for cities seeking expansion teams, and by the Baltimore Orioles. Rather than addressing the many aspects of the sports-cities dynamic, Baltimore once again placed itself at the mercy of professional sports leagues. It accepted the idea that cities had to meet the demands of the leagues and franchises. Baltimore was only reactive during the next series of dealings with the professional sports industry.

Defensive Politics: The Twin Stadiums

Sports politics in Maryland changed dramatically when it became clear that Baltimore could not force the Colts to return. With the conversion of William Donald Schaefer to the cause, the drive for a new facility had irresistible momentum. . . .

Schaefer had always argued against a new stadium on the grounds that other municipal problems were too pressing and the city budget too limited. Schaefer called Memorial Stadium one of the best sports facilities in the country. Typical was his comment in 1983, when Baltimore was still competing with Indianapolis and its brand-new Hoosier Dome to host the Colts: "We're not going to build a new stadium. We don't have the bonding capacity. We don't have the voters or the taxpayers who can support a $60 million stadium. One-third of the people in Baltimore pay taxes. Unless private enterprise builds it, we won't build it." But by the time Schaefer ran a successful campaign for governor in 1986, he was a vocal proponent of a new stadium—and perhaps even two new stadiums.

Schaefer wanted new facilities in Camden Yards, a warehouse district near Baltimore's revitalized business district and Inner Harbor tourist attractions. That site had the virtue of downtown location and proximity to the increasingly important Washington, D.C., market. It also abutted a warehouse recently bought by a group of investors that included Schaefer's leading fundraiser. . . .

By March 1987, barely three months into his term, Governor Schaefer had secured state funding for "twin stadiums." The governor used his overwhelming election victory the previous November as political capital, and he threatened and cajoled opponents of stadium building across the state. Schaefer was not bashful about offering material rewards to the legislators who cooperated—and deprivation to those who resisted.

The Orioles' negotiating strength clearly got a big boost from the Colts' departure. Being the only team in town is more significant than being one of two. The Colts had proved that a franchise could leave whenever it wanted; attention turned to a possible Orioles exit. When Edward Bennett Williams, a prominent Washington attorney, bought the team in 1979, it was feared that he would transfer the team to the capital's Robert F. Kennedy Stadium. Baltimore would have to respond or it would risk losing the team without any legal or political recourse.

Williams made vague and contradictory statements that gave him extraordinary leverage. Williams rarely talked about moving the team, and in fact vowed to stay in the city; but by refusing to sign a long-term lease, he assured that the team's departure was always a possibility. Williams was in the driver's seat. . . . It became clear that only a new stadium could entice Williams into a long-term relationship. Even when the city agreed to build a new stadium, the Orioles would agree to only a fifteen-year lease (the standard sports lease prior to the 1980s was twice that duration). . . .

The Politics of Numbers

Reports filled with promises of economic benefits, backed by a steady stream of debatable numbers, paved the way for a new stadium. . . .

The reports gave the campaign for a new facility an aura of scientific objectivity and legitimacy. . . . Official reports use a number of strategies. First, they emphasize the city as a whole, in order to submerge a project's impact on specific interests. Second, the reports focus on statistics and technical concerns that drown out qualitative considerations. . . . Third, the appearance of officialness enables those who wield these report to depict even the most perfunctory encounters with citizens as serious deliberation.

The reports' major argument was that a new stadium would produce substantial economic benefits to the city and region. The Butta report, for example, maintained that a stadium at Camden Yards would have a larger economic impact than Memorial Stadium had, but it based this conclusion on the assumption that the Orioles would attract 20 percent more fans at the new site. The report did not submit the estimate to any analysis, but rather derived it from "information provided during discussions with local government officials, Baltimore Orioles management, and other community representatives"—that is, the promoters of the new facility. The report also projected a "new stadium bonus," an attendance increase of 400,000 in the first year and 200,000 in the second year due to the excitement of a new stadium. While the estimate turned out to be correct, it did not take into account other factors considered more crucial to attendance, like team performance and population base.

The Butta report also understated the costs of building a new stadium, most notably by excluding the costs of financing (as much as $10 million a year for thirty years) and by ignoring property tax revenues lost to the tax-free stadium (as much as $16 million annually). Other miscalculations characterize the Butta report. The stadium authority, for example, budgeted $7.4 million for relocation of all the businesses and homes on the construction site—a low estimate, as events would eventually demonstrate. . . . The multiplier effect was often offered as a major justification for building the new stadium, even though a new Baltimore stadium would simply transfer an operation from one part of the city to another, and even push some businesses out of the city.

This quantitative blanket smothered the expression of intangible concerns, such as the fabric of neighborhoods and the need to balance sports with other urban concerns. The neutral-sounding words of planning officials reduced the ability of the affected parties to respond. . . .

Stadium opponents had a difficult time overcoming the steady beat of arguments not only in consultant reports but also in the local news media. When these reports did not tout the economic gains for the whole city, they underscored the project's inevitability. Governor Schaefer, it was said, was too powerful a public figure to confront on the stadium issue. Community resistance to the stadium plans was practically impossible. There was no way to shift the issue from small-scale skirmishes fought against overwhelming odds to a larger debate involving the priorities of the city as a whole.

A City of Neighborhoods

. . . But the neighborhoods did not shape their own destinies in the case of Baltimore's stadium politics. The sports industry's ability to control the pace and tempo of the deliberations reduced neighborhood participation to a few quixotic battles mostly irrelevent to the decision-making process.

People in both the current and the proposed stadium neighborhoods opposed the new stadium because of the way it would affect the fabric of their communities, but they failed to involve a wide variety of community groups in a broad-based debate. The discussion, therefore, proceeded according to the logic and demands of the sports industry.

As is often the case with large public projects, some neighborhoods felt they had to accept the basic premise that a new stadium was necessary. When a new stadium appeared inevitable, neighborhoods organized to protect their own parochial interests. . . .

The new stadium site, Camden railroad yards, is on a choice wedge, two blocks to the west of the Inner Harbor. . . . The site is directly connected to the suburban and Washington markets by the Baltimore-Washington Expressway, the Baltimore Beltway, and a number of major downtown arteries. . . .

Public support for construction of new stadiums in Baltimore was doubtful, especially in the state at large. While 53 percent of persons surveyed in the Baltimore City area said they supported building a new stadium, 45 percent said it was not important whether Baltimore had a professional football team. The survey did not include the opinions of residents of the rest of the state, which was overwhelmingly opposed to the stadium. . . . The data seemed to suggest that the stadium might fail if the question of its construction were opened up for public debate.

Despite the bitterness that lingered after the Colts' departure, many Marylanders saw little reason to believe that the Orioles would leave the city. The Orioles drew more fans than ever at Memorial Stadium, even when the team suffered bad seasons on the playing field. In 1987 and 1988, for example, the team finished in the last place but still managed to draw close to 2 million paying customers; in 1988, the team set all-time records for ineptitude but still drew 1.6 million fans. The stadium was located in a charming part of town, the franchise's promotion efforts were successful inside and outside the city, and the team seemed to have won a place in the hearts and routines of the city.

Even though the public was lukewarm about the need to build a new stadium, Governor Schaefer decided to act, for three reasons. First, Schaefer did not want to be the public official held responsible for "losing" another major league franchise. Schaefer avoided blame for the Colts' departure because Irsay was the target of enmity, but losing a second team could be the municipal equivalent of "losing China." Schaefer also wanted to attract a new NFL team to restore the city's damaged pride. Second, big public works projects involve big contracts and public works jobs. Third, large projects provide visible signs of life for the state and city. Schaefer promoted a stadium for the same reasons he had, as mayor, championed the Harborplace development, downtown construction projects, and various gentrification schemes. They gave the city an image of renaissance and action.

Governor Schaefer put his proposal for a new stadium at the top of his legislative agenda. His resounding victory in the previous year's primary and general election campaigns, and his own energy, gave him that executive "power to persuade" that he needed to get stadium legislation through the general assembly. . . .

The mechanism that the state adopted to implement the plan for new stadiums was the quasi-public authority, with its politically advantageous quasi-accountability. The authority would coordinate the many aspects of stadium construction—from running the state lottery that would raise funds to evicting the residents of the neighborhood that would be the site of the new facility. . . .

The Maryland Stadium Authority was designed to operate above the tangled politics of the Baltimore City. It had the power to select a stadium site and to condemn property in the area without negotiations. The authority did not consider renovation of the existing Memorial Stadium or a wide range of alternative sites for building a new stadium. Its extensive powers liberated it from the inconvenience of arguing with local interests. . . .

Opposing the stadium authority was difficult. The authority was an instrument of the state but also separate from the state. Its fund-raising capacity lay in the sale of tax-exempt bonds and the operation of lotteries. These devices avoided the direct coercion of taxes but were provided the state's fiscal backing. Because the public financial burden was indirect, challenges could be blunted. The state could claim that the authority did not impose a financial burden on the public; it could then turn around and claim the opposite, that the authority was a full-fledged part of the government, which is exactly what it did during the battle over the state referendum process. In short, the device of the authority could so blur the distinctions between public and private that a meaningful public discourse could not develop. . . .

Quixotic Resistance

Once the authority had the legal and financial wherewithal to condemn land and build stadiums, there was little room for public debate. Neighborhoods and other opponents could make claims for benefits from the stadium but could not question the project's validity. Given the existence of other urban problems needing state support, most decided that opposing a new stadium was not worth crossing the governor, especially since William Donald Schaefer is well known for his grudges and tit-for-tat style of politics. Working through the stadium authority enabled the state to avoid demands for democratic access, procedures, and debate. The public space was closed. Stadium politics was restricted to the course determined by the tightly controlled authority and the sports industry.

Without the referendum process, which San Francisco and New Jersey used to defeat major stadium projects the same year, opponents of the Baltimore stadiums had little recourse. The stadiums were not popular, but the issue of whether or not they should be built did not justify the kind of massive and concerted activism that would have been needed to defeat the proposal. . . . The belief that the stadium controversy was not important enough to risk activism underscores the fragmentation of local politics. Even though the Camden Yards stadium had the potential to affect the makeup and even the existence of many neighborhoods, residents consciously decided to treat the stadium as an isolated matter. Urbanites are used to coping with numerous and difficult problems, and the kinds of problems that might result from the stadium—such as increasing traffic and driving out middle-income families and small businesses—were not immediate enough threats to prompt an all-out, coordinated fight. . . .

Marker's organization did not faze the stadium juggernaut. Pitted against the city's power structure and Governor Schaefer's enormous power in Annapolis, MASS [Marylanders for Sports Society] had little impact. It also failed to tie the issue to the broader historical picture. Chicago neighborhood activists, by contrast, argued that their displacement by a new stadium was just one event in a long series of policies that segregated the city. Camden Yards stadium opponents might have argued that, combined with the earlier displacement of nearby residents and small businesses to make way for the Harborplace development, the stadium represented a complete takeover by commercial interests of a large part of the city.

In the final analysis, MASS and the neighborhoods failed to extend their battle beyond the immediate circumstances. The feeling of inevitability and the failure to see the linkages to other problems doomed the anti-stadium effort. Camden Yards was selected as the site of a new stadium, among other reasons, to minimize conflict. The area's isolation from more political neighborhood, and its proximity to the downtown area, made it a natural appendage to the already extensive downtown development. . . .

After creation of the stadium authority, there was little that could be done to control it. The responses to the authority's early cost overruns indicate just how much the authority was in charge. State Senator Laurence Levitan said he was "shocked" by the cost overruns; "I'd say they did a lousy job" in estimating the costs of the project. . . .

As Oriole Park at Camden Yards neared completion in the spring of 1922, some of the doubts about the project faded. The team spent $175,000 to celebrate the previously derided Memorial Stadium on its final day in 1991, tapping emotional springs and helping to ease the transition to the new facility. Breaking with the standard "cookie-cutter" approach to stadium design of the 1970s and 1980s, the stadium authority selected an architectural design that recalled the sport's traditional neighborhood parks. An irregular field shape, fewer seats, the use of a historic warehouse as a back drop to the right field fence, and art deco ornamentation made the park feel lived-in before it even opened. One wag commented that he had heard so much about the park's old-fashioned atmosphere that he "expected to see Harry Truman throw out the first pitch." Complaints about cost overruns, favoritism, and political pressure tactics did not seem to matter amidst the national and local media celebrations of the new facility.

The Baltimore elite's constant concern about professional sports can be attributed to a desire to counter the image of decline in the city. Such a concern is reactive, so it was predictable that the monopolistic sports industry would control the way issues were deliberated. With issues discussed in a narrow, sequential style, an open, public dialogue was prevented. The public may have financed the show, but it never managed to land a significant speaking part.

FURTHER READING

Bud Andelman, *Stadium for Rent: Tampa Bay's Quest for Major League Baseball* (1993)

Joan Chandler, *Television and National Sport: The United States and Britain* (1988)

Michael N. Danielson, *Home Team: Professional Sports and the American Metropolis* (1997)

David Harris, *The League: The Rise and Fall of the NFL* (1986)

Thomas S. Hine, "Housing, Baseball and Creeping Socialism: The Battle of Chavez Ravine, Los Angeles, 1949–1959," *Journal of Urban History* 8 (February 1982), 123–43

Kenneth Jennings, *Balls and Strikes* (1990)

James E. Miller, *The Baseball Business: Pursuing Pennants and Profits in Baltimore* (1990)

Barney Nagler, *James Norris and the Decline of Boxing* (1964)

Jeff Neal-Lunsford, "Sport in the Land of Television: The Use of Sport in Network Prime-Time Schedules, 1946–50," *Journal of Sport History* 19 (1992), 52–76

Michael O'Brien, *Vince: A Personal Biography of Vince Lombardi* (1987)

James Quirk and Rodney D. Fort, *Pay Dirt: The Business of Professional Team Sports* (1992)

Benjamin G. Rader, *Baseball* (1992)

Benjamin G. Rader, *In Its Own Image: How Television Has Transformed Sports* (1984)

Peter Richmond, *Ballpark: Camden Yards and the Building of an American Dream* (1993)

Steven A. Riess, "Only the Ring Was Square: Frankie Carbo and the Underworld Control of American Boxing," *International Journal of the History of Sport* 5 (May 1988), 29–52

Randy Roberts and James Olson, *Winning Is the Only Thing: Sports in American Society Since 1945* (1989)

Jeffrey Sammons, *Beyond the Ring: The Role of Boxing in American Society* (1988)

Gerald Scully, *The Business of Baseball* (1989)

Paul Staudohar and James A. Mangan, eds., *The Business of Professional Sports* (1991)

Neil J. Sullivan, *The Dodgers Move West* (1987)

David Q. Voigt, *American Baseball,* vol. 3, *From the Post-War Expansion to the Electronic Age* (1983)

Andrew Zimbalist, *Baseball and Billions* (1992)

TEXT CREDITS